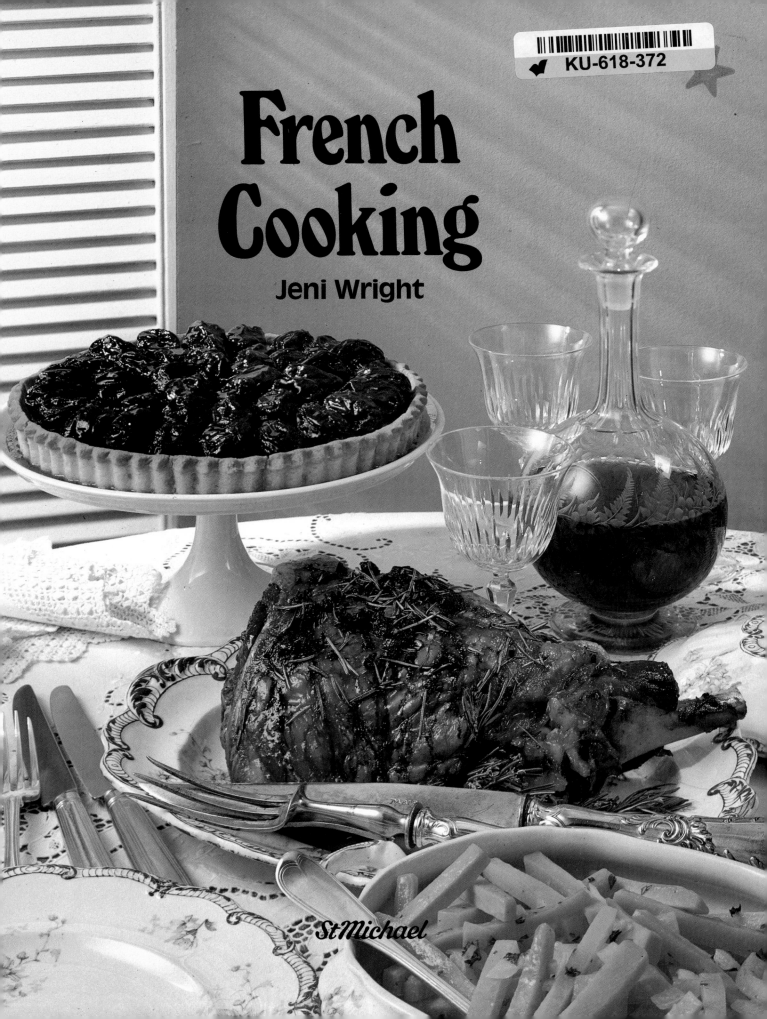

French Cooking

Jeni Wright

St Michael

Contents

Published exclusively for Marks and Spencer p.l.c.
in 1982 by Octopus Books Limited
59 Grosvenor Street, London W1

Fourth impression, 1983

© 1982 Hennerwood Publications Limited

ISBN 0 86273 033 3

Printed in Hong Kong

INTRODUCTION

To the French, cooking is an art, and eating is one of the greatest pleasures in life. The high-class Parisian restaurant specializing in haute cuisine, the corner bistro with its regional specialities, the French housewife preparing a meal for her family, each has its or her own impeccably high standard of preparation and cooking, and each one cooks with the same care and attention.

To understand the French attitude to food, it is essential to start at the beginning with the raw ingredients, because to the French cook these are as important as the cooking itself. No amount of practise or skill can disguise inferior ingredients, and quality is always the order of the day. To shop in France is a joy in itself, not only to see the abundance of fresh produce, from the market stalls of brilliantly coloured vegetables and fruit to the impeccable displays of regional cheeses in the fromageries. Even though excellent modern supermarkets and hypermarkets cater for customers' tastes, most serious French cooks still prefer to go to the local market, charcuterie, poissonerie, etc., because in these specialist shops they can discuss their exact needs and the day's best purchases with the shopkeeper.

YOUR CHOICE OF INGREDIENTS

Shops and markets in Britain are obviously different from those in France, but if you are cooking French-style, do not be discouraged by the thought that you may not be able to buy the right ingredients here. French produce is imported into this country on a large scale, and most supermarkets stock the majority of items you will need. Delicatessens and delicatessen counters within supermarkets stock the more specialist items, and Continental greengrocers can be relied upon for high-quality imported vegetables. The ingredients for the recipes in this book can all be found in any good supermarket or delicatessen, butcher, fishmonger and greengrocer – and where an unusual ingredient might have been used in a similar French recipe, the recipe in this book has been adapted to suit the tastes and availability of ingredients in this country.

To help select the more unusual ingredients with which you may not be so familiar, the following checklist will be helpful.

Bacon Although bacon rashers are not used in France for frying and grilling as they are here, bacon is used to give flavour to many casseroles, stews and pâtés. Buy streaky bacon in the piece or thick belly pork rashers, and dice the meat or cut it into strips, depending on the dish. If available, salt pork gives added flavour, and is more similar in flavour to the French smoked belly of pork which is often used in preference to bacon, an expensive item in France.

Bouquet Garni A handy way to give a subtle flavour of herbs to casseroles, stews and soups, etc., a traditional bouquet garni (bunch of herbs) is made of sprigs of thyme and parsley and one or two bay leaves tied together with string. If fresh herbs are obtainable, then so much the better (many supermarkets sell these three fresh herbs packed together as a bouquet garni), but failing this, dried sachets are widely available. Look for the muslin bags which have string or ribbon attached, as these are the easiest to remove before serving.

Cheeses Many good French cheeses are exported to Britain, and with the advancements made in refrigerated transport their condition and quality is not dissimilar from their equivalents in France. Supermarkets sell the most popular varieties, which are most often imported pre-packaged straight from France. Whilst these are invariably of good quality, a Continental delicatessen will usually have a larger selection of cheeses for sale by the kilo/lb.

Brie, Camembert, and in particular Gruyère, are used often in this book. Brie and Camembert are unique French cheeses for which there are no substitutes, although since the two have a similar appearance and texture they are virtually inter-changeable in recipes – try them both and find which one you prefer. Gruyère in this country is usually imported from Switzerland rather than France, but this will make no difference to the recipes. If Emmental is more readily available, this can be used instead of Gruyère, but no other cheese will give quite the same melting qualities and distinctive flavour as these two, so it is inadvisable to use other alternatives. Goat's milk cheese, or chèvre, used for Tartelettes au Chèvre (page 19) is not so easy to obtain as other French cheeses, but can be found in some supermarkets and delicatessens with good cheese counters. This type of cheese is usually tangier in flavour than cow's milk cheese, and some varieties are very salty.

The French love of cheese far exceeds that of any other country in the world. Cheese is almost always served at every French meal, after the main course. French bread (without butter) may be broken into small pieces and eaten with the cheese, but it is often eaten on its own with any remaining wine and perhaps a few grapes as accompaniments. The French cheeseboard is rarely elaborate, and for most family meals there will be only one, or at the most two, cheeses served – at exactly the right degree of ripeness. In general, desserts are not so popular as they are here (except perhaps with children who often eat yogurt for dessert or a soft white cheese topped with fruit and sugar), and so the cheese marks the end of the meal.

Cream In France there is no equivalent to our single or double cream, and cream is seldom served with puddings and desserts. Fresh cream (crème fraîche) in France has an altogether sharper or tarter flavour than our creams and is more often used in cooking, both in sweet and savoury dishes. Many of the recipes in this book use cream as a thickening agent just before serving – this is a favourite French method of enriching and thickening sauces, particularly if they are to be served with meat, poultry and fish. Crème fraîche is ideal for this because it is not sweet; it also reduces and thickens sauces beautifully without curdling. Because it is not available in this country, the recipes in this book specify double cream wherever crème fraîche might have been used in France. However greater care must be taken with double cream because it has a lower fat content than crème fraîche, and is more likely to separate and become oily. When adding it to a sauce or other liquid, use a heavy-based pan (cast iron is best) and whisk it in with a wire balloon whisk. Bring slowly to the boil and simmer until the liquid reduces and thickens, whisking vigorously all the time. The amount of time this will take varies according to the pan used and the amount of liquid and cream, but it can take as long as 15 minutes. The important thing to remember is to stand over it all the time and to whisk constantly. Double cream will never have quite the body and piquancy of crème fraîche, but used carefully it is a perfectly acceptable substitute.

Garlic To many people in this country, the word garlic is synonymous with French cooking! Garlic is used all over France (especially in the south along the Mediterranean coast and towards the Spanish and Italian borders). Although the French do love garlic, it is not necessary for it to be included in every dish to give it a 'French' flavour. When garlic is used in the recipes in this book, the quantities given are intended only as a guide, and you can use as much or as little as you like. In summer and early autumn look for the purple-skinned varieties imported from France as these tend to be milder.

If you are unused to the flavour of garlic, treat it with caution at first until you and your family have grown accustomed to it. A bulb of garlic is made up of several individual sections or cloves. To separate them, place the bulb on a board or work surface and bang it firmly with the heel of your hand. Peel individual cloves with your fingers, then cut into small pieces with a sharp knife. Put about 2.5 ml/½ teaspoon salt on the board and, working with the flat of the blade of a large cook's knife, crush the garlic and salt to a paste. If you crush garlic in this way,

5

it becomes absorbed much easier and is therefore more digestible. For a more subtle flavour of garlic, simply cut a clove in half and rub the cut surface around the inside of cooking pans and salad bowls, etc. Or 'bruise' a clove of garlic by flattening it with a pestle or blade of a knife, then add it to a sauce, soup or casserole and remove it before serving. A tip for avoiding 'garlic breath' is to chew a sprig or two of fresh parsley!

Herbs Used extensively, fresh herbs are always preferred to dried and are more readily available in France than they are here. Chervil, chives, parsley, rosemary, savory and tarragon are commonly used in French dishes, and all are relatively easy to grow in a sunny sheltered spot in the garden. Tie sprigs together and add to liquids as for a bouquet garni, or chop finely and sprinkle into dishes before cooking; chopped herbs are also often sprinkled over savoury dishes as a garnish. Bay leaves are frequently added to casseroles, sauces and soups to give a subtle flavour, but remember always to remove before serving. Wherever possible in the recipes in this book, try to use fresh herbs; dried can be used as a substitute, but they are more pungent and only half the quantity given for fresh should be used. Dried herbs do not keep their aroma and flavour for long (about 3 months), so it is best to buy them in small quantities and check before use – stale dried herbs can impart a bitter, even musty flavour to a dish.

Mustard The French are great mustard lovers, and there are many different French mustards imported into this country. Although British mustard manu-facturers make jars of 'French mustard' in paste form, it is preferable to use one of the more specific French mustards. French mustards are not sold in powder form like some English mustards, but they are very convenient to use in cooking to add piquancy and sharpness to sauces and casseroles, etc. Many different varieties of Dijon mustard are sold in Britain; sharp rather than hot, they are always smooth-textured and vary in colour from pale yellow ochre through to greeny yellow (this type is made from green peppercorns), and light muddy brown. The pale-coloured varieties are most suitable for cooking, especially in sauces. Another popular French mustard is Moutarde de Meaux, a whole-grain type which tends to be milder in flavour than Dijon, but the granular texture is not always suitable for dishes with smooth sauces. When adding any mustard during cooking, never let it boil or it will impart an overriding bitterness to the finished dish. The best way to avoid this is to stir in the mustard off the heat, just before serving.

Oil For frying, the French tend to use oil in preference to butter and other fats (except perhaps in Normandy and neighbouring northern regions where locally churned butter is popular). Light vegetable oils with little flavour are preferred for most dishes, and any corn, safflower, sunflower or soya bean oil can be used. For salads, mayonnaise and salad dressings, however, olive oil is the one to choose, and the fruitier and greener it is the better. Provençal olive oil is considered one of the best – in Provence it adds its unique fruity flavour to all cooked dishes as well as salads. Olive oil is expensive in Britain, but there is no substitute for its thick consistency and flavour. Buy the best quality you can afford or your salads and dressings may be disappointingly flavourless. Although it is very expensive, the distinctive nutty flavour of walnut oil is becoming increasingly popular in France for salad dressings.

Shallots When glancing through any French cookery book it seems that almost all savoury dishes start by frying shallots, in oil. One of the mildest members of the onion family, the shallot is not so widely used here in Britain as it is in France. If you do not grow your own, look for them in spring and summer at specialist greengrocers and markets, because their mild flavour is more suited to French dishes than other pungent onions. Wherever shallots are used in a recipe and you find them difficult to obtain, use spring onions or half the quantity of mild Spanish onions instead.

Successful Pastry

The French method of making pastry is slightly different from our own in that a higher proportion of fat to flour is used, resulting in a richer, shorter and crisper finish. Pâte brisée is the closest French equivalent to our shortcrust pastry. Sweet shortcrust pastry (pâte sucrée) for flans and tarts, has sugar added during the making of the dough, before cutting in the butter, and for an even richer pastry known as pâte sablée or French flan pastry, one or more egg yolks are added.

The high fat content of these pastries makes them more difficult to handle than other less rich mixtures, therefore extra care should be taken when making them. Always work in the coolest possible temperature and make sure that your work surface and utensils are cold (marble is the best work surface for pastry-making). Warm hands can ruin the rubbing-in process, so before starting to make pastry, hold your hands under cold running water to ensure they keep cool, then dry them quickly. Work quickly and lightly, using only your fingertips and lifting the mixture high above the bowl to aerate it. After rubbing-in, form the dough into a ball with one hand only, taking great care not to overwork the mixture or it will become oily – simply gather it together loosely without pressing and kneading. Once formed into a ball, cover with cling flim or foil and chill in the refrigerator for at least 30 minutes to let the dough cool and relax.

To roll out rich doughs, place the ball on a lightly floured surface and flatten with a floured rolling pin. Shape by rolling in short sharp strokes, working from the centre outwards, taking care not to press down too hard. Turn the shape round frequently as you roll, but do not turn the dough over. Transfer to the flan tin or ring by carefully lifting on to the rolling pin, then ease into the tin with the fingertips, making sure you do not stretch the dough. (If the dough is too sticky to handle it is often easier not to roll it out at all, but simply to place the ball of dough in the tin or ring and press it gently into shape with the fingertips. Patch any cracks with trimmings, pressing them neatly to seal. To help prevent rich doughs shrinking chill again for about 30 minutes before baking.

FIRST COURSES

Invariably simple, at least for family meals, the French serve delicious first courses to whet the appetite in preparation for what is to follow. A simple salad, one or two cooked vegetables tossed in a well seasoned dressing, maybe a slice or two of pâté, ham, salami or other cooked meat from the local charcuterie, a fillet of smoked fish – these are the kinds of things you might be offered in a French home. The first courses and soups in this chapter are more likely to be served at dinner parties or on other special occasions, but many will serve as light supper dishes for fewer people, and the hearty type of soups are often eaten as meals in themselves, with chunks of fresh French bread.

Salade parisienne
Parisian salad

Metric	*Imperial*
100 g button mushrooms, halved or sliced if large	*4 oz button mushrooms, halved or sliced if large*
175 g piece garlic sausage, diced	*6 oz piece garlic sausage, diced*
100 g Saint Paulin or Tomme de Savoie cheese, rind removed, diced	*4 oz Saint Paulin or Tomme de Savoie cheese, rind removed, diced*
50 g shelled walnut halves (optional)	*2 oz shelled walnut halves (optional)*
1 lettuce, separated into leaves	*1 lettuce, separated into leaves*

Dressing:	*Dressing:*
6 × 15 ml spoons walnut oil	*6 tablespoons walnut oil*
2 × 15 ml spoons cider vinegar	*2 tablespoons cider vinegar*
2 × 5 ml spoons light Dijon mustard	*2 teaspoons light Dijon mustard*
salt	*salt*
freshly ground black pepper	*freshly ground black pepper*

Preparation time: 10 minutes

Walnut oil is available in bottles from good delicatessens. Alternatively, make your own by crushing 50 g/2 oz shelled walnuts in a mortar and pestle, or with a rolling pin, and adding 120 ml/4 fl oz olive oil.

Put all the ingredients for the dressing in a screw-topped jar, and shake well to mix.
Put the mushrooms, garlic sausage, cheese and walnuts in a bowl, pour over the dressing and toss gently. Arrange the lettuce leaves around the bottom and sides of a salad bowl. Spoon the salad mixture in the centre and serve immediately.

Salade parisienne; Tomates farcies aux crevettes

Tomates farcies aux crevettes
Tomatoes stuffed with prawns

Metric
8 medium tomatoes
salt
225 g peeled prawns, defrosted if frozen
2 hard-boiled eggs, finely chopped
2 × 15 ml spoons finely chopped parsley
finely grated rind of 1 lemon
freshly ground black pepper
8 unpeeled prawns, to garnish (optional)

Aïoli (garlic mayonnaise):
2 large garlic cloves, peeled
1 × 1.25 ml spoon light Dijon or other French mustard
1 egg yolk
300 ml olive oil

Imperial
8 medium tomatoes
salt
8 oz peeled prawns, defrosted if frozen
2 hard-boiled eggs, finely chopped
2 tablespoons finely chopped parsley
finely grated rind of 1 lemon
freshly ground black pepper
8 unpeeled prawns, to garnish (optional)

Aïoli (garlic mayonnaise):
2 large garlic cloves, peeled
¼ teaspoon light Dijon or other French mustard
1 egg yolk
½ pint olive oil

Preparation time: 25–30 minutes

In France, a mortar and pestle are commonly used when making mayonnaise. An electric blender or food processor can be used, following the same instructions given here, but using 1 whole egg in addition to the egg yolk.

Cut the tops (stalk ends) off the tomatoes and reserve. Scoop out all the flesh and seeds from the insides of the tomatoes with a teaspoon, taking care not to break the shells. Sprinkle a little salt inside the tomatoes, then stand them upside down on a board and leave for 10–15 minutes to drain.

Meanwhile, make the aïoli. Put the garlic cloves in a mortar with 1 × 2.5 ml spoon/½ teaspoon salt. Crush the garlic and salt with a pestle, then work in the mustard and egg yolk. Add the olive oil a drop at a time until the mixture begins to thicken, then add the oil in a thin, steady stream until all is incorporated and the aïoli is very thick, working constantly with the pestle to amalgamate the egg yolk and oil. Set on one side.

Dry the prawns thoroughly with paper towels, then chop roughly. Fold into the aïoli with the chopped eggs, parsley and lemon rind. Add salt and pepper to taste.

Stand the tomatoes upright on a serving plate. Spoon the prawn mixture into them and place the reserved tops on the slant. Garnish each tomato with an unpeeled prawn, if using. Serve at room temperature.

Saumon fumé à la mousse de fromage
Stuffed smoked salmon rolls

Metric	Imperial
1 envelope (15 g) powdered gelatine	*1 envelope (½ oz) powdered gelatine*
3 × 15 ml spoons lemon juice	*3 tablespoons lemon juice*
1 × 15 ml spoon water	*1 tablespoon water*
225 g full-fat soft cheese	*8 oz full-fat soft cheese*
1 bunch spring onions, trimmed and finely chopped	*1 bunch spring onions, trimmed and finely chopped*
2 × 15 ml spoons chopped chives	*2 tablespoons chopped chives*
4 × 15 ml spoons thick mayonnaise or double cream, lightly whipped	*4 tablespoons thick mayonnaise or double cream, lightly whipped*
salt	*salt*
freshly ground black pepper	*freshly ground black pepper*
8 thin slices smoked salmon (total weight about 225 g)	*8 thin slices smoked salmon (total weight about 8 oz)*
2 lemons, cut into wedges, to serve	*2 lemons, cut into wedges, to serve*

Preparation time: 30 minutes, plus chilling

Sprinkle the gelatine over the lemon juice and water in a heatproof bowl. Leave until spongy, then place the bowl in a pan of gently simmering water. Heat gently until the gelatine has dissolved, stirring occasionally. Leave to cool slightly.

Meanwhile, put the cheese in a bowl and beat with a wooden spoon until soft. Beat in the spring onions and chives, then the mayonnaise or double cream and salt and pepper to taste.

Fold in the gelatine liquid until evenly blended, then cover and chill in the refrigerator until the mixture is firm, but not set.

Lay the salmon slices flat on a board or work surface. Divide the cheese mixture equally between them, placing it at one end of each slice, then rolling the salmon up around the filling as neatly as possible.

Place the salmon rolls on a serving platter and chill in the refrigerator for at least 4 hours, preferably overnight. Before serving, sprinkle with pepper and garnish with lemon wedges. Serve chilled.

Crème Du Barry
Cream of cauliflower soup

Metric	Imperial
40 g butter	*1½ oz butter*
1 onion, peeled and finely chopped	*1 onion, peeled and finely chopped*
1 × 450 g cauliflower, divided into florets	*1 × 1 lb cauliflower, divided into florets*
600 ml chicken stock	*1 pint chicken stock*
2 × 5 ml spoons freshly chopped chervil or 1 × 5 ml spoon dried chervil	*2 teaspoons freshly chopped chervil or 1 teaspoon dried chervil*
salt	*salt*
freshly ground black pepper	*freshly ground black pepper*
600 ml milk	*1 pint milk*

Preparation time: 15 minutes, plus cooling
Cooking time: about 40 minutes

This is a simpler version of the classic French soup of the same name.

Melt 25 g/1 oz butter in a heavy-based pan, add the onion and fry gently until soft. Add the cauliflower florets, reserving a few tiny sprigs for the garnish. Cook the cauliflower over gentle heat for about 5 minutes, stirring all the time until coated in the butter and onion.

Stir in the stock and bring to the boil. Lower the heat, add half the chervil, and salt and pepper to taste, then half cover with a lid. Simmer gently for 20 minutes until the cauliflower is tender, stirring occasionally.

Remove from the heat and leave to cool slightly, then purée in an electric blender or work through a sieve until smooth.

Return the purée to the rinsed-out pan and stir in the milk. Bring to just below boiling point, stirring constantly, then simmer gently for about 5 minutes. Check the consistency of the soup, stirring in a little extra milk if it seems too thick.

Meanwhile, melt the remaining butter in a separate pan, add the reserved cauliflower sprigs and toss gently in the butter for 1–2 minutes.

Taste and adjust the seasoning of the soup, then pour into a warmed tureen or 4 individual bowls. Place a few cauliflower sprigs in each serving, then sprinkle with the remaining chervil. Alternatively, leave a few pieces of chervil whole for garnishing. Serve immediately.

Saumon fumé à la mousse de fromage; Crème Du Barry; Crème de courgettes au brie

Crème de courgettes au brie
Courgette and Brie cream soup

Metric
350 g courgettes, sliced
3 small potatoes, peeled
  and quartered
1 × 15 ml spoon olive oil
salt
100 g soft ripe Brie
  cheese, rind removed,
  diced
freshly ground white
  pepper
4 × 15 ml spoons double
  cream

Imperial
12 oz courgettes, sliced
3 small potatoes, peeled
  and quartered
1 tablespoon olive oil
salt
4 oz soft ripe Brie
  cheese, rind removed,
  diced
freshly ground white
  pepper
4 tablespoons double
  cream

Preparation time: 15 minutes, plus cooling
Cooking time: about 30 minutes

Put the courgettes in a large pan with the potatoes, oil and 1 × 5 ml spoon/1 teaspoon salt. Cover with water and stir well. Bring to the boil, then lower the heat and simmer for 15–20 minutes until the potatoes are tender. Leave to cool slightly.

Remove the courgettes and potatoes with a slotted spoon and place in an electric blender. Add the diced Brie and 300 ml/½ pint of the cooking liquid from the vegetables. Blend until smooth.

Return the mixture to the rinsed-out pan and add a further 150 ml/¼ pint cooking liquid from the vegetables. Bring to just below boiling point, stirring all the time, then add salt and pepper to taste. Check the consistency of the soup and add more vegetable liquid or water if it is too thick.

Pour into 4 warmed individual bowls and swirl a spoonful of cream into each. Serve immediately with French bread.

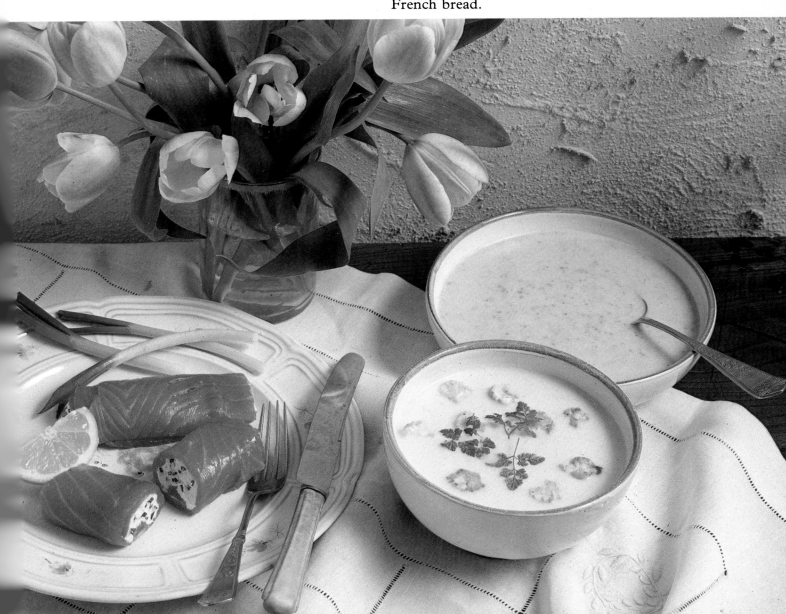

Champignons Kiev
Fried mushrooms with garlic butter

Metric
24 cup mushrooms
100 g unsalted butter,
    softened
2–3 garlic cloves, peeled
    and crushed with
    1 × 2.5 ml spoon salt
2 × 15 ml spoons finely
    chopped parsley
freshly ground black
    pepper
2 eggs
75 dried breadcrumbs
vegetable oil for deep-
    frying

Imperial
24 cup mushrooms
4 oz unsalted butter,
    softened
2–3 garlic cloves, peeled
    and crushed with
    ½ teaspoon salt
2 tablespoons finely
    chopped parsley
freshly ground black
    pepper
2 eggs
3 oz dried breadcrumbs
vegetable oil for deep-
    frying

Preparation time: about 1 hour, plus chilling
Cooking time: about 20 minutes

It is important to use deep, cup-shaped mushrooms so that they will contain the garlic butter. Cup mushrooms are the medium-sized cultivated mushrooms as opposed to the small button or large open (flat) mushrooms.

Wipe the mushrooms clean with a damp cloth, but do not wash or peel them. Carefully pull out the stalks, keeping the caps whole. Dry the caps with paper towels. Chop the stalks very finely.
Put the softened butter in a bowl with the chopped mushroom stalks, garlic, parsley and pepper to taste. Beat together well. Spoon into the mushroom cavities, then sandwich the mushrooms together in pairs. Use cocktail sticks to secure them.
Beat the eggs lightly in a bowl and spread the breadcrumbs out on a plate. Dip the mushroom pairs one at a time into the beaten egg, then roll them in the breadcrumbs. Repeat this process once more until the mushrooms are evenly and thoroughly coated. Chill in the refrigerator for at least 1 hour.
Heat the oil in a deep-fat fryer to 190°C/375°F, or until a stale bread cube turns golden in 40–50 seconds. Fry the mushrooms a few at a time for about 5 minutes, turning them frequently with a slotted spoon until golden brown and crisp on all sides. Drain on paper towels and keep hot while frying the remainder. Remove the cocktail sticks and serve immediately.

Champignons Kiev; Salade de riz provençale

Salade de riz provençale
Provencal rice salad

Metric
450 g fresh mussels,
  scrubbed, with beards
  removed
225 g long-grain rice
900 ml water
pinch of saffron powder
  (optional)
salt
2 shallots or 1 small
  onion, peeled and
  finely chopped
½ red pepper, cored,
  seeded and finely
  chopped
½ green paper, cored,
  seeded and finely
  chopped
3 tomatoes, skinned,
  seeded and chopped
50 g black olives, halved,
  pitted and chopped

Dressing:
2 garlic cloves, peeled
  and crushed with
  1 × 2.5 ml spoon salt
1 egg yolk
6 × 15 ml spoons olive oil
2 × 15 ml spoons wine
  vinegar
2 × 15 ml spoons Pernod
  (optional)
2 × 15 ml spoons freshly
  chopped parsley
freshly ground black
  pepper

Imperial
1 lb fresh mussels,
  scrubbed, with beards
  removed
8 oz long-grain rice
1½ pints water
pinch of saffron powder
  (optional)
salt
2 shallots or 1 small
  onion, peeled and
  finely chopped
½ red pepper, cored,
  seeded and finely
  chopped
½ green pepper, cored,
  seeded and finely
  chopped
3 tomatoes, skinned,
  seeded and chopped
2 oz black olives, halved,
  pitted and chopped

Dressing:
2 garlic cloves, peeled
  and crushed with
  ½ teaspoon salt
1 egg yolk
6 tablespoons olive oil
2 tablespoons wine
  vinegar
2 tablespoons Pernod
  (optional)
2 tablespoons freshly
  chopped parsley
freshly ground black
  pepper

Preparation time: about 45 minutes, plus soaking
Cooking time: 35–40 minutes

To save time, and when fresh mussels are not available, use frozen mussels. These are sold on the half shell by freezer centres and large supermarkets, and are precooked. Simply defrost them according to the package instructions and fold them straight into the salad.

Soak the fresh mussels in cold water for about 1 hour. Put the rice in a large pan with the water, saffron and a pinch of salt. Bring to the boil, stir once, then cover with a tight-fitting lid and lower the heat. Simmer gently for 15–20 minutes, until the rice is tender yet firm to the bite.
Meanwhile, drain the mussels and discard any which are open. Place the closed mussels in a large saucepan with a little water. Bring to the boil, cover and simmer for 10 minutes, shaking the pan frequently. Drain, and discard any unopened mussels. Remove the mussels from their shells, reserving a few in their shells for the garnish.
Drain the cooked rice and make the dressing. Put the garlic and egg yolk in a bowl and whisk with a fork. Whisk in the oil gradually, then the wine vinegar and Pernod, if using. Add the chopped parsley, and salt and pepper to taste.
Turn the warm rice into a large salad bowl and pour in the dressing. Fork the dressing evenly through the rice, then leave until cold.
Add the vegetables and olives to the rice and fork in gently. Fold in the shelled mussels, slicing them in halves or quarters if they are large. Taste and adjust the seasoning. Serve at room temperature, garnished with the reserved mussels left in their shells.

Variation:
Instead of mussels, use 1 × 200 g/7 oz can tuna, drained and flaked, and 1 × 50 g/2 oz can anchovies, drained, soaked in milk for 20 minutes, then drained and chopped.

Garbure
Bean and cabbage soup

Metric	Imperial
225 g dried haricot beans, soaked in cold water overnight	8 oz dried haricot beans, soaked in cold water overnight
450 g belly pork rashers	1 lb belly pork rashers
1 small ham knuckle	1 small ham knuckle
1 bouquet garni	1 bouquet garni
3 carrots, peeled and thickly sliced	3 carrots, peeled and thickly sliced
2 leeks, thickly sliced	2 leeks, thickly sliced
2 turnips, peeled and thickly sliced	2 turnips, peeled and thickly sliced
1 onion, peeled and sliced	1 onion, peeled and sliced
3 garlic cloves, peeled	3 garlic cloves, peeled
1 × 1.25 ml spoon cayenne pepper	¼ teaspoon cayenne pepper
salt	salt
450 g firm cabbage, sliced	1 lb firm cabbage, sliced
freshly chopped parsley, to garnish	freshly chopped parsley, to garnish

Preparation time: about 30 minutes, plus soaking
Cooking time: 1¾ hours

Garbure is a main course soup, popular in country districts. You may use salt pork if preferred (in which case it should be soaked in cold water overnight). The vegetables used can be varied according to the time of year—in summer, for example, fresh French beans may be substituted for the dried haricot beans. Potatoes can be included for a thicker consistency.

Drain the beans and place in a large pan with the pork, ham knuckle and bouquet garni. Cover with fresh cold water and bring to the boil, skimming off any scum. Lower the heat, half cover with a lid and simmer for 30 minutes.
Add the vegetables (except the cabbage), the garlic, cayenne, and salt to taste, then add enough cold water to cover all the ingredients. Bring to the boil, then lower the heat, half cover and simmer for 1 hour until all the meat and vegetables are very soft. Stir in the cabbage and continue cooking a further 15 minutes.
Remove the pork and ham from the soup, then cut the meat into small pieces, discarding all bones and rinds. Discard the bouquet garni, then return the meat to the pan and heat through, adding more water if the soup is too thick. Taste and adjust the seasoning, then serve hot, sprinkled with parsley.
Serves 4–6

Soupe à la bière
Beer soup

Metric	Imperial
25 g butter	1 oz butter
1 × 15 ml spoon olive oil	1 tablespoon olive oil
2 large onions, peeled and finely sliced	2 large onions, peeled and finely sliced
pinch of soft brown sugar	pinch of soft brown sugar
75 g fresh white breadcrumbs	3 oz fresh white breadcrumbs
600 ml light ale	1 pint light ale
600 ml chicken stock or water	1 pint chicken stock or water
salt	salt
freshly ground black pepper	freshly ground black pepper

To finish:	To finish:
4 slices French bread	4 slices French bread
4 × 5 ml spoons brandy (optional)	4 teaspoons brandy (optional)
about 50 g Gruyère or Parmesan cheese, finely grated	about 2 oz Gruyère or Parmesan cheese, finely grated

Preparation time: about 25 minutes, plus cooling
Cooking time: about 55 minutes

In the northern regions of France bordering on Belgium, beer is as popular a drink as wine is in other parts of France. Since French beers are not available in Britain, a light ale is our nearest equivalent.
Use the Parmesan cheese for a sharper flavour.

Melt the butter with the oil in a heavy-based pan, add the onions. Cover and cook gently for 15 minutes, stirring and checking that they do not burn.
When the onions are soft and lightly coloured, sprinkle in the sugar. Stir for 1–2 minutes, then add the breadcrumbs. Stir again for a few minutes until lightly coloured, then stir in the light ale and chicken stock or water with salt and pepper to taste.
Bring to the boil, then lower the heat, half cover the pan and simmer gently for 30 minutes, stirring occasionally. Leave to cool slightly.
Purée the soup in an electric blender or work in a mouli-legumes (vegetable mill) until smooth. Return the purée to the rinsed out pan and bring to just below boiling point, stirring constantly. Simmer gently for about 5 minutes, then check the consistency, stirring in a little water if it seems too thick. To finish, place 1 slice of bread in each of 4 warmed individual bowls. Pour the soup into the bowls, then sprinkle 1 × 5 ml spoon/1 teaspoon brandy into each serving, if using. Serve immediately, with the grated cheese handed separately.

Goujons de sole au fromage
Deep-fried sole with cheese

Preparation time: about 45 minutes, plus chilling
Cooking time: 15–20 minutes

Make the breadcrumbs from bread that is stale (at least 2 days old) or they will not adhere to the egg. If sole is unavailable use plaice instead.

Cut each sole fillet horizontally in half to make 16 strips of fish. Sprinkle with salt and pepper. Cut the cheese into strips or cubes the same width as the fish. Place 1 strip of cheese at one end of a strip of fish, then roll the fish up round the cheese. Secure with 1 or 2 wooden cocktail sticks. Repeat with the remaining fish and cheese.

Coat the fish parcels lightly in flour. Put the beaten eggs in a wide, shallow bowl. Spread the breadcrumbs out on a plate. Dip the fish in the egg, then in the breadcrumbs until evenly coated. Repeat these layers once more to ensure that the fish and cheese are completely covered, pressing the coating on firmly to adhere. Chill in the refrigerator for at least 30 minutes.

Heat the oil in a deep-fat frier to 190°C/375°F or until a stale bread cube turns golden in 40–50 seconds. Deep-fry the goujons in batches for 3–5 minutes until golden brown and crisp, turning them over during frying. Drain on paper towels and keep hot while frying the remainder. Serve at once, with lemon wedges and tartare sauce.

Metric
2 Dover or lemon sole, divided into 8 fillets, skinned
75–100 g Gruyère cheese
about 2 × 15 ml spoons plain flour, for coating
2 eggs, beaten
100–175 g white breadcrumbs
salt
freshly ground black pepper
vegetable oil, for deep-frying

To serve:
lemon wedges
tartare sauce

Imperial
2 Dover or lemon sole, divided into 8 fillets, skinned
3–4 oz Gruyère cheese
about 2 tablespoons plain flour, for coating
2 eggs, beaten
4–6 oz white breadcrumbs
salt
freshly ground black pepper
vegetable oil, for deep-frying

To serve:
lemon wedges
tartare sauce

Garbure; Soupe à la bière; Goujons de sole au fromage

Pâtes d'anchois
Anchovy pastries

Metric
1 × 50 g can anchovies, drained and soaked in milk for 20 minutes
2 hard-boiled eggs, very finely chopped
2 tomatoes, skinned, seeded and very finely chopped
2 × 15 ml spoons very finely chopped parsley
2 × 5 ml spoons tomato purée
1 × 2.5 ml spoon anchovy essence (optional)
freshly ground black pepper
1 × 400 g packet frozen puff pastry, defrosted
1 small egg, beaten, to glaze
cayenne pepper

Imperial
1 × 2 oz can anchovies, drained and soaked in milk for 20 minutes
2 hard-boiled eggs, very finely chopped
2 tomatoes, skinned, seeded and very finely chopped
2 tablespoons very finely chopped parsley
2 teaspoons tomato purée
½ teaspoon anchovy essence (optional)
freshly ground black pepper
1 × 14 oz packet frozen puff pastry, defrosted
1 small egg, beaten, to glaze
cayenne pepper

Preparation time: about 50 minutes, plus soaking
Cooking time: 15 minutes
Oven: 200°C, 400°F, Gas Mark 6

Drain the anchovies, pat dry with paper towels, then chop roughly. Put the anchovies in a bowl with the chopped eggs, tomatoes and parsley, the tomato purée, anchovy essence, and pepper to taste. Mix thoroughly, then set aside.

Roll out half the pastry thinly on a floured surface, then cut into 14–16 'fish' shapes, each one about 10 cm/4 inches long and about 4 cm/1½ inches at the widest point. (If you find it helpful use a paper pattern.) Spread a spoonful of the anchovy mixture on each piece of pastry, piling it up in the centre and leaving a narrow margin around the edge. Place the shapes on dampened baking sheets and brush the exposed edges of the pastry with water.

Roll out the remaining pastry and cut into the similar shapes, but a little larger, to make lids. Place over the anchovy filling and press the edges down firmly to seal. Brush with beaten egg, then make 3 slashes in the top of each pastry and sprinkle with a little cayenne.

Bake the pastries in a preheated oven for 15 minutes or until they are puffed up and golden brown. Transfer carefully with a spatula to a wire rack to cool for 5 minutes. Serve warm.
Makes 14–16

Chaussons
Spinach and cheese puffs

Metric
100 g frozen chopped spinach, defrosted
1 × 400 g packet frozen puff pastry, defrosted
100 g full-fat soft cheese flavoured with garlic and herbs
freshly ground black pepper
vegetable oil, for deep-frying
1 egg, beaten, to glaze

Imperial
4 oz frozen chopped spinach, defrosted
1 × 14 oz packet frozen puff pastry, defrosted
4 oz full-fat soft cheese flavoured with garlic and herbs
freshly ground black pepper
vegetable oil, for deep-frying
1 egg, beaten, to glaze

Preparation time: about 30 minutes
Cooking time: about 25 minutes

Put the spinach in a heavy-based pan and cook over a low heat until completely dry, stirring frequently. Leave to cool.

Meanwhile, roll out the pastry thinly on a floured surface and cut into about 20 × 7.5 cm/3 inch circles. Beat the cheese in a bowl until soft, then beat in the spinach and pepper to taste. Put about 1 × 5 ml spoon/1 teaspoon spinach and cheese filling in the centre of each pastry circle and fold the pastry over. Pinch the edges together at the top to seal.

Heat the oil in a deep-fat fryer to 190°C/375°F or until a stale bread cube turns golden in 40–50 seconds. Dip the chaussons in the beaten egg until evenly coated, then deep-fry a few at a time for 3–4 minutes until puffed up and golden. Remove with a slotted spoon and drain on paper towels. Keep hot while frying the remainder. Serve at once, using cocktail sticks, if preferred.
Makes about 20

Moules farcies à la crème
Stuffed mussels baked with cream

Preparation time: about 45 minutes, plus soaking
Cooking time: 55 minutes
Oven: 190°C, 375°F, Gas Mark 5

Metric
48 mussels, scrubbed,
    and beards removed
150 ml dry white wine
150 ml water
1 bouquet garni
100 g unsalted butter
2 shallots or 1 small
    onion, peeled and very
    finely chopped
1–2 garlic cloves,
    peeled and crushed
    with 1 × 2.5 ml spoon
    salt
175 g button mushrooms,
    very finely chopped
2 × 15 ml spoons freshly
    chopped parsley
75 g fresh white bread-
    crumbs
150 ml double cream
freshly ground black
    pepper
about 2 × 15 ml spoons
    grated Parmesan cheese
    (optional)

Imperial
48 mussels, scrubbed,
    and beards removed
¼ pint dry white wine
¼ pint water
1 bouquet garni
4 oz unsalted butter
2 shallots or 1 small
    onion, peeled and very
    finely chopped
1–2 garlic cloves,
    peeled and crushed
    with ½ teaspoon
    salt
6 oz button mushrooms,
    very finely chopped
2 tablespoons freshly
    chopped parsley
3 oz fresh white bread-
    crumbs
¼ pint double cream
freshly ground black
    pepper
about 2 tablespoons
    grated Parmesan cheese
    (optional)

This is an ideal dish for using frozen mussels on the half shell. Simply defrost, chop and stuff them, then bake in a sauce made from half white wine and half fish or chicken stock.

Soak the mussels in cold water for about 1 hour. Drain the mussels and discard any which are open. Place the closed mussels in a large saucepan with the wine, water and bouquet garni. Bring to the boil, cover with a tight-fitting lid and simmer for 10 minutes, shaking the pan frequently during this time. Meanwhile, melt 25 g/1 oz butter in a pan, add the shallots, or onion, and garlic and fry gently until soft and lightly coloured. Add the mushrooms and fry for a further 1–2 minutes, stirring constantly, then transfer to a bowl.

Drain the mussels, reserving the cooking liquid. Discard the bouquet garni and any mussels which have not opened. Remove all the mussels from their shells, reserving half the shells. Chop the mussels finely, then add to the mushroom mixture with the remaining butter, the parsley and breadcrumbs. Beat well to mix, then stir in 2 × 15 ml spoons/2 tablespoons cream, and pepper to taste.

Divide the mixture equally between the reserved mussel shells, pressing it firmly into each one. Place the shells, stuffed sides facing upward, in individual ovenproof serving dishes.

Strain the reserved cooking liquid and make up to 300 ml/½ pint with wine or water, if necessary. Pour into a clean pan, stir in the remaining cream and pepper to taste, then bring to the boil, stirring. Pour the sauce carefully around the stuffed mussels, then sprinkle each mussel with a little Parmesan cheese, if using. Bake in a preheated oven for 30 minutes, then serve immediately.

Pâtes d'anchois; Chaussons; Moules farcies à la crème

Crudités avec anchoïade
Raw vegetable hors d'oeuvre

Metric
1 head celery, trimmed,
with sticks halved
and cut into even
lengths
1 small cauliflower,
divided into florets
4 carrots, peeled and
cut into thin sticks
½ cucumber, cut into
sticks, with seeds
removed
1 large red or green
pepper, cored, seeded
and sliced into rings
1 bunch radishes, topped
and tailed

Anchoïade
(*Anchovy Dip*):
2 × 50 g cans anchovies
in oil, drained and
soaked in milk for 20
minutes
2 tomatoes, skinned,
seeded and chopped
2 garlic cloves, peeled
and crushed
1 × 15 ml spoon tomato
purée
2 × 15 ml spoons wine
vinegar
about 300 ml olive oil

Imperial
1 head celery, trimmed,
with sticks halved
and cut into even
lengths
1 small cauliflower,
divided into florets
4 carrots, peeled and
cut into thin sticks
½ cucumber, cut into
sticks, with seeds
removed
1 large red or green
pepper, cored, seeded,
and sliced into rings
1 bunch radishes, topped
and tailed

Anchoïade
(*Anchovy Dip*):
2 × 2 oz cans anchovies
in oil, drained and
soaked in milk for 20
minutes
2 tomatoes, skinned,
seeded and chopped
2 garlic cloves, peeled
and crushed
1 tablespoon tomato
purée
2 tablespoons wine
vinegar
about ½ pint olive oil

Preparation time: about 50 minutes, plus soaking

It is great fun to serve these crudités and dips for a dinner-party starter, either handing them round with drinks before guests sit down at the table, or serving them as a first course with everything arranged as a centrepiece in the middle of the table. Guests help themselves to the vegetables and a spoonful or two of dip and eat with their fingers. The selection of vegetables can vary according to personal taste and seasonal availability, as long as they are fresh and crisp. Serve the dip suggested here with either a thick homemade mayonnaise or Aïoli (page 9) for contrast. If you enjoy a stronger flavoured anchoïade, use 3 × 50 g/2 oz cans anchovies.

To prepare the anchoïade, drain the anchovies and pat dry with paper towels. Put the anchovies in an electric blender or food processor with the tomatoes, garlic, tomato purée and wine vinegar. Work to a smooth purée, then add the oil a drop at a time until the mixture begins to thicken, as when making mayonnaise. Continue adding the oil in a thin, steady stream until a thick, smooth paste is formed, then turn into a serving bowl. Cover and leave to stand at room temperature until serving time.

To serve, arrange the prepared vegetables in groups in a large salad bowl or basket, with the dip placed around in separate serving bowls or place a bowl of the dip in the centre of a large tray or platter and arrange the groups of vegetables around the outside. Serve immediately the vegetables are prepared or they will lose their crispness.

Tartelettes au chèvre; Crudités avec anchoïade

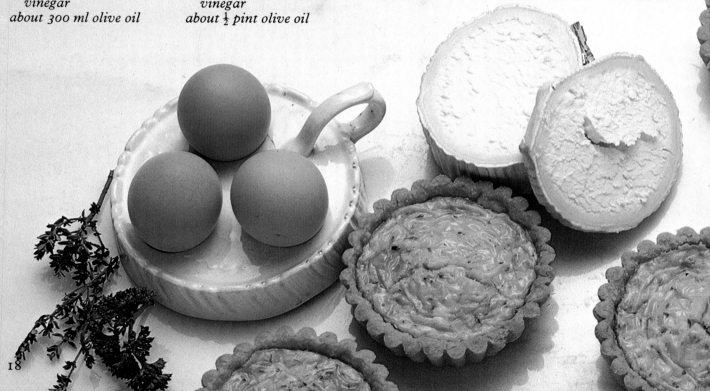

Tartelettes au chèvre
Goat's cheese tartlets

Metric
125 g plain flour
pinch of salt
100 g butter, chilled
1 egg yolk
1 × 5 ml spoon water
*a little beaten egg
    white*

Filling:
*225 g chèvre (goat's milk
    cheese), rind removed*
2 eggs, beaten
*2 × 15 ml spoons brandy
    (optional)*
*1 × 5 ml spoon freshly
    chopped thyme or
    1 × 2.5 ml spoon dried
    thyme*
*1 × 5 ml spoon freshly
    chopped marjoram or
    1 × 2.5 ml spoon dried
    marjoram*
*freshly ground black
    pepper*

Imperial
5 oz plain flour
pinch of salt
4 oz butter, chilled
1 egg yolk
1 teaspoon water
*a little beaten egg
    white*

Filling:
*8 oz chèvre (goat's milk
    cheese), rind removed*
2 eggs, beaten
*2 tablespoons brandy
    (optional)*
*1 teaspoon freshly
    chopped thyme or
    ½ teaspoon dried
    thyme*
*1 teaspoon freshly
    chopped marjoram or
    ½ teaspoon dried
    marjoram*
*freshly ground black
    pepper*

Preparation time: 30 minutes, plus chilling
Cooking time: 25–30 minutes
Oven: 190°C, 375°F, Gas Mark 5

Chèvre, or goat's milk cheese, is available at good Continental delicatessens and some large supermarkets. It makes a strong, flavoursome filling for these tartlets which can be served on their own as a starter or with a selection of salads for lunchtime or a picnic.

To make the pastry, sift the flour and salt into a bowl. Cut the butter into the flour in small pieces, then rub in lightly with the fingertips. Mix the egg yolk and water together, then stir into the flour mixture with a round-bladed knife until the mixture draws together. Form into a smooth ball with one hand, then chill in the refrigerator for 30 minutes.

Meanwhile, make the filling. Put the cheese in a bowl and beat with a wooden spoon until soft and creamy. Beat in the remaining filling ingredients with pepper to taste and set aside.

Roll out the dough on a floured surface and use to line 4 loose-bottomed 10 cm/4 inch flan tins or tartlet moulds. Prick the base of the dough in several places with a fork, then line with foil or greaseproof paper and fill with baking beans.

Bake the pastry cases 'blind' in a preheated oven for 10 minutes, then remove the paper and beans and brush the base of the dough with beaten egg white. Return to the oven and bake for a further 5 minutes. Remove the sides of the tins, then pour the prepared filling into the pastry cases. Bake for 10–15 minutes until the filling is set. Serve warm.

Avocat au crabe
Baked avocado stuffed with crab

Metric
25 g butter
25 g plain flour
300 ml warm milk
salt
1 × 1.25 ml spoon cayenne
  pepper
225 g fresh or frozen
  crabmeat, flaked
2 large ripe avocado pears
juice of ½ lemon

Imperial
1 oz butter
1 oz plain flour
½ pint warm milk
salt
¼ teaspoon cayenne
  pepper
8 oz fresh or frozen
  crabmeat, flaked
2 large ripe avocado pears
juice of ½ lemon

To finish:
25–50 g Gruyère cheese,
  grated
a little cayenne pepper

To finish:
1–2 oz Gruyère cheese,
  grated
a little cayenne pepper

Preparation time: 25 minutes
Cooking time: 20–25 minutes
Oven: 180°C, 350°F, Gas Mark 4

Melt the butter in a pan, stir in the flour and cook for 1–2 minutes, stirring all the time. Remove from the heat and gradually add the milk, beating vigorously after each addition. When all the milk is incorporated, return to the heat and bring slowly to the boil, beating constantly. Lower the heat and simmer until thick, then stir in salt to taste and the cayenne. Remove from the heat, then fold in the flaked crabmeat. Set aside. Halve the avocados, remove the stones and sprinkle the exposed flesh with the lemon juice. Spoon the crab sauce into the avocado cavities and over the top to cover the flesh completely. Stand the avocado shells facing upright in an ovenproof dish. (If they are difficult to stand upright, place each one on a base of crumpled kitchen foil.) Sprinkle the tops with grated cheese, and a little cayenne pepper, then bake in a preheated oven for 15–20 minutes. Transfer carefully to individual serving bowls and serve immediately.

Champignons de Dijon
Mushrooms marinated in mustard

Metric
450 g small white button
  mushrooms
juice of ½ lemon
4 × 15 ml spoons light
  Dijon mustard
4 × 5 ml spoons freshly
  chopped tarragon or
  2 × 5 ml spoons dried
  tarragon
salt
freshly ground black
  pepper
120 ml soured cream
lettuce leaves, to serve

Imperial
1 lb small white button
  mushrooms
juice of ½ lemon
4 tablespoons light Dijon
  mustard
4 teaspoons freshly
  chopped tarragon or
  2 teaspoons dried
  tarragon
salt
freshly ground black
  pepper
4 fl oz soured cream
lettuce leaves, to serve

Preparation time: about 25 minutes, plus marinating

Dijon mustard is a smooth-textured French mustard with a mild flavour. The quantity in this recipe can be adjusted according to taste, but the flavour of the mustard should be predominant. In France, crème fraîche would be used for the dressing rather than soured cream. It is a fresh cream with a high butterfat content and a sharp, slightly cheesy flavour. Soured cream is a good equivalent.

Wipe the mushrooms with a damp cloth, but do not wash them. Halve or slice any large mushrooms.
Put the mushrooms in a bowl and sprinkle with the lemon juice. Add the mustard, half the tarragon, and salt and pepper to taste, then stir gently until the mushrooms are evenly coated in the mustard. Cover and leave to marinate for up to 4 hours.
Line 4 individual serving bowls with lettuce leaves and sprinkle with salt and pepper. Fold all but 4 × 15 ml spoons/4 tablespoons soured cream into the mushrooms, taste and adjust the seasoning, then divide the mixture equally between the dishes.
Top each serving with a spoonful of soured cream and sprinkle with the remaining tarragon. Serve immediately, with hot garlic bread.

Avocat au crabe; Champignons Dijon; Salade verte au roquefort

Salade verte au roquefort
Green salad with Roquefort dressing

Metric
50 g Roquefort cheese
6 × 15 ml spoons olive oil
2 × 15 ml spoons garlic
   vinegar
2 × 15 ml spoons double
   cream (optional)
freshly ground black
   pepper
½ Webb's or Iceberg
   lettuce, shredded
¼ curly endive, separated
   into sprigs

Imperial
2 oz Roquefort cheese
6 tablespoons olive oil
2 tablespoons garlic
   vinegar
2 tablespoons double
   cream (optional)
freshly ground black
   pepper
½ Webb's or Iceberg
   lettuce, shredded
¼ curly endive, separated
   into sprigs

Preparation time: about 20 minutes

Roquefort cheese is available at Continental delicatessens, and some large supermarkets. Otherwise, another French blue cheese with a creamy texture can be substituted, such as Bresse Bleu or blue Brie.

To make the dressing, crumble the cheese into a bowl, then mash with a fork, adding the oil a drop at a time to make a paste. Whisk in the vinegar and cream (if using), then add pepper to taste. Set aside in a cool place.

Put the lettuce and endive in a large wide salad bowl and toss until evenly mixed.

Whisk the dressing vigorously, taste and adjust the seasoning, then pour over the salad. Toss with salad servers until the salad is evenly coated with the dressing. Serve immediately.

PÂTÉS AND TERRINES

The French are masters in the art of pâté making – from the coarse-textured pork and liver pâtés heavily laced with garlic, to their elegant and subtly-flavoured fish terrines. The French pâtés and terrines you find in your local shops rarely match the flavour of those made at home, and though they may seem time-consuming to make, your efforts will be well rewarded when you proudly present them to family and friends. Serve the lighter ones as a first course with hot toast, Melba toast or crispbreads and crackers; the more substantial mixtures are best as meals in themselves, for lunches, suppers and picnics with fresh French bread, a bottle of wine and maybe a salad or two.

Top: Pâté de campagne; Below: Terrine de canard à l'orange

Terrine de canard à l'orange
Duck and orange terrine

Metric	*Imperial*
1 × 2–2.25 kg oven-ready duck	1 × 4½–5 lb oven-ready duck
2 × 15 ml spoons brandy	2 tablespoons brandy
225 g chicken livers	8 oz chicken livers
225 g pork sausagemeat	8 oz pork sausagemeat
50 g fresh white breadcrumbs	2 oz fresh white breadcrumbs
finely grated rind and juice of 1 orange	finely grated rind and juice of 1 orange
6 juniper berries, crushed	6 juniper berries, crushed
1 × 1.25 ml spoon ground allspice	¼ teaspoon ground allspice
salt	salt
freshly ground black pepper	freshly ground black pepper
1 egg, beaten, to bind	1 egg, beaten, to bind
1 orange, thinly sliced	1 orange, thinly sliced

Preparation time: 1–1¼ hours, plus chilling
Cooking time: 1½ hours
Oven: 160°C, 325°F, Gas Mark 3

Bone the duck, removing as much meat as possible from the bones by scraping them with a small, sharp knife. Cut 75–100 g/3–4 oz breast meat into thin slivers, place in a dish and pour over the brandy.
Mince all the remaining duck meat with the liver from the duck and the chicken livers. Place in a bowl with the sausagemeat, mix well, then add the breadcrumbs, orange rind and juice, crushed juniper, allspice, and salt and pepper to taste. Mix well again. Drain the brandy from the slivers of duck and stir the brandy into the mixture. Bind with beaten egg.
Brush a 900 ml/1½ pint terrine or mould lightly with oil. Arrange the orange slices neatly in the base, then spoon in half the minced mixture, packing it down well. Arrange the drained slivers of duck breast evenly over the top, then spoon in the remaining minced mixture and press down firmly.
Cover the mould with lightly oiled foil, then stand it in a bain marie (roasting tin half filled with hot water). Cook in a preheated oven for 1½ hours or until the juices run faintly pink and the terrine has shrunk away from the sides of the mould.
Remove from the bain marie and pour off the excess fat and juices that have collected in the bottom of the mould. Leave until cold, then chill in the refrigerator overnight until firm.
Turn out the terrine carefully on to a serving plate and serve chilled, cut into thick slices.
Serves 6–8

Pâté de campagne
Country-style pâté

Metric	*Imperial*
8 streaky bacon rashers, rinds removed	8 streaky bacon rashers, rinds removed
450 g pig's liver	1 lb pig's liver
450 g chicken livers	1 lb chicken livers
225 g pork back fat or fatty belly pork	8 oz pork back fat or fatty belly pork
175 g fresh white breadcrumbs	6 oz fresh white breadcrumbs
2 eggs, beaten	2 eggs, beaten
2 garlic cloves, peeled and crushed with 1 × 2.5 ml spoon salt	2 garlic cloves, peeled and crushed with ½ teaspoon salt
75 ml red wine	3 fl oz red wine
2 × 15 ml spoons brandy (optional)	2 tablespoons brandy (optional)
2 × 5 ml spoons freshly chopped thyme or 1 × 5 ml spoon dried thyme	2 teaspoons freshly chopped thyme or 1 teaspoon dried thyme
40–50 g pistachio nuts, coarsely chopped	1½–2 oz pistachio nuts, coarsely chopped
freshly ground black pepper	freshly ground black pepper

Preparation time: 30 minutes, plus cooling and chilling
Cooking time: 2½ hours
Oven: 160°C, 325°F, Gas Mark 3

This is a moist, coarse-textured pâté, perfect spread on chunky slices of French bread.

Brush the inside of a 1 kg/2 lb loaf tin or a 1.2 litre/2 pint earthenware dish with oil. Stretch the bacon rashers with the blade of a knife, then use to line the base and sides of the tin or dish. Set aside.
Mince together the pig's liver, chicken livers and pork, then place in a bowl. Add the remaining ingredients with pepper to taste, and stir well.
Spoon into the prepared tin and level the surface. Cover with foil, then stand the tin in a bain marie (roasting tin half filled with hot water). Bake in a preheated oven for 2½ hours until the pâté and the juices are just faintly pink.
Remove from the oven and pour off the excess fat from the tin, leave until cool, then place heavy weights on top of the foil to press the pâté into a firm shape for slicing. When completely cold, place in the refrigerator and chill overnight.
To serve, run the blade of a knife around the edge of the pâté to release the bacon from the sides of the tin, invert a serving plate on top of the tin, then turn out on to the plate. Serve chilled, cut into thick slices.
Serves 8–10

Jambon persillé
Ham and herbs in wine jelly

Metric

1 × 25 g packet aspic jelly
  powder
150 ml warm water
300 ml dry white wine
25 g butter
2 shallots or 1 small
  onion, peeled and very
  finely chopped
1–2 garlic cloves, peeled
  and crushed
25 g fresh parsley, very
  finely chopped
25 g fresh chervil or
  chives, very finely
  chopped
freshly ground black
  pepper
225–350 g cooked ham,
  diced
thick Aïoli (page 9), or
  plain mayonnaise, to
  serve

Imperial

1 × 1 oz packet aspic jelly
  powder
¼ pint warm water
½ pint dry white wine
1 oz butter
2 shallots or 1 small
  onion, peeled and very
  finely chopped
1–2 garlic cloves, peeled
  and crushed
1 oz fresh parsley, very
  finely chopped
1 oz fresh chervil or
  chives, very finely
  chopped
freshly ground black
  pepper
8–12 oz cooked ham,
  diced
thick Aïoli (page 9), or
  plain mayonnaise, to
  serve

Preparation time: about 30 minutes, plus chilling
Cooking time: 10 minutes

Dissolve the aspic jelly powder in the warm water and wine according to packet instructions, then leave until cold.

Meanwhile, melt the butter in a pan, add the shallots or onions and garlic, and fry gently until soft and lightly coloured. Remove from the heat, stir in the herbs and pepper, then stir into the liquid aspic jelly. Rinse out a 450 g/1 lb loaf tin with water. Pour in a little of the liquid aspic to cover the bottom of the tin, then chill in the refrigerator for about 30 minutes until just beginning to set.

Place about one-quarter of the ham pieces on top of the layer of aspic jelly, pressing it into the jelly slightly. Return to the refrigerator for a further 30 minutes or until completely set.

Pour another layer of aspic jelly over the ham and continue making and refrigerating these layers, finishing with a layer of jelly. If the jelly in the pan sets during this time, place the pan over gentle heat and stir until the jelly becomes liquid again.

Chill in the refrigerator overnight, then run a sharp knife around the top edge of the tin and unmould on to an inverted serving plate. Serve chilled, with mayonnaise or aïoli handed separately.
Serves 6

Jambon persillé; Galantine de poularde

Galantine de poularde
Boned stuffed chicken

Metric

1 × 1.5 kg oven-ready
  chicken
25 g butter
1 large onion, peeled and
  finely chopped
3 celery sticks, finely
  chopped
225 g chicken livers,
  roughly chopped
175 g button mushrooms,
  finely chopped
4 rashers back bacon, rind
  removed, roughly
  chopped
100 g fresh white
  breadcrumbs
2 × 15 ml spoons freshly
  chopped parsley
1 × 5 ml spoon dried
  mixed herbs
finely grated rind of 1
  lemon
salt
freshly ground black
  pepper
1 egg, beaten
1 garlic clove, peeled and
  halved
juice of ½ lemon

Imperial

1 × 3½ lb oven-ready
  chicken
1 oz butter
1 large onion, peeled and
  finely chopped
3 celery sticks, finely
  chopped
8 oz chicken livers,
  roughly chopped
6 oz button mushrooms,
  finely chopped
4 rashers back bacon, rind
  removed, roughly
  chopped
4 oz fresh white
  breadcrumbs
2 tablespoons freshly
  chopped parsley
1 teaspoon dried mixed
  mixed herbs
finely grated rind of 1
  lemon
salt
freshly ground black
  pepper
1 egg, beaten
1 garlic clove, peeled and
  halved
juice of ½ lemon

Preparation time: 1¼ hours, plus cooling and chilling
Cooking time: 2¼ hours
Oven: 180°C, 350°F, Gas Mark 4

Put the chicken on a board or work surface, breast side down. With a sharp, pointed knife, cut down the back of the bird, working from the neck to the tail end to expose the backbone. Scrape the flesh away from the carcass on one side of the backbone, keeping the knife facing towards the bones, not the flesh. Scrape down to the ball joint of the leg, then repeat on the other side of the carcass. Bone the legs by cutting through the sinew that joins them to the carcass, then scraping away all the flesh from the main leg bone, holding it firmly by the tip and working down to meet the carcass at the ball joint. Discard all bones from the legs. Bone the wings in the same way, cutting them through at the point where they join the body. Continue scraping away the flesh from the carcass and rib cage of the bird until the breastbone at the front is reached on both sides. Remove the carcass by carefully cutting along the breastbone, taking great care not to slit the thin flesh or skin over the breastbone.

Melt the butter in a pan, add the onion and celery and fry gently until lightly coloured. Stir in the chicken livers and mushrooms and fry for a further 5 minutes, stirring constantly, then transfer to a bowl. Add the bacon, breadcrumbs, parsley, herbs, lemon rind, and salt and pepper to taste. Mix well together, then bind with the beaten egg.

Lay the chicken flat on the board or work surface, skin side down. Place the stuffing mixture in the centre, shaping it with your hands into a neat rectangle. Wrap the chicken around the stuffing to make a neat parcel shape, tucking the legs and wings inside. Sew with thread or fine string, then place on a rack in a roasting tin. Rub the cut surfaces of the garlic all over the skin of the chicken, then sprinkle with the lemon juice and salt and pepper. Cover with foil and roast in a preheated oven for 2 hours, removing the foil for the last 30 minutes to brown the skin. Leave to go cold.

Wrap tightly in cling film or foil, then chill in the refrigerator overnight. Remove the thread or string, then slice neatly.
Serves 8

Terrine de légumes
Courgette and spinach terrine

Preparation time: about 1 hour
Cooking time: about 1¾ hours
Oven: 160°C, 325°F, Gas Mark 3

Metric
2 × 15 ml spoons olive oil
1 onion, peeled and thinly
   sliced
350 g courgettes, sliced
350 g frozen chopped
   spinach, thawed
salt
freshly ground black
   pepper
1 × 2.5 ml spoon freshly
   grated nutmeg
225 g curd cheese
50 g fresh white
   breadcrumbs
2 × 5 ml spoons freshly
   chopped basil or 1 × 5
   ml spoon dried basil
2 × 5 ml spoons freshly
   chopped marjoram or
   1 × 5 ml spoon dried
   marjoram (optional)
1 egg, beaten
melted butter for greasing
   tin

Imperial
2 tablespoons olive oil
1 onion, peeled and thinly
   sliced
12 oz courgettes, sliced
12 oz frozen chopped
   spinach, thawed
salt
freshly ground black
   pepper
½ teaspoon freshly
   grated nutmeg
8 oz curd cheese
2 oz fresh white
   breadcrumbs
2 teaspoons freshly
   chopped basil or 1
   teaspoon dried basil
2 teaspoons freshly
   chopped marjoram or
   1 teaspoon dried
   marjoram (optional)
1 egg, beaten
melted butter for greasing
   tin

Heat the oil in a frying pan, add the onion and courgettes and fry gently until soft and lightly coloured. Remove from the pan with a slotted spoon, then place in a single layer on paper towels. Cover with more paper towels and press to remove excess oil.

Put the spinach in a heavy-based pan and heat gently until thoroughly dry, stirring frequently. Remove from the heat and stir in generous amounts of salt, pepper and the nutmeg.

Work the courgettes and onions to a purée in an electric blender or vegetable mill, then place in a heavy-based pan and dry out over gentle heat as with the spinach. Transfer to a bowl, then beat in the curd cheese, breadcrumbs, basil, marjoram (if using), and salt and pepper to taste. Bind with the beaten egg.

Brush the inside of a 450 g/1 lb loaf tin liberally with butter, line the base with greaseproof paper, then brush with more butter. Put half the courgette mixture in the bottom of the tin, pressing it down firmly and levelling the surface. Spread the spinach in an even layer over the top, then press in the remaining courgette mixture.

Cover the tin with buttered foil, then stand it in a bain marie (roasting tin half filled with hot water) and bake in a preheated oven for 1¼ hours or until the mixture feels firm and set when a knife is inserted in the centre.

Remove from the bain marie, leave the terrine in the tin until completely cold, then chill in the refrigerator overnight until firm.

Loosen the sides of the terrine from the tin with a knife, then carefully turn out on to a serving plate and peel off the greaseproof paper. Serve chilled, cut into thick slices.
Serves 6

Terrine de légumes; Rillettes de porc

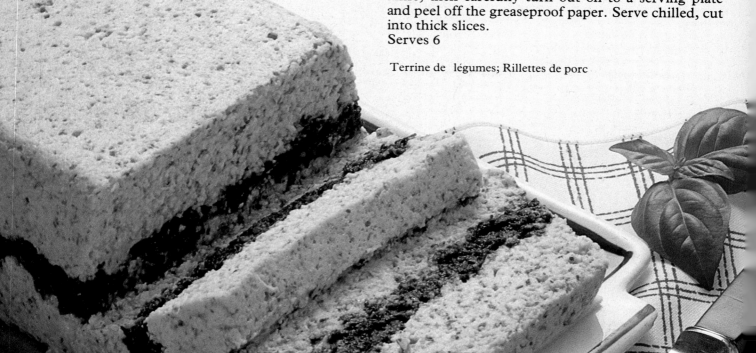

Rillettes de porc
Potted pork

Preparation time: about 45 minutes, plus chilling
Cooking time: 5 hours
Oven: 150°C, 300°F, Gas Mark 2;
 140°C, 275°F, Gas Mark 1

Metric	Imperial
1.25 kg belly pork, boned and rind removed	*2½ lb belly pork, boned and rind removed*
225 g pork back fat	*8 oz pork back fat*
120 ml water	*4 fl oz water*
2 garlic cloves, peeled and crushed with 1 × 2.5 ml spoon salt	*2 garlic cloves, peeled and crushed with ½ teaspoon salt*
1 × 2.5 ml spoon ground allspice	*½ teaspoon ground allspice*
freshly ground black pepper	*freshly bround black pepper*
1 bouquet garni	*1 bouquet garni*
1 bay leaf	*1 bay leaf*

Rillettes de porc are a familiar sight in charcuteries all over France, although they are a speciality of the Loire region. Although slightly tricky to prepare, served with crusty French bread they make an excellent lunch or picnic dish. The proportion of pork to fat can be varied according to individual taste.
Stored in the refrigerator with the seal of fat unbroken, rillettes keep for up to 2 weeks.

Cut the belly pork and back fat into small 5 mm/¼ inch cubes and place in an earthenware casserole dish. Add the water, garlic, allspice and pepper to taste. Stir well to mix, then bury the bouquet garni and bay leaf in the centre.
Cover the casserole tightly with a lid, then cook in a preheated oven for 2½ hours. Reduce the oven temperature and cook for a further 2½ hours. Stir occasionally to prevent the pork or fat sticking.
After 5 hours' cooking, tip the contents of the casserole into a sieve standing over a bowl. Discard the bouquet garni and bay leaf and any large pieces of solid fat, then shred the meat thoroughly with the forks (it should be so soft and tender that it will literally fall apart). Taste and adjust the seasoning.
Pack the shredded meat tightly into 4 individual ramekin dishes, pressing it down firmly with the back of a metal spoon. Leave the strained fat and juices in the bowl until cool and just beginning to thicken, then pour over the top of the meat, leaving behind any sediment that has settled at the bottom of the bowl. Leave until completely cold, by which time the fat will have solidified on top of the meat to seal it, then chill in the refrigerator overnight before serving.

EGGS, CHEESE AND FISH

At lunchtime the French often eat a simple omelette or quiche with bread and a salad. Together with their hundreds of regional cheeses to choose from, there is no lack of variation on this midday theme.

Fresh fish in France is a joy to eat; shellfish from Normandy and Brittany, oysters and mussels from breeding ground bordering on the Atlantic, seawater fish from the Mediterranean, and an abundance of freshwater fish from the many inland rivers and streams. For everyday meals fish is cooked as simply as possible, usually grilled or fried in butter then sprinkled with herbs, freshly ground pepper and lemon juice.

Truite au vin blanc
Trout with white wine

Metric	*Imperial*
4 × 225 g frozen rainbow trout, defrosted	*4 × 8 oz frozen rainbow trout, defrosted*
4 bay leaves	*4 bay leaves*
2 lemons, thinly sliced	*2 lemons, thinly sliced*
salt	*salt*
freshly ground black pepper	*freshly ground black pepper*
300 ml dry white wine	*½ pint dry white wine*
juice of 1 lemon	*juice of 1 lemon*
150 ml double cream	*¼ pint double cream*
1 × 15 ml spoon light Dijon mustard	*1 tablespoon light Dijon mustard*
1–2 × 15 ml spoons freshly chopped parsley	*1–2 tablespoons freshly chopped parsley*

To garnish:	***To garnish:***
few lemon slices	*few lemon slices*
few parsley sprigs	*few parsley sprigs*

Preparation time: 15 minutes
Cooking time: about 40–45 minutes
Oven: 160°C, 325°F, Gas Mark 3

Wash the trout inside and out under cold running water, then pat dry with paper towels. Place in a single layer in a buttered flameproof dish. Insert 1 bay leaf and a few lemon slices inside each fish.

Sprinkle the fish with salt and pepper, then pour over the wine, adding enough water just to cover the fish. Cover with foil and bake in a preheated oven for 20–25 minutes until the fish flakes easily when tested with a fork.

Drain the liquid from the fish into a heavy-based pan. Remove the lemon and bay leaves, place the fish on a warmed serving platter, cover with foil and keep warm in the lowest possible oven.

Stir the lemon juice into the liquid in the pan. Bring to the boil and boil vigorously until the liquid is reduced by about one-third of its volume. Stir in the cream and continue boiling for a further 5–10 minutes until the sauce is thickened and just beginning to turn golden, whisking continuously with a wire balloon whisk. Remove from the heat and add the mustard, parsley and salt and pepper to taste.

Pour a little sauce over the fish, and garnish with lemon slices and parsley. Serve immediately, with the remaining sauce in a warmed sauceboat.

Timbale au jambon
Pasta mould with ham

Metric	Imperial
150 g macaroni	*5 oz macaroni*
salt	*salt*
50 g butter	*2 oz butter*
50 g plain flour	*2 oz plain flour*
450 ml warm milk	*¾ pint warm milk*
100 g Gruyère cheese, grated	*4 oz Gruyère cheese, grated*
2 eggs	*2 eggs*
1 egg yolk	*1 egg yolk*
2 × 15 ml spoons freshly chopped parsley	*2 tablespoons freshly chopped parsley*
freshly ground black pepper	*freshly ground black pepper*
100 g boiled ham, diced	*4 oz boiled ham, diced*

Tomato sauce:	Tomato sauce:
2 × 15 ml spoons olive oil	*2 tablespoons olive oil*
1 small onion, peeled and chopped	*1 small onion, peeled and chopped*
2 garlic cloves, peeled and crushed with 1 × 2.5 ml spoon salt	*2 garlic cloves, peeled and crushed with ½ teaspoon salt*
350 g tomatoes, skinned, seeded and chopped	*12 oz tomatoes, skinned, seeded and chopped*
2 × 15 ml spoons tomato purée	*2 tablespoons tomato purée*
pinch of sugar	*pinch of sugar*
300 ml dry white wine or water	*½ pint dry white wine or water*

From left: Timbale au jambon; Truite au vin blanc

Preparation time: 30 minutes
Cooking time: about 1½ hours
Oven: 190°C, 375°F, Gas Mark 5

Cook the macaroni in boiling salted water for about 8 minutes until 'al dente' (tender yet firm to the bite). Drain thoroughly, then rinse under cold running water. Leave to drain.

Meanwhile, melt the butter in a pan, stir in the flour and cook for 1–2 minutes, stirring all the time. Remove from the heat and gradually add the milk, beating vigorously. Return the pan to the heat and bring slowly to the boil, beating constantly. Lower the heat and simmer until thick, then add the cheese and heat gently until melted.

Leave the sauce to cool slightly, then stir in the whole eggs and egg yolk, parsley, and salt and pepper. Combine the macaroni and sauce, then fold in the ham. Turn the mixture into a well-buttered 900 ml/1½ pint charlotte or savavin mould, pressing it down firmly and levelling the surface. Cover with foil, then bake in a preheated oven for 50 minutes or until set.

Meanwhile, make the tomato sauce. Heat the oil in a pan, add the onion and garlic and fry gently until soft. Stir in the tomatoes, tomato purée, sugar and salt and pepper, and fry for a further 5 minutes, stirring constantly. Stir in the wine or water and bring to the boil, then lower the heat and simmer gently for 20 minutes, stirring occasionally.

Allow the sauce to cool slightly, then purée in an electric blender or work through a sieve. Return to the rinsed-out pan and heat through gently. Adjust the consistency of the sauce – if it is too thick, stir in more wine or water, if too thin, boil vigorously until reduced. Taste and adjust the seasoning.

Remove the mould from the oven and leave to stand in a warm place for 10 minutes. Unmould on to a warmed serving platter and pour over a little of the tomato sauce. Serve immediately, with the remaining sauce handed separately in a warmed sauceboat.

Soupe de poissons marseillaise
Marseille fish soup

Metric	Imperial
2 × 15 ml spoons olive oil	*2 tablespoons olive oil*
1 large onion, peeled and thinly sliced	*1 large onion, peeled and thinly sliced*
2 tomatoes, skinned, seeded and chopped	*2 tomatoes, skinned, seeded and chopped*
1 × 15 ml spoon tomato purée	*1 tablespoon tomato purée*
1 litre fish stock	*2 pints fish stock*
300 ml dry white wine	*½ pint dry white wine*
1 bay leaf	*1 bay leaf*
1 strip orange peel	*1 strip orange peel*
1 sprig fresh fennel or 1 × 5 ml spoon dried fennel	*1 sprig fresh fennel or 1 teaspoon dried fennel*
salt	*salt*
freshly ground black pepper	*freshly ground black pepper*
1 kg mixed white fish (e.g., mullet, cod, haddock, plaice, turbot), skinned, boned and cut into chunks	*2 lb mixed white fish (e.g., mullet, cod, haddock, plaice, turbot), skinned, boned and cut into chunks*
100 g peeled prawns (optional)	*4 oz peeled prawns (optional)*
150 ml Aïoli (page 9)	*¼ pint Aïoli (page 9)*
slices of hot toast, to serve	*slices of hot toast, to serve*

Preparation time: about 25 minutes
Cooking time: 30 minutes

As this recipe requires a mixture of white fish you can ask the fishmonger for the fish heads and tails to make the stock. If you are buying ready-prepared or frozen fish and have no trimmings to make stock, chicken stock may be substituted.

In France the broth from a soup such as this one is served as a first course. Each person helps himself to toast, and pours the broth over the toast in his own plate. The aïoli is stirred in according to individual taste. The fish is then eaten separately as a main course, with more aïoli.

Heat the oil in a large flameproof casserole or heavy-based pan. Add the onion and fry gently until soft Stir in the tomatoes and tomato purée and fry for a further 5 minutes, stirring constantly.

Stir in the fish stock and wine and bring to the boil. Lower the heat, add the bay leaf, orange peel, fennel, and salt and pepper. Add the firm fleshed white fish (such as cod, haddock and mullet), and simmer for 10 minutes, then add the more delicate fish (such as plaice and turbot). Simmer for a further 5 minutes, then add the prawns, if using, and continue cooking for a further 5 minutes, until all the fish is tender and flakes easily when tested with a fork.

To serve, remove the bay leaf, orange peel and fennel sprig (if using). Taste and adjust the seasoning of the soup, then transfer to a warmed tureen or individual plates. Serve immediately, handing round the aïoli separately and served with toast.

Matafam
Cheese and bacon pancake

Metric	Imperial
100 g plain flour	*4 oz plain flour*
pinch of salt	*pinch of salt*
4 eggs, beaten	*4 eggs, beaten*
100 g Gruyère cheese, grated	*4 oz Gruyère cheese, grated*
100 g streaky bacon, rinds removed, cut into strips	*4 oz streaky bacon, rinds removed, cut into strips*
freshly grated nutmeg	*freshly grated nutmeg*
salt	*salt*
freshly ground black pepper	*freshly ground black pepper*
50 g butter	*2 oz butter*

Preparation time: 25 minutes, plus 30 minutes for standing
Cooking time: about 15 minutes

Originally a Spanish dish, the word matafam means 'to kill hunger' in Catalan. Serve hot with fried eggs, grilled bacon or sausages as a lunch or brunch dish, or cold with pickles, cooked meats and cheeses.

Sift the flour and salt into a bowl and make a well in the centre. Put the eggs in the well with the cheese and bacon, then gradually work in the flour with a wooden spoon, drawing it in from the sides of the bowl until evenly mixed. Add nutmeg, salt and pepper to taste, then cover and leave the batter at room temperature for 30 minutes.

Melt half the butter in a heavy-based crêpe or frying pan. Pour in the batter and fry over moderate heat for 7 minutes until the underside is set and golden.

Meanwhile, melt the remaining butter in a separate pan. Drizzle evenly over the top of the matafam, then slide the pan under a preheated hot grill and cook for about 5 minutes until the top is golden brown. Serve immediately, cut into wedges.

From left: Matafam; Soupe de poissons marseillaise; La râpée

La râpée
Egg and grated potato gratin

Preparation time: 20–25 minutes
Cooking time: 35–40 minutes
Oven: 200°C, 400°F, Gas Mark 6

Metric	**Imperial**
50 g butter	2 oz butter
2 × 15 ml spoons olive oil	2 tablespoons olive oil
2 shallots or 1 small onion, peeled and finely chopped	2 shallots or 1 small onion, peeled and finely chopped
1 garlic clove, peeled and crushed with 1 × 2.5 ml spoon salt	1 garlic clove, peeled and crushed with ½ teaspoon salt
4 eggs	4 eggs
150 ml double cream	¼ pint double cream
100 g Gruyère cheese, grated	4 oz Gruyère cheese, grated
salt	salt
freshly ground black pepper	freshly ground black pepper
4 medium potatoes, peeled	4 medium potatoes, peeled

Such dishes, known as 'gratins' in France, are popular for light lunches or suppers, and can be made with different vegetables such as leeks and chicory. Sometimes, ham and anchovies are added for extra flavour and body.

Melt half the butter with the oil in a pan, add the shallots and garlic and fry gently until soft. Transfer to a bowl, add the eggs and beat well. Stir in the cream, Gruyère cheese, salt and pepper. Set aside.
Grate the potatoes coarsely, squeeze them with your hands to extract as much moisture as possible, then pat dry with paper towels. Stir into the egg mixture.
Put the remaining butter in a shallow ovenproof dish and heat in a preheated oven until melted and very hot.
Pour in the egg and potato mixture, then bake for 25–30 minutes or until firm, with a crisp golden crust on top. Serve immediately.

Gougère aux foies de volailles
Choux pastry ring with chicken livers

Preparation time: about 30 minutes
Cooking time: 45–50 minutes
Oven: 200°C, 400°F, Gas Mark 6

Metric
300 ml water
100 g butter, cut into
  small pieces
salt
150 g plain flour
4 eggs, beaten
100 g Gruyère cheese,
  grated
about 1 × 1.25 ml spoon
  cayenne pepper

Imperial
½ pint water
4 oz butter, cut into small
  pieces
salt
5 oz plain flour
4 eggs, beaten
4 oz Gruyère cheese,
  grated
about ¼ teaspoon cayenne
  pepper

Filling:
25 g butter
1 medium onion, peeled
  and thinly sliced
1–2 garlic cloves, peeled
  and crushed with 1 ×
  2.5 ml spoon salt
225 g chicken livers, sliced
2 × 5 ml spoons freshly
  chopped marjoram or 1
  × 5 ml spoon dried
  marjoram
1 × 5 ml spoon tomato
  purée
4 × 15 ml spoons dry
  sherry
4 × 15 ml spoons single
  cream
freshly chopped parsley,
  to garnish

Filling:
1 oz butter
1 medium onion, peeled
  and thinly sliced
1–2 garlic cloves, peeled
  and crushed with ½
  teaspoon salt
8 oz chicken livers, sliced
2 teaspoons freshly
  chopped marjoram or 1
  teaspoon dried
  marjoram
1 teaspoon tomato
  purée
4 tablespoons dry
  sherry
4 tablespoons single
  cream
freshly chopped parsley,
  to garnish

Put the water in a large heavy-based pan with the pieces of butter and a pinch of salt. Bring to the boil, then remove from the heat and add the flour all at once. Return to gentle heat and beat vigorously with a wooden spoon until the mixture forms a ball and leaves the sides of the pan clean.

Remove from the heat and gradually beat in the eggs, until the mixture becomes smooth and glossy, reserving a little egg for glazing. Beat in the grated cheese and salt, and cayenne to taste.

Place spoonfuls of the dough on a greased baking sheet to make a circle or crown shape 20–23 cm/8–9 inches in diameter. Brush with the reserved beaten egg, then bake in a preheated oven for 30–35 minutes until puffed up and golden brown.

Meanwhile make the filling. Melt the butter in a frying pan, add the onion and garlic and fry gently until soft. Add the chicken livers and fry until lightly coloured on all sides, then stir in the marjoram and tomato purée. Fry for 1–2 minutes, then stir in the sherry and continue cooking for a further 5 minutes, or until the chicken livers are cooked to your liking. Add salt, then stir in the cream and heat through gently without boiling.

When the gougère is cooked, transfer carefully to a warmed serving platter and spoon the chicken liver filling in the centre. Sprinkle with parsley and serve immediately.

Gougère aux foies de volailles; Quiche au camembert

Quiche au camembert
Camembert quiche

Metric
175 g plain flour
pinch of salt
100 g butter, chilled
1 egg yolk
1 × 5 ml spoon water
a little egg white, lightly
  beaten

Filling:
350 g soft ripe Camembert
  cheese, rind removed
2 eggs, beaten
150 ml double cream
salt
freshly ground black
  pepper

Imperial
6 oz plain flour
pinch of salt
4 oz butter, chilled
1 egg yolk
1 teaspoon water
a little egg white, lightly
  beaten

Filling:
12 oz soft ripe Camembert
  cheese, rind removed
2 eggs, beaten
¼ pint double cream
salt
freshly ground black
  pepper

Preparation time: about 40 minutes, plus chilling
Cooking time: about 45 minutes
Oven: 190°C, 350°F, Gas Mark 5

This quiche can equally well be made with Brie cheese. Many supermarkets and delicatessens sell a blue-veined Brie which would make a stronger-tasting filling than plain Brie or Camembert.

To make the pastry, sift the flour and salt into a bowl. Cut the butter into the flour in small pieces, then rub in lightly with the fingertips. Mix the egg yolk and water together, then stir into the flour mixture with a round-bladed knife until the mixture draws together. Form into a smooth ball with one hand, then chill in the refrigerator for 30 minutes.

Roll out the dough on a floured surface and use to line a loose-bottomed 23 cm/9 inch fluted flan tin. Place the tin on a baking sheet, prick the base of the dough in several places with a fork, then line with foil or greaseproof paper and fill with baking beans. Bake the pastry case 'blind' in a preheated oven for 10 minutes, then remove the paper and beans and brush the base with the beaten egg white. Return to the oven and bake for a further 5 minutes then carefully remove the sides of the flan tin. Set the pastry case aside on the baking sheet.

To make the filling, cut the Camembert cheese into small pieces and place in a heatproof bowl. Stand the bowl in a pan of gently simmering water and heat gently, stirring constantly until the cheese has melted and is runny. Remove the bowl from the pan of water and gradually stir in the beaten eggs and cream until evenly mixed. Add a little salt, and pepper to taste.

Pour the filling into the pastry case, return to the oven and bake for 20 minutes or until the filling is puffed up and golden brown. Remove from the oven, quickly place on a serving plate and serve immediately.

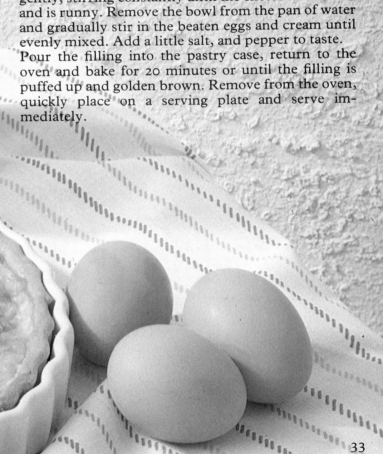

Quiche au crabe
Crab quiche

Preparation time: about 40 minutes, plus chilling
Cooking time: about 50 minutes
Oven: 190°C, 375°F, Gas Mark 5

Metric
125 g plain flour
pinch of salt
100 g butter, chilled
1 egg yolk
1 × 5 ml spoon lemon juice
a little egg white, lightly
   beaten

Filling:
25 g unsalted butter
1 onion, peeled and finely
   chopped
1 × 15 ml spoon tomato
   purée
225 g fresh or frozen
   crabmeat, flaked
3 eggs
150 ml milk
salt
cayenne pepper

Imperial
5 oz plain flour
pinch of salt
4 oz butter, chilled
1 egg yolk
1 teaspoon lemon juice
a little egg white, lightly
   beaten

Filling:
1 oz unsalted butter
1 onion, peeled and finely
   chopped
1 tablespoon tomato
   purée
8 oz fresh or frozen
   crabmeat, flaked
3 eggs
¼ pint milk
salt
cayenne pepper

Sift the flour and salt into a bowl. Cut the butter into the flour in small pieces, then rub in lightly with the fingertips. Mix the egg yolk and lemon juice together, then stir into the flour mixture with a round-bladed knife until the mixture draws together. Form into a smooth ball, then chill in the refrigerator for 30 minutes.

Roll out the dough on a floured surface and use to line a plain 20 cm/8 inch flan ring set on a baking sheet. Prick the base of the dough in several places with a fork, then line with foil or greaseproof paper and fill with baking beans.

Bake the pastry case 'blind' in a preheated oven for 10 minutes, then remove the paper and beans and brush the base of the dough with the beaten egg white. Return to the oven and bake for a further 5 minutes, then remove and set aside.

To make the filling, melt the butter in a pan, add the onion and fry gently until soft. Transfer to a bowl and stir in the tomato purée and flaked crabmeat. In a separate bowl, lightly beat the eggs together with the milk and salt and cayenne to taste. Pour over the crabmeat mixture and fold gently to mix.

Pour the filling into the pastry case, then return to the oven and bake for 25 minutes until the filling is just set. Remove the flan ring carefully, then return to the oven for a further 5 minutes to crisp up the edges of the pastry. Leave to cool for about 15 minutes, then transfer the quiche to a serving plate. Serve warm or cold.

Tarte aux oignons
Onion tart

Preparation time: about 40 minutes, plus chilling
Cooking time: about 2 hours
Oven: 190°C, 375°F, Gas Mark 5

Metric
25 g butter
4 medium Spanish onions,
   peeled and thinly sliced
1 × 5 ml spoon soft brown
   sugar
2 × 15 ml spoons plain
   flour
1 × 15 ml spoon brandy
   (optional)
1 egg
2 egg yolks
4 × 15 ml spoons double
   cream
salt
freshly ground black
   pepper

Pastry:
125 g plain flour
pinch of salt
100 g butter, chilled
1 egg yolk
1 × 5 ml spoon water
a little egg white, lightly
   beaten

Imperial
1 oz butter
4 medium Spanish onions,
   peeled and thinly sliced
1 teaspoon soft brown
   sugar
2 tablespoons plain
   flour
1 tablespoon brandy
   (optional)
1 egg
2 egg yolks
4 tablespoons double
   cream
salt
freshly ground black
   pepper

Pastry:
5 oz plain flour
pinch of salt
4 oz butter, chilled
1 egg yolk
1 teaspoon water
a little egg white, lightly
   beaten

Melt the butter in a large heavy-based pan, add the onions and fry very gently for about 1 hour until very soft and golden (almost a puréed consistency). Stir the onions frequently during frying to prevent them from browning and sticking to the pan.

Meanwhile, make the pastry. Sift the flour and salt into a bowl. Cut the butter into the flour in small pieces, then rub in lightly with the fingertips. Mix the egg yolk and water together, then stir into the flour mixture with a round-bladed knife until the mixture draws together. Form into a smooth ball with one hand, then cover and chill in the refrigerator for 30 minutes.

Roll out the dough on a floured surface and use to line a 20 cm/8 inch flan tin or flan ring set on a baking sheet. Prick the base of the dough in several places with a fork, then line with foil or greaseproof paper and fill with baking beans.

Bake the pastry case 'blind' in a preheated oven for 10 minutes, then remove the paper and beans and brush the base of the dough with the beaten egg white. Return to the oven and bake for a further 5 minutes. Set aside. When the onions are cooked, stir in the sugar and cook for 1 minute, then sprinkle in the flour and cook for a further 2 minutes, stirring constantly with a wooden spoon.

Transfer the onions to a bowl and stir in the brandy (if using). Beat the whole egg and egg yolks together, then stir into the onions with the cream and salt and pepper to taste.

Pour the filling into the pastry case, then place in the oven and bake for 30–35 minutes until the filling is set. Leave to cool for about 15 minutes, then remove the flan tin or ring and place the quiche on a serving plate. Serve warm or cold.

Quiche au crabe; Tarte aux oignons

Sardines grillées à l'ail
Grilled sardines with garlic

Metric	Imperial
1 kg (about 30) fresh sardines	*2 lb (about 30) fresh sardines*
6 × 15 ml spoons olive oil	*6 tablespoons olive oil*
juice of 1 lemon	*juice of 1 lemon*
4 garlic cloves, peeled and crushed with 1 × 5 ml spoon salt	*4 garlic cloves, peeled and crushed with 1 teaspoon salt*
2 × 15 ml spoons finely chopped parsley	*2 tablespoons finely chopped parsley*
freshly ground black pepper	*freshly ground black pepper*
lemon wedges, to serve	*lemon wedges, to serve*

Preparation time: 30 minutes, plus marinating
Cooking time: about 8 minutes

In France, fresh sardines are often cooked over charcoal and are usually left whole, with the heads on; for English tastes, they are more palatable if gutted and cleaned before cooking.

Serve for a light lunch dish (cooked on the barbecue in summer) with French bread or garlic bread, and a tossed green salad or tomato, basil and onion salad, and a thick plain, or garlic-flavoured mayonnaise such as Aïoli (page 9). For a starter, serve with bread and mayonnaise only, and allow 4–6 sardines for each person.

To gut and clean the sardines: insert the point of a small, sharp knife in the centre of the belly and cut along the belly to the gills. Cut off the head behind the gills, gently pulling the entrails of the fish away with it. Cut along the belly towards the tail, then gently open out the fish. Locate the backbone at the head end with the point of the knife, and gently ease it away from the flesh. With thumb and forefinger, pull the backbone away towards the tail. Cut off the backbone with the tail.

Rinse the sardines inside and out under gently running water, then pat dry with paper towels. Place in a single layer in a shallow dish. Mix together the remaining ingredients with plenty of pepper, then pour over the fish. Leave to marinate for at least 1 hour, turning the fish over frequently.

Place the sardines in a single layer on a grill rack covered with foil. Reserve the marinade. Cook under a preheated hot grill for about 4 minutes on each side or until the skin is charred and the flesh cooked through each side, basting frequently with the reserved marinade. Transfer to warmed individual serving plates and pour over the pan juices and any remaining marinade. Serve immediately, with lemon wedges.

Maquereau en concombre vinaigrette
Mackerel in creamy vinaigrette

Metric	Imperial
4 mackerel (about 275 g each), gutted	*4 mackerel (about 10 oz each), gutted*
salt	*salt*
freshly ground black pepper	*freshly ground black pepper*
½ large cucumber, thinly sliced	*½ large cucumber, thinly sliced*
juice of 1 lemon	*juice of 1 lemon*
50 g unsalted butter	*2 oz unsalted butter*

Dressing:	Dressing:
120 ml olive oil	*4 fl oz olive oil*
3 × 15 ml spoons cider vinegar	*3 tablespoons cider vinegar*
2 × 15 ml spoons Aïoli (page 9) or plain mayonnaise	*2 tablespoons Aïoli (page 9) or plain mayonnaise*
2 × 15 ml spoons freshly chopped parsley	*2 tablespoons freshly chopped parsley*

Preparation time: 20–30 minutes
Cooking time: 25–30 minutes
Oven: 200°C, 400°F, Gas Mark 6

Place each mackerel on a piece of foil. Sprinkle the insides of the fish with salt and pepper, then tuck the cucumber inside, reserving a few slices for the garnish. Sprinkle more salt and pepper over the tops of the mackerel, pour over the lemon juice and dot with the butter.

Fold the foil over the fish, tucking in the ends to make 4 individual parcels. Place the fish in a single layer in a large baking dish and bake in a preheated oven for 25–30 minutes or until the fish is cooked through.

Meanwhile, make the dressing. Put all the ingredients in a screw-topped jar with salt and pepper to taste. Shake well to mix, then chill in the refrigerator.

When the mackerel are cooked, unwrap carefully, drain off all the cooking juices and place the fish on a warmed serving platter. Pour over the chilled dressing and serve immediately, garnished with the reserved cucumber twists and accompanied by slices of bread.

From the top: Maquereau en concombre vinaigrette; Sardines grillées à l'ail; Coquilles au cidre

Coquilles au cidre
Scallops with cider

Metric	Imperial
8 scallops (total weight about 350 g), defrosted if frozen	8 scallops (total weight about 12 oz), defrosted if frozen
100 g button mushrooms, finely sliced	4 oz button mushrooms, finely sliced
300 ml dry cider	½ pint dry cider
1 bay leaf, halved	1 bay leaf, halved
2 shallots or 1 small onion, peeled and finely chopped	2 shallots or 1 small onion, peeled and finely chopped
cayenne pepper	cayenne pepper
salt	salt
150 ml double cream	¼ pint double cream
40 g butter	1½ oz butter
40 g fresh white breadcrumbs	1½ oz fresh white breadcrumbs
40 g Gruyère cheese, grated	1½ oz Gruyère cheese, grated

Preparation time: about 30 minutes
Cooking time: about 35 minutes

If using fresh scallops, scrub and scald the shells, for 1 minute in boiling water with 1 × 5 ml spoon/1 teaspoon lemon juice. Frozen scallop meat is available off the shell from good freezer centres, supermarkets and fishmongers. Empty scallop shells (for serving) can be obtained from fishmongers or bought at specialist kitchen shops.

Wash the scallops and coral thoroughly under cold running water, then slice thinly. Put them in a pan with the mushrooms, cider, bay leaf, shallots or onion and a pinch each of cayenne and salt. Bring to the boil, then skim off the scum with a slotted spoon and lower the heat. Simmer gently for 4–6 minutes until the scallops are tender, then strain the liquid into a clean pan, discarding the bay leaf halves.
Boil the liquid vigorously until reduced by about half of its volume. Stir in the cream and continue boiling for a further 5–10 minutes until the sauce is thickened and just beginning to turn golden, whisking continuously with a wire ballon whisk.
Meanwhile, divide the scallops and coral mixture equally between 4 buttered scallop shells. When the sauce is thick, remove from the heat and whisk in half the butter. Taste and adjust the seasoning, then pour over the scallop mixture.
Mix together the breadcrumbs and cheese and sprinkle evenly over the scallops. Dot with the remaining butter and sprinkle with cayenne to taste. Put under a preheated hot grill for about 5 minutes until golden brown and bubbling. Serve hot.

Moules en brochette
Mussel kebabs

Metric	*Imperial*
1.5–1.75 kg fresh mussels, scrubbed, with beards removed	*3–4 lb fresh mussels, scrubbed, with beards removed*
150 ml dry white wine	*¼ pint dry white wine*
150 ml water	*¼ pint water*
1 medium onion, peeled and chopped	*1 medium onion, peeled and chopped*
1 bouquet garni	*1 bouquet garni*
225 g unsmoked back bacon, rind removed, cut into chunks, or bacon rashers, cut into lengths and folded double	*8 oz unsmoked back bacon, rind removed, cut into chunks, or bacon rashers, cut into lengths and folded double*
1 red pepper, cored, seeded, and cut into chunks	*1 red pepper, cored, seeded, and cut into chunks*
1 green pepper, cored, seeded and cut into chunks	*1 green pepper, cored, seeded and cut into chunks*
100 g unsalted butter, softened	*4 oz unsalted butter, softened*
2 garlic cloves, peeled and crushed	*2 garlic cloves, peeled and crushed*
2 × 15 ml spoons freshly chopped parsley	*2 tablespoons freshly chopped parsley*
salt	*salt*
freshly ground black pepper	*freshly ground black pepper*

Preparation time: 30 minutes, plus soaking
Cooking time: 25–30 minutes

Soak the mussels in cold water for about 1 hour. Drain the mussels and discard any which are open. Place the closed mussels in a large saucepan with the wine, water, onion and bouquet garni. Bring to the boil, cover with a tight-fitting lid and simmer for 10 minutes, shaking the pan frequently during this time. Drain and discard any mussels which have not opened. Remove the mussels from their shells.
Thread the mussels on to oiled long kebab skewers, alternating them with pieces of bacon and red and green pepper.
Put the softened butter in a bowl with the garlic, parsley, and salt and pepper to taste. Beat well to mix, then brush over the kebabs to cover them thickly.
Cook the kebabs on a rack under a preheated hot grill for 10–15 minutes until sizzling hot. Turn them frequently during this time, brushing and basting them with any remaining butter and the juices from the grill pan. Serve immediately.

Sole au whisky
Pan-fried sole with whisky sauce

Metric	*Imperial*
40 g butter	*1½ oz butter*
2 Dover or lemon sole, divided into 8 fillets and skinned	*2 Dover or lemon sole, divided into 8 fillets and skinned*
1 small fennel bulb (about 175 g), trimmed and thinly sliced	*1 small fennel bulb (about 6 oz), trimmed and thinly sliced*
1 garlic clove, peeled and crushed with 1 × 2.5 ml spoon salt	*1 garlic clove, peeled and crushed with ½ teaspoon salt*
4 × 15 ml spoons whisky	*4 tablespoons whisky*
100 g peeled prawns	*4 oz peeled prawns*
2 large firm tomatoes, skinned, seeded and chopped	*2 large firm tomatoes, skinned, seeded and chopped*
150 ml double cream	*¼ pint double cream*
salt	*salt*
freshly ground black pepper	*freshly ground black pepper*

Preparation time: 20 minutes
Cooking time: 25–35 minutes

For a special occasion main course, garnish with a few whole unpeeled prawns.

Melt 25 g/1 oz butter in a large non-stick frying pan. Add the sole in a single layer, 4 fillets at a time, and fry very gently for 2–3 minutes on each side until cooked through but not browned. Remove from the pan with a fish slice and keep hot in the lowest possible oven.
Melt the remaining butter in the pan, add the fennel and garlic and fry gently for about 5–10 minutes until the fennel has softened, stirring occasionally.
Increase the heat, add the whisky and stir until reduced slightly, then lower the heat and stir in the prawns and tomatoes. Simmer gently for 5 minutes, then stir in the cream. Heat through, then taste and adjust the seasoning.
To serve, arrange the sole on a warmed serving platter. Remove the prawns and tomato mixture from the pan with a slotted spoon and arrange on top of the fish. Pour over the remaining sauce and serve immediately.

Turbot au champagne
Turbot with sparkling white wine

Metric	Imperial
50 g butter	*2 oz butter*
3 shallots or 1 medium onion, peeled and finely chopped	*3 shallots or 1 medium onion, peeled and finely chopped*
1 bunch watercress	*1 bunch watercress*
300 ml warm milk	*½ pint warm milk*
salt	*salt*
freshly ground black pepper	*freshly ground black pepper*
4 large fillets turbot, skinned	*4 large fillets turbot, skinned*
1 bay leaf	*1 bay leaf*
300 ml sparkling white wine	*½ pint sparkling white wine*

Preparation time: 10–15 minutes
Cooking time: 35–40 minutes
Oven: 180°C, 350°F, Gas Mark 4

Brill or halibut can be used with equal success in this recipe; both are smaller and more economical fish, and more widely available than turbot. Although Champagne is used in cooking in France, sparkling white wine is a good substitute.

Melt the butter in a pan, add the shallots or onion and fry gently until soft. Reserve a few sprigs of watercress to garnish, finely chop the rest (stalks removed) and fry for a further 2 minutes, stirring constantly. Stir in the milk and salt and pepper to taste, bring to the boil, then lower the heat, cover and simmer gently for 15 minutes.

Meanwhile, place the fish in a single layer in a well-buttered ovenproof dish, sprinkle with salt and pepper and place the bay leaf on top. Pour in the wine, then cover with buttered foil and bake in a preheated oven for 10–15 minutes, or until the fish flakes easily with a fork.

Remove the fish with a slotted spoon, discarding the bay leaf, and place on a warmed serving platter. Cover with foil and keep hot.

Allow the milk and watercress mixture and the cooking liquid to cool slightly then purée in an electric blender. Taste and adjust the seasoning of the sauce, then drizzle a little over the fish on the serving platter. Pour the remaining sauce into a warmed sauceboat. Garnish the turbot with watercress sprigs and serve immediately, with the sauce handed separately.

Moules en brochette; Sole au whisky; Turbot au champagne

MEAT AND POULTRY

In France the choosing of meat, poultry and game is not a task to be taken lightly. To watch a French housewife buying meat in her local bouchier, charcuterie or market, to see her discuss the cut, size and cooking method with the shopkeeper or stallholder is evidence in itself. Meat is expensive in France, but at the same time it is of exceptionally high quality, and French butchers have a way of dividing a carcass that leaves the cook with very little wastage and a cut that both looks and tastes superb.

Tournedos de Dijon
Caramelized mustard steaks

Metric	Imperial
4 tournedos steaks, each weighing about 150 g	4 tournedos steaks, each weighing about 5 oz
freshly ground black pepper	fresh ground black pepper
6 × 15 ml spoons Dijon mustard	6 tablespoons Dijon mustard
50 g butter	2 oz butter
4 × 15 ml spoons demerara sugar	4 tablespoons demerara sugar
4 × 15 ml spoons brandy	4 tablespoons brandy
salt	salt

Preparation time: 5 minutes
Cooking time: 6–10 minutes

Tournedos steaks are so tender that they need very little cooking. They are usually sold tied with a strip of fat round them—snip the string and remove this fat before serving.

Sprinkle the steaks liberally on one side with pepper, then spread this side with one-third of the mustard. Melt the butter in a heavy-based frying pan and, when foaming, fry the steaks over brisk heat for 2 minutes, mustard side down. Spread the top side with half the remaining mustard, turn the steaks over and cook for a further 2 minutes for rare, 3 minutes for medium, and 4 minutes for well-done steaks.
Remove the steaks with a slotted spoon and place on a sheet of foil over the grill rack. Spread one side of each steak with the remaining mustard, then sprinkle with the sugar. Put under a preheated hot grill for about 2 minutes until caramelized and bubbling.
Meanwhile, heat the brandy gently in a small pan, remove from the heat and ignite. When the flames have subsided, pour the brandy into the steak juices in the frying pan. Stir vigorously, and add salt and pepper. Serve the steaks with the juices poured over.

Epaule d'agneau aux asperges
Lamb with asparagus sauce

Metric	Imperial
25 g butter	1 oz butter
1 medium onion, peeled and thinly sliced	1 medium onion, peeled and thinly sliced
1–2 garlic cloves, peeled and crushed with 1 × 2.5 spoon salt	1–2 garlic cloves, peeled and crushed with ½ teaspoon salt
1 kg boneless shoulder of lamb, trimmed of fat and cut into cubes	2 lb boneless shoulder of lamb, trimmed of fat and cut into cubes
juice of 1 lemon	juice of 1 lemon
300 ml chicken stock	½ pint chicken stock
freshly ground black pepper	freshly ground black pepper
1 × 225 g packet frozen asparagus spears, defrosted	1 × 8 oz packet frozen asparagus spears, defrosted
salt	salt
150 ml double cream, to finish	¼ pint double cream, to finish

Preparation time: 15 minutes
Cooking time: 2–2½ hours
Oven: 160°C, 325°F, Gas Mark 3

You will need a 2 kg/4 lb shoulder of lamb in order to have 1 kg/2 lb boneless meat. Ask the butcher to bone it for you as it can be a time-consuming task.

Melt the butter in a large flameproof casserole, add the onion and fry gently until soft. Add the garlic and lamb and fry over moderate heat until the lamb is lightly browned on all sides.
Stir the lemon juice into the pan, together with the stock and pepper to taste. Bring to the boil, then lower the heat and simmer gently for 5 minutes. Trim the tips off the asparagus spears and reserve. Stir the spears into the lamb mixture, then cover and transfer to a preheated oven. Cook for 1½–2 hours or until the lamb is tender, stirring occasionally. Meanwhile cook the reserved asparagus tips in simmering water for 3–5 minutes. Drain and set aside.
Return the casserole to the top of the stove and spoon away any fat from the surface. Taste and adjust the seasoning of the sauce. Mix together the cream and reserved asparagus tips, then pour carefully over the surface of the casserole in a thin, even layer. Heat through gently, without stirring, then serve.

Tournedos de Dijon; Epaule d'agneau aux asperges

Paupiettes de boeuf
Beef rolls with anchovy and capers

Preparation time: 40 minutes, plus soaking
Cooking time: 1–1¼ hours

Metric
4 thin slices rump
    steak, 100–175 g each
salt
freshly ground black
    pepper
2 × 15 ml spoons
    vegetable oil
4 rashers streaky bacon,
    rinds removed, chopped
3 shallots or 1 medium
    onion, peeled and
    finely chopped
300 ml full-bodied red
    wine
300 ml beef stock or
    water
1 bouquet garni

Stuffing:
1 × 50 g can anchovies,
    drained and soaked in
    milk for 20 minutes
100 g fresh white
    breadcrumbs
2 × 15 ml spoons capers,
    drained and crushed
2 shallots or 1 small
    onion, peeled and
    very finely chopped
2 × 15 ml spoons finely
    chopped parsley
finely grated rind and
    juice of 1 lemon
1 egg, beaten

To finish:
1 × 15 ml spoon softened
    butter
2 × 15 ml spoons plain
    flour

Imperial
4 thin slices rump
    steak, 4–6 oz each
salt
freshly ground black
    pepper
2 tablespoons vegetable
    oil
4 rashers streaky bacon,
    rinds removed, chopped
3 shallots or 1 medium
    onion, peeled and
    finely chopped
½ pint full-bodied red
    wine
½ pint beef stock or
    water
1 bouquet garni

Stuffing:
1 × 2 oz can anchovies,
    drained and soaked in
    milk for 20 minutes
4 oz fresh white
    breadcrumbs
2 tablespoons capers,
    drained and crushed
2 shallots or 1 small
    onion, peeled and
    very finely chopped
2 tablespoons finely
    chopped parsley
finely grated rind and
    juice of 1 lemon
1 egg, beaten

To finish:
1 tablespoon softened
    butter
2 tablespoons plain
    flour

For a more economical dish, use thin slices of silverside. Ask your butcher to beat the silverside with a mallet to tenderize it, or do this yourself with a rolling pin. Allow an extra 15 minutes' cooking time.

To make the stuffing, drain the anchovies, pat dry with paper towels, then chop roughly. Mix the anchovies with the remaining stuffing ingredients and pepper to taste, adding a few drops of milk if the mixture seems dry.

Spread the slices of beef flat on a board or work surface and cut each lengthwise into two halves. Sprinkle with salt and pepper. Divide the stuffing equally between the 8 pieces of meat, placing it at one end and rolling the meat neatly round it. Tie with string or trussing thread and set aside.

Heat the oil in a flameproof casserole, add the bacon and fry over moderate heat until lightly browned. Lower the heat, add the shallots or onion and fry gently until soft. Remove with a slotted spoon and drain on paper towels.

Add the paupiettes and fry until browned on all sides. Add the bacon and onions and pour in the wine and stock. Tuck the bouquet garni amongst the paupiettes, then sprinkle lightly with salt and pepper. Cover and simmer gently for 45 minutes–1 hour until the beef is tender.

Remove the paupiettes with a slotted spoon and cut off the string or thread. Place on a warmed serving platter, cover with foil and keep warm.

To finish, work the butter and flour to a paste (beurre manié) in a small bowl. Remove the bouquet garni from the liquid in the pan. Add the beurre manié a little at a time, whisking vigorously over high heat until the sauce thickens. Taste and adjust the seasoning, then pour over the paupiettes. Serve immediately.

Boeuf au poivre vert
Beef with green peppercorns

Metric
2 × 15 ml spoons
vegetable oil
1 kg chuck steak,
trimmed of excess
fat and cut into
large chunks
1 large onion, peeled
and chopped
2–3 celery sticks,
chopped
1 garlic clove, peeled
and crushed with 1 ×
2.5 ml spoon salt
4 rashers streaky bacon,
rinds removed, chopped
3 × 15 ml spoons green
peppercorns, drained
3 × 15 ml spoons freshly
chopped parsley
300 ml dry white wine
150 ml beef stock or
water
2 bay leaves
salt

Imperial
2 tablespoons vegetable
oil
2 lb chuck steak,
trimmed of excess
fat and cut into
large chunks
1 large onion, peeled
and chopped
2–3 celery sticks,
chopped
1 garlic clove, peeled
and crushed with ½
teaspoon salt
4 rashers streaky bacon,
rinds removed, chopped
3 tablespoons green
peppercorns, drained
3 tablespoons freshly
chopped parsley
½ pint dry white wine
¼ pint beef stock or
water
2 bay leaves
salt

Preparation time: 30 minutes
Cooking time: 2–2½ hours
Oven: 160°C, 325°F, Gas Mark 3

Heat the oil in a large flameproof casserole, add the meat and fry over brisk heat until browned on all sides. Remove with a slotted spoon and drain on paper towels.

Lower the heat and add the onion, celery, garlic and bacon to the casserole. Fry gently until the vegetables are softened and the bacon lightly coloured, stirring constantly with a wooden spoon.

Crush 2 × 15 ml spoons/2 tablespoons peppercorns in a mortar and pestle, then stir into the casserole with 2 × 15 ml spoons/2 tablespoons parsley. Fry for 2–3 minutes, stirring, then return the beef to the casserole.

Stir in the wine and stock or water and bring to the boil. Add the bay leaves and salt to taste, then cover with a tight-fitting lid. Transfer to a preheated oven and cook for 1½–2 hours or until the beef is tender.

Remove from the oven and discard the bay leaves. Taste and adjust the seasoning, then sprinkle with the remaining peppercorns and parsley.

Left: Paupiettes de boeuf; Below: Boeuf au poivre vert

Filet de porc tourangeau
Pork with prunes and white wine

Preparation time: 15 minutes, plus soaking
Cooking time: 50 minutes

Metric
16 prunes
300 ml dry white wine
50 g butter
750 g pork fillet
    (tenderloin), cut
    into bite-sized pieces
salt
freshly ground black
    pepper
2 × 15 ml spoons
    redcurrant jelly
1 × 5 ml spoon lemon
    juice
150 ml double cream

Imperial
16 prunes
½ pint dry white wine
2 oz butter
1½ lb pork fillet
    (tenderloin), cut
    into bite-sized pieces
salt
freshly ground black
    pepper
2 tablespoons
    redcurrant jelly
1 teaspoon lemon
    juice
¼ pint double cream

Put the prunes in a shallow bowl, pour in the wine, cover and soak overnight.
Drain the prunes, reserving the liquid, and remove the stones.
Melt the butter in a flameproof casserole, add the pork and cook over brisk heat until lightly coloured on all sides. Sprinkle with salt and pepper. Add the prunes, pour over the reserved liquid and bring to the boil. Lower the heat, cover and simmer gently for 30 minutes or until the pork is tender.
Remove the pork and prunes from the pan with a slotted spoon and place on a warmed serving platter. Keep hot at the lowest possible setting in the oven.
Add the redcurrant jelly and lemon juice to the pan and stir until the jelly has melted. Stir in the cream and bring to the boil. Continue boiling for 5–10 minutes until the sauce is thickened and just beginning to turn golden, whisking continuously with a wire ballon whisk. Taste and adjust the seasoning, then pour over the pork. Serve immediately.

Porc au lait
Pork in milk

Metric	Imperial
1 × 1.5 kg loin of pork, skinned and boned	1 × 3 lb loin of pork, skinned and boned
2 × 15 ml spoons light Dijon mustard	2 tablespoons light Dijon mustard
4 garlic cloves, peeled and cut into thin slivers	4 garlic cloves, peeled and cut into thin slivers
salt	salt
freshly ground black pepper	freshly ground black pepper
50 g unsalted butter	2 oz unsalted butter
900 ml milk	1½ pints milk
150 ml double cream	¼ pint double cream

Preparation time: 15 minutes
Cooking time: 2 hours
Oven: 160°C, 325°F, Gas Mark 3

Ask your butcher to bone the pork for you and to cut away all the skin and most of the fat underneath the skin. If you make a slit horizontally through the centre of the joint before spreading with mustard, it will be much easier to roll the meat into a neat shape.

Place the meat on a board or work surface, fat side downward. Spread half the mustard over the meat, then dot with the slivers of garlic and sprinkle with salt and pepper. Roll the meat as neatly as possible, then tie with fine string or trussing thread.
Melt the butter in a flameproof casserole, add the pork and fry over moderate heat until lightly browned on all sides. Pour in the milk and bring to the boil, then lower the heat and sprinkle with salt and pepper. Cover the casserole and transfer to a preheated oven. Cook for 1½ hours or until the pork is tender, then remove from the casserole, discard the string and place on a warmed serving platter.
Strain the milk and cooking juices into a heavy-based pan and stir in the cream. Bring to the boil and continue boiling for 5–10 minutes until the sauce is thickened and just beginning to turn golden, whisking continuously with a wire balloon whisk. Remove from the heat, stir in the remaining mustard, taste and adjust the seasoning. Serve the pork cut into thin slices, with the sauce handed separately in a warmed sauceboat.

Porc en sanglier
Pork marinated in red wine

Metric	Imperial
1 × 1.5 kg leg of pork	1 × 3¼ lb leg of pork
40 g lard or butter	1½ oz lard or butter
2 × 15 ml spoons redcurrant jelly	2 tablespoons redcurrant jelly
Marinade:	**Marinade:**
300 ml red wine	½ pint red wine
1 carrot, peeled and sliced	1 carrot, peeled and sliced
1 onion, peeled and sliced	1 onion, peeled and sliced
2 celery sticks, chopped	2 celery sticks, chopped
1 × 15 ml spoon juniper berries, crushed	1 tablespoon juniper berries, crushed
2 garlic cloves, peeled and crushed with 1 × 2.5 ml spoon salt	2 garlic cloves, peeled and crushed with ½ teaspoon salt
2 bay leaves, halved	2 bay leaves, halved
1 bouquet garni	1 bouquet garni
freshly ground black pepper	freshly ground black pepper

Preparation time: about 30 minutes, plus marinating
Cooking time: about 2 hours
Oven: 160°C, 325°F, Gas Mark 3

Remove the rind and most of the fat from the pork and cut out the bone from the centre of the meat. The bone can be left, but it is easier to carve without it. Put the marinade ingredients in a large bowl. Add the pork, baste well, then cover tightly and marinate in the refrigerator for up to 3 days, turning the meat and basting frequently during this time.
Remove the pork from the marinade and pat thoroughly dry with paper towels. Tie the joint securely with string, as neatly as possible. Strain the marinade, reserving the vegetables and discarding the bouquet garni and bay leaves.
Melt the lard or butter in a large flameproof casserole, add the pork and fry briskly until browned on all sides. Remove and set aside. Lower the heat, and gently fry the reserved vegetables until lightly coloured.
Place the meat on top of the vegetables and pour over the reserved marinade. Cover with a tight-fitting lid and cook in a preheated oven for 1¾–2 hours, basting frequently.
Lift the pork out of the casserole, remove the string and place on a warmed serving platter. Keep warm. Transfer the casserole to the top of the stove and stir in the redcurrant jelly. Heat through until the jelly has melted. Taste and adjust the seasoning, then serve with the sauce in a warmed sauceboat.

Filet de porc tourangeau; Porc en sanglier; Porc au lait

Epaule d'agneau aux haricots
Lamb with haricot beans

Metric
3 garlic cloves, peeled
1 × 2 kg shoulder of
  lamb, boned, rolled
  and tied
salt
freshly ground black
  pepper
2 × 15 ml spoons olive
  oil
2 onions, peeled
225 g tomatoes, skinned,
  seeded and chopped
150 ml dry white wine
  or water
2 × 5 ml spoons freshly
  chopped rosemary or
  1 × 5 ml spoon dried
  rosemary
225 g dried haricot
  beans, soaked in cold
  water overnight
1 whole clove
1 carrot, peeled and
  quartered
1 bouquet garni

Imperial
3 garlic cloves, peeled
1 × 4½ lb shoulder of
  lamb, boned, rolled
  and tied
salt
freshly ground black
  pepper
2 tablespoons olive
  oil
2 onions, peeled
8 oz tomatoes, skinned,
  seeded and chopped
¼ pint dry white wine
  or water
2 teaspoons freshly
  chopped rosemary or
  1 teaspoon dried
  rosemary
8 oz dried haricot beans,
  soaked in cold water
  overnight
1 whole clove
1 carrot, peeled and
  quartered
1 bouquet garni

Preparation time: about 20 minutes, plus soaking
Cooking time: about 1¾–2¼ hours
Oven: 160°C, 325°F, Gas Mark 3

Ask your butcher to bone, roll and tie the lamb as this can be a time-consuming task to do yourself at home. Alternatively, a leg of lamb can be used.

Cut 2 garlic cloves into slivers. Make several incisions in the lamb with a sharp, pointed knife and insert the garlic slivers. Rub salt and pepper into the skin of the lamb.

Heat the oil in a large flameproof casserole, and brown the lamb on all sides over brisk heat. Lower the heat, remove from the pan and set aside.

Chop 1 onion, add to the pan and fry gently until soft and golden. Crush the remaining garlic clove with a little salt, then add to the onion with the tomatoes, wine or water, rosemary and pepper to taste. Bring to the boil, stirring, then lower the heat and return the lamb to the pan. Cover, transfer to a preheated oven and cook for 1½–2 hours or until the lamb is cooked to your liking.

Meanwhile, drain the beans and place in a pan. Stick the clove into the remaining whole onion, then add to the beans with the carrot and bouquet garni. Cover with fresh cold water and bring to the boil, then lower the heat, half cover with a lid and simmer for 1½–2 hours or until the beans are tender.

When the lamb is cooked, lift out of the casserole and remove the string. Place the lamb on a warmed serving platter and cover with foil. Turn the oven down to its lowest possible setting and place the lamb in the oven to keep warm.

Drain the beans, discarding the onion, carrot and bouquet garni. Stir the beans into the cooking liquid in the casserole and simmer on top of the stove for a few minutes. Taste and adjust the seasoning, then spoon around the lamb on the platter. Serve immediately.

Serves 4–6

Epaule d'agneau aux haricots; Gigot de mouton au genièvre

Gigot de mouton au genièvre
Roast leg of lamb with juniper

Metric
1 × 1.5 kg leg of lamb
4 garlic cloves, peeled
3 × 15 ml spoons juniper
   berries
salt
75 ml olive oil
3 × 15 ml spoons cider
   or wine vinegar
2 × 5 ml spoons freshly
   chopped rosemary
2 × 5 ml spoons freshly
   chopped marjoram
freshly ground black
   pepper

Imperial
1 × 3¼ lb leg of lamb
4 garlic cloves, peeled
3 tablespoons juniper
   berries
salt
3 fl oz olive oil
3 tablespoons cider or
   wine vinegar
2 teaspoons freshly
   chopped rosemary
2 teaspoons freshly
   chopped marjoram
freshly ground black
   pepper

Preparation time: 15 minutes, plus marinating
Cooking time: about 1½ hours
Oven: 190°C, 375°F, Gas Mark 5

The lamb is marinated in this recipe for up to 3 days and the longer you leave it to marinate, the better it will taste when cooked.

Cut deep incisions in the lamb with a sharp pointed knife, making as many as possible close to the bone. Into these incisions insert 2 garlic cloves cut into thin slivers, adding a juniper berry with each garlic sliver. Crush the remaining garlic and juniper berries in a mortar and pestle. Rub 1 × 5 ml spoon/1 teaspoon salt all over the surface of the lamb, then rub in the crushed garlic and juniper mixture.

Place the lamb in a large shallow dish. Mix the oil and vinegar in a small bowl with the herbs and pepper to taste. Brush all over the lamb. Cover and leave to marinate in the refrigerator for up to 3 days, turning the meat over and brushing it with the marinade as often as possible.

Place the lamb in a roasting tin, pour over the marinade from the dish, then roast in a preheated oven for 1½ hours or until the lamb is cooked to your liking. Turn the joint over frequently during the roasting time and baste with the marinade and cooking juices. Transfer the cooked joint to a warmed serving dish, then leave to stand in a warm place for 5 minutes before carving. Serve hot.

Variation:
In France the lamb would be served as it is, with only the juices from the roasting tin. If you prefer to serve a gravy, place the roasting tin on top of the stove after removing the lamb and stir in 2 × 15 ml spoons/2 tablespoons plain flour. Cook over moderate heat for 2 minutes until browned, stirring constantly, then gradually stir in 150 ml/¼ pint full-bodied red wine and 300 ml/½ pint water. Bring to the boil, then lower the heat and simmer gently for a few minutes until thickened. Add salt and pepper to taste, then pour into a warmed sauceboat.

Rognons au madère
Kidneys in Madeira

Preparation time: 15 minutes
Cooking time: 35 minutes

If you do not have Madeira, and do not want to go to the expense of buying a bottle specially for this dish, use a dry or medium sherry instead.

Metric
75 g butter
12 lamb's kidneys skinned and sliced, with cores removed
100 g button mushrooms, thinly sliced
salt
freshly ground black pepper
2 shallots or 1 small onion, peeled and finely chopped
1 garlic clove, peeled and crushed with 1 × 2.5 ml salt
1 × 15 ml spoon plain flour
4 × 15 ml spoons Madeira
2 × 15 ml spoons freshly chopped parsley
2 × 15 ml spoons Moutarde de Meaux

Imperial
3 oz butter
12 lamb's kidneys skinned and sliced, with cores removed
4 oz button mushrooms, thinly sliced
salt
freshly ground black pepper
2 shallots or 1 small onion, peeled and finely chopped
1 garlic clove, peeled and crushed with ½ teaspoon salt
1 tablespoon plain flour
4 tablespoons Madeira
2 tablespoons freshly chopped parsley
2 tablespoons Moutarde de Meaux

Melt 50 g/2 oz butter in a large heavy frying pan. Add the kidneys and mushrooms with salt and pepper and fry over moderate heat for about 8 minutes, shaking the pan constantly until the kidneys are lightly browned on all sides and the juices run faintly pink. Remove the kidneys and mushrooms from the pan with a slotted spoon and keep warm in the lowest possible oven. Pour the cooking juices into a jug.
Melt the remaining butter in the pan, add the shallots or onion and garlic and fry gently until soft and lightly coloured. Sprinkle in the flour and fry for a further 1–2 minutes, stirring constantly, then gradually add the Madeira and the reserved cooking juices. Bring to the boil, then lower the heat and return the kidneys and mushrooms to the pan. Stir to coat them in the sauce, then lower the heat and simmer very gently for 15 minutes until the kidneys are tender. Remove from the heat and stir in the parsley and mustard. Taste and adjust the seasoning, then transfer to a warmed serving dish. Serve immediately.

Estouffat de boeuf
Brisket of beef with red wine

Preparation time: about 30 minutes
Cooking time: about 3½ hours
Oven: 150°C, 300°F, Gas Mark 2

Metric
2 × 15 ml spoons beef
   dripping or vegetable
   oil
1–1.125 kg joint brisket
   of beef
1 large onion, peeled
   and chopped
1 garlic clove, peeled
   and crushed with
   1 × 2.5 ml spoon salt
2 large carrots, peeled
   and sliced
2 leeks, sliced
300 ml full-bodied red
   wine
300 ml beef stock or
   water
1 bouquet garni
1 × 1.25 ml spoon ground
   cinnamon
1 × 1.25 ml spoon ground
   allspice
salt
freshly ground black
   pepper

To finish:
1 × 15 ml spoon
   Armagnac or brandy
   (optional)
1 × 15 ml spoon softened
   butter
2 × 15 ml spoons plain
   flour

Imperial
2 tablespoons beef
   dripping or vegetable
   oil
2–2½ lb joint brisket of
   beef
1 large onion, peeled
   and chopped
1 garlic clove, peeled
   and crushed with
   ½ teaspoon salt
2 large carrots, peeled
   and sliced
2 leeks, sliced
½ pint full-bodied red
   wine
½ pint beef stock or
   water
1 bouquet garni
¼ teaspoon ground
   cinnamon
¼ teaspoon ground
   allspice
salt
freshly ground black
   pepper

To finish:
1 tablespoon
   Armagnac or brandy
   (optional)
1 tablespoon softened
   butter
2 tablespoons plain
   flour

Melt the dripping or oil in a large flameproof casserole, add the beef and fry over brisk heart until browned on all sides. Remove from the pan and set aside.

Lower the heat, add the onion and garlic to the pan and fry gently until soft. Add the carrots and leeks and fry for a further few minutes, stirring until lightly coloured.

Stir in the wine and stock or water and bring to the boil. Lower the heat, add the bouquet garni, cinnamon, allspice and salt and pepper to taste, then return the beef to the pan. Cover and transfer to a preheated oven and cook for 3 hours or until the beef is tender, basting occasionally.

Remove the beef from the pan and remove any strings or threads. Place the beef on a warmed serving platter. Warm the Armagnac gently in a small pan, remove from the heat and ignite. When the flames have subsided, pour the brandy over the beef. Keep the meat warm.

Work the butter and flour to a paste (beurre manié) in a small bowl. Remove the bouquet garni from the liquid in the pan. Add the beurre manié a little at a time, whisking vigorously over high heat until the sauce boils and thickens. Taste and adjust the seasoning, then pour a little sauce over the beef. Pour the remaining sauce into a warmed sauceboat.

Rognons au madère; Estouffat de boeuf

Sauté de veau au vermouth
Veal with vermouth and orange

Metric	Imperial
4 veal escalopes, weighing about 100 g each	4 veal escalopes, weighing about 4 oz each
2 × 15 ml spoons plain flour	2 tablespoons plain flour
salt	salt
freshly ground black pepper	freshly ground black pepper
50 g butter	2 oz butter
2 × 15 ml spoons olive oil	2 tablespoons olive oil
juice of 2 oranges	juice of 2 oranges
150 ml dry white vermouth	¼ pint dry white vermouth
2 × 5 ml spoons dark soft brown sugar	2 teaspoons dark soft brown sugar
1–2 oranges, skinned and thinly sliced in rings	1–2 oranges, skinned and thinly sliced in rings

Preparation time: 10 minutes
Cooking time: about 25 minutes

For this dish the escalopes should be sliced very thin.

Beat the escalopes with a mallet or rolling pin. Pat them dry with paper towels, then coat evenly in the flour seasoned with salt and pepper. Melt 25 g/1 oz butter with the oil in a large heavy-based frying pan. Add the escalopes and fry over moderate heat for about 3 minutes on each side until lightly browned. Measure the orange juice and make up to 150 ml/¼ pint with water, if necessary. Pour over the escalopes, then simmer gently for about 8 minutes or until the veal is tender, turning it over once during this time. Remove the veal from the pan with a slotted spoon, arrange on a warmed serving platter and keep hot in a very low oven. Pour the vermouth into the pan, stir in the sugar and increase the heat. Boil vigorously until the sauce has thickened and reduced, stirring continuously with a wooden spoon to loosen any sediment from the bottom and sides of the pan.
Remove the pan from the heat, stir in the remaining butter in pieces, then whisk until the butter has dissolved and the sauce has a shiny glaze. Taste and adjust the seasoning, then pour over the veal. Garnish with orange rings and serve immediately.

Sauté de veau au vermouth; Sauté de veau marengo

Sauté de veau marengo
Sautéed veal with mushrooms

Preparation time: 30 minutes
Cooking time: about 2 hours

Metric

*4 × 15 ml spoons olive
oil*
*1 kg pie or stewing
veal, cut into bite-
sized pieces*
*1 medium onion, peeled
and finely chopped*
*2 garlic cloves, peeled
and crushed with 1 ×
2.5 ml spoon salt*
*2 × 15 ml spoons plain
flour*
*225 g tomatoes, skinned,
seeded and chopped*
300 ml dry white wine
*150–300 ml chicken stock
or water*
1 bouquet garni
1 strip of orange peel
salt
*freshly ground black
pepper*
*12 small pickling
onions, peeled*
*12 small button
mushrooms*
*freshly chopped parsley,
to garnish*

Imperial

*4 tablespoons olive
oil*
*2 lb pie or stewing
veal, cut into bite-
sized pieces*
*1 medium onion, peeled
and finely chopped*
*2 garlic cloves, peeled
and crushed with ½
teaspoon salt*
*2 tablespoons plain
flour*
*8 oz tomatoes, skinned,
seeded and chopped*
½ pint dry white wine
*¼–½ pint chicken stock
or water*
1 bouquet garni
1 strip of orange peel
salt
*freshly ground black
pepper*
*12 small pickling
onions, peeled*
*12 small button
mushrooms*
*freshly chopped parsley,
to garnish*

Heat 3 × 15 ml spoons/3 tablespoons oil in a large flameproof casserole, add the veal and fry over brisk heat until browned on all sides. Remove from the pan with a slotted spoon and set aside.

Lower the heat, add the chopped onion and garlic to the pan and fry gently until soft. Stir in the flour and fry for a further 2 minutes, stirring constantly. Stir in the tomatoes and fry for about 5 minutes, crushing them into the onion and garlic with a wooden spoon.

Return the veal to the pan and stir in the wine and 150 ml/¼ pint stock or water. Bring to the boil, then add the bouquet garni, orange peel and salt and pepper. Lower the heat, cover the pan and simmer gently for 1 hour or until the veal is barely tender, stirring occasionally.

Meanwhile, heat the remaining oil in a separate pan, add the whole onions and fry gently until lightly coloured on all sides. Add the mushrooms and fry for a further 2 minutes, then remove both onions and mushrooms from the pan with a slotted spoon and drain on paper towels.

Remove the veal from the casserole with a slotted spoon and set aside. Pass the cooking liquid through a sieve, pressing firmly to extract all the juices. Return the veal and sieved cooking juices to the rinsed-out casserole, then stir in the small onions and mushrooms. Stir in more stock or water if the sauce seems too thick.

Return the casserole to the heat, bring to the boil, then lower the heat and simmer gently for a further 30 minutes or until the veal is tender. Taste and adjust the seasoning of the sauce, then sprinkle liberally with chopped parsley.

Poulet à l'estragon
Chicken with tarragon butter sauce

Metric	Imperial
100 g butter	4 oz butter
1 × 2 kg oven-ready chicken	1 × 4 lb oven-ready chicken
4 garlic cloves, peeled	4 garlic cloves, peeled
2 × 15 ml spoons freshly chopped tarragon or 1 × 15 ml spoon dried tarragon	2 tablespoons freshly chopped tarragon or 1 tablespoon dried tarragon
salt	salt
freshly ground black pepper	freshly ground black pepper
2 × 15 ml spoons plain flour	2 tablespoons plain flour
450 ml dry white wine and water, mixed	¾ pint dry white wine and water, mixed

Preparation time: 10 minutes
Cooking time: 1 hour 40 minutes
Oven: 190°C, 375°F, Gas Mark 5

Use as much white wine as you can spare for the sauce, and for a dinner party main course swirl in 150 ml/¼ pint double cream just before serving. For an economical meal, the sauce can be made with chicken stock rather than the mixture of white wine and water.

Put half the butter inside the cavity of the chicken with 2 whole garlic cloves, half the tarragon and salt and pepper to taste. Truss with thread or fine string, then put in a roasting tin.
Crush the remaining garlic cloves with 1 × 2.5 ml spoon/½ teaspoon salt. Beat into the remaining butter with the rest of the tarragon until soft, then spread the mixture all over the skin of the chicken. Sprinkle with salt and pepper.
Roast in a preheated oven for about 1½ hours or until the juices of the chicken run clear when the thickest part of the thigh is pierced with a skewer. Turn the chicken over a quarter turn every 15 minutes during roasting, and baste with the cooking juices.
Transfer the chicken to a warmed serving platter and keep hot in the lowest possible oven. Pour off all but 2 × 15 ml spoons/2 tablespoons of the excess fat and juices from the roasting tin. Place the roasting tin on top of the stove over moderate heat and sprinkle in the flour. Cook for 1–2 minutes until golden brown, stirring constantly, then gradually stir in the wine and water mixture. Bring to the boil, then lower the heat and simmer until thickened, stirring all the time. Taste and adjust the seasoning, then pour into a warmed sauceboat. Serve the chicken immediately, with the sauce handed separately.

Poulet basquaise
Chicken Basque-style

Metric	Imperial
4 × 15 ml spoons olive oil	4 tablespoons olive oil
4 chicken portions, skinned	4 chicken portions, skinned
1 medium onion, peeled and finely chopped	1 medium onion, peeled and finely chopped
1 garlic clove, peeled and crushed with 1 × 2.5 ml spoon salt	1 garlic clove, peeled and crushed with ½ teaspoon salt
½ red pepper, cored, seeded and finely chopped	½ red pepper, cored, seeded and finely chopped
½ green pepper, cored, seeded and finely chopped	½ green pepper, cored, seeded and finely chopped
350 g tomatoes, skinned, seeded and chopped	12 oz tomatoes, skinned, seeded and chopped
150 ml chicken stock	¼ pint chicken stock
4 × 15 ml spoons brandy or medium sherry	4 tablespoons brandy or medium sherry
2 × 5 ml spoons freshly chopped rosemary or 1 × 5 ml spoon dried rosemary	2 teaspoons freshly chopped rosemary or 1 teaspoon dried rosemary
2 × 5 ml spoons freshly chopped thyme or 1 × 5 ml spoon dried thyme	2 teaspoons freshly chopped thyme or 1 teaspoon dried thyme
salt	salt
freshly ground black pepper	freshly ground black pepper

Preparation time: 30 minutes
Cooking time: about 1¼ hours

In the south-western corner of France, customs and cuisine are very closely linked with the Basque country across the border in Spain and onions, garlic, peppers and tomatoes are dominant features.

Heat the oil in a large flameproof casserole, add the chicken and fry gently until browned on all sides. Remove from the pan and set aside.
Add the onion to the pan and fry gently until soft. Add the garlic and peppers and fry for a further few minutes, then stir in the tomatoes, chicken stock or water and brandy and bring to the boil.
Lower the heat, add the rosemary, thyme, and salt and pepper to taste, then return the chicken to the pan. Simmer gently, uncovered, for 45 minutes or until the chicken is tender and the liquid and vegetables are reduced. Serve immediately.

Top: Poulet à l'estragon; Below: Poulet basquaise

Poulet au foie gras
Chicken with foie gras sauce

Metric
4 chicken breasts, boned
   and skinned
1 garlic clove, peeled
   and halved
50 g butter
2 × 15 ml spoons olive oil
salt
freshly ground black
   pepper
150 ml full-bodied red
   wine
1 × 150 g can pâté de
   foie gras
150 ml single cream
175–225 g button mush-
   rooms, finely sliced

Imperial
4 chicken breasts, boned
   and skinned
1 garlic clove, peeled
   and halved
2 oz butter
2 tablespoons olive oil
salt
freshly ground black
   pepper
$\frac{1}{4}$ pint full-bodied red
   wine
1 × 5 oz can pâté de
   foie gras
$\frac{1}{4}$ pint single cream
6–8 oz button mushrooms,
   finely sliced

Preparation time: about 20 minutes
Cooking time: 45 minutes

Rub the chicken all over with the cut surfaces of the garlic. Melt half the butter with the oil in a large frying pan. Add the chicken and fry over moderate heat until golden on all sides. Sprinkle with salt and pepper to taste, pour in the wine and bring to the boil. Lower the heat, cover and cook gently for about 30 minutes or until the chicken is tender.

Meanwhile, put the pâté in a bowl and beat until smooth with a wooden spoon or electric beater. Gradually beat in the cream.

Remove the chicken from the pan with a slotted spoon and keep warm on a serving platter in the lowest possible oven. Stir the pâté mixture into the cooking juices in the pan a little at a time, whisking vigorously until a smooth sauce is formed. Add salt and pepper to taste, if necessary, then simmer gently for 5 minutes, stirring occasionally.

Meanwhile, melt the remaining butter in a separate pan. Add the mushrooms and fry over brisk heat for 1–2 minutes, shaking the pan constantly.

Pour the sauce over the chicken and garnish each portion with a cluster of mushroom slices. Serve immediately.

Poulet au fromage
Chicken with cheese and wine sauce

Metric	Imperial
4 chicken portions, skinned	4 chicken portions, skinned
1 × 15 ml spoon lemon juice	1 tablespoon lemon juice
salt	salt
freshly ground black pepper	freshly ground black pepper
75 g butter	3 oz butter
50 g plain flour	2 oz plain flour
150 ml dry white wine	¼ pint dry white wine
200 ml milk	⅓ pint milk
100 g Gruyère cheese, grated	4 oz Gruyère cheese, grated
1 × 1.25 ml spoon ground mace	¼ teaspoon ground mace
100 g button mushrooms, thinly sliced	4 oz button mushrooms, thinly sliced

Preparation time: 10–15 minutes
Cooking time: 50 minutes–1 hour 5 minutes
Oven: 180°C, 350°F, Gas Mark 4

Put the chicken portions in a single layer in a shallow flameproof casserole. Sprinkle over the lemon juice, and salt and pepper to taste, then dot with 25 g/1 oz butter. Cover with foil and cook in a preheated oven for 45 minutes to 1 hour until the chicken is just tender. Baste occasionally with the cooking juices during this time.

Fifteen minutes before the end of the cooking time, make the sauce. Melt the remaining butter in a heavy-based pan, add the flour and stir over low heat for 1–2 minutes. Remove from the heat and gradually add the wine and then the milk, beating with a wire balloon whisk after each addition. Return to the heat and bring to the boil, stirring constantly, then lower the heat and simmer until thick and smooth. Add 75 g/3 oz cheese, the mace, and salt and pepper to taste, and stir until the cheese has melted. Remove from the heat and stir in the mushrooms.

When the chicken is tender, drain off the cooking juices and stir into the cheese sauce. Pour the sauce over the chicken and sprinkle with the remaining cheese. Put under a preheated hot grill for 5 minutes until the cheese is melted and bubbling.

Clockwise from top: Poulet au foie gras; Lapin à la moutarde; Poulet au fromage

Lapin à la moutarde
Rabbit smothered in mustard

Metric	Imperial
4 rabbit portions (total weight about 1 kg)	4 rabbit portions (total weight about 2 lb)
6 × 15 ml spoons light Dijon mustard	6 tablespoons light Dijon mustard
4 × 15 ml spoons oil	4 tablespoons oil
225 g shallots or 2 medium onions, peeled and finely chopped	8 oz shallots or 2 medium onions, peeled and finely chopped
3 × 15 ml spoons plain flour	3 tablespoons plain flour
1 × 5 ml spoon freshly chopped rosemary or 1 × 2.5 ml spoon dried rosemary	1 teaspoon freshly chopped rosemary or ½ teaspoon dried rosemary
1 × 5 ml spoon freshly chopped thyme or 1 × 2.5 ml spoon dried thyme	1 teaspoon freshly chopped thyme or ½ teaspoon dried thyme
300 ml dry white wine or cider	½ pint dry white wine or cider
salt	salt
freshly ground black pepper	freshly ground black pepper
1 bunch watercress, to garnish	1 bunch watercress, to garnish

Preparation time: 15 minutes, plus marinating
Cooking time: 1¼–1½ hours

The quantity of mustard in this recipe can be adjusted to suit individual tastes, although it should be quite strong to be authentic.

Spread the rabbit with 4 × 15 ml spoons/4 tablespoons mustard, then cover and leave in a cool place for at least 4 hours, preferably overnight.

Heat the oil in a large flameproof casserole, add the rabbit pieces and fry over moderate heat until browned on all sides. Remove from the pan with a slotted spoon and set aside.

Add the shallots or onions to the pan and fry gently until soft. Stir in the flour, rosemary and thyme and fry for a further 1–2 minutes, stirring constantly. Stir in the wine or cider, bring to just below boiling point, then return the rabbit to the pan. Add salt and pepper to taste, cover and simmer gently for 45 minutes–1 hour or until the rabbit is tender.

Remove the rabbit from the sauce with a slotted spoon. Place in a warmed serving dish and keep hot. Stir in the remaining mustard, heat through, then taste and adjust the seasoning. Spoon the sauce over the rabbit pieces and garnish with watercress sprigs. Serve immediately.

Perdreaux aux raisins
Partridge with green grape sauce

Metric
50 g butter
2 partridges
salt
freshly ground black
pepper
2–3 celery sticks,
finely chopped
2 shallots or 1 small
onion, peeled and
finely chopped
225 g seedless green
grapes, stalks
removed
2 × 15 ml spoons brandy
(optional)
300 ml dry white wine

To finish:
1 × 15 ml spoon
softened butter
1 × 15 ml spoon plain
flour

Imperial
2 oz butter
2 partridges
salt
freshly ground black
pepper
2–3 celery sticks,
finely chopped
2 shallots or 1 small
onion, peeled and
finely chopped
8 oz seedless green
grapes, stalks
removed
2 tablespoons brandy
(optional)
½ pint dry white wine

To finish:
1 tablespoon softened
butter
1 tablespoon plain
flour

Preparation time: 15 minutes
Cooking time: about 1¼–1½ hours

In France partridges are immensely popular birds for the table although their season is confined to September to January. Oven-ready partridges are available fresh from butchers specializing in game. However, excellent-quality frozen birds are available from large supermarkets all year round. Defrost them for 24 hours in the refrigerator before cooking.

Cut half the butter into 2 equal pieces and place 1 piece inside each partridge. Sprinkle inside and out with salt and pepper.
Melt the remaining butter in a large flameproof casserole, add the partridges and fry over moderate heat until lightly browned on all sides. Remove and drain on paper towels.
Add the celery and shallots or onion to the casserole and fry gently until softened. Stir in the grapes and fry gently for a further 1–2 minutes, then place the partridges on top of the grapes.
If using the brandy, warm it gently in a small pan, remove from the heat and ignite. When the flames have subsided, pour the brandy over the partridges.
Pour the wine into the casserole and bring to boil. Lower the heat, add salt and pepper to taste, then cover and simmer gently for 45 minutes–1 hour until the partridges are tender when pierced with a skewer. Baste the partridges occasionally with the cooking liquid during this time.
Remove the partridges and discard the barding fat and trussing strings. Place the birds on a warmed serving platter, cover with foil and keep warm.
To finish, work the butter and flour to a paste (beurre manié). Add to the sauce in the pan a little at a time, whisking vigorously over high heat until the sauce thickens. Taste and adjust the seasoning, then pour a little sauce over each partridge breast. Serve with the remaining sauce in a warmed sauceboat.

Perdreaux aux raisins;
Canard aux cerises à l'aigre-doux

Canard aux cerises à l'aigre-doux
Duck with sweet and sour cherries

Preparation time: 15 minutes
Cooking time: about 2¼ hours
Oven: 220°C, 425°F, Gas Mark 7;
    180°C, 350°F, Gas Mark 4

Metric	Imperial
1 × 2–2.25 kg duck	1 × 4½–5 lb duck
salt	salt
freshly ground black pepper	freshly ground black pepper
2 oranges	2 oranges
1 onion, peeled and quartered	1 onion, peeled and quartered
1 bouquet garni	1 bouquet garni
25 g butter, softened	1 oz butter, softened
1 × 425 g can sweetened red or black cherries	1 × 15 oz can sweetened red or black cherries
3 × 15 ml spoons red wine vinegar	3 tablespoons red wine vinegar
finely grated rind and juice of 1 orange	finely grated rind and juice of 1 orange
2 × 15 ml spoons cherry brandy (optional)	2 tablespoons cherry brandy (optional)
1 × 15 ml spoon arrowroot	1 tablespoon arrowroot

Sprinkle the inside of the duck with salt and pepper. Cut 1 orange into quarters, then place inside the duck with the onion quarters and the bouquet garni. Truss with thread or fine string.

Place the duck on a rack in a roasting tin and prick the fattiest parts of the skin with the point of a fine skewer. Spread the softened butter all over the bird, then sprinkle with salt and pepper and the juice of the remaining orange.

Cover the duck with foil and roast in a preheated oven for 30 minutes. Reduce the oven temperature and roast for a further 1¾ hours or until the duck is tender and the juices run clear when the thickest part of the thigh is pierced with a skewer. Remove the foil for the last 30 minutes of the cooking time so that the skin becomes crisp and golden brown, sprinkling with more salt if necessary.

During the last 15 minutes of the cooking time, make the sauce. Drain the cherries, reserving half the juice from the can. Put the cherry juice, wine vinegar, orange rind and juice in a measuring jug with the cherry brandy, if using. Make up to 450 ml/¾ pint with water.

In a separate jug, mix the arrowroot to a paste with a little of the measured liquid. Pour the remaining measured liquid into a pan and bring to the boil. Stir in the arrowroot paste and boil vigorously until the sauce thickens. Lower the heat, add the cherries and salt and pepper to taste, then simmer gently for 2–3 minutes until the cherries are heated through.

Remove the thread or string from the duck and place on a warmed serving platter. Pour a little of the sauce over the breast. Serve with the remaining sauce in a warmed sauceboat.
Serves 3–4

VEGETABLES

The vegetable in France holds an exalted place in culinary terms. Rarely will you be served a vegetable on the same plate as the main course, for the French like to savour their vegetables on their own, after the main course. This is why such a great deal of care and attention goes into their selection, preparation and cooking. Usually only one (or at the most two) vegetables are served during the main meal of the day, plus one of the many different potato dishes. Fresh vegetables are always preferred to frozen and canned, and the younger and fresher they are the better, because they are almost always cooked for the shortest possible time, in the minimum amount of liquid.

Fèves à la saucisse à l'ail; Artichauts farcis parisiens

Fèves à la saucisse à l'ail
Broad beans with garlic sausage

Metric	Imperial
1¾ kg fresh broad beans, shelled, or 450 g frozen broad beans	4 lb fresh broad beans, shelled, or 1 lb frozen broad beans
salt	salt
25 g butter	1 oz butter
2 shallots or 1 onion, peeled and finely chopped	2 shallots or 1 onion, peeled and finely chopped
100 g piece garlic sausage, roughly chopped	4 oz piece garlic sausage, roughly chopped
2 × 5 ml spoons freshly chopped savory or 1 × 5 ml spoon dried savory	2 teaspoons freshly chopped savory or 1 teaspoon dried savory
freshly ground black pepper	freshly ground black pepper
150 ml single cream	¼ pint single cream

Preparation time: 5–10 minutes
Cooking time: 20–25 minutes for fresh beans;
      10–15 minutes for frozen

Cook the beans in boiling salted water, allowing 15–20 minutes for fresh beans, 6–8 minutes for frozen or according to packet instruction.
Meanwhile, melt the butter in a heavy-based pan, add the shallots or onion and fry gently until soft and lightly coloured. Add the garlic sausage and fry for 2–3 minutes, stirring frequently.
Drain the beans and add to the onion and garlic sausage with the savory, and salt and pepper to taste. Fold the ingredients together well, then stir in the cream and heat through gently without boiling. Transfer to a warmed serving dish and serve immediately. Serve with lamb or pork dishes, especially grilled or roasted meat.

Artichauts farcis parisiens
Braised stuffed artichokes

Preparation time: about 40 minutes
Cooking time: about 1 hour
Oven: 180°C, 350°F, Gas Mark 4

Metric

4 young globe artichokes
½ lemon
1 × 15 ml spoon lemon
    juice
2 × 15 ml spoons olive oil
1 medium onion, peeled
    and chopped
2 carrots, peeled and very
    thinly sliced
salt
freshly ground black
    pepper
25 g butter
300 ml dry white wine

Stuffing:
50 g unsalted butter
50 g button mushrooms,
    finely chopped
50 g fresh white
    breadcrumbs
2 × 15 ml spoons freshly
    chopped parsley
2 × 5 ml spoons freshly
    chopped thyme or 1 × 5
    ml spoon dried thyme
2 garlic cloves, peeled
    and crushed with 1 ×
    2.5 ml spoon salt
finely grated rind of 1
    lemon

Imperial

4 young globe artichokes
½ lemon
1 tablespoon lemon
    juice
2 tablespoons olive oil
1 medium onion, peeled
    and chopped
2 carrots, peeled and very
    thinly sliced
salt
freshly ground black
    pepper
1 oz butter
½ pint dry white wine

Stuffing:
2 oz unsalted butter
2 oz button mushrooms,
    finely chopped
2 oz fresh white
    breadcrumbs
2 tablespoons freshly
    chopped parsley
2 teaspoons freshly
    chopped thyme or 1
    teaspoon dried thyme
2 garlic cloves, peeled
    and crushed with ½
    teaspoon salt
finely grated rind of 1
    lemon

Serve this substantial vegetable dish as an accompaniment to plain roast or grilled meat, or on its own as a starter before a light main course.

Cut the stems off the artichokes and level the bases so that they will stand upright. Remove the tough outer leaves, then cut off the tops of the remaining leaves about one-third of the way down to expose the chokes in the centre. Rub the cut surfaces immediately with the cut lemon to prevent them discolouring.

Plunge the artichokes into a pan of boiling water to which the lemon juice has been added. Bring back to the boil, then lower the heat and simmer for 10 minutes. Remove the artichokes from the pan with a slotted spoon, then stand them upside down in a colander to drain.

Meanwhile, make the stuffing. Melt the butter in a pan, add the mushrooms and fry gently for 2–3 minutes. Transfer to a bowl with the cooking juices and add all the remaining stuffing ingredients with salt and pepper to taste. Mix together well.

Stand the artichokes the right way up and carefully remove the chokes from their centres with a sharp-edged teaspoon. Fill the cavities with the stuffing.

Heat the oil in a large flameproof casserole into which the artichokes will just fit. Add the onion and carrots with salt and pepper to taste, and fry gently until lightly coloured. Stand the artichokes in the casserole, dot the top of each one with butter, then pour the wine around them and bring slowly to the boil.

Cover the casserole with a lid and transfer to a pre-heated oven. Cook for about 40 minutes or until the artichokes are tender. Serve immediately.

Tomates niçoises
Tomatoes with basil and cream

Metric	Imperial
3 × 15 ml spoons olive oil	3 tablespoons olive oil
1 large onion, peeled and thinly sliced	1 large onion, peeled and thinly sliced
10 large tomatoes, skinned and thinly sliced	10 large tomatoes, skinned and thinly sliced
2 × 5 ml spoons sugar	2 teaspoons sugar
1 × 15 ml spoon freshly chopped parsley	1 tablespoon freshly chopped parsley
2 × 5 ml spoons freshly chopped basil or 1 × 5 ml spoon dried basil	2 teaspoons freshly chopped basil or 1 teaspoon dried basil
salt	salt
freshly ground black pepper	freshly ground black pepper
300 ml double cream	½ pint double cream
75 g fresh white breadcrumbs	3 oz fresh white breadcrumbs
25 g butter	1 oz butter

Preparation time: 30 minutes
Cooking time: 45–50 minutes
Oven: 180°C, 350°F, Gas Mark 4

Heat 2 × 15 ml spoons/2 tablespoons oil in a frying pan, and fry the onion slices gently until soft.
Brush a baking dish with the remaining oil. Put one-third of the tomato slices in the bottom of the dish, sprinkle with a little sugar, parsley and basil, and salt and pepper to taste. Top with a few onion slices, then pour in about one-third of the cream.
Repeat these layers twice more, then sprinkle over the breadcrumbs to cover the cream completely. Dot with the butter. Bake, uncovered, in a preheated oven for 35–40 minutes, until golden.

Aubergines à l'ail
Aubergines roasted with garlic

Metric	Imperial
4 medium aubergines (175–225 g each), tops removed	4 medium aubergines (6–8 oz each), tops removed
6 × 15 ml spoons olive oil	6 tablespoons olive oil
4 garlic cloves, peeled and cut into thin slivers	4 garlic cloves, peeled and cut into thin slivers
4 tomatoes, skinned and thinly sliced	4 tomatoes, skinned and thinly sliced
4 × 5 ml spoons freshly chopped basil or 2 × 5 ml spoons dried basil	4 teaspoons freshly chopped basil or 2 teaspoons dried basil
salt	salt
freshly ground black pepper	freshly ground black pepper
150 ml dry white wine or water	¼ pint dry white wine or water

Preparation time: 20 minutes
Cooking time: 1½ hours
Oven: 180°C, 350°F, Gas Mark 4

Make 4 deep lengthways incisions in each aubergine with a sharp knife. Brush 1 × 15 ml spoon/1 tablespoon olive oil over the cut flesh of each aubergine, then insert the garlic slivers in them, allowing 1 garlic clove for each aubergine. Insert the tomato slices into the incisions on top of the garlic, then sprinkle in the basil, and salt and pepper to taste.
Stand the aubergines in a single layer in a baking dish into which they just fit. Pour the wine into the bottom of the dish, drizzle the remaining oil over the top, and sprinkle with more salt and pepper.
Cover with foil, then bake in a preheated oven for 1½ hours or until the aubergines are tender.
Serve with any roast or grilled meat.

Pommes de terre soufflées
Souffléed baked potatoes

Metric	Imperial
4 large potatoes	4 large potatoes
1 medium cooking apple	1 medium cooking apple
50 g unsalted butter, softened	2 oz unsalted butter, softened
2 eggs, separated	2 eggs, separated
1 × 5 ml spoon dried sage	1 teaspoon dried sage
salt	salt
freshly ground black pepper	freshly ground black pepper

Preparation time: about 40 minutes
Cooking time: 1¼–1¾ hours
Oven: 200°C, 400°F, Gas Mark 6

Prick the potatoes all over with a fine skewer, then place directly on the shelf of a preheated oven. Bake for 1–1½ hours or until the potatoes are soft and tender when gently squeezed between your fingers.
Remove the potatoes from the oven and slice each one in half lengthways. Scoop out the flesh into a bowl and mash well. Reserve the skins.
Peel, core and grate the apple, then beat into the potato flesh with the butter, egg yolks, sage and salt and pepper to taste.
In a separate bowl, beat the egg whites until stiff, then fold into the potato mixture. Spoon the mixture into the reserved potato skins, dividing it equally and moulding it into a domed shape. Return to the oven, on a shelf above the centre, and bake for a further 15 minutes or until puffed up and golden brown.
Serve with casseroles, barbecued meat or with cold meats and a salad.

Beignets de pommes de terre
Potato fritters with cream cheese

Metric	Imperial
1 kg potatoes, peeled	2 lb potatoes, peeled
100 g cream cheese	4 oz cream cheese
2 eggs	2 eggs
2 × 15 ml spoons snipped chives or freshly chopped parsley	2 tablespoons snipped chives or freshly chopped parsley
salt	salt
freshly ground black pepper	freshly ground black pepper
vegetable oil, for shallow frying	vegetable oil, for shallow frying

Preparation time: about 30 minutes
Cooking time: about 15–20 minutes

Grate the potatoes, squeeze them in your hands to extract as much moisture as possible, then pat dry with paper towels.
Put the cream cheese in a bowl and beat until soft. Beat in the eggs, then the grated potatoes, chives or parsley, and salt and pepper to taste.
Pour enough oil into a deep frying pan to come about 2.5 cm/1 inch up the sides of the pan.
Place the pan over moderate heat until the oil is sizzling hot, then drop the potato mixture into the hot oil 1 × 15 spoon/1 tablespoon at a time, spacing them well apart. Fry for about 5 minutes until golden brown on each side, turning them once, then remove from the oil with a slotted spoon. Drain on paper towels and keep hot while frying the remainder.
Serve instead of French fries with grills, fried fish or Tournedos Dijon (page 41).
Makes 20–24

Tomates niçoises; Aubergines à l'ail; Pommes de terre soufflées; Beignets de pommes de terre

Beignets de chou-fleur
Cauliflower fritters

Metric	Imperial
1 × 1 kg cauliflower, stalks removed and divided into florets	1 × 2 lb cauliflower, stalks removed and divided into florets
salt	salt
1 × 15 ml spoon lemon juice	1 tablespoon lemon juice
vegetable oil, for deep-frying	vegetable oil, for deep-frying

Fritter batter:	Fritter batter:
115 g plain flower	4½ oz plain flour
1 × 1.25 ml spoon cayenne pepper	¼ teaspoon cayenne pepper
2 eggs, beaten	2 eggs, beaten
150 ml milk	¼ pint milk
1 × 15 ml spoon melted butter	1 tablespoon melted butter

Preparation time: 15 minutes, plus standing
Cooking time: about 20 minutes

For a starter serve these fritters with tartare sauce or a freshly made tomato sauce which has plenty of flavour – the tomato sauce recipe with Timbale au Jambon (page 29), which is made with onions and garlic, is ideal.

Plunge the cauliflower florets into a large pan of boiling salted water, swirl in the lemon juice, then bring the water back to the boil. Lower the heat and simmer for 2 minutes. Drain thoroughly and cool.
Meanwhile, make the fritter batter. Sift the flour, cayenne and a pinch of salt into a bowl and make a well in the centre. Pour in the eggs, then whisk vigorously with a wire balloon whisk, gradually whisking in half the milk and incorporating the flour from the sides into the centre. Pour in the remaining milk and whisk again until the batter is smooth. Stir in the melted butter.
Stir the cooled cauliflower into the batter, cover and leave to stand for 15–20 minutes, stirring frequently. Heat the oil in a deep-fat frier to 190°C/375°F or until a stale bread cube turns golden in 40–50 seconds. Remove a few of the cauliflower florets from the bowl of batter with a slotted spoon and deep-fry in the hot oil for 2–3 minutes until light golden in colour. Drain on paper towels and keep hot while quickly frying the remainder. Serve immediately, together with the crisp pieces of batter that collect in the pan during frying.
Serve with roasts or as a starter.
Serves 4–6

Epinards aux pignons
Spinach with pine nuts and raisins

Metric	Imperial
1 kg fresh spinach	2 lb fresh spinach
salt	salt
3 × 15 ml spoons olive oil	3 tablespoons olive oil
50 g pine nuts or flaked almonds	2 oz pine nuts or flaked almonds
100 g seedless raisins	4 oz seedless raisins
freshly ground black pepper	freshly ground black pepper

Preparation time: about 30 minues
Cooking time: about 25 minutes

If fresh spinach is not available, use 450 g/1 lb frozen whole leaf spinach; defrost and cook according to packet instructions, then add to the pan of nuts and raisins as with the fresh spinach.

Wash the spinach carefully under cold running water, discarding tough discoloured leaves and large coarse stalks. Put in a large pan with only the water clinging to the leaves. Sprinkle with 1 × 5 ml spoon/1 teaspoon salt and heat gently until the juices flow from the spinach. Cover the pan with a tight-fitting lid and cook gently for about 8 minutes, shaking the pan constantly.
Drain the spinach very thoroughly, then turn on to a board or work surface and chop roughly.
Heat the oil in a large frying pan, add the pine nuts, or almonds, and raisins and fry over moderate heat for about 5 minutes. Stir constantly until the nuts turn golden.
Add the spinach to the pan and stir to mix with the nuts and raisins. Add salt and pepper to taste and continue frying and stirring until the spinach is heated through. Transfer to a warmed serving dish.
Serve with all meats, especially Filet de Porc Tourangeau (page 44), Porc au lait (page 45), and Tournedos Dijon (page 41). This vegetable dish also goes well with omelettes.

Epinards aux pignons; Beignets de chou-fleur; Haricots verts au lard

Haricots verts au lard
French beans with bacon

Metric	Imperial
450 g French beans, topped and tailed	*1 lb French beans, topped and tailed*
salt	*salt*
4 rashers streaky bacon, rinds removed, cut into thin strips	*4 rashers streaky bacon, rinds removed, cut into thin strips*
2 shallots or 1 small onion, peeled and finely chopped	*2 shallots or 1 small onion, peeled and finely chopped*
2 eggs	*2 eggs*
1 × 15 ml spoon wine vinegar	*1 tablespoon wine vinegar*
freshly ground black pepper	*freshly ground black pepper*
freshly chopped savory or parsley, to garnish (optional)	*freshly chopped savory or parsley, to garnish (optional)*

Preparation time: about 15 minutes
Cooking time: about 30–35 minutes

Plunge the beans into a large pan of boiling salted water, bring quickly back to the boil, then lower the heat and simmer for about 15 minutes or until the beans are tender.

Meanwhile, put the bacon pieces in a heavy-based pan and fry over gentle heat until the fat runs from the bacon. Add the shallots or onion and continue frying until both bacon and shallots are lightly coloured. Put the eggs and vinegar in a bowl with 1 × 15 ml spoon/1 tablespoon boiling water from the beans. Beat well to mix.

Drain the beans, then stir them into the bacon and onions. Pour in the egg mixture and stir over moderate heat until the mixture is creamy and coats the beans. Add salt and pepper to taste, then transfer to a warmed serving dish.

Serve with egg and cheese dishes, chicken or meat, and especially Paupiettes de Boeuf (page 42) and Filet de Porc Tourangeau (page 44).

Croquettes de panais
Parsnip croquettes

Metric
450 g parsnips, peeled and
  cut into chunks
2 medium potatoes, peeled
  and halved
salt
50 g plain flour
25 g butter, softened
freshly ground black
  pepper
vegetable oil, for deep
  frying

Coating:
about 2 × 15 ml spoons
  plain flour
1 large egg, beaten
75 g dried breadcrumbs
25 g blanched almonds,
  finely chopped

Imperial
1 lb parsnips, peeled and
  cut into chunks
2 medium potatoes, peeled
  and halved
salt
2 oz plain flour
1 oz butter, softened
freshly ground black
  pepper
vegetable oil, for deep
  frying

Coating:
about 2 tablespoons plain
  flour
1 large egg, beaten
3 oz dried breadcrumbs
1 oz blanched almonds,
  finely chopped

Preparation time: about 45 minutes, plus chilling
Cooking time: about 35 minutes

Cook the parsnips and potatoes in a pan of boiling salted water for about 20 minutes until tender. Drain thoroughly, then return to the rinsed-out pan and place over gentle heat to remove excess moisture. Stir constantly to prevent the vegetables catching on the bottom of the pan.

Transfer the vegetables to a bowl and leave to cool slightly, then mash until smooth. Beat in the flour, butter, and salt and pepper to taste until evenly mixed. With well-floured hands, form the mixture into 8 croquette shapes. Coat with the flour, dip first into the beaten egg, then into the breadcrumbs mixed with the chopped almonds. When evenly and thoroughly coated, chill the croquettes in the refrigerator for at least 1 hour.

Heat the oil in a deep-fat fryer to 190°C/375°F or until a stale bread cube turns golden in 40–50 seconds. Lower a few of the croquettes carefully into the hot oil, then deep-fry for about 5 minutes until they are golden brown on all sides. Drain on paper towels and keep hot while frying the remainder.

Serve immediately with roasts and grills, particularly beef and steaks.

Topinambours aux tomates
Jerusalem artichokes with tomatoes

Metric
1 kg Jerusalem artichokes
salt
juice of 1 lemon
25 g butter
2 × 15 ml spoons olive oil
1 medium onion, peeled
  and thinly sliced
1–2 garlic cloves, peeled
  and crushed with 1 ×
  2.5 ml spoon salt
225 g tomatoes, skinned,
  seeded and chopped
2 × 5 ml spoons freshly
  chopped basil or 1 × 5
  ml spoon dried basil
freshly ground black
  pepper

Imperial
2 lb Jerusalem artichokes
salt
juice of 1 lemon
1 oz butter
2 tablespoons olive oil
1 medium onion, peeled
  and thinly sliced
1–2 garlic cloves, peeled
  and crushed with ½
  teaspoon salt
8 oz tomatoes, skinned,
  seeded and chopped
2 teaspoons freshly
  chopped basil or 1
  teaspoon dried basil
freshly ground black
  pepper

Preparation time: 30 minutes
Cooking time: about 50 minutes

Put the artichokes in a large pan of salted water to which the lemon juice has been added. Bring to the boil, then lower the heat, cover and simmer for 7 minutes. Drain and leave until cool enough to handle. Meanwhile, melt the butter with the oil in a separate pan, add the onion and garlic and fry gently until soft and lightly coloured. Stir in the tomatoes, basil, and salt and pepper to taste, then simmer over very gentle heat for about 5 minutes, stirring occasionally to break up the tomatoes.

Peel the artichokes and slice thickly. Stir into the tomato mixture until coated, then cover and simmer very gently for about 30 minutes or until the artichokes are tender. Stir occasionally during this time to prevent the artichokes from catching on the bottom of the pan, and if necessary stir in a little water from time to time. Taste and adjust the seasoning. Put into a warmed serving dish and serve immediately.

Serve with roast lamb, pork and beef.

Clockwise from top left: Croquettes de panais; Carottes vichyssoises; Topinambours aux tomates

Carottes vichyssoises
Carrots with Vichy water

Metric	Imperial
25 g butter	1 oz butter
1 onion, peeled and finely chopped	1 onion, peeled and finely chopped
450 g carrots, peeled and cut into matchstick strips	1 lb carrots, peeled and cut into matchstick strips
300 ml Vichy water	½ pint Vichy water
1 × 5 ml spoon sugar	1 teaspoon sugar
salt	salt
4 × 15 ml spoons double cream	4 tablespoons double cream
2 × 15 ml spoons freshly chopped parsley	2 tablespoons freshly chopped parsley
freshly ground black pepper	freshly ground black pepper

Preparation time: about 20 minutes
Cooking time: about 40 minutes

This is a classic recipe in which carrots are cooked in natural spring water from Vichy in France. It is an ideal way to use up Vichy water from bottles which have been opened.
Alternatively use half the amount of Vichy water and make up the full quantity of liquid with chicken stock.

Melt the butter in a large heavy-based pan. Add the onion and fry gently until soft and lightly coloured, then add the carrots and stir until coated in the butter and onion. Pour in the Vichy water.
Bring to the boil, then lower the heat and add the sugar and 1 × 2.5 ml spoon/½ teaspoon salt. Simmer continuously for about 30 minutes or until the carrots are tender and all the liquid has been absorbed.
Stir in the cream and parsley, then add salt to taste and plenty of pepper. Transfer to a warmed serving dish. Serve immediately with roast meat, particularly lamb or with chops.

Courgettes au citron vert
Courgettes with lime

Metric	Imperial
25 g butter	1 oz butter
2 × 15 ml spoons olive oil	2 tablespoons olive oil
1 medium onion, peeled and thinly sliced	1 medium onion, peeled and thinly sliced
1–2 garlic cloves, peeled and crushed with 1 × 2.5 ml spoon salt	1–2 garlic cloves, peeled and crushed with ½ teaspoon salt
450 g courgettes, sliced	1 lb courgettes, sliced
juice of 1 lime	juice of 1 lime
salt	salt
freshly ground black pepper	freshly ground black pepper

Preparation time: 10–15 minutes
Cooking time: 15 minutes

If fresh limes are are difficult to obtain, bottled lime juice for cooking is available at some large supermarkets and good delicatessens. You will need about 2 × 15 ml spoons/2 tablespoons. Do not be tempted to cook the courgettes for longer than the exact time stated – they should have a 'bite' to them.

Melt the butter with the oil in a large frying pan. Add the onion and garlic and fry gently until soft and lightly coloured.
Add the courgettes, increase the heat and fry briskly for 10 minutes only, turning them over and shaking the pan constantly. Stir in the lime juice, add salt to taste and plenty of pepper, then turn into a warmed serving dish.
Serve with rich meat dishes, especially pork and veal in creamy sauces, or with oily fish.

Gratin de chou
Cabbage and bacon pie

Metric	Imperial
1 medium white cabbage (about 1 kg)	1 medium white cabbage (about 2 lb)
salt	salt
3 × 15 ml spoons olive oil	3 tablespoons olive oil
225 g back bacon, rind removed, chopped	8 oz back bacon, rind removed, chopped
1 medium onion, peeled and finely chopped	1 medium onion, peeled and finely chopped
1–2 garlic cloves, peeled and crushed with 1 × 2.5 ml spoon salt	1–2 garlic cloves, peeled and crushed with ½ teaspoon salt
2 eggs	2 eggs
150 ml milk	¼ pint milk
50 g fresh white breadcrumbs	2 oz fresh white breadcrumbs
100 g Gruyère cheese, grated	4 oz Gruyère cheese, grated
freshly ground black pepper	freshly ground black pepper

Preparation time: 40 minutes
Cooking time: about 1¼ hours
Oven: 190°C, 375°F, Gas Mark 5

Remove 8 large unbroken leaves from the outside of the cabbage. Plunge into a pan of boiling salted water, bring back to the boil and boil for 5 minutes. Drain thoroughly.
Heat 1 × 15 ml spoon/1 tablespoon oil in a large frying pan, add the bacon and fry over moderate heat until the fat begins to run from the bacon. Add the onion and garlic and continue frying over moderate heat until the bacon and onion are both lightly coloured, stirring constantly. Remove from the pan with a slotted spoon and set aside on paper towels.
Chop half the inner leaves from the cabbage. Heat the remaining oil in the pan, add the chopped leaves and fry for a further 5 minutes, stirring frequently.
Meanwhile, put the eggs in a bowl and beat together lightly with the milk, breadcrumbs, cheese, and salt and pepper to taste. Remove the cabbage mixture from the pan with a slotted spoon and stir into the egg mixture with the bacon and onion.
Place 6 drained outer cabbage leaves in the bottom of a well-buttered shallow 1.2 litre/2 pint baking dish. Overlap them slightly so that they line the dish. Spoon the stuffing mixture into the dish, then fold the leaves over the stuffing. Cover with the remaining 2 cabbage leaves to enclose the stuffing completely.
Bake, uncovered, in a preheated oven for 45 minutes or until the cabbage mixture is set in the centre when pierced with a knife. Remove from the oven and leave to stand for 5 minutes, then unmould on to a warmed serving platter.
Serve hot with sausages or a mixed grill as a lunch or supper dish.

Courgettes dauphinoises
Courgettes with cheese and cream

Preparation time: about 15 minutes
Cooking time: 40–45 minutes
Oven: 200°C, 400°F, Gas Mark 6

Metric
50 g butter
1 medium onion, peeled
   and thinly sliced
450 g courgettes, sliced
2 eggs
300 ml double cream
1 × 1.25 ml spoon freshly
   grated nutmeg
salt
freshly ground black
   pepper
50 g Gruyère cheese,
   grated

Imperial
2 oz butter
1 medium onion, peeled
   and thinly sliced
1 lb courgettes, sliced
2 eggs
½ pint double cream
¼ teaspoon freshly grated
   nutmeg
salt
freshly ground black
   pepper
2 oz Gruyère cheese,
   grated

Melt half the butter in a large frying pan, add the sliced onion and fry gently until soft. Remove with a slotted spoon and place in a buttered ovenproof dish. Melt the remaining butter in the pan, add the courgette slices and fry for about 10 minutes until golden brown on both sides, turning them frequently. Transfer to the dish and mix with the onions.

In a bowl, beat the eggs well to mix, then beat in the cream, nutmeg, and salt and pepper to taste. Pour over the courgettes and onions, then sprinkle the Gruyère cheese evenly over the top. Bake uncovered in a preheated oven for 20–25 minutes or until the custard is set and the topping is golden and bubbling. Serve hot with any meat, or simply with French bread for a lunch dish.

Clockwise from top: Courgettes dauphinoises; Courgettes au citron vert; Gratin de chou

DESSERTS AND PÂTISSERIE

Glancing in the window of any pâtisserie in France, it seems hard to believe that the French prefer to end most everyday meals with cheese and fresh fruit! The spectacular looking tarts with their rows of fresh soft fruits glistening with sweet, shiny glaze, and the gorgeous gâteaux and pâtisserie simply oozing with cream, these are reserved for special occasions only. Not that the French cook never makes his or her own desserts and gâteaux, it is simply an admission that these things are, in the main, best left to the experts. Custards and compôtes are made at home, however, so too are crêpes and mousses, but generally only at weekends and on holidays. For the rest of the year the family is more than content with fresh fruit and cheese.

Sorbet au cassis
Blackcurrant sorbet

Metric	Imperial
100 g sugar	4 oz sugar
300 ml plus 2 × 15 ml spoons water	½ pint plus 2 tablespoons water
1 × 2.5 ml spoon powdered gelatine	½ teaspoon powdered gelatine
225 g fresh or frozen blackcurrants, topped and tailed	8 oz fresh or frozen blackcurrants, topped and tailed
2 × 5 ml spoons lemon juice	2 teaspoons lemon juice
1 egg white	1 egg white
wafers or dessert biscuits, to serve (optional)	wafers or dessert biscuits, to serve (optional)

Preparation time: 30 minutes, plus freezing
Cooking time: 25–30 minutes

This sorbet can be made in a home freezer, or in the freezing compartment of the refrigerator, turned to the coldest setting about 1 hour before starting the recipe. When breaking up the half-frozen mixture, use a fork, not an electric or rotary beater, as these overbeat the mixture which will increase the volume too much and give a diluted or runny result.

Put the sugar and 300 ml/½ pint water in a heavy-based pan and heat gently until the sugar has dissolved, stirring occasionally. Bring to the boil and boil for 10 minutes until syrupy, then remove from the heat and leave to cool.
Sprinkle the gelatine over the remaining 2 × 15 ml spoons/2 tablespoons water in a heatproof bowl. Leave until spongy, then place the bowl in a pan of gently simmering water. Heat gently until the gelatine has dissolved, stirring occasionally, then remove from the heat and stir into the sugar syrup.
Put the blackcurrants in a pan with the lemon juice and heat gently for 5–10 minutes until softened. Cool slightly, purée in an electric blender, then push through a sieve to remove all seeds and skins.
Combine the sugar syrup and blackcurrant purée in a bowl until well mixed, then transfer to a freezer-proof container. Freeze, uncovered, for about 3 hours until firm round the edges.
Remove the mixture from the freezer and break up with a fork. Whisk the egg white until stiff and standing in peaks, then fold into the blackcurrant mixture until evenly incorporated. Return to the freezer container, cover and freeze overnight.
To serve, remove from the freezer and leave to stand at room temperature for about 30 minutes until soft enough to scoop. Serve in individual glasses, with wafers or dessert biscuits such as langues de chats.

Sorbet cassis; Tonille aux framboises

Tonille aux framboises
Almond shortcake with raspberries

Metric	Imperial
75 g flaked almonds, toasted	3 oz flaked almonds, toasted
100 g unsalted butter	4 oz unsalted butter
75 g caster sugar	3 oz caster sugar
150 g plain flour	5 oz plain flour

Filling:	Filling:
450 ml double cream	¾ pint double cream
50 g icing sugar, sifted	2 oz icing sugar, sifted
finely grated rind of 1 orange	finely grated rind of 1 orange
2 × 5 ml spoons orange juice	2 teaspoons orange juice
350 g fresh or frozen raspberries, hulled	12 oz fresh or frozen raspberries, hulled

Preparation time: about 1 hour, plus chilling
Cooking time: 15–20 minutes
Oven: 190°C, 375°F, Gas Mark 5

Ground toasted hazelnuts can replace the almonds and strawberries or peaches can be used instead of raspberries.

To make the shortcake, grind the almonds in an electric grinder or food processor. Set aside.
Put the butter and sugar in a bowl and beat together until light and fluffy. Beat in the flour, then the almonds to make a smooth dough, then form into 3 equal balls. Wrap in foil or cling film and chill in the refrigerator for at least 30 minutes until firm.
With floured fingers, press each ball of dough flat into a 20 cm/8 inch round on a baking sheet lined with non-stick silicone paper, using 2 or 3 baking sheets if necessary.
Bake in a preheated oven, in batches if necessary, for 15–20 minutes until the shortcake is light golden in colour. Remove from the oven and cut 1 round into 6 equal triangles, spacing them slightly apart. Leave to cool on the baking sheets for 10 minutes, then carefully transfer to a wire tray to cool completely.
To make the filling, whip the cream until stiff with 40 g/1½ oz icing sugar, the orange rind and juice. Crush the raspberries lightly, reserving a few whole ones for decoration, then fold lightly into the cream.
To serve, place 1 shortcake round on a serving plate and spread with half the raspberry cream. Place another shortcake on top and spread with the remaining cream. Arrange the triangles of shortcake on top, tilting them upward in the centre so that they fit neatly and a little of the raspberry cream is visible between each triangle. Decorate with the reserved raspberries and dust with the reserved icing sugar.
Serves 6

Clafoutis
Cherry batter pudding

Metric
450 g black cherries, pitted
4 × 15 ml spoons brandy or Kirsch
75 g plain flour
pinch of salt
75 g caster sugar
2 eggs
2 egg yolks
about 450 ml milk
2 × 15 ml spoons melted butter
icing sugar, to serve

Imperial
1 lb black cherries, pitted
4 tablespoons brandy or Kirsch
3 oz plain flour
pinch of salt
3 oz caster sugar
2 eggs
2 egg yolks
about ¾ pint milk
2 tablespoons melted butter
icing sugar, to serve

Preparation time: 20 minutes, plus soaking
Cooking time: 25–30 minutes
Oven: 200°C, 400°F, Gas Mark 6

If fresh black cherries are not available, use 2 × 425 g/15 oz cans of cherries, well drained, and if they are sweetened, decrease the amount of sugar to 25 g/1 oz. Use a cherry pitter to remove the stones because the fruit will not hold its shape during cooking if it is halved.

Put the cherries in a bowl and sprinkle over half the brandy or Kirsch. Leave to soak for 1 hour.
Sift the flour and salt into a bowl and stir in the sugar. Make a well in the centre, add the whole eggs, egg yolks and 300 ml/½ pint milk, and beat, gradually drawing in the flour from the sides of the bowl, until smooth.
Drain the cherries and make up the juice to 150 ml/¼ pint with milk. Whisk this mixture into the batter until smooth, then whisk in the melted butter.
Place the cherries in a shallow baking dish. Pour on the batter, then bake in a preheated oven for 25–30 minutes until puffed up and light golden.
Remove from the oven, sprinkle with the remaining brandy or Kirsch, then leave in a warm place for about 15–20 minutes, by which time the clafoutis will have shrunk slightly. Serve warm, dusted lightly with the icing sugar.

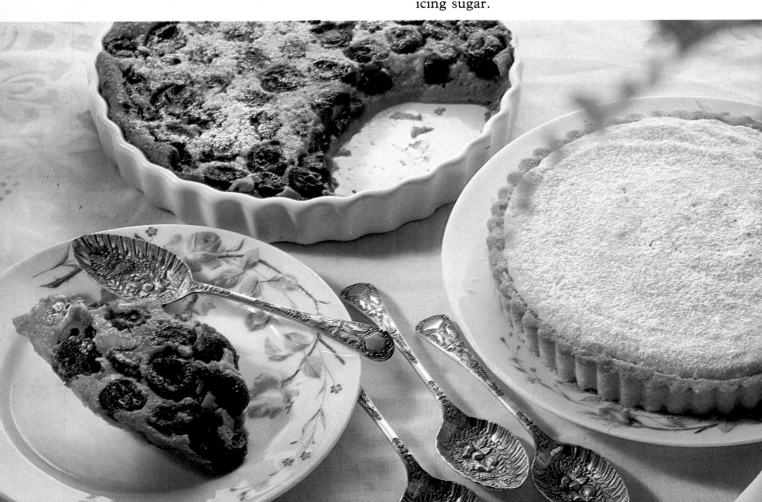

Tarte au citron
Lemon tart

Metric
125 g plain flour
pinch of salt
2 × 15 ml spoons caster
  sugar
100 g butter, chilled
1 egg yolk
1 × 5 ml spoon lemon
  juice
1–2 × 5 ml spoons icing
  sugar, to finish

Imperial
5 oz plain flour
pinch of salt
2 tablespoons caster
  sugar
4 oz butter, chilled
1 egg yolk
1 teaspoon lemon
  juice
1–2 teaspoons icing
  sugar, to finish

Filling:
75 g unsalted butter
75 g caster sugar
100 g ground almonds
2 egg yolks
finely grated rind and
  juice of 1 large lemon
3 egg whites

Filling:
3 oz unsalted butter
3 oz caster sugar
4 oz ground almonds
2 egg yolks
finely grated rind and
  juice of 1 large lemon
3 egg whites

Preparation time: 45 minutes, plus chilling
Cooking time: 35–40 minutes
Oven: 190°C, 375°F, Gas Mark 5;
        160°C, 325°F, Gas Mark 3

With its sharp, tangy flavour, this lemon tart is excellent served warm as a dessert or cold as pâtisserie with coffee. The pastry base, known as pâte sablée in French, is extra rich and sweet, more of a biscuit crust than a pastry. Because of its richness it is difficult to roll out; and it is sometimes easier, therefore, to press it into the flan tin or ring with the fingertips.

Sift the flour and salt into a bowl and stir in the sugar. Cut the butter into the flour in small pieces, then rub in lightly with the fingertips. Mix the egg yolk and lemon juice together, then stir into the flour mixture with a round-bladed knife until the mixture draws together. Form into a smooth ball with one hand, then cover and chill in the refrigerator for 30 minutes.
Roll out the dough on a floured surface and use to line a loose-bottomed fluted 20 cm/8 inch flan tin or flan ring set on a baking sheet. Prick the base of the dough in several places with a fork, then line with foil or greaseproof paper and fill with baking beans.
Bake the pastry case 'blind' in a preheated oven for 10 minutes, then remove the paper and beans. Lightly beat a little egg white from the filling and brush over the base of the dough. Return to the oven and bake for a further 10 minutes, then remove and set aside. Reduce the oven temperature.
To make the filling, put the butter and sugar in a bowl and beat together until light and fluffy. Beat in the almonds, egg yolks and lemon rind and juice until evenly mixed. In a separate bowl, whisk the egg whites until stiff and standing in peaks. Fold the egg whites gently into the lemon mixture then spoon into the pastry case.
Bake in the oven for 15–20 minutes until a skewer inserted in the centre comes out clean. Remove from the oven and sift icing sugar evenly over the top. Leave to cool slightly, then remove the flan tin or ring and place on a serving plate. Serve warm or cold.
Serves 4–6

Clafoutis; Tarte au citron

Gâteau pithiviers
Puff pastry gâteau

Metric
100 g unsalted butter,
  softened
100 g caster sugar
1 egg, beaten with 1 egg
  yolk
100 g ground almonds
2 × 15 ml spoons rum
1 × 400 g packet frozen
  puff pastry, defrosted

Imperial
4 oz unsalted butter,
  softened
4 oz caster sugar
1 egg, beaten with 1 egg
  yolk
4 oz ground almonds
2 tablespoons rum
1 × 14 oz packet frozen
  puff pastry, defrosted

Glaze:
1 egg, beaten
a little icing sugar

Glaze:
1 egg, beaten
a little icing sugar

Preparation time: 45 minutes
Cooking time: 30–35 minutes
Oven: 220°C, 425°F, Gas Mark 7

Put the butter and sugar in a bowl and beat together until light and fluffy. Beat in the egg and egg yolk mixture, then beat in the almonds and rum until evenly mixed. Set aside.

Roll out half the pastry on a floured surface to a 23 cm/9 inch circle. Place the circle on a dampened baking sheet. Spread the filling over the circle to within about 1 cm/½ inch of the edge, mounding it up in the centre. Brush the exposed edge of the pastry with water.

Roll out the remaining pastry to a 25 cm/10 inch circle. Cut away a narrow strip all round the edge of this circle. Press this strip around the moistened edge of the circle on the baking sheet. Brush the strip with water. Cover the filling with the second circle of pastry, pressing it down firmly at the edge to seal. Knock up the edge with the back of a knife, then give the edge a scalloped effect by pressing your thumb around it at regular intervals and marking in between each thumb mark with the back of the knife. Make a hole in the centre of the gâteau with a skewer, and brush all over the pastry with the beaten egg, taking care not to brush the decorated edge or the pastry will not rise. With a sharp knife, make shallow semi-circular cuts in the pastry all round the top of the gâteau, working from the centre towards the outside edge.

Bake in a preheated oven for 25–30 minutes until puffed up and golden brown, then sift the icing sugar evenly over the top of the gâteau and return to the oven for a further 5 minutes until glazed and shiny. Leave to stand on the baking sheet for a few minutes, then carefully transfer to a wire rack. Serve warm or cold with cream.
Serves 4–6

Tarte tatin
Upside-down apple pie

Metric
125 g plain flour
pinch of salt
2 × 15 ml spoons caster
  sugar
100 g butter, chilled
1 egg yolk
3 × 5 ml spoons lemon
  juice
1 kg cooking apples
100 g unsalted butter
100 g sugar

Imperial
5 oz plain flour
pinch of salt
2 tablespoons caster
  sugar
4 oz butter, chilled
1 egg yolk
3 teaspoons lemon
  juice
2 lb cooking apples
4 oz unsalted butter
4 oz sugar

Preparation time: about 45 minutes, plus chilling
Cooking time: 55 minutes
Oven: 190°C, 375°F, Gas Mark 5

Sift the flour and salt into a bowl and stir in the sugar. Cut the butter into small pieces, then rub lightly into the flour. Mix the egg yolk and 1 × 5 ml spoon/1 teaspoon lemon juice together, then stir into the flour mixture with a round-bladed knife until the mixture draws together. Form into a smooth ball with one hand, then chill in the refrigerator for 30 minutes.

Meanwhile, peel and core the apples and slice thinly. Place them in a bowl of ice-cold water and stir in the remaining lemon juice. Melt the butter gently in a 1 litre/2 pint flameproof pie dish. Pour off all but about 2 × 15 ml spoons/2 tablespoons melted butter and reserve. Brush the butter remaining in the dish around the base and sides of it. Sprinkle the base with about one-quarter of the sugar, then continue heating gently until the butter and sugar mixture sizzles and turns a golden-brown, caramel colour.

Drain the apple slices thoroughly. Arrange a single layer of apple slices in the dish, overlapping them in circles. Drizzle over a little of the reserved melted butter and sprinkle with sugar. Continue these layers, finishing with a layer of sugar.

Roll out the dough on a floured surface and use to cover the top of the pie dish, tucking the edges inside the rim of the dish to enclose the apples completely. Make a small hole in the centre of the pastry, then bake in a preheated oven for about 45 minutes until the apples are tender. If the pastry becomes over-brown during baking, cover it with foil.

To serve, leave the pie to stand in a warm place for 5–10 minutes. Loosen the edges by carefully running a knife between the pie and the dish. Invert on to a warmed serving plate and serve immediately, with pouring cream.

Compôte de trois fruits
Three-fruit compôte

Metric	Imperial
100 g sugar	*4 oz sugar*
300 ml dry white wine	*½ pint dry white wine*
150 ml water	*¼ pint water*
1 vanilla pod	*1 vanilla pod*
4 ripe cooking pears	*4 ripe cooking pears*
1 medium pineapple (about 1 kg)	*1 medium pineapple (about 2 lb)*
175 g black grapes, pips removed	*6 oz black grapes, pips removed*
2 × 15 ml spoons brandy (optional)	*2 tablespoons brandy (optional)*

Preparation time: 30 minutes, plus chilling
Cooking time: 40–45 minutes

Put the sugar, wine, water and vanilla pod in a large heavy-based pan. Heat gently until the sugar has dissolved, stirring occasionally, then bring to the boil. Boil vigorously for 5 minutes, then lower the heat and simmer gently.

Peel, core and quarter the pears. Poach them gently in the syrup in the covered pan for 10–15 minutes, spooning the liquid over them occasionally.

Meanwhile, slice the pineapple into rings, discarding the crown. Peel and core the pineapple rings. Add the pineapple to the pan with the grapes, cover again and poach gently for a further 10 minutes until all the fruits are tender. Leave to cool, covered.

Remove the vanilla pod, then sprinkle in the brandy (if using). Carefully transfer the fruit to a serving bowl. Serve warm or cover with cling film and chill in the refrigerator for at least 4 hours before serving.

Gâteau pithiviers; Compôte de trois fruits; Tarte tatin

Charlotte au chocolat
Chocolate charlotte

Metric	Imperial
225 g plain dessert chocolate, broken into pieces	8 oz plain dessert chocolate, broken into pieces
about 6 × 15 ml spoons rum	about 6 tablespoons rum
100 g unsalted butter, softened	4 oz unsalted butter, softened
225 g ground almonds	8 oz ground almonds
oil for preparing mould	oil for preparing mould
about 20 sponge fingers	about 20 sponge fingers
300 ml double cream	½ pint double cream

Decoration:	Decoration:
120 ml double or whipping cream	4 fl oz double or whipping cream
25 g plain dessert chocolate, grated	1 oz plain dessert chocolate, grated

Preparation time: about 1 hour, plus chilling
Cooking time: about 5 minutes

Use the best quality dessert chocolate available; good delicatessens and some large supermarkets sell blocks of French dessert chocolate, which are ideal.
For a prettier effect, and to help keep the sponge fingers in place before serving, tie a ribbon around the middle of the charlotte, finishing with a bow.

Put the chocolate and 2 × 15 ml spoons/2 tablespoons rum in a heatproof bowl standing over a pan of gently simmering water. Heat gently until the chocolate has melted, stirring once or twice. Remove from the heat and work in the butter gradually until melted, then stir in the almonds. Leave to cool.
Meanwhile, line the base of a 900 ml/1½ pint charlotte mould with non-stick silicone or greaseproof paper. Brush the paper and inside the rim of the mould lightly with oil. Dip the sponge fingers one at a time into the remaining rum, then use to line the sides of the mould, standing them sugared side outward and as close together as possible. Trim them to fit if necessary.
Whip the cream until just firm, then fold into the chocolate mixture. Spoon into the mould and level the surface, then cover and chill in the refrigerator overnight.
The next day, turn the charlotte out of the mould on to a serving plate. Whip the cream for decoration and pipe or swirl decoratively on top and round the charlotte. Sprinkle the grated chocolate over the top, then chill in the refrigerator until serving time. Serve chilled with single cream.
Serves 8

Chocolat bavarois à l'orange
Chocolate cream with orange

Metric	Imperial
600 ml milk	1 pint milk
100 g plain dessert chocolate, finely grated	4 oz plain dessert chocolate, finely grated
4 egg yolks	4 egg yolks
75 g caster sugar	3 oz caster sugar
grated zest of 2 oranges	grated zest of 2 oranges
1 envelope (15 g) powdered gelatine	1 envelope (½ oz) powdered gelatine
juice of 1 large orange	juice of 1 large orange
2 × 15 ml spoons orange-flavoured liqueur	2 tablespoons orange-flavoured liqueur
150 ml double cream	¼ pint double cream

Preparation time: 30 minutes, plus cooling and chilling
Cooking time: about 30 minutes

For the flavour of this sumptuous dessert cooking chocolate or chocolate cake covering are not suitable; buy the best quality dessert chocolate available. If preferred, you can fold in 2 stiffly beaten egg whites after the cream for a lighter, less rich result.

Put the milk and chocolate in a heavy-based pan and heat gently, stirring, until the chocolate has melted. Meanwhile, put the egg yolks, sugar and orange zest in a large bowl and beat until the sugar has dissolved. Gradually pour the hot milk and melted chocolate into the egg yolk mixture, stirring constantly. Return this mixture to the pan and heat very gently until the custard thickens and coats the back of a wooden spoon. Stir constantly and do not let the custard boil or it will separate. Remove from the heat and set aside. Sprinkle the gelatine over the orange juice in a heatproof bowl. Leave until spongy, then place the bowl in a pan of gently simmering water. Heat gently until the gelatine has dissolved, stirring occasionally. Remove from the heat and leave to cool slightly, then stir gradually into the chocolate custard with the liqueur. Leave until the custard is completely cold and just beginning to thicken, whisking occasionally to prevent a skin forming on the top.
Whip the cream until just firm, then fold into the cold custard. Pour into a wetted 1.2 litres/2 pint mould, cover and chill in the refrigerator overnight.
To serve, loosen the custard by pulling the top edge away from the mould with your fingertips, then invert the custard on to a serving plate. (If it is difficult to unmould, dip the base of the mould into a bowl of hot water for a few seconds.) Serve chilled.
Serves 6

Top: Chocolat bavarois à l'orange; Charlotte au chocolat

Pêches à la bordelaise
Peaches marinated in red wine

Metric	**Imperial**
300 ml red Bordeaux wine	½ pint red Bordeaux wine
100 g sugar	4 oz sugar
1 cinnamon stick	1 cinnamon stick
4 ripe peaches	4 ripe peaches
25–50 g flaked almonds, toasted	1–2 oz flaked almonds, toasted
dessert biscuits, to serve	dessert biscuits, to serve

Preparation time: 20 minutes, plus chilling

Put the wine in a pan, add the sugar and heat gently until the sugar has dissolved, stirring occasionally. Add the cinnamon stick and bring to the boil. Remove from the heat and cool.

Plunge the peaches into a bowl of boiling water, leave for 10 seconds, then remove with a slotted spoon and peel off the skins. Halve the fruit, remove the stones and slice the flesh thickly. Place the slices in a bowl, then strain in the wine. Cover the surface of the liquid closely with a saucer or small plate (to prevent the peaches floating in the liquid), then chill in the refrigerator for at least 4 hours.

Divide the peaches and wine amongst 4 glasses and sprinkle with the almonds. Serve chilled, with dessert biscuits such as langues de chats.

Fraises cardinales
Strawberries with raspberry sauce

Metric	**Imperial**
450 g fresh raspberries or 350 g frozen raspberries, defrosted	1 lb fresh raspberries or 12 oz frozen raspberries, defrosted
finely grated rind and juice of 1 orange	finely grated rind and juice of 1 orange
4 × 15 ml spoons orange-flavoured liqueur (optional)	4 tablespoons orange-flavoured liqueur (optional)
450–700 g fresh strawberries, hulled	1–1½ lb fresh strawberries, hulled
50–75 g caster sugar	2–3 oz caster sugar
4 orange slices, to decorate	4 orange slices, to decorate

Preparation time: about 20 minutes, plus chilling

Work the raspberries through a fine sieve, or purée in an electric blender, then sieve to remove the seeds. Stir the orange rind and juice into the purée, with the liqueur (if using).

Halve the strawberries or slice them if large. Place a few strawberries in the bottom of 4 individual glasses or bowls and sprinkle with sugar to taste. Pour over a little of the raspberry sauce. Repeat these three layers until all the ingredients are used. Decorate the top of each glass with a twist of orange, then chill in the refrigerator for at least 2 hours. Serve chilled.

Gâteau de crêpes aux abricots
Apricot pancake gâteau

Metric	Imperial
100 g plain flour	*4 oz plain flour*
pinch of salt	*pinch of salt*
1 egg	*1 egg*
300 ml milk	*½ pint milk*
about 2 × 15 ml spoons vegetable oil, for frying	*about 2 tablespoons vegetable oil, for frying*

Filling:	**Filling:**
50–75 g sugar, or to taste	*2–3 oz sugar, or to taste*
150 ml water	*¼ pint water*
4 × 15 ml spoons brandy	*4 tablespoons brandy*
1 kg fresh apricots, halved and stoned	*2 lb fresh apricots, halved and stoned*
50 g ratafias	*2 oz ratafia*
pouring cream, to serve	*pouring cream, to serve*

Gâteau de crêpes aux abricots; Pêches à la bordelaise; Fraises cardinales

Preparation time: about 35 minutes, plus resting
Cooking time: 35–45 minutes

You can use the pancake batter in this recipe to make the classic Crêpes Suzette, as shown on the cover of this book. Add 1 × 5 ml spoon/1 teaspoon each tangerine or orange juice and Curaçao to the batter before frying. When the pancakes are made, spread each one with tangerine or orange butter made by creaming together equal quanties of butter and sugar with tangerine or orange juices, zest and Curaçao to taste. Fold the pancakes over the filling and place in a serving dish. Warm a little Curaçao, then pour over the pancakes and set alight. An alternative method of serving crêpes is to make a syrup from 100 g/4 oz each butter and sugar, with tangerine or orange juice, zest and Curaçao to taste. Fold the pancakes plain after frying, heat them in this syrup, then pour over warmed Curaçao and set alight.

Sift the flour and salt into a bowl. Make a well in the centre, add the egg, then gradually whisk in the milk until the batter is smooth. Cover and leave to stand for 30 minutes.
Meanwhile, make the filling. Put 50 g/2 oz sugar in a heavy-based pan with the water. Heat gently until the sugar has dissolved, then stir in half the brandy. Add the apricots and simmer gently for 10–15 minutes or until they are just tender. Remove with a slotted spoon, reserving the apricot syrup. Leave the apricots to cool slightly, then purée in an electric blender, reserving 6 whole ones for decoration.
Crush the ratafias finely, reserving a few whole ones. Make the pancakes. Heat a few drops of oil in a 15 cm/6 inch crêpe or frying pan until very hot. Pour in about one-eighth of the batter, tilting the pan so that the batter covers the base evenly. Cook for 1–2 minutes until set, then turn the crêpe over and cook for 1 minute on the other side. Slide the crêpe out of the pan on to a warm plate and cover with a sheet of greaseproof paper. Keep warm while making the remaining 7 crêpes, adding more oil when necessary. To assemble the gâteau, heat the apricot purée and the reserved apricot syrup gently in separate pans. Taste the purée for sweetness and add more sugar if necessary. Place one crêpe on a warmed serving platter and spread with about 1 × 15 ml spoon/1 tablespoon hot apricot purée. Sprinkle a little of the crushed ratafias over the top. Repeat these layers until all the pancakes, purée and crushed ratafias are used, finishing with a pancake.
Decorate the top of the gâteau with the reserved whole apricots and ratafias. Stir the remaining brandy into the hot apricot syrup. Serve the gâteau immediately, cut into wedges, with the sauce and cream handed in separate jugs.

Savarin aux fruits
Yeast ring cake with fruit

Preparation time: about ¾ hour, plus rising
Cooking time: 25–30 minutes
Oven: 200°C, 400°F, Gas Mark 6

Metric
15 g fresh yeast
3 × 15 ml spoons
  lukewarm milk
100 g strong white flour
pinch of salt
1 × 5 ml spoon sugar
2 eggs, beaten
50 g butter, softened

Sugar syrup:
225 g sugar
300 ml water
4 × 15 ml spoons Kirsch,
  or to taste

Fruit filling:
2 bananas
100 g fresh strawberries,
  hulled and sliced
100 g fresh raspberries,
  hulled

Imperial
½ oz fresh yeast
3 tablespoons
  lukewarm milk
4 oz strong white flour
pinch of salt
1 teaspoon sugar
2 eggs, beaten
2 oz butter, softened

Sugar syrup:
8 oz sugar
½ pint water
4 tablespoons Kirsch,
  or to taste

Fruit filling:
2 bananas
4 oz fresh strawberries,
  hulled and sliced
4 oz fresh raspberries,
  hulled

The savarin ring can be soaked in the sugar syrup overnight, and then filled with the fruit just before serving.

Cream the yeast in a bowl with the lukewarm milk, then gradually work in 25 g/1 oz flour. Leave to stand in a warm place for about 20 minutes until frothy, then add the remaining flour, salt, sugar, eggs and butter. Beat with a wooden spoon or whisk until an elasticated dough forms.
Put the mixture into a buttered and floured 20 cm/8 inch savarin or ring mould, then leave in a warm place for about 45 minutes until the mixture has risen almost to the top of the tin. Bake in a preheated oven for 25–30 minutes or until the savarin is golden on top and has shrunk away slightly from the sides of the tin. Meanwhile, make the sugar syrup. Put the sugar and water in a heavy-based pan and heat gently until the sugar has dissolved, stirring occasionally. Bring to the boil, simmer without stirring for 5 minutes until syrupy. Remove from the heat and stir in the Kirsch. When the savarin is cooked, turn it out of the tin immediately, and place it the right way up on a wire tray placed over a tray. Prick all over the savarin with a fine skewer, then slowly spoon over the hot sugar syrup. Continue spooning the syrup over the savarin until the cake becomes saturated, using the syrup that drips into the tray underneath. Leave to cool.
To serve, peel the bananas and slice thinly. Toss them immediately in the sugar syrup which has collected in the tray together with the strawberries and raspberries. Place the savarin on a serving plate, spoon the fruit into the centre and serve immediately.
Serves 6

Savarin aux fruits; Tarte aux pruneaux

Tarte aux pruneaux
Prune flan with pastry cream

Metric	Imperial
175 g plain flour	*6 oz plain flour*
pinch of salt	*pinch of salt*
100 g butter, chilled	*4 oz butter, chilled*
40 g ground almonds	*1½ oz ground almonds*
2 × 15 ml spoons caster sugar	*2 tablespoons caster sugar*
1 egg yolk	*1 egg yolk*
1 × 5 ml spoon water	*1 teaspoon water*
350 g prunes★	*12 oz prunes★*
150 ml dry white wine	*¼ pint dry white wine*
6 × 15 ml spoons redcurrant jelly	*6 tablespoons redcurrant jelly*
juice of ½ lemon	*juice of ½ lemon*

Crème pâtissière:	Crème pâtissière:
2 × 15 ml spoons cornflour	*2 tablespoons cornflour*
2 eggs	*2 eggs*
2 egg yolks	*2 egg yolks*
50 g caster sugar	*2 oz caster sugar*
450 ml milk	*¾ pint milk*
15 g butter	*½ oz butter*

Preparation time: about 1 hour, plus chilling
Cooking time: about 1 hour
Oven: 190°C, 375°F, Gas Mark 5

★ Buy prunes that need no soaking before cooking – they are available in packets from most supermarkets. Other fruits can be used instead of prunes but if using pale-coloured fruits substitute sieved apricot jam for the redcurrant jelly. Do not use the glaze more than 2 hours before serving or it will seep into the custard.

Sift the flour and salt into a bowl. Cut the butter into the flour in small pieces, then rub in lightly with the fingertips. Stir in the almonds and sugar. Mix the egg yolk and water together, then stir into the flour mixture with a round-bladed knife until the mixture draws together. Form into a smooth ball with one hand, then cover and chill for 30 minutes.
Meanwhile put the prunes in a large heavy-based pan with the wine. Simmer very gently for 20–30 minutes until the prunes are plump and tender and have absorbed most of the wine. Shake the pan occasionally to stop the prunes sticking to the bottom. Remove the prunes with a slotted spoon and set aside to cool. Reserve any liquid in the pan.
Roll out the dough on a floured surface and use to line a loose-bottomed fluted 24 cm/9½ inch flan tin or flan ring set on a baking sheet. Prick the base of the dough in several places with a fork, then line with foil or greaseproof paper and fill with baking beans.
Bake the pastry 'blind' in a preheated oven for 10 minutes, then remove the paper and beans, and bake for a further 8–10 minutes until the pastry is set and lightly golden. (Take care the pastry does not burn; the addition of sugar and almonds makes it susceptible to scorching.) Set aside to cool.
Meanwhile, make the crème pâtissière. Put the cornflour in a bowl and gradually beat in the eggs, egg yolks and sugar. Beat with a wire balloon whisk or rotary beater until thick and frothy. Heat the milk to just below boiling point, then gradually beat into the egg mixture. Return the mixture to the rinsed-out pan and gradually bring to the boil, whisking constantly and vigorously with a balloon whisk until thick and smooth. Simmer for 2–3 minutes, whisking, then leave to cool for a few minutes.
Remove the flan tin or ring carefully from the pastry case and place the case on a serving plate. Pour in the crème pâtissière and dot with flecks of butter to prevent a skin forming. Allow to cool. Slit the prunes carefully along one side, then ease out the stones. Arrange the prunes in a circular pattern on top of the crème pâtissière. Put the redcurrant jelly and lemon juice into the pan containing the liquid reserved from the prunes, heat gently until the jelly has melted, then simmer for a few minutes until thickened, stirring constantly with a wooden spoon. Strain, then brush evenly over the prunes. Leave to cool before serving.
Serves 6–8

INDEX

PDO 83-122

Brief Contents

Effective Instructional Strategies

From Theory to Practice

SECOND EDITION

Kenneth D. Moore

Henderson State University (Retired)

Los Angeles • London • New Delhi • Singapore

For information:

SAGE Publications, Inc.
2455 Teller Road
Thousand Oaks, California 91320
E-mail: order@sagepub.com

SAGE Publications Ltd.
1 Oliver's Yard
55 City Road
London EC1Y 1SP
United Kingdom

SAGE Publications India Pvt. Ltd.
B 1/I 1 Mohan Cooperative Industrial Area
Mathura Road, New Delhi 110 044
India

SAGE Publications Asia-Pacific Pte. Ltd.
33 Pekin Street #02-01
Far East Square
Singapore 048763

Printed in the United States of America

Library of Congress Cataloging-in-Publication Data

Moore, Kenneth D.
Effective instructional strategies : from theory to practice / Kenneth D. Moore. —2nd ed.
    p. cm.
Includes bibliographical references and index.
ISBN 978-1-4129-5644-4 (pbk.)
    1. Effective teaching. 2. Teacher effectiveness. 3. Teachers—Training of. I. Title.

LB1025.3.M662 2009
371.102—dc22   2008003530

This book is printed on acid-free paper.

08   09   10   11   12   10 9 8 7 6 5 4 3 2 1

Acquisitions Editor:	Diane McDaniel
Editorial Assistant:	Leah Mori
Production Editor:	Astrid Virding
Copy Editor:	Gillian Dickens
Typesetter:	C&M Digitals (P) Ltd.
Proofreader:	Dennis W. Webb
Indexer:	Molly Hall
Cover Designer:	Gail Buschman
Marketing Manager:	Christy Guilbault

SECOND
EDITION

Effective
Instructional
Strategies

DETAILED CONTENTS

PREFACE

The second edition of *Effective Teaching Strategies: From Theory to Practice* is designed to prepare students for the complex world of the school classroom. The aim is to prepare prospective teachers to meet the challenges of today's changing classrooms. Becoming an effective teacher requires extensive knowledge and skills, as well as hard work, commitment, an inquiring mind, and the ability to learn from experiences. The quest for excellence will be difficult, but the satisfaction is worth the effort. This book, therefore, is designed to provide you with the tools for facilitating the quest and the means for achieving excellence. It was further designed to expand the pedagogical teaching knowledge of teachers and their instructional repertoires.

I have described in detail proven instructional methods, coupled with the best in planning and instructional theory, to prepare preservice teachers for entry into the classroom. The textbook will not only help prospective teachers analyze their own teaching but also will provide the means for translating this thinking into effective practice, which will lead to the accomplishment of our society's educational goals. In short, it is my hope that future teachers will find this book valuable as a guide to sound educational practices. This text is intended for use in undergraduate general methods courses, but it could be a useful reference for a variety of courses and for inservice teachers.

Theory to Practice Approach to Instruction

This text embraces a theory to practice theme that runs throughout the book. It takes the latest research on teaching and applies it to the classroom. The book emphasizes the intelligent use of teaching theory and research to improve classroom instruction. Whenever possible, specific examples and teacher viewpoints are presented, not just suggestions for things to try.

No one can deny that teachers matter or that their skills will have a profound impact on student achievement. To make that impact positive, teachers must have both a deep understanding of the powerful principles of teaching as they apply to effective teaching and a clear sense of how these principles can be applied to the classroom. The effective teacher is one who constantly reflects on his or her practices and makes instructional decisions based on a clear conception of how theories and practices affect students. Effective teaching is neither a bag of tricks nor a set of abstract principles; rather, it is intelligent application of research-based teaching principles to address the reality of the classroom. This text will provide the theoretical knowledge and help you develop the practical skills needed to do the most important job you will ever do—teach.

New to the Second Edition

There have been a number of refinements and additions to the second edition of *Effective Instructional Strategies: From Theory to Practice*. All chapters have been updated with new information, and several have been modified to reflect the latest educational issues and theory. The text chapter format and sequence have been reorganized to be more reader-friendly; INTASC standards, NCATE standards, and Praxis exam areas have been aligned with text chapters; the appendix has been enhanced; Technology and Education and Deconstructing the Standards end-of-chapter activities have been added; a second Reflection on Teacher Practice has been added to each chapter; the student Web site has been upgraded; and special icons have been inserted within the chapters to emphasize key topics.

A number of modifications have been made to individual chapters:

- **Chapter 1: Getting Ready for the Classroom** has been reorganized with some sections moved to other chapters and modified to include sections on No Child Left Behind (NCLB), educational law, historical perspectives of education, and theorists' thoughts that shaped teaching.
- **Chapter 2: Planning and Organizing for Teaching** has been reorganized to include the section from Chapter 1 on time in schools and classrooms and modified with the addition of a reflective step to the Model of Teaching and new sections on learning styles and multiple intelligences.
- **Chapter 3: Setting Goals and Objectives** has been expanded to include information on the "new" taxonomy terminology and to include material on alignment of state and national standards with objectives.
- **Chapter 4: Developing Unit and Daily Lesson Plans** has been modified to include information on state mandates and standards, block schedule planning, and modification of the unit and daily lesson planning format.
- **Chapter 5: Using Direct Teaching Methods, Chapter 6: Using Indirect Teaching Methods, Chapter 7: Using Integrated Teaching Methods,** and **Chapter 8: Teaching Effective Thinking Strategies** have been reorganized and updated to provide more examples and activities and greater detail on inquiry teaching and cooperative learning and to include a new section on integrating computers into the classroom.
- **Chapter 9: Evaluating and Measuring Learning** has been reorganized to include the section from Chapter 1 on student performance and modified with new material on rubric construction and a new section on student work samples.
- **Chapter 10: Constructing and Grading Tests** has been upgraded with new sections on recordkeeping and reporting student progress.
- **Chapter 11: Communicating With Students and Parents** has been enhanced with additional information related to the development of a parental involvement plan and a new section on working with difficult parents.
- **Chapter 12: Motivating Students** has been upgraded to provide additional information on appropriate rewards for the different grade levels and motivational methods.
- **Chapter 13: Managing the Classroom Environment** has been expanded to include additional material on classroom leadership and teacher stress and managing the classroom environment.

Features of the Text

Several special features make the second edition of *Effective Teaching Strategies: From Theory to Practice* more accessible to you. Each chapter begins with an overview, objectives, and a reflective classroom case related to the key aspects of the chapter. Scattered throughout each chapter are innovative focal points. A second reflective classroom case, summary, discussion questions and activities, technology and education, deconstructing the standards, and connection with the field at the end of each chapter provide materials that address your present and future professional needs.

A CD array of video clips of excellent teachers and interviews—each tied to a course topic within a chapter and highlighted by a special icon—has been bound with the text to help you understand, analyze, and apply chapter concepts. Three appendices have also been developed to provide information on microteaching and reflective teaching, state licensure/certification and reciprocity, and the Praxis II case history exam format.

Overview

The overview provides an outline of what is covered in the chapter. It provides you with a cognitive set for the chapter content. The overview gives you the major concepts covered in the chapter and the organization of the chapter. As such, it represents a quick reference to the chapter content.

Objectives

The objectives inform you of the instructional intent of the chapter. It gives you an idea of the main information to be learned. It tells you exactly what to expect and what you should be able to do upon completion of the chapter.

Reflections on Teacher Practice

Another opening and closing feature of each chapter gives you the opportunity to hear directly from teachers in the field about topics to be explored. These cases show the major principles in the chapter in action. Each case is an experience taken from a real-life situation. The case describes how principles were applied in classroom settings and the results of each application. They represent brief words of wisdom, strategies, and philosophy from teachers in our elementary, middle, and high schools.

Apply and Reflect

This feature encourages you to stop at key points within the chapter narrative and think carefully and reflect about the issues being presented. They are designed to help you begin to identify and analyze your beliefs about learning and teaching. They deal with important or controversial information or provide thought-provoking exercises pertinent to the subject under discussion. These apply-and-reflect features reinforce the content, examine contentious topics, and challenge you to explore how your own ideas and beliefs inform your teaching practice.

Web Link

This feature is designed to encourage you to explore links to Web sites where you can learn more about the teaching profession by researching issues, learning more about research application, and looking at the practical application of the material presented in the text. These links will help you think more deeply about the issues and questions posed.

Expansion Activity

This feature gives you the opportunity to spend additional time investigating current issues and topics that affect teaching and learning. Each issue or topic highlighted has been chosen because of its direct impact on schooling and its potential for affecting teaching and learning.

Review and Reflective Exercise

These exercises present the most important ideas of the chapter for review and study. Major focus questions provide the framework around which the sections were built. Each exercise uses a series of thought-provoking review questions embedded directly in the text material and reflective questions to help you develop deeper insights into the issues and concepts being discussed.

Summary

This feature provides a complete summary review of each chapter's main points. This summary is an excellent resource for study and review. The information is presented in bulleted form under each major chapter heading to make it easier to access the information in the chapter.

Discussion Questions and Activities

The discussion questions and activities that follow each chapter will help you pursue further topics introduced in the chapter. This section provides critical and creative thinking activities that allow you to work with the issues brought up in the chapter and to think about the ideas the chapter has explored. It gives you a chance to take what you have learned in the chapter and apply it to real-world teaching issues or problems in the classroom.

Technology and Education

This feature gives you the opportunity to further explore the use of technology in the classroom and to assist teachers in the management of the classroom. Each exercise has been designed to help you identify and analyze techniques to better use technology to enhance student learning and to help classroom teachers with the many tasks required in the overall management of a classroom.

Deconstructing the Standards

This feature is designed to explore the links between the chapter content and INTASC standards, to prepare you for the Praxis II and/or state-related exams, and to help you identify portfolio exhibits related to the INTASC standards. These links and activities will provide additional insight and practice in meeting your teacher education program requirements and for passing state licensure/certification examinations.

Connection With the Field

These connections are suggested field experiences to introduce you to the profession from many perspectives, providing suggestions for classroom observation of teaching and learning, interviews with teachers and administrators, and interactions within the schools. Questions provide opportunities for reflection and allow you to gain additional insights into the classroom.

Praxis II Connection

These Praxis II connections are short-answer questions formatted to connect chapter content with relevant sections of the Praxis II: Principles of Learning and Teaching and other state pedagogical exams. These questions provide additional insight and practice in exam areas. They also direct you to material that will be very important in passing licensure examinations.

Organization of the Text

Part I: Setting the Stage for Successful Learning provides an orientation to teaching. In Chapter 1, we will get ready for the classroom. The chapter focuses on the art and science of teaching, effective teaching skills, constructivism, expectations and standards, accountability, and the licensing of teachers. The second chapter deals with the school curriculum. A comprehensive model of teaching is presented and discussed. Chapter 2 provides coverage of planning instruction, with a focus on identifying content, student needs, and technology in the classroom.

Part II: Sequencing and Organizing Instruction deals with establishing instructional intent and planning instruction. Chapter 3 provides comprehensive coverage of setting goals, writing objectives, and the backward design approach to identifying instructional intent. Chapter 4 focuses on developing unit and daily lesson plans. Course, unit, weekly, and daily lesson planning are presented and discussed. Team teaching and teaching special education and gifted and talented students are also covered. Several practical lesson plan formats are illustrated.

Part III: Designing Instruction to Maximize Student Learning relates to selecting instructional strategies. These chapters focus on using the direct, indirect, and integrated teaching methods for instructional delivery. This part also includes a pertinent chapter on skills instruction, which stresses the importance of critical thinking and the development of creative thinking as part of the school curriculum.

Part IV: Monitoring and Evaluating Student Learning addresses student evaluation, test construction, and grading and presents various techniques and procedures. Chapter 9 focuses on evaluation types, systems of evaluation, and information sources. Chapter 10 covers types of assessment, grading systems, and assigning grades.

Part V: Leading the Dynamic Classroom covers the implementation of instruction. The focus is on communication, motivation, and classroom management. The importance of classroom management cannot be overemphasized. Indeed, a classroom must be well managed if learning is to take place. Several management models are covered.

Supplements

Instructor's Resource CD

An instructor's manual is available on CD to help instructors plan and teach their courses. These resources have been designed to help instructors make the classes as practical and interesting as possible for students.

Student Resources CD

Materials are available on the CD at the back of the book to help students better understand course content. For each chapter, this supplement includes video clips that elaborate on or demonstrate identified chapter concepts.

Web-Based Student Study Site

www.sagepub.com/eis2study
This Web-based study site provides a variety of additional resources to enhance students' understanding of the book content and take their learning one step further. The site offers the comprehensive study materials such as practice tests, flashcards, Web resources, test preparation resources, and more. Also included are special features such as recommended readings, links to U.S. Department of Education Web sites, and links to state standards, and "Learning From SAGE Journal Articles." These resources can also be used by the instructor to supplement instruction.

Acknowledgments

I am, indeed, grateful to hundreds of students and teachers who provided critical feedback and served as invaluable sources in the preparation of this text. Moreover, I would like to thank the many educators who helped identify the major ideas presented in this textbook. Special gratitude also goes to the school districts that opened their doors to me and offered their support.

I would like to thank those who reviewed the text for both the first and second editions. Instructors who reviewed the first edition include Jimmy Ames, LeTourneau University; Holly L. Anderson, Boise State University; Sally Beisser, Drake University; Paulette Patterson Dilworth, Indiana University–Bloomington; Vicki Ferguson, University of Science and Arts of Oklahoma; James Haynie, North Carolina State University; W. Scott Hopkins, University of South Alabama; Cynthia J. Hutchinson, University of Central Florida; Andrew C. Kemp, University of Louisville; John Kiraly, Western Kentucky University; Chris Merrill, Illinois State University; Susie Oliphant, Bowie State University; David Peterson, Morehead State University; Lucy Snead, Columbia College; and Jared Stallones, Cal Poly Pomona.

Instructors who reviewed the second edition include Patricia L. Clow, Brevard College; Richard A. Giaquinto, St. Francis College, Brooklyn Heights, New York; Susan Gratz, Lincoln Memorial University; H. Carol Greene, East Carolina University; Andolyn B. Harrison, Grambling State University; Gail B. Hartin, Southern Methodist University; Nancy A. Hill, Southeastern Oklahoma State University; Courtney A. Howard, Claflin University; Andrew L. Hunt, University of Arkansas at Little Rock; D. John McIntyre, Southern Illinois University Carbondale; Annette Nelson, Northland College; Mary Podlesny, Northland College; Mary Ransdell, The University of Memphis; Phillip S. Riner, University of North Florida; Molly Romano, University of Arizona; Carolyn Schmidt-Bova, SUNY College at Buffalo; Sam L. Sullivan, Sam Houston State University; and Russ Whyte, Missouri Valley College.

Many colleagues contributed to this textbook. I am especially indebted to Dr. Sally Beisser at Drake University, who developed three of the lesson plan formats presented in Chapter 4 and wrote the Chapter 4 section on Teaching the Gifted and Talented Student, and to Dr. Chris Merrill at Illinois State University, who wrote the Chapter 6 section on Systemic Problem Solving. Finally, I would like to thank my wife, Susan, for all the support and for acting as a sounding board for many of the ideas presented in the text. The textbook is much stronger, due to the innovative ideas and efforts of these talented colleagues.

I would also like to thank the staff at Sage who helped bring this textbook to life. Diane McDaniel, who got the project started and kept it on track, deserves special thanks. Her leadership will always be remembered and appreciated. Special thanks also go to Leah Mori, Editorial Assistant, who provided much technical and research assistance.

—*K.D.M.*

Interstate New Teacher Assessment and Support Consortium (INTASC) Correlation Chart

This chart has been designed to indicate how the chapter text relates to sections of the Praxis II: Principles of Learning and Teaching (PLT) Assessment. The left-hand column of the chart lists the INTASC Knowledge standards. The center column contains the topics assessed in the PLT test. The right-hand column contains the chapters that correspond to the INTASC standards and the PLT tests.

INTASC Standard	Description of Teacher Performance	PRAXIS Topic	Text Chapter/Connection
Principle 1	Understands the central concepts, tools of inquiry, structure of the disciplines taught; creates learning experiences to make them meaningful to students.	IV. Profession and Community	Chapter 1 Getting Ready for the Classroom Chapter 2 Planning and Organizing for Teaching Chapter 3 Setting Goals and Objectives Chapter 5 Using Direct Teaching Methods
Principle 2	Understands how children learn and develop; provides learning opportunities that support their development.	I. Students as Learners A. Student Development and the Learning Process	Chapter 1 Getting Ready for the Classroom Chapter 2 Planning and Organizing for Teaching Chapter 3 Setting Goals and Objectives Chapter 5 Using Direct Teaching Methods Chapter 8 Teaching Effective Thinking Strategies Chapter 11 Communicating With Students and Parents
Principle 3	Understands how students differ in their approaches to learning; creates instructional opportunities adapted to diverse learners.	I. Students as Learners B. Students as Diverse Learners	Chapter 1 Getting Ready for the Classroom Chapter 2 Planning and Organizing for Teaching Chapter 3 Setting Goals and Objectives Chapter 5 Using Direct Teaching Methods

INTASC Standard	Description of Teacher Performance	PRAXIS Topic	Text Chapter/Connection
Principle 4	Understands and uses a variety of instructional strategies.	II. Instruction and Assessment A. Instructional Strategies	Chapter 4 Developing Unit and Daily Lesson Plans Chapter 5 Using Direct Teaching Methods Chapter 6 Using Indirect Teaching Methods Chapter 7 Using Integrated Teaching Methods Chapter 8 Teaching Effective Thinking Strategies
Principle 5	Creates a learning environment that encourages positive social interaction, active engagement in learning, and self-motivation.	I. Students as Learners C. Student Motivation and the Learning Process	Chapter 2 Planning and Organizing for Teaching Chapter 6 Using Indirect Teaching Methods Chapter 7 Using Integrated Teaching Methods Chapter 8 Teaching Effective Thinking Strategies Chapter 12 Motivating Students Chapter 13 Managing the Classroom Environment

Principle 6	Uses knowledge of communication techniques to foster active inquiry, collaboration, and supportive interaction.	I. Students as Learners
		  B. Students as Diverse Learners
		III. Communications Techniques
		  A. Basic, effective verbal and nonverbal communication techniques
			Chapter 5 Using Direct Teaching Methods
			Chapter 6 Using Indirect Teaching Methods
			Chapter 7 Using Integrated Teaching Methods
			Chapter 11 Communicating With Students and Parents

Principle 7	Plans instruction based on knowledge of subject matter, students, the community, and curriculum goals.	II. Instruction and Assessment B. Planning Instruction	Chapter 2 Planning and Organizing for Teaching Chapter 3 Setting Goals and Objectives Chapter 4 Developing Unit and Daily Lesson Plans Chapter 5 Using Direct Teaching Methods Chapter 6 Using Indirect Teaching Methods Chapter 7 Using Integrated Teaching Methods Chapter 8 Teaching Effective Thinking Strategies
Principle 8	Understands and uses formal and informal assessment strategies.	II. Instruction and Assessment C. Assessment Strategies	Chapter 4 Developing Unit and Daily Lesson Plans Chapter 9 Evaluating and Measuring Learning Chapter 10 Constructing and Grading Tests
Principle 9	Reflects on teaching.	III. Profession and Community	Chapter 1 Getting Ready for the Classroom Chapter 9 Evaluating and Measuring Learning Chapter 10 Constructing and Grading Tests
Principle 10	Fosters relationships with colleagues, parents, and agencies in the larger community.	I. Students as Learners B. Students as Diverse Learners III. Profession and Community	Chapter 1 Getting Ready for the Classroom Chapter 3 Setting Goals and Objectives Chapter 11 Communicating With Students and Parents Chapter 13 Managing the Classroom Environment

National Council for Accreditation of Teacher Education (NCATE) Correlation Chart

This chart has been designed to indicate how the chapter text relates to NCATE standards. The left-hand column of the chart lists the NCATE standards. The right-hand column of the chart contains the chapters that correspond to the NCATE standards.

NCATE Standard		Chapter
Standard 1	Candidate knowledge, skill, and disposition	Chapter 2 Planning and Organizing for Teaching
		Chapter 3 Setting Goals and Objectives
		Chapter 4 Developing Unit and Daily Lesson Plans
		Chapter 5 Using Direct Teaching Methods
		Chapter 6 Using Indirect Teaching Methods
		Chapter 7 Using Integrated Teaching Methods
		Chapter 8 Teaching Effective Thinking Strategies
		Chapter 11 Communicating With Students and Parents
		Chapter 12 Motivating Students
		Chapter 13 Managing the Classroom Environment
Standard 2	Assessment system and unit evaluation	Chapter 3 Setting Goals and Objectives
		Chapter 4 Developing Unit and Daily Lesson Plans
		Chapter 5 Using Direct Teaching Methods
		Chapter 6 Using Indirect Teaching Methods
		Chapter 7 Using Integrated Teaching Methods
		Chapter 9 Evaluating and Measuring Learning
		Chapter 10 Constructing and Grading Tests
Standard 3	Field experiences and clinical practice	Presented and discussed throughout the text
Standard 4	Diversity	Chapter 1 Getting Ready for the Classroom
		Chapter 2 Planning and Organizing for Teaching
		Chapter 11 Communicating With Students and Parents
		Chapter 12 Motivating Students
		Chapter 13 Managing the Classroom Environment
Standard 5	Faculty qualifications, performance, and evaluation	Presented and discussed throughout the text
Standard 6	Governance and resources	Chapter 2 Planning and Organizing for Teaching
		Chapter 5 Using Direct Teaching Methods
		Chapter 6 Using Indirect Teaching Methods
		Chapter 7 Using Integrated Teaching Methods
		Chapter 13 Managing the Classroom Environment

SETTING THE STAGE FOR SUCCESSFUL LEARNING

W hat is the purpose of education? Careful consideration of this question should be one of the first concerns of a prospective teacher. Historically, education has undergone constant change. Changes in society are often reflected in more demands being placed on our educational system.

Teaching is a challenge that requires long hours of work and preparation. Part I addresses the constantly changing field of education. The purpose of this first section is to help you gain insight into the process of teaching and to put that process into a framework that will assist you in preparing to teach.

Prospective teachers need to understand teaching as a profession. Thus, Chapter 1 presents some background information on where education is coming from and how it is constantly changing. On the other hand, because schools function to bring about learning, prospective teachers need a basic understanding of effective teaching, effective teaching skills, accountability, professional standards, educational law, and licensure requirements. Chapter 1 covers these essential topics.

Chapter 2 deals with the school curriculum. The key to success as a teacher is a well-designed curriculum based on student needs and societal needs. The program design must be based on sound research and state and national standards. It is the teacher, however, who has the final say in what will be taught. As such, a comprehensive model of teaching is presented and discussed. Chapter 2 also provides comprehensive coverage of planning a course of instruction.

CHAPTER 1

Getting Ready for the Classroom

The human contribution is the essential ingredient. It is only in the giving of oneself to others that we truly live.

—ETHEL PERCY ANDRUS

OVERVIEW

Teachers must be mentors, effective subject matter experts, counselors, and social psychologists. Teachers must also understand the social forces and theoretical thoughts that have shaped schools and teaching to be more effective in the classroom. Effective teachers must (a) engage in quality planning and preparation, (b) prepare a positive classroom environment, (c) use proven instructional techniques, and (d) exhibit professional behavior.

Teachers teach students. The intent is to bring about learning. Therefore, to maximize learning, one must take into account student needs, differences, and abilities. Many factors will influence development, teaching, and learning; I will focus my attention, however, on those that are relevant to the classroom.

Becoming a teacher requires that you meet state and national standards. Most states require that you demonstrate that you are a highly qualified teacher by passing a state or national exam.

Finally, teachers must be knowledgeable of educational law. Teacher must have a working knowledge of students' rights and teachers' rights and responsibilities.

OBJECTIVES

After completing your study of Chapter 1, you should be able to do the following:

- Describe some of the historical changes and major theoretical influences that have helped shape American education.
- Define teaching and explain the concept of teaching as an art and as a science.
- Describe the characteristics and skills associated with effective teaching and reflective teaching as well as the constructivist approach to learning.
- Explain why teachers need an understanding of students.

- Explain the role of parents and the community in the learning process.
- Explain the purposes of accreditation agencies and analyze the benefits of accreditation for various constituencies.
- Give an overview of students' and teachers' major rights and related court litigation.
- Explain the purpose of the state licensure/certification process.

What makes a "good" teacher, an "effective" teacher, a "successful" teacher? Are there certain identifiable skills that make one an effective teacher? Let's set the stage for our study of effective methods by focusing on what it means to teach and on standards for preparing effective teachers.

Teaching

What does it mean to teach? Moore (2001) defines **teaching** as "the actions of someone who is trying to assist others to reach their fullest potential in all aspects of development" (p. 5). The personal characteristics and skills needed to accomplish this noble task have been debated for years. Generally, the argument centers on the following questions: (a) Is teaching an art or a science, and (b) exactly what is effective teaching?

Historical Perspective on Teaching

The American public schools have always been dedicated to the concept of providing an education to the children and youth of the nation. Schools will continue to change, but if history is a guide, this change will come slowly. A brief overview of the important historical changes in the role of American education can be found on the Web-based student study site (http://www.sagepub.com/eis2study). Schools will likely continue to be based in communities, and teachers will continue to provide instruction to diverse groups of children in self-contained classrooms. However, expectations for teachers and students are factors that likely will change drastically in the decades ahead.

Teaching as an Art and a Science

Do some teachers have better instincts for teaching than others? If so, can these instincts be identified and taught? Some educators argue that teachers are born and not made and the ability to be an effective teacher cannot be taught. Conversely, other educators argue that teaching is a science with specific laws and principles, which can be taught.

Those who think *teaching is an art* may argue that good teaching is primarily a creative act. That is, teachers create learning in a spontaneous manner by combining individual pieces of education and experience into a new whole that is specially made for the circumstances they see in their situation. These individuals may recognize the need for a strong educational background but believe that once you are in the classroom, you operate from a gut-level feeling that leads you to know how to put theory into practice. This theory of teaching suggests that there are some who possess a special sense of knowing what to do and when to do it that cannot be taught. And although this idea doesn't leave the prospective teacher with a list of tangible options for putting together the pieces of education, it does explain a mysterious aspect of teaching that many spend a lifetime seeking. Indeed, this may be the mystery that has motivated so much research in the hope that perfect formulas will be discovered to direct us in our search for best practices and methods in education.

Those holding that *teaching is a science* believe that good teaching is the result of having a deep knowledge of the subject matter and a solid understanding of the principles of teaching and learning. They believe it is possible to learn and master the skills and strategies needed to be a successful teacher. Decades of research have provided specific information about how learning occurs, what influences motivation, and which particular teacher skills produce learning. Promoters of the teaching as a science theory offer specific methods and skills that are attainable for the prospective teacher. It is believed that persons who learn to use these skills will be successful.

Today, most educators are in agreement with Gagne (1985), who argues that there is a scientific basis for the art of teaching. Experienced teachers know it is not simply a matter of sharing what they know with their students. Teaching is a complex and challenging profession. A good teacher must be able to transform knowledge into learning activities that motivate students to learn. Thus, teaching can be viewed as having both artistic and scientific elements. Essentially, educators are accepting the viewpoint that individuals who have an interest in teaching fall somewhere along a continuum like that shown in Figure 1.1. Furthermore, many agree that specific artistic and scientific elements can be transmitted effectively.

Theorist Thoughts That Shaped Teaching

The search for effective teaching is not a new one. Good teaching requires a large repertoire of skills and the ability to put these skills to use in different situations. However, human beings are complicated. Few theories explain and predict perfectly. Because no one theory offers all the answers to effective teaching, this text will address only some of the commonly agreed on thoughts.

For many years, it was believed that a teacher's personal qualities were the most important attributes for effective teaching. Teachers who were warm and loving were thought to be more effective than those who lacked such attributes. This belief has a measure of truth to it, but it also gives an incomplete picture of effective teaching.

When we consider what effective teachers do, we think of the day-by-day instruction of students. The overall framework for thinking about effective teaching comes mainly from two sources: the teaching strategies and procedures that research has produced over the past 50 years and the wisdom of practice of experienced teachers.

Figure 1.1
Teaching as an Art and a Science

Art   Science

Natural   Learned
teaching   teaching
instincts   principles

John Dewey (1859–1952) was an educational reformer during what was known as the Progressive Era. Dewey was arguably the most influential American educator in the 20th century. He was instrumental in developing modern education theory.

Dewey's theory of schooling emphasized students and their interests rather than subject matter. From this theory came child-centered curriculum and child-centered schools. The progressive movement also maintained that schools should be concerned with preparing students for the realities of today rather than some vague future time. Dewey believed that learning activities about life and the skills necessary for living should come out of daily life.

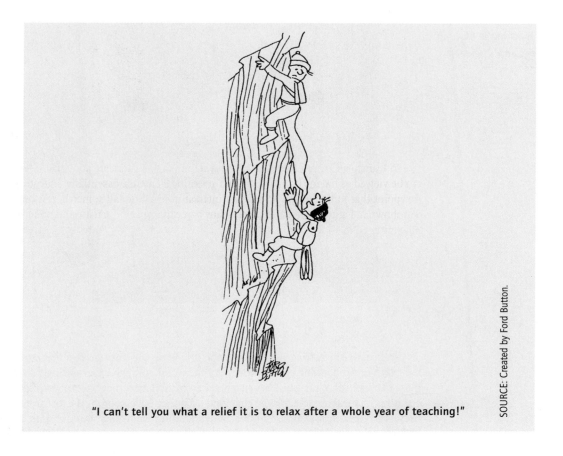

"I can't tell you what a relief it is to relax after a whole year of teaching!"

SOURCE: Created by Ford Button.

APPLY AND REFLECT 1.1	Dewey indicated that school is not preparation for life, but school is life. What do you suppose Dewey is suggesting by this statement? Share your thoughts with your class. Do they agree with your conclusions?

A relatively new theory of learning and teaching has recently emerged—constructivism. Constructivism constitutes a paradigm shift in how teaching is viewed. The essence of the **constructivist approach** to learning is the idea that learners individually discover and build their own knowledge (Anderson, Greeno, Reder, & Simon, 2000; Brooks & Brooks, 1999; Waxman, Padron, & Arnold, 2001). Learners construct a unique mental image by combining information in their heads with the information they receive from their sense organs. With the constructivist approach, students control some of the learning focus and activities; teacher-centered strategies, such as lectures, are minimized; multiple ways of knowing (through arts, for example) are honored; learning activities and assessments are often rooted in authentic situations; and much learning occurs in groups. The constructivist theory views learners as active participants in their own learning, not passive recipients of information. Learners construct their own meaning by negotiating that meaning with others, making connections with and modifying prior conceptions, and addressing content in a variety of contexts. This approach calls for a more active role for students in their own learning than is typical in many classrooms. Learning is a search for meaning. This constructivism perspective can be conveyed through the ancient Chinese proverb: "I hear and I forget; I see and I remember; I do and I understand."

Teaching is both an
art and a science.

Constructivism is basically a theory about how people learn. It says that students will construct their own understanding and knowledge of the world, through experiencing things and reflecting on those experiences. When students encounter something new, they have to reconcile it with their previous ideas and experiences, maybe changing what they believe, or maybe discarding the new information as irrelevant. Meaning requires understanding wholes as well as parts. And parts must be understood in the context of wholes. The learning process focuses on primary concepts, not isolated facts. In any case, students will be active creators of their own knowledge. To do this, they must be allowed to ask questions, explore, and assess what they know. The purpose of learning is for an individual to construct his or her own meaning, not just memorize the "right" answers and regurgitate someone else's meaning.

Teachers must focus on making connections between facts and fostering new understanding in students. They must tailor their teaching strategies to student responses and encourage students to analyze, interpret, and predict information. Teachers must rely heavily on open-ended questions and promote extensive dialogue among students. Students cannot be treated as though their brains are *blank slates* to be written upon or *empty vessels* to be filled up. Learners are not, in other words, passive. Rather, they often are quite active in learning. Students need to use and test ideas, skills, and so on through relevant activities. Often, this involves concrete experiences that combine with abstract ideas that have just been presented to learners.

The constructivist view of learning requires a reconceptualization of teaching. Teachers must focus on helping students construct understanding of concepts themselves. Instead of spending time memorizing material, filling in the blanks on worksheets, and repeating large numbers of similar problems, students need to learn to solve novel problems, integrate information, and create knowledge for themselves. The teacher's role is to foster and direct this work on the part of students. The teacher encourages students to use active techniques (experiments, real-world problem solving) to create more knowledge and then to reflect on and talk about what they are doing and how their understandings are changing. The teacher makes sure he or she understands the students' preexisting conceptions and guides the learning to address them and then build on them. Constructivist teachers encourage students to constantly assess how the learning activity is helping them gain understanding. By questioning themselves and their strategies, students in the constructivist classroom ideally become "expert learners." This gives them ever-broadening tools to keep learning. With a well-planned classroom environment, the students learn HOW TO LEARN. Teaching is getting students to see things in new ways. One of the biggest jobs becomes *asking good questions.*

Joyce and Weil (1996) and Joyce, Weil, and Calhoun (2003) have identified and described more than 20 major approaches to teaching. Each model differs in its basic rationale or philosophical base and in the goals it is designed to achieve. Obviously, it is unrealistic to ask a teacher to be this prescriptive in a single classroom when he or she must deal with such a wide diversity of students. However, each model shares many effective procedures and strategies, such as the need to motivate, define expectations, and involve students in their own learning. This text will address many of these shared procedures and strategies from the work of Joyce, Weil, and Calhoun that are based on traditional perspectives about teaching and learning. The text will also focus on the wisdom of practice of experienced teachers.

APPLY AND REFLECT 1.2	How would you answer the following question: What is a school and what is it for? Discuss your answer with your classmates.

Effective Teaching

The search for the elements of effective teaching is not a new one. Teaching requires a large repertoire of skills and the ability to put these skills to use in different situations. Good teachers improvise: No one approach works equally well all the time and in all situations. In short, effectiveness depends on the subject, students, and environmental conditions.

Effective teaching is complicated. The better teachers, however, are proactive; that is, they are active information processors and decision makers. They are strongly committed to the importance of content delivery and tend to be task oriented. They understand the demands of teaching their content, the characteristics of their students, and the importance of decision making in keeping students on task. Research suggests that teacher knowledge of subject matter, student learning, and teaching methods are important elements of effective teaching. Indeed, according to *What Matters Most: Teaching for America's Future* (National Commission on Teaching & America's Future, 1996), teacher knowledge and what teachers do are the most important influences on what students learn.

Contrasting ideas about effective teaching have recently emerged. No matter what view of effective teaching is held, however, the dynamic and complex nature of teaching warrants that teachers be prepared to be self-monitoring individuals. Self-monitoring requires that teachers have skills that enable self-analysis of teaching episodes; they reflect and focus on events rather than on personalities, as well as on systematic observations for patterns and trends in teaching and learning behavior. These contrasting ideas suggest that to be effective, teachers must inquire into students' experiences and build an understanding of learners and a capacity to analyze what occurs in classrooms and in the lives of their students. In effect, you change your orientation from a view of teaching as static, with simple formulas and cookbook rules, to teaching as dynamic and ever changing. This change requires that you become a reflective teacher.

Reflective teachers learn all they can about teaching from both theory and practice. They teach and reflect on the teaching. They think deeply about the theory and practice of teaching. Such teaching requires that you be sensitive to the diversity of students' needs and family background. Reflective teaching requires that you ask basic, but often difficult, questions about the appropriateness and success of your teaching. If a lesson is unsuccessful, you should be asking how you could change your teaching to make it successful. If students aren't motivated, what can you do to motivate them? If grades are poor, how can you improve achievement? Reflective teaching, then, is the continued self-monitoring of satisfaction with effectiveness. Valuable insight into your reflective and self-monitoring efforts can be provided by Web sites such as that established by ProTeacher (www.proteacher .com), Middle-Web (www.middleweb.com), and Teachers At Risk (www.teachersatrisk.com) and by resources such as *Best Practices for High School Classrooms* (Stone, 2002). The following Through the Eyes of Teachers interlude gives an overview of the ProTeacher site.

THROUGH THE EYES OF TEACHERS

ProTeacher Community (www.proteacher.net)

A popular and carefully moderated discussion site for elementary schoolteachers, ProTeacher is host to hundreds of active and changing discussions and tens of thousands of teaching ideas contributed by teachers nationwide.

Professional classroom teachers, specialists, substitute teachers, student teachers, and administrators working in early childhood, elementary, and middle school are invited to participate—and many do. Although ProTeacher has been designed primarily for elementary schoolteachers, the discussions and ideas are often applicable to all grade levels.

Participation is free of charge and no registration is required. All newcomers, however, should first read their "tips and guidelines" page, which contains helpful advice for first-time visitors, as well as established rules and policies. Special rules apply to student teachers.

The ProTeacher motto is "By sharing ideas and being helpful, we're encouraging others to do the same!" With experienced teachers from across the country doing just that, ProTeacher is definitely worth a visit!

Effective teachers know that good teaching is more than simply explaining, lecturing, and discussing. To be effective, teachers must be well organized.

APPLY AND REFLECT 1.3 The debate continues as to whether teaching is a profession similar to law and medicine. Or is teaching a semi-profession? Or is teaching a calling? What is your view of the professionalism of teaching? Discuss your views with your class.

Effective Organization

Classrooms can be organized or disorganized. Better quality instruction is structured around appropriate content, materials and methods, and interaction patterns. The thoughtfully structured classroom is one in which students engage in meaningful tasks. Matching of instructional tasks with all the interacting variables in a classroom, however, is not easy because of the differences in student ability and potential for learning.

Well-organized classrooms are businesslike. Classes get started on time, and students know what they are to do with class time. Moreover, students know when it is time to get back to work, and they understand the reasons behind and importance of assignments.

Finally, when a lecture is presented or a group activity is conducted, it should be well organized, with clear, well-illustrated explanations. Lesson content should be constructed and presented in logical order, with ideas that are interrelated and interwoven. In effect, thoughtful lessons are designed so students have meaningful and coherent material to learn. Outlines, schematic diagrams, and hierarchies are effective techniques for organizing and presenting lesson content. Complete Web Link 1.1: The World Wide Web to explore some Web sites that you may find useful.

WEB LINK 1.1   The World Wide Web

The World Wide Web offers educators unlimited resources for increasing their effectiveness in the classroom. Examine a couple of Web sites for educators. How could the available resources contribute to your effectiveness as a teacher?

Skills of Effective Teachers

Effective teaching is a complex occupation requiring the development of knowledge and essential teaching skills, as well as continuous professional growth. After a thorough analysis of current research, Danielson (1996) suggested four main skill areas for effective teaching. Effective teachers (1) engage in quality planning and preparation, (2) prepare a positive classroom environment, (3) use proven instructional techniques, and (4) exhibit professional behavior. These skill areas are derived from the work of the Educational Testing Service (ETS) in the development of Praxis III. Praxis III: Classroom Performance Assessments is used to assess actual teaching skills and classroom performance. The Danielson skill areas are grounded in the constructivist approach to learning and are based on formal analyses of important tasks required of beginning teachers: reviews of research, analyses of state regulations for teacher licensing, and extensive fieldwork.

Quality Planning and Preparation

Many people assume all you really need to be an effective teacher is an understanding of content. They assume that once you know your content, it is simply a matter of telling others what you know. In reality, knowing your subject is only part of the instructional process. Effective teachers must spend considerable time and energy planning the activities, materials, and evaluation elements associated with teaching the content. Danielson (1996) found that effective teachers need

- a knowledge of content and pedagogy (know their subject and how to teach it),
- a knowledge of students (know how students learn and develop),
- the ability to select instructional goals (set appropriate expectations),
- a knowledge of resources (can locate materials and people that will enhance instruction),
- the ability to design instruction (can plan effective lesson plans), and
- the ability to design student evaluation (can design fair and meaningful evaluation).

Effective teachers must carefully orchestrate these elements into a coherent teaching plan of instruction.

The Classroom Environment

Effective teachers must create and maintain an environment in which learning can take place. Danielson (1996) found planning classroom environments that allow for positive student learning experiences requires skill at

For material related to this concept, go to Clip 1.1 on the Student Resource CD bound into the back of your textbook.

- creating an environment of respect and rapport (create caring teacher-student and peer relationships),
- establishing a culture for learning (create an environment in which learning is valued and meaningful experiences occur),
- managing the classroom (success at management of the business of the classroom),
- managing student behavior (effectively responding to appropriate and inappropriate student behavior), and
- organizing physical space (positive use of classroom space).

It is especially important that teachers have expertise in classroom management to be successful. Classrooms are multidimensional and crowded with people, tasks, and time pressures. Teachers, therefore, must be effective at managing this multidimensional environment. They must be able to create and maintain a positive learning environment, establish classroom rules and procedures, and establish effective communication with students, parents, and school administrators.

Instructional Techniques

For material related to this concept, go to Clip 1.2 on the Student Resource CD bound into the back of your textbook.

Instructional techniques must be planned that will captivate the interest of students and motivate them to learn. Techniques would include such skills as questioning, using student ideas and contributions, and reinforcing. Danielson (1996) found that effective teachers plan and use instructional techniques that

- communicate clearly and accurately (use strong verbal and written communication skills),
- use effective questioning and discussion techniques (use different types of questions and responses),
- engage students in learning (actively involve students in learning),
- provide feedback to students (provide information on progress), and
- are flexible and responsive (spontaneously modify lessons based on feedback).

Professional Behavior

Teaching often goes beyond traditional classroom instruction. Effective teachers embrace these extra tasks and strive to improve their knowledge and skills in instruction while working to make significant contributions to their school and community. They work to become true professionals. Danielson (1996) found that true professional teachers

- reflect on their teaching (thoughtfully consider what was taught and how well it was taught),
- maintain accurate records (keep written records to document student learning),
- communicate with families (stay in written and verbal contact with families to support student progress),
- contribute to the school and district (support functions of the school and district),
- grow as professionals (take courses and workshops and consult with others), and
- show professionalism (serve as advocates for students and families).

Teachers, like other professionals, must continue to grow professionally. To this end, teachers have established a number of professional organizations that are vitally concerned with issues of special interest to teachers. Professional teachers are involved in such organizations and strive to continuously improve their skills and make teaching a profession. The professional teacher is dedicated to continuous learning—both about the teaching-learning process and about the subject(s) taught.

APPLY AND REFLECT 1.4	Are effective teachers "born," or can an individual be taught to be an effective teacher?

To be effective, you must be well organized. However, your orientation, dispositions, and attitudes toward students and learning will often affect students.

Dispositions and Attitudes

The National Council for Accreditation of Teacher Education (NCATE) defines dispositions as the values, commitments, and professional ethics that influence behaviors toward students, families, colleagues, and communities and affect student learning, motivation, and development, as well as the educator's own professional growth. Dispositions are guided by beliefs and **attitudes** related to values such as caring, fairness, honesty, **responsibility,** and social justice.

REFLECTIONS ON TEACHER PRACTICE 1.1   Making Education Meaningful

1. Are schools today setting students up for failure? If so, how must schools change to provide success for all students?

2. What is the attitude of most parents regarding school involvement? How can teachers involve parents and the community to a greater extent in our schools?

◆ ◆ ◆

Education should be painless. I believe the education of students should be a partnership between teacher and student and it is the greatest gift we can give a student.

Students approach education in different ways. Some are easily stimulated and are easily taught. Others are harder to reach. The trick is to balance the teaching approach to benefit each student as an individual. Education should encompass a variety of experiences that add up to a complete entity, the educated person.

Students need encouragement, a stable classroom/school environment, and a chance to succeed. In our modern world of fast-moving images and strong media influence, a student's ability is often taken for granted. Since we are inundated with information, it is easy to assume students are being educated when they are out of the classroom. In most cases, however, this is not the case. Students need a stable classroom environment in which to be the students they are and learn what they need to know.

Students deserve the chance to succeed. By manipulating some situations, it is possible to give each student the satisfaction of being a success.

Effective teachers should be flexible and should be able to wear a lot of different hats. Sometimes these different hats have to be worn at once, so flexibility is paramount. Flexibility allows for trial and error. If one teaching method or strategy isn't working, something new should be tried. A teacher isn't just a teacher anymore, which accounts for the many hats. A teacher has to assume the role of parent, counselor, and disciplinarian. An effective teacher should be able to assimilate these roles into one package. In addition to flexibility and juggling hats, an effective teacher has to be both receptive and perceptive. A receptive teacher is open to new ideas, which is important when trying to teach a variety of different students. A perceptive teacher is able to see the student. By keeping a close watch on students and student performances, you open up opportunities to reach them.

Teachers should involve families and the community in the school. Parents should be seen as partners in the education of students. Parents should be kept informed of progress both good and bad. The old adage, "No news is good news" is outdated. Parents need to be made a part of the education of students. When possible, parents should be used as a classroom resource. Many parents have skills or experiences that can be tapped for classroom use as a speaker or helper.

The community should be welcome in the school. The community supports public schools financially through taxes and fund-raising and should feel a part of the school. In most cases, the school is a central focus in the community. This focus should be a good thing, not a bad one. The community has vast resources for schools both financial and academic. Through programs like "adopt a classroom" and others, the community can be brought into the school for a purpose and both school and community benefit. The education of students should not occur behind closed schoolhouse doors. The community and parents should feel a connection to the school and feel they are part of the education of our children.

—RACHEL, elementary school teacher

SOURCE: Reprinted with permission from ProTeacher, a professional community for elementary school teachers (http://www.proteacher.net).

ON YOUR OWN 1.1 **Reflections on Teacher Practice**

Read and reflect on the viewpoints expressed in Making Education Meaningful. Log on to the Web-based student study site at http://www.sagepub.com/eis2study and react to the related activities.

Although every teacher holds his or her own dispositions and attitudes, there are several common dispositions and attitudes that effective teachers hold. First of all, effective teachers are real. Within reason, they share their true selves with students. Second, effective teachers have positive expectations for *all* students. They have realistic, yet challenging, expectations for *all* of their students. Third, effective teachers are caring about their students. They have an attitude of acceptance and trust. Fourth, effective teachers are excited about teaching and learning. They demonstrate love of teaching and learning. Fifth, effective teachers value diversity. They treat *all* students equally and fairly. Finally, effective teachers are willing to collaborate. They see themselves as part of an educational team and community. Great teachers do not just love kids. They facilitate a love of learning in the students they teach.

APPLY AND REFLECT 1.5

What are the dispositions of your teacher education program? Do you agree they are dispositions that effective teachers should possess?

Students

Students are the intended audience for the curriculum. Therefore, you must have some general information about the nature of the students in the schools in which you will be teaching.

For material related to this concept, go to Clip 1.3 on the Student Resource CD bound into the back of your textbook.

Children do not look and act like they did 20 or 30 years ago, and the differences are not only the result of changes in dress and hairstyles. Today, schools are showing major increases in non-White student populations. Moreover, the need to acculturate newly arrived immigrants is still an important part of the schooling process. But the faces of immigrant youth are no longer predominantly European faces. They are increasingly the faces of Asians, Hispanics, and others. A large percentage of the Asians are from Southeast Asia, and a large percentage of the Hispanics are from Latin America. As a result of this new influx of immigrants, more foreign languages are being spoken in our schools than ever before, and many of these languages have yet to become a part of the **formal curriculum.**

As a teacher, you will be required to plan very carefully to meet the needs of such a diverse student population. Failure to recognize and address the needs of these students could result in a large portion of the future adult population of this country that cannot participate successfully in the marketplace or as citizens.

APPLY AND REFLECT 1.6

How are students and families different than they were a decade ago? Have you seen many changes in your state? If so, what kinds?

Parent and Community Involvement

Parent and community involvement is an important factor in improving the academic learning of students. Parent and community involvement is a process wherein parents and educators are encouraged to cooperate in and support the education of students. This involvement can come in four different forms and levels: instruction at school, instruction at home, school governance, and community service.

Getting parents involved in the educational process is not always easy. Parents and teachers live in different worlds that are often separated by psychosocial barriers. Indeed, parents frequently have preconceived and sometimes biased views of schools and teachers. Even with these constraints, however, parent and community involvement will generally positively affect the educational process.

Ultimately, educators must find ways to open and support culturally responsive communication between parents and schools. Too often, low-income and minority families face sustained isolation from the school culture. Such isolation can result in an "us" versus "them" mentality. Teachers then often blame parents for student academic failures. Keep in mind, however, that because of changes in modern families (e.g., non-English-speaking, single-parent families, decreasing family size, both parents working, and increased poverty), it often takes a whole community to educate our young people. To further explore parent involvement in the schools, complete Expansion Activity 1.1: Parent Involvement.

EXPANSION ACTIVITY 1.1   Parent Involvement

Research shows that parent involvement greatly influences students' school attitudes, interest, attendance, and academic achievement. Develop an action plan for involving parents in your classroom in a variety of ways. What are some barriers you must overcome to involve parents? How are you going to overcome those barriers? Why should parents, families, and community members be recognized and encouraged to participate in the elementary school program? Secondary school programs?

This completes my introduction to teaching. Table 1.1 summarizes the concepts addressed in this section. Review the summary and complete Review and Reflective Exercise 1.1.

TABLE 1.1   Teaching Concepts

Concept	Description
Teaching as art	Effective teachers have natural instincts for teaching.
Teaching as science	Effective teaching comes from learned laws and principles of teaching.
Organized classroom	Classroom is structured around a businesslike atmosphere and well-planned appropriate lessons.
Transfer	The ability to use information acquired in one situation in new situations.

REVIEW AND REFLECTIVE EXERCISE 1.1   Define teaching and describe the skills associated with effective teaching.

REVIEW

- Is teaching an art or a science?
- Are there specific skills that effective teachers should develop? What standards should we have for teachers? Students?
- How is time used in the classroom?

REFLECTION

- Teachers have many different responsibilities in today's schools. Do you think teachers are asked to do too many things? If so, what can be done to improve the working conditions of teachers? Do you feel qualified to carry out the diverse roles of a teacher? Do you have strong areas? Weak areas? Understanding and willingness to adapt (to be responsive) are often suggested as attributes of the successful teacher. Do you possess these attributes? What other attributes do you feel are important to teachers?

- Write a short essay explaining what effective teachers must know and be able to do. Explain how the following terms are related to effective teaching: (a) knowledge of subject, (b) time, (c) teaching skills, and (d) standards.

ON YOUR OWN 1.2 View From the Classroom

Log on to the Web-based student study site at http://www.sagepub.com/eis2study. Review the Chapter 1 teacher surveys and react to the related activities.

Professional Teaching Standards

Research shows that what teachers know, do, and value has a significant influence on the nature, extent, and rate of student learning. Recognition of the critical teacher impact and relationship between teacher and learner highlights the need to better define and build on what constitutes effective teaching. Professional teaching standards provide a powerful mechanism for achieving this aim.

Challenges in Preparing to Teach

Many new regulations from local, state, and federal agencies have brought new challenges to teaching. As you prepare for a career in teaching, you will become familiar with rules that govern such things as length of time spent on subjects taught, textbooks used for instruction, guidelines for teacher conduct and interactions with students, and requirements for student promotion. Regulating agencies also require institutions, like the university or college you are attending, to meet rigid standards within teacher education programs that are preparing teachers for the classroom. There are standards and benchmarks used to measure instruction and student learning that will affect you as you prepare to learn the necessary skills of a beginning teacher. Although there are a growing number of new requirements guiding the profession, many teachers express satisfaction with the amount of control they have in presenting instruction within their classrooms. On the other hand, some teachers may feel somewhat isolated and miss adult interaction. Has your state or subject area established standards that you must meet as a teacher? Complete Web Link 1.2: Educational Standards to answer this question.

WEB LINK 1.2 Educational Standards

Access the following Internet URL site: http//www.academicbenchmarks.com. Analyze the educational standards for your state and for your subject area. How are they useful for improving teaching and learning? How can the standards be used to enhance the opportunity to learn? How will the standards lead to higher student achievement? Share your conclusions with the class.

No Child Left Behind (NCLB)

On January 8, 2002, President Bush signed the No Child Left Behind (NCLB) Act of 2001 into law (U.S. Department of Education, 2004). The act was enacted to ensure accountability and flexibility as well as to increase federal support for education. The major goal of NCLB is to ensure all public schools provide each student with a solid education. The central tenet is to test students, and schools should pay a penalty when their kids don't meet state performance targets. Except, not every student's exam score counts in the evaluation of a school's performance (limited English speakers and learning-disabled students are sometimes not included). Moreover, NCLB requires that test scores be broken down by group—forcing schools to publicly document the performance of minority groups and low-income students. NCLB requires yearly gain among all students, regardless of race, income, or English ability. The law requires that every child in America be proficient in reading and mathematics by 2014. Schools must assess 95% of their students' academic skills in reading and writing annually in Grades 3 through 8 and

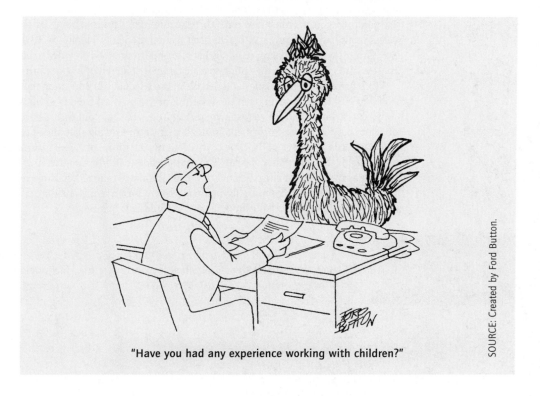

"Have you had any experience working with children?"

SOURCE: Created by Ford Button.

at least once in Grades 10 through 12. Schools also must assess 95% of all major subgroups of students, such as minority or disabled students. Schools not assessing 95% or more of eligible test takers may be identified as needing academic improvement—as are schools in which students do not meet minimum test score requirements. Schools identified as academically troubled and in need of improvement face consequences ranging from having to permit students to transfer to other, higher achieving schools or paying for tutoring to replacing the faculty. NCLB is seen as an aggressive response to a national problem with the reading and mathematics performance of fourth graders and eighth graders. However, some states are lowering their standards and benchmarks so schools can avoid consequences that come with missing annual progress goals (Zuckerbrod, 2007).

NCLB couples testing requirements with a push for qualified teachers in all core academic subjects (English, math, science, social studies, art, music, and foreign language). The original act mandated that states require all teachers to (a) hold at least a bachelor's degree, (b) hold a license or certificate to teach in the state of his or her employment, and (c) have proven knowledge in core academic subjects they teach. States have been asked to establish a plan for improving the quality of teachers and increasing the number of highly qualified teachers. However, some states are finding it difficult to meet this mandate. Also, due to extensive criticism and extreme shortages in certain areas, the federal Department of Education has become more flexible in how a teacher can be considered highly qualified. Many states are increasing the number of highly qualified teachers by implementing more alternative paths toward licensure or certification. Some states also have turned to online alternative paths toward receiving full licensure or certification. Still others are bringing in teachers from foreign countries to fill shortage areas.

NCLB also requires schools that receive Title I funding to notify parents at the beginning of each school year if their child has been taught for 4 consecutive weeks by a teacher who is not highly qualified. NCLB also requires that paraprofessionals who are funded with Title I funds and who provide instructional support complete 2 years of study at an institution of higher education, obtain an associate's degree, or meet a rigorous standard of quality and demonstrate knowledge of certain core subjects. New paraprofessionals must now meet these requirements prior to being employed, and current paraprofessionals had until January 2006 to meet the requirements. Finally, NCLB targets resources to support learning in the early years, requires that more information be provided to parents about their child's progress, and gives parents the option to transfer their child out of low-performing schools.

NCLB has opened new issues and debate on the adequacy of education in the United States. Issues related to NCLB continue to be at the forefront of the political agenda at both the national and state levels (Zuckerbrod, 2007). As a result, modifications in the law continue to be implemented, and states continue to develop and implement strategic plans for ensuring that all students are meeting grade-level standards. However, at the time of this writing, the future of NCLB is uncertain. NCLB continues to be a highly debated political issue. The next president and/or Congress may seek major changes in NCLB, may make minor changes in it, or try to eliminate it altogether. However, educational accountability will continue to be a highly political issue. Complete Expansion Activity 1.2: No Child Left Behind to further explore your thoughts on No Child Left Behind.

APPLY AND REFLECT 1.7

No Child Left Behind legislation requires that every classroom have a highly qualified teacher. States define *highly qualified teacher* differently. How would you define highly qualified teacher?

EXPANSION ACTIVITY 1.2   No Child Left Behind

No Child Left Behind (NCLB) calls for a fully qualified teacher in every classroom. Do you agree with this regulation? Why do you support or not support such a requirement? What about areas with teacher shortages? Should we bring teachers in from other countries to have a fully qualified teacher in every classroom? Why is this a good idea or bad idea? Discuss these issues in class with classmates.

Several national groups and professional associations have invested considerable time, energy, and resources in establishing a rationale for teaching standards and in working with classroom practitioners to design and test various models and approaches to professionalize teaching. These efforts resulted in the recommendation and establishment of standards and **teacher testing.** Playing a central role in these efforts were NCATE, the National Board for Professional Teaching Standards (NBPTS), the Interstate New Teacher Assessment and Support Consortium (INTASC), and the Educational Testing Service (ETS). Most teacher preparation programs are specifically aligned with the INTASC standards at the undergraduate level (initial licensure) and with the NBPTS at the graduate level (advanced licensure). In addition, some states require teacher education programs that prepare teachers (early childhood, English, mathematics, science, special education, etc.) and other school personnel (counselors, principals, superintendents, etc.) to meet specific Specialized Professional Association (SPA) standards. A brief discussion of NCATE, NBPTS, and INTASC can be found on the Web-based student study site (www.sagepub.com/eis2study).

Assessment of Standards

To ensure that the INTASC standards are being met, many states are requiring all teacher candidates to successfully pass a standardized test that assesses their understanding of the subject they will teach and knowledge of teaching and learning. One exam that is commonly used for the purpose is the Praxis II, which was developed by the ETS. Some states, however, have developed state tests to assess whether candidates meet INTASC standards. Forty states now use the Praxis Series to assess the national standards.

The ETS developed the Praxis Series to assist state education agencies in making licensing decisions. The Praxis Series: Professional Assessments for Beginning Teachers is a set of rigorous and carefully validated assessments designed to provide accurate, reliable licensing information. An overview of the Praxis Series can be accessed at the ETS Web site (www.ets.org/praxis). The Praxis Series is used by nearly 80% of states that include tests as part of their licensing process. Access www.ets.org/praxis/prxstate.html to check Praxis test requirements for specific states.

The three categories of **assessment** in the Praxis Series correspond to the three decision points in teacher preparation:

- Entry into a teacher training program: Praxis I: Academic Skills Assessments
- Requirement for initial licensure into profession: Praxis II: Subject and Pedagogy Assessments
- Requirement for permanent licensure: Praxis III: Classroom Performance Assessments

Only the Praxis I and II are used extensively by states in their licensure process. The Praxis I: Academic Skills Assessments (Pre-Professional Skills Tests, or PPST) tests candidates relative to their reading, writing, and mathematics abilities. The Praxis II: Subject and Pedagogy Assessments contains two types of tests: Multiple Subjects Assessments and Principles of Learning and Teaching Assessments.

The Praxis II: Multiple Subjects Assessments tests the subject matter knowledge of teacher candidates. Some of these subject area tests include multiple exams, and some include a pedagogy exam. For example, the social studies and English exams consist of two content exams and a pedagogy exam. Most of the exams are 1 or 2 hours in duration.

The Praxis II: Principles of Learning and Teaching Assessments is designed to assess pedagogical knowledge in such areas as educational psychology, human growth and development, classroom management, instructional design and delivery techniques, evaluation and assessment, and other preparation. The assessments are divided into early childhood, Grades K to 6, Grades 5 to 9, and Grades 7 to 12 to reflect the different levels of licensure. Each assessment includes four case histories each followed by three short-answer questions about the case and 24 multiple-choice questions. The multiple-choice questions cover candidate knowledge in the following areas:

Students as Learners

Student Development and the Learning Process

Students as Diverse Learners

Student Motivation and the Learning Environment

Instruction and Assessment

Instructional Strategies

Planning Instruction

Assessment Strategies

Communication Techniques

Basic, effective verbal and nonverbal communication techniques

Effect of cultural and gender differences on communications in the classroom

Types of communications and interactions that can stimulate discussion in different ways for particular purposes

Profession and Community

The Reflective Practitioner

The Larger Community

Because you will probably be required to demonstrate competency relative to the INTASC standards during your initial teacher preparatory program and perhaps to the NBPTS in an advanced program, I will focus on these standards throughout this text. I will also indicate how the text content relates to sections of the Praxis II: Principles of Learning and Teaching Assessments. Before turning to the next section, complete Expansion Activity 1.3: Becoming a Teacher, which will let you explore your self-concept of teaching.

EXPANSION ACTIVITY 1.3   Becoming a Teacher

After some thinking, write a personal statement about the following. What kind of teacher do you want to become? How will national (NCATE , NBPTS, INTASC, and SPA) standards help you become that teacher? What strengths do you want to have? What potential weaknesses might you need to overcome?

APPLY AND REFLECT 1.8

Most states now require that prospective teachers pass licensure/certification exams. Is this a good idea? Why do you support or oppose a testing requirement for teachers? Some states grant a teaching license/certificate to anyone who holds a degree and a passing score on a state-required teacher exam. Why should individuals with only a degree and no teacher preparation training be allowed to teach by simply passing a test? What potential problems do you see with this policy?

REFLECTIONS ON TEACHER PRACTICE 1.2   The Standards Movement

1. Why should schools have to meet national and state standards? Do standards really lead to more effective teaching and learning?

2. What benefits and problems do you associate with high-stakes testing?

◆ ◆ ◆

The establishment of standards has changed how most teachers teach. However, one problem with the "standards movement" is that advocates of standards-based classrooms have lost control of their message, as high-stakes state testing advocates have seized the "standards" language—tacking it onto the state accountability system without sufficient thought and certainly regarding the needed major investment in professional development required to make standards a meaningful tool to raise student achievement.

I've had the opportunity to observe standards-based classrooms where teachers are improving teaching and learning through the use of standards. In every case, the standards were developed or modified by the school system, with active teacher participation, and were accompanied by "performance standards" that showed teachers and students what is "good enough." The standards-based initiative was accompanied by lots of professional development that linked standards to teaching practice, classroom assessment, etc. In these classrooms and schools, the decision to measure student progress against standards provoked deep conversations about the quality of lessons and teaching strategies, about the meaning of grades, and about the need to deepen content. Also, in every case, teachers were using all the provided creative teaching strategies.

Even with help, grasping and applying the standards-based approach to teaching and learning is very hard work. But in dozens of interviews with teachers in these schools, I heard over and over again that the standards-based approach to teaching was improving the curriculum, reducing duplicative teaching across grades in every subject area, and causing teachers to ask some difficult but important questions about the value of favorite projects that kids enjoyed but that did little to increase their skills and knowledge.

In many cases, the process of examining lessons from a standards perspective made it possible for teachers to modify those "favorite units," retaining the fun and excitement while strengthening the academic purpose and the learning outcomes. None of this will have an impact unless teachers move beyond the point of simply trying to "match" a list of standards to their existing lesson plans.

I know there are teachers who have experienced the positives of standards-based teaching. However, in some schools, the growing pressure to perform on standardized state tests has actually stymied the move toward standards-based teaching, as principals and teachers have given in (understandably) to pressure from above to drill, drill, drill—to narrow curriculum and make the state test the Alpha and Omega of schooling.

I don't believe excellent teachers are afraid to ask tough questions about their own teaching and the teaching in their schools. That's what standards should be all about. Unfortunately, politicians and other folks who seek to gain an advantage by leveling blanket attacks on educators, without much clue about the realities of school, are turning the standards movement into a bludgeon. That's a dead-end strategy that won't help teachers, schools, or, most important of all, kids.

In closing, I believe it is possible to criticize the negative effects to high-stakes testing, champion constructive teaching, and still support the proposition that standards-based teaching can raise student achievement.

—JOHN NORTON, education writer

SOURCE: Reprinted with permission from MiddleWeb.

ON YOUR OWN 1.3 **Reflections on Teacher Practice**

Read and reflect on the viewpoints expressed in The Standards Movement. Log on to the Web-based student study site at http://www.sagepub.com/eis2study and react to the related activities.

Educational Law

Education is a serious responsibility and is often controversial. Argument over the most appropriate aims, the most propitious means, and most effective control continue to rage. Responsibility for and control of education, as it operates in the United States, is a state function under the Tenth Amendment, which provides that powers not delegated by the Constitution to the federal government are passed on to the states. It is important to note, however, that education is not a constitutional right but, rather, a privilege granted to people through state government. The federal Constitution does, however, affect public education.

The U.S. Supreme Court has increasingly been asked to resolve issues relating to education. This rise in educational litigation reflects the fact that education has assumed an importance in our society that it did not have a few decades ago. The growth in litigation has been paralleled by an increase in state and federal legislation affecting education and the need to provide a quality education to *all* children (Hollingsworth, 2005). Teachers face the dilemma of balancing the need for order in the school environment and classroom with the need to respect the legal rights of students and parents.

Student Rights

Student rights have been at the forefront of educational litigation over the past 50 years. Generally, Supreme Court decisions have reflected favorably on the rights of students and mandated substantive guarantees to protect students' rights and to establish equity (Looney, 2004). The Supreme Court addressed equity in the case *Brown v. Board of Education of Topeka,* which stated that separate (segregated) but equal is not equal (Brown, 2004). Subsequently, the Civil Rights Act of 1964 (PL 88–352) authorized the U.S. Commissioner of Education to support both state and local school districts to assist in their efforts to racially desegregate public schools. New meaning was given to *Brown v. Board of Education of Topeka* with the enactment of Public Law 94–142, the Education of All Handicapped Children Act (1975), and its amendment in 1990 by Public Law 101–476, the Individuals with Disabilities Education Act (IDEA). Public Law 94–142 granted students with disabilities and their families many powerful rights. Public Law 94–142 mandated free and appropriate public education services to *all* school-age children and youth, regardless of disability.

The Vocational Rehabilitation Act was passed in 1973. While the intent was to provide job opportunities and training to disabled adults, the act also addressed the failure of the public schools to educate disabled students. The single paragraph that is referred to as Section 504 of the Vocational Rehabilitation Act focuses on nondiscrimination. Through Section 504, all school-age children are ensured an equal opportunity to participate in school activities. The provisions of Section 504 broadly prohibit the denial of a public education or enjoyment of the benefits offered by public school programs because of a disability. The language of Section 504 provides for a free, appropriate public education to qualifying disabled students whose disabilities are not so severe as to create IDEA eligibility. To encourage compliance, Congress made future receipt of federal funds conditional on a district's compliance with Section 504 provisions.

Child Abuse and Neglect

Laws in all 50 states have enacted mandatory child abuse and neglect reporting in some form to satisfy the Child Abuse Prevention and Treatment Act (CAPTA) (January 1996 version). All states require certain professionals to report suspected child abuse, including teachers and other school personnel. Eighteen states have broad statutes requiring "any person" to report child abuse. The extent of the knowledge triggering the requirement to report often varies. Some states require reporting upon a mere "reasonable cause to believe" or a "reasonable suspicion," while others call for the reporter to "know or suspect." Failure to report suspected child abuse can result in criminal liability. However, in most states, it is a misdemeanor punishable by a fine. Keep in mind, however, that failure to report child abuse can result in civil liability.

CAPTA requires states to enact legislation that provides immunity from prosecution for reporting abuse and neglect. CAPTA also requires states to enact legislation for prosecution for false reporting of abuse and neglect. To report suspected child abuse and neglect, call your local Child Protective Service (CPS) agency or the CPS agency in the state in which the abuse or neglect occurred. Complete Web Link 1.3: Abuse and Neglect to explore the reporting of abuse and neglect in your state.

WEB LINK 1.3   Abuse and Neglect

Using one of the available search engines, investigate the reporting of child abuse and neglect in your state. Do you think the process is teacher-friendly and adequate? How would you change the process? Discuss the reporting system in class.

Student Privacy

Students have the right to privacy. Student privacy is provided through the Family Educational Rights and Privacy Act (FERPA), also known as the Buckley Amendment. FERPA also gives students the right to inspect their own records. FERPA applies to any public or private elementary, secondary, or postsecondary school and any state or local education agency that receives federal funds.

FERPA has two parts. First, it give students the right to review and inspect their own educational record, request corrections, halt the release of personally identifiable information, and obtain a copy of their institution's policy concerning access to educational records. Second, it prohibits educational institutions from disclosing "personally identifiable information in education records" without the written consent of the student or, if the student is a minor, the student's parents. However, several exceptions allow the release of student records to certain parties or under certain conditions. Records may be released without the student's consent (a) to school officials with a legitimate educational interest, (b) to other schools to which a student seeks or intends to enroll, (c) to education officials for audit and evaluation purposes, (d) to accrediting organizations, (e) to parties in connection with financial aid to a student, (f) to organizations conducting certain studies for or on behalf of a school, (g) to comply with a judicial order or lawfully issued subpoena, (h) in the case of health and safety emergencies, and (i) to state and local authorities within a juvenile justice system.

Some records maintained by schools are exempt from FERPA, including (a) records in the sole possession of school officials, (b) records maintained by a law enforcement unit of the educational institution, (c) records of an educational institution's nonstudent employees, and (d) records on a student who is 18 years of age or older or who attends a postsecondary institution that is maintained by a health professional. FERPA also allows, but does not require, schools to release "directory information," including students' names and addresses, to the public. High schools, however, are now required to provide students' names, addresses, and telephone numbers to military recruiters unless a student or parent opts out of such disclosure.

Corporal Punishment

The United States, Canada, and one state in Australia are the only industrialized countries in the world that allow school corporal punishment. In the United States, 27 states and the District of Columbia presently ban corporal punishment through state regulation, by every local school board in the state, or by rescinding authorization to use. However, the debate on corporal punishment continues (Reese, 2005). Some advocates argue that such discipline is required to maintain order in our schools. Other opponents insist that such action is cruel and unusual punishment. It appears the pendulum is now swinging toward the abolishment of corporal punishment.

The U.S. Supreme Court addressed the issue of corporal punishment in a 1977 Florida case in which two junior high students were severely paddled. The students claimed the use of such punishment was a violation of the Eighth Amendment, which bars cruel and unusual punishment. The U.S. Supreme Court, in a five-to-four decision, ruled that the punishment was both severe and unreasonable yet was not a violation of the Eighth Amendment. Thus, the Court has supported the right of a teacher to use corporal punishment even over parental objections.

Corporal punishment may take other forms than striking or spanking a student. It is sometimes interpreted as any action that could cause emotional or physical damage to a student, such as taping a student's mouth or having a student stand with a book on his or her head.

The courts also generally oppose punishing all students for the misbehavior of one when the culprit cannot be identified. Such mass discipline affects the innocent as well as the guilty. To explore the status of corporal punishment in your state, complete Web Link 1.4: Corporal Punishment.

WEB LINK 1.4   Corporal Punishment

Since states are split on the issue of corporal punishment, teachers need to know the laws within their specific state, as well as within the district they teach. Using one of the available search engines, investigate the use of corporal punishment in your state. Is it still used? Do you think it should be used? Do your classmates agree?

Teachers' Rights

The First Amendment clearly sets forth a person's right to freedom of expression (Looney, 2004). Before the 1960s, however, teachers were commonly dismissed or disciplined for expressing their opinions. A landmark case in 1968 changed this policy. It recognized public schoolteachers' rights to free speech when the issue is of public concern. Moreover, the Supreme Court confirmed that teachers do not leave their constitutional rights when they enter the school. Although the Court clearly indicated that teachers are protected under the First Amendment, court decisions since have ruled that not all speech is protected, especially when it includes threats or vulgar language or if it endangers others.

Teachers have advanced considerably since the days when they were forbidden to drink or smoke and married women were not permitted to teach. Teachers are presently granted a great many privileges, but their behavior is still sometimes challenged and brought before the courts. Grooming, dress, and sexual behavior usually come under a teacher's right to privacy, unless it can be proved that the teacher's appearance or lifestyle affects his or her teaching.

At one time, teachers were considered role models and could be dismissed for almost any reason. Today, however, the laws are much broader and grant teachers the same constitutional protection as nonteachers. Teachers within the public schools system have the right to privacy, freedom of religion, and freedom of association. Of course, such rights are limited in some situations. Regardless of the limitations, teachers, like students, have more rights than they did in years past.

ON YOUR OWN 1.4   Public View of Education

Log on to the Web-based student study site at http://www.sagepub.com/eis2study. Review the public surveys relative to Chapter 1 and react to the related activities.

Licensure/Certification

Licensure/certification is the process by which teachers receive state permission to teach (see Appendix B). Moreover, in some cases, large cities (e.g., New York, Chicago, Buffalo) have their own licensure/certification requirements that must be met.

The licensure of teachers is as old as the nation. Licensing is generally viewed as absolutely essential to ensure the quality of our teaching force. The goal is to have a fully qualified licensed teacher in every classroom. To receive a teaching license, all states require successful completion of an approved teacher education program that culminates with at least a bachelor's degree.

Teacher shortages in some areas and the growing criticism of current traditional teacher education practices have combined to spawn a wide movement toward alternative teacher certification. Every state in the nation has implemented or is now seriously working on the challenge of creating alternatives to the traditional undergraduate college teacher education program route for certifying teachers. These programs are designed for people who already have at least a bachelor's degree in a field other than education and want to become licensed to teach. More information on alternative teacher certification for each state can be obtained at the following sites:

http://teach-now.org

http://www.ed.gov/admins/tchrqual/recruit/altroutes/index.html

http://www.ncei.com/Alt-Teacher-Cert.htm

Complete Expansion Activity 1.4: Alternative Routes to Certification to explore the status of alternative routes to licensure in your state.

Preparing quality teachers is a complex and challenging process. Complex standards have been implemented to make sure teacher education programs are preparing teachers who can meet the challenges of our rapidly changing and diverse society. Complete the Review and Reflective Exercise 1.2 to check your understanding of this process.

Teachers and school personnel must meet state licensure/certification requirements.

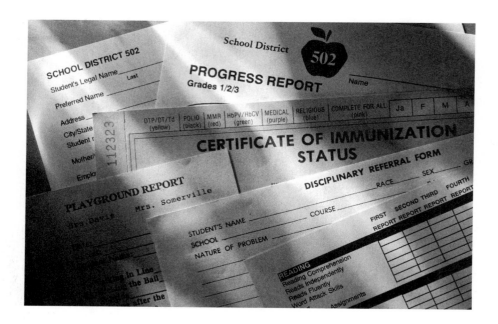

EXPANSION ACTIVITY 1.4   Alternative Routes to Certification

Due to a growing shortage of teachers, many states are now offering alternative and/or fast routes to teacher certification. Does your state offer such routes? What are the requirements? Do you see any potential problems with alternative certification? Discuss this practice with classmates. What do the majority of your classmates think of alternative routes to licensure? If possible, interview some public school teachers and administrators. What do they think of alternative certification?

A good understanding of teaching will greatly facilitate one of the major missions of education—literacy. To fully realize this mission will be difficult, but along with a greater knowledge of all aspects of education comes success. Now, let's develop a teaching model to complete the picture of effective teaching.

REVIEW AND REFLECTIVE EXERCISE 1.2   Outline the professional standards for preparing teachers.

REVIEW

- What is the purpose of professional standards?
- Why is it important that teachers be knowledgeable of educational law?

REFLECTION

- What are the assessment requirements for teacher candidates to be licensed in your state? Does your state require teacher candidates to pass a test series? Is it a state-developed test or the Praxis Series? Do you think teacher candidates should be held accountable and be required to pass a test to be licensed?
- Do you agree with the policy on corporal punishment in the state you plan to teach?

SUMMARY

This chapter introduced you to teaching and professional teaching standards. The main points were as follows:

Teaching

- The historical changes in American education and earlier theoretical thoughts laid the foundation for our modern schools and teaching.
- Effective teaching is an art as well as a science.
- Constructivism focuses on actively involving students in their own learning. Students construct their own meanings.
- Teaching requires a repertoire of skills and the ability to put these skills to use.
- Effectiveness depends on the subject, students, and environmental conditions.
- Danielson (1996) suggests four skill areas are needed for effective teaching: (1) quality planning and preparation, (2) preparation of a positive classroom environment, (3) use of proven instructional techniques, and (4) professional behavior.
- Forty-nine states have adopted state-mandated testing.
- Parent and community involvement is an important factor in improving the academic learning of students.

Professional Teaching Standards

- No Child Left Behind (NCLB) presents a rigorous plan for the reform of education. The future of NCLB is uncertain.
- The Educational Testing Service (ETS) developed the Praxis Series to assist state education agencies in making licensing decisions.
- Students and teachers do not lose their rights when they enter the schoolhouse door. They are protected under state and federal law.
- Licensure/certification is the process by which teachers receive state permission to teach. Licensure regulations vary a great deal among states.

DISCUSSION QUESTIONS AND ACTIVITIES

1. **Teaching platform.** Develop a "teaching platform" that describes your current thinking about teaching, learning, and teacher effectiveness.
2. **The challenge.** Think about the grade level you expect to teach. Consider at least two ways that your classroom at that grade level is likely to be challenging. Write about how you will cope with this.
3. **Teaching knowledge.** Some teaching knowledge is gained only through experiences and cannot be found in a textbook or in a college course. Do you agree with this statement? Give some examples.
4. **Personal traits.** Make a list of personal traits you possess that will assist you in teaching at your planned grade level. If you plan to be an elementary level teacher, compare your list with a future secondary teacher, and if you are planning to be a secondary teacher, compare your list with a future elementary teacher. Are there differences? In what areas do differences exist?

5. **Teacher effectiveness.** What do you think is the ultimate measure of a teacher's effectiveness? Explain your response.

6. **Teaching all students.** Remember that a teacher's job is to teach all students and assume an attitude that all students can learn. Research techniques and strategies that can be used to accomplish this task. Sources of information include the library, the Internet, current journals, and recent books.

TECHNOLOGY AND EDUCATION

We have identified some characteristics of effective teachers. How can technology contribute to effective teaching? What technology-related knowledge and skills do effective teachers need? Many states and teacher education programs require that prospective teachers demonstrate technology competence. What technology competencies does your state require? What technology competencies does your teacher education program require? What technology competencies do you now possess?

DECONSTRUCTING THE STANDARDS

Chapter 1 content addresses topics related to INTASC Standards 1, 2, 3, and 6.

- ◆ INTASC Standard 1 states: *Knowledge of Subject Matter:* The teacher understands the central concepts, tools of inquiry, and structures of the subject being taught and can create learning experiences that make these aspects of subject matter meaningful for students.
- ◆ INTASC Standard 2 states: *Knowledge of Human Development and Learning:* The teacher understands how children learn and develop and can provide learning opportunities that support their intellectual, social, and personal development.
- ◆ INTASC Standard 3 states: *Adapting Instruction for Individual Needs:* The teacher understands how students differ in their approaches to learning and creates instructional opportunities that are adapted to diverse learners.
- ◆ INTASC Standard 6 states: *Communication Skills:* The teacher uses knowledge of effective verbal, nonverbal, and media communication techniques to foster active inquiry, collaboration, and supportive interaction in the classroom.

For each of these four standards, write your response to the following:

- Which part(s) of each standard does this chapter address?
- How does this chapter address this standard?
- How will the concepts in this chapter help you apply this standard as a teacher?

The complete INTASC standards can be found at http://ccsso.org/pdf/standards.pdf. I suggest you download the complete standards because you will use them in each chapter.

PRAXIS CONNECTION

Log on to the Web-based student study site at http://www.sagepub.com/eis2study. Access the Praxis II: Principles of Learning and Teaching assessments and/or state-related exams and complete the Chapter 1 test preparation exercises.

PORTFOLIO CONNECTION

Log on to the Web-based student study site at http://www.sagepub.com/eis2study. Access the Portfolio Connection. Complete the Chapter 1 portfolio link to INTASC activities.

CONNECTION WITH THE FIELD

1. **Classroom observation.** Observe a kindergarten, elementary, middle school, and high school classroom and focus on teaching and learning effectiveness, the use of classroom time, and the characteristics of students. Collect and analyze data with regard to your observations.

2. **Teachers' view of effective teaching and learning.** Interview several teachers. How do they define effective teaching and learning? How do they know when it has occurred in their classrooms? How would they measure effective teaching and learning? Are there differences at the elementary and secondary levels?

3. **Principals' view of effective teaching and learning.** Interview two elementary and two secondary school principals. How do they view effective teaching and learning? Is their view the same as that of the teachers? If not, which view do you tend to support?

4. **Evaluation of effective teaching and learning.** Visit at least two local school districts. Do these school districts evaluate their teachers? If so, who does the evaluation? What criteria are used? What do teachers think of the evaluative process? What do you think of the criteria? Would you want to be evaluated using the criteria?

5. **Parent and community involvement.** Interview several teachers from local schools about how they foster parent and community involvement. Try to visit with a kindergarten teacher, an elementary teacher, a middle school teacher, and a high school teacher. Summarize your discoveries.

CHAPTER 2

Planning and Organizing for Teaching

The extent to which you are able to transform your "self-concern" into "other-concern" will determine your effectiveness in getting others to follow along.

—Anonymous

OVERVIEW

Good teaching requires planning and the effective use of classroom time. A seven-step cyclic teaching model is presented to assist you in this most important planning process. The curriculum is one of the most important ingredients in a school program. Indeed, the curriculum often makes or breaks a school. Therefore, a school curriculum must be identified and selected with care.

An effective education is achieved when the learning situation is accurately diagnosed as to the appropriateness of the curriculum to be taught. In other words, content must be selected for the appropriate entry level of students. This selection process cannot occur by chance: It must thoughtfully weigh the needs of both the students and the society, and it must be based on the structure of the subject itself.

The final decision as to what will be taught in the classroom will be up to you as the classroom teacher. In some cases, assistance in making curriculum decisions will be available from curriculum committees or from curriculum specialists. In most cases, however, you alone will make the curriculum decisions.

Once students' entry level has been determined, courses must be planned. Specific units must be formed, sequenced, and time allotments made for the units. These plans must remain flexible so adjustments can be made as the year progresses.

American classrooms are changing. Teachers must now plan for a multicultural classroom. The elimination of racism, sexism, and ethnic prejudice has become a challenge for our schools. Moreover, not all students are the same, which calls for differentiation of instruction to some extent.

To maximize learning, planning must address learning styles and **multiple intelligences.** All students don't learn through the same modality and/or aren't intelligent in the same areas.

The use of technology in the classroom offers a viable alternative to traditional classroom instruction. The use of **computers** in the classroom has proven to enhance student motivation to learn.

OBJECTIVES

After completing your study of Chapter 2, you should be able to do the following:

- Describe the seven steps to teaching excellence.
- Differentiate among the five categories of time found in schools.
- Define *curriculum* and describe the teacher's responsibility associated with school curriculum.
- Describe the *backward design model* for curriculum design.
- Outline and explain the influences of students' abilities, society issues, the subject structure, and brain research on the school curriculum.
- List and explain the areas that must be addressed in planning a course for the year.
- Discuss the changing nature of American classrooms.
- Define *learning style* and describe its various dimensions.
- Explain the concept of multiple intelligences and describe Gardner's eight areas of intelligence.
- Explain how technology can be used in the classroom.

Soon you will have a classroom of students to get to know, lessons to launch, routines to establish, and a host of other activities to get under way. To do all this, you must be organized. You will soon learn that organization is central to effective teaching. Let's begin our look at organizing for teaching with a model for good teaching.

A Model of Teaching

Good teaching requires that you make a constant series of professional decisions that affect the probability that students will learn. Thus, good teaching is a multifaceted quest to help students achieve mastery of a subject. Basically, this quest is a seven-step cyclic process. The seven sequential steps in a model of effective teaching follow:

1. Diagnosing the learning situation

2. Planning the course

3. Planning the instruction

4. Guiding learning activities

5. Evaluating learning

6. Reflection

7. Following up

Figure 2.1
A Model of Teaching:
The model is
sequential and cyclic
in nature.

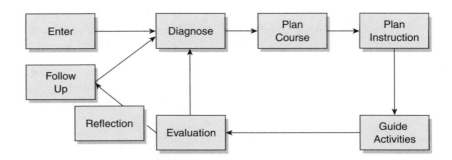

This sequential teaching process is illustrated in Figure 2.1.

Step 1 involves selecting the curriculum to be taught. This selection process is based on the needs of students, the society, and the subject. Essentially, you must diagnose the situation to find out what students already know. You may want to strengthen some areas and reteach some concepts.

Once the situation has been diagnosed, Step 2 is to plan and outline exactly what will be taught in the course. That is, you identify the curriculum areas to be addressed and the amount of time allotted to the areas outlined.

In Step 3, unit and daily plans are developed. In other words, you decide exactly what students should know and plan the activities that will bring the desired results. Essentially, objectives are written and the instructional **strategy** is selected.

Step 4 involves teaching the planned activities. You guide the students through the planned sequence of activities, using your knowledge of students, learning theory, and effective teaching techniques.

In Step 5, you determine whether you have accomplished the instructional intent; that is, you must evaluate students' mastery of the specifics taught. The results of the evaluation tell you what to do next. If students show mastery, you start the next planning cycle (Step 1). If mastery is not demonstrated, follow-up will be needed.

Once a lesson has been taught, Step 6 is to reflect on the success of the lesson. You must determine whether the lesson accomplished its intended purpose. You must analyze all available information and address reteaching needs and make changes in the lesson if it is to be taught again.

The follow-up (Step 7) can be a relatively brief summary of the material covered, while at other times extensive reteaching may be necessary. The extent of your follow-up will depend on the findings of the evaluation analysis.

As you can see, achieving teaching excellence is a major undertaking. The steps in the model of good teaching will be highlighted in subsequent chapters.

APPLY AND REFLECT 2.1   Good teachers plan well and are organized. Does this sound like you? Do you plan well and are you organized? What area(s) do you need to work on to be a better planner?

Time in Schools and Classrooms

Time is a valuable and limited classroom resource that must be used wisely. It is often divided into five distinct categories: mandated time, allocated time, instructional time, time on task or engaged time, and academic learning time. Figure 2.2 illustrates how the five time categories relate to each other.

The total time available for all activities carried out in a school is established by the state. Typically, schools are in session approximately 7 hours a day for 180 to 190 days. This **mandated time** must be used for academic, as well as for nonacademic, activities.

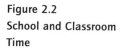

Figure 2.2
School and Classroom
Time

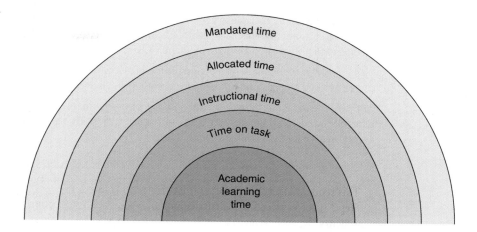

State-mandated time must be divided among a variety of subjects that must be taught, with time allotted for other school activities, such as lunch, announcements, recess, transitions between classes, and so on. The time appropriated for each of these activities is often called **allocated time.** For example, 45 minutes of each day may be used for lunch, and 50 minutes may be needed for changing classes. An important school goal is to expand the amount of allocated time available for learning.

Teachers must translate the available allocated time into learning through **instructional time.** Despite your best efforts, however, not all students will stay on task or pay attention all the time. For example, some students may be daydreaming when you are explaining, some may be goofing off, and others may simply be thinking about other things they would rather be doing. As a result, educators refer to another area within instructional time called time on task.

Time on task, or **engaged time,** differs from mandated, allocated, and instructional times in that it is the actual time individual students engage in learning. In effect, students are actively (physically or mentally) participating in the learning process during time on task. This active participation may simply involve listening to you explain something, reading, writing, or solving problems. If students are not actually on task in the learning process, they do not learn; so another important goal of the instructional process is to improve the quality of time use by keeping students on task. Time on task depends on routine classroom practices, student motivation, and the quality of instruction. Typically, time on task varies from lows of 50% in some classrooms to as high as 90% in others (Berliner, 1987).

Time on task isn't always productive. Indeed, students often engage in class activities at a superficial level, with little understanding or retention taking place. For example, they could be watching a film while actually concentrating very little on what is being shown. Thus, you must plan your instruction to make the time on task more productive. In other words, you must maximize **academic learning time.** For some educators (Block, Efthim, & Burns, 1989), academic learning time ideally should reflect student performance on assigned tasks at an 80% level or better.

A lot of instructional time is lost in today's classrooms. In fact, some educators contend that as many as 50 to 60 days are wasted each year. Some common time wasters are listed as follows:

1. *Starting classes.* Many teachers take 5 to 10 minutes per class to record attendance and make announcements. Systems should be devised for speeding up these housekeeping chores. The use of assigned seats or seating diagrams, for instance, will speed up this duty.

2. *Excessive use of films.* Films are often shown that have little instructional value or are simply used as time fillers—especially on Fridays. Instructional tools, such as films and computer activities, should be justified in terms of their classroom value.

3. *Discipline time.* Disciplinary actions take time and often interrupt instruction. The use of nonverbal actions in curbing misbehavior allows a lesson to proceed without interruption. The use of nonverbal methods will be discussed at length in Chapter 13.

4. *Early finishes.* Much instructional time is lost when lessons are finished early. This tendency can be avoided by planning more instruction than you'll need.

5. *Extracurricular activities.* Students are often dismissed early for athletic events, plays and rehearsals, music and band activities, and other such activities. Schools should schedule special events on activity days or after school hours.

How can you tell when students are off task? This is not easy. Sharpen your observation skills. Watch students' eyes: Are they watching you during your presentations, or do their eye movements suggest that they are engaged in other interests? Finally, do they ask or answer questions? Be sensitive to the signal indicators that indicate that students are engaged and on task. Keeping students engaged and on task isn't always easy.

REFLECTIONS ON TEACHER PRACTICE 2.1 | Computing in the Classroom

1. What benefits relative to academic achievement and/or personal behavior can be gained from the effective use of computers in the classroom?

2. How can teachers use the Internet to provide better instruction? What pitfalls do you foresee in using the Internet in the classroom?

◆ ◆ ◆

I recommend task computing as an effective way to use computers in your classroom. You will be using your computers to enhance the curriculum and your students' learning. Please do not use the computer as a reward for early finishers and good behavior (the strugglers and behavior problems might be the students who need computer time the most). I just completed my thesis on how this valuable form of technology is being ineffectively used in so many classrooms. Basically, I found that poorer and lower-ability kids get less classroom computer time (and often use it for drill and practice) and richer and higher-ability kids get more classroom computer time (and are doing media presentations and problem solving).

Think of the computer as another area you need to plan for weekly. Plan daily or weekly tasks that every student needs to accomplish. For example, they may have to visit the website of an author whose novel you are reading and find five interesting facts about him or her. The next day, they might take that information and construct a paragraph in Microsoft Word. The next task might be to copy the author's picture onto their document and print it (or e-mail it to the teacher). There are great math sites with problems of the day or week. I especially like Math Maven's Mysteries, where the students read a story and problem solve. The science-related sites are incredible. The possibilities are endless. With task computing, your computers will be in use more time than they are idle. Check out this website: www.framingham.k12.ma.us/k5/task.htm.

—JOAN, elementary school teacher

SOURCE: Reprinted with permission from ProTeacher, a professional community for elementary school teachers (http://www.proteacher.net).

ON YOUR OWN 2.1   **Reflections on Teacher Practice**

Read and reflect on the viewpoints expressed in Computing in the Classroom. Log on to the Web-based student study site at http://www.sagepub.com/eis2study/and react to the related activities.

The Curriculum

What is curriculum? That is, what exactly is the curriculum of a typical elementary or secondary school? Schools are similar in many respects, but they also vary in some important ways. The curriculum, student body, and teaching strategies of a school will reflect the values, attitudes, beliefs, and goals of the community in which it exists. If we define the **curriculum** as all the learning, intended and unintended, that takes place under the sponsorship of the school, then we have set the stage for a broad interpretation of curriculum, and of schooling. Specialists have suggested, however, several different definitions for the term *curriculum* (Armstrong, 2002; Oliva, 2000). For our purposes, let us define *curriculum* as all the planned and unplanned learning experiences that students undergo while in a school setting.

The teacher's responsibility involves selecting the curriculum on both a long-term and short-term basis. To accomplish this task, the teacher must consult a variety of sources, including state curriculum frameworks, district curriculum guides, school guidelines, and relevant adopted textbooks. These plans become the blueprint for instruction.

Curriculum Mapping

There can be a large gap between what is specified in a district curriculum guideline and what is actually taught in classrooms. The gap can represent a challenge to personnel trying to improve the curriculum in a district. Unless they know what is really being taught, they are working in the dark. *Curriculum mapping* can help.

Curriculum mapping is a technique for gathering data on what is actually being taught through the course of a school year (Jacobs, 1997). When operationalized, all teachers at a school enter information about their classroom curricula for the year into a computer database. Teachers enter major activities related to three types of data: content, specific skills, and assessments. The process should be totally nonjudgmental about the teacher's styles, techniques, and materials. By carefully analyzing the maps, schools can detect and fix curriculum gaps, address repetitions in the curriculum, and refine scope and sequence connections. The school can also identify potential areas for curriculum integration, better align their assessments with state and district standards, and even consider ways to upgrade teaching strategies and materials.

Instruction should be based on accurate student information.

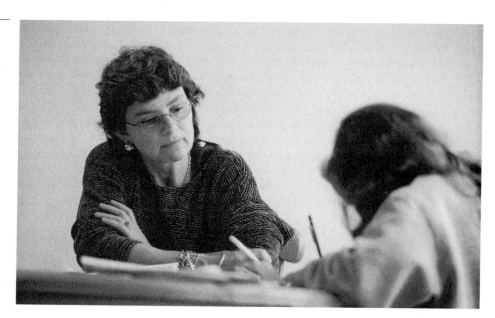

Backward Curriculum Design

Wiggins and McTighe (2005) offer an alternative approach to curriculum design. Unlike many instructional design models, the Wiggins and McTighe *backward design model* is well suited for the academic community. The backward design model centers on the idea that the design process should begin with identifying the desired results and then "work backwards" to develop instruction rather than the traditional approach, which is to define what topics need to be covered. The Wiggins and McTighe framework identifies three main stages (see Figure 2.3):

Figure 2.3
Backward Design
Process

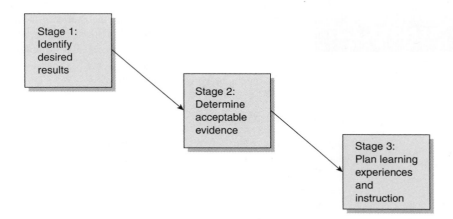

- Stage 1: Identify desired outcomes and results.
- Stage 2: Determine what constitutes acceptable evidence of competency in the outcomes and results (assessment).
- Stage 3: Plan instructional strategies and learning experiences that bring students to these competency levels.

Stage 1. Identify Desired Results

In traditional design models, Stage 1 would be defining goals and objectives. Wiggins and McTighe (2005), however, ask that teachers identify not only course goals and objectives but also the *enduring understanding. Enduring understanding* is the learning that should endure over the long term. Backward design uses a question format rather than measurable objectives. These questions focus on the line of inquiry leading to the desired learning. The desired learning is determined by national standards and state standards or benchmarks. These standards and benchmarks are turned into question form. Possible examples are "Is there enough water to go around?" or "Does art reflect culture or shape it?" Asking such inquiry-based questions facilitates the students finding the answers.

The backward approach to curricular design departs from common school practice. Instead of starting with a textbook to determine the curriculum, the teacher starts with the end—the desired results (goals, standards, or benchmarks). The curriculum is derived from the evidence of learning (performance) called for by the standard or benchmark.

Stage 2. Assessment

The second stage in the design process is to define what forms of assessment will demonstrate that students have acquired the desired knowledge, understanding, and skill. Wiggins and McTighe (2005) define three types of assessment: performance task (an authentic task of understanding), criteria-referenced assessment (quiz, test), and unprompted assessment and self-assessment (observations, dialogues, etc.).

Stage 3. Plan Learning Experience and Instruction

In this stage, it is determined what sequence of teaching and learning experiences will equip students to develop and demonstrate the desired understanding. This will include the research-based repertoire of learning teaching strategies. These are the activities students will do during the unit and what resources and materials will be needed.

APPLY AND REFLECT 2.2	Many experienced teachers use the backward curriculum model. What rationale can you see for this decision?

Curriculum Reform

The curriculum taught in American schools has changed in recent years. In general, reform efforts can be seen as focusing on either a subject-centered approach to curriculum planning or a student-centered one. The pendulum has swung from one extreme to the other in an attempt to create either relevant or rigorous content for students at all levels within the K–12 system. New views of learning and teaching require changes in other components of schooling, namely, curriculum and assessment. The new curriculum and teaching strategies ask that students not only master factual information but also learn to apply that information by reasoning and solving novel problems.

Recent studies of the brain and how it learns have also given educators new insights about teaching and learning. New findings indicate, for example, that the idea of learners being predominantly left or right brained is misleading. The brain is much more complex than that. We do not operate in one function for science and mathematics and another for the fine arts.

Brain research indicates that the brain needs 6 to 12 glasses of water per day. Without enough water, we don't learn as well. Hannaford (1995) identifies dehydration as a common classroom problem that can lead to impaired learning. Researchers further suggest that the school environment should challenge brain development in nonthreatening ways by making use of the arts for teaching thinking and for building emotive expressiveness and memory. Findings indicate that physical activity is also essential in promoting the growth of mental functions. Jensen (2005) suggests that learning is enhanced by daily stretching, walking, and dancing, as well as other physical movement.

For material related to this concept, go to Clip 2.1 on the Student Resource CD bound into the back of your textbook.

Researchers agree that an optimal learning environment requires comfortable temperatures and protection from distracting sounds. Noise and physical discomfort often send distress messages to the brain, which limits the brain's normal operations. Researchers suggest that the significance of the learning environment cannot be underestimated. The brain learns faster in challenging, creative, accommodating, relaxed, and healthy environments. Suggested teaching strategies that enhance brain-based learning include the use of manipulatives, active learning, field trips, guest speakers, and real-life projects that allow students to use many learning styles and multiple intelligences (addressed later in this chapter). Integrated and interdisciplinary curriculum also reinforces brain-based learning because the brain can better make connections when material is presented in an integrated way, rather than as isolated bits of information.

Curriculum Structure

Generally, a school district has the flexibility to pattern its curriculum any way it chooses (Oliva, 2000). Typically, these organizational patterns tend to range between the extremes of being subject centered on one side to student centered on the other (see Figure 2.4). The subject-centered curricular organization tends to be content oriented; conversely, if a curriculum follows a student-centered

Figure 2.4
Curriculum Patterns

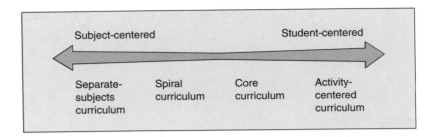

pattern, it is learner oriented. In general, most districts organize their curriculum (a) as an eclectic combination of several patterns, (b) with most programs somewhere toward the middle of the continuum, and (c) with a good deal of variety from class to class and teacher to teacher. The organization of the curriculum is influenced strongly by the district's philosophical position on the purpose of education.

Subject-Centered Curriculum

The **subject-centered curriculum** is still the most widely used curriculum pattern in United States schools. It regards learning primarily as cognitive development and the acquisition of knowledge and information. With this approach, all the subjects for instruction are separated. In general, the content areas are taught in isolation, with no attempt at integration.

The subject-centered curriculum places emphasis on oral discourse and extensive explanations. It expects teachers to plan instruction before teaching begins and to organize it around the content, and it assumes that certain content should be taught to all students. The subject-centered curriculum usually consists of a study of specific facts and ideas. The teaching methods usually include the direct strategies: lectures, discussions, and questions (see Chapter 5).

The most widely used subject-centered curriculum is the separate-subjects curriculum. The separate-subjects curriculum content is divided into fairly discrete areas of study—reading, language arts, algebra, history, composition, chemistry, literature, and so forth. The required subjects (general education) usually make up most of the school program, and students are given little choice in selecting courses. Some districts, however, are giving students more opportunity to select electives.

Some feel that the subject-centered curriculum does not adequately foster critical or creative thinking or develop an understanding of societal issues. This approach often places emphasis on the memorization of facts and ideas and, moreover, tends to focus on the past. For example, social studies instruction often consists of the study of the past and the related facts.

Supporters and defenders of a subject-centered curriculum argue that the approach has stood the test of time and that not all subjects can be studied at once—as other curriculum approaches propose to do. They further argue that study cannot be all-inclusive: There is simply too much information, and it must be ordered as well as segmented.

A second type of subject-centered curriculum is referred to as a spiral curriculum. The spiral curriculum is organized around the material to be taught. It is similar to the separate-subjects pattern but differs in two notable ways. First, the spiral curriculum puts more emphasis on the concepts and generalizations; in other words, it emphasizes the structure of knowledge. Second, it is designed to fit sequentially with students' developmental thinking stages.

Student-Centered Curriculum

A **student-centered curriculum** can be described as an activity curriculum. In effect, a student-centered curriculum focuses on student needs, interests, and activities. In its purest form, a student-centered curriculum operates with students as the center of the learning process. Activities are planned jointly by the teacher and students. The teacher is seen as a stimulator and facilitator of student activity. The student-centered curriculum is the most appropriate curriculum pattern for the elementary school level but has never secured a firm foothold at the secondary level.

One kind of student-centered curriculum is the core curriculum. The core curriculum is a student-centered pattern with several subject-centered characteristics. Typically, it combines subjects into broad fields of study. This pattern of organization is most frequently found in middle and junior high schools. The subjects most often combined in core curricula are social studies and language arts, mathematics and science, and social studies and science.

Still another type of student-centered curriculum is called activity-centered curriculum. Like the core curriculum pattern, the activity-centered curriculum is patterned around the needs and interests of students. The content coverage, however, is more flexible than in the core curriculum. Learning by doing and problem solving are emphasized. As such, detailed lessons often are not planned because the teacher cannot anticipate what student interests will surface or where their inquiry will take them. The subject-centered curriculum and the student-centered curriculum patterns represent two opposite ends of a curriculum continuum. Table 2.1 contrasts the two curriculum patterns.

Curriculum Integration

Curriculum integration is one of several reforms designed to enhance the quality of student learning. **Curriculum integration** is a form of teaching and learning that draws upon the knowledge and skills of a variety of discipline areas as they become necessary in problem solving (Beane, 1995). It is argued that such a strategy better reflects real-world problem solving than does single-subject instruction. It is maintained that an integrated curriculum provides holistic, problem-based learning that leads to a greater ability to make connections and to solve problems.

Ross and Olsen (1993) offer five models for implementing an integrated curriculum. Each provides foundation for the model that follows.

1. *Single-Subject Integration:* A teacher presents a single subject and requires students to solve real problems.

2. *The Coordinated Model:* Two or more teachers cooperate in teaching integrated single subjects.

3. *The Integrated Core Model:* A single teacher remains with students for two or three periods. A teacher might teach science in the context of math or social studies as the "core" around which the rest of the school day is planned.

TABLE 2.1   Contrasting Curriculum Patterns

Subject-Centered Curriculum	Student-Centered Curriculum
Focus on subject matter	Centered on learner needs
Centered on subjects	Centered on cooperative determination of subject matter
Subject matter organized by teacher before instruction	Emphasis on variability in exposure to learning
Emphasis on facts, knowledge, and information	Emphasis on skills
Generally lower-level learning	Emphasis on immediate meanings of learning
Emphasis on uniformity of exposure	Emphasis on indirect strategies
Emphasis on direct strategies	

4. *The Integrated Double Core Model:* Two teachers teach integrated "cores" to the students. One might teach math in the context of science, while the other teaches language arts within the context of social studies.

5. *The Self-Contained Core Model:* A single teacher with multiple credentials teaches one group of students all day within a single meaningful context.

Each of these five models offers teachers useful, logical, and flexible ways to organize and offer an integrated curriculum and engage students in meaningful and functional learning activities.

Curriculum Selection

Students and, ultimately, society will be the consumers of the school curriculum. As such, both deserve to supply input as to what should be taught. Moreover, the structure of a subject often dictates the content to be taught, as well as the sequence of teaching that content. The well-planned curriculum, then, will take into account student and societal **needs** as well as the subject itself. Keep in mind, however, that students, society, and the subject structure are influenced by other factors, as depicted in Figure 2.5.

Recently, the structure of a subject has been dictated in terms of competencies to be demonstrated by learners. These competencies are sometimes called standards or skills or outcomes or benchmarks or some other state standard term. They are statements of what all students, pre-K through 12, should know and be able to do at various grade levels. For example, the state of Oklahoma has established learning outcomes for students completing all grades and subjects, whereas Arkansas has established benchmarks for all subjects and grades. In Alaska, curriculum frameworks in CD-ROM format and "Framework Resource Kits" in specific subjects are given to teachers by the Department of Education and Early Development. These standards relate to the basic principles that undergird the different curriculum areas. Basically, the standards represent the minimum knowledge and skills individual students need at their respective grade levels. When teachers make decisions about what to teach, they look to the state standards. However, keep in mind that states sometimes change these standards and the associated assessment system in response to changing needs—or sometimes they raise the bar when significant improvement has occurred. While these standards are not and should not be the only curriculum teachers teach, they are the starting points. Thus, these standards are the basis for teaching and testing. Complete Web Link 2.1: State Standards to identify and review the state-mandated learning intent in the state in which you intend to teach.

Figure 2.5
Influences on
Curriculum Selection

Needs of curriculum

Needs of society

Needs of students

Needs of school

Curriculum

A more enriching classroom curriculum is one that supplements the textbook content with issues related to student interests.

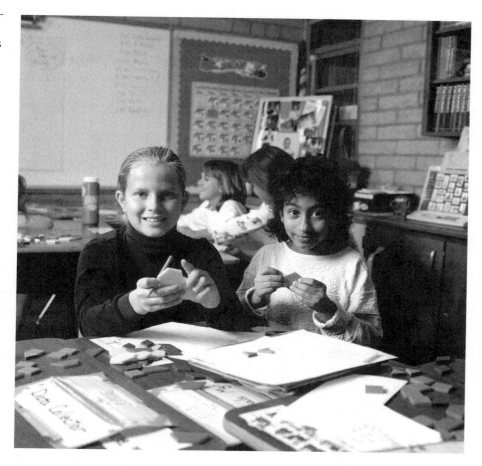

WEB LINK 2.1   State Standards

Access the state department Web site for the state in which you plan to teach. Download the state standards, competencies, outcome, skills, or benchmarks for the subject(s) you plan to teach. Compare your state standards, competencies, outcomes, skills, or benchmarks with those of two other states. Are they generally the same? If they are different, why do you suppose there are differences? Compare your findings and reflections with classmates.

Teachers, schools, and states are evaluated and rewarded on how well students perform on local and state tests. Many states now rank their schools on how well students achieve. For example, Florida grades its schools much like teachers grade their students (on a letter scale from A to F), while Texas rates its schools as Exemplary, Recognized, Academically Acceptable/Acceptable, and Academically Unacceptable/Low Performing. The ranking of schools is spreading across the nation.

Schools must pay particular attention to their curricula, and curriculum developers need to direct their attention to three major areas of need: the learner, the society, and the subject. Keep in mind that curricula, student needs, and societies change over time—and no curriculum has reached a state of perfection. Therefore, you need to decide the appropriate content to be taught in your classroom. Complete Expansion Activity 2.1: The Curriculum, which will let you further your understanding of the content you will be teaching.

EXPANSION ACTIVITY 2.1   The Curriculum

With four or five other students in your class, decide how much of the curriculum should include group activities and how much should involve individual activities at each of these grades.

Kindergarten

Elementary school

Middle school

High school

Also, discuss whether some subject areas might lend themselves better than others to group activities. Evaluate whether some children might benefit more than others from group work.

Most school districts offer at most only limited curriculum assistance to teachers. As such, teachers are often obliged to undertake course planning on their own. We will look at procedures for accomplishing this task in the next section.

Table 2.2 summarizes the concepts related to school curriculum and areas of curriculum need. Before you continue with the next section, review Table 2.2 and complete Review and Reflective Exercise 2.1.

"Yes, your findings are correct. No, I don't believe you should publish your findings."

SOURCE: Created by Martha Campbell.

TABLE 2.2   The Classroom Curriculum

Concept	Description
Curriculum	Planned and unplanned experiences that students undergo in school settings
Subject-centered curriculum	Curriculum pattern wherein subjects are separated into separate courses of study
Student-centered curriculum	A curriculum that focuses on student needs, interests, and activities
Needs	Academic and social areas in which students have weaknesses, limitations, or deficiencies

REVIEW AND REFLECTIVE EXERCISE 2.1   Define curriculum and how it affects the classroom.

REVIEW

• What factors influence curriculum decisions?

• What is the difference between subject-centered and student-centered curricula?

• In what ways do textbooks influence curricula in schools?

• How has increased emphasis on diversity issues affected school curricula?

REFLECTION

• Many factors affect curriculum decisions in a school district, school, and classroom. Think about how you will make curriculum decisions for your classroom. Will you alone make the decisions? Will you ask for assistance in making the decisions? Will you consult district, state, and national guidelines in making your decisions?

• Think back on your own K–12 learning experiences and recall the curriculum (formal curriculum and hidden curriculum) that had the greatest impact on your life.

Planning the Course

All teachers are responsible for the instructional emphasis within their classrooms. They are responsible for organizing instruction in such a way that students receive instruction in, and achieve mastery of, the state-mandated curricula. But state-mandated curricula do not complete the picture of those things deemed important for students to learn. There are "generic" lessons that take place in the classroom that are rarely found in the curriculum documents of the state or the district. There also are worthy "enrichment" activities that the teacher and students deem important. Decisions must be made about the time, personnel, energy, and resources allocated to each of these important components of the curriculum.

APPLY AND REFLECT 2.3   It is suggested that you learn as much as possible about the school and community in which you teach. How will this make you a better teacher?

Figure 2.6
Allocating Curricular
Time.

Mastery Curriculum	
60–75% of time Highly structured	
Generic Curriculum	**Enrichment**
Unstructured	

Planning Instruction

Glatthorn (1987) suggests that 60% to 75% of instructional time should be allocated to the state-mandated curriculum. Glatthorn calls this the **mastery curriculum** and defines it as the learning considered essential for all students to know. He further states that the teaching of the mastery curriculum requires highly structured, well-planned, sequenced units and lessons that produce measurable results. The generic curriculum comprises the interpersonal and intrapersonal attitudes, beliefs, skills, and knowledge that do not tend to lend themselves to a highly structured plan of instruction. Enrichment includes the things that are nice to know but are not essential for all students. A graphic model of curricular allocation as suggested by Glatthorn is shown in Figure 2.6.

The procedures for identifying the content for a complete school program (K–12) can be quite sophisticated. Essentially, such procedures should be left to textbook writers in deciding what to include in a textbook series or to developers of curriculum programs for a school district. Only rarely will the classroom teacher be expected to develop the scope and sequence of a program. As noted earlier, however, teachers should plan their courses in terms of student needs, district goals, and the needs of society. Complete Web Link 2.2: Instructional Resources to explore some of the resources available to teachers on the Internet.

WEB LINK 2.2   Instructional Resources

Access teachers.net at http://www.teachers.net. Review the various site resources and the Explore Teachers.net options. How useful would this site and other similar sites be to you as a teacher? Share your thoughts and conclusions with your classmates.

Frequently, your first task as a teacher will be to plan your course(s) for the school year (Posner & Rudnitsky, 2000). Basically, you must lay out your instruction for the year for each subject you teach. To do so, you must address the following questions:

1. What major topics (chapters) will be covered? Can you justify your selections?
2. Should the class textbook content (chapters) be supplemented?
3. How should the topics (chapters) be grouped to form units of study? Why?
4. In what sequence should the planned units be taught? Why?
5. How much emphasis should each unit receive? In a 35-week course, how much time should each unit receive (in weeks and fractions of weeks)?

Your answers to such questions should result in a systematic layout of your course for the year. You will need to consult the curriculum guidelines of your state and school district and any standardized tests your students are required to take. Most teachers use an adopted course textbook as the core for planning. Such a procedure could, for example, yield a unit sequence of study and time allotments for a course as follows:

Unit 1 The Universe (3 weeks)

| Chapter 1 | Stars |
| Chapter 2 | Galaxies |

Unit 2 The Solar System (4 weeks)

| Chapter 4 | The Earth |
| Chapter 5 | The Moon |

Unit 3 The Earth's Atmosphere (4½ weeks)

Chapter 6	Atmosphere
Chapter 8	Sun, Water, and Wind
Chapter 9	Weather

Unit 4 The Earth's Crust (5 weeks)

Chapter 11	Rocks
Chapter 12	Volcanoes
Chapter 13	Earthquakes

Unit 5 The Changing Crust (4 weeks)

Chapter 14	Weathering
Chapter 15	Erosion
Chapter 10	Mountain Building

Unit 6 The Earth's History (4 weeks)

| Chapter 16 | Geologic Time |
| Chapter 17 | Stories in Stone |

Unit 7 Animal Life (4 weeks)

| Chapter 3 | Place and Time |
| Chapter 18 | Development of Life |

Unit 8 Human Life (4½ weeks)

| Chapter 20 | Human Life Begins |
| Chapter 19 | The Human Environment |

Your course plan should be flexible so changes can be made during the year. As you analyze the textbook and select chapters to be covered, recognize that not all chapters need to be covered, that the textbook chapters may not include all the content areas you want to teach, that the text sequence is not always the best sequence for every class, and that not all chapters are equally important. Also, make time allotments based on your intended methods and procedures and on the importance you place on the topic.

Finally, leave open a couple of weeks at the end of the year, in case more time is required than originally planned to finish some of your units. The extra time can always be used for review or enrichment if it is not needed for unit instruction.

One of the chief values of course planning is that it permits you to better anticipate desirable media and instructional materials (e.g., films, special equipment, computer programs, and special books). In fact, some school districts even require that all special materials be requested at the beginning of the year. In such districts, course planning will be essential.

Course planning is essential to effective teaching.

Multicultural Classroom

For material related to this concept, go to Clip 2.2 on the Student Resource CD bound into the back of your textbook.

The face of many American classrooms is changing. The United States has always been a multicultural society, and the growth of minority populations is projected to increase rapidly in the next few decades. Presently, 37% of school-age children are minorities, a figure that will continue to increase in the coming years. It is projected that, by the year 2040, children of color will compose more than half the children in classrooms. In 2002, the U.S. Census Bureau announced that Hispanics had overtaken African Americans as the largest minority group. The fastest growing states have high percentages of minority youth. For example, Texas, Florida, California, and New York will have more than one third of the nation's young people by 2010, and the youth population of each of these states will be more than 52% minority. By this same year, about 12 states will have more than 50% minority youth populations. Along with ethnic and racial diversity, we will have linguistic diversity. Increasing numbers of children are entering school from minority language backgrounds and have little or no competence in English. As might be expected, teachers will encounter more students whose ethnic and cultural backgrounds reflect a Hispanic or Asian heritage. Also, as a result of Public Law 94–142 and its successors, students with a variety of disabilities now spend increasing amounts of time in traditional classrooms while still receiving the services they need.

Multicultural education is being implemented widely in our schools. Indeed, more classroom teachers have studied the concepts of multicultural education than in past years. Textbook publishers are now also integrating ethnic and cultural content into their books. Despite the growing successes, however, multicultural education faces serious challenges.

Banks (2002) suggests there are two broad goals for multicultural education. First, educational equality should be improved for students from various ethnic and cultural groups and for students with special needs. Second, multicultural education should help all (including those who are Caucasian) build the knowledge, skills, and attitudes they need to be successful in a diverse society.

A variety of strategies should be planned for the classroom to meet these goals. Campbell (2000) identifies four major components to multicultural education:

APPLY AND REFLECT 2.4	Multiculturally aware teachers learn about students, respect all students, avoid using stereotypes, use culture-fair and gender-fair language, and integrate multicultural perspectives throughout the curriculum. What qualities and experiences do you possess or lack that might affect your ability to be a multiculturally aware teacher?

1. **Making the curriculum more inclusive of different cultural perspectives and contributions.** For example, a course in science should include information and discussion of the contributions of African American, Native American, and Hispanic peoples.

2. **Raising the academic achievement of minority groups.** Teachers must be committed to helping all students academically, regardless of race and ethnicity.

3. **Improving intergroup relations.** Teachers need to break down thinking and actions that are prejudicial, stereotypic, and discriminatory.

4. **Helping students understand and deal with social and structural inequities in society.** Discuss racism, sexism, and class prejudice.

The goal of creating a multicultural classroom is to eliminate racism, sexism, and ethnic prejudice while providing equal educational opportunities for all students. To reach this goal and to meet the challenge of teaching in a multicultural classroom, you should let three general principles guide your teaching. First, know your students, students' families, and communities. Try to spend time outside of school with students and parents. Also, teachers should try to find and read books, magazines, and research articles or take coursework or workshops that relate to a better understanding of multiculturalism. Ask parents to help in class or to speak to your students about their hobbies, jobs, or history and heritage of their ethnic group. Second, respect your students. Know the struggles they face and the obstacles they must overcome. Show genuine acceptance. Help your students maintain a sense of pride in their cultural group and who they are. Finally, teach all students to read, write, speak, compute, think, and create. Instead of simply adding on information about particular groups, leaving the rest of the curriculum untouched, real multicultural education presents multiple perspectives and viewpoints to help students understand how events can be interpreted differently by various groups. Above all, teachers should connect the world of students and their cultures to the world of the school and the classroom. Multicultural education should pervade all aspects of school life. Don't limit the goals for low-SES (social economic status) or minority students. Hold high standards for all students. Now complete Expansion Activity 2.2: Multicultural Education to explore your thoughts on multicultural education.

EXPANSION ACTIVITY 2.2 Multicultural Education

In the context of education, are racial and ethnic differences negative? Come up with some differences that might be positive in your classroom. In terms of multicultural education, what do you hope to do differently as a teacher than what your former teachers did?

ON YOUR OWN 2.2 **Public View of Education**

Log on to the Web-based student study site at http://www.sagepub.com/eis2study/. Review the public surveys relative to Chapter 2 and react to the related activities.

Differentiated Instruction

Not all students are alike. As such, teachers need to be flexible in their approach to teaching and adjust the curriculum and presentation of content to learners rather than expecting students to modify themselves for the curriculum. **Differentiated instruction** is a teaching theory based on the premise that instructional approaches should vary and be adapted in relation to individual and diverse students in the classroom. Differentiated instruction means that classroom teachers make vigorous attempts to meet students where they are in the learning process and move them along as quickly and as far as possible in the context of a mixed-ability classroom (Tomlinson, 1995).

To differentiate instruction is to recognize students' varying background knowledge, readiness, language, preferences in learning, and interests and to react responsively. Differentiated instruction is a way to approach teaching and learning for students of differing abilities in the same class. The intent of differentiating instruction is to maximize each student's growth and individual success by meeting each student where he or she is and assisting in the learning process.

In differentiated classrooms, teachers are able to reach students by appealing to differing interests and by using varied rates of instruction along with varied degrees of complexity. Teachers in differentiated classes use time flexibly and use a range of instructional strategies. Teachers can differentiate at least four classroom elements based on students' readiness, interest, or learning profile.

1. **Content.** What the student needs to learn or how the student will get access to the information. Teachers can use reading materials at varying readability levels, put text on tape, present ideas through both auditory and visual means, and reteach an idea or skill in small groups to struggling learners or extend the thinking or skills of advanced learners.

2. **Process.** Activities in which the students engage to make sense of or master the content. Teachers can provide interest centers; offer different activities with different levels of support, challenge, or complexity; offer manipulatives or other hands-on supports; and vary the length of time a student may take to complete an activity.

3. **Products.** Culminating projects that ask the students to rehearse, apply, and extend what they have learned in a unit. Teachers can give students options on how to express required learning (e.g., write a letter or use a computer), use rubrics that match and extend students' varied skill levels, allow students to work alone or in small groups on projects, and encourage students to create their own product assignments.

4. **Learning Environment.** The way the classroom works and feels. Teachers can make sure there are quiet places in the room to work, provide materials that reflect a variety of cultures and home settings, set clear guidelines for independent work, and help students understand that some students have to be active to learn.

There is ample evidence that students are more successful in school, and find it more satisfying, if they are taught in ways that are responsive to their readiness levels, interests, and learning profiles.

APPLY AND
REFLECT 2.5

Students bring particular needs to the classroom, in part because of different racial, ethnic, cultural, and socioeconomic backgrounds. Based on the geographic area where you plan to teach, what area of need do you need to learn most about? How will you tailor your approaches to teaching to respond to the unique needs in your future classroom?

Students who are gifted and talented also need an appropriately differentiated curriculum designed to address their individual characteristics, needs, abilities, and interests. An effective curriculum for students who are gifted is essentially a basic curriculum that has been modified to meet their needs. Developing curriculum that is sufficiently rigorous, challenging, and coherent for students who are gifted can be a challenging task. A class is not differentiated when assignments are the same for all learners and the adjustments consist of varying the level of difficulty of questions for certain students, grading some students harder than others, or letting students who finish early play games for enrichment. It is not appropriate to have more advanced learners do extra math problems, extra book reports, or after completing their "regular" work be given extension assignments. Karnes and Bean (2000) suggest several ways in which the learning environment should be modified for gifted students in order to facilitate effective teaching and learning:

- Create a learner-centered environment that allows for student choice, flexibility, and independence.
- Focus on complexity rather than simplicity.
- Provide for high mobility within the classroom and various grouping arrangements.
- Express openness to innovation and exploration.

APPLY AND
REFLECT 2.6

Is acceleration (skipping grades) a useful approach with gifted students? What problem do you see with the strategy?

There is no recipe for differentiation. Rather, it is a way of thinking about teaching and learning that values the individual and can be translated into classroom practice in many ways.

APPLY AND
REFLECT 2.7

It is suggested that you learn as much as possible about students' home lives (without exceeding a reasonable right to privacy). How will this information affect your ability to better work with students and parents?

Learning Styles

Students learn more and retain it longer when the material they are learning is taught in a manner that is comfortable to them. Thus, students learn through different channels; that is, they have different **learning styles.** Some are visual learners, or those who learn best by seeing or reading; some are auditory learners, or those who learn best by hearing; and some are physical learners, or those who learn best through the manipulation of concrete materials. Some students learn quickly, others rather slowly. Some require substantial teacher help; others are able to learn independently. Most of us have taken on each of these learning styles at one time or another, depending on the circumstances; however, we tend to favor one style over another. Differences in learning styles are often due in part to differences in our **cognitive**

For material related to this concept, go to Clip 2.3 on the Student Resource CD bound into the back of your textbook.

style—that is, differences in how we respond to the environment and differences in the way information is processed and organized (Green, 1999; Riding & Rayner, 1998).

Researchers have produced vital information for teachers regarding the relationship between learning and learner characteristics. Dunn and Dunn (1993) describe learning styles as a person's preference in four main areas:

1. *Environmental:* the light, sound, temperature, and physical room preferences when learning

2. *Emotional:* the responsibility and persistence shown and the level of structure and supervision needed when involved in learning

3. *Sociological:* preference for a large or small group, for being alone, or for adult assistance when learning

4. *Physical:* sensory mode preference (e.g., visual, auditory, tactile, and kinesthetic) in learning and the need for movement, food intake, and a specific time of day

Factors in these four areas have a major impact on student learning. For example, some students prefer dim lighting, whereas others prefer brightly lit environments. Frequently, room temperature and noise level are the first learning style preferences communicated by students. Teachers who are unaware of the environmental effects on learning may interpret this communication as simple complaining. Informed teachers have come to realize that, just as students are unique, each learns in a unique way.

Sensitive teachers can sometimes identify the learning preferences of students through careful observations. However, a learning styles record form, such as the four-category form shown in Figure 2.7, can be helpful for this purpose. Interviews are an excellent way to have students talk about their experiences as learners and often will provide more accurate information regarding their learning styles. Teachers, however, sometimes have difficulty identifying students' learning styles accurately without some type of instrumentation. Some characteristics simply are not observable, even to the experienced teacher. Moreover, teachers can misinterpret students' behaviors and misunderstand their symptoms. An instrument often used to determine learning style that has high reliability and validity is the Dunn, Dunn, and Price Learning Style Inventory (LSI), with subtests for students in Grades 3 to 12. Teachers can have students take the LSI and receive a formal report on their styles. According to Dunn (Shaughnessy, 1998), the LSI does the following:

1. Allows students to identify how they prefer to learn.

2. Recommends a classroom environment that will complement students' learning styles.

3. Provides the group arrangement in which each student is likely to learn most effectively (e.g., alone, with two or more classmates, with a teacher, or, depending on the task, with students with similar interests or talents; it also describes whether all or none of those combinations is acceptable for a particular student).

4. Tells which students need direction and high structure and which students should be given options and alternatives.

5. Sequences and then reinforces the perceptual strengths individuals use to begin studying new and difficult information.

6. Tells how each student should study and do homework.

7. Outlines methods through which individuals are most likely to achieve (e.g., programmed learning, contracts, tactual manipulatives, multisensory resources, kinesthetic games, or any combination of these).

8. Tells which children are conforming and which are nonconforming and explains how to work with both types.

9. Provides information relative to the best time of day for each student to be scheduled for difficult subjects (thus, it shows how to group students for instruction based on their learning-style energy-highs).

10. Indicates those students for whom movement or snacks, while the students are learning, may accelerate learning.

11. Provides information regarding those students for whom analytic versus global approaches are likely to be important.

**Figure 2.7
Sample Learning
Styles Record Form**

Learning Styles Record Form		

Directions: For each student, record your observations regarding the following items related to the student's preferred style of learning.

Student's name: _____

Learning Style Attribute		**Findings (check when applicable)**	
		No	**Yes**
1. Style of working:	Prefers to work alone	_____	_____
	Prefers to work with others	_____	_____
2. Learning modality:	Listening	_____	_____
	Reading	_____	_____
	Watching	_____	_____
	Writing	_____	_____
	Discussing	_____	_____
	Touching	_____	_____
	Moving	_____	_____
3. Need for structure:	Low	_____	_____
	High	_____	_____
4. Details versus		_____	_____
generalities		_____	_____

APPLY AND REFLECT 2.8

Should teachers match instruction to individual learning styles? Do you see any problems associated with this attempt?

Some student differences in learning styles can be accommodated; others are more problematic. The number of different learning styles often is too varied to make it practical for teachers to accommodate every student's learning style. As much as possible, however, you should see that students' learning needs are met. If sound is needed, you can allow students to use a CD player. When classroom resources fail, use personalized computer software packages. If verbal interaction is important, block off a portion of the room for conversation. If complete silence is needed, provide noise filters. For unmotivated students, make sure you work with them, check on them, and give them encouragement. For motivated students, leave them alone and monitor as needed. Finally, work with the administration and schedule students' toughest classes when they are in their prime. Some students will be morning learners, while others will learn better in the late afternoon. Teacher flexibility and willingness to experiment with different techniques will provide opportunities to maximize learning. Complete Web Link 2.3: Learning Styles for ideas on being flexible.

WEB LINK 2.3 Learning Styles

Access search engine Yahoo, Northern Light, Google, or AltaVista on the Internet and conduct a "Lesson Plan" search or access URL http://www.microsoft.com and do a lesson plan search. Select a lesson plan that addresses at least two different learning styles. Share and discuss these styles with the class.

Multiple Intelligences

Intelligence is usually defined as the ability to answer items on a traditional IQ test. Howard Gardner has argued that humans have at least eight distinct intelligences. According to Gardner, individuals differ in their strengths in the various intelligences. Gardner (Armstrong, 1994; Checkley, 1997) has shown not only insight but also compassion with the development of the concept of multiple intelligences. These eight areas of intelligence relate to the individual's abilities linguistically, mathematically, spatially, kinesthetically, musically, interpersonally, intrapersonally, and naturally (see Table 2.8). Gardner (2003) also is investigating whether a spiritual or existential intelligence may satisfy his criteria for individual intelligences. Gardner's multiple intelligence theory gives classroom teachers two extremely valuable tools that will make learning more focused on individual abilities. First, it gives teachers assistance in assessing where students' abilities and strengths lie. Second, it is a guide for teachers in the design of classroom activities that will give students an opportunity to experience working in different areas of intelligence. This will help students discover talents that may otherwise have gone unnoticed or untapped. The teachers of younger children function in a vulnerable position because these young children are experiencing a bombardment of developmental changes. Thus, many times, Gardner's multiple intelligences approach is especially important when assessing these younger children to attempt to discover who they are, where their strengths lie, and what talents might be able to help them develop a greater concept of self. Teachers must avoid thinking about children as smart or not smart since there are many ways to be smart.

Traditionally, schools have reinforced a learning profile emphasizing verbal/linguistic and logical mathematical abilities and de-emphasizing or excluding other possible intelligences. However, to address these other intelligences, Gardner emphasizes learning in context, particularly through apprenticeships. For example, student development in an area of nature should be fostered through hands-on experiences with nature. However, even traditional subjects should be taught in a variety of ways to address the varied intelligences of both students and teachers. For example, state history might be taught through a number of media and methods, ranging from field trips to biographies to films to art and architecture to reenactments of state events.

This concludes our discussion of planning a course. But before I leave the topic of organizing for teaching, let's take a brief look at an area that has been receiving attention by educators—technology in the classroom.

APPLY AND REFLECT 2.9

Evaluate your own intelligence profile according to Gardner. In what frames of mind (intelligence areas) do you come out strongest?

Figure 2.8
Gardner's Eight
Areas of Intelligence

Intelligence	Core Components	Teaching Activities
Linguistic	Ability to use language, either oral or written. Sensitivity to the sounds, structure, meanings, and functions of words and language.	Activities related to word games, e-mail discussions, choral reading, card games, journal writing, Internet searches, etc.
Logical-mathematical	Ability to use mathematics and numbers. Sensitivity to and capacity to discern logical or numerical patterns; ability to handle long chains of reasoning.	Activities related to problem solving, mental calculations, classification, number games, critical thinking, solve puzzles, etc.
Spatial	Ability to perceive the spatial world. Capacity to perceive the visual-spatial world accurately and to perform transformations on one's initial perceptions.	Visual activities related to graphic art, mind mapping, visualization, maps, pictures, imagination games, models, etc.
Bodily-kinesthetic	Ability to use one's body movement. Ability to control one's body movements and to handle objects skillfully.	Hands-on activities, drama, pantomime, dance, sports that teach, tactile activities, etc.
Musical	Ability to undertake musical endeavors. Ability to produce and appreciate rhythm, pitch, and timbre; appreciation of the forms of musical expressiveness.	Songs that teach, rapping, learn tunes, create rhymes, superlearning, enhance ability to learn, etc.
Interpersonal	Ability to understand other people. Capacity to discern and respond appropriately to the moods, temperaments, motivations, and desires of other people.	Cooperative learning activities, lead discussions, community involvement, dramatic activities, social activities, simulations, etc.
Intrapersonal	Ability to understand oneself. Access to one's own feelings and the ability to discriminate among one's emotions; knowledge of one's own strengths and weaknesses.	Individual instruction, read books, journal writing, independent study, self-esteem activities, play activities, cooperative groups, etc.
Naturalist	Ability to understand nature. Ability to make distinctions in the natural world; capacity to recognize flora and fauna.	Activities related to the natural world and the biological sciences, exploration of nature, find origins, study nature objects, etc.

REFLECTIONS ON TEACHER PRACTICE 2.2 | The Curriculum

1. How can teachers emphasize both breadth and depth when teaching the required school curriculum? Why are both breadth and depth needed for understanding?

2. How can teachers planning and teaching as a team result in more effective teaching? How would such teaming make schools more of a challenge for students?

◆ ◆ ◆

I find it very difficult to "cover" my curriculum by myself, but with the cooperation of other teachers (not just core teachers), I am able to cover and practice much more. We often think of related arts classes as being nonacademic, but they are only nonacademic if we teach them that way.

The science teacher on my team has partnered with the FACS teacher on the human body, hygiene, and rocks/fossils/minerals content very successfully. Likewise, the science teacher on my team is having her students reply to response-like questions in the same way I have been requiring them to answer in my classroom. We are already making plans for next year's first

quarter to be sure our students are able to take notes and present research effectively as well as other overlapping skills.

We need more time to plan together as well as the openness of others to include/hook into each others' subject concepts. It takes time to see the connections, but it is vital if we are ever to live up to the grand expectations of those who write our curriculum.

Breadth is wonderful, but not if it is at the expense of understanding and deep knowledge.

—ELLEN, middle school teacher

SOURCE: Reprinted with permission from MiddleWeb.

ON YOUR OWN 2.3 **Reflections on Teacher Practice**

Read and reflect on the viewpoints expressed in The Curriculum. Log on to the Web-based student study site at http://www.sagepub.com/eis2study/ and react to the related activities.

Technology in the Classroom

Technology is evolving at an astonishing rate. There is growing consensus that today's technologies possess incredible potential to improve and even revolutionize our schools. As such, **technology literacy** must be integrated into the school curriculum. To explore the competencies associated with technology literacy, complete Web Link 2.4: Technology Literacy.

WEB LINK 2.4 **Technology Literacy**

The International Society for Technology in Education (ISTE) has created six broad categories of standards for technological literacy. These standards can be accessed at http://www.iste.org. Many teacher education programs and school districts have adopted these standards for prospective teachers and students. Download and review the standards. Do you think it is realistic for all prospective teachers and students to meet the ISTE standards? Discuss your reflections with classmates.

Most students now have access to computers and the **Internet** in their classrooms, nearly all students have access somewhere in their schools, and a majority of teachers report using computers or the Internet for instructional purposes. Technology is changing the way teachers teach and students learn. It is also offering new ways for all involved in education to be openly accountable to parents, communities, and students. Children have grown up with technology. They have been raised in a world of instant access to information, a world where vivid images embody and supplement information formerly presented solely through text. They are used to an environment where they control information flow and access, whether through toys or a video game controller, remote control, mouse, or touch-tone phone.

The most dramatic area of technology growth has occurred in the use of computers. The decreasing cost and increasing availability of microcomputers and other technologies in schools have led educators to become more interested in technology, particularly as a means of meeting students' diverse needs. Technology, particularly computers, is being viewed as an essential part of instruction to help students develop basic and critical thinking skills.

Instructional use of computers varies from helping students learn basic facts to teaching them complex thinking strategies. Their value to students along the learning continuum from disabled to gifted and talented comes from their ability to adapt instruction to meet the diverse needs of students.

The idea behind **computer-based instruction (CBI)** is to use the computer as a tutor to present information, give students practice, and assess their level of understanding. CBI programs generally share the following characteristics: (a) using a structured curriculum; (b) letting students work at their own pace; (c) giving students controlled, frequent feedback and reinforcement; and (d) measuring performance quickly and giving students information on their performance.

The benefits derived from the classroom use of technology remain mixed. Review of 133 research studies on educational technology from 1990 to 1994 showed that technology had a significant positive impact on achievement in all subject areas, across all school levels, and in regular classrooms as well as those for special-needs students (Healy, 1998; Kirkpatrick & Cuban, 1998). Other studies have varied the benefits derived from using word processing, the Internet, and other classroom technology (Aviram, 2000; Lewin, 2001; Linn & Slotta, 2000). However, other critics (Becher & Ravitz, 2001; Cuban, 2001; Green, 1999; Salpeter, 2000) claim that technology is having little impact on classroom learning. Clearly, more research is needed on the impact of technology on student learning (Becher & Ravitz, 2001; Cuban, 2001).

Most teachers also use computers to enhance instruction. Word processing is the most common instructional use of computers by teachers. Teachers can create handouts for students, write letters to parents, and respond to administrators' requests for information. Computers are also commonly used for recordkeeping, creating grade books, and storing standardized test results and lesson plans. Most teachers also use computer technology for communicating via e-mail, generating exams for students, and using the Internet as a resource for lesson planning.

Although computers are one of the most important technological advances, technology actually includes much more than this. Technology in the classroom makes possible the instant exchange of information between classrooms as well as individual students; it allows instant access to databases and online information services and provides multimedia technical resources such as interactive audio and video. Technology also allows for the repurposing of preexisting educational materials across media formats: Print, static illustrations, still and digital photographs, digital audio, still and motion video, still and motion film, animations, computer graphics, and hypermedia can all be accessed and combined in novel ways.

To incorporate technology more fully into the classroom, teachers must be provided with the time and support to explore technology on their own. Administrators must provide the time for teachers, who now suffer from larger classes and more responsibility than ever, to take a break from teaching to start learning.

Whatever the format, technology has a motivating quality for students. They often work longer and harder than they would with comparable paper-and-pencil tasks. Complete the Web Link 2.5: Computers in the Classroom. It should generate an array of potential computer activities for your classroom.

APPLY AND REFLECT 2.10   Are you technology literate? What are your strengths and weaknesses relative to technology?

WEB LINK 2.5   Computers in the Classroom

Browse the World Wide Web to locate examples of K–12 uses of computers in the classroom. What types of activities are the most common? Discuss the benefits gained from your findings. Include benefits to students and teachers.

This completes our study of planning courses and the use of technology in the classroom. Review the planning and technology topics in Table 2.3 and complete Review and Reflective Exercise 2.2 to explore related concepts.

ON YOUR OWN 2.4   View From the Classroom

Log on to the Web-based student study site at http://www.sagepub.com/eis2study/. Review the Chapter 2 teacher surveys and react to the related activities.

TABLE 2.3   Classroom Planning

Concept	Description
Course planning	Establishing the curriculum and instructional emphasis of a course for a year
Multicultural classroom	Valuing the ethnic, racial, and linguistic diversity of cultural groups
Differentiated instruction	Modifying instruction in the classroom to reflect the different abilities of students
Technology	Using multimedia in the classroom to enhance instruction

REVIEW AND REFLECTIVE EXERCISE 2.2   Outline the process you would follow and the issues you would address in designing a course.

REVIEW

- What is involved in planning a course for a year?
- How do cultural differences affect teaching and learning?
- How has the increased emphasis on diversity issues affected school curricula?
- What is the impact of technology on teaching and learning?

REFLECTION

- How important is it to plan a course for the year? Can't you just adopt and follow a good textbook for your course plan? What problems could develop if you covered only the content in the adopted textbook?
- There has been much debate in the media over possible bias in the school curriculum. What can you as a teacher do to reduce or eliminate school curriculum bias and its effects?
- What are the strengths and limitations of technology in individual classrooms? Should classroom computers be connected to the Internet?

A Model of Teaching

- Effective teachers must diagnose, plan the course, plan instruction, guide planned activities, evaluate, reflect, and, when necessary, follow up.

- Time mandated by the state must be allocated both to instructional and noninstructional uses. Instructional time must be organized so that time on task is maximized. Time on task must be turned into academic learning time (performance on assigned tasks at 80% or better) for teachers to be truly effective.

The Curriculum

- The curriculum of a school consists of all the planned and unplanned experiences students undergo in the school setting.

- Curriculum mapping can be used to identify gaps in the curriculum being taught.

- The backward design model offers an alternative approach to curriculum design.

Curriculum Structure

- The curriculum pattern can be subject centered, student centered, or an integrated combination of both forms.

Curriculum Selection

- Content selection should be planned so that instruction fulfills the needs of students, society, and the structure of the subject.

Planning the Course

- Chapter topics are often combined into units, and a sequence for the units along with unit time allotments is then established.

- A course plan should remain flexible so needed modifications can be made during the year.

- Teachers must plan for a multicultural classroom.

- Not all students are alike, which calls for differentiated instruction in the classroom.

- Students learn through different channels; they have different learning styles. Teachers must be sensitive to these different learning styles and modify their instruction as much as possible to accommodate the differences in learning style.

- Gardner suggests that humans have eight different intelligences: linguistical, mathematical, spatial, kinesthetical, musical, interpersonal, intrapersonal, and natural. Teachers need to focus instruction on these different abilities.

Technology in the Classroom

- Technology is changing the way teachers teach and students learn.

DISCUSSION QUESTIONS AND ACTIVITIES

1. **The curriculum.** Obtain a state and district curriculum guide for elementary or secondary education. How would you improve the curriculum at the level you plan to teach? Should teachers be free to determine what they will teach? What forces commonly influence the school curriculum? The formal curriculum? The hidden curriculum?

2. **School and classroom time.** How could you improve academic instructional time? Academic time on task? What procedures and/or rules would you implement for changing activities or starting (and ending) your class to increase instructional time?

3. **Planning a course.** Select a basic textbook from your area of specialization. Using the selected textbook, plan a 35-week course. Select the topics (chapters) to be covered, supplement the textbook where needed, combine the topics (chapters) into appropriate units of study, and make unit time allotments.

4. **Textbook examination.** Examine some elementary and secondary textbooks and other materials for the classroom. Do you see any racial, gender, or ethnic biases?

5. **Technology.** Think about how you can use e-mail and chat rooms to help you and your students learn.

6. **Diversity.** What other elements of diversity will you find in your students that have not been discussed in this chapter? How will you be sensitive to these differences?

TECHNOLOGY AND EDUCATION

Use one of the available search engines to explore the Web for technological tools such as lesson planning software, worksheets and puzzle tools, poster and bulletin board production tools, and time management tools that will assist you in planning. Share your findings with your class.

DECONSTRUCTING THE STANDARDS

Chapter 2 content addresses topics related to INTASC Standards 1, 2, 3, 5, and 7.

- ◆ INTASC Standard 1 states: *Knowledge of Subject Matter:* The teacher understands the central concepts, tools of inquiry, and structures of the subject being taught and can create learning experiences that make these aspects of subject matter meaningful for students.
- ◆ INTASC Standard 2 states: *Knowledge of Human Development and Learning:* The teacher understands how children learn and develop and can provide learning opportunities that support their intellectual, social, and personal development.
- ◆ INTASC Standard 3 states: *Adapting Instruction for Individual Needs:* The teacher understands how students differ in their approaches to learning and creates instructional opportunities that are adapted to diverse learners.
- ◆ INTASC Standard 5 states: *Classroom Motivation and Management:* The teacher uses an understanding of individual and group motivation and behavior to create a learning environment that encourages positive social interaction, active engagement in learning, and self-motivation.
- ◆ INTASC Standard 7 states: *Instructional Planning Skills:* The teacher plans instruction based on knowledge of subject mater, students, the community, and curriculum goals.

For each of these five standards, write your response to the following:

- Which part(s) of each standard does this chapter address?
- How does this chapter address this standard?
- How will the concepts in this chapter help you apply this standard as a teacher?

PRAXIS CONNECTION

Log on to the Web-based student study site at http://www.sagepub.com/eis2study/. Access the Praxis II: Principles of Learning and Teaching assessments and/or state-related exams and complete the Chapter 2 test preparation exercises.

PORTFOLIO CONNECTION

Log on to the Web-based student study site at http://www.sagepub.com/eis2study/. Access the Portfolio Connection. Complete the Chapter 2 portfolio link to INTASC activities.

CONNECTION WITH THE FIELD

1. **The teaching model.** Visit several schoolteachers. Discuss their planning. Do they follow the seven-step planning model presented in this chapter or a modification of the model? Describe the models used by the teachers.

2. **The school curriculum.** Examine the documents that outline the curriculum at a nearby school. Interview several students about the school curriculum. Ask them what they are learning. What attitudes do the students have about their school experiences? Determine if there is a parallel relationship between what the school teaches and the career aspirations of students.

3. **Classroom observation.** Complete several classroom interaction observational activities in different classrooms. Focus the collection of information on
   a. actions that help you better understand students and their behaviors;
   b. information gained from conversations within the classroom environment that help you understand students' needs, likes, and dislikes; and
   c. student weaknesses and strengths gained from verbal examination of students' class work and homework.

4. **Barriers**. Interview teachers at the grade level you expect to teach in a local school district. What barriers must they contend with in their efforts to include technology in the curriculum? What are the implications of these barriers for you as a teacher?

Sequencing and Organizing Instruction

The central focus of Part II is preparing for teaching. Effective teachers must plan and plan well. They identify lesson learning intent, select appropriate media, and select and implement appropriate teaching strategies and methods. A major purpose of this section is to assist you in becoming a better planner. To do so, you must decide where you want to go and the best method of getting there. The backward design approach to identifying instructional intent is also presented and discussed.

Chapter 3 covers the process of determining and organizing the intended goals of a course for different students. This chapter relates to determining where you want to go in terms of developing your skill at writing well-stated objectives.

Chapter 4 centers on how to design and carry out course, unit, weekly, and daily planning. It shows you how to plan presentations that achieve the stated objectives and focuses on teaching content and thinking skills. Chapter 4 also explores how to plan for students with different abilities. Teaching special education students and gifted and talented students is covered. Finally, several practical lesson plan formats are illustrated and discussed.

CHAPTER 3

Setting Goals and Objectives

The aim [of education] should be to teach us rather how to think, than what to think.

—JAMES BEATTIE

OVERVIEW

Selecting the curriculum is only the beginning in planning for instruction. You must now clarify your purpose and your instructional intent: You must decide exactly what you want students to learn, how they will learn it, and how you will know they have learned it. Generally, these three steps occur simultaneously with the setting of priorities regarding time, objectives, materials, and methods of instruction.

This chapter will address student expectations and standards and the establishment of goals and objectives, whereas Chapters 4, 9, and 10 will be devoted to lesson planning, evaluation of student learning, and testing and grading, respectively.

OBJECTIVES

After completing your study of Chapter 3, you should be able to do the following:

- Describe the expectations and standards associated with teaching and learning.
- Explain the provisions of Public Law 94–142, IDEA, Section 504 of the Vocational Rehabilitation Act, and No Child Left Behind.
- Give valid rationales for stating instructional goals and objectives.
- Contrast the terms *educational goals, informational objectives,* and *instructional objectives.*
- Prepare (write) educational goals.
- Describe the four components that make up a properly written instructional objective.
- Describe the three domains of learning.
- Classify objectives into cognitive, affective, and psychomotor domains and rate them as higher or lower level within each domain.
- Prepare (write) informational objectives and instructional objectives at different levels of cognitive, affective, and psychomotor sophistication.
- Describe the *backward design* approach to stating instructional intent.

The intent of teaching is learning. **Learning** can be defined as a change in an individual's capacity for performance as a result of experience. Changes that come about through development (such as sexual maturity or growing taller) are not considered to be learning. People are constantly absorbing information, both intentionally and unintentionally. For example, students may intentionally learn to read but may unintentionally learn to fear the dentist. Of course, your main concern will be with intentional learning. Don't totally discount unintentional learning, however, because as you teach, students are determining that the subject is interesting or dull, useful, or useless. This learning, although unintentional, is important to the learning process.

Standards for Student Performance

Standards for student performance have changed as expectations about what exactly education should *do* have changed. One unresolved problem of schools is how to provide equal educational opportunity to learn while ensuring the public that a high-quality education is being provided.

Despite the increased focus on the diversity among K–12 students, studies suggest that many schools and teachers still often treat girls, racial- and language-minority students, and working-class students differently from boys, nonminority students, and middle- and upper-class students and have lower expectations for them (Kaufman, Westland, & Engvall, 1997; McCall, 1995; Padron, 1994). Factor into this equation the 1970s legislation that mandated equal opportunities for children with handicapping conditions (to take place in an integrated setting), and you can begin to appreciate the competing expectations and demands with which schools and teachers must contend.

Most schools are organized around a set of expectations or benchmarks regarding the purposes of education. The public has sought, even demanded, that schools focus on the needs of more and more groups of young people. In addition, the public has demanded that schools include coursework that addresses health, economic, and societal issues as well as the "basics." Funding for these needs has been sporadic and inadequate, yet the public has also demanded **accountability** for student performance, particularly in the area of basic skill acquisition.

The attempt to control quality in the public schools and ensure some form of standardization has resulted in an **accreditation** process that mandates review at the state level and rewards approval at the regional level. All states require periodic review of programs for accreditation. A few states have used this process to declare some schools "educationally bankrupt" and have assumed control of such schools. Often, students who wish to attend more prestigious institutions of higher education must attend regional accredited schools. Moreover, school choice plans (students choose the school they attend) and No Child Left Behind legislation are likely to increase the demand for careful scrutiny of school programs as parents "shop" for schools for their children.

Needs of Students

The more you know about your students, the easier will be your task of bringing about the desired learning. In short, to be an effective educator, you must identify your students' needs—their strengths, weaknesses, aspirations, limitations, and deficiencies. These student needs can be academic or social. Some students may be lacking in reading or in mathematics, whereas others may be gifted, academically talented, or creative. An awareness of these differences is needed so you can devise ways to provide adequate instruction. In addition, you must take into account differences in social and cultural background, as well as different student abilities.

Some of your students will be academically able or even bright, whereas others will be slower, **disabled,** or **handicapped.** Student differences often require that you adapt the classroom's physical environment and your instructional strategies to better accommodate the unique needs of mainstreamed or special students. In other words, you must learn to modify your instruction to fit the unique needs of special students.

Physical development
is an important aspect
of schooling.

APPLY AND REFLECT 3.1

Many states have established benchmark standards for the different subject content areas and grade levels. Do you support this policy? Why or why not?

Public Law 94–142 (PL 94–142), the Education for All Handicapped Children Act, was enacted to require that every school system in the nation provide a free, appropriate public education for every child between the ages of 3 and 21. In 1990, PL 94–142 was recast as the Individuals With Disabilities Education Act (IDEA). IDEA spells out broad mandates for services to all children with disabilities. These include evaluation and eligibility determination, appropriate education and an individualized education plan (IEP), and education in the least restrictive environment (LRE). The IEP must state present levels of functioning, long- and short-term educational goals, services to be provided, and plans for initiating and evaluating the services. Carrying out IEP goals and objectives may require lesson modifications, such as adapting assigned work, developing special reproduced materials for teaching difficult concepts, planning and writing special study guides, and obtaining and using special equipment. Some districts assist teachers with their instructional modifications by developing classroom modifications plans. Figure 3.1 shows a sample plan with three categories. The teacher checks those items that will apply to a specific student.

In 1997, the Individuals With Disabilities Education Act Amendments of 1997, or IDEA '97, was passed to reauthorize and strengthen the original act. Among the goals of this law are raising educational expectations for children with disabilities, increasing the role of parents in the education of their children with disabilities, ensuring that regular classroom teachers are involved in planning for and assessment of these children, including students with disabilities in local and state assessments, and supporting professional development for all who educate children with disabilities.

In 1973, the federal government passed the Vocational Rehabilitation Act. Section 504 of the law prevents discrimination against individuals with disabilities in any program that receives federal

Schools must focus on state and national standards.

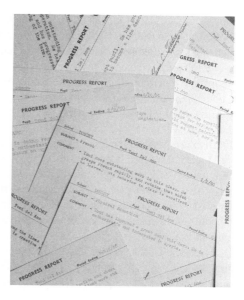

money, such as public schools. If a student has a condition that substantially limits participation in school, the school must develop a plan for giving that student access to education. Section 504 offers accommodations to two major groups: students with medical or health needs, such as diabetes, drug addition, severe allergies, communicable diseases, temporary disabilities resulting from accidents, or alcoholism, and students with **attention-deficit/hyperactivity disorder (ADHD).** Complete Web Link 3.1: Individual Education Plan (IEP) to review some sample IEPs.

WEB LINK 3.1   Individualized Education Plan (IEP)

Teachers who work with children with special needs are generally involved in the development of an IEP for each child. Review sample IEPs online, and discuss how all students could benefit from receiving the type of feedback present in an IEP.

Under the IDEA, children with disabilities must be educated in the least restrictive environment (LRE). This means an environment as similar as possible to the one in which children who do not have a disability are educated. The education of children with a disability in the regular classroom was referred to as *mainstreaming*. This term, however, has been replaced by the term *inclusion*, which means educating a child with special educational needs full-time in the regular classroom with other children (Idol, 1997). One recent study found that the achievement of students with learning disabilities benefited from inclusion (Rea, McLaughlin, & Walther-Thomas, 2002).

Limited English Proficiency (LEP)

A major problem facing many school districts in some areas of the country is learning a second language, English. In many communities today, it is not uncommon for more than half the students to come from homes where the first language is not English. In the Los Angeles Unified School District,

For material related to this concept, go to Clip 3.1 on the Student Resource CD bound into the back of your textbook.

for example, more than 81 languages are spoken in the homes. Big city school districts in New York City, Miami, and Houston, as well as many smaller districts, now have populations of ethnic minorities that equal or exceed non-Hispanic students. Nationwide, the number of students whose first language is not English is expected to increase during the next couple of decades. By 2026, it is projected that about one fourth of all students will come from homes in which the primary language is not English. Yet Standard English will continue to be a necessity for success in school and society.

Learning to communicate reasonably well in English will be a major task for many limited English students. They will need your encouragement and help. The terms **limited English proficient (LEP)** and **English language learners (ELL)** are used for students who have not yet attained an adequate level of English to succeed in an English-only program. These students are learning **English as a second language (ESL)** and may attend special classes for English language learners. Some schools use a pullout system, in which part of the student's day is spent in special bilingual classes and part in the regular classroom. Students in these special programs usually receive anywhere from 30 minutes to several hours of instruction per week in their primary language, but at least half of their instruction is generally in English. Other schools place students in sheltered classes consisting of specific cultural groups where the teacher is specially trained to work with LEP students. Whatever system is used, teaching students who have limited proficiency in English should include the use of hands-on learning activities and cooperative learning (see Chapter 6). At the elementary level, these hands-on learning activities may include playing action games at recess, drawing and painting, and viewing displays and demonstrations. At the secondary level, the hands-on learning activities may include almost all aspects of physical education class or some vocational classes and viewing displays and demonstrations in other areas. You should attempt to communicate with LEP students through gestures, pictures, and any words you know from their language. Whatever you do, even though attempting to communicate with LEP students may be frustrating, always be positive. Also, encourage other students to include LEP students in their activities, explaining that they can make the new students comfortable by helping them learn the standard procedures and popular activities.

Some of the students in most regular classrooms will be gifted and talented (G/T). These students also are entitled to be served by teachers who are prepared to differentiate instructional content and methods and who possess personal and professional traits that promote successful learning for G/T students in their classroom (see Chapter 4).

APPLY AND REFLECT 3.2	As a classroom teacher, you will have students with special needs mainstreamed into your classes. Do you support or not support the inclusion concept? Why?

The use of differentiated assignments is a must when working with mainstreamed special-needs students and G/T students. This is accomplished by individualizing the curriculum as much as possible. Many of the suggestions in Figure 3.1 can be adapted to the gifted and talented.

Rationale for Objectives

Almost anything you try in the classroom will result in some type of learning, but it is not always desirable learning. To be effective, learning must have direction; it must have purpose. For example, your school might want to focus on reading and writing skills. Your task would then be to decide on the specific learning that will lead to the attainment of this goal. Thus, even though they are broad and basic skills, reading and writing would be integrated into course content and related specific objectives. Viewed in this context, your objective can be defined as a clear and unambiguous description of instructional intent. It is finite and measurable. Its accomplishment can be verified.

Figure 3.1
Classroom
Modification Plan

Student: _____ Teacher: _____

School: _____ Grade/Course: _____

A. Exam Modification

_____ 1. Reduce the number of exams to _____

_____ 2. Open-book exams

_____ 3. Allow more time for regular exam

_____ 4. Reduce the length of the regular exam

_____ 5. Use more objective items (fewer essay items)

_____ 6. Give same exam orally

_____ 7. Write down test items for students

_____ 8. Read test items to student

_____ 9. Substitute assignment for test

_____ 10. Enlarge test item print

_____ 11. Allow use of computer

_____ 12. Other (specify) _____

B. Assignment Modification

_____ 1. Provide more detailed directions

_____ 2. Repeat instructions

_____ 3. Give instructions through several channels (oral, written, etc.)

_____ 4. Provide materials that are programmed/self-checking

_____ 5. Brief student on major points before starting an assignment

_____ 6. Allow more time for regular assignments

_____ 7. Reduce length of regular assignments

_____ 8. Break assignment into a series of smaller assignments

_____ 9. Reduce reading level of the regular assignment (edit, reword)

_____ 10. Change format of the instructional materials

_____ 11. Use different format materials to teach the same content

_____ 12. Provide study aids (hints, cue cards, guides, calculators, computers)

_____ 13. Provide hands-on activities/physical assignments

_____ 14. Oral presentations/reports/projects/games, etc.

_____ 15. Other (specify) _____

C. Presenting Content Alternatives

_____ 1. Make cassette or CD or DVD recordings of lectures for individual playback

_____ 2. Allow teacher aide/volunteer to take notes for student

_____ 3. Allow classroom peers to make carbon copies of classwork for the student

_____ 4. Use visual (DVDs, charts, pictures, etc.) and/or audio materials (CDs, tapes, records)

_____ 5. Use individualized learning contract or learning centers

_____ 6. Use computer learning packages

_____ 7. Provide hands-on/learning by discovery experiences

_____ 8. Use self-checking materials

_____ 9. Other (specify) _____

An **objective** is not a statement of what you plan to do; instead, it is a statement of what your students should be able to do after instruction. For example, if the purpose of instruction is to foster student understanding of the conditions that led to our focus on the exploration of space, the objective would *not* be "The *teacher will present* information about our ventures into space." It does not matter at all what the teacher does if students do not learn. Remember the purpose of instruction is to get students to learn. Therefore, the objective should be "The *student will discuss* world conditions that led to our focus on the exploration of space." Objectives, then, should place the emphasis on student outcome or performance.

There are a number of approaches to writing objectives. The behavioral objectives approach proposed by Robert Mager (1997) and the general/specific objectives approach proposed by Norman Gronlund (1999) are the most common. Mager proposes writing specific statements about observable outcomes that can be built up to become a curriculum (an inductive approach). An example of a behavioral objective would be

Given 3 minutes of class time, the student will solve 9 out of 10 addition problems of the type: $5 + 4 = $ _____.

Gronlund (1999), on the other hand, proposes starting with a general statement and providing specific examples of topics to be covered or behaviors to be observed (a deductive approach). An example of a general/specific objective would be

The student can perform simple addition:

a. can define what addition means, in his or her own words.

b. can define relevant terms such as *addend* and *sum.*

c. can solve problems of the type $5 + 4 = $ _____.

While there are advantages and disadvantages to each approach, this text will focus on Mager's (1997) approach, because it is the most widely used and perhaps the most inclusive.

Teaching, as noted in Chapter 2, can be envisioned as a seven-phase process (review Figure 2.1). Once the content to be taught has been selected, objectives must be written related to the selected content. The written objectives will then set the framework for the instructional approach and the student evaluation.

Objectives establish the framework for instruction: They compel you to provide the environment and sequence of activities that will allow students to reach the stated intent. For example, if your objective is the instant recall of specific information (such as the elements in the periodic table), your activities must include practice in the recall of the information. If, on the other hand, the objective is related to the use of information in problem solving, practice in problem-solving procedures must be provided. Thus, objectives spell out general strategies and specific activities for their attainment.

Objectives also prescribe exactly what skills and knowledge students must manifest as a result of instruction. In other words, your objectives will set the framework for the evaluation process.

ON YOUR OWN 3.1   View From the Classroom

Log on to the Web-based student study site at http://www.sagepub.com/eis2study. Review the Chapter 3 teacher surveys and react to the related activities.

Communication of Intent

Objectives also serve an important communication function. Clear and measurable objectives need to be stated for the benefit of students, parents, and program accountability. Through the use of properly written objectives, educators can show where students are, as a group or as individuals, with respect to the stated objectives. Administrators can communicate similar information to school boards or the community at large.

Objectives make clear to students your expectations prior to instruction. This communication eliminates guesswork related to students' learning (e.g., "Will this be on the test?"). Thus, when you communicate your objectives, students know exactly what is expected of them, and they no longer have to guess what is important. They know whether it will be on the test.

An essential part of planning is writing the objectives that set the framework for the total instructional process.

Objectives are being widely used in education today. Public Law 94–142 (**PL 94-142**) and its successors, for example, require that an IEP be written for every handicapped student in your class. And, for each of these plans, specific objectives must be written for the students. When writing objectives for IEPs, you should start with standards for regular education students and design modifications and interventions to accommodate the student's needs. The IEP should describe the student's educational needs, identify learning and developmental deficiencies, and propose a set of achievements for the student. It is a guide to the professional staff responsible for implementing it or supervising its implementation. The value of any IEP depends on the quality of its communication. Poorly written objectives pose problems for the teacher, who is held accountable for implementing the plan, and for the administrator, who must justify the plan to state IEP auditors. Therefore, well-written goals and objectives are crucial to IEP success. The school must make sure that the student's IEP is being carried out as it is written. If parents do not agree with an IEP or the placement, they can ask for additional evaluation, mediation, or a due process hearing or file a complaint with the state education agency.

With the 2004 reauthorization of the federal IDEA, states and school districts were given more options for how to evaluate public school students for specific learning disabilities (LD). One new approach to evaluation that has gained increasing interest is responsiveness to intervention (RTI). RTI emphasizes "student outcomes instead of student deficits" (Kavale, Holdnack, & Mostert, 2005) and makes a clear connection between identification and instruction. This strategy improves the ability of students with disabilities to participate and progress in the general education curriculum. RTI is used to identify students with LD and to determine early intervention. This is accomplished through evaluation of student responses to targeted, higher quality instruction that has been demonstrated as effective for most students (Batsche et al., 2005). It has also been argued that RTI can be used for all students, not just those with LD. It is focused on providing early and more immediate support for student needs by screening students as early as kindergarten (Vaughn & Fuchs, 2003).

Finally, individualized program and mastery learning techniques, as well as some state and district regulations, require the specification of objectives. Thus, you, as a prospective teacher, must understand and develop the skills for prescribing and writing your instructional intent (objectives).

APPLY AND REFLECT 3.3	What should be the goals of American education and education in your state? Should we have a national and/or state agenda that shapes our instructional objectives?

Teacher Accountability

Finally, the movement for teacher accountability has become a simple extension of objectives, testing, and evaluation. Teacher accountability means that teachers are responsible for the quality of their instruction and the progress of their students. Generally, teacher performance related to planning and instruction is measured through classroom-based observation and evaluation by administrators. Typically, student progress is measured by performance on nationally normed standardized tests.

"What did I learn today? My mother will want to know."

SOURCE: Created by Ford Button.

A three-stage accountability model is depicted in Figure 3.2. The first stage in the model is the establishment of objectives—that is, learning intent. In Stage 2, instructional activities designed to develop student mastery are implemented. The final stage is a determination of whether the intent was accomplished. In other words, did you do the intended job? You must show that the intended learning outcome has taken place. You are being held accountable for students' acquisition of the desired learning as stated in the objectives.

APPLY AND REFLECT 3.4

Do you think teachers should be held accountable for the progress of their students? Why or why not? Should teacher salary increases or merit pay be related to student test scores?

Figure 3.2
A Three-Stage
Accountability Model

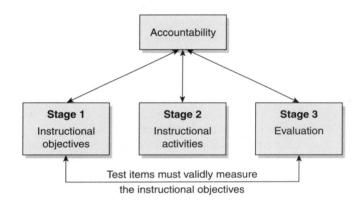

As shown in Figure 3.2, objectives drive the entire instructional process. Therefore, it is essential that objectives be clear and measurable because the evaluation will be determined by the objectives. That is, the evaluation must measure the outcome that is specified in the objective. The following examples illustrate incorrect and correct evaluation of intended learning outcomes.

Objective: The student will use geometric formulas.

Wrong Evaluation: Derive geometric formulas.

Better Evaluation: Please find the area and volume.

Objective: The student will swim 100 yards in boiling oil.

Wrong Evaluation: Explain the theory and philosophy of oil swimming.

Better Evaluation: Please swim.

Note that the first objective calls not for being able to derive geometric formulas but for using them. Likewise, the second objective does not require that students explain the theory and philosophy of oil swimming but, rather, that they actually swim. Obviously, your evaluation must assess what was specifically stated in your objectives. These specifics were the learning intent.

Instructional intent can be stated at varying levels of specificity. At the general level, statements of instructional intent are presentations of the broad goals of instruction. At the more specific level, instructional intent tells what students will be able to do following instruction. When writing instructional intent, you begin by identifying your goals at a broad level and follow these with the more specific objectives. Thus, movement is from a general frame of reference to a more specific frame. Let's now look at this deductive process in greater detail.

ON YOUR OWN 3.2 **Public View of Education**

Log on to the Web-based student study site at http://www.sagepub.com/eis2study. Review the public surveys relative to Chapter 3 and react to the related activities.

Objective Specificity

There is a difference in the level of specificity at which instructional intent should be written. Whereas **goals** are usually broad statements used to describe the purposes of schooling or the purposes of a course, objectives are narrower statements of the intended learning of a unit or specific lesson. A nomenclature that makes a distinction between goals and objectives has been developed; however, there is little agreement about terminology. The terms *educational aims, educational goals,* and *general objectives* are often used to denote broad instructional intent, whereas the terms *performance objectives, informational objectives, behavioral objectives,* and *instructional objectives* are often used to denote the more specific instructional intent.

This text will address three levels of specificity: educational goals, informational objectives, and instructional objectives. Educational goals and the more specific instructional objectives can be thought of as forming a continuum from general to specific, with goals being written for a school course or unit, followed by (in descending order) informational and instructional objectives written for specific lessons and exercises. Examples of these three levels of specificity are shown in Table 3.1. Note that the level of specificity increases as you move down through the examples, with the informational objective being subordinate to the educational goal and the instructional objective being subordinate to the informational objective.

Educational goals are broad and may take an extended period of time to be accomplished. Note how the goal in Table 3.1 is the actual intent of the course: It is what the teacher wishes to accomplish in the broadest sense—in this case, computer literacy. The informational and instructional objectives, then, support the educational goal. They tell what the student will do to show that they are computer literate. Following are other examples of educational goals:

1. The students will develop a command of Standard English.
2. The students will expand their leisure activities.
3. The students will develop good ethical character.
4. The students will formulate an appreciation for all people.
5. The students will develop good health habits.

Note that these statements are so general that they appear to give us little help in instruction. Yet, on closer examination, they do give us general direction and, therefore, represent the first step in deciding what to teach. They set the general direction we wish to go with our instruction. To this end, educational goals are usually concerned with covert (nonobservable), internal changes, which are less clearly measurable than are the behaviors associated with the more specific objectives. Some handy verbs that should prove helpful in writing educational goals are listed in Table 3.2. Notice that many of the verbs used in writing educational goals are rather vague and open to interpretation. They lack the specification of exactly what, in observable terms, the student is to do to show that the intended learning has taken place. Complete Expansion Activity 3.1: Educational Goals, which will let you explore goals for your expected grade level or content area.

TABLE 3.1   Examples of Educational Goal and Objective Specificity

Type	Example
Educational goal	The student will develop computer literacy.
Informational objectives	The student will be able to use a word-processing software program.
Instructional objective	Given a set of specific requirements, the student will be able to use a word-processing program to write a one-page paper with no errors.

EXPANSION ACTIVITY 3.1   Educational Goals

Educational goals give direction to our instructional intent. Research the national, state, and district goals of the grade level or content area you expect to teach. What are some of the broad goals for instruction for the grade or content subject you expect to teach? List them.

TABLE 3.2   Some Illustrative Verbs for Writing Goals

A apply appreciate	E enjoy	L like
B believe	F familiarize fully appreciate	R realize recognize
C comprehend cope	G grasp	T think
D demonstrate develop	I imagine	U understand
	K know	V value

Our next step in the planning process is to decide the specifics related to our goals. That is, we must now decide more precisely what students should know and, consequently, do to demonstrate that they have accomplished these goals. These decisions are stated in our more specific objectives: informational and instructional.

APPLY AND REFLECT 3.5

Educational goals should be written to set the framework for writing the more specific instructional intent. What sources and guides should be used to establish your goals?

REFLECTIONS ON TEACHER PRACTICE 3.1   Setting Goals

1. Why is it sound practice to ask students to set realistic goals? To ask teachers to set goals?

2. How does the setting of goals motivate students?

◆ ◆ ◆

Students need to learn to set realistic goals. When I talk about setting goals with my students, I talk about the value of setting goals. Setting goals gives you control over your life. Many of my at-risk students have few or no goals. To be honest, most haven't even thought much about the future. They have some vague sense that they'll work at something, or they'll play pro basketball in the NBA or something. They just drift through life, day after day letting others make goals for them. When they realize that by making their own goals they can take charge of their lives, they are more open to the topic of goal setting.

First, goals need to be realistic. They have to be doable. In order to be able to set realistic goals, my students need to know themselves. What strengths do they have? What weaknesses do they have? What do they like doing? What do they hate doing? Are they people smart, self-smart, body-smart, word-smart, number-smart, music-smart, nature-smart, or spatial-smart? There's no point in wanting to play basketball at the NBA level if you're not

body-smart. There's no point in getting a job that involves heavy duty number crunching if you aren't number smart. How do students discover their "smarts"? I have them complete a questionnaire based on Gardner's Multiple Intelligences. There are many versions of the test available. Once they determine their strengths, they can set more realistic goals.

One more thing. It's important for students to set short-term, medium-term, and long-term goals. By setting and meeting short-term goals, my at-risk students quickly come to realize that they have some choice in their lives and that motivates them to take more ownership of their lives. Setting medium- and long-term goals helps them see that they can have a say in what happens in the future. Perhaps more importantly, they see they have a future.

—*Special at-risk teacher*

SOURCE: http://www.teachersatrisk.com/category/goals/. Reprinted with permission.

ON YOUR OWN 3.3   **Reflections on Teacher Practice**

Read and reflect on the viewpoints expressed in Setting Goals. Log on to the Web-based student study site at http://www.sagepub.com/eis2study and react to the related activities.

Stating Objectives

The primary purpose of school is to cause students to learn. Thus, as a result of your instruction, there should be a change in state within your students. This change in state must be overt (observable), with students acting differently than they did before being involved in the learning process.

Objectives must lay out everything you intend but must not imply things you do not want to say. Consequently, informational and instructional objectives must be unambiguous as well as being testable and measurable. Table 3.3 suggests some verbs that are appropriate for informational and instructional objectives. Note the difference in clarity of language between the verbs listed in Tables 3.2 and 3.3.

TABLE 3.3	Illustrative Verbs for Writing Informational and Instructional Objectives	
A	**E**	**P**
add	evaluate	pick
adjust	explain	plan
analyze		point
appraise	**G**	pronounce
arrange	graph	
assess		**Q**
	I	question
B	identify	
build	infer	**R**
	inspect	read
C		recite
calculate	**J**	run
chart	judge	
choose	justify	**S**
circle		select
cite	**L**	sing
classify	label	sort
compare	list	state
construct	locate	support
contrast		
critique	**M**	**U**
	make	underline
D	manage	use
define	measure	
describe		**V**
diagnose	**N**	validate
draw	name	
		W
	O	write
	operate	
	order	
	organize	

Elements of Instructional Objectives

Instructional objectives precisely communicate learning intent. Mager (1997) outlines three components to instructional intent: behavior, conditions, and criterion. This book, however, recommends that an expression of instructional intent comprise these four elements:

1. Spell out the terminal behavior, or *performance,* that details the actions that will be accepted as evidence that the intent has been achieved.

2. Specify the *product* or what is to be produced by the student actions.

3. Describe the *conditions* under which the student action is to be expected.

4. State the *criteria* of acceptable performance; you are describing how well you want the students to perform.

At times, not all of these elements are necessary. The object is to clearly communicate your intent. Thus, sometimes informational objectives (addressed later in this chapter) will suffice, and sometimes not.

A well-written objective clearly defines the mastery level. How well students achieve this level tells the teacher whether the instructional plan has been successful.

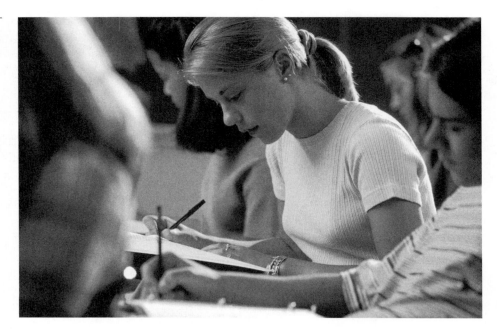

Element One: The Performance

The first element of an instructional objective is the specification of what students are expected to do after they receive instruction. This action is clarified in your selection of a word, usually a verb that indicates what students are to do or produce. Because the purpose of instruction is to elicit a predetermined action, instructional objectives should always be written in terms of observable student performance. Special care must be taken in selecting the proper verb, so that you achieve clarity of language with no ambiguity in meaning. You, your interested colleagues, and your principal must interpret the same meaning from each verb used in your objectives. Subjective terms, such as *know, realize,* and *understand,* should not be used as performance verbs in writing your objectives. These terms are open to interpretation and have different meanings to different individuals. In a word, you should use terms that denote observable (overt) actions or behaviors. Verbs—for example, *list, name, state, bisect,* and *graph*—prompt observable behaviors that, in turn, will help you evaluate your instructional intent. The action associated with the selected verb should describe an anticipated measurable performance that will demonstrate the student has acquired the knowledge, skills, or values related to the overall goal of the lesson. It allows you to be able to see, hear, or examine a student's action or work project. Review Table 3.3 for further examples of appropriate verbs for writing instructional objectives.

Element Two: The Product

The second element of an instructional objective is to specify what is to be the result of the students' performance. It is this product of students' actions that you will evaluate in determining whether the objective has been mastered. This product can be a written sentence, a written sum, listed names, a demonstrated skill, or a constructed object. Students, for example, could be asked to produce a 300-word essay, a list of nouns, an analysis of the characters in a play, or the solutions to a set of basic addition facts.

The product is the outcome that you've planned to result from the instructional process. In other words, it is what you want students to be able to do after your instruction that they (supposedly) couldn't do prior to instruction.

Element Three: The Conditions

The third element in the statement of an instructional objective is to establish the conditions under which the learner is to perform the prescribed action. Conditional elements can refer to the materials, information, or special equipment that will or will not be available to students; any special restrictions as to time and space; and any other applicable requirements. Consider this example: "Given the formula, the student will be able to calculate the attractive force between two masses." This objective tells students that they need not memorize the formula—that they will be given the formula and they should simply know how to use it. Note the use of "Given the formula" for the conditional statement. Terms and phrases such as "Given" or "With (Without) the aid of" are commonly used in conditional statements.

Conditions must be realistic and clearly communicate expectations to students. They should make your desires more explicit. Following are other examples of conditions that might be included in an instructional objective:

Given a list of verbs . . .

After reading Chapter 10 . . .

Using class notes . . .

With a ruler, protractor, and compass . . .

Within a 10-minute time interval and from memory . . .

On an essay test . . .

Given the necessary materials . . .

During a 5-minute interval . . .

From a list of compound sentences . . .

Without the aid of references . . .

These are a few examples of how conditions can be included as elements in instructional objectives. Essentially, you should attempt to visualize under what conditions you want students to show mastery and prescribe these conditions in your objectives. As shown in the examples, conditions are usually written as the first component in the objective, but their placement can be anywhere in the objective. For example, the objective "The student will identify, on a multiple-choice test, Newton's laws of motion with 100% accuracy" has the conditional component (on a multiple-choice test) toward the middle of the objective.

Element Four: The Criterion

The fourth, and last, element of an instructional objective is the level of acceptable student performance. This is where you state the lowest level of performance that you will accept as showing mastery. It is the product evaluation. This evaluation can be established in terms of time limits, percentage of correct answers, minimum number of correct answers, ratios of correct to incorrect responses permitted, an acceptable tolerance, and other observable operations. For example, it may be measured by rubric scoring, the percentage of correct items on a test/quiz, check sheets, score on homework assignments, score on a paper or project, and so on. This standard, or criterion, should be stated clearly so that students know in advance exactly what the standards are by which their performance will be judged. In other words, criterion levels should be stated as in the following specific examples:

. . . at least three reasons . . .

. . . 9 of the 10 cases . . .

. . . with no spelling errors.

. . . with 80% accuracy.

. . . 90% of the 20 problems.

. . . within plus or minus 10%.

. . . to the nearest hundredth.

. . . correct to the nearest percent.

. . . within 10 minutes.

. . . in less than 5 minutes.

. . . at least two problems within a 5-minute period.

. . . within 20 minutes with 80% accuracy.

Each of these criterion levels represents well-defined standards toward which students can strive. Usually, such standards are selected rather arbitrarily on the basis of past experiences and class expectations.

Carefully defined levels of desired performance are essential for effective instruction. You should take care, however, not to set standards that are too high. You should also guard against watering down your expectations. You should know your students so you can set reasonable levels of performance.

Now that you know the four elements of an instructional objective, you are ready to differentiate between informational and instructional objectives.

Informational Objectives

Frequently, you will want 100% of the class to attain 100% of the objective—that is, 100% mastery. Furthermore, objectives often have no special conditions. In these cases, informational objectives usually meet your instructional needs.

Informational objectives are abbreviated instructional objectives. Whereas instructional objectives contain the four elements noted earlier, informational objectives specify only the student performance and the product. Consider, for example, the following instructional and informational objectives written for the same instructional intent.

Instructional Objective: Given the voltage and resistance, the student will be able to calculate the current in a series and parallel circuit with 100% accuracy.

Informational Objective: The student will be able to compute the current in a series or parallel circuit.

Notice that the informational objective is an abbreviation of the instructional objective in that it omits the conditions ("given the voltage and resistance") and the criterion for judging minimum mastery ("100% accuracy"). The informational objective contains only the performance ("to calculate") and the product ("the current in a series or parallel circuit"). Frequently, the conditions are such that they are understood. In the cited example of an informational objective, it is understood that the necessary information must be provided to calculate the current. Moreover, it should be understood that only 100% accuracy would be desired.

Informational objectives are often adequate when you share your instructional intent with students. If you feel more information is needed to communicate the exact intent, however, you should write instructional objectives, or perhaps informational objectives with the conditions or the criterion added. Let's now look at the communication of objectives.

APPLY AND REFLECT 3.6	Objectives are generally used as an aid in designing evaluation procedures. Some teachers, however, feel this process should be reversed. Which order do you think is the most educationally sound? Why? Which order do you prefer? Why?

REFLECTIONS ON TEACHER PRACTICE 3.2 | Establishing Objectives

1. What advantages do you see in having students involved in determining educational intent?

2. What impact will student attitudes have on the desire to learn?

◆ ◆ ◆

My fifth-grade class goes to a physical education teacher once a week. The physical education teacher was complaining about the performance of my students during their once-a-week physical education class. My first response was, "What do you expect me to do?" Yet, I began noticing student attitudes toward their physical education class were very negative and getting progressively worse. Some were bringing notes from home asking that they be excused from physical education for various reasons. The physical education teacher indicated he would give students an unacceptable grade if they had any further notes from home.

I decided to schedule additional physical education time into our daily schedule in an effort to find out what was going on. I perceived that my students needed to somehow develop a deeper appreciation for physical activity so I decided to take them out to play kick ball and see for myself what was going on. I selected kick ball because it is the simplest, physical game I know. It has simple rules, requires little or no setup time, and the only materials I needed was a ball for them to kick and bases. I required everyone to participate while I observed.

On our first day of kick ball, there was much arguing, intentional cheating by some, disgruntled players, reluctant/discouraged players, and a few (two or three) eager students. The attitudes were awful! Even the eager students had no sense of fair play or team spirit. Some of the students were unable to kick the ball without falling down. Several couldn't run. I mean they really didn't know how to run or even where to run. Some didn't know the correct base order to tag bases. Two students didn't speak English. Furthermore, name calling and negative remarks were

the general basis for communication. Indeed, the frustration level for the group was extremely high. Obviously, they were finding very little satisfaction from their learning time. Of course the big question was, "Are they learning anything?" I certainly learned a lot from them. First, I learned that when students do not have explicit objectives for their activities, they tend to devise their own. I asked my group what our objectives should be to justify our time outside each day. Each of them had different ideas about the goals and objectives of physical education time. No wonder they seemed to be going in 20 different directions.

With the help of my class, we made a list of objectives that would address our immediate needs in an effort to focus the group. We made a list of skills needed to be successful at kick ball. The list of objectives gave the group a focus and gave me a tool for evaluation of each student's progress. Students began to focus less on winning and losing and more on skills needed for the game to run smoothly. Certainly, there is nothing wrong with focusing on winning as long as prerequisite skills are not neglected.

The result of having specific objectives focused everyone and the assessment was built into the accomplishment of the objectives. The results were astounding! I've never been more pleased with my work. First, I learned that many of my students honestly didn't know how to run. I guess I thought that was something that just came naturally to children. I learned many of my students rarely played outside. As a result of this, I began communicating more with parents to find out more about my students. My teaching became more personable and I began to realize the connection

(Continued)

(Continued)

between what my students could learn and what was going on in their personal lives. I watched each student become more and more proficient with the physical skills needed for their physical education class. Their attitudes about themselves and each other improved dramatically. Many students expressed pride in their accomplishments and began to talk about how they now liked physical education. Getting to know my students on a personal level along with the use of specific, obtainable objectives made a huge difference.

—*SUSAN MOORE, 5th grade, Pike Elementary School, Fort Smith, AR*

SOURCE: Courtesy of Susan Moore, Van Buren, AR. Used with permission.

ON YOUR OWN 3.4   Reflections on Teacher Practice

Read and reflect on the viewpoints expressed in Establishing Objectives. Log on to the Web-based student study site at http://www.sagepub.com/eis2study and react to the related activities.

Communication of Objectives

As noted earlier in the chapter, you should spell out objectives for students if you are to get maximum value from the objectives. This communication is usually presented at the beginning of a unit of study in written form. One useful format that is recommended for stating multiple objectives is to use an introductory statement to communicate common needed conditions and/or a criterion level. The remainder of each individual objective is then listed with the performance verb, the product, and additional desired conditions—for example, upon completion of "The Earth in the Universe" unit, you should be able, on an end-of-unit exam, to perform the following with 70% proficiency:

1. Identify the various stars discussed in class.

2. Use constellations to locate stars.

3. Identify three current ideas about how the universe originated and developed.

4. Describe nebulas, where they occur, and how they may form.

5. Find latitude and longitude of places from globes or maps, and locate places on globes or maps from latitude and longitude.

6. Name the planets in their order from the sun.

7. Identify some of the physical characteristics of each of the planets.

8. Describe the actual and relative sizes of the Earth and its moon, as well as the paths they follow around the sun.

The exact format used in communicating objectives is not critical, but they should be spelled out in precise terms. You should tailor your communication of objectives to the specific needs of your students. With younger children, you usually want to communicate your intent orally.

This concludes our formal discussion of goals and objectives. Table 3.4 summarizes the key concepts covered to this point. Review the summary and complete Review and Reflective Exercise 3.1, which will check your understanding of goals and objectives.

TABLE 3.4   Instructional Intent

Concept	Description
Educational goal	Broad statement of instructional intent used to describe general purpose of instruction.
Instructional objective	A narrow four-component statement of learning intent. The components include the performance, a product, the conditions, and the criterion.
Informational objective	Abbreviation of the instructional objective with only the performance product specified.

REVIEW AND REFLECTIVE EXERCISE 3.1   Define an instructional objective and write different kinds of objectives.

REVIEW

- What expectations should we have for students?
- What is an objective?
- Differentiate between an educational goal and an instructional objective.
- What are the components (elements) of a well-written instructional objective?

REFLECTION

- What goals should be generic to all students and schools? Should goals be different for different students? Should goals be different for elementary and secondary schools?
- How important are instructional objectives? Should teachers be required to submit weekly objectives?
- When writing objectives, do you really need all four elements? Which would you eliminate?
- How will you communicate your objectives to students?

Taxonomies of Objectives

Objectives can be classified into three primary categories on the basis of their instructional focus: thinking, attitudes, and physical skills. These areas of focus represent the three domains of learning: cognitive, affective, and psychomotor. In reality, however, the domains do not occur in isolation. Whereas some behaviors are easily classifiable into one of the three domains, others will overlap a great deal. This overlap is diagrammed in Figure 3.3. A good example of this overlap is seen when students are required to complete an assignment that involves a written response. In so doing, they must recall information and think (cognitive), they will have some emotional response to the task (affective), and they must use fine motor skills to make the necessary writing movements (psychomotor).

The three domains for objectives were designed to form hierarchical taxonomies of student learning—from simple to complex—with each level making use of and building on the behaviors addressed in the preceding level. The levels do not imply, however, that behaviors must be mastered sequentially from the lowest level to the highest level. Indeed, instruction can be directed toward any level of complexity.

Don't write objectives at specific taxonomy levels just to have objectives at all levels. Although it is possible to write objectives at any of the taxonomy levels of the three domains of learning, Mager (1997) suggests that, once you have made a suitable analysis of your instructional intent, you will know what you want your students to learn and you will automatically write your objectives at the intended

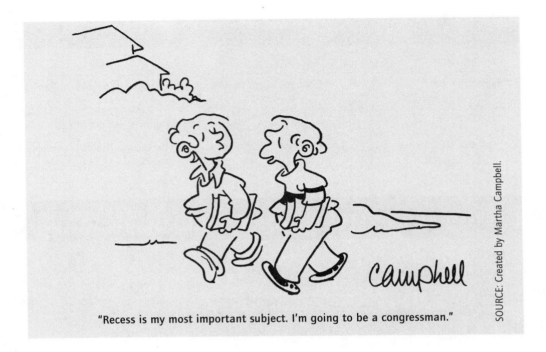

"Recess is my most important subject. I'm going to be a congressman."

SOURCE: Created by Martha Campbell.

levels. Furthermore, you must guard against falling into the habit of writing objectives only for the lower levels of learning within a particular domain because writing higher level learning objectives is more difficult. A working knowledge of the taxonomy of the domains can prevent this pitfall to some extent. In other words, you can use your knowledge of the taxonomies to formulate the best possible objectives for your teaching intent, to not write objectives at a particular level, and to ensure that your teaching is not focused totally on the lower levels.

Although an overview of the three domains of learning and the associated major categories of each taxonomy follows, a more detailed description of the domains can be found by referring to one of the objective references. The information presented about cognitive taxonomy levels is adapted from the work of Bloom, Engelhart, Furst, Hill, and Krathwohl (1956); the material on affective taxonomy levels, from the work of Krathwohl, Bloom, and Masia (1964); and the coverage of the psychomotor taxonomy, from the works of Harrow (1972) and Jewett and Mullan (1977).

Cognitive Domain

Objectives in the **cognitive domain** are concerned with the thinking and reasoning ability of students. Because the ability to think can range from simple recall of information to more complex thinking behaviors, Benjamin Bloom and his associates (1956) developed a hierarchical classification system, or taxonomy, to help teachers gain a better perspective on the behaviors to be emphasized in instructional planning.

Bloom's Taxonomy classifies cognitive ability into six categories, ranging from the fairly simple recall of information to the complex assimilation of information and evaluation. These categories, along with verbs commonly used to express the required behaviors, are listed in Table 3.5. Let's now briefly examine the six levels of Bloom's Taxonomy.

Level One: Knowledge

The term *knowledge* learning refers to the simple recall or recognition of previously learned materials. This may involve the recall of terminology, basic principles, generalizations, and specific facts such as

Figure 3.3
The Three Domains

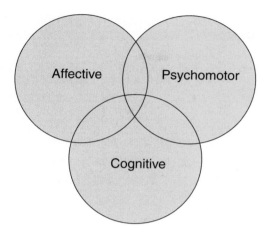

dates, events, persons, and places. For the most part, no manipulation or interpretation of the learned material is required of students. The information is usually retrieved in the same form that it was stored. Students, for example, could be required to remember the names of major scientists, to memorize a poem, to recognize chemical symbols, or to recall basic mathematics facts.

Knowledge-level objectives usually focus on the storage and retrieval of information in memory. In other words, the thinking ability required is in tapping the appropriate signals, cues, and clues to find and retrieve knowledge from memory. In a sense, the knowledge-level category lays a foundation for the higher thinking ability categories in that it provides the basic information needed for thinking at the higher levels. At times, however, teachers overuse the knowledge category. An example of an informational knowledge-level objective follows:

The student will be able to identify the major characters in an assigned short story.

Level Two: Comprehension

Comprehension represents the first level of understanding. The handling of information extends beyond the memorization of previously learned material to changing its form or making simple interpretations. Comprehension activities could require that students translate material to new forms, explain and summarize material, or estimate future trends. For example, you could ask students to interpret given information, translate information from one medium to another, or simply describe something in their own words. An example of an informational comprehension level objective follows:

Given a graph of economic data, the student will be able to interpret the information in his or her own words.

Level Three: Application

Application entails putting learned information to use in reaching a solution or accomplishing a task. Students are asked to use remembered principles or generalizations to solve concrete problems. The process may require the application of rules, general ideas, concepts, laws, principles, or theories. For example, students apply the rules of grammar when writing a term paper, or they apply geometrical theorems when solving geometry problems. To be categorized as an application activity, a problem must be unique—that is, it must not be one that was addressed in class or in the textbook. An example of an instructional application-level objective follows:

Given a simple sentence, the student will be able to determine its noun and verb.

TABLE 3.5	Bloom's Taxonomy and Illustrative Action Verbs
Level	**Student Action**
Knowledge	Identify, define, list, match, state, name, label, describe, select
Comprehension	Translate, convert, generalize, paraphrase, rewrite, summarize, distinguish, infer, alter, explain
Application	Use, operate, produce, change, solve, show, compute, prepare, determine
Analysis	Discriminate, select, distinguish, separate, subdivide, identify, break down, analyze, compare
Synthesis	Design, plan, compile, compose, organize, conclude, arrange, construct, devise
Evaluation	Appraise, compare, justify, criticize, explain, interpret, conclude, summarize, evaluate

Level Four: Analysis

Analysis can be defined as breaking down complex material into its component parts so it can be better explained. This may involve subdividing something to explain how it works, analyzing the relationships between parts, or recognizing motives or organizational structures. A science teacher, for example, might ask how the circulatory system works, a second-grade teacher might ask for ideas on how to use a word in a sentence, or a social studies teacher might ask for a description of the national attitude toward the environment. An example of an informational analysis-level objective follows:

> Given a chemical compound, the student will be able to correctly break it down into its simplest elements.

Level Five: Synthesis

Synthesis occurs when components are combined to form a new whole. With synthesis, a new and unique form must be produced from available elements. This may involve the creation of a unique composition, communication, plan, proposal, or scheme for classifying information. The unique creation may be in verbal or physical form. Students, for example, could be asked to use the British and American forms of government to create a completely unique governmental system. The key to synthesis-level activities is the incorporation of known ideas to form unique patterns or to create new ideas. A possible instructional synthesis level objective follows:

> Given a societal problem, the student will be able to propose at least two possible solutions to the problem.

Level Six: Evaluation

Evaluation means that a judgment is required as to the value of materials or ideas. Students are required to make quantitative and qualitative judgments on the extent to which an internal or external criterion is satisfied. To accomplish this end, students must (a) set up or be given appropriate criteria or standards and (b) determine to what extent an idea or object meets the standards. For example, students could be asked to decide who was the greatest president, or they could be asked to determine the best source of energy for the United States. Indeed, most questions that ask students to decide the best/worst or identify the least/most important require thinking and reasoning at the evaluation level. An example of an informational evaluation-level objective follows:

Given a video of a tennis match, the students will rate the match in terms of the tennis tactics and skill outlined in class.

The advantage of the Bloom Taxonomy is its utility in different subjects. The body of work by Orlich et al. (1990); Arons (1988); Haller, Child, and Walberg (1988); Wittrock (1986); Nickerson (1985); and Beyer (1984), however, has led to a novel interpretation of how the cognitive taxonomy may operate. Instead of the six major categories viewed as a ladder (Figure 3.4) that must be climbed one level at a time, a three-dimensional model (Figure 3.5) can be offered. This model is analogous to an apple. The outward peel represents knowledge, the first level. The meat of the apple is analogous to the comprehension (understanding) level, and the higher levels of thinking represent the core of all understanding. This model views the cognitive categories as interactive, with the comprehension level being the key to unlocking the other levels. That is, once you truly understand the knowledge, then you can branch into any of the remaining four categories—application, analysis, synthesis, or evaluation. There is no need for one to move through the categories one step at a time. Students can move from comprehension to evaluation, from comprehension to analysis thinking, from comprehension to synthesis, or from comprehension to application.

Bloom's cognitive taxonomy was recently revised to make it more relevant for today's students and teachers (Anderson & Krathwohl, 2001). Lorin Anderson, a former student of Bloom, led a group of educators in revision of Bloom's Taxonomy to make the taxonomy more consistent with the present theories on levels of thinking. Basically, the revision changed the six major categories from noun to verb form and changed the structure of the taxonomy with the addition of a knowledge product dimension. Several excellent sources are available that detail the revisions and reasons for the changes. The revised categories, along with student actions associated with each category, are presented in Table 3.6. Some educators suggest the revised taxonomy provide a better tool for alignment between standards and educational goals, objectives, products, and activities.

Figure 3.4
Traditional Model of Cognitive Taxonomy as a Ladder

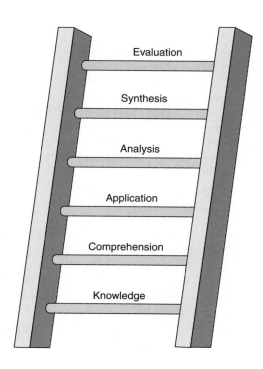

Figure 3.5
Three-Dimensional
Model of the
Cognitive Taxonomy

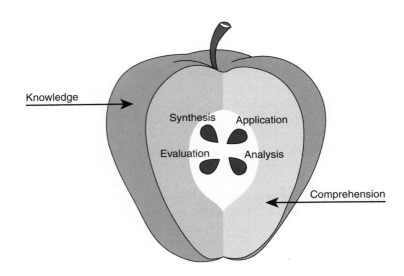

Affective Domain

Objectives in the **affective domain** are concerned with the development of students' attitudes, feelings, and emotions. They can vary according to the degree of internalization of the attitude, feeling, or emotion.

Clearly, because teachers must be concerned with the total development of students, not just development in the cognitive domain, the writing of objectives for the affective domain should be an integral part of the planning process. Yet, because of the difficulty of writing objectives for the affective domain, this has not been the case. Affective domain objectives are difficult to write because attitudes, feelings, and emotions are hard to translate into overt, observable behaviors. For example, the affective objective "The student will value the need for rules" is not properly written. The behavior "value" is not observable or measurable. The verb *value* must be replaced with an action that shows observable behavior: "The student will support the school rules during class discussions on class rules." This objective would be one, and only one, of many possible indicators that the student "values" the need for rules.

Behaviors related to the affective domain must take place in a "free-choice" situation if they are to give a true indication of student attitudes, likes and dislikes, and feelings. If not out of free choice, students may exhibit the desired behaviors for a reward or because they want to please you. For example, students who attend class every day may not be doing so because they like coming to your class or because they like the subject but because of the grade. But the objective "The student will eagerly participate in class discussions" would specify one possible indicator that the student likes the class.

Another free-choice technique sometimes used to reveal attitudes, feelings, emotions, and interests is the administration of various affective domain inventories. These instruments will be discussed at length in Chapter 9.

David Krathwohl and associates (1964) developed a classification system for categorizing affective responses into five levels, according to the degree of internalization. That is, it is organized as to the degree to which an attitude, feeling, value, or emotion has become part of the individual. The taxonomy levels and some illustrative verbs commonly used for revealing the extent of internalization are given in Table 3.7. In a sense, the taxonomy forms a hierarchical continuum of internalization—ranging from a person's merely passive awareness to an individual's being characterized by certain values and attitudes. Let's now take a brief look at the taxonomy levels.

TABLE 3.6	Revised Bloom's Taxonomy and Category Definitions
Level	**Student Action**
Remembering	Retrieve, recognize, and recall relevant knowledge
Understanding	Construct meaning from oral, written, and graphic messages through interpreting, exemplifying, classifying, summarizing, inferring, comparing, and explaining
Applying	Carry out or use a procedure through executing or implementing
Analyzing	Break material into constituent parts; determine how the parts relate to one another and to an overall structure or purpose through differentiating, organizing, and attributing
Evaluating	Make judgments based on criteria and standards through checking and critiquing
Creating	Put elements together to form a coherent or functional whole; reorganize elements into a new pattern or structure through generating, planning, or producing

Level One: Receiving

Receiving can be defined as being aware of and willing to attend freely to stimuli and messages in the environment (listen and look). All teachers want their students to listen to and be aware of classroom stimuli. At this level, students are attending to what the teacher is presenting, but the attention is not active involvement. An example of an informational receiving-level objective follows:

The student will follow given directions, without their needing to be repeated because of student inattentativeness.

Note that the student must be attentive and make a conscious effort to pay attention to the classroom environment rather than to other stimuli. The attention, however, can be rather passive.

Level Two: Responding

Responding requires active participation: A person is not only freely attending to stimuli but also voluntarily reacting to those stimuli. This involves physical, active behavior, where students make choices about issues. An example of an informational responding-level objective follows:

TABLE 3.7	Affective-Domain Taxonomy and Illustrative Action Verbs
Level	**Student Action**
Receiving	Follow, select, rely, choose, point to, ask, hold, give, locate, attend
Responding	Read, conform, help, answer, practice, present, report, greet, tell, perform, assist, recite
Valuing	Initiate, ask, invite, share, join, follow, propose, read, study, work, accept, do, argue
Organization	Defend, alter, integrate, synthesize, listen, influence, adhere, modify, relate, combine
Characterization by a value or value complex	Adhere, relate, act, serve, use, verify, question, confirm, propose, solve, influence, display

The student will willingly assist other students with their homework when they encounter problems.

At this level, students have developed an interest and make a choice to participate. Furthermore, they are satisfied with this participation.

Level Three: Valuing

Valuing refers to voluntarily giving worth to an idea, a phenomenon, or a stimulus. Behaviors at this level are selected even when there are alternatives. Students not only accept the worth of a value, but they also internalize that worth. An example of an instructional value-level objective follows:

When given alternatives, the student will share concerns about the need for clean air and water on at least two occasions.

Note that students are given alternatives and the opportunity to repeat the choice. Also notice that the choice must be made freely.

Level Four: Organization

The term *organization* refers to building an internally consistent value system. At this level, a set of criteria is established and applied in choice making. The individual takes on value positions and is willing to defend them. An example of an informational organization-level objective follows:

The student will voluntarily seek information related to career opportunities and will prepare for selected career goals.

Organization means one has made a commitment. In a sense, a "philosophy of life" has been internalized.

Level Five: Characterization by a Value or Value Complex

If behaviors reveal that an individual has developed a value system and acts consistently with the internalized values, then *characterization by a value* or *value complex* has been established. At this level, the person displays individuality and self-reliance. An example of an informational objective at the level of characterization by a value or value complex follows:

In a class discussion, the student will defend the rights of *all* individuals to express their ideas and opinions.

Demonstration of this behavior would reveal that an individual is acting consistently with an established value system.

Psychomotor Domain

Objectives in the **psychomotor domain** relate to the development of muscular abilities that range from simple reflex movement to precision and creativity in performing a skill. The psychomotor domain is especially relevant in physical education, music, drama, art, and vocational courses, but all subjects will relate to this domain to some degree.

Although the psychomotor domain was the last to have a taxonomy developed for it, several systems have now been developed. The four-level system presented here is based on and adapted from the work of Harrow (1972) and Jewett and Mullan (1977). As you read through the levels and illustrative verbs presented in Table 3.8, notice how the processes can be applied to such areas as physical education, music, art, and vocational education.

Level One: Fundamental Movement

Fundamental movements are those that form the basic building blocks for the higher level movements—for example, the ability to track objects, grasp objects, or crawl and walk. A sample informational objective for the fundamental-movement level follows:

> The student will be able to hold a tennis racket properly for the backhand.

Notice that this objective deals with the fundamental movement of the proper grasp of a tennis racket. Indeed, it is basic to the higher level tennis movements.

Level Two: Generic Movement

Generic movement refers to the ability to carry out the basic rudiments of a skill when given directions and under supervision. At this level, effective motor patterns, timing, and coordination are being developed and refined. Awareness of the body in motion and of the arrangement and use of the body parts is learned. The total act, however, is not performed with skill. An example of an instructional generic movement-level objective follows:

> Under supervision, the student will be able to perform a required musical score with no more than five errors.

This level of motor skill requires supervision in that it represents the initial learning of a series of movements.

Level Three: Ordinative Movement

Ordinative movement marks the competence in performing a skill ably and independently. The entire skill has been organized and can be performed in sequence. Conscious effort is no longer needed: The skill has been mastered, and there is precision of performance. At this level, the skill can be carried out

The development of motor skills is an essential part of the learning intent in many classrooms.

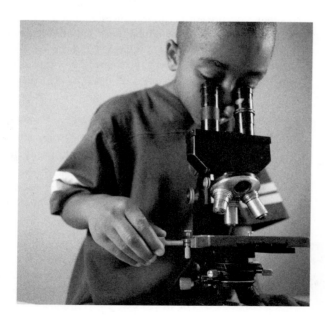

TABLE 3.8 Psychomotor Domain Taxonomy and Illustrative Action Verbs

Level	Student Action
Fundamental movement	Track, crawl, hear, react, move, grasp, walk, climb, jump, grip, stand, run
Generic movement	Drill, construct, dismantle, change, hop, clean, manipulate, follow, use, march
Ordinative movement	Play, connect, fasten, make, sketch, weigh, wrap, manipulate, play, swim, repair, write
Creative movement	Create, invent, construct, manipulate, play, build, pantomime, perform, make, compose

by habit under complex conditions. An example of an informational ordinative movement-level objective follows:

> Given a dive to perform, the student will be able to carry out the step-by-step technique without pausing to think.

Level Four: Creative Movement

Creative movement, which calls for the ability to produce and compose, serves the personal purposes of the performer. That is, the individual should be able to invent unique motor options, improvise originality into a movement, combine several movements into a personal unique motor design, or invent a new movement pattern. An example of an informational creative movement-level objective might be as follows:

> Given a dance routine, the student will be able to make appropriate changes to incorporate personal dance strengths.

Instruction and learning in the classroom frequently contain elements of all three domains. Nevertheless, your objectives usually will place primary emphasis on the cognitive, affective, or psychomotor domain. Furthermore, remember that the three domain taxonomies can be valuable tools for upgrading your writing of objectives. But don't become a slave to the taxonomies; instead, base your objectives on the needs of your class and use the taxonomies as a guide. Finally, strive to incorporate the higher levels of each taxonomy in your learning experiences. Before finishing this chapter, complete Web Link 3.2: Examples of Objectives to further refine your understanding of objectives.

WEB LINK 3.2   Examples of Objectives

Access the examples of instructional objectives and student activities on Internet URL sites www.adprima.com/examples.htm and http://adprima.com/usermenu.htm. Analyze the objectives. Are objectives written for all three domains? Are they clear? How could they be improved?

APPLY AND REFLECT 3.7

You should analyze your instructional intent prior to writing your objectives; then focus your objectives on the appropriate domain and taxonomy level. What domain and taxonomy levels will be emphasized in the area you expect to teach?

This concludes our discussion of the three learning domains and their respective taxonomies. Before leaving this chapter, however, let's look at using state content standards in writing objectives and the new backward design concept for identifying instructional intent. Many of the best teachers use the backward design.

Linking Standards and Objectives

Standards have become a common fixture in the education landscape. Under No Child Left Behind (NCLB), legislation has placed responsibility on states to implement accountability systems that are aligned with state standards. States must be able to accurately and efficiently measure whether students are meeting the standards, competencies, or benchmarks expected of them; diagnose problems; and offer immediate intervention. As a result, schools and teachers must translate state standards into effective instruction with a valid assessment process. This accountability system requires that schools and teachers align all components (state learning expectations, instruction, and assessment) into a verifiable teaching/learning system. Therefore, teachers must clearly link state expectations, classroom objectives, instruction, and assessment. One way to be sure these links have been established is to write a behavior content chart. This is simply a chart that shows how state learning expectations are aligned with a course objective(s) and assessments. A simple behavior content chart is shown in Figure 3.6.

For material related to this concept, go to Clip 3.2 on the Student Resource CD bound into the back of your textbook.

Figure 3.6
Simple Behavior Content Chart

Competency	Objective	Assessment
(Geography) Locate and identify on maps the continents of the world, the 50 states of the United States, and the major physical features of Texas.	1. After studying and discussing the world map, the student will know the names of the continents and their relative size, shape, and location with 100% accuracy.	Label correctly continents on blank world map.
	2. After reading and discussion, the student will locate and label major rivers and land regions of Texas with 100% accuracy.	Label major rivers and land regions on blank Texas map.
(Mathematics) Create charts, tables, and graphs and use statistics to summarize data, draw inferences, and make predictions.	1. After reading and discussing and examining a handout, students will compare precipitation in their own area with precipitation in other areas and show understanding by creating a bar graph with 85% accuracy.	Give students precipitation data and have them graph the data.

Backward Design Approach

The *backward design* approach to instruction offers an alternative view to the traditional way of determining intent (see Figure 2.3). The backward design begins with the end in mind, the enduring understandings that you want students to learn and apply. In other words, what knowledge is *worth* understanding? Examples of enduring understandings might include an understanding of community

Table 3.9	Objective Domains
Domain	**Description**
Cognitive	Category of learning that focuses on the ability to think and reason, consisting of six cognitive taxonomy levels: knowledge, comprehension, application, analysis, synthesis, and evaluation
Affective	Category of learning concerned with emotional development, encompassing five affective domain taxonomy levels: receiving, responding, valuing, organization, and characterization by a value or value complex
Psychomotor	Category of learning related to muscular and motor skill development, consisting of four psychomotor domain taxonomy levels: fundamental movement, generic movement, ordinative movement, and creative movement

helpers by kindergarteners, an understanding of the digestive system by 5th graders, an understanding of the role of technology in people's lives by 7th graders, and an understanding of proper writing techniques by 10th graders. District, state, and national standards are often used in establishing enduring understandings.

After establishing the enduring understandings, related essential questions are developed that cover the full range of the understandings. These questions should be geared to help students take an inquiry approach toward the various learning experiences that will be designed. Good essential questions should

- Be open-ended with no simple or single right answer.
- Be deliberately thought provoking, counterintuitive, and/or controversial.
- Require students to draw upon content knowledge and personal experience.
- Be framed to provoke and sustain student interest.
- Engage students in evolving dialogue and debate.
- Lead to other essential questions posed by students.

The essential questions should focus on the key knowledge and skills students should acquire.

Take a few minutes to complete Review and Reflective Exercise 3.2, which will check your understanding of the concepts presented in this section. Before doing so, however, review the concepts presented in Table 3.9.

REVIEW AND REFLECTIVE EXERCISE 3.2
Define a taxonomy and the three domains of learning.

REVIEW

- Name the three learning domains of objectives and the levels within each.

REFLECTION

- What learning domain will be the focus of most of your instruction?
- Do you think it is important to know the domains of learning and write objectives for each?

SUMMARY

The intent of teaching is learning.

Standards for Student Performance

- Public Law 94–142, IDEA, and Section 504 of the Vocational Rehabilitation Act focus on nondiscrimination against the disabled.
- Limited English proficiency (LEP) is a major problem in some parts of the country. In some schools, more than half the students have a first language other than English.
- Forty-nine states have adopted state-mandated testing.
- The No Child Left Behind Act was designed and enacted to help low-income and minority students perform at the same achievement level as their peers.

Rationale for Objectives

- Objectives specify your instructional intent to students. They specify what your students should be able to do following instruction. Objectives are finite and measurable.
- Objectives set the framework for your instructional approach and the evaluation of student learning. They serve an important communication function.
- Objectives also serve an accountability function.

Objective Specificity

- The specificity of instructional intent varies from broad educational goals to very narrow specific objectives.
- The three levels of learning intent, in order of specificity, are educational goals, informational objectives, and instructional objectives.

Stating Objectives

- The actions called for by educational goals are overt, nonmeasurable behaviors, whereas the actions called for by informational and instructional objectives are overt and measurable.
- Instructional objectives consist of four components: (1) the performance, (2) the product, (3) the conditions, and (4) the criterion.
- Informational objectives specify only the performance and the product; the conditions and criterion are usually not specified.

Communication of Objectives

- Objectives should always be communicated to students. This communication is usually in written form at the beginning of a unit of study.

Taxonomies of Objectives

- Objectives can be written at any of the levels within the three domains of learning: cognitive, affective, and psychomotor. Each domain is arranged in hierarchical order from simple to complex.

Linking Standards and Objectives

- States are required to establish accountability systems that align state learning expectation with student assessment.

Backward Design Approach

- The backward design approach to instructional planning offers an alternative view to the traditional way of determining intent. The backward design begins with the establishment of enduring understandings.

DISCUSSION QUESTIONS AND ACTIVITIES

1. **Analysis of textbook objectives.** Review the teacher's edition of a school textbook from the grade level and/or subject you expect to teach that lists the unit and/or chapter objectives. Address the following questions in your review.
   a. Are informational objectives given for the chapters? Are instructional objectives? Are the objectives the same for all students?
   b. Are objectives written for all three domains of learning?
   c. Are the objectives written at the different taxonomy levels within each of the learning domains?
2. **Writing goals and objectives.** Consider your planned teaching grade level and/or subject and write a broad educational goal that you feel should be addressed at the identified level. Now write at least three different informational and instructional objectives that tell what students should do to show you that the goal has been accomplished.
3. **Writing cognitive, affective, and psychomotor domain objectives.** Write 10 cognitive and psychomotor domain objectives for a topic from your area. Make the objectives at various taxonomy levels of sophistication. Now write five affective domain objectives at various taxonomy levels for the same class. Let your classmates review and critique your objectives.
4. **Backward design.** Write an enduring understanding for an area you expect to teach. Write guiding essential questions that cover the enduring understanding.

TECHNOLOGY AND EDUCATION

How have recent developments in technology affected planning instruction? Use one or more of the available search engines to conduct a search relative to this question. Does technology enhance the teacher's ability to plan instruction? To what technology should students have access? Do you have any educational concerns about the use of these technologies in schools?

DECONSTRUCTING THE STANDARDS

Chapter 3 content addresses topics related to INTASC Standards 1 and 7.

- INTASC Standard 1 states: *Knowledge of Subject Matter:* The teacher understands the central concepts, tools of inquiry, and structures of the subject being taught and can create learning experiences that make these aspects of subject matter meaningful for students.

♦ INTASC Standard 7 states: *Instructional Planning Skills:* The teacher plans instruction based on knowledge of subject matter, students, the community, and curriculum goals.

For each of these two standards, write your response to the following:

- Which part(s) of each standard does this chapter address?
- How does this chapter address this standard?
- How will the concepts in this chapter help you apply this standard as a teacher?

PRAXIS CONNECTION

Log on to the Web-based student study site at http://www.sagepub.com/eis2study. Access the Praxis II: Principles of Learning and Teaching assessments and/or state-related exams and complete the Chapter 3 test preparation exercises.

PORTFOLIO CONNECTION

Log on to the Web-based student study site at http://www.sagepub.com/eis2study. Access the Portfolio Connection. Complete the Chapter 3 portfolio link to INTASC activities.

CONNECTION WITH THE FIELD

1. **Teacher interviews.** Interview several teachers. Are they required to write objectives? Do they write the same objectives for all students or do they take into account the abilities of the students? Do they write objectives for all three learning domains? Do they write objectives at different levels within each domain? Do they use the backward design?

2. **Principals' view of objectives.** Interview two elementary and two secondary principals. What is their view of objectives? Are their views similar to that of the teachers? Are objectives a district requirement?

CHAPTER 4

Developing Unit and Daily Lesson Plans

The object of education is to prepare the young to educate themselves throughout their lives.

—ROBERT MAYNARD HUTCHINS

OVERVIEW

Why do teachers plan? This chapter will focus on this question and on techniques for effective planning. I will explore some of what is known about the processes of planning and decision making.

Because planning is essential to achieving excellence in instruction, the planning processes that result in the successful delivery of knowledge, attitudes, values, and skills will be explored. I will consider the different levels of planning, as well as personnel associated with the planning processes. Finally, this chapter will focus attention on the basic components of unit and daily lesson planning. This examination will include a rather detailed explanation of specific planning procedures and several different formats.

OBJECTIVES

After completing your study of Chapter 4, you should be able to do the following:

- Describe the four levels of planning.
- Identify and describe the key components of a unit and daily lesson plan.
- Differentiate between teacher-centered and student-centered instruction and name various methods associated with each.
- Explain the importance of daily lesson planning in the learning process.
- Operationally define set induction and lesson closure and explain their importance to effective teaching.
- Outline procedures for modifying lessons to accommodate special-needs and gifted and talented students.
- Operationally define instructional strategy and name its two components.

- Describe the four variables that should be considered in the selection of an appropriate instructional method.
- Develop a course plan and unit plan for a given area within your area of specialization.
- Develop daily lesson plans for a unit or series of units.

No two teachers teach in the same way; similarly, no two teachers plan in exactly the same way. Planning serves two practical functions: It allows you to anticipate instructional needs in advance so materials can be gathered and organized, and it provides a plan that directs classroom interactions. The excellent lesson delivery of effective teachers often appears spontaneous. These teachers, however, have planned—formally or informally—each daily lesson with care. They have the lesson content and the related teaching skills mastered to the extent that their delivery is poised and automatic.

Planning for instruction is one of the most important things a teacher or group of teachers can do. Even experienced teachers spend time planning. They replan the presentation of lessons they have taught many times to avoid becoming stale and routine.

Planning Instruction

As shown in Figure 4.1, teachers should engage in four levels of planning. Course and unit planning are broader in scope than weekly and daily planning. Course and unit plans determine the direction you will take and what the general impact of the entire curriculum will be.

No matter what the level of planning, decisions must be made with respect to the coordination of course content, instructional materials, and the special needs of students. Therefore, before I look at the levels of planning in greater detail, I will focus on state mandates, teacher-student planning, and the selection of instructional materials.

State Mandates

As the public and government have demanded increased accountability of how effectively schools are educating our nation's youth, state-mandated curriculum and assessment have taken on a more powerful role. As a result, efforts began to connect state-endorsed instructional outcomes to state-mandated assessment. Most states have now or are in the process of identifying outcomes that every student in the state is expected to meet. Some states label these outcomes standards; others call them essential skills; others call them competencies; still others label them benchmarks. Whatever term is used, these outcomes must be integrated into your planning and instruction. In many states, these outcomes will be reflected in achievement tests that are given to every student in the state. Some states also require students to pass exit or end-of-course exams covering state outcomes to receive a high school diploma. Complete Expansion Activity 4.1: State Mandates to explore accountability in your state.

| APPLY AND REFLECT 4.1 | Do you think we should have a national curriculum? A national assessment system? |

EXPANSION ACTIVITY 4.1   State Mandates

Revisit the state outcomes (standards, competencies, skills, or benchmarks) downloaded in Chapter 2. Investigate the outcome and assessment issues in your state. What are the expectations with regard to outcomes, assessment, and accountability for schools and teachers?

Over the past 20 years, national attention has focused on the establishment of national goals, a mandated curriculum, and national subject-matter examinations. However, so far, Congress has consistently resisted the establishment of national mandates, although the No Child Left Behind Act will create a national requirement that states test their students' achievement in key subject areas.

Instead of federally mandated standards, standards have been developed by discipline-specific national groups of scholars and educators. Many of these groups identify not just *what* students all over the United States should learn at each grade level but, in some cases, *how* students should be taught. For example, national standards have been established in such areas as science, mathematics, reading, and writing. Other national projects are under way in most subject matter areas, including geography, history, and the arts. Some states have found these standards to be useful as they developed or as they presently develop statewide curriculum guides and state-mandated tests.

Teacher-Student Planning

Students as well as teachers can be engaged in the planning process. The extent to which students participate in the planning of their own learning activities varies greatly from classroom to classroom. In many classrooms, the only involvement students have is the selection of class projects, reports, and outside readings. By engaging students, however, the teacher gains insights into student interests and areas of weakness and strength. A **teacher-student planning** process promotes "ownership" of the curriculum. If students communicate that they already understand intended instructional material, they could be tested on the material. If, in fact, they do have a good understanding of the material in question, then valuable time and resources could be reallocated to other areas. How many times has each of us studied the colonial period of American history but failed to spend any time on the period following World War II?

Figure 4.1
Levels of Planning

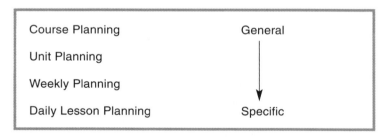

APPLY AND
REFLECT 4.2

Do you support teacher-student planning? How much student involvement in the planning process do you feel is feasible at the grade level you expect to teach?

Instructional Materials

Essential to effective planning are the survey and preparation of available media and materials for instruction. Textbooks, audiovisual materials, supplementary reading materials, and supplies and

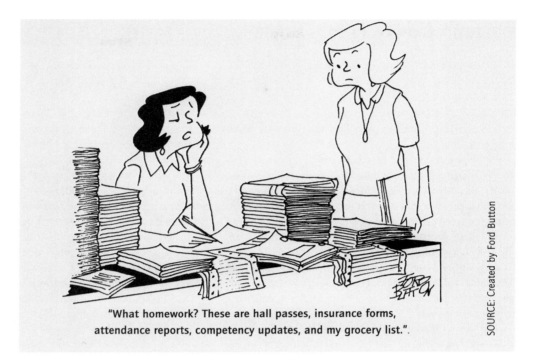

SOURCE: Created by Ford Button

"What homework? These are hall passes, insurance forms,
attendance reports, competency updates, and my grocery list.".

equipment for group and individual projects should be examined and coordinated with your lesson. Time spent on reviewing what is available in the district will be time well spent. You should preview films and computer software, review printed materials, and learn to use the latest instructional technology.

The incorporation of a wide variety of instructional materials will improve your lessons and heighten students' attention and interest. The use of videotapes, the Internet, and computer software in presenting examples and nonexamples of concepts, for instance, will serve as a lesson stimulus. I will address the effective use of various motivational techniques in Chapter 12.

Having looked at some of the general planning of instruction, it is time to look at the four planning levels in greater detail. However, before you do so, complete ■ Web Link 4.1: Classroom Resources.

WEB LINK 4.1 Classroom Resources

Access the classroom resources at www.teachertools.org/index.html. Review the available resources for appropriateness at the grade level you expect to teach. Select two resources that you think will be of most use for you. Write a short summary for each on how you would use the resource in your classroom. Share your summaries with your classmates.

ON YOUR OWN 4.1 View From the Classroom

Log on to the Web-based student study site at http://www.sagepub.com/eis2study. Review the Chapter 4 teacher surveys and react to the related activities.

REFLECTIONS ON TEACHER PRACTICE 4.1   Rethinking Unit Planning

1. How does unit planning result in more effective teaching?

2. Should students be given long-term class projects to complete or shorter projects? Why?

♦ ♦ ♦

I teach middle school and have been rethinking the whole way I do units.

In the past few years, I have been writing units that span nearly a full quarter. Each unit included many learning objectives, smaller assignments that helped students learn content along the way, and a large, final assessment at the end of the quarter. I have been pretty proud of my units because of the time and practice allotted to my students to master concepts before formal assessment. If you had asked me a month ago, I would have told you I would never teach another way. But the thing about teaching I have found is to never say never. Faced with only 5 weeks to complete my fairy tale unit, I had to revamp the unit to fit into the smaller space of time.

In 5 weeks, my students completed two projects. One was to work with a partner to identify five characteristics of fairy tales, develop a definition of a fairy tale, and present using PowerPoint.

While the results for some were poor (largely because of off task behavior), the overall motivation, attitude, and thoughtfulness of my students increased dramatically. No one was asking me "What PowerPoint presentation?" like other students had asked me "What magazine article?" in the previous unit. It seemed this project was more important to them.

The second project was to rewrite a fairy tale of the students' choice from the evil character's point of view. We read several examples, including *The True Story of the Three Little Pigs* by Jon Scieza and *Interview,* a poem by Sara Henderson Hay that presents Cinderella's stepmother's point of view. Students had 2 weeks to write, revise, and type their stories. As a bonus, we sent each student's story in to Barry Lane's writing contest for recycled fairy tales.

With this project, I had very little problem with students being off task at any point, and all but maybe five students turned their stories in on time. I have not begun to assess them, but after reading through several of the stories during the past week, I am

encouraged. I witnessed once again a positive attitude about the task, and students seemed very mindful of the scoring guide and task deadline.

With the results I have been getting, I have to pause to reflect upon why. Why are my students more focused? Why are they more likely to turn in their work? Why are they more interested and excited? I think the shorter project time has a lot to do with the results I am getting. Middle school students seem to be in a time vacuum; without the immediacy of a task deadline to guide them, I think they are more apt to procrastinate. Students live in the here and now, not in the hazy, distant end of the quarter.

I have decided this realization does not mean I have to give up my longer projects; to the contrary, I think as long as I create intermediate deadlines with tangible products that will be assessed along the way to the larger assessments at the end of the unit, I can create the same sense of urgency and importance as with these smaller units. It is a matter of breaking down the task into manageable parts.

A second reason I think the past two projects have been so successful is that I have made a conscious effort to start first with what my students need to know in a backward design sort of approach. I have tried to do this with my larger units, but using Grant Wiggins's process on a smaller task helped me understand the process a little better, producing better results in task design.

The recycled fairy tale task was designed in response to my students' struggle with point of view, both in class and on a variety of district and state assessments. It felt good to be responsive to my kids, to remember I am teaching kids, not curriculum.

Just when I think I have task design mastered, I find I have much left to learn.

—*ELLEN, middle school English/language arts teacher*

SOURCE: www.middleweb.com. Reprinted with permission.

ON YOUR OWN 4.2   Reflections on Teacher Practice

Read and reflect on viewpoints expressed in Rethinking Unit Planning. Log on to the Web-based student study site at http://www.sagepub.com/eis2study and react to the related activities.

Students can be directly involved in planning academic and nonacademic activities.

Course Planning

The most general type of planning you will perform as a classroom teacher is **course planning** (Posner & Rudnitsky, 2000). Although in most cases, the textbook forms the basic structure for course plans, it should not be the main premise of instruction. Beginning teachers should use state curriculum suggestions and their textbooks as instructional guides and should integrate supplementary material into the basic text structure. Experienced teachers, however, often structure their courses on the basis of experience and use state curriculum suggestions and the textbook to supplement their experience base. To further explore course planning, complete Expansion Activity 4.2: Course Planning.

Unit Planning

Courses are usually divided into a sequence of manageable units of study that represent discrete segments of the year's work. Each unit is organized around a specific theme or a cluster of related concepts. For example, a unit in earth science might be titled "Plants" or a unit in kindergarten might be titled "Community Helpers." Units provide a framework for the design of a course. In effect, a unit is a series of many intended learning activities and experiences, unified around the theme or a cluster of related concepts.

For material related to this concept, go to Clip 4.1 on the Student Resource CD bound into the back of your textbook.

Unit planning can be deemed more critical than other levels of planning. The **unit plan** links the goals, objectives, content, activities, and evaluation you have in mind. As noted earlier, you should align your objectives with state and national standards. These plans should be shared with students to provide the overall road map that explains where you are going. Such communication expresses to students what they are expected to learn.

The unit plan has several components. The plan is titled by the topic that represents the unifying theme for the unit. These topics may follow the chapter headings in your textbook or the areas within your subject that the various curriculum guides direct you to cover. These topics could be derived through teacher planning or through teacher-student planning. As discussed in Chapter 2, unit topics generally are taken from the headings of course plans. The plan should spell out your goals and specific instructional objectives. A somewhat detailed outline of the content should be included, as should learning activities appropriate to the content and to the learners. A list of needed instructional

---

EXPANSION ACTIVITY 4.2   Course Planning

Obtain the teacher's edition of a textbook for a subject that you hope to teach and the learning outcomes for that subject that you downloaded in Chapter 2. Using the textbook and the learning outcomes as guides, structure two different course plans for a year. Outline the content units to be taught and unit time allotments for each plan. Share your plans with classmates.

---

materials and resources should be provided. Finally, the methods you intend to use for evaluating student learning need to be specified and what constitutes acceptable evidence of mastery. In addition, you should indicate accommodations that will be made for exceptional students and a reflection section that should be completed after the lesson has been taught. More specifically, a well-constructed unit should include the following components:

1. *A topic:* presumably the subject suggested by a course outline, a textbook, or a state curriculum guide.

2. *Goals and objectives:* a list of your learning intentions in broad and specific terms.

3. *Content outline:* an outline of the material to be covered—with as much detail as you feel is needed—which should help clarify the subject and help you with the sequence and organization.

4. *Learning activities:* teacher and students activities—comprising introductory, developmental, and culminating activities—that, when arranged into a series of daily lessons, will lead to the desired learning outcomes.

5. *Resources and materials:* a list of materials to be selected and prepared for the unit.

6. *Evaluation:* an outline of your evaluation procedure—including homework, tests, and special projects—which should be planned and prepared prior to instruction.

7. *Accommodations:* the plans you have made to accommodate students who would have difficulty meeting your objectives or already can perform the lesson intent or know what the lesson teaches.

8. *Reflection:* a self-evaluation on the effectiveness of the lesson and needed changes if the lesson is to be taught again. This section is completed following execution of the lesson.

Units vary greatly in scope and duration, depending on the grade level and subject. Generally, they range in duration from a few days to a few weeks. Other examples of typical units are the court system in government, astronomy in the 10th grade, and geometry in the 5th grade.

A unit structure now being emphasized in many schools is the **thematic unit** (Roberts & Kellough, 2003), the organizational structure of interdisciplinary/curriculum-integrated teaching. Thematic units offer teaching teams a useful, logical, and flexible way to organize for interdisciplinary/cross-curricular teaching over a block of time. It is a curriculum plan that provides opportunities for more relevant, less fragmented, and more stimulating experiences for students. Thematic units may focus on a specific content area or they may be global in nature. For example, in language arts, the focus of a theme may be on realistic fiction, or it may center on a global topic such as conflict. The team plans so that insights and understandings from one discipline, such as science, relate to other disciplines, such as literature and social studies. The planning of thematic units requires the identification of a team of teachers and students and the model to be implemented (see Chapter 2);

the identification of a unit theme, including objectives, activities, and evaluative methods; and sufficient planning time made available for team teachers.

There are several sources available for assisting teachers with their unit plans. In some states, the curriculum is quite explicit, and the goals and topics that must be covered are mandated. When this is the case, the prescribed goals and topics are usually presented in terms of minimum requirements, so there is still plenty of justification for the careful planning of additional learning units. Even when a good deal of the course content has been predetermined, it is still necessary to plan the sequence, present the content, and test the outcomes. Many school districts also have a mandated curriculum that must be included in any course plan. These demands for covering specific content do not preclude the need for planning.

The course textbook offers clues for unit planning. Content must be selected and organized, however, with regard to your goals and learners. You must recognize that a particular author's view of sequence, for instance, may not serve your needs or the needs of your students. Textbooks are written for a wide audience and should be viewed as one of the tools for teaching a course, not as the course itself.

The information to be presented forms the bulk of a unit. This material should generally extend beyond the concept contained in the textbook and should be correlated with the unit objectives. Once you have determined the topics, sequence, and time for each topic, you must develop unit objectives that relate to the selected content. The goals should be your guide in determining unit objectives. You must then designate the specific student outcomes desired, as well as the level of behavioral complexity. Of course, keep in mind that the level of complexity sets the framework for your lesson activities and the evaluative process. Since Chapter 3 was devoted to the writing of goals and objectives, I will not discuss them further here.

Learning activities must then be identified that will support the unit. You need to choose the learning activities carefully to ensure that the objectives can be met. In addition, you should group your unit objectives and activities into daily lessons for implementation. Selecting of activities and groupings of your unit objectives and activities require you to decide how best to accomplish your planned goals. If you intend to illuminate the court system at work, you might plan a variety of activities, such as having students read about the court system in their textbooks, holding a mock trial, showing a film about a court case, or taking a trip to a nearby courtroom to observe a trial in session. Indeed,

" . . . and the reason we have summer vacation is so you can go home
to help with the crops."

SOURCE: Created by Ford Button.

EXPANSION ACTIVITY 4.3   Unit Planning

Obtain the teacher's edition of a textbook for a grade level and subject that you expect to teach. Using the textbook as a guide, outline two units you would teach and the unit time allotment for each unit. Write a rationale for each unit.

---

you might decide that a visit from a district attorney or a judge may be in order. These are all decisions you need to make early in the planning process to allow time for arranging these activities.

Always keep in mind that a unit consists of a series of daily lessons. The unit can be viewed as the whole, with the individual lessons as its parts. Thus, the individual lessons must be selected so they are interrelated and address the learner outcomes that are specified in the objectives of the unit as a whole.

Planning for instructional materials is an important part of the entire planning process. You need to familiarize yourself with the materials available in your school building and school district. You also need to investigate your community for possible sources of learning materials. A field trip to a courtroom may be problematic if the nearest court is several miles away and you have failed to contact the court or to arrange for permissions and transportation. Beginning teachers need to establish contact with experienced teachers in their building who are willing to share information with them about how to accomplish these kinds of tasks. As you plan for instructional materials, it is a good idea to keep a notebook or journal of available materials and resources.

Finally, how will you know if the students have learned what you intended in your carefully planned unit? The answer lies in carefully planning for evaluation. Will you give paper-and-pencil tests? If so, how often? Will student participation enter into the evaluation process, and how will you determine the value of each student's participation? These questions and others must be answered in the planning phase. The evaluation process will be addressed in detail in Chapters 9 and 10. Now complete Expansion Activity 4.3: Unit Planning, which will further develop your unit planning skills.

Weekly Plans

Most school districts ask that teachers submit a weekly lesson plan so that, in the event the teacher is absent, the substitute teacher has some idea of what was to be covered that day. A typical **weekly plan,** as shown in Figure 4.2, outlines each day's lesson for 1 week. These weekly lesson plans vary greatly in detail from school to school. They essentially are short, watered-down copies of the week's daily lesson plans, written on special forms provided by the school.

Daily Lesson Plans

The most detailed and specific type of plan is a **daily lesson plan,** which simply defines the objectives and class activities for a single day. Thus, unit planning does not eliminate daily planning; rather, because the objectives, activities, experiences, and necessary materials have been specified in the unit plan, the daily lesson plan flows naturally out of the unit plan. The exact structure of the daily lesson plan, however, depends on the type of lesson being designed. Lesson plans should reflect the individual needs, strengths, and interests of the teacher and the students. Lesson planning should never be dictated by rigid standards that prevent and stifle creativity. Indeed, you will rarely carry out a lesson entirely as planned. You must anticipate what is likely to happen as you teach your planned lessons, and you must make modifications as needed. Good teachers expect to adjust their plans as they move along, and they have alternatives in mind in case they are needed. The fact that most plans must be modified as they are taught does not justify the avoidance of

Figure 4.2
Weekly Lesson
Plan Form

Teacher: _____ Subject: _____ Grade/Room: _____

Period(s)/Block(s) (Time): _____ Week of: _____

Accommodations for
504/Special Students:

1. Small Group
2. Extended Time
3. Test Read Aloud
4. Modified Assignments
5. Preferential Seating
6. Oral Testing
7. Other

Day _____ Date _____
Unit: _____

Materials:

Transparency, manipulatives, dry erase board, informational resources, software, etc.

Technology: YES   NO

Assessment:

Formal   Informal   Alternative

Objective(s) and/or State Standard(s):

Content:

Teacher Procedure: *Reteaching/Enrichment:*

Accommodations: (circle)   1   2   3   4   5   6
7 Other _____

Day _____ Date _____
Unit: _____

Materials:

Transparency, manipulatives, dry erase board, informational resources, software, etc.

Technology: YES   NO

Assessment:

Formal   Informal   Alternative

Objective(s) and/or State Standard(s):

Content:

Teacher Procedure: *Reteaching/Enrichment:*

Accommodations: (circle)   1   2   3   4   5   6
7 Other _____

Day _____ Date _____
Unit: _____

Materials:

Transparency, manipulatives, dry erase board, informational resources, software, etc.

Technology: YES   NO

Assessment:

Formal   Informal   Alternative

Objective(s) and/or State Standard(s):

Content:

Teacher Procedure: *Reteaching/Enrichment:*

Accommodations: (circle)   1   2   3   4   5   6
7 Other _____

Figure 4.2 (Continued)

Teacher: _____ Subject: _____ Grade/Room: _____

Period(s)/Block(s) (Time): _____ Week of: _____

Accommodations for   1. Small Group   2. Extended Time
504/Special Students: 3. Test Read Aloud   4. Modified Assignments
                         5. Preferential Seating 6. Oral Testing   7. Other

Day _____ Date _____ Unit: _____	Objective(s) and/or State Standard(s):
Materials: Transparency, manipulatives, dry erase board, informational resources, software, etc. **Technology:** YES NO **Assessment:**	**Content:**
	Teacher Procedure: *Reteaching/Enrichment:*
Formal Informal Alternative	**Accommodations: (circle)** 1 2 3 4 5 6 7 Other _____
Day _____ Date _____ Unit: _____	Objective(s) and/or State Standard(s):
Materials: Transparency, manipulatives, dry erase board, informational resources, software, etc. **Technology:** YES NO **Assessment:**	**Content:**
	Teacher Procedure: *Reteaching/Enrichment:*
Formal Informal Alternative	**Accommodations: (circle)** 1 2 3 4 5 6 7 Other _____

thorough initial planning. Few teachers can "wing it." Planning, however, does not ensure success. The delivery counts for a great deal.

Postlesson Evaluation

Student evaluation should be an integral part of every lesson taught. As described here, evaluation entails postinstructional assessment of student performance. During evaluation, you determine the degree to which learners have attained the anticipated outcomes of the lesson.

Once a lesson has ended, a clear picture of how well students have mastered the stated objectives must be in your grasp. If there is a discrepancy between the intent and what was achieved, then you must decide whether reteaching is necessary.

The postlesson assessment that emerges from a lesson can vary widely in specificity and level of formality. Sometimes it will come from information gained during question-and-answer sequences. Sometimes it consists of information gleaned from student group work, individual seatwork, or completion of class activities. At other times, the assessment is formal (quiz or test).

Postlesson assessments help ensure that students are not pushed on to new content before they have mastered prerequisite skills. In effect, they help you identify learning problems at the end of a unit, when a unit evaluation is usually administered. You can often avoid many classroom problems if you will conduct and use information obtained in postlesson assessments. It is generally wiser to plan reteaching for students who are having difficulty with lesson concepts and to design enrichment activities for those having no difficulty rather than having them proceed to the next lesson.

Planning establishes a proposed course of action that serves as your guide, from which appropriate deviations can be made. Following are some sample daily lesson plans. These formats differ somewhat in style, but each focuses on the type of learning desired.

Lesson Formats

Lesson Plan Format 1. A lesson plan should provide needed structure to a lesson but should be general enough to allow for flexibility. Writers in the area of planning (Jacobson, Eggen, & Kauchak, 1989; Orlich et al., 1990) suggest the following basic lesson plan format:

For material related to this concept, go to Clip 4.2 on the Student Resource CD bound into the back of your textbook.

1. *Objectives:* the specific learning intent for the day, selected from the unit plan

2. *Introduction (set induction):* an activity used at the beginning of the lesson to attract student attention and interest

3. *Content:* a brief outline of the content to be covered in the lesson

4. *Methods and procedure:* a sequential listing of developmental activities for the day, selected from the unit plan

5. *Closure:* the lesson wrap-up activity

6. *Resources and materials:* a list of instructional materials needed for the lesson

7. *Evaluation procedure:* an activity or technique that determines how well students have mastered the intended learning outcomes of the lesson

8. *Assignment:* the in-class or homework assignment to be completed for the next class period

Lesson Plan Format 2. The second format has been suggested by advocates of the Madeline Hunter instructional design. It is a detailed and prescriptive seven-component plan with a highly structured format that emphasizes student involvement and success (Hunter, 1980). It is appropriate for skill learning and many forms of teacher-centered instruction, such as lecturing, lecture recitation, and Socratic questioning. The more student-centered lessons, such as discussions and problem solving, would not fit into this format (Shulman, 1987). The seven components of this format follow:

1. *Anticipatory set:* a teacher activity designed to prompt students to focus on the lesson before the lesson begins

2. *Objective and purpose:* teacher statements that explicitly inform students as to what will be learned in the coming lesson and how it will be useful

3. *Input:* the new knowledge, processes, or skills students are to learn

4. *Modeling:* the examples used in developing an understanding of the knowledge, processes, or skills being taught—including the techniques used to illustrate the new knowledge, processes, or skills

5. *Checking for understanding:* a method for determining whether students understand the learning intent that may occur before or during the teacher-directed activity (modeling) or during the student-guided activity

6. *Guided practice:* student practice of new knowledge, processes, or skills under teacher supervision (in-class)

7. *Independent practice:* unsupervised practice of new knowledge, process, or skill (assigned seat-work or homework)

Lesson Plan Format 3. This format is suggested for use with the small-group learning strategy. Small-group strategies generally require that students be prepared for their task and be debriefed once the assigned task has been addressed. Therefore, the planning process is a student-centered format with the following components:

1. *Objectives:* statements of the specific learning intents or what students should be able to do upon completion of the lesson

2. *Initial focus (set induction):* teacher-directed activity to get student attention and interest focused on the required assigned task

3. *Major task:* teacher-directed presentation of assigned group task, directions for group work, and options available to students

4. *Group activity:* students' task assigned by the teacher, who can offer strategy options or require that students develop their own

5. *Debriefing:* students' analysis and presentation of the product of the assigned task, as well as of the strategies that were and were not effective

6. *Resources and materials:* listing of the materials needed for groups to work on and complete the assigned task

7. *Evaluation:* formal and informal techniques to be used to check whether students have achieved task and objectives

Lesson Plan Format 4. This format is suggested for the backward design approach to instruction. It is based on the concept that a firmer and clearer grasp of where learning is going will be presented when goals or assessments are clearly articulated right from the beginning.

1. *Enduring understanding(s):* knowledge and skills worth being familiar with and important to know and do

2. *Essential questions:* related questions that fully cover the enduring understanding(s) that will guide and focus teaching/learning

3. *Assessment/acceptable evidence:* how students will demonstrate understandings, knowledge, and skills

4. *Strategies/best practices used to explicitly teach understandings:* sequence of teaching/learning experience that will equip students and demonstrate the desired understandings designed to hook students and hold their interest

5. *Resources and materials:* listing of materials needed to accomplish tasks

The plans presented are intended to be illustrative, not all-inclusive. Note the different terms commonly used for the lesson introductory activity, including *set induction, focus,* and *anticipatory set.* Some alternate lesson plan formats are shown in Figures 4.3 through 4.7. Each alternate format has been logically structured for a specific type of lesson. Note the adaptation and extension planning section in the formats presented in Figures 4.5 through 4.7. You should select the format that will lend direction to your lesson but not be a manuscript from which to read statements verbatim.

As the lesson formats presented in this section suggest, teachers vary widely in their approaches to daily planning. Some develop detailed daily plans, whereas others merely write out a few notes as reminders. The sample lesson plans presented in Figures 4.8 through 4.12 illustrate how the various components can be constructed.

Figure 4.3
Outline of Key
Questions/Discussion
Lesson Plan Format

1. **Unit Topic:** _____

2. **Objectives:** _____

    _____

3. **Set Induction:** _____

    _____

4. **Procedures for Discussion:** _____

    _____

5. **Key Questions** _____

    A. _____

    Possible Answers: _____

    _____

    Summary: _____

    _____

    B. _____

    Possible Answers: _____

    _____

    Summary: _____

    _____

    C. _____

    Possible Answers: _____

    _____

    Summary: _____

    _____

Figure 4.3
(Continued)

6. Conclusions: _____

_____

_____

_____

_____

7. Closure: _____

_____

_____

_____

_____

8. Evaluation: _____

_____

_____

_____

_____

9. Assignment: _____

_____

_____

_____

_____

Figure 4.4
Outline of Inquiry and
Problem-Solving Lesson
Plan Format

1. **Lesson Topic:** _____

2. **Objectives:** _____

   _____

3. **Set Induction:** _____

   _____

4. **Procedures or Steps**

   A. Problem Identification: _____

   _____

   B. Data Collection: _____

   _____

   C. Formulation of Hypotheses or Assumptions: _____

   _____

   D. Analysis of Data or Materials: _____

   _____

   E. Testing Hypotheses or Assumptions: _____

   _____

   F. Conclusion or Judgment: _____

   _____

5. **Closure:** _____

   _____

6. **Evaluation:** _____

   _____

7. **Assignment:** _____

   _____

Figure 4.5
Concept Attainment
Lesson Plan

Your Name: Grade Level: (circle one) K   1   2   3   4   5   6

Subject: (circle one) Language   Arts   Social Studies   Mathematics   Science

Lesson Title:

Materials Needed:

Prerequisite Skills:

Lesson Objective(s):

Concept Label:

Critical Attributes: [yes] Non-Critical Attributes: [no]

A feature of a certain concept that   Features found in some but not all
distinguishes it from other concepts   members of a category

Definition of Concept

1. **Present objectives:** (What are students going to learn?) Time:

2. **Provide examples and nonexamples to the class:** (Input/modeling)
   Time:

3. **Test for attainment: (Do the students understand the concept?)**
   Time:

4. **Analyze student thinking processes and integration of learning:**
   (Are they able to provide additional examples and nonexamples?) Time:

5. **Assessment/closure:** (How do you evaluate student progress or provide
   closure for this lesson?) Time:

6. **Adaptation for students who need extra help, time, or attention?**

AND

Extension for students of high ability? Time:

TOTAL LESSON TIME: _____

References Consulted (Curriculum books, teacher resources, websites, etc):

SOURCE: Developed by Dr. Sally Beisser, School of Education, Drake University. ©Beisser, 2000. Used with permission.

**Figure 4.6
Cooperative Learning
Lesson Plan**

Your Name: Grade Level: (circle one) K   1   2   3   4   5   6

Subject: (circle one) Language   Arts   Social Studies   Mathematics   Science

Lesson Title:

Materials Needed:

Prerequisite Skills:

Lesson Objective(s):
  a. Academic
  b. Social

Cooperative Learning Grouping Structure

  1. **Present objectives:** (What are students going to learn?) Time:

  2. **Present information for the academic goal:** Time:

  3. **Organize students into learning teams:** Time:
      (What is the social goal?)
      (How will you organize the groups?)
      (What group roles will you have?)

  4. **Assist team work and study:** Time:
      (How will you monitor progress of the academic and the social goals?)

  5. **Provide recognition:** Time:
      (How will students know they have met both academic and social goals?)

  6. **Assessment/closure:** Time:
      (How do you evaluate student progress or end this lesson?)

  7. **Adaptation for students who need extra help, time, or attention?**

AND

Extension for students of high ability? Time:

TOTAL LESSON TIME: _____

References Consulted (Curriculum books, teacher resources, websites, etc):

SOURCE: Developed by Dr. Sally Beisser, School of Education, Drake University. ©Beisser, 2000. Used with permission.

Figure 4.7
Direct Instruction
Lesson Plan

Your Name: Grade Level: (circle one) K   1   2   3   4   5   6

Subject: (circle one) Language   Arts   Social Studies   Mathematics   Science

Lesson Title:

Materials Needed:

Prerequisite Skills:

Lesson Objective:

1. **Provide objectives:** (What are students going to learn?) Time:

2. **Demonstrate knowledge or skill:** (Input/modeling by the teacher) Time:

3. **Provide guided practice:** (Guided practice with the teacher) Time:

4. **Check for understanding and provide student feedback:** (How will you know students understand the skill or concept? How will they know they "get it"?) Time:

5. **Provide extended practice and transfer:** (Independent practice of the skill) Time:

6. **Assessment/closure:** (How do you evaluate student progress or provide closure to this lesson?) Time:

7. **Adaptation for students who need extra help, time, or attention?**

AND

Extension for students of high ability? Time:

TOTAL LESSON TIME: _____

References Consulted (Curriculum books, teacher resources, websites, etc):

SOURCE: Developed by Dr. Sally Beisser, School of Education, Drake University. ©Beisser, 2000. Used with permission.

**Figure 4.8
Creativity Lesson Plan**

Topic: Creating a School

Objectives:

The students will be able to:

1. Give examples of the special features of different secondary schools.
2. Apply terms associated with secondary schools to an original student project.

Introduction (Set Induction):

Spend 10 minutes using pictures to review various secondary school terms. Students create a glossary of important secondary school terms in the form of a three-column chart giving terms (e.g., curriculum, hidden curriculum, extracurricular activities, administration, scheduling, minicourses, flexible scheduling, modules, learning centers, staff, discipline, and school district), definitions, and examples (e.g., the principal is an administrator).

Content: None

Procedure:

1. Divide class into groups of four or five. Group members are to work cooperatively on planning and drawing an imaginary secondary school.
2. Students are to give their school a name and decide on its main function (prepare students for the workforce, college, or vocational school).
3. Each school should feature a curriculum, disciplinary process, class time scheduling, administration setup, and so forth.
4. Students are to decide on other special features of their school (music programs, sports, busing of students, clubs, etc.).

Closure:

Each group presents its proposed secondary school. The class will discuss the drawbacks and advantages of each group's presented proposal.

Materials:

School pictures, textbooks, glossary, large pieces of drawing paper or poster paper, felt pens or markers

Evaluation:

Observe student participation as they work on assigned project. Check each group's imaginary secondary school and its main function.

Assignment:

Outline problems that must be overcome to implement the secondary school that your group created. Be prepared to discuss the identified problems in class.

Accommodations:

Will depend on needs of special students in class.

Figure 4.9
A Sample Language
Arts Lesson

Topic: The Elements of Story Writing

Objectives:

Given a picture stimulus, students will be able to write a short fiction story that contains the needed elements for a short story.

Introduction (Set Induction):

Read aloud a short fiction story that will be of interest to the class. (Jumping Mouse, a short myth, demonstrates the elements in an interesting but condensed form.)

Content:

The Elements of a Short Story

    I. Short Story Beginnings
        A. Describe the setting
        B. Introduce the main character
        C. Introduce the plot (problem or goal the main character attempts to solve or achieve)

   II. Middle Story Elements
        A. First roadblock (character's attempt to reach goal)
        B. Second roadblock
        C. Climax of story (character reaches goal)

  III. Story Endings
        A. Make conclusions
        B. Wrap up any loose ends

Procedure:

1. After the oral reading, ask students to explain when and how the author introduced the main character.

2. Discuss the promptness that authors use to introduce the main character, setting, and plot in short stories. Record responses on the chalkboard using the bell-shaped curve to portray the elements of short stories. (Bell curve not shown here.)

Figure 4.9
(Continued)

3. At this point, ask students to summarize the elements needed in a short story's beginning. (They should be able to identify introduction of the main character, description of the story setting, and introduction of the story's plot.) It is important to convey to students that the order in which the elements are introduced is not important; but rather, that the inclusion of these elements is a crucial feature of the short story.

4. Next, ask students to recall the first roadblock (or difficulty the main character had in attempting to reach the intended goal). Record response on bell curve and stress that the middle of a story includes the majority of the story—including the story's climax.

5. As students recall the roadblocks presented in the short book, continue to record these on the bell-shaped curve to demonstrate the rising tension presented in the story.

6. Ask students to describe how the main character finally confronted and solved the problem presented in the introduction of the story. Explain that this element is called the climax of the story. The climax should be placed at the top of the bell-shaped curve to demonstrate it as the peak of the story.

7. Ask students to summarize the elements that constitute the middle parts of a short story. (The bell-shaped curve on the chalkboard should reveal that the middle story elements are composed of roadblocks in the main character's attempt to reach a goal, and the climax or the reaching of that goal is at the peak of the bell curve.)

8. Finally, ask students to talk about the brevity the author uses to end the story once the main character has reached his or her goal. (Again, this is demonstrated by the falling line of the bell curve drawing on the board.)

Closure:

Ask students to make an outline of the elements of a short story using the information presented on the bell-shaped curve.

Evaluation:

Answers to questions during class discussions. Check students' outline of short story as work is being completed.

Assignment:

Let each student choose a picture from a magazine and instruct them to use the outline for short stories as a guide to write a short story about the picture selected.

Accommodations:

Will depend on needs of special students in class.

**Figure 4.10
Sample Small-Group
Strategy Lesson Plan**

Topic: Classifying Information

Objective:

At the completion of this lesson, the student will be able to classify information into groups on the basis of similar or common attributes.

Initial Focus:

Why should we learn to classify information into categories or groups? Discuss at least three reasons for classifying information.

Major Task:

Skim text (pages 107–121) for important ideas or items that might be classified. Agree on categories (groups or labels) that could be used to classify text information. Choose three unused practice items in the text and have individual students label the items accordingly. Ask individual students to share their label with the class to ensure understanding. Form groups of three. Instruct the groups to classify the items listed below, in at least two ways.

Items: Wichita, chair, Dallas, Denver, mule, Boston, horse, New York, house, Chicago, deer, bed, picture, Lincoln, elephant, and Oklahoma City

Group:

Students work on classification activity. Each group will produce two schemes. Schemes are to be recorded on transparency film.

Debriefing:

Each group will present their two classification schemes to the class. Class will react and make recommendations.

Resources and Materials:

Textbook, transparency film (two sheets per group), transparency pen (one per group), and classification item list

Evaluation:

Check for students' ability to classify practice items during major task phase of lesson, participation in group activity, and appropriateness of the two classification schemes by each group.

Accommodations:

Will depend on needs of special students in class.

Figure 4.11
Sample Key
Question/Discussion
Lesson Plan

Topic: A Cashless Society

Objectives:

The students will:

1. Explain their feelings about the effects of electronic funds transfer (EFT) systems on society.

2. Participate in group discussion and decision making.

Set Induction:

Money isn't going to be needed in the future. You will have no use for cash in everyday life.

Procedure for Discussion:

Questions will be presented to the class for discussion. Responses will be recorded on board. A summary of the responses will be made.

Key question 1: What effect will a cashless society have on daily life?

Possible answers: Computers will deal with money. Everyone will use checks and/or credit cards. Vending machines will change. Some types of crime will decrease while other types will increase.

Summary: We will have to change surprisingly little to become a cashless society.

Key question 2: How do you think EFT systems will change consumer behavior?

Possible answers: Problems with budgeting money may result. Buying by television, the Internet, catalog, and telephone will increase. People will be less concerned about prices and money.

Summary: EFT systems will create many problems in society.

Key question 3: Where do you think EFT systems will have the greatest impact?

Possible answers: More checking accounts will be opened. Banks will issue more credit cards. All stores will take checks and credit cards. Prices will increase because of bad checks and fraud.

Summary: Bank and consumer interaction will increase, as will the incidence of some types of crime.

Conclusions:

A cashless society would have positive and negative effects on society. An EFT system likely would lead to less individual privacy and more control over people and their daily lives.

Closure:

Review responses recorded on board. Ask pertinent questions regarding recorded responses.

Evaluation:

Consider students' participation in discussion and decision making. Also evaluate question-and-answer sequences.

Assignment:

Keep track of the number of times and the type of transaction in which cash is needed in a 24-hour period. What effect would an EFT system have on your life?

Accommodations:

Will depend on needs of special students in class.

Figure 4.12
A Sample Block
Pattern Lesson

Grade Level(s): 11, 12

Subject: Science/Physics

Duration: One 90-minute block

Description: A basic first look at gravity.

Goal: The students will understand the basic interaction between two massive bodies.

Objectives:

The student will be able to scientifically explain why the human body is attracted by the Earth.

Materials Needed:

Ball bearings, marker, hoop, jar, meter stick, vacuum cylinder containing a penny and a feather, computers, lab sheet (not included here)

Set Induction (Focus):

Demonstration: Two ball bearings will be dropped off the edge of a table. One will be dropped straight down from the edge, and the other one will be given a slight horizontal push. Both balls will hit the ground at the same time.

Procedure:

1. Experiment: The students will be given a meter stick with premeasured reaction lines. They will then measure each other's reaction time.

2. Experiment: Set up a marker on a hoop balanced on a jar. The student will pull the hoop out and the marker will drop into the jar.

3. Demonstration: Show that in a vacuum cylinder a feather and stone fall with the same acceleration.

4. Computer activity: With two students assigned to each computer, have the students use one of the search engines to locate and summarize information relative to the law of gravity and relative to one of the following: Sir Isaac Newton, Galileo, Copernicus, Johannes Kepler, or Albert Einstein. Students are to present their findings on the last class period of the unit.

Closure:

Discuss the finding relative to the demonstrations and experiments and explain the law of gravity.

Accommodation: Experimental groups and computer pairs will be formed so that special-needs students work with higher ability students. Will be sensitive to possible apprehensions.

Lesson Analysis: To be completed after lesson has been taught.

<table>
<tr><td>**APPLY AND**
REFLECT 4.3</td><td>Would the planning formats presented in this chapter be appropriate for all grade levels and/or subject areas? Why or why not?</td></tr>
</table>

EXPANSION ACTIVITY 4.4   Planning Format

A lesson plan serves as an organizational tool that ensures that you cover the material you wanted to. Develop a lesson plan format that will best fit your teaching philosophy and style. Share your format with classmates.

As the sole person responsible for your classroom, you must make sure it runs smoothly. This will take thorough planning. Complete Expansion Activity 4.4: Planning Format to further develop your planning skills.

Some school districts have adopted block-of-time schedules, and teachers must plan for this pattern while other teachers must plan as a team. Teachers should also always make provisions for students who have special needs. Here is a brief look at these areas.

Block Scheduling

Block scheduling is an instructional delivery pattern that divides school time into instructional blocks ranging from 20 to 110 minutes. There is no single, standard form of block schedule. However, all have basically the same premise: A school need not be organized into the traditional 7- or 8-period day but should allow for longer classes in most subjects. Many **middle schools** have used longer block scheduling for some time. High schools have also begun to implement block schedules to address curriculum fragmentation.

Block scheduling offers many simple advantages. First, because there are fewer class changes, chaos in the halls is reduced. Second, teachers prepare for fewer classes and work with far fewer students each day. Third, students have the opportunity for in-depth study of subject matter. Finally, teachers tend to revise their teaching methods to be more student centered to accommodate the longer class periods.

When traditional schedules are restructured into larger blocks of time, teachers soon learn that they cannot take the simplistic approach of using the same methods they did before, only for a longer time, since nothing will disengage a group of students from the learning process more quickly than lecturing for an entire class block. Numerous creative instructional approaches are possible within longer time frames; therefore, teachers should be cautious about relying too heavily on familiar daily instructional routines. As a general strategy, teachers should consider planning three to four activities during the instructional block. For example, block-of-time lessons could be structured in the following manner:

Review Previous Learning. Through such means as checking homework, teacher questioning, and student self-assessment in learning pairs, teachers can quickly assess student mastery of previously taught concepts and engage in appropriate reteaching strategies.

Instructional Input. Important new concepts should be delivered with primary concern for active student involvement. Direct teaching, demonstrations, multimedia presentations, concept attainment, and inquiry methods are a sampling of effective approaches for ensuring that students receive instruction on the day's concepts. Teachers who have previously employed traditional direct instruction methods should feel fairly proficient with this portion of the lesson provided, of course, that they include opportunities for direct student involvement.

Student Performance. Group experiences provide students with an opportunity to master the lesson content while engaging in hands-on activities. Experiments, cooperative learning, role-playing, case studies, and computer simulations can each be used to provide effective experiences.

Guided Practice/Reteaching. Individual student mastery remains the foundation of effective teaching. Guided practice (individually or with a group) should be provided so teachers can assess levels of student understanding. This component is especially critical for schools with alternate-day schedules since students will most likely not have an opportunity to correct learning errors for 2 or more days. Teachers should reteach and reinforce the day's objectives, provide closure, and assign homework.

Longer periods of teaching time will require longer range and more thoughtful planning. Informal learning activities that enrich and supplement the formal instructional objectives of the class should be readily available and carefully planned, especially for classes that include diverse and special-needs students, or for those times when students are just not ready to engage in additional formal learning activities. Educational games of various kinds, whether commercially prepared or student created, can often be used to relieve the stress of long periods of intense instruction while also supporting the learning goals of the class. Finally, students can work in pairs or teams to review curricular content and to develop cooperative learning skills.

Team Planning

Team planning can have tremendous value. For example, if all the social studies teachers were to coordinate their course plans, then the possibility of duplicating efforts or of leaving out important lessons would be reduced. Careful planning as a team can increase the time for enrichment activities. Team planning also facilitates coordination efforts among disciplines. The American literature teacher and the American history teacher, for example, could design their courses so that they were covering the same time frames simultaneously. Students would have the opportunity to see the connectedness of the two disciplines. Moreover, reading and writing assignments could be planned to enhance student understanding of how the milieu influenced the writers of a particular era.

Many middle schools are organized around interdisciplinary teams that plan as a group. These planning teams usually consist of a mathematics teacher, a science teacher, a language arts teacher, and a social studies teacher. In some middle schools, a reading teacher, a gifted education teacher, and a special education teacher may also be part of the team. These teachers plan for a common group of students.

Elementary teachers in some schools will work together as grade-level teams. These teams work together in developing lessons and designing activities and materials for their lessons. The joint teamwork of the group of teachers will generally lead to better and more effective teaching.

Opportunities for teachers to engage in critical thinking and analysis are greatly enhanced through team planning. A team approach calls upon teachers to critically analyze the content of their respective courses so the concepts can be merged into a unified, workable whole. Teaming demands careful attention to details so that each team member knows what to do, how to do it, and when to do it. In addition, it requires that evaluation be carefully thought out to ensure that plans are executed properly and are accomplishing their intended function.

Some of your students will have limited academic abilities, whereas others will be advanced; some will be skilled socially, whereas others will be less poised. You must, however, plan your instruction to fit the individual needs and interests of all students. Let's take a brief look at two special groups.

Teaching Special Education Students

Teachers with special students or mainstreamed students (handicapped students placed in regular classes) must learn to modify their plans and give differentiated assignments. You can do this by modifying or varying the length or difficulty of assignments. For example, in a science class, you might assign two experiments to your slow students, three experiments to the average students, and four—or perhaps more demanding—experiments to high-achieving and exceptional students. Similarly, you might require only half as much writing from English students who experience motor difficulties. Other examples of lesson modifications might include developing special worksheets to help teach difficult concepts, modifying assigned work, developing special study guides, giving oral exams, and obtaining and using special equipment with the physically handicapped.

Another approach to differentiated assignments is to vary the type of work students do. For example, some students can be allowed to complete and submit their written assignments on a word processor. Students occasionally might be allowed to assist each other or work together in groups.

Some planning guidelines for working with students who have special needs follow:

1. Gather information about the nature of the exceptional student's difference and how that difference might affect the learning process.

2. Get help from district special education or resource experts.

3. Gather the equipment needs (typewriters, computers, VCR, print enlarger, Braille material, etc.) of exceptional students to allow them to function at an optimum level.

4. Adapt the curriculum and your teaching strategies to better serve the needs of the exceptional students.

5. Individualize the curriculum as much as possible in your classroom.

6. Provide for the removal of barriers, both physical and psychological, that limit the full functioning of exceptional students in your classroom.

Teaching the Gifted and Talented Student

In addition to students who need time and attention in order to meet regular curricular expectations, teachers will have gifted learners in their classrooms with exceptional general intellect, specific academic ability, creative productive thinking, leadership ability, or visual and performing art talents (Tomlinson, 1999). **Gifted and talented (G/T) students** often progress through their education with insufficient levels of challenge due to myths and controversy surrounding gifted education. Table 4.1 presents some of these myths.

Characteristics of Gifted and Talented Students

How will you know when you have an exceptionally gifted or talented learner in your class? Look for characteristics that distinguish students in your class, such as the following:

1. *Advanced intellect.* Curious; asks intriguing questions; reads avidly; understands abstract concepts and ideas; learns rapidly; memorizes easily; reads rapidly; follows and completes multiple and complex instructions; focuses on problem solving, processes, and explanations; retains information; has interests, knowledge, or hobbies different from peers of similar age; has advanced understanding of mathematical reasoning

2. *High verbal skills.* Has a keen sense of humor; uses advanced vocabulary; explains complex ideas in unique and creative ways; fluently exchanges ideas and information; easily completes word games and puzzles; influences thinking of others

3. *Keen power of concentration.* Engages in activities for long periods of time; pays attention to novelty and complexity; becomes totally absorbed in an activity; is quickly observant and responsive; maintains interests and activities different from peers

4. *Atypical response behaviors.* May be more sensitive or creative than their peers regarding issues or concerns; may take high-level risks; comes up with original ideas and relationships often missed by

Table 4.1 Gifted and Talented Student Myths and Facts

Myth	Fact
Gifted learners can "make it on their own" because they are bright. Other students need teacher attention more than gifted and talented (G/T) students.	Gifted students need specific interventions and educational programs designed to meet their complex learning needs. Without special considerations, gifted students are unlikely to reach their full potential.
All kids are gifted.	Each student is a special person. Some are, however, distinguishably different in talent, ability, or motivation. Some kids are measurably higher (gifted) in one or more areas in comparison to their age peers.
It is undemocratic or "elitist" to give special attention to the gifted learner.	All students need appropriate levels of challenge and should receive educational programming suitable for their needs and abilities. To provide G/T students with inadequate curriculum or low levels of support from teachers or administration is unjust.
Gifted students are unaware of their differences unless they are identified in special programs.	On the contrary, gifted students are often keenly aware of their differences from others. They may hide their talents to escape peer ridicule. Many seek older friends with advanced vocabulary and similar intellectual interests.
All gifted students want to participate in special gifted programs with high levels of challenge for which they have been identified.	Unfortunately, some gifted students do not participate because they go unnoticed or unidentified in school. Others avoid extra work that comes with challenge. Some have never experienced demanding work and may confront such opportunities negatively. Teachers, administrators, and parents can encourage success in programs commensurate with student needs.
Gifted students placed in special programs will have adjustment or social-emotional problems.	The opposite of this myth is more often accurate. If gifted students do not receive essential enrichment and/or accelerated learning opportunities, then poor study habits, social-emotional discontent, or behavioral problems often result.
It is too much work for regular classroom teachers to plan instruction for gifted learners.	Initially, it is time-consuming for teachers to differentiate instruction or plan specifically for gifted learners. Ultimately, many teachers find results worth the effort for both the G/T learners and their peers (Renzulli & Reis, 1997).
Gifted students take pleasure in being good examples for other students.	On the contrary, most G/T students thrive with goals of their own, rather than setting examples for others. Gifted students may be "introverts" who prefer an environment with internal, not public thinking and reasoning (Silverman, 1986). Many G/T students find cooperative learning tasks, with high-medium-low ability groupings, exasperating (Kulik & Kulik, 1992). They need opportunities to share ideas with intellectual peers, not necessarily in the role as tutor or teacher.
Gifted students should strive to fit in conventional classrooms since they will join a majority workforce in their futures.	Mediocre education is inappropriate whenever excellence is necessary to compete in an ever-changing world, where bright minds contribute ideas and solve problems.

others; may exhibit perfectionism or procrastination behaviors (or both); displays a strong sense of self; influences behavior of others; identifies with adults or older peers; can display advanced inter- and intrapersonal skills along with leadership and motivational ability

5. *Performance ability.* Displays high-level mastery in visual, physical, and performing arts; masters physical and artistic skills beyond their peers

Not all gifted students possess each one of these characteristics. They vary widely in characteristics and potential, just as special education students are different. Some G/T students are well-balanced, personable school leaders, whereas others are socially awkward or have serious emotional problems. Not all G/T students enjoy learning at school. Finally, many students from diverse backgrounds have been historically underrepresented in gifted education programs. Therefore, regular classroom strategies are critical for G/T learners.

Strategies for Teaching Gifted Students

What can you do with gifted and talented learners who exhibit one or more of these characteristics? Numerous strategies (Beisser, 1998) can be employed in the regular classroom where students spend the majority of school time.

Differentiated Instruction. As noted earlier, differentiation refers to instruction or curriculum that has been modified from a standard approach to meet the needs of particular students (Tomlinson, 1999). Although often used to accommodate special-needs students, this approach also works well for gifted students. This means the teacher modifies the lesson or unit to address the needs of G/T students by variation of the process, content, or product required.

Vary Instructional and Grouping Strategies. An effective whole-class strategy is to use problem solving, inquiry-based lessons, or group investigation where G/T learners can thrive in their ability to think, reason, and do research independently. Use flexible grouping such as small cluster groups (Renzulli, Gentry, & Reis, 2003) to provide bright students with opportunities to learn and work together within the structure of whole-class or cooperative learning group assignments. Advanced use of technology (e.g., multimedia and Web site design) for instruction and communication is another technique that motivates and challenges gifted learners.

Varied Questioning. Use higher levels of questioning at various times for gifted students so they can provide fluent or elaborate explanations, learn to think abstractly, and are not able to get by with quick answers.

Compact the Curriculum. Why make the G/T students review material or complete tasks they have already accomplished? If they have a sound grasp of skills and content, provide opportunities to demonstrate proficiency (e.g., assign the most difficult problems first or allow completion of the end-of-chapter test in advance) and then move on to more complex concepts and skills (Winebrenner, 2002).

Acceleration. Gifted students require faster paced instruction for content, skills, and processes so they can move rapidly through the curriculum. Perhaps they can read above grade-level materials (e.g., supplying chapter books for a kindergarten child), leave the class to work with an upper grade level (e.g., a second grader going to fourth-grade math), or take classes earlier than their peers (e.g., taking college algebra while in high school). Many high school students take college-level courses through local institutions or online offerings.

Independent Study. Challenge gifted students to explore individual topics of interest. Let them investigate a central question, gather multiple and varied resources, make inferences, provide a hypothesis, explain findings, and cite the sources. An important step in independent study is to share results with an appropriate audience that will appreciate the work they have completed (e.g., a research project on the extinction of the Siberian tiger should be shared with a naturalist or environmentalist).

Tiered Activities. Tomlinson (1999) suggests that teachers can focus on the same understanding and skills but at different levels of abstraction and complexity. For example, all students may be reading books with "chocolate" as a central theme but will use texts with a variety of reading levels and engage in tasks differing in complexity associated with each book level.

Interest Centers. Renzulli and Reis (1997) suggest that students don't know what interests them until they explore various topics. Establish classroom interest centers with frequently changing themes that may focus on timely events, such as presidential elections or the Olympics, as well as diverse themes derived from students, such as exploring Stonehenge, techniques of playing chess, or serving people in poverty.

Apprenticeships. Because gifted learners may have interest and skill areas outside of your classroom curriculum, you may find community resource personnel a valuable asset. For example, arrange for a stockbroker to work with a small group of students interested in investing in the stock market or encourage students to be mentored by field area specialists at a local university after school hours.

Teacher Advocacy. If nothing else, provide educational and emotional support for the gifted student within a rich classroom environment with advanced activities resources, technology, and choices (Beisser, 1998). Hold high standards that help bright students reach their potential. Accept gifted learners in your class, as they have individual needs for challenge and support. The power of a positive, supportive teacher is immense. Learn through the parents of gifted students. They have lived many years with the gifted child who has been placed in your classroom. Speak out on behalf of gifted and talented students at educational meetings and programs. Become informed of local and state curriculum planning decisions or budget allotments for gifted learners. It is easier to have an impact on key decisions before they are made, rather than trying to undo unfavorable determinations. Seek professional information from your state and national gifted education organizations such as the National Association for Gifted Children (NAGC). They have numerous materials and professional growth opportunities such as conferences and workshops. NAGC has a Curriculum Studies Division that focuses on issues, models, and practices related to the development, implementation, and evaluation of curricula for the gifted (see www.nagc.org).

Gifted learners are entitled to be served by teachers with expertise in appropriate differentiated content and instructional methods, involvement in ongoing professional development, and who possess personal and professional traits that promote successful learning for gifted students in their classroom.

APPLY AND REFLECT 4.4	Since you will have low-ability, average-ability, and high-ability students in your classes, how will you design your units and lessons to meet the needs of these different ability levels?

Having looked at the general planning of instruction, let us look next at the four planning levels in greater detail.

Table 4.2 offers a summary of the planning concepts covered in this section. Before you move on to the next section, review Table 4.2 and complete Review and Reflective Exercise 4.1.

Teachers must often plan for special students.

Lesson Plan Structure

As a teacher, you will probably imitate a favorite teacher in your initial planning. Later, you will modify the initial structure to fit your individual style. Regardless of the amount of detail in or the general format of lesson plans, an examination of the various lesson plan formats reveals that each contains three common elements: the set induction (cognitive set), the lesson itself (instructional strategies), and the lesson closure.

Set Induction (Focus)

The **set induction** is what you do at the outset of a lesson to get students' undivided attention, to arouse their interest, and to establish a conceptual framework for the information that follows.

Until your students are attentive and prepared to listen (until they have a **cognitive set**), it is usually unwise to begin a lesson. Your opening activity—frequently related to the homework assignment or some recent lesson—will have to be repeated if you have not gained their attention.

You must plan some strategies for getting the students' undivided attention. Keep in mind that you will be competing with a host of other attention getters: student body elections, an assembly, the "big game," a change in weather, and a recent or pending holiday. Whatever the distractions, it is pointless to proceed without the students' attention.

One way to get attention is to do nothing. Stand quietly. Students will soon focus their attention on you. Students are accustomed to teachers' frequent talk. Absence of teacher talk will attract their attention. This is particularly useful if only a few students are inattentive. Another technique is to begin talking in a very low tone, gradually increasing volume. Most of us want to hear what we cannot hear. The low tone of the teacher's voice will attract attention. Some teachers turn the lights on and off. This is generally done in elementary schools but can sometimes be effective at the middle and secondary levels. If you use one of these techniques on a regular basis to cue the students to attention, chances are they will

TABLE 4.2 Planning Concepts

Type	Description
Team planning	Group or team of teachers organizing instruction so that each supplements the other
Teacher-student planning	Involvement of students in planning process. Learning activities are based on students' interests and their involvement promotes ownership.
Course planning	Broad planning of instruction for year or term
Unit planning	Discrete segment of a year's work organized around a specific theme or cluster of related concepts
Weekly planning	Short-form outline of instruction for 1 week on a single sheet of paper
Daily lesson planning	Detailed description of objectives and activities for one instructional period. Daily plans should flow naturally out of the unit plan.

REVIEW AND REFLECTIVE EXERCISE 4.1   Explain what is involved in unit and daily planning.

REVIEW

- What role does state mandates have in the planning process?
- Why do unit, weekly, and daily plans need to be planned and developed?
- Why is planning for special students important for effective teaching?

REFLECTION

- Do state mandates put too much pressure on teachers for student success? What impact does state requirements have on classroom instruction?
- In your own experiences, did you ever have a teacher who did not plan well? What was it like for students?

begin to look for your cue even before you start. The lesson is guaranteed to be more successful if everyone is ready to learn.

Although getting student attention is important for cognitive set, it is also instrumental in sparking student interest and involvement in the lesson. Provide a tickler. Pose a perplexing problem. Share a story. These are all possibilities for setting the stage to teach.

Motivating student interest is not always an easy task. Be ready and willing to be creative. Let your topic and known student interests provide clues for creating lesson motivators. If the hottest rap group around is doing a concert nearby, use that news to spark a discussion of freedom of expression as you study the Bill of Rights. A recent oil spill could serve as a catalyst for a lesson on pollution problems. A plastic sack filled with a Styrofoam cup, a disposable diaper, a lipstick in three layers of packaging, a can of motor oil, a can of aerosol hairspray, and a bottle of toxic weed killer could serve as an introduction to a lesson on environmental pollution. Several magazine advertisements could provide a springboard for a persuasive writing lesson.

Suspense can generate excitement, interest, and involvement. Begin the class with a discrepant event or an interesting demonstration. For example, build a working model of a volcano in earth science, show pictures of the Old West in social studies, or mix paints to create various paint colors in art. Make the discrepant events or demonstration as surprising or novel as possible. Even better, involve the students directly in showing the discrepant events or in conducting demonstrations.

Models, diagrams, or pictures situated in visible spots will capture attention and interest. You might begin the lesson by soliciting student comments. For example, you might ask the class to guess what a diagram or picture represents or how a model functions.

Posing a provocative question and presenting a hypothetical problem are also effective lesson starters. Be careful to use truly thought-provoking questions and hypothetical situations that present interesting dilemmas. Superficial use of these techniques provides little motivation for students to become engaged in the learning process. Questions such as "What would happen if . . . ?" and "How do you account for . . . ?" have the potential to spark student interest and participation, whereas questions like "What was the date of . . . ?" or "Who was the author of . . . ?" are likely to bring any interest to a halt after the one "right" answer is given. A hypothetical situation is best used when it can provide a dilemma: "Given the power and the money, how would you solve the problem of . . . ?" is such an example. Used strategically, both of these techniques are promising in their potential for promoting student interest and involvement.

Students generally learn more from a lesson when they know what is expected of them. Thus, to maximize learning, you should plan introductory remarks that provide students with what Ausubel (1963) calls an **advance organizer:** Plan remarks that give students a "what to look for" frame of reference. Basically, the concept of the advance organizer is related closely to the establishment of student interest but is usually more specific. Advance organizers can be generalizations, definitions, or analogies (Orlich et al., 1990). For example, a science teacher might start a lesson about light with a generalization about the major characteristics of light. A social studies teacher might start a lesson on war by relating it to a football game. No matter what form it takes, an advance organizer serves the purpose of giving students needed background information for the upcoming lesson or of helping them remember and apply old information to the lesson. Thus, the advance organizer acts as a kind of conceptual bridge between the new and old information.

Colorful models can often get a lesson started.

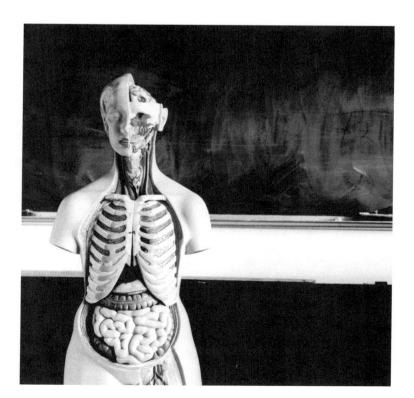

Some teachers use a verbal statement of lesson objectives as the advance organizer. You must take care, however, to translate the written objectives into a form that is both understandable and interesting to students—for example,

Objective: The students will be able to correctly describe the effect of gravity on different objects.

Translation: [*Teacher holds a heavy and light object overhead.*] When I drop these objects, watch them closely. [*Teacher drops objects.*] There was a continuous increase in their speed as they fell, which requires that some force be acting upon them. What is this force and how strong is it? Why do both objects hit the ground at the same time? [*Silence.*] Today, we are going to answer these questions.

You must set the stage for the learning process. If you fail to arouse student attention and interest and to establish a framework for your lesson, the remainder of the lesson may be wasted. Listen to your students' conversations for topics that you can use to start your lessons. A simple remark related to the topic is all that is needed to get the discussion started. Complete Web Link 4.2: Sets, which will let you develop some set inductions for your future classes.

WEB LINK 4.2   Sets

Access the lesson plans at URL Web sites www.lessonplanspage.com and www.teachnology.com/teachers/lesson_plans. Locate five lesson plans relative to the grade level and subjects you expect to teach. Analyze and modify the sets to make them more effective for your future students. Do all the lessons include a set? If the selected lesson does not have a set, design one.

APPLY AND REFLECT 4.5   Teachers must plan interesting ways of introducing their lessons. What interesting ways of introducing lessons do you foresee using? What techniques have you seen other teachers use?

Strategies and Procedures

How will you teach the objectives you have targeted? What will the students read? Is a short lecture the best method for presenting the information, or would an inquiry lesson better suit your purposes? Should the students work individually or in groups? Would a guest speaker be beneficial, or would a field trip serve your objectives better? These are the kinds of questions you must ask as you prepare daily lessons. Once again, the unit plan and the nature of the material, as well as the resources available, will guide these decisions.

A well-planned lesson consists of the content to be taught, as well as the **instructional strategy** to be employed in teaching it. The instructional strategy consists of two components: the methodology and the lesson **procedure.** The instructional strategy is the global plan for teaching a particular lesson. It can be viewed as analogous to the overall plan for winning a tennis match or basketball game.

The **methodology** acts as the student motivator and sets the tone for the lesson. It consists of planned patterned behaviors that are definite steps by which the teacher influences learning. The methodology should be designed and organized so that it captures and holds students' attention and involves them as much as possible in the learning situation.

The **lesson procedure** is the sequence of steps that has been designed for leading students to the acquisition of the learning objectives. For example, you may decide on the following sequence for a lesson on atomic energy.

1. Present a short introductory lecture on atomic energy.

2. Show a film on splitting the atom.

3. Conduct a summary discussion on the content of the film.

4. Conduct a question-and-answer session on major points covered in the lecture and in the film.

As you see, the procedure consists of the sequenced teacher and student activities used for achieving the lesson objectives.

When you plan, don't overlook student practice. Students must have the opportunity to test themselves on the content. Providing these opportunities must be a regular part of the daily lesson plan. Two types of practice are important and should take place during the course of each lesson: (1) *guided practice,* or practice with the help and encouragement of the teacher, and (2) *independent practice,* or practice without the help and encouragement of the teacher.

Practice opportunities need not be meaningless worksheets. Guided practice can be oral. Guided practice can be geared for group participation or for group creation of a product or set of ideas. The important thing is to furnish a "safety net." It is through guided practice that the teacher can observe whether the students understand the concepts to be learned. Concepts that students have not fully understood can be retaught immediately. Reteaching could be accomplished by allowing the peer group to restate the concepts in the students' language. Immediate reteaching is more effective than trying to return to a previous topic several days later. If the unit requires that learning be cumulative, one misunderstood lesson can have serious consequences for later learning. Once the teacher is confident that students can proceed without the safety net, it is time to provide for independent practice.

Independent practice generally is homework. But homework need not be meaningless worksheets, either. The exploration of one concept in depth; the interview of one appropriate expert; the building of one model, one drawing, one map, one idea—all these avenues for discovery can be more valuable than copying definitions from the textbook.

Finally, you may want to evaluate your daily lesson objectives. You have set the stage, identified the objectives, developed the strategies, and planned for practice. Now you may want to include in your plan a daily evaluation of student learning. There are several techniques for assessing student learning. These will be discussed in detail in Chapters 9 and 10. Always refer to the lesson objectives when determining how you will evaluate student progress. If the objectives are well written, the methods for evaluation are more easily determined.

Your instructional strategy is the actual presentation of the lesson content. It consists of your techniques for giving students the information. Deciding on a methodology requires that you choose from a wide variety of methods, activities, and learning experiences—the techniques you feel will best lead to the desired learning outcomes.

Methodology Selection

Instructional methods can influence students directly through focused, teacher-directed instruction or influence them indirectly by actively involving them in their own learning. Most instruction can be categorized into two basic types: teacher centered and student centered. Comparisons of these two methods of instruction are given in Table 4.3. The teacher-centered instructional approaches are more "traditional" or didactic, with students acquiring knowledge by listening to the teacher, by reading a textbook, or both. In the teacher-centered instructional approach, students are passive recipients of information. In contrast, student-centered approaches to instruction invite students to participate actively in their own learning experiences. The two instructional approaches are equally effective in bringing about learning. Concepts in math, for example, can be taught through a teacher-centered approach, such as the lecture method, or through a student-centered approach, such as cooperative learning.

With all these possible methods, which method should be selected for a particular lesson? Suffice it to say that the best choice is often based on experience. The lesson procedure, as well as other factors, however, must be considered in your selection of methods. Indeed, some writers (Orlich et al., 1990) suggest there are four factors that affect the selection of the appropriate instructional method

For material related to this concept, go to Clip 4.3 on the Student Resource CD bound into the back of your textbook.

TABLE 4.3 Comparison of Teacher-Centered and Student-Centered Methodologies

Method	Amount of Teacher Control	Intent and Unique Features
Teacher-Centered Instructional Approaches		
Lecture	High	Telling technique: Teacher presents information without student interaction
Lecture-Recitation	High to Moderate	Telling technique: Teacher presents information and follows up with question-and-answer sessions
Socratic	Moderate	Interaction technique: Teacher uses question-driven dialogues to draw out information from students
Demonstration	High to Moderate	Showing technique: Individual stands before class, shows something, and talks about it
Modeling	High	Showing technique: Teacher or individual behaves/acts in way desired of students. Students learn by copying actions of model
Student-Centered Instructional Approaches		
Discussion	Low to Moderate	Interaction technique: Whole class or small group interact on topic
Panel	Low	Telling technique: Group of students present and/or discuss information
Debate	Low	Telling technique: Competitive discussion of topic between teams of students
Role Playing	Low	Doing technique: Acting out of roles or situations
Cooperative Learning	Low	Doing technique: Students work together in mixed-ability group on task(s)
Discovery	Low to Moderate	Doing technique: Students follow established procedure in an attempt to solve problems through direct experiences
Inquiry	Low	Doing technique: Students establish own procedure to solve problem through direct experiences
Simulations/Games	Low	Doing technique: Involvement in an artificial but representative situation or event
Individualized Instruction	Low to Moderate	Telling/doing technique: Students engage in learning designed to fit their needs and abilities
Independent Study	Low	Telling/doing technique: Learning carried out with little guidance

SOURCE: Moore, K. D. (2001). *Classroom Teaching Skills* (5th ed.). New York: McGraw-Hill. Used with permission.

for a particular lesson: content and objectives of the lesson, teacher characteristics, learner characteristics, and the learning environment.

Your lesson must have a purpose. Are you trying to teach in the cognitive, affective, or psychomotor domain? The selection of a methodology and related experiences depends on the teaching domain. In addition, your selection should be related to such factors as goals, specific learning objectives, and content. For example, if you are trying to teach a psychomotor skill or develop an attitude, the lecture method is not a desirable approach.

Like all teachers, you have a unique set of personal experiences, background knowledge, teaching skills, and personality traits that make you more comfortable and more effective with certain methodologies than with others. Obviously, you will select the methods that have proven most successful in the past. Because teachers are inclined to select the methodology that makes them feel most comfortable, it is easy to get into a teaching rut. Therefore, you should be prepared to experiment with different methods. You cannot become comfortable or even familiar with methods you have not used.

Your selected methodology must also match the maturity level and experiences of your students. You would not use the lecture method with slower students or young children who have trouble paying attention to verbal messages. Just as teachers often prefer one teaching style, students feel comfortable and learn better when the method fits their abilities, needs, and interests. Keep in mind that when your method is mismatched with students' preferred style, learning does not take place at the maximum level. Thus, you should select the best method for a particular class.

Obviously, your selected method may not always be the best one for all students in a single class, but it should be the best method for the class as a whole. Indeed, to fit the abilities, needs, and interests of every student in a class, you must individualize the instruction. Individualizing instruction does not mean, however, that you leave students on their own at all times. Some direct instruction (active teacher-centered instruction) should be used even when individualizing. After all, you are responsible for organizing the content and directing the learning process.

The environment and related environmental factors also must be taken into account when you select your methodology. Factors such as the space available, time of day, and weather can influence a lesson greatly. For example, you should not select a method such as the discovery method, which requires a great deal of space, when little space is available and when you have a large class.

Finally, how much time should you devote to each of the two approaches to instruction? This is a complex question. This decision varies depending on the subject, the grade level, the amount of time students have available for the lesson, the materials available, and the philosophy of the teacher and school. Indeed, whenever possible, try to vary your method and become skilled in combining a variety of methods into a total lesson strategy.

APPLY AND REFLECT 4.6	Teachers should always use appropriate vocabulary. Why is this important? Shouldn't we use the language of our students?

Procedure Selection

As noted earlier, the lesson procedure is your outline, or model, of instruction for the implementation of the lesson, and it generally takes one of two basic forms: the teacher-centered or student-centered model. These approaches differ in the amount of structure offered students. The traditional model (teacher centered) involves all students in all activities at the same time, whereas the interactive model (student centered)—through its diagnostic-corrective-enrichment activities—provides a high degree of individualization because it enables students to learn at different paces and to use different materials. These two models will be addressed at length in Chapters 5, 6, and 7.

No matter whether you are an experienced teacher or a novice or how much detail is included in a written lesson plan, the lesson must be well structured to be successful. The structure should incorporate instructional strategies and techniques that will keep students interested and motivated. Some commonly used techniques include the following:

- Making your activities meaningful through active involvement of students
- Making the content as relevant as possible
- Keeping the instructional atmosphere as safe and informal as possible
- Being enthusiastic about the material you are teaching
- Challenging students by pointing out problems, inconsistencies, and contradictions throughout your lessons
- Sharing your lesson goals, objectives, and procedures with students, so that they will know where they are going and how they are going to get there
- Whenever feasible, using the ideas, suggestions, and opinions expressed by students so they will feel you value their input

Attention to these above suggestions and to the factors that should be considered in selecting an instructional strategy will lead to more effective instruction.

Closure

For material related to this concept, go to Clip 4.4 on the Student Resource CD bound into the back of your textbook.

How will the lesson end? Will the bell ring and the students file out to begin another lesson in a different subject area? Will you simply tell students to put their reading books away and take out their social studies books? These are not very satisfactory ways for lessons to end. A **closure** activity should provide a logical conclusion; it should pull together and organize the concepts learned. Once your lesson has been concluded, the lesson closure consolidates the main concepts and ideas and integrates them within the students' existing cognitive structure.

Closure should be more than a quick review of the ideas covered in the lesson. It should be designed to enable students to organize the new material in relation to itself and to other lessons. It should show the relationship among the major ideas and tie together the parts of the lesson. Closure is a vital, and often overlooked, component in the teaching-learning process. Indeed, it is as vital as your set induction and your lesson itself.

Closure isn't something that takes place only at the conclusion of a lesson: Sometimes you may want to achieve closure during the course of a particular lesson. Closure can be appropriate in the following situations:

- Following up a film, record, play, or television program
- Summarizing the presentation of a guest speaker
- Closing a group discussion
- Summarizing experiences of a field trip
- Consolidating the learning of a new concept
- Ending a science experiment
- Concluding a long unit of study

Many methods of providing closure are available. Having students relate the material learned back to the general theme is one way to achieve closure. Examples of methods that can be implemented to initiate closure discussions include such statements as "The characteristics of this play make it an excellent example of a comedy," "These proofs tend to support our original generalization that a negative number times a positive number results in a negative number," and "This form of government fits our model of a dictatorship."

Cueing is another technique used to provide closure. Have students fill in an outline you have provided that includes the main points of the lesson. Use cueing questions or statements. Examples of cueing questions are "What are some things we found in our study of rocks?" and "Which governmental agencies can we credit with primary involvement in environmental issues?" Cueing statements might include "There are four major environmental issues that society must address, and they are . . ." and "You learned the following things about community helpers: one . . . " Cueing is an important skill to develop. In a courtroom, cueing is called "leading the witness." In the classroom, cueing is a necessary tool for organizing conceptual learning.

You can also draw attention to the completion of the lesson through the use of summary questions. A question such as "What were the four major ideas covered in today's lesson?" or "Joe, can you summarize today's lesson?" or "Let's see if we can draw any conclusions from our discussion?" can effectively close a lesson.

Connecting new and previously learned material can help students reach closure. A structured statement can be used, such as "Let's relate this to yesterday's study of the nervous system," "This form of art is similar to the other forms of art we have studied," and "Can we relate this example to examples we have studied in the past?"

Another commonly used way for achieving closure is to have students demonstrate or apply what they have learned. If they cannot demonstrate or apply the new concept or skill, then learning is questionable. Examples of this technique include teacher questions such as "Can you give me other examples of verbs and adverbs?" or statements such as "Let's diagram the two sentences at the top of page 123, as the textbook did in its examples" and "Let's do the oral exercises on page 97 together." Demonstrating or applying new information at the conclusion of a lesson has the added advantage of providing needed immediate feedback to the students. Many teachers have students do in-class assignments to achieve closure by application and to provide the needed feedback.

Every student in your class must achieve closure on a lesson. One student's achievement of closure does not indicate that all students have achieved it. Just because one student is able to answer closure questions correctly does not mean that all can. Therefore, you must take care to ensure that all students achieve closure. Complete Web Link 4.3: Closure to gain additional skill at planning closures for lessons.

WEB LINK 4.3   Closure

Access the lesson plans at URL Web site www.eduref.org/Virtual/Lessons. Locate five lesson plans relative to the grade and subjects you expect to teach. Analyze and modify the closures to make them more effective for your future students.

Lesson Planning for Everyday Use

The formats described in this chapter are probably more detailed than the formats you will use in the schools. Experienced teachers use an abridged format—commonly found in planning books—like that shown earlier in Figure 4.2.

Planning book formats that are blocked out in terms of days and periods are useful for keeping track of a week's class activities. Because of the limited space available in these books, however, teachers usually list only major activities or topics for a class period, as is shown in Figure 4.13. A quick glance tells the teacher the major activities for the period of the day. This is often helpful in keeping track of where a unit is going.

The use of a planning book does not mean that thorough planning is unnecessary. Every lesson should be thoughtfully planned in detail. The shortened plan can be helpful for communication with

Figure 4.13
Activities for Class
Period

Period 1	Review homework
	Introduce film
	Show film
	Discuss film
	Give assignment

school administration; in fact, some teachers submit a copy of this planning book format for the required weekly lesson plan.

The planning approach typically recommended in textbooks on instruction and by methods course instructors involves developing objectives, selecting subject matter and associated materials, choosing strategies and methods to be employed, and deciding how to evaluate the achievement of intended outcomes. Preservice students, student teachers, and beginning teachers need to comply with this rational model to develop and/or refine their planning skills. Research indicates, however, that experienced teachers often modify this approach. Objectives, as such, play a very little part in initial planning (although they are subsequently useful for communicating intentions to students and other parties). Instead, experienced teachers focus on the content to be taught and specific instructional activities. Objectives do, however, provide valuable direction for lesson development for experienced teachers.

Planning also goes on more in the mind than on paper for many experienced teachers. Experienced teachers tend to be involved in planning every free thinking moment of the day. They also rely to an extent on incidental planning.

APPLY AND REFLECT 4.7

What would you do if a planned lesson went badly? Would you stick with the plan no matter what or improvise? Should teachers always have a backup plan ready in case a lesson doesn't go well?

REFLECTIONS ON TEACHER PRACTICE 4.2   A Year Plan

1. What are the benefits of having teachers plan for the year at the beginning of school?

2. How will technology make teachers better planners? Better teachers?

◆ ◆ ◆

I spend many hours at the beginning of the year making a Year Plan, with the objectives and concepts, topics, or stories that I plan to teach each week, trying to make sure all objectives will be covered and introduced in some sort of logical or sequential manner. I've written my plans on the computer for the past several years, just setting up a table and copying the master to a new document each week, saving by date and main topic. Like the other savers, I find this to be a great resource in later years—especially now that I have them on computer I can just search and find my topics so easily. Since my schedule and

special things change throughout the year, my table/template will also change as needed. Since Texas has made such a push to cover all of the objectives and to retain children who can't pass state tests, I have started writing the state objective numbers after each entry in my plans. At first this was a real pain, but I found that it actually turned out to be an excellent training for learning exactly what my objectives are. I believe that I am much better at including things that I might have left out in the course of teaching because I do know objectives better. I usually look at my plans at the first and last of the day, and occasionally to check for a page number or other specific detail. I don't feel bound by the plans, and give myself the freedom to go with the flow if the lesson leads . . . but with plans I know I won't stray too far for too long. Unless you are following a textbook or other pre-planned series or routing, I would question whether or not a person could keep in mind where they were going, what they had covered, and what hadn't been addressed without some sort of reference I probably go to the extreme in detailing my plans, but I have had a few weeks when they just didn't get made. Those have never been weeks that I would count as my most effective. I think you can be an excellent teacher without lesson plans, but don't see how having them could do anything but make you even better. (The clearer the target, the more precise the hit.)

—SJ, elementary teacher

SOURCE: Reprinted with permission from ProTeacher, a professional community for elementary teachers (http://www .proteacher.net).

ON YOUR OWN 4.3 **Reflections on Teacher Practice**

Read and reflect on viewpoints expressed in A Year Plan. Log on to the Web-based student study site at http://www.sagepub.com/eis2study and react to the related activities.

Reflective Teaching

A model that is receiving much attention is the concept of the teacher as a reflective decision maker. Donald Cruickshank (1987), the primary architect of **reflective teaching,** suggests that reflective teachers consider their teaching carefully and, as a result, are more thoughtful and alert students of teaching. Essentially, according to Cruickshank, careful reflections on past experiences result in teacher growth and lead to more effective planning and teaching. Reflective teachers ask themselves such questions as, "What am I doing and why?" "How can I better meet my students' needs?" "What are some alternative learning activities to achieve my objectives?" "How could I have encouraged more involvement or learning on the part of the students?"

Self-knowledge and self-assessment are hallmarks of reflective practice. Good teachers are constantly evaluating their own behavior and finding better ways of doing thing. Even when lessons go well, reflective teachers analyze the lesson to determine what went well and why and how else things might have been done. Teaching practices tend to become routine with time and are repeated with very little or no forethought. Through reflective teaching, however, a teacher might examine student satisfaction with a lesson or examine whether all students were actively involved in a lesson. Reflective teachers learn to formulate their own rules, principles, and philosophies that can guide them to better practices. In other words, teachers who reflect on their practices—who submit them to examination—become better decision makers and, consequently, better planners and more successful teachers. Think about your teaching, test new ideas, and evaluate the results—and you will improve your teaching practice.

APPLY AND REFLECT 4.8   Reflection takes time and effort. Is reflective teaching worth this investment of time and effort? Do you think the reflective teaching process will make you a better teacher?

This concludes the discussion of lesson plan structure. Table 4.4 gives a summary of section concepts. Review Table 4.4 and complete Review and Reflective Exercise 4.2, which will check your understanding of the concepts presented in this section.

TABLE 4.4 Lesson Plan Structure Concepts

Component	Description
Set induction	Activity at outset of a lesson to get students' undivided attention, to arouse their interest, and to establish a conceptual framework
Instructional strategy	The methodology and procedure. It is the global plan of a lesson.
Methodology learning	Planned patterned behaviors that are definite steps by which the teacher influences
Procedure	Sequence of steps designed to lead students to the acquisition of the desired learning
Closure	An activity designed to pull a lesson together and bring it to a logical conclusion

ON YOUR OWN 4.4   Public View of Education

Log on to the Web-based student study site at http://www.sagepub.com/eis2study. Review the public surveys relative to Chapter 4 and react to the related activities.

REVIEW AND REFLECTIVE EXERCISE 4.2   Discuss lesson planning in terms of set induction, instructional strategy, and closure.

REVIEW

- What is the purpose of the lesson set induction and closure?
- What is the lesson instructional strategy?

REFLECTION

- What kinds of lesson plans would be most appropriate for the grade and/or subject you expect to teach? How will you approach the introduction and closure?

SUMMARY

Effective teaching requires planning. Novices, as well as experienced teachers, must plan and plan well.

Planning Instruction

- Teachers engage in four levels of planning: course, unit, weekly, and daily.
- Course planning is the broadest and most general type of planning.
- Comprehensive unit plans that include a title, goals and instructional objectives, an outline of content, learning activities, resources and materials, and evaluation strategies are necessary for coherent instruction. Accommodations for exceptional students and reflections should also be important components of unit plans.
- The planning of daily lessons should be viewed as one of the most important components of effective teaching.

Lesson Plan Structure

- A strong set induction (focus) is crucial for a lesson. It sets the tone and establishes a conceptual framework for the coming activities.
- The methodology and procedure form the lesson instructional strategy. The method used forms the heart of a lesson where you decide which will be most appropriate, a teacher-centered or a student-centered mode of delivery.
- When selecting a lesson method, students should actively respond in some manner or should at least be mentally alert.
- Lessons should have a well-planned ending. This is your lesson closure.
- Teachers should be reflective decision makers. Reflective teachers encompass past experiences in planning their teaching.

DISCUSSION QUESTIONS AND ACTIVITIES

1. **Set induction techniques on television.** Watch the beginnings of several television programs, and notice how the concept of cognitive set is used to get viewers interested in the upcoming program. Can you use the same techniques in the classroom environment?
2. **Closure techniques on television.** Watch the endings of several television programs, and notice whether closure is achieved. If so, how?
3. **Textbook.** Examine the teacher's guide for a textbook in your field at the grade level you expect to teach. Are the units and lessons organized as you would like to teach them? How would you change the sequence if you had to use this text for teaching? Are there things you would like to leave out or add?
4. **Research.** Collect as many examples of unit and lesson plan models as you can find in the library. Try to think of one lesson in your field that is particularly suited to each model you discover. Develop a few lesson plans using the models you have collected.
5. **Planning a lesson.** Plan a lesson presentation for the topic of your choice for the grade level or content you expect to teach. Include in the plan the three key ingredients that make up a well-written lesson plan.

TECHNOLOGY AND EDUCATION

An excellent Internet resource for teachers is the ERIC Resource Information Center (http://www.eric.ed.gov/), which provides a wide range of free information about educational topics. Access the site and review the information available. What information on the site would be useful to you at the grade level you expect to teach? Summarize the information and share it with your classmates.

DECONSTRUCTING THE STANDARDS

Chapter 4 content addresses topics related to INTASC Standards 4, 7, and 8.

- ◆ INTASC Standard 4 states: *Multiple Instructional Strategies:* The teacher uses various instructional strategies to encourage students' development of critical thinking, problem solving, and performance skills.
- ◆ INTASC Standard 7 states: *Instructional Planning Skills:* The teacher plans instruction based on knowledge of subject mater, students, the community, and curriculum goals.
- ◆ INTASC Standard 8 states: *Assessment of Student Learning:* The teacher understands and uses formal and informal assessment strategies to evaluate and ensure the continuous intellectual, social, and physical development of the learner.

For each of these three standards, write your response to the following:

- Which part(s) of each standard does this chapter address?
- How does this chapter address this standard?
- How will the concepts in this chapter help you apply this standard as a teacher?

PRAXIS CONNECTION

Log on to the Web-based student study site at http://www.sagepub.com/eis2study. Access the Praxis II: Principles of Learning and Teaching assessments and/or state-related exams and complete the Chapter 4 test preparation exercises.

PORTFOLIO CONNECTION

Log on to the Web-based student study site at http://www.sagepub.com/eis2study. Access the Portfolio Connection. Complete the Chapter 4 portfolio link to INTASC activities.

1. **Classroom Interviews.** Visit with teachers at local schools. Find out how the standards, assessment, and accountability movement has affected these schools and how the teachers are affected in their classrooms.

2. **Classroom observation.** Observe in several classrooms. Note the structure of the lessons being presented. Can you identify the elements that constitute the lesson plan? How is set induction achieved? How is closure achieved? Can you draw any conclusions as a result of your observations?

3. **Teacher interviews.** Interview several teachers. Are they required to write and submit lesson plans? Do they include the three major components of a lesson plan?

Designing Instruction to Maximize Student Learning

Effective teaching methods often make or break a lesson. The chapters in Part III focus on helping you choose and use appropriate methods for specific learning intent. The strengths and limitations of various teaching strategies and methods are the focus of these chapters.

Effective teachers must keep students involved in their lessons if they are to accomplish their intent. Thus, teachers must master a variety of teaching strategies. They must be able to establish and maintain student attention. They must be able to elicit responses from students so as to keep them involved. Therefore, Chapters 5, 6, 7, and 8 focus on selecting teaching strategies, questioning, and reinforcement that will help accomplish this task.

Chapters 5, 6, and 7 focus on using the direct, indirect, and integrated teaching methods for instructional delivery. Chapter 8 focuses on developing thinking skills as part of the school curriculum.

CHAPTER 5

Using Direct Teaching Methods

Not only is there an art in knowing a thing, but also a certain art in teaching it.

—CICERO

OVERVIEW

I will now engage in a study of actions and skills that produce learning. In this chapter, you will study direct approaches that can be used to organize and present integrated bodies of knowledge for instruction. Direct teaching and exposition approaches to teaching integrated bodies of knowledge provide us with direct instructional alternatives.

Effective questioning patterns have long been associated with good teaching. As such, it is important that prospective teachers recognize and use behavior patterns related to the productive use of the different levels of questions, as well as the different kinds of questions and proven questioning techniques. Thus, in this chapter, I will focus special attention on questioning and its effective use in the classroom.

OBJECTIVES

After completing your study of Chapter 5, you should be able to do the following:

- Discuss factors that should be considered in selecting teaching techniques and strategies.
- Define *direct teaching* and *exposition teaching* and discuss the strengths and weaknesses of the various methods within these teaching strategies.
- Describe the *direct teaching* format and its appropriate uses.
- Explain the importance of and techniques for improving the lecture method.
- Explain the importance of incorporating different levels and types of questions.
- Identify and differentiate between the different categories of questions, as well as the levels within these categories.
- Identify and differentiate between focusing, prompting, and probing questions.
- Define wait time 1, wait time 2, halting time, and silent time.
- Define and explain the benefits derived from the use of the redirecting technique, wait times, and halting time.
- Identify guidelines that should be followed in effective questioning.

Children often need help in learning how to learn. Basically, you will have three types of students in your classes: students who can learn on their own, students who need some help in learning, and students who need a lot of help in learning. Your job will be to provide training to those students who need help with the skills needed in building concepts. Thus, your instructional purposes will be to make information meaningful, to help students develop learning and study skills, and to teach so knowledge can be applied or transferred to other areas.

Successful teachers draw from a variety of strategies (methods and procedures) in accomplishing their instructional purposes. Strategies should be selected that best serve the delivery of content and achievement of the purposes and objectives. If strategies are just arbitrarily chosen, then their emphases are on themselves, rather than on content, purposes, or objectives.

Strategies, then, should be viewed as utilitarian: They achieve the instructional intent. For example, if the intent of a social studies lesson is to share views on some controversial issue, it is obvious that the discussion method and applicable procedures should assist in achieving this objective. The lecture method, or simply showing a film, would not support the intent of the lesson.

For material related to this concept, go to Clip 5.1 on the Student Resource CD bound into the back of your textbook.

With all the possible strategies, how do you decide which is best? Experience can often be the best basis for selection; however, other factors often must be considered in your selection of strategies:

- What are the students' needs?
- What age are the students?
- What are the students' intellectual abilities?
- What are the students' physical and mental characteristics?
- What are the students' attention spans?
- What is the lesson purpose?
- What content is to be taught?

You should take such factors into account when you consider teaching strategies and, above all, select those strategies that should best serve the teaching situation.

Some strategies influence students directly, whereas others influence students indirectly; that is, some strategies emphasize focused, teacher-directed instruction, whereas others involve students actively in their own learning. Thus, there are two major ways of delivering instruction: directly or indirectly. The direct delivery of instruction ("telling") is the "traditional" or didactic mode, in which knowledge is passed on through the teacher, the textbook, or both. The indirect avenue of instruction ("showing") provides students with access to information and experiences whereby they develop knowledge and skills.

The main strength of the direct instructional strategy is that it is efficient, especially in quickly providing information to the students. It is also an effective way to allow students to achieve mastery when learning fundamental facts, rules, formulas, or sequences. The direct instructional strategy is not an effective way to teach higher level thinking, analysis, or evaluation. It cannot be used to teach material over a long period of time or present additional details to students who have already mastered the basic concepts. In contrast, the indirect instructional strategy presents students with instructional stimuli in the form of materials, objects, and events and requires students to go beyond the basic information that they are given to make their own conclusions and generalizations. Indirect instruction allows teachers to engage their students in activities that require the students to learn independently. Students take an active role in their learning by developing ideas, testing their own conclusions, and discussing their results. This allows students to independently discover patterns and relationships in their learning and knowledge. Students go beyond the basic problems presented to them, allowing them to develop advanced levels of thinking analysis.

Although instructional strategies can be categorized as direct or indirect, the distinctions are not always clear-cut. For example, a teacher may provide information through the lecture method (from the direct instructional strategy) while using a small-group discussion method to ask students to determine the significance of information that was presented (from the indirect instruction strategy).

How much time should be devoted to each of the two modes of instruction? This is a complex question. At this point, suffice it to say that the amount of time spent varies, depending on the subject, grade level, students, time, and material available, as well as the philosophy of the teacher and the school. Experience suggests, however, a compelling relationship between method of instruction and student retention, depicted in Table 5.1, in which a blend of "telling" and "showing" techniques results in greater retention. Furthermore, varying the strategy can positively affect student motivation to learn. It is a fortunate situation when you have a choice of equally effective strategies for achieving your instructional intent. In such instances, it is possible to choose a method and procedure (strategy) that will foster motivation, improve classroom control, or cost less to implement. Indeed, you should become skilled in combining various strategies into a total lesson package.

TABLE 5.1 Relationship Between Method of Instruction and Retention (in Percentages)		
Methods of Instruction	Recall 3 Hours Later	Recall 3 Days Later
Telling when used alone	70	10
Showing when used alone	72	20
Blend of telling and showing	85	65

Often, too much classroom learning is rote; that is, it is the memorization of facts or associations, such as math facts, rules of grammar, words in foreign languages, or presidents and vice presidents of the United States. Optimal learning takes place when information is made meaningful. Essentially, information must be well organized and tied into an existing cognitive structure. To accomplish this task, students must be encouraged to think about new material in ways that connect it to information or ideas already in the students' minds and to generate their own questions about the material.

The ultimate goal of teaching and learning is to develop students' ability to apply classroom-acquired information outside the classroom or in different subjects. For example, students should be able to write a letter outside the classroom, and they should be able to use mathematical skills in their science class. This ability is referred to as **transfer.** With transfer, you are trying to develop the ability to apply knowledge acquired in one situation to new situations. Presumably, students in a Spanish class will be able to communicate with people who speak Spanish. The likelihood of transfer can be enhanced by making the original learning situation as similar as possible to the situation to which information or skills will be applied. For instance, science should be taught through the use of realistic problems from your students' daily lives. Of course, another means for accomplishing transfer is through learning: Students cannot use information they do not thoroughly understand. Finally, similarity and thoroughness make it more likely that students will be able to apply newly acquired information in real-life problem situations.

The remainder of this chapter will elaborate on the direct modes of instruction: direct teaching, exposition teaching, and exposition with interaction teaching. These are modes of instruction with which you have had much experience. I will review the more indirect modes and procedures in Chapters 6 and 8 and some of the integrated direct approaches and procedures in Chapter 7.

APPLY AND REFLECT 5.1	How much time should be devoted to direct teaching and to indirect teaching at the grade level you expect to teach? Which mode of delivery do you favor? Why?

ON YOUR OWN 5.1 **View From the Classroom**

Log on to the Web-based student study site at http://www.sagepub.com/eis2study. Review the Chapter 5 teacher surveys and react to the related activities.

Direct Teaching

Direct teaching, sometimes called systematic teaching or active teaching, is a teacher-centered, skill-building instructional model with the teacher being a major information provider. The teacher's role is to pass facts, rules, or action sequences on to students in the most direct way possible. This usually takes a presentation with explanations format (modified lecture), examples, and opportunities for practice and feedback. The direct teaching format calls for teacher-student interactions involving questions and answers, review and practice, and the correction of student errors. The direct teaching strategy works best with teaching skill subjects such as reading, writing, mathematics, grammar, computer literacy, and factual parts of science and history. Young children, slower learners, and students of all ages and abilities during the first stages of learning informative material or material that is difficult to learn will benefit most from direct teaching.

Different authors describe the specific elements of direct teaching differently (see Evertson, Emmer, Clements, Sanford, & Worsham, 1994; Hunter, 1995; Rosenshine & Stevens, 1986). They generally agree, however, as to the sequence of events that characterize effective direct teaching lessons. First, the teacher brings students up-to-date on any skills they might need for the lesson and tells them what they are going to learn. Then, the teacher devotes most of the lesson time to teaching the skills or information, giving students opportunities to practice the skills or express the information,

REFLECTIONS ON TEACHER PRACTICE 5.1 **Answering Questions**

1. How can you encourage students to find their own answers to all questions?

2. Why is it important that teachers work on improving students' listening skills? How are listening and questioning related?

◆ ◆ ◆

I teach sixth grade and was going home each and every day mentally wiped out because I think I answered 9,000 questions. Questions like "Should I put my name on my paper?" (Of course.) "Can I write in red pen?" (Never.) I started calling these "self explanatory questions" because they pertained to policy that they should have had under control by now—and I think some of them just liked to hear themselves talk. Anyway, I started with discussing strategies of how they could find answers to their questions before asking me—basically just wanting to work on their listening skills. (Hey, isn't that a standard?!) I even went so far as to give them each three tickets for the day—if they had a question to ask me (not content related) that they could have found the answer for themselves, I took a ticket away in exchange for an answer. Some kids didn't even make it through first period.

As a result, I had a parent COMPLETELY flip out and call our assistant principal. She totally supported me to this

parent, but I had to write a "letter of explanation" about why I had to use the ticket system in my classroom. I made sure that I filled it with things like "listening is a skill that will benefit all students" and "by answering fewer self-explanatory questions I have more time for one-on-one instruction with students" and so forth and so on. It just made me angry that they would even waste time questioning it. At any rate, the ticket system has worked. If students make it to the end of the day with a ticket, they get a piece of candy. Now, we have stretched it to three tickets for the week— make it to Friday and you get candy. My days go much smoother!

—*MICHELLE, elementary teacher*

SOURCE: Reprinted with permission from ProTeacher, a professional community for elementary school teachers (http://www.proteacher.net).

and questioning or quizzing students to determine whether they are learning what is intended. The general lesson structure will vary in different subject areas and at different grade levels. Teachers of older students may take several days for each step in the process, ending with a formal test or quiz. Teachers of younger children may go through the entire process in one instructional period, using informal assessments at the end.

ON YOUR OWN 5.2　Reflections on Teacher Practice

Read and reflect on the viewpoints expressed in Answering Questions. Log on to the Web-based student study site at http://www.sagepub.com/eis2study and react to the related activities.

A brief description of the parts of direct teaching follows:

1. *State learning objectives and orient students to the lesson.* Tell students what they will learn and what will be expected of them. State the goals and objectives of the lesson. Establish a mental set or attitude of readiness to learn in students. This is your set induction.

2. *Review prerequisites.* Go over any skills or concepts students will need to understand the lesson. Provide advance organizers to give students a framework for understanding the new material.

3. *Present new material.* Teach the lesson, presenting information, giving concrete and varied examples and nonexamples, demonstrating concepts, and so on. Present the material in small steps. Present an outline when material is complex.

4. *Provide guided practice and conduct learning probes.* Pose questions to students to assess their level of understanding and correct their misconceptions. Give students practice problems and check for misconceptions and misunderstanding. Have students summarize in their own words. Reteach as necessary.

5. *Provide independent practice.* Give students an opportunity to practice new skills or use new information on their own, in seatwork, or in cooperative groups.

6. *Assess performance and provide feedback.* Review independent practice work or give a quiz. Give feedback on correct answers, and reteach skills as needed.

7. *Provide distributed practice and review.* Assign homework to provide distributed practice on the new material.

Madeline Hunter's "Mastery Teaching" contains many of the features of the direct teaching strategy and has been implemented in many parts of the country. Mastery teaching includes the following five steps:

1. *Anticipatory set.* The teacher presents a short activity to get students' minds ready for the planned lesson.

2. *Instruction or providing information (input).* Information is presented, including modeling and checking for understanding.

3. *Guided practice.* Students practice new learning under direct teacher supervision.

4. *Closure or checking for performance.* The teacher reviews or wraps up the lesson by posing questions for the class.

5. *Independent practice.* The teacher releases students to practice new materials on their own.

Keep in mind, however, that not all elements of the direct teaching strategy belong in every lesson, although they will occur in a typical unit plan composed of several lessons. Complete Expansion Activity 5.1: Direct Instruction to explore your thoughts on the implementation of the direct instruction strategy.

Let's now look at the various components of direct instruction in more detail. Expository teaching (lecture and explanations) and questioning hold key roles in the success of direct instruction.

EXPANSION ACTIVITY 5.1   Direct Instruction

List the sequence of steps that you feel should characterize a direct instruction lesson at the grade level you expect to teach. Is it the same as those present in this section? Why did you make the changes? Share your steps with several classmates. Do they agree?

Exposition Teaching

Exposition teaching is considered to be the best way to communicate large amounts of information in a short period of time. Exposition techniques comprise the methods in which an authority—teacher, textbook, film, or microcomputer—presents information without overt interaction between the authority and the students.

Lecture

The **lecture** is probably the most widely used exposition teaching method. Virtually every teacher employs it to some degree, and some use it almost exclusively. Though much criticized by current educators, the lecture does possess some unique strengths.

Strengths of the Lecture

The lecture is an excellent way of presenting background information when building a unit frame of reference or when introducing a unit. Indeed, it often can be just the tool for setting the atmosphere or focusing for student activities. Moreover, a short lecture can effectively wrap up a unit, an activity, or a lesson. Finally, the lecture is time-efficient; that is, planning time is devoted to organizing content, rather than to devising instructional procedure. Thus, the lecture affords the teacher ample opportunity to collect related materials, assemble them into a meaningful framework, and present the information to students in a relatively short period of time. The teacher simply plans a lecture for the entire instructional period.

Weaknesses of the Lecture

The lecture has several serious flaws, however. First, it is passive learning, with very low student involvement. Students are expected, and even encouraged, to sit quietly, listen, and perhaps take notes. Thus, it is not a good approach for helping students develop skills in thinking, problem solving, and creativity.

Second, lectures are often boring and do not motivate. For this reason—except in unusual cases—very little of a lecture is retained by students. Indeed, because lectures tend to focus on the lowest level of cognition, understanding and transfer are often limited.

Finally, the lecture method may lead to the development of discipline problems. Most lectures generate little interest, and student attention soon wanes and turns to more stimulating and often undesirable activities. Thus, not only does the lecture lose the attention of those involved in these

"It's difficult to reprimand some children for inattention in class."

SOURCE: Created by Martha Campbell.

unwanted activities, but the lecture itself is often disrupted. The wise teacher should always remember that most students are easily bored and usually have a low tolerance for boredom.

Textbook Lecture

Lecturing from the textbook could well be the most common teaching method used in today's schools. The content of such lectures usually is structured directly from the course textbook, progressing from Chapter 1 to the end of the book without deviation, as illustrated in Table 5.2.

Textbook teaching requires very little teacher preparation when the structure of the textbook is strictly followed. Indeed, when one is teaching in a content area without adequate academic preparation in that area and does not wish to spend the time to become content competent, textbook teaching is an ideal technique. Thus, the lack of time needed for preparing lesson plans and lack of content mastery are reasons for the popularity of this method of instruction.

Textbook teaching suffers from all the problems of lecturing, but it has a couple of unique flaws. First, the content of the course often becomes rigid; normally, no new content is added to the lecture, and the course content is determined entirely by an external author who is not in complete harmony with the needs of students, the school, and the community. Second, the lectures can get extremely boring, because the teacher usually is lecturing about the material students were assigned to read. If no new content is added to the lesson, students tend to either read the text or listen to the lectures—seldom both.

Planning the Lecture

Planning is essential for a good lecture. Lectures must be well crafted to be clear and persuasive. The lecture must be designed to gain—and maintain—student attention throughout the lesson, to instill motivation, and to accomplish lesson objectives. Let's now look at some techniques that can help achieve these ends.

The most successful lectures should be relatively short. Even older, brighter students probably won't listen to a lecture for more than about 20 minutes. Therefore, limit your lectures to short

TABLE 5.2	Sample Table of Contents Used in Textbook Lecturing

Chapter 1 The Science of Biology

Chapter 2 The Nature of Living Matter

Chapter 3 The Beginning of Life on the Earth

Chapter 4 Units of Living Matter

Chapter 5 The Classification of Living Things

Chapter 6 The Bacteria

Chapter 7 Microbes and Disease

Chapter 8 The Seed Plants

Chapter 9 The Higher Plant Body

Chapter 10 One-Celled Animals—The Protozoa

Chapter 11 The Mammals

Chapter 12 Muscles and Their Actions

Chapter 13 Life of the Past

Chapter 14 Human Life of the Past

periods of time and periodically change to other activities (preferably to those that require active student involvement). For example, the subdivisions of a lesson (with time allotted for each activity) might be as follows:

1. Overview of topic (10 minutes)*

2. Show a film (20 minutes)

3. Discussion of film (10 minutes)

4. Demonstration (5 minutes)

5. Wrap up and review (5 minutes)*

*Denotes activities where the teacher is lecturing.

Although this plan uses lecturing where appropriate, it relies on other techniques to augment the learning—namely, discussion and demonstration. Only three tenths of the time is devoted to lecturing; most of the time allows for more student involvement.

In planning, give careful attention to the start of your lecture. Determine the specific objectives of the lecture and share them with students at the beginning. Research (Wulf & Schane, 1984) shows that, when objectives are shared, intentional learning tends to increase. Moreover, your lecture introduction should arouse student interest, be motivational, and establish a framework for the lesson (see Chapter 4 for a review of these topics).

In preparing the lecture, you must decide what students are to do while you lecture. Will students be asked to take notes? Will students be involved in some assigned seatwork? If yes, instructions and guidelines must be planned accordingly. Using the chalkboard and passing out written instructions are often the best ways for establishing these guidelines.

A lecture must have closure (see Chapter 4). Once given, the lecture theme should be related to the course and/or to what has already been taught. This can be accomplished through a review of the major points of the lecture.

In summary, a good lecture must be well planned if it is to be clear and persuasive. Try following this good planning formula:

- Tell students what you are going to tell them.
- Tell them.
- Tell them what you have told them.

The proper application of this formula will result in a logical, well-organized lecture with a firm introduction and a well-planned wrap-up.

Presenting the Lecture

An effective lecture must maintain student interest and attention from beginning to end. Factors such as the tempo, audiovisual aids, stimulus variation, and language can exert major influence on student interest and attention.

Tempo

The tempo, or pacing, of your lecture should be moderate (not too slow or too fast). If the pace is too fast, students become discouraged with their inability to understand and keep up; if the pace is too slow, they become bored and look elsewhere for stimulation. Use feedback checks to ascertain whether students understand your material and adjust your pace according to the feedback you obtain.

Instructional-Media Learning Tools

Visual aids should accompany all lectures. The use of the chalkboard, models, pictures, transparencies, diagrams, and PowerPoints can greatly enhance a lecture. Use any media that can be used to help convey your message; they should stimulate and maintain student interest. Indeed, make your lectures as multisensory as is feasible. Multisensory input will usually result in better learning.

When appropriate, teach students to take notes. A good lecturer, for example, outlines the major points on the chalkboard or on an overhead projector. Such outlines provide students with the structure and time needed for developing their note-taking skills. Once students have become skilled note takers, the practice of supplying an outline can be discontinued.

Stimulus Variation

As you plan your lecture, create an introduction that will grab students' attention and augment your lecture with actions that will maintain this attention. **Stimulus variation** techniques, such as gestures, pauses, and teacher movement, can help keep student attention directed toward your lecture. As student attention wanders, a tap on the board, a hand gesture, sudden silence (a pause), or physical movement often will refocus attention back to your lecture.

Enthusiasm is contagious. If you express a high level of interest and sense of importance about your topic, students often become spellbound, anxious to find out what is so interesting. But be a bit careful: Too much enthusiasm can direct attention toward you, the teacher—and away from the lecture topic.

Humor and rhetorical questions can also attract and keep student attention. Humor can help reduce anxiety, whereas rhetorical questions, used in conjunction with pauses, give students the opportunity to consider and think about the information presented.

Finally, eye contact can help maintain attention. Eye contact gives students the feeling that you are addressing each of them personally. Indeed, eye contact can provide a teacher with valuable feedback on how well a lecture is being received. Look at your students; glance around and move about the room, based upon what you see.

The use of instructional materials and media enhances most lectures and stimulates student interest.

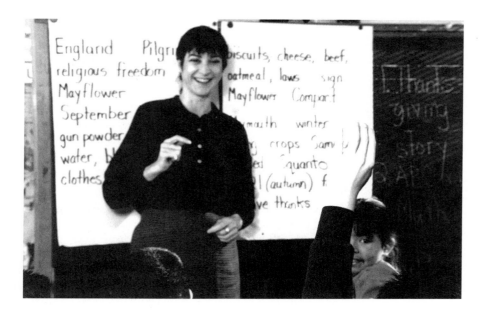

Voice and Language

Delivery can make the difference between a boring lecture and a stimulating one. Keep your voice low-pitched, be expressive, and make sure all students can hear. Your voice can bring words to life. Voice volume, rate, tone, inflection, and pitch can all communicate valuable information.

Deliver your lectures in Standard English, and use vocabulary that students will understand. That is, don't talk over your students' heads. Also, avoid using slang expressions and street language in your lectures. Such language will only confuse your students.

Balancing the Lecture

Lecturing to students is inevitable for most teachers; however, it should be used sparingly, especially with younger students, and mixed with other appropriate methods. For example, a teacher could follow up a short lecture by having students complete a worksheet, by conducting a small-group discussion, or by asking students to conduct an investigation.

Indeed, a lesson or 50-minute class period can often be divided into a number of short lectures, with a distinct change in modality between lectures. These changes retain students' attention and hold their interest for the instructional period. Above all, adjust your lecture time and style to students' attention span. Break up your lecture with other methods and activities. Devise a questioning sequence, give students a problem to solve, or give students a short break.

APPLY AND REFLECT 5.2	Lectures can be boring. How have your past teachers who used the lecture method made them more interesting? If you plan to use the lecture method extensively, how will you keep your students interested and involved?

Variants of the Lecture

Let's now examine some of the commonly used variants of the lecture. Two such variants are the tel-electure and prerecorded lecture.

Telelecture

Normally, the lecturer and students are in the same room. In some rural areas, however, an insufficient number of students needing or desiring a course in one district may not warrant the hiring of a teacher for that course. Through technology, however, it is possible for several districts to "hire" a needed teacher and to transmit lectures from a studio classroom to other locations by means of telephone, cable, or microwave. This **telelecture** enables students who are not in the immediate classroom to hear the lectures. The remote students may talk to the lecturer and ask questions by means of a telephone link. Special science, mathematics, and language courses are being taught in this manner across the nation.

Prerecorded Lecture

A lecture is easily captured on tape or film. Such tapes and films often are prepared by local school districts and by commercial publishers. Prerecorded lectures, however, have several disadvantages when compared with live lectures. First, and perhaps most important, there is *no* direct contact between students and lecturer; no minute-by-minute adjustments can be made based on feedback and questions. In addition, student attention becomes a major problem when the lecture is on tape or film; attention lags more quickly than when a person is actually present. Finally, tapes and films quickly become obsolete as new information is gleaned regarding content and teaching techniques.

Despite the flaws, prerecorded lectures have some merits. Most important is their capacity for individualized instruction because a tape or film can be played as many times as desirable. I will address individualization of instruction in greater detail in the next chapter.

Table 5.3 summarizes the different direct teaching and the exposition teaching methods. Review the summary and complete Review and Reflective Exercise 5.1.

Exposition With Interaction Teaching

For material related to this concept, go to Clip 5.2 on the Student Resource CD bound into the back of your textbook.

Exposition with interaction teaching is a method of teaching in which an authority presents information and follows it up with questioning that determines whether that information has been understood. Essentially, this method is a two-phase technique: First, information is disseminated by the teacher or through students' study of written material. Second, the teacher checks for comprehension by asking questions to assess student understanding of the material explained or studied.

TABLE 5.3	Exposition Teaching
Method	**Description**
Direct teaching	Teacher controls instruction by presenting information and giving directions to the class; associated with teacher-centered, teacher-controlled classrooms; an instructional procedure for teaching content in the most efficient, straightforward way
Lecture	Teacher presents information, with no overt interaction with students
Telelecture	Lecture transmitted from central-studio classroom to distant classrooms
Textbook lecture	Lecturing directly about material presented in the textbook
Prerecorded lecture	Lecture that has been recorded on videotape or film

Lectures need not be passive learning. They can be made stimulating.

The comprehension monitoring phase of this teaching technique requires that the teacher be knowledgeable and an effective questioner. Because questioning is so essential to the overall success of exposition with interaction, let's first analyze this important skill in some detail.

The Art of Questioning

Proper questioning is a sophisticated art at which many of us are less than proficient even though we have asked thousands of questions in our lives. Research indicates that questioning is second only to lecturing in popularity as a teaching method. Teachers spend anywhere from 35% to 50% of their instructional time conducting questioning sessions. Teachers ask questions for a variety of purposes, including

- To develop interest and motivate students
- To evaluate students' preparation and check on homework
- To develop critical thinking skills
- To review and summarize previous lessons
- To assess achievement of objectives

Questioning is an important part of the teaching-learning process because it enables teachers and students to establish what is already known, to use and extend this knowledge, and then to develop new ideas. It also provides a structure to examine ideas and information. Questioning is important to developing reflective and metacognitive thinking. It requires students to reflect on their understandings and can lead to changes and improvements in learning, thinking, and teaching.

Good questioners must be skilled in formulating good questions: Questions must be asked at the appropriate level, they must be of the appropriate, and, above all, they must be worded properly. Moreover, the art of questioning requires mastery of techniques for follow-up to students' responses—or lack of response—to questioning. The kinds of questions asked, the way they are asked, and the responses given affect both the self-esteem of the students and their participation. Let's now look at the different levels at which questions may be asked.

REVIEW AND REFLECTIVE EXERCISE 5.1   Describe direct teaching and the lecture method.

REVIEW

- What are the strengths and weaknesses of direct teaching and the lecture method?
- How can you make the lecture method more effective?

REFLECTION

- Reflect on the teaching methods used by your past teachers. Did they use direct teaching? The lecture method? Was it effective?
- Do you plan on using direct teaching or the lecture method in the area you expect to teach? How will you make them effective?

APPLY AND REFLECT 5.3   Do you think questions can be used effectively to promote learning? How?

Levels of Questions

Questions may be categorized as being "narrow" or "broad." Narrow questions usually ask for only factual recall or specific correct answers, whereas broad questions seldom can be answered with a single word. Moreover, broad questions do not have one correct answer and call on students to reach beyond simple memory. Broad questions prompt students to use the thinking process in formulating answers. Both narrow and broad questions contribute to the learning process. Too often, however, teachers rely too heavily on narrow questions when learning would be greatly enhanced through the use of both types of questions.

You must adapt the level of your questions to the purpose for which they are being asked. Consequently, ask questions that reveal whether students have gained specific knowledge, as well as questions that stimulate the thinking process. Because thinking can take place at several levels of sophistication, it is important that you as a teacher be able to classify—and ask—questions at these different levels.

Many effective classification systems have been developed for describing the levels of questions. Most of these systems are useful only to the extent that they can provide a framework for formulating questions at the desired level within a classroom environment. Consequently, some teachers may want to use only a two-level classification system, whereas others may want to use a more detailed system.

This discussion will focus on two systems that will be of most benefit to you as a classroom teacher. The first widely used system classifies questions as either *convergent* or *divergent;* the second categorizes questions according to the mental operation students use in answering them. These two classification systems are only two of the many systems to which you can refer in your classroom. When you prepare questions, however, evaluate them according to some classification system. By so doing, you will significantly improve the quality of your questions.

Convergent and Divergent Questions

One of the simplest and easiest ways of classifying questions is to determine whether they are convergent or divergent. **Convergent questions** allow for only a few right responses, whereas **divergent questions** allow for many correct responses.

Questions regarding concrete facts that have been learned and committed to memory are convergent. Most who, what, and where questions are also classified as convergent:

"Mirror, mirror, on the wall, who's the most sensitive,
open, student-centered, and innovative teacher of all?"

SOURCE: Created by Ford Button.

"What is 2 + 2?"

"Who was the 25th president of the United States?"

"What type of equation is $x^2 + 3x + 3 = 0$?"

"Where is Stratford-upon-Avon located?"

"What was the major cause of the Great Depression?"

Convergent questions may also require students to recall and integrate or analyze information for determining *one expected* correct answer. Thus, the following questions would also be classified as convergent:

"Based on our discussion, what is the major cause of water pollution?"

"By combining the formulas for a triangle and a rectangle, what would be the formula for finding the area of a trapezoid?"

"Based on our definition of a noun, can you name three nouns?"

Most alternate-response questions, such as yes/no and true/false questions, would also be classified as convergent because the responses available to students are limited.

Conversely, questions calling for opinions, hypotheses, or evaluation are divergent in that many possible correct responses may be given:

"Why do you suppose we entered World War II?"

"What would be a good name for this painting?"

"Can you give me a sentence in which this word is used correctly?"

"Why is it important that we speak correctly?"

Divergent questions should be used frequently because they encourage broader responses and, therefore, are more likely to engage students in the learning process. They prompt students to think. Convergent questions, however, are equally important in that they deal with the background information needed in dealing with divergent questions. In the classroom, it is generally desirable to use convergent questions initially and then move toward divergent questions.

Mental Operation Questions

Based on the work of J. P. Guilford and Benjamin Bloom, Moore (2001) developed the Mental Operation system for classifying questions. Table 5.4 shows the relationship between the Mental Operation system, Guilford's Structure of the Intellect model, and Bloom's Taxonomy. The **Mental Operation system** is basically a four-category system that combines the cognitive and memory categories of the Guilford model into a single factual category. In addition, it combines four of Bloom's categories of higher order thinking into two categories (see Chapter 3). The categories of questions that make up the Mental Operation model are factual, empirical, productive, and evaluative.

Factual questions test the student's recall or recognition of information learned by rote. That is, it tests the student's recall or recognition of information that has been committed to memory through some form of repetition or rehearsal. Some examples of factual questions are listed here:

"Who drilled the first oil well?"

"Joe, can you define the short story?"

"Which of these is the chemical formula for salt?"

"What is the formula for the volume of a cylinder?"

Empirical questions require that students integrate or analyze remembered or given information and supply a single, correct *predictable* answer. Indeed, the question may call for quite a lot of thinking, but, once thought out, the answer is usually a single, correct answer. Empirical questions are also narrow questions. Some examples of empirical questions include the following:

"Based on our study of California, what conditions led to its becoming a state?"

"Given that this circle has a radius of 5 centimeters, what is its area?"

"According to the information provided in the text, what is the most economical source of energy presently being used in the United States?"

"Which of these two forms of government is most like the British?"

Note that when answering these questions, students must recall learned information and carry out a mental activity with that information to arrive at the correct answer. There is, however, only one correct, predictable answer.

TABLE 5.4	Categories of Questions		
Mental Operation Questions	**Guilford's Structure of the Intellect**		**Bloom's Taxonomy**
1. Factual	Cognitive/memory		Knowledge/comprehension
2. Empirical	Convergent thinking		Application/analysis
3. Productive	Divergent thinking		Synthesis
4. Evaluative	Evaluative thinking		Evaluation

Productive questions do not have a single, correct answer, and it may be impossible to predict what the answer will be. Productive questions are open-ended and call for students to use their imaginations and think creatively. These questions ask students to develop a unique idea. Although the broad nature of productive questions prompts students to go beyond the simple recall of remembered information, students still need the basic related information to answer them. Following are some examples of productive questions:

"How can we improve our understanding and use of English?"

"What changes would we see in society if we were to eliminate unemployment in the world?"

"What are some possible solutions to the problem of world hunger?"

"What do you suppose the painter's intent was in this painting?"

Finally, **evaluative questions** require that students put a value on something or make some kind of judgment. Evaluative questions are special cases of productive questions in that they, too, are often open-ended. They can, however, be more difficult to answer than are productive questions in that some internal or external criteria must be used; that is, some criteria must be established for making the judgment. The responses to evaluative questions can often be predicted or limited by the number of choices. For example, the question "Which of these two short stories is the best?" limits the responses to two, whereas the question "What is the best automobile made today?" allows a variety of responses. Other examples of evaluative questions are these:

"Who was our greatest scientist?"

"How would you rate our success in controlling government spending in this nation?"

"Do you think the author of the play developed the characters sufficiently?"

"Are Native Americans portrayed accurately in the movies?"

These questions call on students to make judgments based on internal criteria. When student responses are formally evaluated and bear directly on grades, however, you must establish evaluative criteria. The alternative is to rely on students' internalized criteria, which you cannot evaluate, confirm, or refute. You can establish evaluative criteria for your evaluative questions by following them up with an empirical or a productive question that asks for the reasons behind the stated judgment or value or by making sure you develop and ask evaluative questions in a way that includes external criteria.

Use of the Mental Operation system of classifying questions (Table 5.5) should give you the needed framework for improving your questioning skill. You should be asking questions at all four levels of the system, instead of at the factual level only, as many teachers do. To this end, you should plan and ask more productive and evaluative questions than is commonly done by teachers. These questions will give your students the opportunity to think and reason.

| APPLY AND REFLECT 5.4 | Think back to your most recent class. What kinds of questions did your professor ask? What sort of thinking is required? |

TABLE 5.5   Levels of Classroom Questions

Category	Type of Thinking	Examples
Factual	Student simply recalls information "Who was…" "What did the text say…"	"Define…"
Empirical	Student integrates and analyzes given or recalled information "Explain in your own words…" "Calculate the…"	"Compare…"
Productive	Student thinks creatively and imaginatively and produces unique idea or response "What's a good name for…" "How could we…"	"What will life be like…"
Evaluative	Student makes judgments or expresses values "Why do you favor this…" "Who is the best…"	"Which painting is best?"

Types of Questions

As an effective teacher, you must ask the right types of questions. That is, you must adapt the type of question to the specific purpose for which you are asking the question. For example, you may want to ask questions to determine the level of your students' study, to increase student involvement and interaction, to increase clarification, or to stimulate student awareness. These purposes call for different types of questions.

Focusing Questions

Focusing questions, which may be factual, empirical, productive, or evaluative, are used to direct student attention. Focusing questions can determine what has been learned by students, can motivate and arouse student interest at the start of a lesson or during the lesson, can stimulate involvement and check understanding during a lesson, and can check students' understanding of lesson material at the close of a lesson.

Was the assigned chapter read by students? No use discussing the material if it wasn't read! Did the students learn and understand the material assigned? Can students apply the information? Focusing

Questions can often give a lesson life and arouse student interest.

questions can provide valuable information regarding these concerns. Ask factual questions to check on basic knowledge at the beginning of or during a lesson. Use empirical questions to have students figure out correct solutions for problems related to assignments or issues being discussed. Pose productive and evaluative questions for motivating and stimulating thinking and interest in the topic.

When opening a lesson or discussion with a question, it is good practice to use a productive or evaluative question that focuses on the upcoming topic. The question should be such that it arouses students' interest and thinking:

"What do you suppose would happen if I were to drop these two objects at the same time?"

"How could we test the hypothesis suggested by the results?"

"Should we do away with the income tax in the United States?"

These questions should then be followed with questions at all levels to develop understanding and to maintain interest.

Prompting Questions

What should you do when a student fails to answer a question? Most teachers answer the question themselves or move on to another student. This technique will get your question answered, but it fails to involve the original student in the discussion. Rather, it leaves that student with a sense of failure, which, more than likely, will result in even less participation in the future. A better way to address this problem is to use a prompting question as a follow-up to the unanswered question.

Prompting questions use clues that help students answer questions or correct initially inaccurate responses. Thus, a prompting question is usually a rewording of the original question—with clues added. Consider this example of a prompting questioning sequence:

Teacher: What is x^2 times x^3, Pat?

Pat: I don't know.

Teacher:	Well, let's see if we can figure it out. What do we do with the exponents when we multiply variables?
Pat:	Multiply?
Teacher:	No.
Pat:	Add!
Teacher:	Right! So, if we add 2 + 3, what will our answer be?
Pat:	[*Pause*] 5.
Teacher:	So what would x^2 times x^3 be?
Pat:	x^5.
Teacher:	Very good, Pat.

Your use of prompting questions with students should lead to a sense of success when they finally answer correctly. Indeed, the successes could even act as **reinforcers** to students, which result in even greater participation.

Probing Questions

Up to this point I have discussed focusing questions and prompting questions. The former can be used for determining the level of learning and understanding and for increasing student participation, whereas the latter can be used when no response to a question is forthcoming. Another situation with which a teacher must contend occurs when the student's response is incorrect or correct yet insufficient because it lacks depth. In such cases, you should have the student correct the mistake or ask that he or she supply the additional needed information. This is accomplished through the use of probing questions.

Probing questions aim at correcting, improving, or expanding a student's initial response. They compel the student to think more thoroughly about the initial response. Probing questions can be used for correcting an initial response, eliciting clarification, developing critical awareness, or refocusing a response.

You may want to ask a probing question for the purpose of clarification. Students sometimes give flimsily thought-out answers or give only half-answers to questions. These responses should be followed up with probing questions that force the student to think more thoroughly and urge him or her to firm up the response. Here are examples of such probing questions:

"What are you saying?"

"What do you mean by the terms . . . ?"

"Would you say that in another way?"

"Could you elaborate on those two points?"

"Can you explain that point more fully? It lacks clarity."

You sometimes may want students to justify their answers; that is, you may want to foster their critical awareness. This also can be accomplished with probing questions. Probing questions that could be used to develop critical awareness include these:

"What is your factual basis for these beliefs?"

"Why do you believe that?"

"What are you assuming when you make that statement?"

"What are your reasons for those assumptions?"

"Are you sure there isn't more evidence to support that issue?"

Finally, you may want to probe to refocus a correct, satisfactory student response to a related issue. Examples of questions that could serve this function follow:

"Let's look at your answer with respect to this new information."

"Can you relate your answer to yesterday's discussion?"

"What implications does this conclusion have for . . . ?"

"Apply these solutions to . . ."

"Can you relate Mary's earlier answer to this issue?"

The different types of questions will be invaluable to you as a teaching tool. When used effectively, they can increase student participation and involve students in their own learning. You should practice these different questions and become proficient in their use.

APPLY AND REFLECT 5.5	You can use focusing, prompting, and probing questions to determine what has been learned, to arouse interest, and to stimulate involvement. Are these different question types more effective at specific grade levels? If so, what grade level?

Questioning Techniques

Certain techniques associated with asking questions tend to increase the quantity of and enhance the quality of the students' responses. Let's now look at four such techniques.

Redirecting

Redirecting is a technique that is useful for increasing the amount of student participation. It allows you to draw students into a discussion by asking them to respond to a question in light of a previous response from another student. Because this technique requires several correct responses to a single question, the question asked must be divergent, productive, or evaluative. The following is an example of how you might redirect a question:

Teacher: We have now studied the administrations of several presidents. Which president do you think made the greatest contribution?

[*Pause. Several hands go up.*] Cindi?

Cindi: Lincoln.

Teacher: Jeff?

Jeff: Washington.

Teacher: Mary, what is your opinion?

Mary: John Kennedy.

You should note that, if you are using redirecting correctly, you do not react to the student responses. You simply redirect the question to another student. Thus, it is hoped that this technique will lead to greater student participation and involvement and, consequently, to greater learning and increased interest.

The redirecting technique can also be used effectively with students who are nonvolunteers. You should try to involve these nonvolunteers as much as possible because, as noted earlier, participation enhances learning and stimulates interest.

It is important to remember, however, that nonvolunteers should never be forced to answer; rather, they should be given the opportunity to contribute to the discussion. In addition, you should give nonvolunteers ample time to consider a response. This time needed for students in considering their responses to questions is referred to as **wait time.** Let's now look at the appropriate use of wait time in questioning.

Wait Time

For material related to this concept, go to Clip 5.3 on the Student Resource CD bound into the back of your textbook.

Students need time for thinking and pondering the responses they will give to your questions. Research by Rowe (1974a, 1974b, 1978), however, has shown that teachers on the average wait only about 1 second for students to give an answer. Rowe's research also revealed that, when teachers learned to increase wait time from 3 to 5 seconds, the following results occurred:

1. Student response time increased.

2. Failure to respond tended to decrease.

3. Students asked more questions.

4. Unsolicited responses tended to increase.

5. Student confidence increased.

Basically, there are two types of *wait time. Wait time 1* is the time provided for the first student response to a question. *Wait time 2* is the total time a teacher waits for all students to respond to the same question or for students to respond to each other's response to a question. Wait time 2 may involve several minutes. If you are to engage students more in your lessons, you must learn to increase your wait time tolerance so students have more opportunities to think and to ponder their answers.

The typical pattern of questioning in the average classroom can be depicted as follows:

```
Teacher————————————————-> Student A
Teacher————————————————-> Student B
Teacher————————————————-> Student C
```

This pattern represents nothing more than a question-and-answer period. The teacher asks a question of a student, the student answers, the teacher moves to the next student and asks a question, the student answers, the teacher moves to the next student, and so on. Students often receive little time for thinking and expressing themselves and usually no time for reacting to each other's comments. In fact, most of the questions are typically at the lower level. Appropriate use of questioning techniques, higher level questions, and wait time can and should change this sequence to the following:

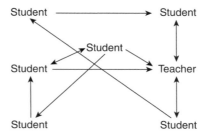

This pattern facilitates student discussion, welcomes extended responses, and provides opportunities for commenting on other students' questions and for asking questions. There is real involvement! Indeed, you will find that extending the time you wait after a question from 3 to 5 seconds—and giving students time to react to your questions and other students' responses—is well worth the added effort.

Halting Time

When presenting complex material, you need to learn to halt in what you are saying and give students time to think. This pause is referred to as **halting time.** No questions are asked, and no student comments are elicited. In using the halting time technique, you present some complex material or complicated directions and then stop momentarily so students have time to consider the information or carry out the directions. During this pause, you visually check with the class to see whether they are with you and understand what you are trying to communicate. If your observations are positive, you continue. If students appear to be confused, you may want to redo the explanation or directions.

Reinforcement

Once you have asked a question and have received an acceptable response, you must react to the response. Should you merely accept the response without comment and continue with the lesson or should you offer praise for a job well done? Your **reinforcement**—that is, your pattern of positive reaction—will have a powerful effect on the direction of the interaction in the classroom.

Rewards and praise often encourage students to participate. Phrases such as "Fine answer," "Great," "What an outstanding idea," and "Super" may be used when rewarding students' correct answers.

Reinforcement is often a good idea, but the too-frequent application of reinforcement can negate the benefits of using wait time. If reinforcement is given too early in an answering sequence, other students may decide not to respond because they fear their answer could not match an earlier response. After all, didn't you say the earlier response was "great"? Rather than give reinforcement early in the questioning-answering sequence, you should allow as many students as possible to respond to the question, then reinforce all of them for their contributions. You can always return to the best answer for further comment.

APPLY AND REFLECT 5.6	You can keep students focused on your lesson through the use of the redirecting technique, wait time, halting time, and reinforcement. Have your past teachers used these techniques? Were they effective? Why or why not?

Tips on Questioning

Asking good questions is an art. It is an art, however, that can be mastered with practice. The improper use of questioning can negatively affect learning. Teachers who strive for higher level questions, for example, may lose interest in the just as important bread-and-butter memory questions. They may even tend to cater to the capacities of superior students. Let's now look at some questioning tips that may prove helpful in avoiding questioning pitfalls.

Questions should be clear, and you should ask the question before designating who is to answer. Ask the question, wait for the class to think about it, and then specify an individual to answer. As usual, there are exceptions to this rule. When you call on an inattentive student, it is often wise to designate the individual first, so that the student is sure to hear the question. Similarly, you should call the name first of slow or shy students so that they can prepare themselves.

Distribute your questions about the class fairly. Avoid directing all questions to a selective few bright students. Also avoid using a mechanical system for asking questions because students soon catch on to such systems—such as going by alphabetical order or row by row—and they will pay attention only when it is their turn.

Do not ask more than one question at a time. Asking too many questions at once often confuses students. Simultaneous questions permit no time to think, and when several questions are asked, students are not sure which question to answer first.

Do not ask too many questions. Often, you need to establish a knowledge base before initiating a questioning sequence. This is especially true when the questions require thinking and reasoning.

Ask questions at all ability levels in the class. Some questions should be easy, whereas others should be more difficult. Also, use questions to help students modify their inaccurate responses. Use prompting and probing questions to help students think more thoroughly about their responses. This approach will increase involvement, will develop better thinking skills, and will reinforce student successes.

Finally, listen carefully to student responses. Wait at least 3 seconds following a student response. This allows the student time for making further comments and gives other students time to react to the initial student's response.

The key to the effective use of exposition with interaction is good questioning. Therefore, you must refine your ability to think, plan, and ask questions throughout your lessons. Let's now look at some methods that contain many of the features of the exposition and exposition with interaction strategies.

APPLY AND REFLECT 5.7	Do you consider effective questioning an art? What are your strengths and weaknesses as a questioner? What types and levels of questions will be the most useful to you as a classroom teacher?

Lecture Recitation

Lecture recitation is an instructional method in which the teacher presents information by telling and explaining and follows up with question-and-answer sessions at periodical intervals. Thus, questions are used for summarizing the content of the lecture and for helping students consolidate and organize the presented information.

The lecture recitation method is often efficient in terms of time, flexibility, and learning while actively involving students in the lesson. Its basic structure of teacher talk/teacher question/student response/teacher talk makes questioning the key component to the method. Moreover, this method is highly adaptable to a large variety of topics and frequently is used as a companion to the lecture method or to the study of a textbook. Indeed, it is a form of recitation.

A hybrid form of the lecture recitation method, in which questions are interspersed throughout the lecture, has proven to be the most popular among classroom teachers (Goodlad, 1984). When proper lecturing is executed and when questions are strategically used, this method is an effective and efficient way of teaching content. That is, the questions can and should be designed to provide feedback on understanding, to add variety to the lecture, and to maintain the students' attention. Moreover, questions from students can also help clarify the content and shed light on how well the lecture is being understood.

APPLY AND REFLECT 5.8	How can being asked a question be viewed as punishment for some students and reward for others?

Textbook Recitation

The **textbook recitation** method is relatively simple: You assign students content to read and study in their textbook and then question them on what they have read and studied. Textbook recitation is an effective technique for teaching basic information simply because students are often motivated to read and study the assignment in anticipation of being called on to recite the information. However, this method does not foster true understanding and the application of the assigned content.

On the other hand, textbook recitation has the added advantages of giving students feedback on the accuracy of the content learned and of providing them with the opportunity to learn from the replies of fellow students. Indeed, these ends can be accomplished by planning higher level questions in advance, with an emphasis on questioning sequences that will develop thinking and reasoning skills.

APPLY AND REFLECT 5.9	You must make sure a knowledge base has been established prior to questioning. How can this knowledge base be established?

The various direct instruction models have strengths and weaknesses. Complete Web Link 5.1: Direct Instruction to explore some of these strengths and weaknesses.

WEB LINK 5.1 Direct Instruction

Choose one of the direct instruction models found in this section and do an Internet search relative to the strengths and weaknesses of the model. Share the results with your class.

REFLECTIONS ON TEACHER PRACTICE 5.2 Motivating Students to Read

1. Why should reading be an important part of the curriculum in all subject areas?

2. How can students be motivated to read?

◆ ◆ ◆

I go to the public library every three weeks and check out high interest picture books that center around whatever I am currently teaching, picture books that are nonfiction, for the most part, and appropriate for middle school students. Lots of DK books, Science Encyclopedias, all-in-one volumes, and Seymour books. They sit in a laundry basket at the front of my room as resources to read.

Here's my one tip that I have used and found wildly successful. Every once in a while, we do a science "read around day." On that day, I take those books from the basket and put them in the middle of the lab tables. When I say, "go"! They have to select a book and read until I say stop. Usually it's about 3–4 minutes. Then they send their book to the next person. This continues until all four people have read the books at that table.

They don't have to start at the beginning; they can just look at pictures, or use the index to find something that interests them. From here each table interviews each person on what they

learned, or what they liked. From here we switch that pile of books with another table and continue with the process.

They love it, and they hate it. They want to read more of at least one book and they can't because it has rotated around. Well, let me tell you, books fly out of the basket in extra time before class, or if they finish early. The afterglow only last a couple of days, but it works. And sometimes, oh how I love those sometimes, someone will ask to have a library pass so they can go see if that book is in our library or if the media specialist can help them interlibrary loan it.

That's what I've tried in science. Now math, well, that's another story. I'm still working on it—mostly working to find read-alouds beyond the standards.

—*MARSHA, middle-level teacher*

SOURCE: www.middleweb.com. Reprinted with permission.

ON YOUR OWN 5.3 **Reflections on Teacher Practice**

Read and reflect on the viewpoints expressed in Motivating Students to Read. Log on to the Web-based student study site at http://www.sagepub.com/eis2study and react to the related activities.

This concludes our discussion of various direct teaching methods. Apply the concepts developed in this chapter in Expansion Activity: Direct Instruction Application.

Table 5.6 gives a review of the direct teaching methods. Review the table and complete Review and Reflective Exercise 5.2.

EXPANSION ACTIVITY 5.2 **Direct Instruction Application**

Teachers work hard and spend a lot of time and effort developing plans, activities, and instructional resources to maximize learning. However, sometimes learning is limited. Create a two-column chart of the direct instructional strategies covered in Chapter 5 and indicate your feelings as to the value of each strategy at the grade level you expect to teach. Use the following three categories to evaluate each strategy for your chart: (1) appropriate and useful, (2) limited usefulness, and (3) not appropriate and not useful.

TABLE 5.6 **Exposition With Interaction Teaching**

Method	Description
Lecture Recitation	Teacher presents information and follows up with questions
Textbook Recitation	Students are assigned content to read and study and are later questioned over information

REVIEW AND REFLECTIVE EXERCISE 5.2 Describe the effective use of questioning in the classroom.

REVIEW

- Describe the exposition with interaction instructional method of teaching. What are the strengths and weaknesses of this instructional approach?
- Why is questioning an art?
- Describe two questioning classification systems.
- Describe the different types of questions.

REFLECTION

- Do you consider yourself a good questioner? How can you improve your skills?
- Should teachers use a question classification system? Why? What system do you plan to use in the area you expect to teach?

SUMMARY

There are two basic approaches to teaching: direct and indirect.

Direct Teaching

- Direct teaching is a teacher-centered skill-building model.

Exposition Teaching

- Exposition teaching offers an effective way to convey a great deal of information in a short period of time.

Exposition With Interaction Teaching

- Exposition with interaction teaching is often more effective than exposition teaching.
- The key to exposition with interaction teaching is questioning. Asking good questions is an art that is essential to the lecture recitation and textbook recitation methods.
- The recall of information requires the use of narrow questions (convergent) while the desire to stimulate thinking and reasoning calls for the use of broad questions (divergent).
- The Mental Operation question system categorized questions as factual, empirical, productive, or evaluative.
- Focusing, prompting, and probing questions can be used to arouse interest and increase involvement.
- Redirecting questions, using wait time and halting time, and using reinforcement can enhance questioning skills.

DISCUSSION QUESTIONS AND ACTIVITIES

1. **Direct instruction.** What aspects of direct instruction might explain its success?
2. **Strategy selection.** You have been assigned a new class to teach. This class consists largely of slow learners. The class is restless, not interested, and hard to manage. What teaching strategies and methods would be best to use with this class if it were the following? Give a valid rationale for your selection.
   a. A 3rd-grade class
   b. A 6th-grade middle school class
   c. A 10th-grade social studies class
3. **The lecture method.** When would it be appropriate to use the lecture method? Consider objectives and purpose. How would one plan an effective lecture? Consider motivation, length, aids, clarity, and interest. How could you tell whether a lecture has been successful?
4. **Preparing questions.** Prepare examples for each level within the following question categories.
   a. Convergent and divergent
   b. Mental Operation system
5. **Textbook questions.** Obtain the teacher's edition of a textbook for a subject you expect to teach. Analyze the questions contained in the text. What levels and types of questions are most frequently suggested?

TECHNOLOGY AND EDUCATION

The quality of instruction can be improved through the use of technology. How would you use technology to improve direct instruction at the grade level you expect to teach? You might want to access the following Internet URL Web sites for ideas: http://www.teachnology.com, http://www.edzone.net/~mwestern, http://wtvi.com/teks, http://www.lessonplanspage.com, and http://www.eduref.org/Virtual/Lessons/index.shtml. Form groups of four or five to share ideas. Share your group's ideas with the class.

DECONSTRUCTING THE STANDARDS

Chapter 5 content addresses topics related to INTASC Standards 1, 2, 3, 4, 6, and 7.

- ◆ INTASC Standard 1 states: *Knowledge of Subject Matter:* The teacher understands the central concepts, tools of inquiry, and structures of the subject being taught and can create learning experiences that make these aspects of subject matter meaningful for students.
- ◆ INTASC Standard 2 states: *Knowledge of Human Development and Learning:* The teacher understands how children learn and develop and can provide learning opportunities that support their intellectual, social, and personal development.
- ◆ INTASC Standard 3 states: *Adapting Instruction for Individual Needs:* The teacher understands how students differ in their approaches to learning and creates instructional opportunities that are adapted to diverse learners.
- ◆ INTASC Standard 4 states: *Multiple Instructional Strategies:* The teacher uses various instructional strategies to encourage students' development of critical thinking, problem solving, and performance skills.
- ◆ INTASC Standard 6 states: *Communication Skills:* The teacher uses knowledge of effective verbal, nonverbal, and media communication techniques to foster active inquiry, collaboration, and supportive interaction in the classroom.
- ◆ INTASC Standard 7 states: *Instructional Planning Skills:* The teacher plans instruction based on knowledge of subject mater, students, the community, and curriculum goals.

For each of these six standards, write your response to the following:

- Which part(s) of each standard does this chapter address?
- How does this chapter address this standard?
- How will the concepts in this chapter help you apply this standard as a teacher?

PRAXIS CONNECTION

Log on to the Web-based student study site at http://www.sagepub.com/eis2study. Access the Praxis II: Principles of Learning and Teaching assessments and/or state-related exams and complete the Chapter 5 test preparation exercises.

PORTFOLIO CONNECTION

Log on to the Web-based student study site at http://www.sagepub.com/eis2study. Access the Portfolio Connection. Complete the Chapter 5 portfolio link to INTASC activities.

CONNECTION WITH THE FIELD

1. **Questioning in the classroom.** Attend a class in a public school or college classroom. Keep a tally of the levels of questions, as well as types of questions, used by the instructor. Did you see any patterns? What other questioning techniques did you observe? Were they successful? Why, or why not?

2. **Teaching.** Prepare and teach a minilesson using a direct methods approach. Use the miniteaching guidelines and forms in Appendix A to plan and analyze your minilesson.

3. **Teaching analysis.** Make a videotape of your miniteaching lesson; then critically analyze it with your peers.

CHAPTER 6

Using Indirect Teaching Methods

What we learn to do, we learn by doing.

—ARISTOTLE

OVERVIEW

Many theorists argue that learning is an active process. Indeed, they suggest that your function as a teacher is to act as a facilitator, a guide. They view your function as a provider of participatory experiences that will result in the desired learning. This chapter will examine indirect approaches to instruction. Discussions, discovery, and inquiry are indirect participatory alternatives.

OBJECTIVES

After completing your study of Chapter 6, you should be able to do the following:

- Discuss reasons for using various participatory teaching techniques as well as advantages and disadvantages associated with their use.
- Describe the primary roles associated with various discussion techniques and the respective responsibilities.
- Explain the four areas that must be addressed in effective discussion planning.
- Identify strengths and limitations associated with various small-group discussion structures.
- Compare and contrast the purpose and function of the small-group structures of brainstorming, buzz groups, task groups, and panels.
- Describe the major purpose, characteristics, teacher role, and desired environment associated with heuristic modes of instruction, namely, discovery and inquiry.
- Differentiate between discovery and inquiry learning.
- Define problem solving and distinguish between the three levels of problem solving.
- Outline and explain the five-step discovery model, or general scientific method of investigation, and the three-step inquiry approach.

- Identify strengths and weaknesses associated with various heuristic methods.

- Explain the basic features of Richard Suchman's inquiry learning and the procedures associated with its use.

- Describe the teacher's function and the appropriate environment conducive to effective implementation of the heuristic methods.

Two major functions of education are the development of students' ability to think critically and the development of their ability to perform independent inquiry. This is often difficult, if not impossible, with the more direct teaching strategies. Fortunately, as a teacher, you have at your disposal a wide range of methods of a more participatory nature. These indirect methods typically are less teacher directed, but they are more time-consuming.

The Discussion Method

An important but infrequently used indirect teaching method is the classroom **discussion.** What all too frequently passes for a classroom discussion is really nothing more than a lecture with periodic questioning-answering sequences. In a true discussion, students should talk more than the teacher. A discussion is not a "bull" session, however, but a carefully structured exchange of ideas directed toward a specific goal.

Two kinds of classroom goals are conducive to the discussion method. First, many subjects pose questions that have no simple answers. For example, is there a simple answer to the cause of war? What can be done about the rising cost of medical care? How was the work of Ernest Hemingway influenced by the politics of that period? Questions of this type are open to interpretation. Through discussion of issues from history, government, economics, literature, and science, students develop understanding of the issues, rather than simply receiving and rehearsing factual information. Thus, discussing controversial issues often increases knowledge about the issues, as well as encouraging deeper understanding of the various sides of an issue (Johnson & Johnson, 1985).

The second type of goal that lends itself to the use of the discussion method involves situations in which issues from the affective domain are being addressed. Indeed, the discussion method usually is far more effective than the lecture method at changing attitudes, values, and behaviors. A discussion about drug use, for example, would likely tap into students' attitudes more than a lecture would. Similarly, discussions on issues such as voting, AIDS, poverty, types of music, and art can lead to the establishment of such attitudes as civic duty, patriotism, public health concerns, and a commitment to the arts.

Open communication and a supportive atmosphere are keys to effective discussions. The classroom should serve as an open forum in which students can feel free to express their opinions as well as review factual material. Certain roles and procedures, however, are essential to the success of the discussion procedure.

First, the teacher's role becomes less a director of learning and more a facilitator of or guide to learning. But an active, purposeful leader is needed in guiding the discussion. This individual can be the teacher or, even better, a student. Leaders should not dominate the discussion but, instead, should see that the discussion starts smoothly by making sure that everyone understands the purpose and topic of the discussion. Once introduced, the discussion must be kept moving and on track. Thus, discussion leaders occasionally must pose questions to the group and to individuals. These questions should be designed for keeping the discussion on track, preventing individuals from dominating the discussion, getting various individuals involved if they are not participating, and making sure alternative viewpoints are addressed. Finally, the discussion leader should be prepared to summarize periodically the major point of the discussion.

Second, discussions need a recorder (or secretary), who will keep notes on the key points made, create a summary of results, and record the group's conclusions. Occasionally, the teacher may want to assume the recorder role and designate a student group leader. The record can even be displayed on the chalkboard or on an overhead projector, which makes it possible for the participants to see and use the record for reference purposes.

Third, the participants are expected to be prepared, and they should peruse the materials provided for the discussion. They should be ready to listen, give each other the opportunity for expressing differing opinions, and ask questions.

APPLY AND REFLECT 6.1	Can the discussion method be used effectively at any grade level? In any subject? Is it more suitable for certain grade levels and/or subject areas? If so, what grade levels and subject areas?

Finally, in a discussion, as the teacher, you can assume the role of leader, recorder, or a consultant—ready to provide needed resources or advice. Whatever role you assume, you must plan the discussion and make sure the plan is executed. Let's now look at the planning phase of the discussion method.

Planning the Discussion

Although few actual materials are usually required in implementing the discussion method, lessons that emphasize the technique must be well organized. If not, most discussions will disintegrate into a sharing of ignorance or into chaos. Basically, four areas must be addressed when planning a discussion activity.

First, you must carefully consider your goals and student preparation needed to achieve these goals. Your goals most likely will be the acquisition of content knowledge or the exploration of attitudes or values. Unlike other methods in which the content or background information is an integral part of the lesson, however, discussions will require that students be thoroughly conversant with the related information prior to the discussion. That is, students must have something to discuss if the discussion method is to work. Thus, it is essential that you direct your students to be prepared with regard to content knowledge or background information prior to the discussion. This preparation may require that they read an assigned chapter, conduct research, or, in the case of attitudes and value-issue discussions, form a personal position to support.

REFLECTIONS ON TEACHER PRACTICE 6.1   Learning by Doing

1. If students learn best by doing, can we teach all subjects, attitudes, and skills "by doing"? Why or why not?

2. Is "learning by doing" more applicable to the elementary, middle school, or high school classroom? Why?

◆ ◆ ◆

It is unfortunate that Columbine High School has changed the reputation of our young people. All the stereotypes of "sex, drugs, and violence" are, after all, true, and we must change our schools to prevent such a disaster from ever taking place again! Fortunately, Columbine is merely an aberration—tragic, but in no way typical of today's young people.

At Shawnee Mission Northwest High School just the opposite has been true since the day it opened in 1969.

The students have collected food, clothing, and even presents for all the men at the state prison. In 1991, it was decided to make this an autonomous class. It was eventually called "Cougars Community Commitment." It is a social science offering for a half-credit per semester. It is open to juniors and seniors, and, with approval of the sponsor, students may enroll for as many as four semesters.

(Continued)

(Continued)

Seventeen students were enrolled the first year, and those 17 set a standard few classes have met. Few in the community took the class seriously: Rake the lawn, mow my grass at no charge?! The class motto was simply "THE DOER OF GOOD BECOMES GOOD!" It was and is our opinion that what we used to take for granted now has to be taught. Goodness needs to be nurtured but never taken for granted.

—*RONALD W. POPLAU,*
high school social studies teacher, Shawnee Mission Northwest
High School, Shawnee, Kansas

SOURCE: Randi Stone's *Best Practices for High School Teachers: What Award-Winning Secondary Teachers Do.* Reprinted by permission.

ON YOUR OWN 6.1   Reflections on Teacher Practice

Read and reflect on the viewpoints expressed in Learning by Doing. Log on to the Web-based student study site at http://www.sagepub.com/eis2study and react to the related activities.

Second, you must decide whether the discussion should be a large-group (whole-class) or small-group activity. Small-group activities might take such forms as buzz groups, brainstorming sessions, or task groups. The particular type of group used is related to the lesson goals. If the goals are the development of better content understanding or abilities to analyze, synthesize, and evaluate, a large-group activity would be most appropriate. The development of leadership skills, social skills, listening skills, or other related skills, however, would probably call for a small-group activity. Whole-group discussions have some definite advantages—the primary one being the ability to keep the discussion focused on the topic. In addition, it is often much easier to maintain control with whole-class discussions. Unlike small-group techniques, however, whole-class discussions do not give students the opportunity for practicing active listening, editing of ideas, idea building, communication, and turn taking. Thus, if such skills are your goals, small-group work might help you accomplish these goals.

Figure 6.1
Large-Class Discussion Seating Arrangements (To maximize interaction, students should be seated in a circular or hollow square arrangement. Arrows pointing through the center indicate that the individual was speaking to the total group. Leader and recorder positions are marked with an X.)

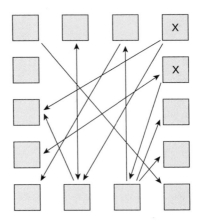

Figure 6.2
Small-Group
Discussion Seating
Arrangements (Leader
and recorder positions
are marked with an X.)

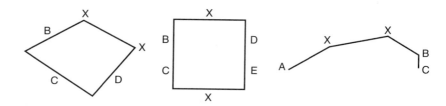

Third, seating must be considered. A productive discussion requires interaction, which often is directly related to the seating arrangement. Seating should be arranged so that students can look directly at each other when they interact. Figure 6.1 shows two possible whole-class arrangements. Note that any student can make eye contact with any other student without turning. Similarly, Figure 6.2 shows three possible small-group arrangements that should maximize interaction.

Finally, you must consider the time allotted for the activity. Plan for about 45-minute discussion periods with older students, shorter periods with younger students. In general, the time given for small-group discussions depends on the type of small group and its function. Small-group discussion time, however, generally is relatively short. Indeed, a good format to follow is to give students very explicit directions as to what is to be accomplished and a time limit for the discussion.

Only careful planning will result in a successful discussion activity. This planning requires that you have a thorough understanding of the characteristics and function of the two basic discussion forms: whole class and small group.

APPLY AND REFLECT 6.2	Did you ever have a teacher who used the discussion method extensively? How successful were they? How would you change his or her roles and procedures?

Whole-Class Discussions

Whole-class discussions are similar in some respects to the class recitation method. You or a designated discussion leader pose questions, listen to student answers, react, and probe for more information. In the true whole-class discussion, however, you try to assume a less dominant role. Rather, you should assume the role of passive moderator and create a pleasant atmosphere conducive to free interaction. Neither you nor any class member should dominate the discussion. Your major task is to make the total class session more interactive.

When carrying out a whole-class discussion, you first should make sure your topic is appropriate for whole-class discussion and that the class has an adequate knowledge base. Next, make up a plan for the discussion that lays out a procedure (agenda), time limits, and discussion ground rules. For example, your procedure might include a teacher introduction session, followed by a 30-minute discussion, followed by a teacher-directed wrap-up. In addition to your 30-minute discussion time limit, you also might set a 2-minute time limit for each student to speak. You also could lay down ground rules such as these: (a) give a summary of the last student's comments before making your own, (b) sarcasm is not allowed, (c) no one will make fun of another student's ideas or comments, and (d) only the discussion topic will be addressed in making comments.

Plan a lively springboard or set that will get the discussion started. For example, you might start the discussion with a short film, a role-playing exercise, an open-ended question, or a contrived situation. Once the discussion has begun, it is the leader's function to keep it on track, summarize as needed, and involve all class members through the use of questions, the redirecting technique, and reinforcement. Finally, the discussion points must be brought to a logical conclusion.

Textbooks are an essential part of most classes, but their value usually suffers through a lack of integration into various teaching strategies. Indeed, in most classrooms, the textbook is integrated into the lecture method only. An effective way of improving student learning, however, is through whole-class discussions built around textbook content. One such strategy, called *listen-read-and-discuss,* begins with a teacher's short overview lecture of the textbook material, which is to be read by students (Alvermann, Moore, & Conley, 1987). This short introductory lecture should serve as an advance organizer and should set the framework for the material subsequently read by the class. A discussion of the content material follows. This procedure allows students to compare their understanding of the reading with the teacher's presentation. Furthermore, it gives the teacher the opportunity for evaluating and getting feedback on students' understanding of the concepts covered.

APPLY AND REFLECT 6.3	Name some topics that would be appropriate for whole-class discussions.

Small-Group Discussions

As with any discussion, *small-group discussions* should follow the presentation of information through teacher-directed lessons, assignments, books, or films. When students are adequately prepared, they should form their groups and start to work.

For material related to this concept, go to Clip 6.1 on the Student Resource CD bound into the back of your textbook.

Successful small-group learning requires very careful planning. The different groups will probably gather and work in different parts of the classroom. Under such conditions, it is impossible for you to be with each group. Therefore, you must provide students with clear guidelines regarding their task and responsibilities. You should appoint a responsible, well-organized student as leader for each group. The leader's function is to keep the group on task, to guide them toward completion of that task, and to ensure that all group members participate. An appointed group recorder should also write down the group's ideas and conclusions. Upon completion of the group activity, each group should be required to report to the rest of the class.

What is the optimal size for small-group learning? There is no easy answer to this question. But some literature suggests that groups of five to seven work best (Dillion, 1987). In larger groups, it is too easy for students to hide and not participate in the interaction, and smaller groups lack the diversity of opinions needed in the interaction.

Small-group instruction has several strengths, chief among which are the development of communication skills, leadership abilities, open-mindedness, persuasive arguing, and other interpersonal skills. In addition, group work often leads to a stronger sense of personal commitment to decisions made by the group than those made by the whole class or individuals. Finally, students involved in small-group work are usually given more opportunity for active verbal participation and, in some cases, for physical movement.

Small-group discussion has its limitations as well as strengths. One of the primary problems is the tendency for students to quickly drift off task, and the activity too often disintegrates into bickering and becomes a waste of time. Another danger of small groups concerns the group composition. It is possible—and quite likely—that some groups cannot work together cooperatively or that they include students with very similar (or very different) points of view or interests. Such groups often have difficulty reaching conclusions. Careful teacher planning and supervision, however, can combat the limitations associated with small groups.

Groups are often formed and structured for achieving specific purposes. The kinds of groups and functions that can be formed in your classroom are limited in scope only by your own creative design capabilities. Let's now look at four such small-group types.

Leadership can often be developed through involvement in small-group activities.

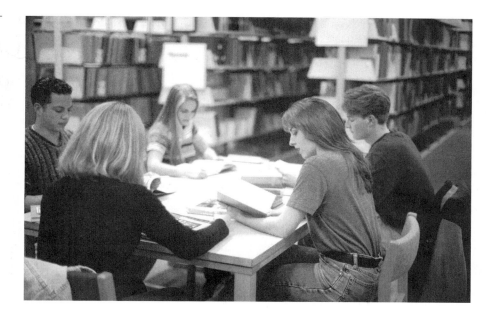

Brainstorming

Brainstorming is a small-group activity used to generate ideas. The brainstorming session is started by the leader, who introduces a topic or problem and asks each small group to generate ideas, solutions, or comments. The topic can be as simple as "What topics should the class study for enrichment?" or as complex as "What can we do about the low class test scores?" All answers, no matter how wrong, should be accepted as possible solutions. No comments about or reactions to contributions should be allowed until all groups have reported their ideas.

Brainstorming sometimes results in a mood of delightful quest. Therefore, you should emphasize the need for decency and decorum. At the same time, participants need to realize that quantity of suggestions is paramount.

Brainstorming is an excellent initiating process for another activity, such as another discussion, research, problem solving, or small-group activities. For example, the brainstorming suggestions can be evaluated, and those deemed worthy of further study can be addressed in follow-up activities.

Buzz Group

A **buzz group** is a work group of relatively short duration. Such a group is established quickly to share opinions, viewpoints, or reactions. The group can be formed easily by counting off or by having those in proximity form a group.

Buzz groups usually consist of from four to seven members and rarely meet for more than 15 minutes. They can be established for a brief discussion of certain ideas or course content. The buzz session then should be followed up with a whole-class discussion of the conclusions or findings.

Task Group

A **task group** sets out to solve a problem or complete a project. Unlike other types of discussion, however, task groups involve students in some kind of work or activity, and each group member has a role or an assignment that is clearly defined for all group members. Their size usually ranges from four to eight members, depending on the problem or project.

Task groups tend to be teacher directed. The teacher selects the tasks and assigns the group members specific responsibilities. The teacher may also find it beneficial to establish a work schedule and monitoring system. In addition, the teacher should make available any resources needed in accomplishing the identified tasks.

For material related to this concept, go to Clip 6.2 on the Student Resource CD bound into the back of your textbook.

Task groups are best suited for a small number of students who are, or can be, fairly self-directed. The students should be able to create an uninhibited, but productive, environment in which discussion can be free and open.

Panels

Panels, which also are referred to as **roundtables,** are a special form of the small-group approach. A group of students—usually five to eight—prepare in advance an informal discussion about an assigned issue to be presented in front of the class. One student usually serves as panel chair and directs the discussion. Each panel member makes an informal opening statement; however, no speeches as such are made. A give-and-take session between panel members and members of the class follows the opening statement and discussion.

The topics for panel discussions can evolve from ongoing class activities, or they can be anticipated and planned by the teacher. Identification of controversial areas within a given unit is often a relatively simple matter; however, the best panel discussions come from issues that are important and meaningful to the students.

Most students will need teacher assistance in preparing for their panels. For most panel issues, the group should be given about a week's preparation time. Part of this preparation time should be given in class so that you can oversee the development of their presentations.

You should brief students carefully on the panel procedure to be followed. The initial panelist presentations should be limited, for example, to about 15 minutes. After this more formal portion of the panel presentation, the discussion should be opened up for a class discussion of the topic or for a question-and-answer session from the audience. This open-ended session then should be followed by a summary of the important points by the panel chairperson.

APPLY AND REFLECT 6.4	Name some topics or tasks that would be appropriate for small-group discussions. What type of small-group structure would be best for each topic or task?

Planning and conducting a discussion lesson can be challenging. Complete Web Link 6.1: Discussions to further explore discussion techniques.

WEB LINK 6.1 Discussions

Search the Web and locate a discussion lesson plan appropriate for the grade level you expect to teach. Dissect the lesson's component parts. Describe the quality of your chosen lesson and how you think it could be improved.

This concludes the examination of the various discussion techniques. Table 6.1 summarizes the different discussion teaching methods. Review the summary and complete Review and Reflective Exercise 6.1.

Heuristic Methods

Teaching can be organized so that it is active, somewhat self-directed, inquiring, and reflective. Such modes of instruction are referred to as *heuristic* teaching methods. In this section, I will address some

TABLE 6.1	Discussion Methods
Method	**Description**
Whole-class discussion	All students in class exchange and share ideas regarding an assigned topic.
Small-class discussion	Five to eight students interact and/or work together in reaching conclusions, generating ideas, or completing a task.
Panels	Five to eight students prepare and discuss topics in front of class.

REVIEW AND REFLECTIVE EXERCISE 6.1   Describe the various discussion techniques and their strengths and limitations.

REVIEW

- Describe the characteristics of the true discussion.
- What are some pros and cons of the discussion teaching method?
- Describe the different discussion formats.

REFLECTION

- How can the discussion approach to learning be adapted to any grade level? What format would work best at the elementary level? Middle level? Secondary level?

modes that are designated as heuristic approaches: discovery, inquiry, and the Richard Suchman inquiry methods of instruction.

Confusion often is expressed when the discovery and inquiry methods are discussed. Some educators use the terms interchangeably, whereas others feel they represent subcategories of each other. For the purposes of this textbook, the discovery and inquiry methods will be considered as unique, yet somewhat related, techniques. Because the **heuristic approach** actively involves students in problem solving, let's begin our study of the heuristic modes by looking at the problem-solving process.

Problem Solving

A problem exists whenever something gives rise to uncertainty. The literature generated by John Dewey from 1884 to 1948 advocated a curriculum that was based on problems. Some contemporary curricula and a large number of textbooks rely heavily on Dewey's problem-solving approach, along with direct experiences. That is, students are required to solve problems through direct experiences provided by the teacher. Therefore, a good working definition of **problem solving** is the intentional elimination of uncertainty through direct experiences and under supervision.

Because preparing students to solve everyday problems is an important function of schools, curricular specialists who advocate a problem-solving instructional approach suggest that schools should develop traits (or behaviors) that enable individuals to be effective problem solvers. Furthermore, the experiences provided by the school should articulate the content and processes needed to produce successful problem solvers.

Problem solving actively involves students in their own learning. The amount of decision making performed by students, however, can be classified according to three levels of involvement. As depicted in Table 6.2, Level I is the traditional teacher-directed method, in which the problem, as well

TABLE 6.2 Levels of Problem Solving

	Level		
	I	II	III
Problem identification	Generated by teacher or textbook	Generated by teacher or textbook	Generated by students
Processes for solving problem	Decided by teacher or textbook	Decided by students	Decided by students
Establishment of tentative solution to problem	Determined by students	Determined by students	Determined by students

as the processes and procedures leading to an intended conclusion, is provided for students. This level of problem solving can also be referred to as guided problem solving. Level I problem solving is highly manageable and predictable. It is probably best for students without the ability to engage in higher mental operations and teaching basic concepts.

In Level II, problems are usually defined by the teacher or the textbook, whereas the processes for solving the problems are left for students to develop. Level II problem solving gives the learners the opportunity, often for the first time, to find out something by themselves through their own independent skills.

Level III represents almost total self-direction. Students generate the problems and then design ways to solve these problems. This level is often referred to as open problem solving.

Ideally, you should have students independently identify some of their class problems and the procedures for solving them. Student-identified national problems, for example, are an excellent source of issues for supplemental inclusion in a social studies, civics, or government class. Care should be taken, however, in the amount of independence given students. Some students will be unable to benefit from such freedom and, therefore, such an activity should be delayed until a later date.

APPLY AND REFLECT 6.5

What level of problem solving would work best at the elementary level? Middle school level? Secondary school level?

Discovery Learning

Discovery learning is a means by which students engage in problem solving in developing knowledge or skills. A good working definition of *discovery learning* is intentional learning through supervised problem solving following the scientific method of investigation. Thus, with discovery, the learning must be planned, it must be supervised, and it must follow the scientific method of investigation (see Figure 6.3). As noted earlier, discovery learning is frequently confused with inquiry.

Actually, both discovery and inquiry are specific kinds of problem solving. Whereas discovery follows an established pattern of investigation, inquiry has no such established pattern: Discovery learning follows the general scientific method for conducting an investigation, shown in Figure 6.3. There is no such method for inquiry learning.

"Earth science, close up."

SOURCE: Created by Martha Campbell.

Discovery learning can take place at three levels, depending on the level of problem solving (review Table 6.2). At Level I, discovery learning is carefully guided (*guided discovery*); at Level II, a moderate amount of guidance is administered (*modified discovery*); and at Level III, it is very casually supervised (*open discovery*).

Discovery Learning Strategies

The degree of success of discovery learning depends in a large part on your ability to plan and execute the problem-solving process effectively. Your role is to provide a situation that lets students identify a contradiction or uncertainty and then to guide and assist them in finding a relationship between what they already know and the newly discovered knowledge. Essentially, you direct the planning, organization, and execution of the general scientific method of investigation (review Figure 6.3).

Selecting the Problem. Although problem solving is emphasized in discovery learning, students often lack the sophistication to identify their own problems (open discovery); that is, students usually lack the expertise for involvement in Level III problem solving (review Table 6.2). Therefore, you must be prepared to suggest problems or areas in which students may seek problems.

Discovery learning works well with many subjects. Science, geometry, social studies, art, and mathematics all provide many opportunities for discovery learning. For example, in a science class, you might suggest an examination of pollution in the local river; in a social studies class, you could suggest an investigation of voter apathy; in an art class, you might have students mix colors; in a mathematics class, a discussion of societal mathematics needs might suggest an examination of the mathematics skills needed by individuals in various occupations.

Language arts and other subjects that are not as obviously discovery oriented can still be presented with the discovery method. Completing crosswords or other puzzles, using a computer spell checker, discussing recently read literature, presenting dramatic plays with specified situations but without

Figure 6.3
General Scientific
Model of
Investigation

Identify problem
1. Be aware problem exists
2. Write problem statement(s)

Develop possible solutions
1. Propose testable hypotheses

Collect data
1. Gather evidence
2. Conduct experiment(s)
3. Survey a sample

Analyze and interpret data
1. Develop data-supported meaningful statements
2. Test hypotheses
3. Establish relationships or patterns
4. Make generalizations

Test conclusions
1. Obtain new data
2. Revise original conclusions

scripts, following maps created by a partner, working in small groups to solve a common problem, and creating and operating puppets are just a few examples. Another example of discovery learning for social studies would be during a lesson about another culture. You could select a traditional cultural recipe. The difficulty of the recipe would depend on the age and ability of the students. The ingredients, tools, and written recipe would be made available to students. You could allow students to make the food according to the recipe directions. Figure 6.4 offers some additional discovery learning activities.

Suitable problems should not be left to chance. Left alone, students often flounder or select problems that are not suitable for your course, or they may select problems whose solution requires materials and equipment that are not available or problems that are too large and unyielding.

Once students have a general grasp of the problem, you must help them clarify and state the problem in clear, precise terms. You should be prepared to make suggestions or ask questions that will assist students in knowing exactly what they want to find out. These suggestions or questions should be such that students are forced to think and analyze the problem situation for clarity; that is, you should help students make sure they are clear on what problem is to be studied.

Clarification of the problem is a crucial step in finding a solution. If this crucial step is neglected, students often have difficulty in knowing exactly where to start in attempting to find a solution.

Proposing Possible Solutions. Once students clearly define the problem, hypotheses and solutions must be generated. Accomplishment of this task requires that data be collected and analyzed. Your function will be to provide materials or make suggestions about where data can be located and to provide resources where information related to the problem area can be obtained.

When students are proposing possible solutions, you should encourage guessing and intuitive thought. Also, encourage healthy skepticism and practice in suspending judgment. Ideally, you want to give students the opportunity to express all their ideas in a nonthreatening environment.

The collection of data is a significant component of discovery learning.

Collecting of Data. Proposed solutions must be tested; that is, each of the generated hypotheses must be checked for validity. Thus, additional data must be amassed. Data collection sometimes requires that experiments be set up and carried out. At other times, surveys must be conducted. Students often need guidance and assistance with their data collection tools and techniques. Experiments must yield valid results, and surveys must provide usable data, which often calls for planning and the development of appropriate instrumentation. Students may need your assistance with such planning and instrumentation.

Data Analysis and Interpretation. Once collected, data must be analyzed and interpreted. Criteria must be established, and the validity of hypotheses must be judged against these criteria. You might need to guide students in making such judgments and in determining their validity. Students often think they have proven a hypothesis when, in fact, they have not.

Based on the interpretation of data, conclusions must be established. Thus, the data must be carefully examined and evaluated so that conclusions are supported by the data. Although you should not establish conclusions for students, you can help in this process by pointing out patterns, showing relationships, and asking questions. With your help, students should develop skill in reaching plausible conclusions to their identified problems.

Testing Conclusions. Once established, conclusions must be tested and revised. Consequently, the final step in the problem-solving component of discovery is the generation of data that will lend support to the identified conclusions or that will lead to revisions of the conclusions.

Benefits of Discovery Learning

Discovery learning is active rather than passive learning. **Active learning** tends to result in a higher degree of intrinsic motivation. With verbal teaching methods, motivation comes only from your comments following class contributions, following correctly answered questions, or from grades received

Figure 6.4
Discovery Learning
Activities

Flashlight Fixing

Materials:

- Shoeboxes
- Working flashlights with bulbs and batteries
- Paper and pencil

Take the flashlights apart. For younger children, simply remove the batteries. For older children, also remove the light bulb. Put the flashlights and the various parts into the shoeboxes. Instruct the children to put the flashlights together so they will work. Children should record their discoveries.

Car Design

Materials:

- Books about automobiles, transportation, and/or simple machines such as the wheel
- Several small boxes such as shoeboxes, tissue boxes, or gift boxes
- Items to create wheels and axles such as paper towel tubes, cardboard, dowel rods, plastic coffee can lids, rubber balls, spools, etc.
- Scissors
- Glue
- Tape
- Crayons, watercolor markers, or paints—optional

Read to the children or have the children read one or more of the selected books. Instruct children to use the craft items or others they find to create cars with wheels that roll.

Baking Bread

Materials:

- A gingerbread or cornbread recipe, or for younger children a mix
- The ingredients for making the bread and all the bowls and utensils
- Adult supervision for the baking

Provide children with all the ingredients and tools needed to make the mix and ready it for the oven. Supervise the baking, placing into and removing the bread from the oven if need be. Once it has baked and is sufficiently cool, have the children serve and taste the results.

on assignments. In discovery learning, motivation comes from the activity itself and the excitement of direct involvement. This activity and excitement have the added advantage of increased learning and better retention. Students tend to learn more and retain information longer when they are actively involved in the learning process. Explore further benefits of discovery learning by completing Expansion Activity 6.1: Discovery Learning.

Discovery learning also fosters the development of positive social skills. Obviously, discovery learning requires that students work cooperatively. They must develop skill in planning, following established procedures, and working together toward the successful completion of common tasks.

EXPANSION ACTIVITY 6.1   Discovery Learning

Write a short essay explaining how discovery learning is related to constructivist theory.

Limitations of Discovery Learning

The greatest limitation associated with discovery learning probably is the demand it places on you and your students. Because discovery learning is a cooperative process rather than a competitive one, it calls for an adjustment—by students and teacher alike—to the very nature of discovery. With the lack of competition, there is little feedback as to how well students are doing and how much learning is taking place. This lack of feedback often leads to uncertainty for you and for students.

Discovery learning can also be an inefficient system for covering large amounts of material. This limitation is a major concern to teachers who feel they are expected to cover all the material in the textbook.

Inquiry Learning

Like discovery, **inquiry** basically is a problem-solving technique. Unlike discovery, however, the emphasis is placed on the process of investigating the problem, rather than on reaching a correct solution. In fact, although inquiry is concerned with problem solving, it does not require solutions to the problems being investigated. Thus, whereas with discovery learning, a set pattern is followed by reaching a solution, no established pattern exists with inquiry learning. Indeed, different students may use different strategies in obtaining information related to a problem. Students may even take intuitive approaches to problems.

As with discovery learning, there are three levels to inquiry learning: guided inquiry, modified inquiry, and open inquiry. Thus, you may want to identify the problem and then decide how to investigate it (guided inquiry), you may want to identify the problem and then have students decide how to go about finding out about it (modified inquiry), or you may want the students to identify the problem and then design ways for obtaining information (open inquiry).

Inquiry Learning Strategies

The inquiry approach is flexible yet systematic. It is systematic in that a basic, three-step problem-solving procedure is followed (review Table 6.2), yet it is flexible in that the activities used in addressing the problem may vary. Let's now look at this three-step procedure.

Identifying the Problem. Inquiry learning is closely related to discovery learning. Thus, the problem selection processes are essentially identical, with either the teacher deciding (as in guided or modified inquiry) or the students deciding (as in open inquiry) the problems or issues to be addressed. This decision, of course, depends on the sophistication of the students. In short, you must decide whether students are ready and have the skill to identify suitable problems for study. In most cases, however, you must continually monitor the problem identification process and provide guidance or suitable alternatives for consideration.

Working Toward Solutions. The second task in an inquiry lesson is to work on a solution to the problem. Again, there should be no set prescription or rules governing the procedure for finding a solution. In fact, decisions regarding strategies directed toward a solution can be teacher orchestrated (guided inquiry) or student orchestrated (modified and open inquiry).

The emphasis in inquiry learning should be placed on the process of finding a *problem's* solution, not on the solution itself. Whenever appropriate and within limits, students should be given the opportunity to devise their own strategies for addressing problem situations. Some may want to attack a problem through the literature and a search of textbooks, whereas others may want to interview experts in the problem area, and others may want to design and carry out experiments. In a word, the teacher should provide the freedom to enable students to develop creative approaches to problem solving. These opportunities show students how inquiry works in the real world.

Establishing Solutions. The success of inquiry learning is not necessarily dependent on reaching a predetermined conclusion. Even when directed by the teacher, inquiry learning should be a highly personal experience for each individual involved. Individuals should be given the opportunities for applying themselves totally—so they may put their fullest talents, ideas, skills, and judgments to work in reaching their own conclusions.

In the process of inquiry, students identify problems (brainstorm and ask questions), work toward solutions (formulate questions, investigate, and analyze), and establish solutions (interpret results, discuss, reflect, make conclusions, and present results) (Bruner, 2004). This sequence of inquiry serves as a general model for teaching an inquiry-based lesson. However, another version of the inquiry-based learning sequence is the five-E model. This five-step inquiry sequence is Engage, Explore, Explain, Elaborate, and Evaluate.

Step 1. Engage. Students first encounter and identify the instructional task. Activities capture students' attention and stimulate their thinking. Questions are asked, connections between past and present learning experiences are made, and a problem is defined.

Step 2. Explore. Students get directly involved with phenomena and materials. They develop a grounding of experience with the phenomena. Students identify and develop concepts, processes, and skills. They actively explore their environment or manipulate materials.

Step 3. Explain. Students are involved in an analysis of their exploration. They put the abstract experiences into a communicable form. They have opportunities to verbalize their conceptual understanding or to demonstrate new skills or behaviors. Students' understanding is clarified and modified because of reflective activities.

Step 4. Elaborate. Students expand on the concepts they have learned, make connections to other related concepts, and apply their understandings to the world around them. These connections often lead to further inquiry and new understandings.

Step 5. Evaluate. The teacher determines whether learners have attained understanding of concepts and knowledge. Evaluation and assessment can occur at all points along the continuum of the instructional process.

The five-E inquiry model is based on the constructivist approach to learning. It can also be used with students of all ages.

Inquiry gives students the opportunity to learn and practice skills associated with critical thinking (see Chapter 8). Helping students develop the ability to think is now being emphasized because of the realization of the importance of thinking in our technological society. Unfortunately, our traditional educational system has worked in a way that discourages the natural process of critical thinking and inquiry. Students become less prone to ask questions as they move through the grade levels. In traditional schools, students learn not to ask too many questions; instead, they are trained to listen and repeat the expected answers. Figures 6.5 and 6.6 offer examples of an inquiry lesson for young children and the five-E inquiry model.

Suchman Inquiry Learning

J. Richard Suchman (1961, 1966) developed a junior high school–oriented program designed entirely around the concept of inquiry. This program, the Inquiry Development Program (IDP), placed

Figure 6.5
Inquiry Lesson for
Young Children

Grade level: K–1

Description: Young children should explore an awareness of themselves in a social setting. This lesson lays the foundation for the study of school and family life.

Prior to this lesson, the children learned about families so they have an understanding about different types of families. In this lesson, children will speculate about where families live, examine pictures of different types of houses and locations, and draw conclusions.

Materials: Dollhouse, flipchart, pictures of different types of homes

Instructional Objectives:

Students will:

- Speculate about where families might live.
- Describe different types of homes based on a set of pictures.
- Describe simple differences and similarities among ways people live in different locations.
- Develop a general statement indicating that families live in a variety of homes that provide for family needs.

Procedures:

1. Introduction and motivation
   a. Place the class dollhouse in the center of the classroom. Ask: If this were a real house, how would a family use it?
   b. Allow children to describe how the rooms might be used. Ask: Why is it important for families to have a place to live? Important reasons may include sleep, eat, keep warm, and play.

2. Have students develop some guesses
   a. Ask: Where do people live?
   b. Students may respond that people live in houses. If so,
      i. Write the word *houses* on the flipchart.
      ii. Stimulate guessing. Ask: Does everyone live in the same type of house?

3. Looking at pictures
   a. Say: Those are really good ideas. Let's look at some pictures of houses and see if we can get some more ideas.
   b. Show pictures: (a) suburban house, (b) complex in city, (c) trailer house, (d) apartment house, (e) farmhouse. After each picture, ask: Tell me about this house. Point out differences in style and location.
   c. Possible problem: Children unfamiliar with apartments may be confused about how families live in these buildings. Use the school as a comparison with the classrooms as apartments. Houses have rooms; apartments have rooms.

4. Adding to our list
   a. Ask: Did we learn about some new houses?
   b. Say: Let's add those homes to our list.

5. Conclusion
   a. Let's go back to our BIG question. Where do people live?
   b. Ask: What can we say about where people live?
   c. Outcome: People live in a variety of homes that provide for family needs.

**Figure 6.5
(Continued)**

6. Assessment
   a. Did the class develop the conclusion?
   b. Who participated in the discussion?

7. Possible follow-up activities
   a. Have children find and cut out pictures from magazines, brochures, catalogs, and old books that show different homes.
   b. Have children draw a picture of their home and have them talk about it with the class.

emphasis on physical science and was designed for developing the basic processes associated with inquiry. These processes varied, with some associated with data generating, some with data organizing, and some with idea building.

The basic feature of the **Suchman inquiry** is the concept of "discrepant event." These discrepant events were filmed physics demonstrations—originally presented in short, silent, color, loop cartridges—whose outcomes were contradictory to what was expected. A common example showed a teacher filling a collecting bottle to the brim with water and placing a 3-by-5-inch piece of cardboard over the mouth of the bottle. The bottle was then inverted, with the cardboard held firmly over the mouth. The hand supporting the cardboard was then taken away. The water remained in the bottle—and the cardboard firmly attached—even though the cardboard was not supported in any

**Figure 6.6
Five-E Inquiry Model
Lesson**

Topic: Earthquakes

Materials: Internet, resources science books

Objectives:

Students will:

1. Explain what earthquakes are and what causes them.

2. Identify events caused by the movement of the earth plates.

Procedures:

Engage: Has anyone in class ever experienced an earthquake or seen one in the news? Have you ever felt the ground move under your feet? Have you ever been involved in an accident?

Explore: In small groups, explore the Internet and/or read the class book and other available books on earthquakes and what causes them.

Explain: Each group presents a summary of what they have found.

Elaborate: What other events are caused by earth plate movement?

Evaluate: Each group will make a formal presentation on plate movement and the ramifications of such movement.

"Mrs. Broderick isn't as user-friendly as our teaching machines."

SOURCE: Created by Martha Campbell.

way. The title of each of these filmed demonstrations asked why the outcome of the demonstration occurred. The teacher's role was to develop an environment where inquiry could take place.

The original Suchman inquiry approach has changed in two ways. First, the episodes to be considered are usually shown directly through materials by the teacher rather than through films. Second, students receive more guidance from the teacher than did the students in the original program. But the basic purposes of the inquiry program, which were the development of skills in searching and data processing and the development of concepts through analysis of concrete problems, have not changed.

The Suchman inquiry approach focuses on the process by which information is acquired, rather than on the final information. The problem-solving process associated with this approach occurs in three steps: analyzing the episode, gathering information, and reaching conclusions.

Analyzing the Episode. A Suchman session is initiated by having students view a discrepant event. The event can be presented by the teacher or by playing one of the Suchman film loops. After the discrepant event has been presented, the teacher asks the class for ideas, guesses, or hypotheses as to what has transpired. Students are allowed to ask the teacher as many questions as they wish in their attempt to develop these explanations. There are three rules, however, that must be followed.

1. All questions to the teacher must be worded so that they can be answered with a yes or no.

2. One student has the floor at a time and can ask as many questions as he or she wants without being interrupted by the class.

3. The teacher will not respond to a question that asks for support of a student-originated theory or hypothesis.

These rules give students the freedom of establishing a sequence and pattern of questions that, in turn, will help lead them to possible hypotheses.

Gathering Information. Once a hypothesis has been presented, it is the class's responsibility to gather data that support or refute this hypothesis. Thus, students formulate their own hypothesis and then collect their own supporting or refuting data. The questions asked during this phase have to be phrased in such a way that allows tests to be set up to verify an answer. "Would the object sink in a different kind of liquid?" and "Would a heavier object sink in the liquid?" are examples of such questions. Also, during this phase, students attempt to determine what conditions were necessary for the final outcome to occur.

The Suchman inquiry approach requires a supportive atmosphere. Students must be given the opportunity to conduct any reasonable tests or experiments to check on the validity of their proposed hypotheses. Although the teacher does provide some information for assistance to students, the class is encouraged to seek data individually or in small groups without help from the teacher. Thus, in the typical Suchman inquiry session, students work independently, conducting experiments, reexamining the discrepant event, engaging in questioning sessions with the teacher, and involving themselves in an evaluation of data.

Reaching Conclusions. Based on the data obtained, students draw their own conclusions and attempt to explain the cause of the observed phenomenon. In addition, they try to determine why the conditions identified were necessary for the final outcome.

The Suchman inquiry technique can be a valuable tool in a teacher's repertoire. By seeing how problems are solved in the classroom, models are provided that can be followed in solving problems in other areas of their lives.

Benefits of Inquiry Learning

The inquiry method of teaching has several unique benefits. First, it encourages students to develop creative solutions to problems: There are no rigid guidelines, so the imagination can be used without penalty. In fact, students sometimes can go off on tangents and address problems that have little to do with the original problem. Thus, investigations can be as original and limitless as students' imaginations. They are allowed to solve a problem any way they can.

Inquiry often stimulates interest and urges students to solve problems to the very limits of their abilities. They are not penalized for lack of content knowledge. Students are free to use the skills they do possess to reach their own solutions.

Last, because of the individuality possible in carrying out the problem-solving procedure, it is impossible to fail in inquiry learning. Students carry out the approach to the best of their abilities and then stop without being penalized for not reaching a predetermined solution. Thus, students' self-confidence is enhanced.

Limitations of Inquiry Learning

Inquiry tends to appear, and sometimes tends to be, chaotic. It is possible in a class of 25 students to have as many as 25 different activities that address a single problem. Although the students involved generally cause few problems, inquiry can appear to be an undisciplined process in which little learning is taking place. Anticipating and locating materials can be a major problem. It is impossible to anticipate all the resources that students will require in one inquiry lesson. Indeed, some students may want to conduct experiments, whereas others may want special reference books in carrying out a literature search. Whatever the need, you must try to anticipate students' needs and make the materials available. This isn't an easy task.

As with discovery learning, a problem associated with inquiry learning is time: Giving students the freedom to engage in problem solving is time-consuming. Moreover, because students investigate to their own limits, some will finish quickly, whereas others will not want to stop their investigations.

A problem unique to inquiry is evaluation. Because you must provide grades, you need some criteria on which to base your evaluation. This problem can be overcome, to some extent, by having students keep records of their activities. From such reports, you can determine your students' progress.

Systemic Problem Solving

Problems that teachers and students face in and out of the classroom are seldom presented in a clearly defined form. Therefore, teachers must undertake a process to solve problems in a systematic, purposeful manner. The International Technology Education Association identified a process used for technological design that can be implemented in the classroom to help teachers and students alike learn how to solve a problem in a procedural-type approach. This technological design and problem-solving process has specific steps to initially follow, similar to the process when using the scientific method. This process, however, allows for criteria, constraints, efficiency, and trade-offs to be intertwined with human creativity. Although this process has steps to follow, it should be understood that the process is iterative. The steps in the design and problem-solving process are

1. Defining the problem
2. Brainstorming
3. Researching and generating ideas
4. Identifying criteria and specifying constraints
5. Exploring possibilities
6. Selecting an approach
7. Developing a design proposal
8. Making a model or prototype
9. Testing and evaluating the design using specifications
10. Refining the design
11. Creating or making the solution
12. Communicating the processes and results

The defining characteristics for the design and problem-solving process are that it is purposeful, based on certain requirements, systematic, and contains many possible solutions. Teachers have often thought that only one answer or solution can be the "right one" to solve a problem. In fact, there can be many different solutions to solve the same problem. Balancing the solution with the criteria, constraints, efficiency, and trade-offs of the design will allow the teacher and the student to solve the problem in the most appropriate manner for the situation. Using problem solving as a teaching method can be a powerful approach to teaching and learning that draws on what students currently know and can explain about a given situation. The problem-solving approach as a teaching methodology, used in conjunction with the constructivist process, may allow the teacher and students to reach a deeper level of understanding for not only the task at hand but also lifelong learning.

This completes the discussion of the various heuristic teaching methods. Table 6.3 summarizes these methods. Review the summary and complete Review and Reflective Exercise 6.2.

Since the teacher and environment are so important to the success of the indirect approaches to instruction, let's take a brief look at these two factors before we go on to thinking skill development.

TABLE 6.3	Heuristic Methods
Method	**Description**
Discovery	Intentional learning through supervised problem solving following the scientific method
Inquiry	Flexible yet systematic process of problem solving
Suchman inquiry	Inquiry approach whereby students are presented with and asked to explain discrepant events

---

REVIEW AND REFLECTIVE EXERCISE 6.2   Outline discovery and inquiry learning and the strengths and limitations associated with each.

REVIEW

- Contrast discovery and inquiry learning.
- Describe the three levels of problem solving.
- What are the strengths and limitations of discovery and inquiry learning?
- What are the teacher's roles in discovery and inquiry learning?

REFLECTION

- Can all students be given the freedom needed to make discovery and inquiry learning successful? If not, why not? If yes, what are some areas of concern for you that must be overcome?

REFLECTIONS ON TEACHER PRACTICE 6.2   Problem Solving

1. How can issues in the life of students be connected to lessons? Which curriculum areas would be most difficult to make life connections?

2. Would researching issues be appropriate at all grade levels? Why? At what grade level is it most appropriate?

♦ ♦ ♦

Try to work in some of your students' personal interests into your teaching. I have been pleasantly surprised by the connections my students could make and the inquiry projects they have done when learning about things that MATTER to them (if they can see WHY and HOW they matter, unlike some school info, which you might need to connect to them more closely).

One interesting research project I did required students to select an event in history (recent, ancient, local, global . . . whatever) and research. The goal was to figure out as much as possible about the event, including how the student's life was affected by the event, positively or negatively, directly or indirectly. They needed to consider the possibilities of how their lives would be different, had the chosen events not taken place.

Another project that involved all students integrated history and science (in many cases), language arts, and technology (they presented their projects on hyper studio). I had students research the building of the local mall, the Holocaust, Columbine, and dozens of other great topics. The only criteria I required for topic selection were: The topic MUST BE appropriate for school; and You MUST show some logical connection to your life. (This helped me to give reasons why Charles Manson was NOT a great choice; I didn't accept "If he hadn't done what he did, I wouldn't be researching him—that's how he affects me.")

—*AMY, middle-level teacher*

SOURCE: www.middleweb.com. Reprinted with permission.

ON YOUR OWN 6.2   **Reflections on Teacher Practice**

Read and reflect on the viewpoints expressed in Problem Solving. Log on to the Web-based student study site at http://www.sagepub.com/eis2study and react to the related activities.

Teacher's Role

When using indirect approaches to instruction, you should function as a facilitator. Accomplishment of your goals, however, will usually call for continuous monitoring of students.

Active participatory methods require a close working relationship between you and your students. You must constantly be alert for hang-ups and stumbling blocks. Students must not simply be turned loose and allowed to flounder around or follow their own whims.

Although the various indirect participatory approaches to instruction are good preventive techniques against discipline problems, there are students in every school who, sometimes because of factors outside your control, will cause you difficulty. If these students won't meet you halfway, there's not much you can do about it. An interactive, constructivist approach that engages students in relevant, meaningful experiences is likely to be good preventive medicine against even the most difficult students. Indeed, this approach can often encourage and empower the most disheartened students. You must take every opportunity to interact with your students one-on-one and to really get to know them as individuals. Find out as much as you can about their experiences/interests, and try to connect to these whenever possible. This will be a challenge, but students who are turned off to school often have special interests and talents that you can tap.

Problem solving often requires special attention. You must help students constantly in their systematic investigation of problems. You must make sure that you or the students define the problem precisely, and then you must make sure problem-solving methodologies focus on and are appropriately applied to the various aspects of the problem. Indeed, the problem must be established, related issues must be clarified, ways of obtaining information must be proposed, and conclusions and discoveries must be formed. In fact, you would be wise to demand that students submit periodic progress reports related to their investigative progress.

A participatory approach to teaching requires in-depth planning. Don't expect to step into the classroom and wing it and be successful. If you don't plan thoroughly and thoughtfully, you will likely have major problems. Don't be discouraged when things don't work as well as you hoped. Make adjustments and try again. Don't fall into the student-blaming trap.

APPLY AND REFLECT 6.7

How would you make problem solving successful? What role would you assume?

Classroom Environment

Now that I have addressed the basic tenets of the various indirect methods and the respective teacher's roles, let's look at the kind of classroom environment that promotes such methods. First, the participatory methods imply a certain amount of freedom for exploring problems and arriving at possible solutions. Such freedom takes time—with a corresponding reduction in the amount of material that can be covered. Indeed, problem-solving episodes may last for a period of days or even weeks. At times, you may opt to conduct ongoing problem-solving episodes and regular, more teacher-directed lessons.

Active, self-directed, inquiring learning requires that students be directly involved in the quest for their own knowledge. To this end, the classroom must contain the necessary materials and equipment needed by students in testing their ideas and hypotheses. In fact, as noted earlier, the classroom may even appear somewhat chaotic at times, what with all the different activities that can be taking place simultaneously.

Indirect methods require openness. Encouragement must be readily available when mistakes are made, and diversity must be encouraged at all times. Permissiveness and sloppy work, however, must not be tolerated. Indirect methods are most effective in classrooms where there is cooperation, trust, self-control, and conviction. This requires that you plan carefully and emphasize systematic skill building.

This completes our discussion of the various indirect teaching strategies. Complete Expansion Activity 6.2: Indirect Instruction Application to further explore the use of indirect instructional strategies at the grade level you expect to teach.

EXPANSION ACTIVITY 6.2   Indirect Instruction Application

Create a two-column chart of the indirect instructional strategies covered in Chapter 6 and indicate your feelings as to the value of each strategy at the grade level you expect to teach. Use the following three categories to evaluate each strategy for your chart: (1) appropriate and useful, (2) limited usefulness, and (3) not appropriate and not useful.

SUMMARY

The Discussion Method

- Discussions can be used to stimulate students' thinking, to help them articulate their own ideas, and to teach them how to listen to the ideas of others.
- The teacher's role in discussion sessions is to be less directive and less obtrusive. Simply set discussions into motion and monitor their progress.
- Discussions can be whole class or small group. One of the major problems of whole-class discussions is that a few students tend to dominate. Small-group discussions result in more student-to-student interactions.

Heuristic Methods

- Heuristic methods actively involve students in their own learning and result in higher degrees of intrinsic motivation.
- The heuristic modes of discovery and inquiry essentially represent different types of problem solving.
- Systemic problem solving represents a systematic, purposeful problem-solving process.

Teacher's Role

- The teacher's role in using indirect methods is to act as a facilitator. However, active participatory methods require a close working relationship between teacher and students.

Classroom Environment

- Indirect methods require a certain amount of student freedom. Indirect methods require openness.

DISCUSSION QUESTIONS AND ACTIVITIES

1. **Indirect methods.** When is it appropriate to use indirect methods? Consider the objectives and purpose of the instruction as well as the students themselves.
2. **Discussion topics.** Generate a list of topics that would be appropriate for discussions. Once you have compiled your topics, separate them as appropriate for whole-class or small-group discussions. Give your reasons and justify them.
3. **Textbook examination.** Examine a textbook or curriculum guide and identify several possible topics for a discussion lesson. What kinds of questions would you use to (a) begin the lesson, (b) keep the discussion rolling, and (c) wrap up the lesson?

TECHNOLOGY AND EDUCATION

The quality of instruction can be improved through the use of technology. How would you use technology to improve indirect instruction at the grade level you expect to teach? You might want to access the following Internet URL Web sites for ideas: http://www.teachnology.com, http://www.edzone.net/~mwestern, http://wtvi.com/teks, http://www.lessonplanspage.com, and http://www.eduref.org/Virtual/Lessons/index.shtml. Form groups of four or five to share ideas. Share your group's ideas with the class.

Chapter 6 content addresses topics related to INTASC Standards 4, 5, 6, and 7.

♦ INTASC Standard 4 states: *Multiple Instructional Strategies:* The teacher uses various instructional strategies to encourage students' development of critical thinking, problem solving, and performance skills.

♦ INTASC Standard 5 states: *Classroom Motivation and Management:* The teacher uses an understanding of individual and group motivation and behavior to create a learning environment that encourages positive social interaction, active engagement in learning, and self-motivation.

♦ INTASC Standard 6 states: *Communication Skills:* The teacher uses knowledge of effective verbal, nonverbal, and media communication techniques to foster active inquiry, collaboration, and supportive interaction in the classroom.

♦ INTASC Standard 7 states: *Instructional Planning Skills:* The teacher plans instruction based on knowledge of subject matter, students, the community, and curriculum goals.

For each of these four standards, write your response to the following:

• Which part(s) of each standard does this chapter address?
• How does this chapter address this standard?
• How will the concepts in this chapter help you apply this standard as a teacher?

PRAXIS CONNECTION

Log on to the Web-based student study site at http://www.sagepub.com/eis2study. Access the Praxis II: Principles of Learning and Teaching assessments and/or state-related exams and complete the Chapter 6 test preparation exercises.

PORTFOLIO CONNECTION

Log on to the Web-based student study site at http://www.sagepub.com/eis2study. Access the Portfolio Connection. Complete the Chapter 6 portfolio link to INTASC activities.

CONNECTION WITH THE FIELD

1. **Classroom observation.** Visit several public school classrooms. Keep a record of the different methods used. What indirect methods did you observe? Was there a pattern?

2. **Inquiry lesson.** Design a lesson for an inquiry lesson. How in the lesson will you initiate the following phases?
   a. Identifying the problem
   b. Working toward solutions
   c. Establishing solution
   d. Teaching the lesson

3. **Teaching.** Prepare and teach a minilesson using an indirect method. Use the microteaching guidelines and forms in Appendix A to plan and analyze your minilesson.

4. **Teaching analysis.** Make a videotape of your miniteaching lesson; then critically analyze it with your peers. Access http://www.sagepub.com/eis2study and use the minilesson analyze forms to analyze the lesson.

CHAPTER 7

Using Integrated Teaching Methods

In doing we learn.

—GEORGE HERBERT

OVERVIEW

I will now engage in a study of techniques for giving students access to information and allowing them to examine the content and help produce their own learning. I will examine instructional approaches that can be used to organize and integrate bodies of knowledge for direct instruction with students engaging in a form of guided learning.

In this chapter, I will focus on the use of the various integrated directed teaching strategies in the classroom. Demonstrations, the Socratic method, concept attainment, cooperative learning, computer integration, simulations and games, individualized instruction, independent study, and mastery learning provide integrated direct teaching alternatives.

OBJECTIVES

After completing your study of Chapter 7, you should be able to do the following:

- Describe the integrated directed teaching concept.
- Describe the purpose, structure, and function of the demonstration method, Socratic method, concept attainment strategy, and cooperative learning method; valid reasons for their use; and techniques for their effective implementation.
- Identify and explain the three-step procedure for role-playing and suggest ways to use role-playing in the classroom.
- Explain how to integrate computers into the curriculum.
- Explain the purposes of simulations and games and the benefits and limitations associated with their use.
- Differentiate between human and person-to-computer simulations as well as between simulations and games.
- Describe the three fundamental individualization strategies: individualized instruction, independent study, and mastery learning.
- Identify the benefits and limitations associated with individualization of instruction.
- Describe the purpose of drill and practice, as well as techniques for their effective use.

The teacher's task in the classroom is to deliver instruction. This task may be accomplished through strategies that influence students directly, indirectly, or by a combination of these. Thus, the teacher may deliver instruction by telling, by showing, and by providing access to the information to be learned. A combination of these options can be viewed as integrated directed teaching. The teacher provides access to information by working with students. Together, teacher and students can blend telling, showing, and self-exploration into a meaningful, intrinsically motivational approach. This approach tends to give students more control over their own learning. To a degree, students become self-directed. The teacher provides access to learning, and it is up to students to engage in the learning. Students become aware of their own learning. They learn to think critically and to derive their own patterns of thought and meaning from the content presented. Self-directed learning is an approach to both teaching and learning that engages students, actively and/or mentally, in the learning process to acquire higher order thinking outcomes. Students learn to construct their own understanding and meaning and learn to reason, problem solve, and think critically.

The way teachers deliver instruction is changing. Technology and the Internet have the potential for effecting fundamental changes in the design of the learning process. Students and teachers will have ubiquitous access to all forms of information sources, demonstrations, library and research materials, and tutorials over high-speed networks from anywhere at any time. Effective use of the Internet as a teaching tool requires that the concept of self-directed learning be understood and developed. Teachers who have learned through direct teaching methods and have been successful in using the direct methodologies must gradually blend teacher-directed and self-directed learning. Students must learn that they can be in charge of their own learning some or most of the time.

APPLY AND REFLECT 7.1	Do you see potential uses for the newer technologies (smart boards, the Internet, online instruction, etc.) in the area you expect to teach? What technologies will be the most useful to you? Discuss your ideas with your classmates. Are their selections similar to yours?

Teachers must nurture student self-direction by providing students with opportunities before, during, and after instruction to exercise some control over their own learning. An emphasis on self-direction means that students must be taught and engaged in strategies that offer them opportunities to make decisions and solve problems on their own without being told what to do at all times. It means providing students with strategies designed to help them process information effectively and be self-confident, believing that they have the ability to succeed. Keep in mind, however, that students will learn more when they are taught in a manner that is comfortable to them. Thus, as teachers make their instruction more student directed, they must remember that their students will have different learning styles (see Chapter 2). And perhaps most important, teachers need to help students become more reflective about their thinking and learning processes.

ON YOUR OWN 7.1 View From the Classroom

Log on to the Web-based student study site at http://www.sagepub.com/eis2study. Review the Chapter 7 teacher surveys and react to the related activities.

Self-direction depends on who makes the learning decision—what is to be learned, who should learn it, what methods and resources should be used, and how the success should be measured. As such, only degrees of self-directedness are possible. Complete Expansion Activity 7.1: Self-Directedness to further explore the levels of self-directedness.

An excellent starting point for developing self-directed learning is through demonstrations, the Socratic method, concept attainment, and cooperative learning. These initial experiences can be followed with simulations and games and individualized instruction, which give students even more control over their own learning.

The Demonstration Method

The **demonstration** is the method in which the teacher or another designated individual stands before the class, shows something, and tells what is happening or what has happened, or asks students to discuss what has happened. A demonstration, then, is a process of teaching by means of using materials and displays to make information accessible to students. Even though the only person usually directly involved with the materials is the teacher or individual conducting the demonstration, students like demonstrations because they are actively engaged in a learning activity rather than merely talking about it. Information and concepts are made accessible to students; it is up to the students to learn. It is often good procedure, however, to have a student conduct the demonstration. This often arouses even more interest and student involvement.

The demonstration can be effective in many subject fields. For example, a teacher could demonstrate the steps in doing a science activity, the steps in writing a business letter, the steps in solving a mathematics problem, or how to adjust a microscope. Essentially, the technique deals mostly, but not totally, with showing how something works or with skill development. The demonstration may be by the teacher, by a student, by film or videotape, by Internet, or even by a sequence of pictures. Whatever technique is chosen, a demonstration should be accompanied by a verbal explanation or follow-up discussion. In an ordinary demonstration, the explanation accompanies the demonstration. One type of demonstration, however, asks students only to observe in silence. This method is referred to as the **inquiry demonstration.**

The inquiry demonstration is similar to the Socratic method (see next section of this chapter) in that students observe the demonstration in silence. These observations are then followed up with teacher questioning or with a discussion of what was observed. Students are asked to think logically, make inferences, and reach conclusions.

REFLECTIONS ON TEACHER PRACTICE 7.1   Seeking Quality

1. How can you help students take responsibility for their own learning and behavior?

2. How can students be taught to objectively evaluate each other and themselves?

◆ ◆ ◆

How do we get kids to work toward quality rather than just completion? I struggled with this for a long time, and this year I finally really and truly got it: AUDIENCE and REFLECTION.

The journey started with a series of PowerPoint presentations to the class. After each group presented, I asked the audience to share each presentation's strengths and areas that needed improvement. It was slow going at first; I had to remind them time and again that their critiques had to be specific so the presenters would know what to repeat and what to avoid in another situation.

(Continued)

(Continued)

I went through this process several more times with various pieces of work. My kids developed better on task behavior, became more likely to use the rubric while they were working, and my students' comments were more specific. Better yet, more students were completing projects, and the projects themselves were of higher quality. The only thing I was not happy with was presentation skills; though the kids would point out lack of eye contact, volume, and so on in their critiques, I didn't see the same sort of improvement as in the projects themselves.

As a result, with the last presentation I had kids work with their partners to score each presentation with the rubric. While content was included, the bulk of the points were focused on volume, enthusiasm, eye contact, speaking clearly, and so forth. The kids filled out the rubrics, made comments at the bottom, and then we shared our thoughts in discussions. As a result, I saw more kids actively working on volume, eye contact, and enthusiasm, among other things.

They have become very good evaluators, and no one wants to be evaluated poorly by their peers. We've developed a common language and understanding of what makes quality work, and the kids are judging solely on the work and not who the presenter is. As they work, I push them to answer the question, "Is this good enough?" themselves, using the scoring guide and their own experiences. I can honestly say it has helped AND, if we don't present something we've done in class, they always want to know why. We put those items on the wall, and the discussion continues after class.

It is a process. I did A LOT of modeling, demonstrating the appropriate way to give praise and make suggestions. If a student made a particularly insightful/ interesting/appropriate comment, I'd point to their comment as the type we were looking for. I ALWAYS start with the positive, no matter how dreadful the presentation is; we found good things to say about students with one slide out of the required eight, incomplete work, and so on. There is always a strength, a place to start, and while I had to connect the dots for them at first, they've gotten really good at doing it themselves. Of course, they still really enjoy pointing out the flaws, BUT they do it in a completely objective, supportive manner. I wonder if they zero in on the negatives so easily because that's what they've seen modeled for them by their teachers through the years?

It is just not Okay to treat others poorly in my classroom or in my presence. I've tried to model what I want from them at all times. We sometimes believe kids know how to act, and while they might be able to describe it, putting it into practice is an entirely separate matter. We must teach, model, and practice how to talk with each other thoughtfully.

As I've thought all of this over, I've realized how important it is to teach kids to become their own evaluators. They came in so dependent on me to tell them what was good and what needed improvement. If I am *really* going to teach them, I need to teach them to evaluate themselves and hold themselves to high standards. In the end, it's not about me, it's about them learning how to recognize and work for quality—for themselves.

—*ELLEN, middle-level English/language arts teacher*

SOURCE: www.middleweb.com. Reprinted with permission.

ON YOUR OWN 7.2   Reflections on Teacher Practice

Read and reflect on the viewpoints expressed in Seeking Quality. Log on to the Web-based student study site at http://www.sagepub.com/eis2study and react to the related activities.

There are at least five major reasons for teachers to use the demonstration in conveying a concept or the content in a subject: Among other things, demonstrations are useful when there is danger involved in students' using equipment or materials, they save time when absolutely necessary, they can show proper use of equipment, they can detail the steps in a particular procedure, and they can get a point across that is not easily expressed in words.

A good demonstration begins with an introduction (cognitive set) that indicates what students are to learn and/or are to look for and, perhaps, defines terms you will use in the demonstration. It is essential that you establish a strong cognitive set prior to conducting an inquiry demonstration. Your introduction should result in a focus of attention on what is to follow, but it should not give the details of what is to take place.

Students should be directly involved in classroom demonstrations and, whenever possible, should perform the actual demonstration.

Following the introduction, the demonstration should be completed as simply and as much to the point as possible. If equipment or a procedure is being demonstrated, you should follow the desired action step-by-step, with pauses and explanations offered as needed in clarifying the actions. Occasionally, when the mere process of listening could interfere with students' observations, you might want to hold comments to a minimum or conduct an inquiry demonstration. In fact, in such cases, you might even want to proceed through the demonstration silently the first time and repeat it with explanations. Finally, in conducting classroom demonstrations, the following guidelines should be followed:

1. Go slowly so students can follow.

2. When procedures are complex, break down the demonstration into small components and demonstrate them separately; once students understand the components, conduct the demonstration in its entirety.

3. Repeat steps of the demonstration until students understand.

4. Remember, left and right are reversed, so set up the demonstration from the students' perspective.

After the demonstration, you should do a follow-up to check for understanding. It may be advantageous to have the students walk through the steps with you to test their competency at using equipment or in using a demonstrated procedure. In fact, you might wish to use the Socratic method (see next section of this chapter) to determine the effectiveness of your demonstration.

Plan your demonstration for success. Try your demonstrations before trying them in class to be certain that they will work and that they take a reasonable amount of time. Set up demonstrations so that they are visible to all students; seating students in a semicircle around the demonstration often works best. You should plan techniques for keeping students attentive. In most cases, presenting demonstrations that are exciting will keep students' interest and attention. But, if needed, questions are often effective at regaining wandering attention.

APPLY AND REFLECT 7.2

Demonstrations can be used in most subject areas and at most grade levels. Demonstrations, however, are more applicable to some areas than others. How useful will demonstrations be as a teaching method in the area(s) you expect to teach?

The Socratic Method

The **Socratic method** derives its name from its ascribed adherent, Socrates. It is a technique of using a questioning-and-interaction sequence designed to draw information out of students, rather than pouring it into them. This method is purely verbal and interactive. Most teachers use the Socratic method to develop content information.

The Socratic method, in general, involves teaching by asking questions and, in so doing, leading students into a logical contradiction. Essentially, the Socratic method follows a general pattern:

1. A broad, open-ended question that most students can answer is asked first.

2. A second questioning sequence begins to narrow the range of responses and focuses the students' thinking onto the topic of the questioning strategy.

3. Review lectures and/or statements are interspersed among the questions in order to keep the salient points in the forefront.

4. A concluding question then brings students to the desired endpoint.

The techniques as originally developed by Socrates must be adapted to the reality of the classroom. The method Socrates conceived requires a one-to-one relationship between the student and teacher, with the teacher posing a series of questions that gradually tangle the student up to the point where ideas and thinking must be carefully scrutinized. In the classroom, the teacher generally does not focus the questioning sequence on one student but, rather, questions one student first, then another, and then another—moving slowly throughout the class. Although this technique usually works well, the pure essence of the Socratic technique is often difficult to capture. Still, the Socratic method can be quite effective, and it works best in small-group sessions and in tutorial sessions.

Richard Paul (1993) outlines the types of questions that can be used in the Socratic dialog sequence to probe the underlying logic or structure of student thinking and enable them to make reasonable judgments. Example questions might include the following:

- Questions of clarification
  –What do you mean by that?
  –Can you give me an example?
  –Why do you say that?

- Questions that probe assumptions
  –What is being assumed?
  –Why would somebody say that?
  –Is that always the case?

- Questions that probe reason and evidence
  –What are your reasons for saying that?
  –What criteria do you base that argument on?
  –Could you explain your reasons?

- Questions that probe implications and consequences
  –What might be the consequences of behaving like that?

–Do you think you might be jumping to conclusions?
–How can we find out?

- Questions about viewpoints or perspectives
  –What would be another way of saying that?
  –How do Judy's ideas differ from Mike's?
  –What is an alternative?
- Questions about the question
  –How is that question going to help us?
  –Can you think of any other questions that might be useful?
  –What is the question?

A Socratic dialog is a collective attempt to find the answer to a fundamental question or issue. The question or issue is the center of the dialog. Consider this dialog relative to choice.

Teacher:	Suppose your school is having a science fair and you can get class credit for presenting a project. Someone offers to do the necessary science project for you for a price. You know that wouldn't be right. What do you do?
Mike:	I would pay them and let them do it for me.
Teacher:	What would you do if a science judge asked if it was your work?
Mike:	I paid for it. I would say it was mine.
Teacher:	But wouldn't that be a lie?
Mike:	I did pay for it. So it is mine.
Teacher:	All right, but you know it wasn't really your work. Suppose the judge asks you to verify that you did the actual work.
Mike:	I'd have no choice but to say I didn't.
Teacher:	Suppose it wasn't the science judge, but rather your science teacher who asked, "Mike, did you do all this good work?"
Mike:	I might say, "Yes, I did it."
Teacher:	Okay, why would you say that?
Mike:	Fear of getting no credit.
Teacher:	Does that mean it is all right to have someone else do your work and lie? Then, doctors should be able to do it, your classmates, the president, and your parents?
Mike:	[*Long pause*] Well, no.
Teacher:	Then it is okay for you, but not others? Are there different rules for you?
Mike:	[*Longer pause*] No.
Teacher:	What would you think of yourself now that you've said that you would lie to your teacher out of fear? Are you that kind of person? You would pay someone else to do your work. What vision would you have of yourself?
Mike:	Well, what with the thought I have given it today, I would feel bad. Before today, I wouldn't have cared.
Teacher:	Do you have a different image of yourself now?

Mike: Yes. I think more of myself today than I would have yesterday. Because I know there's a better me and I should do the right thing.

Essentially, the Socratic method is a process in which ideas are debated in a back-and-forth discussion until some recognizable clarity (the light) is reached. When conducting such a dialog, you must have a clear vision of what you want students to learn from it. It is essential to have your endpoint in mind so that you can always be angling toward it.

APPLY AND REFLECT 7.3	How can the Socratic method be used effectively at the grade level you plan to teach?

Concept Attainment

Concept attainment is an instructional strategy that uses a structured inquiry process. The strategy is based on the research of Jerome Bruner (1977) and his associates, who investigated how different variables affected the concept-learning process. In concept attainment, students figure out the attributes of a group or category that has been provided by the teacher. To do so, students compare and contrast examples that contain the attributes of the concept with examples that do not contain those attributes. By observing these examples, students discuss and identify the attributes of each until they develop a tentative hypothesis (definition) about the concept. Next, students separate the examples into two groups, those that have the attribute and those that don't. This hypothesis is then tested by applying it to other examples of the concept. Examples could be symbols, words, passages, pictures, or objects. This strategy can be used in all curriculum areas. Finally, students demonstrate that they have attained the concept by generating their own examples and nonexamples. Concept attainment, then, is the search for and identification of attributes that can be used to distinguish examples of a given group or category from nonexamples. With carefully chosen examples, it is possible to use concept attainment to teach almost any concept in all subjects.

To illustrate the concept attainment process, consider the concept *proper noun*.

- First, the teacher chooses the concept to be developed (i.e., proper noun).

- Begin by making a list of both positive "yes" and negative "no" examples: The examples can be put on sheets of paper or flash cards or written on the chalkboard.

- *Positive examples:* Positive examples contain attributes of the concept to be taught (e.g., Jane, Houston, John, Settle, United States, George Washington, Honda, Old Testament). Your list of examples should include the idea that a proper noun means a specific person, place, or thing.

- *Negative examples:* Next present negative examples of the concept (i.e., run, is, and, boy, heavy, slowly, town, chair). Note the negative examples differentiate *proper nouns* from *common nouns.*

- Designate one area of the chalkboard for positive examples and one area for negative examples. A chart could be set up at the front of the room with two columns—one marked YES and the other marked NO.

- Present the first card by saying, "This is a YES." Place it under the appropriate column (e.g., Settle is a YES).

- Present the next card and say, "This is a NO." Place it under the NO column (e.g., run is a NO).

- Repeat this process until there are three examples under each column.

- Ask the class to look at the three examples under the YES column and discuss how they are alike. Ask, "What do they have in common?"

- For the next three examples under each column, ask the students to decide if the examples go under YES or NO.

- At this point, there are six examples under each column. Students should begin to hypothesize a name for the concept. These hypotheses are tested with further examples and nonexamples provided by the teacher. Students determine which hypotheses are acceptable and which ones have to be rejected based on the examples. They also can suggest additional hypotheses at this point. The process of presenting examples, analyzing hypotheses, presenting additional examples, and continuing to analyze hypotheses continues until all the hypotheses but one are eliminated.

- Discuss the process with the class. Students should be asked to explicitly define the hypothesis and identify the characteristics. Students are then asked to define a proper noun.

- Next, students are asked to apply the concept by classifying examples or generating examples of their own.

- Students analyze their own thinking (metacognition). Ask questions such as, "Did anyone have to change his or her thinking?" or "What made you change your mind?" or "When did you begin to see this concept?"

The concept attainment strategy is based on the assumption that one of the best ways to learn a concept is by seeing examples of it. Because examples are central to the concept attainment activity, special attention must be paid to their selection and sequencing.

APPLY AND REFLECT 7.4	The concept attainment strategy takes more time to plan, prepare materials, and carry out than some of the other strategies. Do you think the time is well invested, or should this time be used for other more pressing classroom activities? Share your thoughts with your classmates. Do they agree with you?

Cooperative Learning

The evolving constructivist perspectives on learning have fueled interest in collaboration and cooperative learning. As a result, **cooperative learning** has emerged as a promising instructional approach. Several approaches to cooperative learning have been developed (Davidson & O'Leary, 1990; Kagan, 1990); however, most of them share certain characteristics.

Cooperative learning is more than simply putting students in groups. Cooperative learning generally requires that students work together in mixed-ability groups in accomplishing a set of tasks. Students are placed in groups that are mixed in performance level, gender, and ethnicity. The percentage of high, middle, and low learners in each group should represent the appropriate population of each group in the whole class. Rewards to individual students are often based on the performance and accomplishment of the team. Accountability of individual students for the whole group builds an incentive for students to work productively together.

The size of the cooperative learning group varies, depending on the task to be accomplished. The common group size tends to be four. In general, cooperative learning groups are given considerable autonomy. Team members are allowed a great deal of freedom as they decide how to deal with the assigned task.

Individual accountability is an essential characteristic of all cooperative learning. Accountability means that the success of the group is based on the individual learning of each team member. Individual accountability occurs when each student in the group is held responsible for the required learning goals.

Some teachers assign roles and responsibilities to students to encourage cooperation and full participation. Assigned student roles might include recorder, encourager, materials monitor, taskmaster, quiet captain, and coach. If you do decide to assign roles, be sure the roles support the desired learning and that students understand their roles.

Graphic organizers can be a valuable resource when working with cooperative learning groups. Graphic organizers are pictorial or graphical ways to organize written or oral information. Graphic organizers form visual pictures of information and allow people to process information more intensely, which improves recall. They help students organize information into a simple-to-read, structured display that presents complex information in an easy-to-understand manner. Essentially, learning is enhanced because students must prioritize information when they create the graphic organizer and when they determine where each information component is placed on the graphic organizer. Graphic organizers examples include timelines, spider maps, hierarchies, and Venn diagrams. Graphic organizers can be grouped into three main classes and types from simple to more complex: sequential (timeline, flowchart, cyclical, hierarchy), single main concepts (continua, argumentation structure, spider maps), and multiple concepts (Venn diagram, matrix) (Drafke, 1993). Access http://www.cod.edu/people/faculty/drafke/Graphic%200rganizers.htm, http://www.teachervision .fen.com/graphic-organizers/printable/6293.html, and www.eduplace.com/graphicorganizer to review examples of these different classes of graphic organizers. Complete Expansion Activity 7.2: Graphic Organizers and Web Link 7.1: Graphic Organizers to further explore the use of graphic organizers.

EXPANSION ACTIVITY 7.2   Graphic Organizers

Two specific examples of graphic organizers are the K-W-L-H Technique and the Scientific Method Diagrams. Access www.enchantedlearning.com/graphicorganizers/KWHL and www.enchantedlearning.com/graphic organizers/scientificmethod and review these graphic organizers. Analyze both organizers. Would either be useful at the grade level you expect to teach? Why or why not? Share your perceptions with your classmates.

WEB LINK 7.1   Graphic Organizers

Access http://www.enchantedlearning.com/graphicorganizers. Review and analyze the graphic organizers presented on the Web site. Make a list of those formats that you feel would be most useful to you at the grade level you expect to teach. Form groups of four or five and see if there is a relationship between graphic organizers and the subject being taught. Share your group's conclusions with the class.

Cooperative learning takes many forms. The most common approaches include peer tutoring, student teams achievement division (STAD), group investigation, and the jigsaw strategy.

Peer Tutoring. One of the simplest forms of cooperative learning uses students as supplementary instructors in basic skills areas. The teacher presents material as he or she normally would. Pairs of students then use structured exercises and worksheets with answer sheets to reinforce the new material. Students take turns being the tutor and provide each other with immediate, one-to-one feedback (A. D. Miller, Barbetta, & Heron, 1994).

Student teams achievement division (STAD). In STAD, students are paired on evenly matched teams of four or five, and team scores are based on the extent to which individuals improve their

For material related to this concept, go to Clip 7.1 on the Student Resource CD bound into the back of your textbook.

scores on skills tests. Rewards are given to teams whose members improve the most over their past performances, thus encouraging group cooperation. The steps involved in implementing STAD are as follows (Slavin, 1995):

1. Pretest. This can be a unit pretest or work from previous units.
2. Rank students in descending order.
3. Divide students so each team of four has high-, medium-, and low-ability students and those groups are diverse in terms of gender and ethnicity.
4. Present lessons as you normally would.
5. Students study worksheets that focus on the goals and content covered by the teacher.
6. Monitor groups relative to progress on goals.
7. Administer individual quizzes to students.
8. Assign team scores based on individual score gains.

STAD is a popular cooperative learning strategy because of its wide applicability across a variety of subject matter areas (including math, reading, and social studies) and grade levels.

Group Investigation. Cooperative learning can be used to promote higher level learning. Group investigation involves a combination of independent learning and group work. It places students together in teams of three to six to investigate or solve some common problem. Examples might include social studies or a science experiment, a community project, or construction of an art collage. Students are responsible for developing group goals, assigning individual responsibilities, and bringing the projects to completion. Cooperation is encouraged and fostered through common group goals, and grades are assigned to the total project. Designers of group investigation identify six steps in implementing group investigations: (1) topic selection, (2) cooperative planning, (3) implementation, (4) analysis and synthesis, (5) presentation of final product, and (6) evaluation. To accommodate diversity, the teacher should ensure that

Group work gives students the opportunity to learn important social and cognitive skills from each other.

groups are heterogeneous and the different groups' members all contribute to the goals and final product. The teacher's role is to facilitate investigation and maintain cooperative effort.

Jigsaw Strategy. The jigsaw strategy is a cooperative learning plan in which six-member teams work to investigate a common topic. The topics are typically broad enough in scope (for example, the country of Canada in geography, islands in science, and the body in health) that individual members of the team can be assigned subjects within the topic. Individuals are responsible for researching and learning their part. Members of different teams who have studied the same part convene, discuss their part, and then return to their teams, where they take turns teaching their part to other team members. All students are expected to learn all the information on the topic, and comprehensive quizzes can be used to supplement group reports to measure if this happens.

Researchers have found that cooperative learning can be an effective strategy for improving achievement, especially when two essential conditions are met (Johnson & Johnson, 1999, 2002; O'Donnell, 1996; Slavin, 1995):

- Some type of recognition or small reward is provided to groups that do well so that the group members can sense that it is in their best interest to help group mates learn.

- Some method of evaluating each student's individual contribution, such as an individual quiz or individual work, needs to be used. For example, groups might be evaluated on the basis of the average of their members on individual quizzes, or students might be individually responsible for a unique portion of a group task. Without this individual accountability, some students might let others do their work.

APPLY AND REFLECT 7.5	The cooperative learning strategy is being used by many teachers. Based on your experiences and educational observations, what advantages associated with cooperative learning are behind the recent interest in cooperative learning?

When the conditions of group rewards and individual accountability are met, cooperative learning improves achievement across different grades, in tasks ranging from basic skills to problem solving, and in all types of schools (Ellis, 2001; Johnson & Johnson, 1999, 2002). In addition to boosting achievement, cooperative learning fosters a positive impact on intergroup relations, self-esteem, attitude toward school, and acceptance of children with special educational needs (Slavin, 1995).

Cooperative learning is appropriate in many situations. It can be an effective technique for reviewing for tests, for completing laboratory work, and for practicing skills. Remember, however, that you are rewarding cooperative learning. All students are involved in their group grade, and the better students are expected to help pull up the team grade. To get a better perspective of the uses and attributes of cooperative learning, complete Web Link 7.2: Cooperative Learning.

WEB LINK 7.2   Cooperative Learning

Go to the following cooperative learning Web sites:

www.co-operation.org

http://edtech.kennesaw.edu/intech/cooperativelearning.htm

Review the sites relative to cooperative learning uses and techniques. Write a summary of your findings. Share the summary with your classmates.

Table 7.1 summarizes the teaching approaches presented in this section. Review the summary and check your knowledge of this section by completing Review and Reflective Exercise 7.1.

TABLE 7.1   Integrated Methods

Method	Description
Ordinary demonstration	Individual shows and explains something to class
Inquiry demonstration	Individual shows class something without explanation; students observe, make inferences, and reach conclusions
Socratic method	Questioning and interaction to draw information out of students
Concept attainment	Teaching strategy designed to help students learn concepts and practice analytical thinking skills
Cooperative learning	Students work together as a team on assigned tasks

REVIEW AND REFLECTIVE EXERCISE 7.1   Describe integrated directed instructional strategies.

REVIEW

- What are some good demonstration strategies?
- What challenges do demonstrations pose for teachers?
- Describe the Socratic method. What are the strengths and weaknesses of this method?
- Describe the concept attainment and cooperative learning methods of teaching. How do they differ?

REFLECTION

- During a demonstration, how can teachers give students a sense of ownership?
- Is the Socratic method a viable teaching method for the grade level you plan to teach? Why or why not?
- The concept attainment and cooperative learning strategies could result in the development of social skills. How would you use these strategies to develop social skills at the grade level you expect to teach?

REFLECTIONS ON TEACHER PRACTICE 7.2   Cooperative Learning

1. How can students benefit from group work? How can it result in more effective teaching and learning?

2. What potential do you see for group work at the grade level you expect to teach? Is group work more effective at lower or upper grade levels? If so, why? If not, why not?

◆ ◆ ◆

The key to successful cooperative grouping is keeping the kids on task while they are working. If you make the group sizes reasonably small—no more than three, then you will have more constructive work time. I have found that when you have groups of more than three, somebody in the group is coasting, while others are carrying the weight of the work. I also make sure that

(Continued)

(Continued)

each person in the group has an assigned job. I have successfully had kids do maps together. They can also work together in small groups to read the textbook. Each group can pick a section of the text, then report it to the class. Sometimes I have them get together as a small group to play reporter. They report the event as if it happened yesterday. "And in

today's news, the colonists dumped tea into Boston harbor . . ."

—*WANDA, elementary teacher*

SOURCE: Reprinted with permission from ProTeacher, a professional community for elementary school teachers (http://www.proteacher.net).

ON YOUR OWN 7.3   **Reflections on Teacher Practice**

Read and reflect on the viewpoints expressed in Cooperative Learning. Log on to the Web-based student study site at http://www.sagepub.com/eis2study and react to the related activities.

Computer Integration

Computer use in the classroom can be highly motivational. Computers tend to increase student self-confidence and determination. Indeed, when computers are integrated into the content areas, learners are more apt to learn.

Computer use can be incorporated into every content area to some extent and thus truly be integrated into the entire curriculum. Computer use needs to be included in the teaching plan so that students spend part of each day interacting with the computer, being led through exercises that expand on the information being discussed in class.

Computers use can and should be applied in all content areas. For example, many word-processing and reading programs can enhance language arts writing and reading skills. Math, science, and social studies can be integrated quite easily as well. Moreover, the Internet can be used for a variety of tasks ranging from e-mail pen pals to research assignments. Computer use can be incorporated into lab activities and assignments for experiments or projects. There are also many educational games and problem-solving programs that engage students interactively.

If integrating computers use into content areas benefits students, how do you do it? A computer center or computer lab approach to computer integration with some time spent in the center or lab daily offers the most likelihood of success. Students not only have assigned computer time, but learning styles can be addressed. However, if you must use computers within your classroom, here are some tips to help you integrate them.

1. *Start slow.* Start with a weekly 15-minute lesson plan to get familiar with the equipment and test your students' interest and capabilities.

2. *Keep it simple.* Remember that for some students, just using a computer is a lesson in itself. Also, be selective with the computer activities you plan; try to integrate them into your curriculum.

3. *Be selective.* Keep your students' age and abilities in mind. An overwhelming experience with a computer can result in a lasting intimidation.

4. *Be flexible.* If students' interest level on certain projects is lacking, make room for changes.

5. *Allow flexibility in grouping.* Since computers are often limited in the classroom, the majority of your activities will be in groups. For example, you can form research, project, practice, or enrichment groups and have these groups work at the computer during center or morning work time. When computers are limited, many teachers keep student names on index cards and use a mental ring and

hook to display them near their computer(s). Each morning, after lunch, or any chosen time, students take their turn and then flip the card. A computer monitor can be named to remind students when it is their turn or when a student's computer time is up.

Computer use can increase your students' success by providing an avenue for them to explore and reinforce classroom concepts. Your teaching can be enhanced by exciting materials that can be used to reinforce what you are teaching. However, use your computers and technology wisely.

APPLY AND REFLECT 7.6	As a student, have you ever wished that a teacher used more or less computer assignments? Why did you want more or less of this computer time?

Simulations and Games

Simulations and game activities can be most useful as teaching tools. Indeed, they provide a variety of learning opportunities in the classroom. Such activities can create interest and relieve tension in difficult curriculum areas. Furthermore, students often find simulations and games fun.

Simulation is the presenting of an artificial situation or event that represents reality but that removes risk to the individual involved in the activity. Simulations can be viewed as models of what exists or might exist under manageable and controlled conditions.

Two basic types of simulations can be used in the classroom: human simulations and person-to-computer simulations. Human simulations are usually conducted in the form of role-playing and sociodramas, whereas person-to-computer simulations often take the form of simulation games.

What is the distinction between a *simulation* and a *game?* There is no clear-cut answer to this question. Usually, games are played to win, whereas simulations need not have a winner. In fact, in some simulations, it is difficult to determine whether there are winners or losers. Regardless of the label, simulations and games are similar in that there are roles that must be assumed and specific types of activities for the participants. In addition, the purpose of a simulation is to encourage students to act out the behaviors and express in their own words the actions and arguments behind an issue. Thus, whether an activity is a simulation or a game is often a matter of semantics.

Role-playing is the acting out of roles in re-creating historical or future events, significant current events, or imaginary situations (Gilstrap & Martin, 1975, p. 87). The role-playing student tries to "become" another individual and, by assuming the role, to gain a better understanding of the person, as well as the actions and motivations that prompted certain behaviors. Role-playing usually involves a structure, a stated issue to be resolved, and, in some cases, a winner or loser. Essentially, the idea is to become the individual being played as much as possible and, by re-creating the person's actions, to gain a better understanding of the person and the related motivations. A role-playing simulation may involve a limited number of individuals in one-to-one interactions or several students in small-group interactions.

Role-playing is often used for teaching citizenship responsibilities and for group counseling. It gives students opportunities to study human behavior. Students can explore their feelings, gain insights into the perceptions and attitudes of others, and develop their problem-solving skills. Teachers often use role-playing to facilitate learner involvement and interaction in the process of decision making. It teaches the process of decision making. It teaches students to learn through dramatization.

Role-playing can also be a group technique that may include almost any number of participants, depending on the purpose. Role-playing commonly consists of three components: the situation, the role-playing, and the follow-up discussion.

The role-playing episode should be a spontaneous acting out of a situation or an incident, which in the process fosters a deeper understanding of the associated actions, motives, and behaviors. You

"I like educational toys. I like educational TV. I like educational reading
material. It's education I don't like."

SOURCE: Created by Martha Campbell.

should give students a thorough briefing or detailed preparation regarding the situation prior to the
episode. For example, students can assume the role of Einstein and reenact the development of his
theories, or they can reenact the writing of the Declaration of Independence, or they can assume the
role of Shakespeare in the Globe Theater. Indeed, students can bring to life scenes from scientific discoveries, scenes from short stories or plays, events from the lives of different people, courtroom
dramatizations, legal-ethical situations, mock town meetings, or United Nations sessions. Whatever
the episode, describe the situation in detail to your students and set clear guidelines.

A debriefing session should follow any role-playing episode. The class should analyze the episode
with respect to the values and behaviors of the participants, as well as the consequences of the
actions.

The *sociodrama* is a form of role-playing. But it differs in that it focuses on how the group solves a
problem; that is, alternative solutions to problems of concern to the total group are explored. For
example, the problem may be related to an issue before a town meeting, a family problem, or a United
Nations problem.

Educational games involve students in decision-making roles in which they compete for certain
objectives according to specified rules. Thus, educational games should reflect society; they should
offer students the opportunity to experience roles that are common in life. The competitive nature of
games, however, should be kept in perspective. One of the best-known educational games is
Monopoly, a simulation board game of the real estate business.

For material
related
to this concept,
go to
Clip 7.2
on the Student
Resource CD
bound into the
back of your
textbook.

The use of computer simulations and games is increasing. Computer games are now familiar to
everyone; they are often played on home computers and in many classrooms. They come in a myriad
of formats, with the majority of those appropriate for the classroom involving hand-eye coordination
(such as Pac-Man) or problem-solving abilities (such as Dungeons & Dragons). Indeed, computer
games can function as an excellent motivational device when the chance of playing a game is contingent on doing one's work.

The use of simulations and games offers many benefits:

1. They actively involve students in their own learning.

2. They provide immediate feedback to students.

3. They enable students to practice communication skills.

4. They create a high degree of interest and enthusiasm.

5. They allow teachers to work with a wide range of student capabilities at the same time.

6. They promote and reward analytical and critical thinking.

7. They allow experimentation with a model of the real environment.

Basic to any teaching strategy is its motivational value. Simulations and games appear to be quite effective as motivational tools. Students think they are fun, and they even learn.

Several limitations have also been voiced regarding the use of simulations and games:

1. They demand a great deal of imagination on the part of the teacher and students.

2. They often screen out critical elements; for example, the driver education simulator often does not include traffic, noise, and the presence of others.

3. The expense involved in obtaining commercially produced simulations and games can be great.

4. Relationships often develop between the teacher and students that are too informal, which can lead to management problems.

These limitations can be overcome with proper planning. The use of simulations and games offers too many special opportunities to be ignored.

Some of the best simulations and games are those designed by teachers, who develop and adjust the activities according to their own students' needs. Even better, students can develop their own simulations and games.

APPLY AND REFLECT 7.7	What potential do you see for games in the school classroom? Discuss this issue in class.

In using simulations and games, you must be familiar with the desired roles, rules, and conflicts to be followed or addressed. In the case of games, you would be wise to play the game yourself first. In addition, it is a good idea to prepare handouts, materials, and guides for students. Complete Web Link 7.3: Educational Games to further explore the use of games at the grade level you expect to teach.

WEB LINK 7.3   Educational Games

Conduct an Internet search on educational games that would be appropriate for the grade level you expect to teach. Make a resource file of the best games and their sources. Are there any cautions teachers need to be aware of when using games for teaching? If there are, describe them. Share your resource file and cautions with your classmates.

Individualized Strategies

Students do not learn or master skills uniformly. Therefore, individualization is often required in maximizing the potential of each student; this is especially important when students come from different backgrounds and have varying abilities. In this section, I will address three fundamental techniques for individualization: individualized instruction, independent study, and mastery learning. Later, I will take a brief look at the somewhat related topic of drill and practice.

Individualized Instruction

Individualized instruction can take several forms. Ideally, **individualized instruction** engages students in learning plans tailored to meet their interests, needs, and abilities. Accordingly, you might vary one or more of the following: (a) the learning pace, (b) the instructional objectives, (c) the learning method, or (d) the learning materials. Students do not learn at the same pace. Some need more time to attain understanding. Thus, one—and perhaps the simplest—method to individualize instruction is that of permitting students to work on the same assignments at their own pace. This is accomplished by breaking down the instructional materials into a series of short and related activities or lessons. The faster students or high achievers can move through the lessons rapidly without having to wait for classmates to catch up. Students experiencing difficulty can move through the materials at a slower pace, reworking troublesome areas and seeking assistance when unable to master the material.

Another technique that can be used for individualizing instruction is varying your objectives. If you pretest your class on the intended instructional outcomes (objectives), you may find that some have already mastered these outcomes. Thus, instead of insisting that all students work on the same outcomes, you tailor the activities to the needs and abilities of different students or groups of students. Low-ability students might need to work on all your objectives, whereas better students might need to work on a small number. Clearly, you need to break down your instruction into a variety of objectives and related activities to accommodate this type of individualization.

A third individualization technique is to vary the method used in accomplishing the desired outcome. Even when students are working on the same outcome, they can use different means of achieving mastery. One student may rely on a textbook, whereas another may work with tutors. Still other students with learning difficulties may need to work with special teachers. Self-instructional packages, learning centers, and computer-assisted instruction (CAI) are other possible methods that could provide individualized instruction.

The final technique, of varying the materials used in accomplishing your objectives, can also lead to individualized instruction. As just noted, textbooks can be used in individualizing instruction. Some students, however, may read at lower reading levels than their classmates. In fact, some may have severe reading problems, which would hamper the use of any textbook. If reading is a problem, textbooks at different levels can be made available, as can other modes—such as films, audiotapes and videotapes, overheads, and models.

Essays and research projects are also an excellent way of individualizing instruction. They allow students or small groups of students to pursue areas of interest. For example, essays can be assigned on broad topics such as farming, the space program, teenage suicide, or the national debt, whereas research projects can be given in such areas as creating an air car, building classroom models, or writing and/or performing a play. Research projects usually are more challenging than essays; however, students involved in research often gain needed practice in finding and developing materials.

Although the classroom is normally viewed as a place for housing and teaching a class of students, you can often introduce a certain amount of individualization by forming learning groups or through the use of mastery learning. Group organizational structures—sometimes referred to as cooperative or team learning—enable and encourage students to learn and to assist each other, whereas mastery learning can be achieved through individual learning or group learning (see Mastery Learning section of this chapter). Students often learn and retain more when taught by peers. Thus, groups can be formed so that a range of ability levels and skills is represented within the groups. Also, student assistants can be assigned to work with specific groups on problems, to lead seminars, to demonstrate equipment, or to direct discussions.

Independent Study

There is no reason for you to do what students can do for themselves. Older students can often be involved in independent study. **Independent study** can be defined as any educational activity carried out by an individual with little or no guidance. Essentially, independent study is a pure form of self-directed learning.

Teachers often need time for working with individual students or with small groups. Independent study can provide this time. One way to provide this time is structuring the time for students to engage in interesting, creative tasks of their own choosing. For example, students can be allowed to research a topic of personal interest. Other possibilities include reading and reviewing books of interest, acting as tutor to other students, working at learning or interest centers, and working on classroom models. Such activities should be available for students who finish their seatwork quickly. They should not be punished indirectly for their rapid completion of an assignment with more of the same work. You might also want to carefully structure long periods of independent study. Self-directed library research studies on topics of personal interest, for example, make excellent learning experiences. Most students enjoy working independently on gathering facts on concrete problems. These topics need not always be traditional, content-centered topics. Attitude and awareness sometimes can be stimulated by combining factual knowledge with student interests and values.

Mastery Learning

Before focusing on the mastery learning model, let's look at the traditional model of instruction. This traditional model of instruction is shown in Figure 7.1. When you use this model, all of your students are involved in all activities at the same time. The instruction begins with an identification of the unit objectives, and then you present the primary instruction to the entire class. The primary instruction comes in the form of lectures, discussions, reading, media presentations, seatwork, or a combination of these techniques. After the primary instruction, you evaluate student achievement relative to your objectives.

Like the traditional model, the **mastery learning** model takes a group approach to teaching. This model, through its diagnostic-corrective-enrichment activities, provides a high degree of individualization because students often learn at different paces and use different materials. As depicted in Figure 7.2, the mastery learning model essentially represents a six-step pattern.

As with the traditional model, your first step in using the mastery model is identification of your objectives. Before the primary instruction is delivered, however, a preassessment step is carried out. The purpose of this second step is to determine where students are with respect to the objectives. Some students may lack unit prerequisite skills and need to work on them prior to receiving the primary instruction. Other students may have already mastered the unit objectives and should be directed to enrichment activities or to the next unit.

The third step in the mastery learning model is the delivery of the primary instruction. This instruction, as with the traditional model, involves all students except those who have demonstrated mastery in the activities, and it is presented through lectures, discussions, readings, and so on.

At this point—the fourth step—the mastery model parts from the traditional model: A formative assessment (progress check or diagnostic test) takes place. The purpose of this evaluation is to determine which students have achieved the desired mastery level and which students are in need of further instruction. Those at the mastery level are directed to enrichment activities, whereas those below the mastery level are involved in further objective-related activities. These fifth-step enrichments and

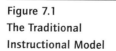

Figure 7.1
The Traditional
Instructional Model

**Figure 7.2
The Mastery Model
of Instruction**

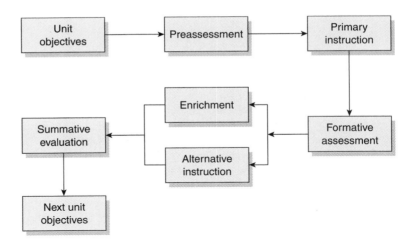

alternatives can be structured as group or individual activities. Further formative evaluations should be an integral part of the alternative instructional sequence.

Once the initial alternative activities have been completed, student progress should be checked once again; this cycle is repeated until mastery is achieved. During this sixth and final phase, all students are given a final, or posttest, evaluation.

The basic structure of the mastery learning model can take two forms. In the first, the enrichments and alternatives parallel each other, with the posttest evaluation providing closure for the unit. As students achieve mastery, they are routed to the enrichment component until the class is ready for the formal evaluation. The sixth step, the posttest evaluation, also may be administered to students at different times. In such situations, students can be tested when the formative evaluation indicates mastery has been achieved. The students who test early can be involved in other types of individualized strategies, or they can work on the next set of unit objectives on an individualized basis.

Effectiveness of Individualization

The evidence supporting the value of the various individualized strategies is mixed. Under certain conditions, for example, research suggests that the mastery learning approach does lead to higher student achievement. When used as the only method of instruction, however, such methods have not proven superior to traditional methods.

Individualization can be successful at any grade level. However, your decision on whether to use individualization should be guided by the nature of your students and their abilities and by the nature of the learning task. Individualized strategies tend to leave students on their own too much. Only the most motivated and self-directed students stay on task for extended periods of time. Therefore, with most students, a lot of time is wasted. Also, most students lack skill at analyzing and thinking reflectively about studied materials. They need the direct teaching and explanations provided by the teacher. Instead, the teacher's time is too often devoted to the preparation of materials and correction of individual assignments.

If carefully designed and monitored, individualization can be effective at providing needed remediation or enrichment. Students can work at their own pace on assignments geared to their ability, for example, but receive direct instruction from the teacher with the rest of the class. This more active involvement in their own learning generally results in a higher level of interest, better motivation, and a feeling of independence and self-discipline.

Efforts at improving individualization will continue. Students can only benefit from such techniques. Therefore, you will want to individualize your instruction at times. Study the various techniques and other self-directed methods and determine how you can incorporate them into your class.

Complete Expansion Activity 7.3: Self-Directed Learning Methods to explore the use of individualization and other self-directed techniques at the grade level you expect to teach. But be sure to remember that students need a teacher: They need your expertise and guidance.

EXPANSION ACTIVITY 7.3 Self-Directed Learning Methods

Do you think individualization and self-directed learning will work at the grade level you expect to teach? Why or why not? If it would, what forms and techniques would work?

APPLY AND REFLECT 7.8

How much individualization do you feel comfortable with in terms of your future classes? What forms would you support?

Drill and Practice

Drill and practice provide (or should provide) exactly what their names indicate—systematic and repeated "workout" in the intended skill areas, with the purpose of achieving automatic accuracy and speed of performance. **Drill** is concerned with the fixation of specific associations for automatic recall, whereas **practice** is concerned with improvement. Thus, one drills on writing the different shorthand symbols but practices on the basic multiplication facts.

Individualized problem-solving processes are the key to drill and practice. They are based on further development of initial whole-class learning. Seen in this light, drill and practice should be basic parts of the curriculum, not merely time fillers. As such, they should give students opportunities to apply their knowledge in solving problems or refining their skills. Such practice and/or drill, when designed properly, will give you good feedback on how students are progressing. Therefore, you should plan your drills and practice carefully and communicate their importance to students.

Students should not have to interrupt drill or practice frequently to get help. Students who are supposed to work independently must understand what they are to do with little or no help. First, make

For material related to this concept, go to Clip 7.3 on the Student Resource CD bound into the back of your textbook.

"We're going to need a new computer in our class today.
I hope I'm the one it replaces."

SOURCE: Created by Martha Campbell.

APPLY AND REFLECT 7.9

How do you feel about drill and practice? Will they be useful at the grade level you expect to teach and in your subject area? Why or why not?

sure assigned drills and practices are appropriate and not too difficult. Next, give clear expectations about what students should do when they finish their work. Last, make sure students are held accountable; when applicable, all seatwork should be checked.

Computers, with their nearly limitless patience and endurance, can be quite effective at providing drill and practice. Computers can drill students as long as the students can hold up. Math programs, for example, use a random-number generator to create new problems—as long as students make requests.

Drill and practice cannot be completely effective without some differentiation. You should always make your drill and practice flexible because they often must be adjusted to meet the differing learning needs of your students (see Chapters 1 and 2). For example, some students may need only one or two drill sessions or practice sessions, whereas others may need more extensive drill or practice. Flexibility and variety should be the keys to drill and practice; don't assume all students learn the same.

Table 7.2 summarizes the self-directed techniques covered in this section. Review Table 7.2 and check your knowledge of this section by completing Review and Reflective Exercise 7.2.

TABLE 7.2   Self-Directed Approaches

Method	Description
Computer integration	Using computers to enhance curriculum learning
Simulations and games	Models of artificial situations and events designed to provide no-risk experiences for students
Individualized instruction	Instruction tailored to interests, needs, and abilities of students
Independent study	Activities carried out with little or no guidance
Mastery learning	Diagnostic-corrective-enrichment model where students work on objectives until mastery is achieved
Drill and practice	Development of automatic and/or improved performance

Computer labs as a supplement to classroom teaching offer students opportunities for practical application of instruction.

REVIEW AND REFLECTIVE EXERCISE 7.2 Describe integrated directed instructional strategies.

REVIEW

- What is computer integration?
- What is individualized instruction?
- Discuss important features of individualized instruction.
- What are some pros and cons of individualized instruction?

REFLECTION

- Should all teachers integrate computers into the curriculum?
- How would you go about teaching individualized learning skills to students?
- Did any of your past teachers involve you in individualized instruction? If so, how successful was it? Did you like this instructional approach?

This completes the discussion of the various integrated teaching strategies. Complete Expansion Activity 7.4: Integrated Instruction Application to further explore the use of integrated instructional strategies at the grade level you expect to teach.

EXPANSION ACTIVITY 7.4   Integrated Instruction Application

Create a two-column chart of the integrated instructional strategies covered in Chapter 7 and indicate your feelings as to the value of each strategy at the grade level you expect to teach. Use the following three categories to evaluate each strategy for your chart: (1) appropriate and useful, (2) limited usefulness, and (3) not appropriate and not useful.

SUMMARY

The integrated directed strategy gives students some control over their own learning.

The Demonstration Method

- Demonstrations can be effective when used appropriately. Before conducting a demonstration, you should practice it in class, have all materials at hand, go slowly, often repeat components, and above all make it simple and to the point.

The Socratic Method

- The Socratic method of teaching is designed to draw information from students through the use of questions. Application of the Socratic teaching method calls for the teacher to focus the questioning sequence on a single student, then another, and then another.

Concept Attainment

- The concept attainment strategy uses a structured inquiry process. Students learn concepts by comparing and contrasting examples and nonexamples of the concepts.

Cooperative Learning

- Cooperative learning has emerged as a promising instructional approach. Forms of cooperative learning include peer tutoring, student teams achievement division, group investigation, and the jigsaw strategy.
- Graphic organizers can be valuable teaching aids when students are working in groups.

Computer Integration

- Computer integration into the curriculum can be highly motivational and will often result in better learning for students.

Simulations and Games

- Simulations are problem situations that are intended to represent reality.
- Role-playing is useful in getting students to look at the motives behind actions and behaviors.
- Educational games involve students in decision-making roles.

Individualized Strategies

- Individualized strategies include individualized instruction, independent study, mastery learning, and drill and practice. They represent techniques tailored to fit students' needs and abilities.
- Individualization can be provided by students working at their own pace on different objectives, working with different materials, and working on essays or projects.
- Mastery learning represents a model of instruction where students continue their work on unit objectives until mastery is achieved.

Drill and Practice

- Drill and practice provide students with needed accuracy and/or speed. Drill is usually concerned with the recall of associations, whereas practice is more often concerned with improvement.

DISCUSSION QUESTIONS AND ACTIVITIES

1. **Demonstration topics.** Generate a list of demonstrations that would be appropriate at the grade level you expect to teach. Once you have compiled your topics, separate them as appropriate only for teachers to do and those that students could do.

2. **Integrated directed methods.** When is it appropriate to use integrated directed teaching methods? Consider your instructional intent, as well as the students themselves. Would mastery learning be appropriate for the students you expect to teach?

3. **Diversity.** Could you use cooperative learning at the grade level you expect to teach? What form would work best? How would you accommodate diversity?

4. **Role-playing.** Identify some core values (American, school, community, etc.) that could be taught using role-playing (e.g., honesty, fairness).

5. **Educational games.** Suppose a parent criticized your use of games in the classroom; prepare a response entitled "Why Our School Uses Games."

6. **Individualized strategies.** If individualized strategies are so important and beneficial, why are they not implemented by all teachers? Give your reasons and justify them.

TECHNOLOGY AND EDUCATION

The quality of instruction can be improved through the use of technology. How would you use technology to improve integrated instruction at the grade level you expect to teach? You might want to access the following Internet URL Web sites for ideas: http://www.edzone.net/~mwestern, http://wtvi.com/teks, http://www.lessonplanspage.com, and http://www.eduref.org/Virtual/Lessons/index.shtml. Form groups of four or five to share ideas. Share your group's ideas with the class.

DECONSTRUCTING THE STANDARDS

Chapter 7 content addresses topics related to INTASC Standards 4, 5, 6, and 7.

- ♦ INTASC Standard 4 states: *Multiple Instructional Strategies:* The teacher uses various instructional strategies to encourage students' development of critical thinking, problem solving, and performance skills.
- ♦ INTASC Standard 5 states: *Classroom Motivation and Management:* The teacher uses an understanding of individual and group motivation and behavior to create a learning

environment that encourages positive social interaction, active engagement in learning, and self-motivation.

♦ INTASC Standard 6 states: *Communication Skills:* The teacher uses knowledge of effective verbal, nonverbal, and media communication techniques to foster active inquiry, collaboration, and supportive interaction in the classroom.

♦ INTASC Standard 7 states: *Instructional Planning Skills:* The teacher plans instruction based on knowledge of subject matter, students, the community, and curriculum goals.

For each of these four standards, write your response to the following:

- Which part(s) of each standard does this chapter address?
- How does this chapter address this standard?
- How will the concepts in this chapter help you apply this standard as a teacher?

PRAXIS CONNECTION

Log on to the Web-based student study site at http://www.sagepub.com/eis2study. Access the Praxis II: Principles of Learning and Teaching assessments and/or state-related exams and complete the Chapter 7 test preparation exercises.

PORTFOLIO CONNECTION

Log on to the Web-based student study site at http://www.sagepub.com/eis2study. Access the Portfolio Connection. Complete the Chapter 7 portfolio link to INTASC activities.

CONNECTION WITH THE FIELD

1. **Teacher interviews.** Visit with several classroom teachers and discuss with them how they use integrated directed instruction. Do they use individualized strategies extensively? Why or why not?

2. **Classroom observation.** Visit several public school classrooms. Keep a record of the different methods used. What integrated directed methods did you observe? Was there a pattern? Were drill and practice used?

3. **Teaching.** Prepare and teach a minilesson using the demonstration method. Use the microteaching guidelines and forms in Appendix A to plan and analyze your minilesson.

4. **Teaching analysis.** Make a videotape of your miniteaching lesson; then critically analyze it with your peers.

CHAPTER 8

Teaching Effective Thinking Strategies

The person with big dreams is more powerful than the one with all the facts.

—ANONYMOUS

OVERVIEW

It is necessary, and even desirable, to provide students with a sound education in basic skills. A complete education, however, must emphasize thinking skills that enable students to function responsibly and to solve problems in ways that are sensitive and caring of others, society, and the world. Undoubtedly, this goal requires teachers of all disciplines to explicitly teach the thinking skills deemed necessary for a lifetime of continuous learning.

In the 1923 work *The Prophet,* Kahlil Gibran (1923/1989) tells us, "If the teacher is indeed wise, he does not bid you enter the house of his wisdom, but rather leads you to the threshold of your mind." These words suggest that thinking skills must be placed high on our agenda as one of the most basic of all skills needed today. In fact, thinking skills can be regarded as essential skills.

This chapter will focus on teaching students how to think. A wide variety of thinking skills will be examined; however, critical and creative thinking will be emphasized. I will attempt to examine some of the ideas, methods, and issues related to critical thinking and creative thinking.

OBJECTIVES

After completing your study of Chapter 8, you should be able to do the following:

- Define *thinking* and differentiate among the various categories of thinking skills.
- Explain creativity as a process and product and describe the four stages of creative thought.
- Describe various difficulties that can hinder the creative process.
- Define and describe *metacognition*.
- Describe different approaches and activities that can be used in teaching thinking skills.
- Explain the eight behaviors that exemplify "nonthinking."
- Explain the role of the teacher and how modeling is used in the teaching of thinking skills.

Research (Sadler & Whimbey, 1985) has led educators to question the meaning of "basic skills" for learning, and many have suggested that "thinking skills" are the basis on which all other skills are developed. That is, individuals need thinking skills for remembering information, incorporating knowledge, learning and using motor skills, and developing values and attitudes. Some of these skills are generic and can be taught as general learning strategies, without reference to content.

The research findings tend to confirm that when thinking skills become an integral part of the curriculum and instructional practice, test scores in academic areas increase. It is now widely accepted that teachers of every discipline must teach thinking skills explicitly in addition to their content area. It is also generally agreed, however, that students must assume much of the responsibility for developing these skills. Students must take an active role in the learning process, but the teacher must provide opportunities for using thinking skills and not inhibit such activity.

Implicit within the notion of thinking is the concept of decision making, which involves making choices from among a number of competing appropriate responses. Not all problems have answers that are clearly "correct." In such situations, a person must choose from among a variety of acceptable alternatives. This process of making choices involves skill at thinking (Beyer, 1988).

To further explore the concept of thinking, complete Expansion Activity 8.1: Thinking.

EXPANSION ACTIVITY 8.1   Thinking

Schools should develop a well-balanced program of personal development for all students. This program should balance academic, social, and personal growth. Can all types of school experiences be accepted as part of the development of student thinking skills? Are school experiences designed to develop thinking skills? If so, have they been successful?

Thinking Skills

What are thinking skills? How does one go about teaching them? These are difficult questions to answer. Indeed, there are as many definitions of *thinking* as there are thinkers. Do not all cognitive acts require thinking? Although it is true that all cognitive acts require thinking, it is also important to distinguish between the ability to use one's mind in simply reproducing rote facts and the creative ability to use higher thinking skills to generate new information.

Many believe that it is possible to teach students the skills that will enable them to produce the creative thoughts that lead to finding solutions to problems—a skill much needed in preparing the youth that will be tomorrow's leaders (Martinez, 1998; Mayer & Wittrock, 1996). In fact, authorities in the field of education have expressed strong feelings about what it means to "think" beyond the mere level of replication of information. For example, in a 1990 Association for Supervision and Curriculum Development (ASCD) video, David Perkins of Harvard University says that **thinking** is "problem solving, its decision making, reading, reflecting, making predictions about what might happen." In the same video, Matthew Lipman (ASCD, 1990) suggests that thinking is processing your experiences in the world; to edit, or rearrange, or examine experiences; and to think about the process of thinking about your experiences. On the other hand, Ernest Boyer (1983), president of the Carnegie Foundation, stated that thinking cannot be separated from good language. Finally, *The Random House College Dictionary* (Stein, 1984) defines thinking as follows: "To employ one's mind rationally and objectively in evaluating or dealing with a given situation; to have a certain thing as the subject of one's thoughts; to consider something as a possible action, choice, etc.; to invent or conceive of something; to have consideration or regard for someone; to have or form in the mind as an idea, conception, etc.; to have an opinion or belief; to consider for evaluation or for possible action upon." All of these reflective thoughts describe many important aspects of the operation of thinking, and there are, indeed, many areas to approach in the teaching of thinking.

Students must learn
to be responsible for
their own learning.

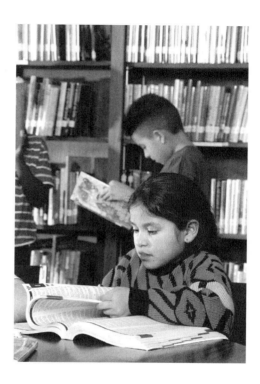

There appear to be many views of thinking. To clearly define *thinking* for teachers searching for ways to create thinking students, this discussion will encompass all of the definitions cited and summarize *thinking* as the act of withholding judgment to use knowledge and experience to find new information, concepts, or conclusions. Let us now look at the different types of thinking.

REFLECTIONS ON TEACHER PRACTICE 8.1   Thinking Games

1. What is "thinking" ability?

2. How do we use our thinking ability everyday? Why might we need to address thinking in school?

♦ ♦ ♦

To engage my students in thinking, I have my class work in pairs to construct a game about our state. I give them a rubric when I explain the lesson that outlines what they are expected to include (for example: game pieces, strategy, at least 15 cities mentioned, at least 15 facts about the state, etc.). An old clothes box makes a great box for storage of the game! The game construction worked out great and the kids had fun working on the project.

I was really impressed with some of the game ideas students came up with. On the day they were due, each pair had to present

their game to the class. Then we had a "game day" and I let them play their games for part of the afternoon. We also kept them in the room for extra things to do during indoor recess. I plan to use the same idea again and students will get to pick different states.

—*TRACY, elementary school teacher*

SOURCE: Reprinted with permission from ProTeacher, a professional community for elementary school teachers http://www .proteacher.net).

ON YOUR OWN 8.1 **Reflections on Teacher Practice**

Read and reflect on the viewpoints expressed in Thinking Games. Log on to the Web-based student study site at http://www.sagepub.com/eis2study and react to the related activities.

Categories of Thinking

Your first task in teaching thinking skills is to determine which skills are appropriate for your class. In doing so, you should consider the maturity level of your students, along with the special needs of your subject. It is commonly believed that it is better to teach a few skills well and thoroughly rather than many skills superficially.

APPLY AND REFLECT 8.1

You should show students that they can be successful thinkers. How could you do this at the grade level you expect to teach? Share your ideas with your class.

All teachers teaching thinking skills should refer to Bloom's Taxonomy of thinking levels for assistance in the formation and understanding of various thinking levels. As noted earlier, Bloom's Taxonomy is generally viewed as a multitiered model of classifying thinking according to six cognitive levels of complexity. The levels have often been depicted as a ladder (see Figure 3.3) that students are encouraged to "climb to reach higher levels of thought." The lowest three levels are knowledge, comprehension, and application. The highest three levels are analysis, synthesis, and evaluation. The taxonomy is hierarchical; each level is subsumed by the higher levels. In other words, a student functioning at the "analysis" level has also mastered the material at the "knowledge," "comprehension," and "application" levels. Almost all content areas can provide instruction at six levels of thinking: knowledge, comprehension, application, analysis, synthesis, and evaluation.

• At the knowledge level, most thinking tasks require students to recognize or remember key facts. The knowledge level calls on students to be attentive to information, or repeat information verbatim, and to recite facts, such as math facts and formulas. Activities that ask students to recall, define, recognize, practice drills, or identify concepts are a few knowledge-level thinking skills.

• Students translate, interpret, and explain given information at the comprehension level. Comprehension thinking tasks involve interpreting the meaning of a graph or diagram or decoding a word. Knowledge and comprehension levels are not representative of the higher order thinking skill levels because students are not required to come up with new information but are called on to translate the information that has been given.

• Students at the application level can transfer known information to applicable situations. In effect, they must think and decide how information can be applied to situations other than those presented. Students are given generalizations and are required to make applications and explain relationships. For example, students could be asked to solve equations by applying a correct formula or transfer known skills to another area in solving a problem.

• At the analysis level, students must think about how to divide a whole into component elements. Generally, this level includes finding comparisons and relationships between the parts to the whole concept. Students are required to break down complex information or ideas into simpler parts.

Thinking tasks that call on students to identify the underlying structure of complex ideas or information and to compare similarities and differences fall into the analysis level.

• Thinking tasks at synthesis levels require that students take parts of previously learned information and create completely new products, or wholes. Both inductive and deductive thinking and reasoning fall in this category. With inductive thinking, students are provided evidence or details and then asked to use thinking skills to make generalizations. Conversely, students using deductive thinking are given a generalization and are asked to provide evidence that explains the generalization. Hypothesizing, predicting, and concluding are examples of deductive thinking.

• Finally, evaluation-level thinking tasks are those in which students judge quality, credibility, worth, and practicality. Student thinking at this level generally must provide evidence, logic, and values in support of conclusions. It is easy to make swift judgments that do not require the evaluation level of thinking. Tasks at this level, however, also demand that students use all the previous levels of thinking. The key in determining whether students are actually at this level lies with their ability to withhold judgments until they are able to explain the logic or provide evidence in support of their judgments.

Critical Thinking

Critical thinking is not the same as intelligence; it is a skill that can be improved in everyone (Walsh & Paul, 1988, p. 13). Also, many educators differentiate between ordinary thinking and thinking critically. According to Lipman (1988b), ordinary thinking is usually simple and lacks standards, whereas critical thinking is more complex and is based on standards of objectivity and consistency. He suggests that students must be taught to change their thinking (a) from guessing to estimating, (b) from preferring to evaluating, (c) from grouping to classifying, (d) from believing to assuming, (e) from inferring to inferring logically, (f) from associating concepts to grasping principles, (g) from noting relationships to noting relationships among relationships, (h) from supposing to hypothesizing, (i) from offering opinions without reasons to offering opinions with reasons, and (j) from making judgments without criteria to making judgments with criteria.

A good way to develop critical thinking skills is by teaching students to recognize propaganda, a form of persuasion that is intended to influence the audience by the use of exaggerations and emotional appeals. Students often enjoy looking for examples of propaganda that are readily found in political promotions and product advertisements. Samples from newspapers, magazines, and television can be analyzed for evidence of misleading statements, biased or one-sided reports, false assumptions, avoidance of issues, exaggerated statements, and emotional appeals.

Critical thinking tends to require higher levels of thinking—that is, more evaluation and synthesis than application or analysis. Indeed, it should be remembered that Bloom's Taxonomy is hierarchical; therefore, operation at the evaluative level requires the use of the previous thinking levels as well.

Creative Thinking

All people have the potential for experiencing those feelings of "Aha!" or "Wow, guess what I just figured out?" Such thinking is creative thinking. It occurs as the result of questioning and learning beyond the gathering of rote information. Research indicates that the "creative" right brain generates ideas and images, whereas the "logical" left brain critiques and evaluates. It is during the creative processes that the two halves of the brain seem to communicate best. Before we can decide how to develop creativity, however, we must discuss what, exactly, creativity is.

Some degree of **creativity** occurs whenever a person assembles information to discover something not previously taught or understood. To the individual, this may be the discovery of a new relationship between two unlike concepts. This concept of creative thinking is often associated with creative thinking as a process.

Open-ended activities, with no single correct answer, can be used to develop thinking skills.

When creativity is defined as a product, the result embraces the idea of the production of a new invention or theory. This type of creative thinking is associated with the realization of an original concept. For the student, this could be the creation of a poem, a song, a game, or an unusual use for a common item. Ideally, all creative thinking takes people "beyond where they have ever gone before."

Curiosity, imagination, discovery, and invention are all equated with creative thinking. Although it may not be possible for one person to teach another person how to be creative, it is possible to provide activities that enhance opportunities for thinking. Frequently, there is a high level of frustration associated with creative thinking as individuals travel through the four stages of creative thought.

Creative thinking is generally thought of as putting together information to come up with a whole new understanding, concept, or idea. The four stages generally identified with the development of creative thought are preparation, incubation, illumination, and verification (see Figure 8.1). Numerous thinking skills are used during each of these stages of the creative process. In fact, the greater the flexibility in thinking, the greater the possibility for developing students' creative thinking ability.

During the first stage, preparation, the creative thinker collects information and examines it, using many of the thinking processes previously mentioned. The creative thinker, however, questions and investigates until a major relationship seems to appear among events, objects, or ideas. Usually a hypothesis emerges in the thinker's mind, which causes the individual to ponder and meditate in a questioning manner. This begins what is known as the second stage of creative thought, incubation. The individual may spend quite some time allowing images from the unconscious to surface. At other times, this stage may be very short-lived, moving the creative thinker into the "Aha!" or illumination stage. Suddenly, the "I've got it" or "Now I know" may emerge. At this stage, the individual may feel confident and regain equilibrium, which can be followed by new questioning and a need for elaboration. Next, the individual begins to seek out ways of verifying and testing the idea. This is called the stage of verification. Figure 8.1 summarizes the four stages of creative thinking.

Eminent creative persons, and others less prominent but no less creative, have expressed frustration and disconcerting feelings while struggling with a puzzling concept that later led them to a discovery or "Eureka!" feeling. The following types of difficulties have been reported (Torrance, 1983) by many who have studied the creative thinking process.

1. Difficulty in finding words to describe original images is one of the frequently reported frustrations given by creative thinkers. Sometimes ideas or images are too complex for them to put into

"Cafeteria duty."

SOURCE: Created by Ford Button.

words. Certainly, not all creative insights must be expressed in words; they can also be expressed visually or kinesthetically.

2. An inability to let the imagination "go" can be a problem. Many cannot permit themselves to "let go" in childlike play even momentarily. The ability to relax, laugh, and play with new ideas with an unrestricted attitude is an important characteristic of creative thought.

3. A tendency to analyze rather than synthesize is a common mistake that can hinder creative thinking. Whereas analysis is helpful during the early stages of creativity, synthesis is necessary in pressing forward through the development of new, original ideas.

4. Creative thinkers sometimes "jump the gun" to synthesize before analysis of the facts is complete. This can create "thinking blocks," which hinder the consideration of other valuable possibilities.

5. Many have communicated fears of expressing new ideas they were generating in their own minds. Some are afraid to let others see their inventions and express doubt that others will appreciate their ideas. It takes courage to be an independent thinker. This does not mean, however, that independent thinkers never experience doubt or misgivings. Even the most eminent creative thinkers of our time have experienced these feelings.

6. A frequent complaint of creative thinkers has been that they get too many ideas at one time. The flood of information becomes a form of stress and gives the individual an "avalanche effect." Successful completion of one or more of these ideas requires the thinker to shelve some of the ideas and focus on what is needed for the moment.

If you are to confront and overcome these difficulties, you must provide students opportunities for creative successes in the classroom. Moreover, you should avoid judging students' creative endeavors and provide support and encouragement for their attempts.

Figure 8.1
Stages of Creative Thinking

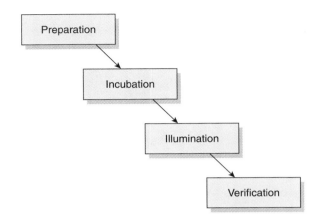

APPLY AND REFLECT 8.2	You should provide instructional materials and support for students' creative endeavors. Generate some ideas for materials and support that would help your future students develop their thinking skills. Share your ideas.

Few people would argue with the importance of improving critical thinking and creative skills of students in subjects such as mathematics, English, and history. Of course, some students will develop learning skills on their own, but most students need assistance.

Metacognition

For material related to this concept, go to Clip 8.1 on the Student Resource CD bound into the back of your textbook.

Metacognition can be simply defined as "thinking about thinking." Thinking skills and study skills are examples of metacognitive skills. They include invisible thinking skills such as self-interrogation, self-checking, self-monitoring, and analyzing, as well as memory aids (called mnemonics) for classifying and recalling content.

Metacognition consists of two processes occurring simultaneously: monitoring progress when engaged in learning and making changes and adapting corrective strategies when problems occur during learning. It involves overseeing whether a cognitive goal has been met. It is about self-reflection, self-responsibility, and initiative. Metacognitive skills include monitoring the progress of learning, correcting errors, analyzing the effectiveness of learning strategies, and changing learning behaviors when necessary. Metacognitive strategies come into play when cognitions fail, such as the recognition that one did not understand what one just read. Such an impasse should activate metacognitive processes as the learner attempts to rectify the situation.

Metacognition enables students to better benefit from instruction. Students don't often stop to evaluate their comprehension of material. They don't generally examine the quality of their work or stop to make revisions as they go along. They too often don't attempt to examine a problem in depth. They don't make connections or see the relevance of material in their lives. Take reading, for example. Students often read a page (or a whole chapter!) in a textbook without comprehending a single thing. They simply go on to the next page, thinking that merely reading the words on a page is enough. They need to learn to reread difficult pages until the main concept is understood, flag difficult pages until the main concept is understood, or flag a difficult passage to ask for clarification from the teacher.

Students can be taught strategies for assessing their own understandings and how to choose effective plans of attack to study or solve problems. For example, in reading a book, students are bound to come across a paragraph that they don't understand on first reading. What do they do? Perhaps they could reread the paragraph more slowly. Perhaps they should look for other clues, such as pictures, graphs, or glossary terms, to help them understand. Perhaps they should read farther back in the chapter to see whether the difficulty arose because they did not fully understand something that came earlier. These are all examples of metacognitive skills; students need to learn how to know when they are not understanding and how to correct themselves (Schunk & Zimmerman, 1997). Another important metacognitive process is the ability to predict what is likely to happen or to tell what is sensible and what is not. Other metacognitive strategies that students can be taught to use include

- Consciously identifying what they already know
- Determining how performance will be evaluated
- Estimating the time required to complete a task
- Planning study time into their schedule and setting priorities
- Making a checklist of what needs to happen when
- Organizing materials
- Taking the necessary steps to learn by using strategies such as outlining, mnemonics, diagramming, and so on
- Reflecting on the learning process, keeping track of what works and what doesn't work
- Monitoring learning by questioning and self-testing
- Providing their own feedback
- Keeping concentration and motivation high

APPLY AND REFLECT 8.3	Use and teach students mnemonic devices for remembering information. How have you used such devices before? If not, research some common ones. Share your findings with your class.

Although many students will develop adequate metacognitive skills, some will not. Teaching metacognitive strategies to students can lead to a marked improvement in their achievement (Alexander, Graham, & Harris, 1998). Students can learn to think about their own thinking processes and apply specific learning strategies to think themselves through difficult tasks (Butler & Winne, 1995; Schunk, 2000). Self-questioning strategies are particularly effective (Zimmerman, 1998). Essentially, students can be taught to talk themselves through activities they are engaged in, asking themselves or each other the questions you would ask.

As students become more skilled at using metacognitive strategies, they gain confidence and become more independent as learners. Students realize they can pursue their own intellectual needs and discover that a world of information is at their fingertips. The task for you as a teacher is to acknowledge, cultivate, exploit, and enhance the metacognitive capabilities of all your students. Complete Expansion Activity 8.2: Thinking Skills to explore the emphasis put on thinking skills in your state.

EXPANSION ACTIVITY 8.2 Thinking Skills

Access the state content standards (competencies, benchmarks) for the grade level and area(s) you expect to teach. What types of thinking skills are stated? What changes would you make in the amount of emphasis put on developing thinking skills in your state? Do your classmates agree?

APPLY AND REFLECT 8.4	You should be a model of critical and creative thinking. How would you do so?

The concepts regarding thinking skills are summarized in Table 8.1. Review the summary and complete Review and Reflective Exercise 8.1.

Thinking Skills Instruction

The teaching of thinking skills requires open-mindedness on the part of those who teach them. Every rock of information must be turned over; every avenue of learning must be explored. You must be willing to explore, question, take risks, and experiment; otherwise, how can you lead students through the same processes?

Many suggest that you begin the teaching of thinking skills by selecting only a few individual lessons that focus on particular skills. Then, as experience and confidence grow, you should consider extending the emphasis on thinking skills and integrate these skills into your content area.

Should you teach thinking skills separately or infuse them into your content area? There are pros and cons to both approaches. Those favoring the separate approach maintain that, like reading and writing, thinking skills are enabling disciplines and deserve separate instruction (Lipman, 1988a, p. 43). Conversely, advocates of the infusion approach argue that certain cognitive skills are specific to particular disciplines and, therefore, should be taught in context (Ashton, 1988, p. 4). Perhaps the answer to this issue is to use both separate instructional programs and infusion programs. Let's look at these two approaches.

The Separate Approach

Reuven Feuerstein (ASCD, 1990), an internationally known cognitive psychologist, points out that many students lack the basic skills and abilities for seeing relationships or comparisons between ideas. He suggests that these students need special programs of focused instruction upon specific skills—that is, separate instruction on thinking skills. Many educators prefer the **separate approach** when introducing a new skill because it may be difficult for students who are unfamiliar with a skill to focus on the learning of a new skill and on learning of content at the same time.

Modeling is an important component in the separate approach. In fact, when using this approach, you should always begin the teaching of a skill by modeling it. For example, when teaching students about classification, you should demonstrate the skill by doing a whole-class classification activity.

TABLE 8.1 Thinking Skills	
Concept	Description
Thinking	The act of withholding judgment to use knowledge and experience in finding new information, concepts, or conclusions
Critical thinking	The ability to analyze complex situations critically, using standards of objectivity and consistency
Creativity	The capacity for producing imaginative, original products or ways of solving problems
Metacognition	The skill of thinking about thinking

Students should be given the opportunity to ponder issues related to classroom instruction and to present alternative ideas.

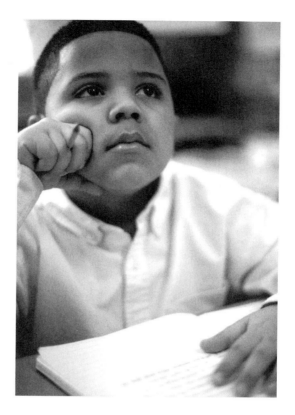

Although you may demonstrate how to classify, you would be wise to create a thinking exercise wherein the students' answers diverge. Guidance can be provided, for instance, by presenting the classification steps on the overhead projector or chalkboard—for example:

- Skim over all the objects to find two that have something alike.
- Choose two that are alike and label them as a group.
- See if any others fit into that group.
- Find two more that have similarities and label them a group.
- Skim over the others to see if they fit into this group.
- Continue the process until all items have been classified.

You should call for whole-class responses to each of the steps, which in turn will demonstrate that the skill allows for many correct responses. Class input is one of the most important aspects of teaching the classification skill as a thinking skill. As students make suggestions and form their own classified groups, you gradually need to release responsibility to students by allowing them to arrive at answers. Afterwards, students should give explanation to the logic that led to their conclusions. Once the initial introductory activity has been completed with the group, you should provide students an opportunity for practicing the skill individually so their understanding of the modeled skill can be evaluated.

The Infusion Approach

The **infusion approach** calls for the use of the desired skill in conjunction with the regular curriculum (Prawat, 1991; Sternberg, 1998; Tishman, Perkins, & Jay, 1995). In effect, this approach requires that students transfer the newly acquired skill to the regular content being studied. If teaching students the skill of classification, for example, after the skill has been taught, it would be applied to the regular curriculum. That is, once students are taught to classify through introductory activities, they are asked to apply it to the content being studied. You might simply ask them to synthesize different ways the content being studied can be classified. If necessary, direct them toward items in your content area in which classifying may be of use. For example, the outlining of a chapter requires grouping information under headings and categories. Once another use has been established, go through the whole-class collaboration steps once again—using the skill in this new context. Afterwards, the procedure of infusing the thinking skill into your content needs can be finalized by assigning students a situation in your content area in which they can apply the skill.

Critical Thinking Instruction

Stephen Brookfield (1987) purports that there are two activities central to critical thinking: (1) identifying and challenging assumptions and (2) exploring and imagining alternatives. Moreover, Brookfield defined *assumptions* as the unquestioned rules that individuals have assimilated into their value system as self-evident truths—"taken-for-granted" truths established by the culture that individuals have accepted as their own. These assumptions influence how we interpret situations and how we perceive solutions to problems. Consequently, one of the basic behaviors we develop through critical thinking is open-mindedness and a willingness to explore other possibilities. In effect, we must teach students to examine old ideas in new ways and to consider alternatives to old ways of thinking. This task is not an easy one because it is often inherently disruptive to personal values and beliefs. This personal disruption may be one reason critical thinking activities are at times so strongly resisted.

Direct, specific instruction is often useful in critical thinking and should be used in assisting students in dealing with assumptions so that a more open-minded attitude toward new modes of thinking can be developed. Without such instruction, there is little hope for dismantling the concepts our society has outgrown—for example, previously held conceptions about racism and sexism. Although many misconceptions about areas such as these still exist, an important aspect of teaching thinking is the modeling of the open-minded attitude you hope to foster. This will not be possible if you become a dictator of your most comfortable ways of thinking and behaving. Indeed, you must provide opportunities for students to think about their views and the views of others; yet, the final decision should be left to students as respected thinkers. Without this atmosphere of respect, it is impossible to model the concepts you desire to teach.

One good way of providing opportunities for students to examine assumptions is by having them work in small groups with a list of "loaded" questions—statements about which the groups must gather responses from each member and then report their areas of agreement and disagreement during a whole-class discussion. The following statements are examples of loaded questions:

1. When we see a person who is wearing shabby clothes, what assumptions might we make about him or her?

2. When we see a picture of a rock star, what assumptions might we make about his or her lifestyle?

3. When we see a classmate get a D on his or her report card, what assumptions might we make about him or her?

4. When we see a woman running for the presidency of the United States, what assumptions might we have about her abilities?

5. If a substitute teacher is in the classroom on a particular day of school, what assumptions might you make about how to conduct your behavior for the day?

6. When we hear someone has AIDS, what do we think?

Developing societal consciousness is a starting point in developing a line of reasoning skills needed for producing thoughtful citizens for our future. Certainly, one of the critical aspects of critical thinking is the challenge of the basic assumptions. A word of caution is in order, lest we isolate the very foundation we desire to develop. Indeed, Stephen Brookfield (1987) points out that challenges of the assumptions underlying our value systems can be both "liberating" and "threatening." He further suggests that questioning internalized truths, whether actually true or not, is a part of one's personality. It may seem demeaning to our capacity for valuing, believing, and developing moral codes, however, when we discover that the absolutes we hold to be true are not necessarily absolutely true. The development of completely new thought patterns that differ from past thinking structures can even create momentary imbalance. Therefore, you might find it necessary to implement ways to help students broaden their thought structures beyond the confines of their own culture, without weakening their desire to believe in, and form, values. The goal is not to destroy but to refine. Above all, remember that, sometimes you too will pass through these disruptive processes as a teacher-learner.

APPLY AND REFLECT 8.5	Develop a plan for integrating direct instruction of critical and creative skills, techniques, and processes into your teaching. Share your plan.

Regardless of the approach you choose for teaching critical thinking skills, there are eight non-thinking behaviors (Raths, Wassermann, Jonas, & Rothstein, 1986) frequently reported by classroom teachers. These eight behaviors will negatively affect the development of thinking skills. As such, you must learn to diagnose and prescribe appropriate thinking activities that will enable your students to overcome the following behaviors:

1. *Impulsiveness.* Students may respond before the question is completed. They do not take time to consider the problem or alternatives. In other words, they "leap before they look" without adequate thought. These students think, but they fail to consider consequences of their inferences, hypotheses, or decisions on information presented. They blurt out the answer without having enough information, or they impulsively base their decision on the first thing that enters their minds.

2. *Overdependence on the teacher.* Students sometimes raise their hands as soon as the teacher finishes explaining the assignment and begins the independent work. These students won't try the concept first but, rather, say, "I don't understand this"—before even attempting to read the instructions. These students often fail to pay attention during group instruction and insist that the teacher provide individual instruction at their desks.

3. *Inattentive behavior.* These students start working but don't stay on task. They need constant prompting, their attention span is short, and their attention constantly wanders, seemingly into "space." These students rarely finish assignments and demonstrate a lack of self-motivation.

4. *Restless rusher.* Restless rushers get very little meaning out of assigned tasks; rather, they rush through their work, concentrating only on turning in the assignment. These students frequently finish the work first but lack accuracy. When asked questions pertaining to the assignment just finished, they pause and reply, "I don't know." If the student is prompted further to redo the work, he or she usually rushes through the second time just as quickly as the first time. These students differ from impulsive students in that they usually don't base their responses on past or similar experiences and jump the gun as impulsive students do; instead, they concentrate only on turning in the work.

5. *Dogmatic, assertive behavior.* These students fail to consider another's point of view. Basic assumptions are never questioned, and they always think their perceptions are the only correct ones. Because they think their views are already perfect, they see no reason for considering or listening for other possibilities.

6. *Rigidity, inflexibility of behavior.* These students are reluctant to give up old strategies that have worked for them in the past, even when they prove inadequate in the new situation. For example, students might be requested to perform a certain task, and they may reply that it's not the way they learned to do it last year.

7. *Fearful, lack of confidence.* These students rarely respond to questions that require anything other than one right answer. They are fearful of expressing their own views and opinions, as they lack confidence in their own thinking. When asked to answer a question that calls for higher order thinking skills or to voice their thoughts during a brainstorming activity, these students are afraid to express themselves. They seem to be the opposite of the overdependent student in that they usually won't seek extra help.

8. *Responsibility forfeiture.* These students want the teacher to provide one right way of accomplishing all learning tasks. Again, fear of taking risks or assuming responsibility is evident. These students are grade-conscious individuals who are not afraid to approach their teacher for specific guidelines; by obligating the teacher in this way, the students shift responsibility to the teacher and relieve themselves from thinking for themselves.

Often, you will need to prescribe thinking activities that alter these behaviors and promote self-confidence and mental growth. Let's now look at some of the activities that could be used in correcting faulty thinking habits.

APPLY AND REFLECT 8.6	It is suggested that teachers build into their lessons time for students to reflect on their learning. Is this a good idea for students at the grade level you expect to teach? Why or why not?

Thinking Skills Activities

Teaching thinking skills requires open-ended activities in which no single, correct answers are sought. Although there are many areas, categories, and thinking operations that could be approached, let's examine some of the concepts that could be prescribed for the eight no-thinking behaviors.

For material related to this concept, go to Clip 8.2 on the Student Resource CD bound into the back of your textbook.

Brainstorming

Brainstorming is an excellent way of promoting fluent thinking (see Chapter 6). It can also be used at any grade level. Students can be given a real or imaginary problem and asked to think of as many ways as they can to solve it. You can use brainstorming to solve real problems, or you may want to use fantasy situations simply to promote thinking skills. Some topics might include the following:

1. What are some things we can do to make our classroom more attractive?

2. How can we better show our appreciation to parents who help in our classroom?

3. In what ways are steam engines and boats alike?

4. How could you change a car to make it more energy efficient?

The goal of brainstorming is to produce as many responses as possible. It is crucial that all responses be accepted and appreciated during the activity. Withhold praise or judgment and provide an accepting atmosphere throughout the activity. Encourage your students to "hitchhike" on each other's ideas. Emphasize that not all responses will be of high quality because the aim is for quantity, and hitchhiking on each other will generate additional ideas. Brainstorming activities of this type can also encourage flexible thinking.

Flexible Thinking

With flexible thinking, activities stretch the mind into considering possibilities beyond the usual responses. During these activities, you need to define the area for examination. Ask students to put their five senses to work in thinking about how many different ways a concept could be used. For example, ask your students questions that help them consider alternate possibilities—perhaps, for the use of a water hose should they be stranded on a deserted island. Inspire them to ask themselves questions that take forms such as these:

What if _____ ?
Suppose that _____ ?
How is _____ like _____ ?
If you were _____ ?

Such questions and statements help define new possibilities and produce flexible thinking.

Another outstanding thinking skill that improves students with impulsive behaviors is cause-and-effect considerations. Forecasting activities can help students generate causes and effects of a given situation.

Forecasting

Instruct students to brainstorm all possible causes and effects of getting good grades. This requires that students make inferences about cause and effect. The idea, once again, is to forecast what could be or might be. Afterwards, students should examine the quality of each prediction and choose the best cause and effect, and then they should provide reasons for their choice. Providing explanations for choices that students determine to be the best helps promote inductive thinking.

Inductive Thinking

Inductive thinking activities can be helpful for students who frequently fail to check their responses to determine whether their generalizations can hold up against data. During **inductive thinking,** students collect, organize, and examine data; then they identify common elements; finally, they make generalizations based on common or general elements. Once students have examined the data, they should be encouraged to state generalizations that are based on inferences found in the data. For example, encourage students to "read between the lines" when reading a selected newspaper article and then to state a generalization based on information known about the article. If possible, provide students with newspaper articles from different areas and by different authors to further check the generalization against data. Making inferences is closely related to finding generalizations.

Inference Making

When a person makes an inference, he or she must provide a possible consequence, conclusion, or implication from a set of facts or premises. Inference making requires that thinkers provide a rationale for their thoughts. These thoughts are personal beliefs about a situation based on similar associations with past experiences. Basic assumptions people hold play a key role in the inferences they make. Questions that call for inference making ask students to provide their personal opinion. "Why do you suppose?" and "What do you think someone should do?" and "What do you suppose was meant by . . . ? Why?" are all questions frequently used in promoting inference making. As with forming generalizations, however, it is important that you ask students to supply evidence or provide reasons for the inference they make. Even when basic assumptions are examined, it may be necessary to determine whether inferences are based on clear, meditative thinking or whether they are the product of assertive, dogmatic rigidity. Therefore, students also need practice in logical thinking.

Logical Thinking

Logical thinking is believed to be a left-brain function that organizes and associates ideas. Activities that require logical thinking begin with assumptions or concepts and generate ideas step-by-step to arrive at an endpoint or a solution. Logical thinking is based on previous knowledge or acquired patterns of thinking. Logic requires that students interpret information in deriving the intended meaning from a source. Students must examine the main idea presented and follow the supporting details to arrive at a conclusion. For example, samples of logic skills can be taught, and then students can develop thinking activities, such as the one shown in Figure 8.2. Indeed, such activities can be developed by students and exchanged with classmates for solving.

Deductive Thinking

Whereas inductive thinking calls on a student to make generalizations based on data, **deductive thinking** asks the student to consider the generalizations given and provide supporting data. Most thinking activities will be incomplete until students provide a rationale for their responses.

Deductive thinking is crucial in a democratic society that demands a responsible citizenry in decision making. Deductive thinking often requires that students evaluate the merit of an activity, object, or idea. Therefore, teaching students to identify possible outcomes, define standards of appraisal, and make judgments based on careful consideration are all-important elements of instruction. When students are called on to decide among objects or alternatives, decision-making and problem-solving steps will be helpful to them in reaching their conclusions.

Problem Solving

Complex thinking processes often involve problem solving and decision making. Problem solving involves six steps: (1) defining the problem, (2) collecting data, (3) identifying obstacles to the goal, (4) identifying alternatives, (5) rating alternatives, and (6) choosing the best alternative. Problem-solving models can be developed that guide students through these important steps. For example, divergent questions might be developed that discourage students from supplying one "right" answer. Also, brainstorming should be an important aspect of each step. Students should consider the following questions as they carry out the problem-solving steps:

1. What is fact and what is opinion?
2. Is there only one right way?
3. Do the examples presented prove the rule?
4. Just because two things happened together, does this prove one is the cause of the other?
5. Is it possible that personal feelings are causing you to rule out possibilities?

Figure 8.2

Sample Logical-
Thinking Activity

CRAWLING CATERPILLARS

1. The caterpillar crew is enjoying an out-of-school crawl.

2. Read the clues below carefully. Then write each crew member's name in logical sequence.

ASSUMPTIONS:
(Clues)

1. Rick Reader loves to read.

2. Rick Reader is between Duff and Shades.

3. Shades is following Carrie the Carrier.

4. Carrie the Carrier is following Headphones Hector.

SOURCE: Raul Acosta, seventh grade, Anadarko Junior High. Used with permission.

Sometimes guides with similar questions help new problem solvers organize problem-solving activities. In using such a guide, students should be asked to record alternatives and then asked to critically consider their choices. A similar process can be followed at almost any level, and it can be integrated into any content area. Examples might include the following:

1. Survey the community to find school tutors. (social studies)
2. Design an attractive display for school accomplishments. (math, art)
3. Find a solution to uneven air conditioning in the school. (physics)
4. Discover why plants die in the school cafeteria and correct the situation. (biology)

Decision Making

Decision making involves the thinking skills needed in choosing the best response from several options. It involves examining advantages and disadvantages, considering all of the steps of problem solving, and evaluating the final decision in relationship to available alternatives and consequences. Basic to decision making are the abilities to observe, interpret, compare, classify, and analyze information. For example, you could work with your students on suitable careers or the best form of energy to use or the best way to catch a groundhog or the best way to spend the $150 given to your class by the school.

Observation

Observation demands that students watch for a purpose and note objective changes, details, or procedures. Students must use their five senses if they are to record data accurately. This activity can help students check the accuracy of a match between what is seen, heard, smelled, and so on. The proposition that you can't believe anything you hear and only half of what you "think you see" becomes a reality, as students not only examine their own perception of things but also attempt to understand the point of view of others. A good way of practicing careful observation techniques is by observing television commercials for underlying messages developed and conveyed through various techniques. Close observations of this type lead students to recognize the power of effective persuasion and help them develop open perceptions when attempting to interpret information.

Interpretation

Interpreting requires that students use their perceptions in examining their assumptions when making a judgment or reaching a conclusion. Perceptions are developed through associations with personal experiences and are, therefore, unique to each individual. Interpreting is an important skill to teach directly, as people tend to generalize on the basis of insufficient evidence in our repertoire of basic assumptions. Our interpretations sometimes become hazy when we experience doubt in our attempts to attribute causation and validity to data. Causation and validity must be closely examined before deriving conclusions. Explain to students that the skill of interpreting depends on drawing inferences from *valid* data. Warn them about the tendency to generalize on the basis of insufficient evidence. Guide them in critically examining information and in differentiating between what is true and what they may believe to be true. Students' first interpretation activities might begin with your presentation of a large poster with a graph or picture. Begin by asking students to list at least four statements that can be made through observing the picture. Afterwards, ask them to share with the class their interpretation of what the picture was telling. After the first student gives personal responses of interpretation, search for other responses that might represent different interpretations. This particular activity prompts examination of the many ways individuals perceive and interpret information. It can further develop students' ability to withhold judgments of absolutes and to consider other alternatives. Thinking skills instruction must include training that fosters open-mindedness, so that students understand that what seems to be unconditionally true in one situation may not be completely true in another.

Comparison

Comparison requires that students examine two or more situations, objects, ideas, or events and seek out relationships, similarities, or differences. The degree of thinking (or level of Bloom's Taxonomy) needed varies with the assignment of tasks for comparison. Once differences and similarities have been determined, designate opportunities for the students to practice the skill independently. Above all, link the thinking skill taught to some practical use and encourage students exhibiting no-thinking behaviors to keep an open mind and compare their answers and beliefs with the opinions expressed by others.

WEB LINK 8.1   Critical Thinking

Select an online lesson plan (www.lessonplanspage.com) and "remodel" it as a critical thinking activity. Describe elements of the remodeled lesson that will develop and reinforce students' critical thinking skills.

Analysis

During analysis, students examine the problem to be solved, taking it apart, identifying its elements, and finding relationships. Instruct students to identify useful ways of breaking problems into parts, ask them to define each part clearly, and request that they organize the data related to each part and examine relationships in determining their conclusions. If you prefer the infusion method of instruction, you should ask students to consider each of these elements in relation to the problem needing solving. If, however, you prefer to step your students through the skill of analyzing before asking them to apply the skill to a real problem for solving, you might simply present an item for analysis and give them four steps to follow—for example: first, identify the whole; second, define each part of the whole; third, organize data related to each part; and fourth, state a conclusion based on your analysis. Keep in mind the difference between asking an analysis question and asking a knowledge-level recall question.

While analysis is an important aspect of problem solving and decision making, it is not intended for confining the individual to categorizing only presented information. That is, students should be encouraged to analyze information for relationships that might otherwise go unnoticed.

Again, the teacher's role in developing students' skills in decision making is to create an atmosphere of acceptance and support in the forming of values and beliefs, lest students experience despair and turn off from a feeling of "overloaded" disequilibrium. Let's look at one scenario in which a teacher successfully shared classroom decision-making responsibilities with students. This teacher felt so overwhelmed by the demands of recordkeeping needed in the classroom that she formulated a shared-responsibility system with her students. Each class was divided into three groups, and student elections were conducted. Each group elected an officer, who handled recordkeeping for his or her group.

Students quickly learned to value honesty and accountability. As a result, each group requested additional officers so they could ensure more of a "check and balance" system. Each of the groups elected three officers—governor, assistant, and secretary—and assigned them each specific responsibilities. For example, the secretary of each group recorded and collected all makeup work for absentees in the group. When students returned after being absent, they were directed to see their secretary for makeup work. Thus, the group held the secretary accountable for all makeup work. Subsequently, another interesting occurrence with this system was that peer responsibility began to expand and be expected among students. Often, secretaries talked with a group member when absenteeism was frequent or was affecting the member's performance in class. Moreover, whenever an officer failed to provide a student member with accurate records, other issues evolved. For instance, should a student be "impeached" from office when found in error? To what extent should peers be tolerant of shortcomings? The classroom teacher in this situation continued to insist on a shared-responsibility role and required students to use problem-solving and decision-making skills in resolving these problems. Thus, the system provided students with opportunities to practice and refine responsibility learning.

APPLY AND REFLECT 8.7	Plan a sequence of learning activities that will lead to successful thinking skills. Share your activities.

When you convey to your students that you view them as responsible persons, you give them an "I can!" sense that helps them view themselves as successful thinkers and, so, nurture different ways of thinking, believing, and acting. Help them develop the vital sense of responsibility for their own accomplishments and for finding solutions to complex problems.

You need to reassure students constantly that, even though it is important to withhold judgments temporarily, it is important to never "bail out" until they feel comfortable with their personal interpretations and perceptions. You, too, may feel some disequilibrium and may be tempted to shut down or bail out because the challenges your students present have become intense. Complete Web Link 8.1: Critical Thinking and Web Link 8.2: Creative Thinking, which will give you some experience at planning for critical and creative thinking.

For material related to this concept, go to Clip 8.3 on the Student Resource CD bound into the back of your textbook.

WEB LINK 8.2 Creative Thinking

Evaluate an online lesson plan for its creative value. Discuss aspects of the lesson that foster students' creative skills with your classmates. Explain how the lesson could be improved to increase its creative value.

REFLECTIONS ON TEACHER PRACTICE 8.2 | Critical Thinking

1. How can critical thinking be taught?

2. What is the connection between critical thinking and learning? Between critical thinking and memory?

◆ ◆ ◆

Critical thinking skills are essential to education and here's a great opportunity for students to develop and use them. How about getting the kids to read the stories and rewrite portions (if not the whole story) to make them "politically correct" by today's standards, such as changing the word "lady" to "woman," or even "womyn," changing job stereotypes, etc. It can lead to interesting dialogues about the changes in societal values and norms. Even if the stories don't need to be run through the "political correctness mill," create an assignment to have them identify specific aspects that make or break a story and why the story (or stories) they have read may or may not be interesting to students of today, as compared to students in 1979.

—Middle school teacher

SOURCE: ProTeacher, a professional community for elementary school teachers. Reprinted with permission. (http://www.proteacher.net)

ON YOUR OWN 8.2 Reflections on Teacher Practice

Read and reflect on the viewpoints expressed in Critical Thinking. Log on to the Web-based student study site at http://www.sagepub.com/eis2study and react to the related activities.

Developing thinking skills requires that you become a more reflective teacher and a model for reflective thinking. You should teach students to be more reflective about what they learn. Students should be taught to approach subject content and unique situations with a thinking orientation. For example, when faced with conflicts, values, practices, or actions, they need to learn to be reflective on more than the content information. They should learn to reflect on the meanings, implications, and consequences of what they are learning. Students should be encouraged to actively construct understanding that is logical and makes sense to them. In other words, you must actively engage student in reflection and in building their thinking. You should encourage them to think about what they are learning and to gradually accept greater responsibility for their own learning and thought processes. Learning how to learn and thinking skills development are essential for dealing with life situations. Complete Expansion Activity 8.3: Thinking Skills Application to explore the use of thinking skills activities at the grade level you expect to teach.

EXPANSION ACTIVITY 8.3 Thinking Skills Application

Create a two-column chart of the thinking skills activities covered in this section (brainstorming, flexible thinking, forecasting, etc.) and indicate your feelings as to the value of each activity at the grade level you expect to teach. Use the following three categories to evaluate each strategy for your chart: (1) useful, (2) limited usefulness, and (3) not useful.

This completes the examination of various activities for developing students' thinking skills. Table 8.2 summarizes the two thinking skills instructional approaches. Review the summary and complete Review and Reflective Exercise 8.2.

Creativity should be encouraged in the classroom.

TABLE 8.2   Thinking Skills Instruction

Concept	Description
Separate approach	Program that focuses instruction on thinking skill development without regard to content
Infusion approach	Development of thinking skills in conjunction with regular curriculum; thinking skill instruction is followed by applying the skill to the content being studied

REVIEW AND REFLECTIVE EXERCISE 8.2   Describe how teachers can foster thinking skills.

REVIEW

- Differentiate between the separate and infusion approaches to teaching thinking skills.
- Describe the eight non-thinking behaviors reported by teachers and activities to overcome them.

REFLECTION

- Should you teach thinking at the grade level you expect to teach? If so, which approach to teaching thinking skills would work best? If not, why?

SUMMARY

Thinking can be viewed as the act of withholding judgment to use knowledge and experience to find new information, concepts, and conclusions.

Thinking Skills

- Thinking can take place at any one of Bloom's Taxonomy levels: knowledge, comprehension, application, analysis, synthesis, and evaluation.
- The thinking level most appropriate to a specific class depends on the maturity of the students and the needs of the content area. The most commonly taught thinking skills are critical and creative thinking.
- Metacognition can be simply defined as thinking about thinking. Metacognition skills enable students to better benefit from instruction.

Thinking Skills Instruction

- Thinking skills can be taught separately (separate approach) or by infusing them into the content (infusion approach).
- Direct, specific instruction often proves useful in fostering critical and creative thinking skills.
- Eight behaviors have been identified that negatively affect the development of thinking skills: impulsiveness; overdependence on the teacher; inattentive behavior; restless rusher; dogmatic, assertive behavior; rigidity, inflexibility of behavior; fearful, lack of confidence; and responsibility forfeiture.

DISCUSSION QUESTIONS AND ACTIVITIES

1. **Teaching methods.** What teaching methods and procedures can be used to improve students' critical thinking abilities? Creative thinking abilities?
2. **Thinking.** What type of thinking is emphasized in most schools? Is critical thinking rewarded? Creative thinking? Is school success based on students' ability to think critically? Creatively?
3. **The environment.** What type of classroom environment would be conducive to developing critical thinking? Creative thinking? What problems can you foresee in establishing this environment?

TECHNOLOGY AND EDUCATION

The quality of instruction can be improved through the use of technology. How would you use technology to improve thinking skills at the grade level you expect to teach? Use available search engines to research ideas for developing thinking skills at the grade level you expect to teach. Form groups of four or five to share ideas. Share your group's ideas with the class.

DECONSTRUCTING THE STANDARDS

Chapter 8 content addresses topics related to INTASC Standards 2, 4, 5, and 7.

- ♦ INTASC Standard 2 states: *Knowledge of Human Development and Learning:* The teacher understands how children learn and develop and can provide learning opportunities that support their intellectual, social, and personal development.

- ♦ INTASC Standard 4 states: *Multiple Instructional Strategies:* The teacher uses various instructional strategies to encourage students' development of critical thinking, problem solving, and performance skills.
- ♦ INTASC Standard 5 states: *Classroom Motivation and Management:* The teacher uses an understanding of individual and group motivation and behavior to create a learning environment that encourages positive social interaction, active engagement in learning, and self-motivation.
- ♦ INTASC Standard 7 states: *Instructional Planning Skills:* The teacher plans instruction based on knowledge of subject mater, students, the community, and curriculum goals.

For each of these four standards, write your response to the following:

- Which part(s) of each standard does this chapter address?
- How does this chapter address this standard?
- How will the concepts in this chapter help you apply this standard as a teacher?

PRAXIS CONNECTION

Log on to the Web-based student study site at http://www.sagepub.com/eis2study. Access the Praxis II: Principles of Learning and Teaching assessments and/or state-related exams and complete the Chapter 8 test preparation exercises.

PORTFOLIO CONNECTION

Log on to the Web-based student study site at http://www.sagepub.com/eis2study. Access the Portfolio Connection. Complete the Chapter 8 portfolio link to INTASC activities.

CONNECTION WITH THE FIELD

1. **Classroom observation.** Visit several public school classrooms at the grade level you expect to teach. Keep a record of the techniques used to develop student critical thinking and creative thinking. Share your record with your class.
2. **Interviews.** Interview several teachers at different grade levels. How do they incorporate critical thinking and creativity into their everyday teaching activities? Make a list of ideas you can use when you become a teacher.

PART IV

MONITORING AND EVALUATING STUDENT LEARNING

Eventually, teachers must evaluate the effectiveness of instruction. Teachers must assess students, evaluate results, and assign grades. To this end, you must have a clear understanding of assessment, evaluation, and measurement. Part IV covers assessment, information sources, test construction, test scoring, and the conversion of test data into grades. The strengths and limitations associated with various test item types and grade assignment techniques are explored.

Chapter 9 focuses on the role of evaluation in the instructional process, evaluation types, and various systems of evaluation. It also focuses on the role of evaluation in the instructional process. Measurement accuracy and source of information are covered and considered. Finally, Chapter 9 provides a framework for making accurate observations to be used in planning, evaluation, and during instruction.

Assessment provides the data to make judgments for grading and assigning grades. Chapter 10 provides a framework for teacher-made test construction and accurately assigning grades. Test design and construction is a major focus of this chapter. Various techniques and systems for assigning grades are presented and discussed. Authentic and portfolio assessment are also covered.

CHAPTER 9

Evaluating and Measuring Learning

If you tell people where to go but not how to get there, you'll be amazed at the results.

—George S. Patton

Overview

Today, assessment occurs more frequently in schools than it did 30 years and more ago. The heavy emphasis on assessment is a result of the accountability and reform movements that have affected this nation's schools. Therefore, it is critical that beginning teachers build a repertoire of effective evaluation strategies for assessment of knowledge, behaviors, skills, and abilities in the cognitive, affective, and psychomotor domains.

Like every other aspect of the teaching-learning process, assessing the outcomes of teaching and learning is a complex and sometimes confusing endeavor. Nonetheless, teachers, administrators, and parents need information about the general impact of their programs and instruction.

Though the terms *assessment, evaluation,* and *measurement* are closely related, they are not synonyms. In this chapter, you will examine the difference between these terms, as well as some of the kinds of assessment, evaluation and measurement techniques. The information presented should make teaching more productive, learning more engaging, and explaining the outcomes more tenable.

Although certain evaluation techniques are beyond the scope of this chapter, many of the basic concepts will be addressed. Thus, it will provide beginning teachers with a basic grasp of evaluative topics and procedures.

Objectives

After completing your study of Chapter 9, you should be able to do the following:

- Define *assessment and evaluation* and explain the purposes of each.
- Distinguish between the concepts of evaluation and measurement.
- Explain the purposes of evaluation.

- Compare and contrast pretest, formative, and posttest (summative) evaluation.
- Create a plan for the appropriate use of the three different kinds of evaluation.
- Differentiate among the competitive, noncompetitive, and performance assessment systems.
- Explain what is meant by the possibility of bias in the assessment process.
- Differentiate among the concepts of reliability, validity, and usability.
- Describe the various sources of evaluative information.
- Identify the advantages and limitations associated with the use of the different sources of evaluative information.
- Explain the purpose of and advantages associated with the use of rating scales, checklists, and questionnaires.
- Define the following evaluative terms: *competitive evaluation, noncompetitive evaluation, performance assessment, norm-referenced evaluation, criterion-referenced evaluation, standard scores, percentile,* and *student work sample.*

There exists a learning gap in this country. As early as fifth grade, U.S. students lag far behind their counterparts in other countries. Reformers are increasingly aware of this learning gap and are seeking ways to address it. The challenge is to find a way to improve classroom teaching so that our educational goals can be realized. Virtually every state is working to develop high student standards, along with means for assessing students' progress. Educators must now find ways of providing students with the learning opportunities they need to reach the new standards.

Forty-nine states in the United States have adopted state-mandated testing that aims to raise standards of performance for children in our schools in a manner that assigns accountability to schools and teachers. No longer does policy permit students to be promoted solely on the basis of completing a particular grade with acceptable grades—even though some teachers continue to do so. An increasing number of states have instituted programs that call for testing at certain grades to determine if students continue to the next grade. One issue that has received considerable attention is the increased use of **minimum competency tests** to award graduation diplomas. At issue is whether such tests are accurate measures of the scope of knowledge and ideas learned in school. For those who fail to pass the tests, a certificate of attendance is usually awarded. Many believe this practice will have a chilling effect on minority students and students with special needs.

In January 2002, a piece of federal legislation called the No Child Left Behind Act was signed into law. One of the major purposes of this act is to help low-income and minority students perform at the same achievement level as their peers. The legislation also couples testing requirements with a push for qualified teachers in all classrooms and strict sanctions when schools fail to improve test scores for *all* students. No Child Left Behind also targets resources to support learning in the early years, requires that more information be provided to parents about their child's progress, and gives parents the option to transfer their child out of low-performing schools.

| **APPLY AND REFLECT 9.1** | Student assessment and testing has become a national issue. What benefits and/or problems do you see with the emphasis on testing in our schools? |

The Evaluation Process

Assessment and evaluation are vital parts of the instructional process. Assessment is the process of documenting, usually in measurable terms, knowledge, skills, attitudes, and beliefs. Evaluation, on the other hand, refers to the process of making judgments, placing value, or deciding on worth. A test, for example, is an assessment device to determine how much students know about a topic. Assigning grades, however, is an evaluation process because values are being assigned to the information.

For material related to this concept, go to Clip 9.1 on the Student Resource CD bound into the back of your textbook.

Assessment is the gathering of information about students, the curriculum, and the school environment. This information can be gathered through information observations and verbal exchanges or through formal assignments or tests. The purpose of assessment, either through observable performance, product development, or traditional paper-and-pencil tests, is to provide data to measure the degree to which a desired outcome has been mastered. That is, assessment provides the information for evaluation. Students can show their learning by writing an essay, painting a picture, constructing a table, baking a pie, or taking a test. However, most assessments in schools are teacher-made tests, standardized test, or quizzes. Assessment can be designed by classroom teachers or by local, state, or national agencies. Information about instruction and the classroom environment can also be an important part of the assessment process. In the evaluation process, the teacher compares the assessment information to some criteria and then makes judgments. Teachers make all kinds of judgments (evaluations). Should I show this film to my ninth graders? Is this book appropriate for a second-grade class? Is John's behavior improving? What textbook should I use this year? Should I give Mary a B or C on her term paper? These judgments are made based on some type of assessment information. In effect, teachers assess any time they collect information and evaluate any time they determine a course of action based on that information.

Evaluation must be conducted to determine whether students are learning, to gauge the appropriateness of the curriculum for a given group of students, to identify what must be retaught, to ensure proper placement of individual students within a program of instruction, and to make sure that state guidelines for achievement have been met. Viewed in this context, evaluation performs a dual function in the educational process. Essentially, it provides not only information about student achievement but also information that can be used in future curriculum planning.

As you can see, evaluation serves many roles in the teaching-learning process. It is important to decide the purpose of every evaluation effort prior to implementing a plan of action. The approach to evaluation you would take if you wished to determine the level of student learning differs from the approach you would take if your purpose of evaluation were to determine the effectiveness of a particular teaching technique. Likewise, you would not use a pencil-and-paper test in ascertaining whether a particular performance skill, such as creating a poster using the computer, has been achieved. How you plan for and carry out evaluation and the methods of measurement you use can help determine how effective you are as a teacher.

Evaluation must also be more than a measurement of academic achievement. It will be necessary to determine the quality of student work beyond a minimum standard. You may want to gauge how well students work in small and large groups. You may want to evaluate students' abilities to work with very little supervision on projects of interest to the students. You may need to identify which students display leadership potential in group situations. Perhaps you will need to know your students' attitudes toward a particular learning experience. There are appropriate strategies for finding out whatever you need to know.

The identification of learner difficulties is a basic skill that successful teachers must possess. No matter how much planning goes into your lessons, some students will experience difficulty in mastering desired learning outcomes. Without proper identification and remediation, such difficulties may compound until the student becomes frustrated and turns off to your subject altogether. Thus, evaluation and measurement are essential components to effective teaching.

No process is more central to teaching than evaluation. But evaluation is not just testing. Evaluation is much broader. It demands that you make a qualitative judgment regarding some type of measure. **Evaluation** is the process of making a judgment about student performance; **measurement** provides the data for making that judgment. Valid evaluations depend on accurate measurement. Evaluation often involves more than simply measuring academic achievement. It requires some type of decision. In other words, information is used in making a decision. Thus, in the classroom, evaluation can be related to how well students carry out specific actions (performance) or to what they can produce (product). Sometimes you will be interested only in how well a student performs, whereas at other times you may only be interested in an end product. For example, you may want to evaluate how well your students participate in group work, how well they can perform algebraic equations, or how they go about adjusting a microscope in an experiment. Also, because attitudes and feelings can have an effect on learning, you may want to focus on such subjective factors in your teaching and in your evaluation.

Evaluation must be viewed as a two-step process. First, you must gather pertinent data regarding the desired outcomes (assess). During this step, the tools and techniques of measurement are applied in gathering relevant information about students' acquisition of the intended instructional outcomes. Second, once the data have been gathered, the information is used in making reasonable judgments concerning students' performance. However, evaluation should not be limited to only the "desired outcome" but must also be sensitive to all factors potentially associated with the course of instruction. The motivational, social, and attitudinal effects associated with the "desired outcome" should be considered in making judgments.

Measurement comes in different types and with different precision. For example, you can compare the loudness of two sounds or the height of two objects, use a scale to find your weight, use a ruler to find the length of an object, or watch a speedometer on a trip. What these measurements have in common is that the perceptual process of hearing and sight are used in gathering data. These measurements, however, differ greatly in terms of their precision.

As a teacher, you will take hundreds of measurements daily. But, like all measurements, they will differ in type and have varying degrees of precision. For example, you will collect data as you observe your students' behaviors, when you ask questions and hear responses, and when you give and analyze an examination. There will be differences in the accuracy of the data, however, because of the difference in what is being measured and how it is being measured.

Evaluation requires that judgments and decisions be made. TenBrink (2003) suggests that the evaluation process consists of four steps:

1. *Preparation.* Determine the kind of information needed, as well as how and when to collect it.

2. *Information collecting.* Select techniques for gathering a variety of information as accurately as possible.

3. *Making judgments.* Compare information against selected criteria to make judgments.

4. *Decision making.* Reach conclusions based on formed judgments.

APPLY AND REFLECT 9.2

Is student evaluation really necessary at the grade level you expect to teach? Why or why not? If so, how would you use the information collected?

Evaluation provides essential information regarding how your students are doing relative to intended outcomes.

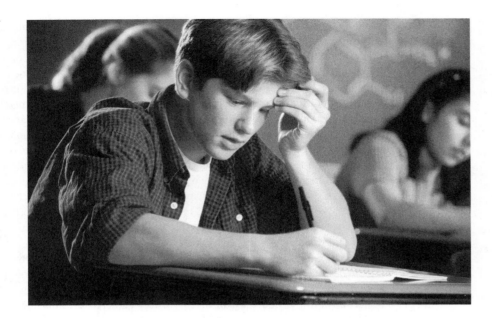

These four steps require that you develop an understanding of the different kinds of evaluation, as well as the different data collection techniques, and that you sharpen your decision-making skills. These understandings and skills will be addressed in this chapter and the next.

The ultimate question in the instructional process is whether you have taught what you intended to teach and whether students have learned what they were supposed to learn. Can they demonstrate the outcomes specified in your original objectives? That is, do they meet the acceptable level of performance as specified in the criteria of your objectives? These objectives call for the demonstration of cognitive skills, performance skills, and in some cases attitudes or feelings. Thus, you may be required to perform evaluations in the cognitive, psychomotor, and affective domains. These different evaluations call for different evaluation techniques.

Evaluation in the three domains of learning demands that you collect different types of information. Before turning our attention to the gathering of evaluation information in the three domains, however, let us briefly look at the evaluation types and the sources of evaluation information available to classroom teachers.

Evaluation Types

Continuous feedback is needed throughout the planning, monitoring, and evaluation of instruction. This feedback may be obtained through any one of three different types of evaluation: pretest, formative, and posttest (summative; see Table 9.1). These three primary types of evaluation differ in terms of their nature and chronological position in the instructional process.

Pretest Evaluation

Diagnostic pretest evaluations normally are administered before instruction to assess students' prior knowledge of a particular topic for placement purposes. Diagnostic pretests can also be used to identify specific deficits that need remediation. More sophisticated assessments can help teachers

TABLE 9.1	Characteristics of Pretest, Formative, and Posttest Evaluation		
	Pretest	**Formative**	**Posttest (Summative)**
Purpose	To identify difficulties and place students	To promote learning through feedback	To assess overall achievement
Nature	Many questions related to general knowledge	Few questions related to specifics of instruction	Many questions related to specific and general knowledge
Frequency of Administration	Varied—usually before instruction	Frequently—usually during instruction	Once—usually final phase of instruction

determine students' cognitive styles and the depth of their understanding of complex concepts. **Diagnostic evaluations,** however, may also become necessary during the course of study when the teacher feels students are having difficulty with the material. The purpose of pretest evaluations generally is to anticipate potential learning problems and, in many cases, to place students in the proper course or unit of study. A common example of pretest evaluation is the assignment of high school students to basic mathematics or remedial English based on entrance assessment. Such preassessments are often designed for checking the ability levels of students in designated areas, so that remedial work can be planned or an instructional starting point can be established.

Pretest evaluation provides valuable information to teachers about the knowledge, attitudes, and skill of students. The results will assist the teacher in planning effective lessons in terms of appropriate activities and the level and pace of class instruction. Pretest evaluation can be based on teacher-made tests, standardized tests, or observational techniques.

Pretest information gives curriculum planners invaluable information regarding the appropriateness of instruction. Unfortunately, most school districts use pretest information for determining the achievement levels of students rather than for evaluating the curriculum. Achievement test scores, for example, are often devoted to making comparisons of school district group scores with national norms, whereas they could be interpreted for the purposes of making needed improvement in curricula and for redesigning curricula in areas found to be below the national norms.

Pretest information can also be used for the correct placement of students in curricula tracks and courses. One critical piece of pretest information often needed by secondary teachers is reading ability and comprehension. If your students have reading difficulties, modification in instruction must be planned to address these deficiencies.

Formative Evaluation

Formative evaluation is carried out during instruction to provide feedback on students' progress and learning. It is used in monitoring instruction and promoting learning. Formative evaluation is a continuous process. But comparatively little use has been made of formative evaluation.

Pretest information should be revised as formative information is gleaned from students' performance on oral and written work. This permits teachers to monitor and modify their instruction as needed. As individual student deficiencies or program problems are noted, remedial work or changes should be planned that will bring the slower learning students up to the level of their peers or that will correct program weaknesses. Thus, although pretest evaluation alone usually is considered diagnostic, formative evaluation is also diagnostic in that it provides information about the strengths and weaknesses of students.

Students sometimes require more assistance than you can provide. On such occasions, you should seek outside assistance from a qualified specialist. Finally, the information gained from formative evaluation might lead you to correct any general misconceptions you observe or to vary the pace of your instruction.

Formative evaluation generally focuses on small, independent pieces of instruction and a narrow range of instructional objectives. Essentially, formative evaluation answers your question "How are you doing?" and uses checkup tests, homework, and classroom questioning in doing so. You should use the results obtained from formative evaluation to adjust your instruction or revise the curriculum, rather than to assign grades.

Posttest Evaluation

Posttest (summative) evaluation is the final phase in an evaluation program. Because posttest evaluation is primarily aimed at determining student achievement for grading purposes, it is generally conducted at the conclusion of a chapter, unit, grading period, semester, or course. Thus, **posttest evaluation** is used for determining student achievement and for judging teaching success. Grades provide the school with a rationale for passing or failing students and are usually based on a comprehensive range of accumulated behaviors, skills, and knowledge.

Posttest evaluation, as the term implies, provides an account of students' performances. It is usually based on test scores and written work related to cognitive knowledge and rarely addresses such areas of learning as values, attitudes, and motor performance.

Student performance on end-of-chapter tests, homework, classroom projects, and standardized achievement tests is commonly used in posttest evaluation. Posttest evaluation can be used in judging not only student achievement but also the effectiveness of a teacher or a particular school curriculum. The data collected and instrumentation used in collecting the data differ, depending on the type of posttest evaluation being considered.

"I can accept and process data, but I have trouble generating it on my own."

SOURCE: Created by Martha Campbell.

Devices such as tests and homework are used most often in posttest evaluation. These devices, however, can also help diagnose learning problems and promote learning. In short, some evaluation devices can be used in diagnosing learning problems, promoting learning, and deriving a grade. For example, tests can identify areas of difficulty (diagnose problems), feedback can be given when you return the examination and discuss the items (promote learning), and test grades should be recorded (derive a grade). Likewise, homework should be analyzed for problem areas; feedback comments written in the margins can promote learning; and, finally, grades can be assigned.

Evaluation should be a continual process as you go about the daily classroom routine. Many times you will gain valuable information regarding achievement, skills, or attitudes prior to or during class. Difficulties can be noted, and on-the-spot feedback can be provided to remedy the situation. Lack of response to questioning, for instance, often reveals that material is misunderstood. Trouble with a written assignment may suggest that students need further instruction. A spot check of student term papers during seatwork might reveal problem areas.

Systems of Evaluation

Evaluation systems can be grouped into two categories: competitive and noncompetitive. **Competitive evaluation** systems force students to compete with other students (norm referenced), whereas **noncompetitive evaluation** systems do not require interstudent comparisons; rather, they are based on established sets of standards of mastery (criterion referenced). We will take a closer look at norm-referenced and criterion-referenced tests later in this chapter. Traditionally, many middle and secondary schools have required competition among students because of the belief that it stimulates motivation.

Figure 9.1
Normal Probability Curve

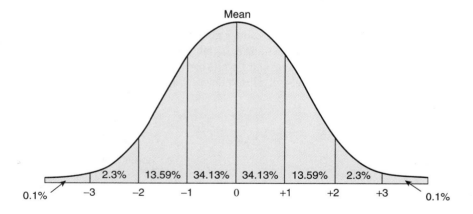

Competitive Evaluation

Most evaluators concerned with students' standing within a group make use of the *normal curve*. This curve is commonly called the *natural curve* or *chance curve* because it reflects the natural distribution of all sorts of things in nature. This distribution is shown in Figure 9.1. Such a curve is appropriately used when the group being studied is large and diversified. Within a classroom, the curve can be used to give teachers an idea of how well a student has performed in comparison with classmates.

An understanding of the normal curve requires a basic knowledge of the concept of variability; that is, you must understand standard deviation. The **standard deviation** is a measure of the extent to which scores are spread out around the mean. The greater the variability of scores around the mean, the larger the standard deviation. A small standard deviation means that most of the scores are packed in close to the mean. A large standard deviation means that the scores are spread out. When all the scores are identical, the standard deviation is zero.

The **normal curve** is a mathematical construct divided into equal segments. The vertical lines through the center of the curve (the mean) represent the average of a whole population on some attribute. For example, in a large population, the average (mean) IQ would be 100. Because this number represents the mean, it would occur most often and appear at the highest point on the curve. To the left of the highest point, each mark represents 1 standard deviation below the average. To the right of the highest point, each mark represents 1 standard deviation above the average. Neither side of the curve would touch the baseline, thus showing that some extreme IQ scores might exist. As shown in Figure 9.1, about 34% of the named population on an attribute will be within 1 standard deviation below the mean, and about 34% of that population will be above the mean. About 13.5% of the identified population will be in the second deviation below the mean, and 13.5% of the population will be in the second deviation above the mean. About 2% of the population will fall in the third deviation below the mean, and an equal portion will fall in the third deviation above the mean. Finally, about 0.1% of the population will fall in the extreme fourth deviation below the mean, and 0.1% will be in the fourth deviation above the mean. Some of the many things that are subject to the normal distribution are weights and heights of animals, average temperatures over an extended period of time, and margins of error on measurements. Indeed, most schools use normal curve and standard scores when reporting the results of standardized tests.

Standard Scores and Percentile

Most schools report student performances in terms of **standard scores** such as z scores, T scores, and stanine scores, as well as in terms of percentile. These methods use the normal distribution curve to show how student performances compared with the distribution of scores above and below the mean. Standard scores provide a standard scale by which scores on different evaluative instruments by different groups may be compared reasonably (see Figure 9.2). The various standard scores and percentile say the same thing in slightly different ways.

Note that z scores and T scores correspond to the standard deviation of the population scores: They tell us how far above or below the mean in standard deviation units raw scores lie. Both z scores and T

Figure 9.2
The Characteristics of the Normal Curve

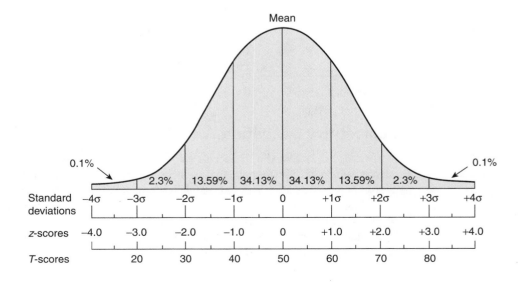

scores indicate the number of standard deviations that a particular raw score is above or below the mean of the raw score distribution. Thus, a score falling 1 standard deviation below the mean would have a *z* score of –1, a score falling two standard deviations above the mean would have a *z* score of +2, and so on. The use of negative numbers is avoided by converting *z* scores to *T* scores. This is done by multiplying the *z* score times 10 and adding a constant of 50.

$$T = 10z + 50.$$

Many schools use stanine (standard nine) when reporting student performance, with a stanine of 1 representing the lowest performance and a stanine of 9 the highest. These nine numbers are the only possible stanine scores a student can receive. Stanines use the normal distribution in grouping scores into nine categories, with a mean of 5 and a standard deviation of 2. Figure 9.3 gives the stanine score distribution and the percentage of scores that will fall into each category.

Figure 9.3 Normal Distribution Curve and Stanine Scores

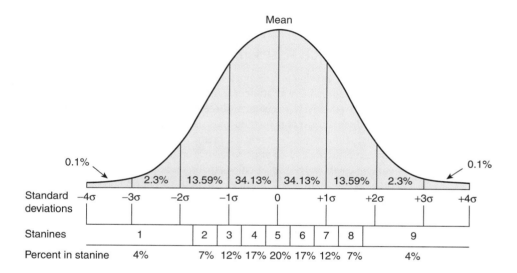

Another type of score is the percentile. Percentile scores are often confused with percentage correct. However, the **percentile score** indicates the percentage of the population whose scores fall at or below that score. A score of 20, for example, would have 20% of the group falling at or below the score and 80% above the score. Of course, the 50th percentile would be the mean (see Figure 9.2). Equal differences between percentile scores do not necessarily indicate equal differences in achievement.

Converting raw scores to standard scores allows you to compare scores on different assessment instruments. You could compare a student's performance in mathematics with science or reading with English or any other tested areas. For example, if a student obtains a score of 65 on his or her math midterm and 70 on his or her history midterm, on which test did he or she do better compared to the rest of the class? If converting the student's scores to standard score yields a *z* score of 1.5 in math (*T* score of 65) and a *z* score of 1.0 in history (*T* score of 60), you can conclude that the student did better in math.

Noncompetitive Evaluation

Some researchers suggest that criterion-referenced evaluation (which does not force competition among students) contributes more to student progress than does norm-referenced evaluation (Fantini, 1986). In effect, these researchers suggest that not all students are motivated through competition. In fact, they suggest that competition can discourage less able students who are forced to compete with more capable students. Competition can even be harmful to more capable students because it often teaches that winning is all-important. Criterion-referenced evaluation focuses on assessing students' mastery of specific skills, regardless of how other students did on the same skills.

Today, many educators feel grades should reflect a student's efforts. No one should receive an A without really trying, nor should students who are exerting themselves to their fullest potential receive an F. There is now a national call for change in how students are assessed. The feeling is that grades should reflect students' progress. Performance assessment and the use of portfolios show promise as a more viable assessment technique.

APPLY AND REFLECT 9.3	What advantages do you see in using competitive evaluation? Noncompetitive evaluation?

Performance Assessment Using Portfolios

Educators are trying to redesign schools to reflect changing world conditions. An essential element of that redesign is the way student learning is assessed. Simply testing isolated skills or retained facts does not effectively measure a student's capabilities. To accurately evaluate what students have learned, an assessment method must examine their collective abilities. This can be accomplished through authentic assessment. Authentic assessment usually includes a task for students to perform and a rubric by which their performance on the task will be evaluated. Authentic assessment presents students with real-world situations that require them to apply their relevant skills and knowledge. In other words, students apply their skills to authentic tasks and projects. In authentic assessment, students

- Make oral reports
- Play tennis
- Write stories and reports
- Solve math problems that have real-world applications
- Do science experiments
- Read and interpret literature

For material related to this concept, go to Clip 9.2 on the Student Resource CD bound into the back of your textbook.

In authentic assessment, assessment drives the curriculum. That is, teachers first determine the tasks that students will perform to demonstrate the desired outcomes, and then a curriculum is developed that will enable students to perform those tasks well, which would include the acquisition of essential knowledge and skills. This has been referred to as planning backwards (see Chapter 2).

Authentic assessment has evolved to encompass a range of approaches, including portfolio assessment, journals and logs, products, videotapes of performances, and projects. Portfolio assessment is presently being widely adopted in many schools.

Some educators use the term *performance assessment* in place of, or with, *authentic assessment.* They call upon students to demonstrate specific skills and outcomes, that is, to apply the skills and knowledge they have mastered but with no reference to the authentic nature of the task. In **performance assessment,** students demonstrate the behaviors that the assessor wants to measure (Airasian, 2001; Meyer, 1992). For example, if the desired behavior is writing, students write; or if the desired behavior is identification of geometric figures, they draw or locate geometric figures. Assessment is done by measuring the individual works against specified criteria that match the objectives toward a specific purpose. In effect, samples of students' work are compiled for evaluation. The students, the teacher, or both can select items for assessment of performance. These items are

"This would be a lot easier if they didn't require such pinpoint accuracy."

SOURCE: Created by Martha Campbell.

often accumulated in portfolios, thus allowing students to display a variety of evidence of performance. The **portfolio** is a purposeful collection of student work that tells the story of the student's efforts, progress, or achievement in a given area. Teachers design activities resulting in student-made products that are collected to make a portfolio for each student. The portfolio of work is then used as the product by which students are evaluated.

A portfolio can be thought of as a systematic, organized collection of evidence that documents growth and development and that represents progress made toward reaching specified goals and objectives. Portfolios enable students to display their skills and accomplishments for examination by others. Portfolio advocates suggest that portfolios are a more equitable and sensitive portrait of what students know and are able to do. They encourage teachers and schools to focus on important student outcomes.

To make the evaluation of portfolios as objective as possible, most teachers develop a scoring rubric to guide the grading process. A **rubric** is a summarization of the performance criteria at different levels of performance. Often, teachers label the different levels as "excellent," "good," "fair," and "poor" or with particular grades to summarize the performance. A sample scoring rubric that can be used to assess a research study is shown in Figure 9.4. As shown in the example, the criteria are usually listed in the column on the left, and the columns to the right of the criteria describe varying degrees of quality. As concise as possible, the columns explain what makes a good piece of work exceptional, good, or bad. A rubric is incomplete unless it contains all of these elements. Generally, there are two types of rubrics: holistic rubrics and analytic rubrics. A holistic rubric makes assessment decisions based on a global look at something. An analytic rubric examines only certain components. For example, you might take an overall global look at a portfolio or an analytical look to examine the portfolio artifacts. To use a scoring rubric, teachers judge which descriptions come closest to the student's performance. Sometimes teachers use a checklist or rating scale in conjunction with the rubric summary performance levels to increase the accuracy of the assessment. Rubrics communicate standards and scoring criteria to students before the performance. Complete Web Link 9.1: Rubrics, which will let you analyze other sample rubrics. Some teachers also require students to include a reflection upon their skills and accomplishments as part of their portfolios. The reflective caption is designed so that the student can explain why he or she chose a particular piece of evidence.

**Figure 9.4
Scoring Rubric for
a Research Study**

Criteria	Excellent (4)	Good (3)	Fair (2)	Poor (1)
Purpose	Explains the key purpose of study in detail	Explains the key purpose of study adequately	Explains purpose but misses key details	Does not refer to the purpose
Content	The student is extremely knowledgeable about the study topic and reveals profound topic insight.	The student has a good understanding of the topic and reveals topic insight.	The student demonstrates some knowledge and understanding of the topic but doesn't show a central insight about topic.	The student shows no knowledge or understanding of topic and doesn't show any insight regarding the subject.
Organization	Well organized and easy to follow	Good organization and fairly easy to follow	Somewhat organized but hard to follow in places	Not organized at all and difficult to follow most of time
Mechanics	There are few or no minor errors. Few careless mistakes.	There are some minor errors. Overall, the student's writing is adequate.	There are numerous major and minor errors, but meaning is still clear.	Errors are so numerous and serious that they interfere with communication.

WEB LINK 9.1   Rubrics

The following Web sites provide examples of rubrics in different subjects and grades.

http://rubistar.4teachers.org/

http://school.discovery.com/schrockguide/assess.html

http://www.teachnology.com/web_tools/rubrics/

Analyze the rubric examples relative to their quality. What makes the good ones good and the bad ones bad?

Constructing a rubric is not an easy task. A clearly defined purpose is essential as each component is developed. With this in mind, follow these steps:

Step 1. Examine the standards or objectives that the product or performance is meant to address.

Step 2. Write or identify the criteria that will be used to judge the student's product or performance and make sure they match the standards or objectives.

Step 3. Design a frame by deciding on the major categories or attributes the rubric will address.

Step 4. Describe the different levels of performance (exceptional, very good, adequate, etc.) that match each criterion. Be sure to choose words or phrases that show the actual differences among the levels. Make sure they are observable.

Step 5. Test the rubric with students to make sure it is understandable.

Step 6. Revise the rubric as necessary.

A well-designed rubric enables students to understand what is expected of them. Furthermore, once students gain experience with rubrics, they can help construct their own rubrics. Now try your hand at developing a rubric of your choice by completing Web Link 9.2: Rubric Development.

WEB LINK 9.2   Rubric Development

Access and analyze the rubrics on the following Web sites: www.rubrics.com/rubric_examples.html and www.rubrics4teachers.com. Using the information gleaned from your analysis of the Internet rubrics, develop a rubric for a student project or activity of your choice. Share your rubric with the class.

Portfolios also provide students with the opportunity to communicate their learning to their parents (Overturf, 1997). Students can be asked to share their portfolios with parents, and parents can provide a written response regarding the contents. Indeed, student-led parent-teacher conferences can be structured to center on student portfolios (Countryman & Schroeder, 1996).

Due to the bulk of hard-copy portfolios and the limitations associated with paper-based portfolios, there has been movement toward the use of digital portfolios (also called electronic portfolios or eportfolios). Digital portfolios give students the ability to use electronic artifacts, photographs, and videotapes and clips as performance evidence. Moreover, digital portfolios have the ability to store multiple media. Graphics, for example, can be incorporated into students' work. Finally, digital portfolios can be communicated across distances—some distances as short as between classrooms, some as long as from a school to parents or to state education departments. Due to data requirements from accreditation bodies such as the National Council for Accreditation of Teacher Education (NCATE), many teacher education programs are using portfolio services such as Chalk and Wire (http://www.chalkandwire.com) or Livetext (http://www.livetext.com) for student portfolio development and assessment.

Efforts to reform education and create a quality teaching force include holding teachers accountable. An approach gaining wide support in many of these accountability systems is the use of teacher portfolios. A teacher portfolio is a collection of work produced by a teacher. Just as artists use portfolios of collected works to illustrate their talents, a teacher portfolio is designed to demonstrate the teacher's talents. Teacher portfolios are developed by teachers to highlight and demonstrate their knowledge and skills as a teacher. A portfolio can also provide a means for showing teacher reflections; it offers teachers the opportunity to show how they critique their work and evaluate their teaching effectiveness. What is actually included or related in a teacher portfolio depends on how the portfolio will be used. A teacher portfolio may include teacher background information, results of written examinations (National Teacher's Exam, state licensure tests), a personal statement of teaching philosophy and goals, documentation of effort to improve one's teaching, implemented lesson plans, video- or audiotape of classroom lessons, colleagues' observation records, and written reflections on teaching. A common misconception is that a teacher portfolio is a folder laden with artifacts and evaluation. A teacher portfolio, rather, is a document created by the teacher that reveals and describes the teacher's duties, expertise, and growth in teaching.

APPLY AND REFLECT 9.4

Many school districts are now using teacher portfolios to evaluate teachers. What do you think of this process? What should be included in a teacher portfolio?

REFLECTIONS ON TEACHER PRACTICE 9.1	Using Portfolios

1. How does the use of portfolios improve teaching and student assessment?

2. How can students be involved in the use of portfolios?

◆ ◆ ◆

I have seen different teachers implement portfolios in many different ways. Some teachers use subject based portfolios, some use an all purpose portfolio, and some even use electronic portfolios (those were the coolest)! As for how often, I saw one teacher do it this way: On the last part of the day on Friday's while students were finishing work or reading, she would have portfolio conferences. After saving ALL work that the child had completed the entire week (either in a work folder or in those cardboard shelving systems with labels for each child), the student and teacher would have a short conference at the desk to decide which pieces of work should be included in the portfolio. The student was allowed to choose one, and the teacher was

allowed to choose one. Both the student and teacher have to explain why they are choosing this piece. Of course, sometimes more than one piece of work was chosen. They actually filled out paperwork on each piece that had title, reason picked, and some other things.

Good luck with portfolios. This is a wonderful authentic assessment, and I think all teachers should implement it in some form.

—*BETH, elementary teacher*

SOURCE: Reprinted with permission from ProTeacher, a professional community for elementary school teachers (http://www.proteacher.net).

ON YOUR OWN 9.1 **Reflections on Teacher Practice**

Read and reflect on the viewpoints expressed in Using Portfolios. Log on to the Web-based student study site at http://www.sagepub.com/eis2study and react to the related activities.

Work Samples

The use of **student work samples** can be used to offer credible evidence of student learning and to provide evidence of teacher effectiveness. They portray the learning process of students over a sufficiently long period of time for appreciable progress in learning to occur. Work samples might include (a) written work such as a report, science experiment results, test, or story; (b) artwork; (c) tape recordings; (d) a constructed project done in art, industrial arts, or an appropriate subject; and (e) other types of finished products depending on the subject area. Work samples collected over sufficiently long periods of time allow teachers to assess and evaluate the success of their teaching, the progress of their students in relation to the objectives and standards delineated in the planning of instruction, and the ability to reflect on student achievement in relation to teaching and make the changes necessary for improved teaching and student success. Work samples also give teachers the opportunity to think reflectively about teaching—planning, instruction, assessment, management of the learning environment, and professionalism. They give teachers the opportunity to demonstrate with hard evidence that they are in fact able to foster learning gains in students.

Accurate information is essential to making sound classroom decisions. Complete Expansion Activity 9.1: Accurate Information, which will let you further explore gathering information for your future classroom.

EXPANSION ACTIVITY 9.1   Accurate Information

Accurate information from the teacher is essential for students' academic progress. Distinguish among competitive, noncompetitive, and performance assessment. Describe the purposes of each and which type would be most applicable to the area you expect to teach.

Problems With Evaluation

We all like to view ourselves as fair, even-handed people. We believe it is possible and desirable to fairly evaluate our students' performance. But, for fairness to prevail in student evaluation, we must recognize and plan for biases built into human nature and into the nature of schooling (Lyman, 1991).

A lot of research evidence suggests that certain groups of students are not assessed fairly because of predetermined notions of primarily White, middle-class teachers about what constitutes successful school performance. Girls fare better than boys in the evaluation process partly because the structure of schools and classrooms favors the more passive socialization often demonstrated by girls. At the same time, some evidence suggests that boys begin to perform better than girls, particularly in mathematics and sciences, beginning in the middle school years (Murphy & Davidshofer, 1991). Many believe that this phenomenon is accounted for partly because boys tend to be given specific feedback regarding their academic performance, whereas girls are more likely to receive nonspecific feedback for both academic performance and classroom behavior (Sadker & Sadker, 1994). Whatever the reasons, girls and boys need to receive equal recognition and feedback for academic performance. Equally important is providing an environment that values individual and group differences within the classroom.

Likewise, poor and minority students often do not fare as well in the classroom setting. Teachers need to be aware of cultural and socioeconomic differences that may negatively influence how students are evaluated and then take every opportunity to reduce the influence of those factors.

Children who are creative, especially in ways not recognized within the ordinary structure of the classroom and the school, are often evaluated unfairly on the basis of pencil-and-paper tests. Children with behavior problems and other special needs are also often assessed unfairly. Poor behavior should never be a factor in determining grades. Special-needs students who have been mainstreamed should be evaluated against their own performance, not against the performance of the class as a whole.

Fairness issues and ethical issues must be considered before methods of assessment are determined. Criteria for evaluation should be related to the learning objectives. Performance standards should be established prior to assessment, not on the basis of the best example you receive. The purpose of the evaluation (pretest, formative, or posttest) should be clear to you and clear to the students before the learning experience takes place. The results of assessment should be shared only with the students and their parents or guardians. Some circumstances will call for sharing results with the principal or a counselor. The point to be made here is that assessment results are not to be shared indiscriminately. Everyone who sees the results of a student assessment should have a legitimate need to know.

Clearly, if you are to make accurate judgments about student performance and the meeting of state standards, you need to have confidence in the data you have collected. In other words, you must develop and/or select measurement devices that provide reliable and valid information and that are usable.

ON YOUR OWN 9.2 **Public View of Education**

Log on to the Web-based student study site at http://www.sagepub.com/eis2study. Review the public surveys relative to Chapter 9 and react to the related activities.

Measurement Accuracy

Reliability, validity, and usability are three important qualities of every measurement device. If a teacher-made test reveals that 50% of an algebra class was unable to solve algebraic equations, should the teacher be concerned? The answer depends on the reliability, validity, and usability of the test—that is, the ability of the test to consistently measure what it is supposed to measure: problem-solving ability. Let's take a brief look at the three essential elements of measurement: reliability, validity, and usability.

Reliability

Reliability is the consistency with which a measurement device gives the same results when the measurement is repeated. In other words, it is the measurement device's trustworthiness or dependability. A reliable bathroom scale, for example, gives identical weights for each of three separate weights taken in a single morning. If, on the other hand, the three weights taken differ by 5 pounds, the scale could not be considered very reliable. Likewise, a true/false test that is so ambiguously worded that students are forced to guess would probably yield different scores from one administration of the test to the next. In short, it would be extremely unreliable.

Measurement devices must provide reliable information if they are to be of value in decision making. No evaluation, however, is perfect. There is always some measurement error—for example, (a) poor construction could affect the score (sampling error), (b) the attribute being measured may vary over time (trait instability), (c) scoring or recording inaccuracies will affect scores (scoring error), and (d) variables such as motivation, health, and luck can cause variance. The extent to which such errors can be minimized determines the reliability of the measurement device. Typically, assessment results will be less reliable for younger children because of their tendency not to follow direction, poor listening skills, and other developmental factors.

How can teachers increase the reliability of their measurement devices? Basically, the reliability of measurement instruments can be improved by incorporating the following suggestions into their construction.

1. *Increase the number of evaluative items.* Reliability can be improved by increasing the amount of data collected. Because you have a larger sample of the trait being evaluated, chance errors will tend to cancel each other out. Thus, a test of 30 items is more reliable than one of 20 items.

2. *Establish optimum item difficulty.* Reliability can be increased by making the items being evaluated (test or observational) of moderate difficulty. In effect, moderate difficulty gives a moderate spread of scores, which allows you to better judge each student's performance in relation to other students. Conversely, difficult and easy items result in bunched scores, which make it more difficult to differentiate among scores. Thus, tests made up of moderate items spread the data over a greater range than devices composed mainly of difficult or easy items. In the case of observational scales, an item with a 5-point scale would give more reliable information than a 7- or 3-point scale because it would give more consistent results than would larger or smaller scales.

3. *Write clear items and directions.* Reliability is improved when students clearly understand what is being asked. Ambiguities and misunderstood directions lead to irrelevant errors.

4. *Administer the evaluative instrument carefully.* Reliability is improved when students are not distracted by noises or when they are not rushed.

5. *Score objectively.* Reliability is greater when objective data are collected. With subjective data, internal differences within the scorer can result in identical responses or behaviors being scored differently on different occasions.

Validity

Validity is the extent to which an evaluative device measures what it is supposed to measure. It measures what was taught and learned. For instance, if social studies content knowledge was taught and learned, but students scored low on the test over the content because they could not understand the questions, then the test is not valid. We all have had teachers who taught one thing and tested over something else, or who have made the test so difficult that we performed poorly.

Although there are several types of validity, the most important one to teachers is content, or face, validity. *Content,* or *face, validity* is established by determining whether the instrument's items correspond to the content that was taught in the course. Teachers sometimes construct tests that seem to address what was taught but, in fact, do not. For example, if instruction focused on developing issues and trends, the test should give students the opportunity to demonstrate their understanding of issues and trends. If the test focuses on names and dates, it does not have content validity. In the case of standardized tests, test inspection is carried out by subject experts. Similarly, the content validity of a teacher-made test should be evaluated by checking the correspondence of the test items with the teacher's stated outcomes. This simple process alone, however, does not guarantee content validity. For example, the objectives may have been prepared by making a superficial examination of the textbook and writing objectives at random, rather than by carefully matching objectives to what was taught in class. In short, content validity requires that a teacher's test items match the actual class instruction.

Any measurement device, whether it is a test or an observation instrument, must be valid to supply usable information. But an instrument is not simply valid or invalid; rather, its validity is a matter of degree, with each instrument having low, satisfactory, or high validity. Thus, the adequacy of an instrument involves a judgment regarding the usefulness of the information it provides for future decision making. Although most teachers lack the expertise or time to do extensive validity checks, they can at least make sure their test items match their stated learning objectives.

Usability

Usability is how well a measurement device is suited for gathering the desired information. For example, a 2-hour science test would not be suitable for a 50-minute class period. A test should be easy to administer and score, fall within budget limitations, be suitable to the test conditions, and have the appropriate degree of difficulty.

Reliability, validity, and usability are all interrelated. In fact, measurement devices must be reliable and suitable for the purposes they are used for before they can be valid. For example, if you cannot get consistent height measurements from a yardstick (not reliable), you cannot expect it to be accurate. The measurements might also be very consistent (reliable) but still not accurate (valid). A pencil-and-paper test would hardly be suitable for evaluating the ability to hit a tennis ball. Clearly, if a measurement device is to be used in making decisions, it is essential that the information be reliable *and* valid, as well as suitable.

This concludes the discussion of the assessment process. Table 9.2 gives a review of the major assessment concepts. Before you continue, review Table 9.2 and complete Review and Reflective Exercise 9.1.

TABLE 9.2	Assessment Concepts
Concept	**Description**
Diagnostic evaluation	Evaluation administered prior to instruction for placement purposes
Formative evaluation	The use of evaluation in supplying feedback during the course of a program
Summative evaluation	A judgment made at the end of a project that determines whether it has been successful or not and commonly used to give grades
Competitive evaluation	Evaluation that forces students to compete with each other
Noncompetitive evaluation	Evaluation that does not force students to compete with each other
Performance assessment	Assessment in which students demonstrate the behaviors to be measured
Student work sample	Collection of students' work over a sufficiently long period of time
Portfolio	A systematic, organized collection of evidence that documents growth and development and that represents progress made toward reaching specified goals and objectives
Standard scores	A score based on the number of standard deviations an individual is from the mean
Percentile	The point on a distribution of scores below which a given percentage of individuals fall
Reliability	The extent to which individual differences are measured consistently, or the coefficient of stability of scores
Validity	The extent to which measurement corresponds with criteria—that is, the ability of a device to measure what it is supposed to measure
Usability	The suitability of a measurement device for collecting desired data

Information Sources

Evaluation is the result of measurement. That is, evaluation requires that a judgment be made, and this judgment requires information. Therefore, you must become familiar with the sources of evaluative information.

Cumulative Record

Cumulative records hold the information collected on students over the school years. These records are usually stored in the guidance center office and contain such things as academic records, health records, family data, vital statistics, and other confidential information, as well as scores on tests of intelligence, aptitude, and achievement. Cumulative records also often contain behavioral comments from past teachers and administrators. These comments can prove useful in understanding the reasons for students' academic problems and disruptive behaviors. Treat these comments with great care, however, because teachers sometimes let them color their judgment or expectations. Indeed, it is recommended that you consult students' cumulative records only with good reason. An awareness of the information contained in students' files may affect your own observations and may lead to the formation of inaccurate judgments. Moreover, exercise care in interpreting student test scores. Many teachers misinterpret test scores because of insufficient training.

REVIEW AND REFLECTIVE EXERCISE 9.1   Discuss the nature of evaluation and measurement.

REVIEW

- What are the purposes of diagnostic, formative, and summative evaluation?
- What are some of the features of performance-based assessment?
- How can portfolios be used in assessment?
- What do fairness, reliability, validity, and usability have to do with the quality of evaluation?

REFLECTION

- How would you go about creating rubrics for assessing answers to the preceding four items?
- Can a test be valid but not reliable? Reliable but not valid? Explain in your own words.

The test scores found in cumulative files are usually those from standardized tests. As such, students' scores are given in terms of how they compare with a large (usually national) group of students used in establishing norms for the test. That is, the scores are generally reported in the form of standard scores, such as z scores, T scores, or stanine scores, or in the form of percentiles.

Individual scores or a group of scores may vary from established norms for many reasons. For example, the content and skills addressed in a course may differ from that examined in the selected standardized test, or the test may be inappropriate for the individual students or a group in terms of difficulty, clarity of instruction, and so forth. Therefore, when you use a standardized test for collecting evaluative information, make sure it is appropriate for the group being evaluated; this isn't always an easy task.

You should also be aware that federal legislation permits the records of any student to be inspected by parents or guardians. Parents or guardians also have the right to challenge any information contained in the file. As a result, some teachers and administrators are reluctant to write comments or reports that may be considered controversial. This reluctance sometimes leads to the omission of important information that would be useful to other teachers and administrators.

Personal Contact

Information can be gathered as you interact with students on a daily basis. Your observations of students as they work and interact and your conversations with students provide valuable information that will be of assistance in planning your instruction. Indeed, observational information is available continuously in the classroom, as you watch and listen to students in numerous daily situations. For example, you can observe your students during guided practice, while they work in small groups, as they use resource materials, and as they participate in questioning sessions.

Accurate observation provides information about work habits, social adjustment, and personality that cannot be collected through pencil-and-paper tests. Observations can help you answer some of your own questions: Are students confused? Can they apply the concepts? Should I plan more activities to teach this concept? Are some students in need of special assistance?

Based on your observations related to your own instruction, you can draw certain conclusions about the academic progress of your students. Your observation during questioning, for example, might reveal that certain students have trouble with a concept, appear to need special help, or need additional activities related to lesson concepts. Therefore, observe your students closely and be alert as they go about their daily activities. In fact, you may want to develop observational devices such as rating scales or checklists to ensure that your observational information is more accurate.

The information obtained through careful observation needs to be recorded and organized in a way that ensures accuracy and ready access, so insights can be gleaned about learning and development. Without a written record, you are often left with only general impressions of classroom actions. Over time, classroom impressions will fade, become distorted, or blend into one another—which will result in an inaccurate and biased picture of what has transpired. The development and use of an anecdotal record form, such as that shown in Figure 9.5, can prove useful in recording some of your observations.

It is important that you include students in the evaluative process. Students can be asked whether they understand material or how they feel about a particular topic of discussion. They can also best report on their beliefs regarding the value of what they have learned, of what they are still unsure, and of their readiness for testing on a topic. In fact, information about student problem areas can often be obtained from casual conversations before and after class. Formal and informal conversations with students may be among the best techniques for gaining diagnostic and formative evaluative information. Therefore, pay close attention to students' comments when they want to talk about needed help or academic concerns. Such exchanges and questions will give you the opportunity for gaining valuable information not readily available from other sources. Exercise caution, however, when considering the reliability of the information gleaned from students: They may choose to tell you what they think you want to hear, so combine your observations with the students' self-reports before making instructional judgments.

The use of observation is not without its critics. Many believe that observation is too subjective to provide reasonable evaluation and, furthermore, that keeping good observational records is too time-consuming to be practical. Simple observational instruments, however, can be devised prior to the lesson under observation, which in turn reduces recordkeeping concerns. The simple instrument of making several copies of the classroom layout could be used for a variety of purposes (see Figure 9.6). You could record the physical movement of students during seatwork time.

Who was out of their seats and why? Did they go to the pencil sharpener? The stack of dictionaries? The wastebasket? The teacher's desk for help or materials? In this way, you would be able to analyze potential problem areas that might keep students from remaining on task.

The same instrument (Figure 9.6) could be used to follow the flow of a questioning session. By devising a simple code, you could indicate who answered and who asked questions. You could break it down further by noting whether the questions answered were higher or lower order questions. Later analysis could reveal which students demonstrated understanding of the material and at what level of

**Figure 9.5
Anecdotal Record
Form**

Student: _____ Date: _____

Description of environment/class: _____

_____

_____

Description of incident: _____

_____

_____

_____

_____

Reported by: _____

**Figure 9.6
Seating Chart Record
of Classroom
Behaviors**

1 – 1 – 1 1 – 1 – 4 Sherry	1 – 1 – 2 2 – 1 – 2 Julie	2 – 1 – 2 1 – 2 – 1 Sue	2 – 1 –2 3 – 3 – 3 Chad	1 – 3 – 1 3 – 3 – 3 Paul	1 – 3 – 1 5 – 1 – 2 Mary
1 – 1 – 1 1 – 1 – 2 Joe	2 – 2 – 2 2 – 2 – 1 Mike	1 – 2 – 1 1 – 4 – 1 Sally	3 – 3 – 2 2 – 3 – 1 Conrad	3 – 3 – 1 1 – 1 – 1 Aaron	1 – 2 – 2 2 – 2 – 2 Scott
Empty Seat	2 – 2 – 2 2 – 3 – 3 Jan	1 – 1 – 1 2 – 2 – 2 Billie	5 – 5 – 1 1 – 2 – 1 Susan	1 – 1 – 1 3 – 3 – 3 Pat	1 – 1 – 1 3 – 3 – 3 Jean
2 – 1 – 1 1 – 1 – 1 Lisa	2 – 1 – 1 1 – 3 – 3 Lila	2 – 1 – 1 1 – 1 – 4 Dawn	3 – 1 – 1 1 – 1 – 4 Skip	3 – 1 – 1 2 – 2 – 5 Ben	Empty Seat

Legend: 1. Quiet and on task
2. Quiet, not working
3. Talked to other student
4. Finished work early
5. Talked with teacher

performance. It also might indicate the level of interest in the topic if, for example, the questions were answered on an all-volunteer basis. Thus, once teachers have refined their observational skills, the objectivity of personal contact information can be greatly enhanced through appropriate instrumentation. (I will address this issue later in the chapter.) Moreover, the time committed to personal contact recordkeeping can be kept under control by opening a portfolio for each student and adding a few descriptive phrases periodically. Examples might include such phrases as "Mary has difficulty remembering to bring her book to class," "John must be continuously reinforced to study," and "Ron has trouble with fine motor adjustments in chemistry lab."

The point to keep in mind is that observation is productive only if it has a clear purpose (e.g., determining if students are on task), if all students have the opportunity to be observed equally, if the rating of performance is consistent with previously established criteria, and if the information gathered is later contemplated, analyzed, and used for improving instruction and learning.

Analysis

Teachers monitor students' work on a regular basis; that is, they analyze it for possible errors. Analysis of students' work can take place during or following instruction, and, as with other techniques we have discussed, analysis has the advantage of not being a formal test with its accompanying pressures. Analysis is, however, more formal than personal contact.

Analysis is important in that it provides the opportunity for correcting faulty beliefs or practice. A teacher can reteach skills during the learning process by analyzing the students' work as it is produced, probing for understanding, and suggesting new approaches to problem solving. This practice can enhance the students' abilities to self-analyze their performances. When combined with observation

Evaluation is
a continuous process
fostered by daily
teacher-student
interaction.

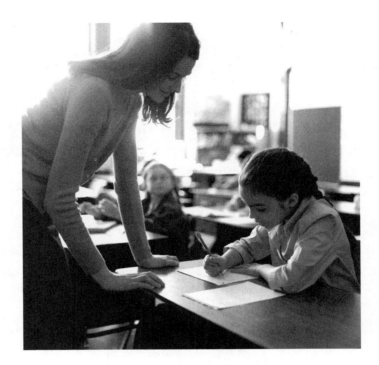

and inquiry, analysis can provide useful clues into the students' thinking processes and skills acquisition. For this reason, a good rule to follow is not to assign work unless it is going to be graded immediately by the teacher, another student, or the student himself or herself.

Students can and should be involved in the evaluation process. They can be called on to reflect about and critique their own work and the work of their peers. If this type of evaluation is to be successful, the criteria for performance should be clearly outlined prior to the exercise. The teacher must determine if the students understand the criteria for review before allowing such an exercise to take place. Peer critiques are especially effective in a cooperative learning exercise. After a peer review session, students should be afforded the opportunity to revise their work before a grade is assigned.

Analysis is a useful tool for demonstrating progress or the lack of progress to parents. Samples of each student's work should be kept in a file. This file can be reviewed periodically, and progress can be noted. Students should have the opportunity to review and critique previous work. Many students enjoy the chance to improve on something they did earlier in the year. Both samples should be kept to show improvement. Any written critique or analysis done by the teacher needs to be as objective as possible. Once again, planning and determining criteria prior to analysis improves the quality of the analysis.

Open-Ended Themes and Diaries

Teachers have long been aware of the influences that peer groups and out-of-school activities have on classroom learning. Therefore, knowledge about the social climate and activities in which students live can be indispensable in the evaluation process. This information will make it possible to adjust the curriculum so that it better addresses out-of-school differences in students' lives. For example, if most of the students in your class have after-school jobs, it is not wise to assign a lot of homework.

One technique that can be used for gaining valuable information about students is simply to ask them to write about different in-school and out-of-school topics. You might ask students to react to questions such as these:

Assessment information should be shared with students.

1. What profession would you most like to make your life work? What profession would you least like to make your life work?

2. What do you want to do with your life?

3. What is your favorite leisure pastime? Why?

4. With whom do you most like to spend your free time? Why?

5. How do you feel about the students in this school?

Of course, many of the comments and views expressed in students' writing will be distorted to some extent; nevertheless, students' views of reality will often be revealed when their writing is analyzed.

Diary writing on a periodic schedule (for example, once a week) is another method for obtaining evaluative information. A diary can consist of a record book in which students write about their concerns and feelings. Under conditions of good positive rapport, students often communicate their true concerns and feelings openly and freely.

Conferences

Students do not exist in isolation; they are affected by the environment in which they live. Students are influenced first and foremost by their families but also by neighborhoods and communities. Accordingly, schools must find new ways to involve parents in the education of students. Many times you can understand classroom problems better after observing and visiting with parents. Objective parental discussions can often reveal much.

Parental conferences may be needed for gathering evaluative information. Parents sometimes can shed needed light on students' social and academic problems. Parent conferences, however, are most beneficial when they are scheduled ahead of time and well planned. Table 9.3 offers a helpful framework for approaching parental conferences. Such conferences should not be a time for lecturing parents or for giving them advice on the proper rearing of the student. The overall atmosphere should be positive.

Traditional parent-teacher conferences are 15- to 20-minute discussions about their child. At times, what the parents hear at home from the youngster is quite different from the picture the teacher paints at the conference. Parents are then in the difficult position of wondering whether to believe their child or the teacher. This often places the teacher and/or parents on the defensive, blocking open communications. One solution to this dilemma is to have the student join the conference. This is often not productive, however, because the student becomes nothing more than a silent partner or a martyr chastised for little effort. An answer to this problem is the establishment of student-led conferences (Countryman & Schroeder, 1996). Student-led conferences give teachers and parents a better opportunity to get to know and understand each other.

TABLE 9.3	Framework for a Successful Conference
Step 1	*Plan ahead.* Establish your purpose. Plan what you intend to say, what information you want to obtain, and what your concerns are. Plan what your next step will be in the classroom as a result of the conference.
Step 2	*Starting the conference.* Be positive. Begin the conference with a positive statement.
Step 3	*Holding the conference.* Establish a positive sharing relationship. Be an active listener. Be accepting with regard to input and advice. Establish a partnership, so all concerned can work toward a common goal.
Step 4	*Ending the conference.* End the conference on a positive note. Communicate the fact that in working together, the common goals will be reached.
Step 5	*Conduct follow-up contact.* Keep all parties informed. Send notes and make phone calls to share successes and/or further concerns.

Information useful in making evaluative judgments can often be obtained from other teachers who have had your students in their classes. These colleagues can share difficulties these students had in their classes, some techniques that were used to correct problems, and evaluative judgments. Like conferences with parents, however, conferences with other teachers should be scheduled and well planned so that sufficient time will be available for productive meetings.

Finally, the school's support personnel—such as counselors, assistant principals, and secretaries—can be an excellent source of information. For example, counselors can help interpret and shed light on test results, as well as on personality factors that might affect student performance.

Testing

All of you have taken tests. You have taken weekly exams in English or history, and you have taken state-mandated achievement tests during most of your school years. If you examine the purposes of tests, then you have some idea of how testing can be used most effectively. You will also develop an understanding of the limitations of testing for determining some aspects of learning.

A **test** may be defined as a task or series of tasks used to obtain systematic information presumed to be representative of an educational attribute or series of attributes. This definition implies that a test must be developed systematically (using specific guidelines) and must provide a specific description of the traits or attributes being measured, as well as an established procedure for responding and scoring. Tests are classified according to (a) how they are administered (individually or in groups), (b) how they are scored (objectively or subjectively), (c) the emphasis of the response (speed or accuracy), (d) the type of response (performance or pencil and paper), and (e) the comparison groups (teacher made or standardized).

Tests are generally constructed to provide one of two types of interpretations: norm referenced or criterion referenced. A **norm-referenced test** interpretation is made when you compare a student's score with that of a norm group (a large, representative sample) in obtaining meaning. That is, a norm-referenced test compares individuals with one another. This comparison is made when you need to know how your students perform in relation to others at the same age or grade level. A **criterion-referenced** test interpretation is made when you compare an individual's score against a predetermined standard. In effect, students are compared with an absolute standard, such as 60% or 80% correct. Teacher-made tests generally belong in the criterion-referenced group because students are compared with criteria specified by the teacher.

Tests are used for many reasons. The most common reason is for determining cognitive achievement. Tests are also often used to measure attitudes, feelings, and motor skills.

There are many types of tests carried out in the classroom, including pretests, posttests, chapter exams, unit exams, midterms, final exams, standardized tests, and quizzes. The type of testing depends on your needs and the purpose for collecting the data. There are two general types of tests: (1) objective, which require students to select the correct response from several alternatives or to supply a word or short phrase to answer a question or complete a statement, and (2) subjective or essay items, which permit students to organize and present an original answer. Objective tests include multiple choice, true/false, matching, and completion, while subjective tests include short-answer essay, extended-response essay, problem solving, and performance. Essay tests are more subjective in nature due to their susceptibility to scoring influences and are generally easier and less time-consuming to construct than are most objective tests. Subjective tests generally require clear thinking more so than objective tests. Because of problems associated with reliability, validity, and usability, however, extra care must be taken in selecting tests that measure attitudes, feelings, and motor skills.

Good tests are carefully constructed and administered but have certain limitations. For example, most tests do not measure environmental factors or student motivations. Moreover, you must guard against tests that are poorly administered and vulnerable to student guessing. It is important to realize that certain test types are better suited than others for measuring particular learning objectives. For example, learning objectives requiring the student to demonstrate, show, or perform or that induce a student to explain or describe may be better measured by essay test. The matching of product may be better measured by performance tests, whereas objectives requiring the learning objective expectations with certain test types can help you select an appropriate kind of test for your classroom exam as well as provide a higher degree of test validity (i.e., testing which is supposed to be tested). Unless tests are carefully constructed and administered, the danger of testing superficial learning exists. Even under the best of conditions, pencil-and-paper tests—which are used more often than other kinds of assessment techniques—tend to place more value on knowing than on thinking, on verbalizing than on doing, and on teacher expectations than on student beliefs and values. With careful thought, however, you can construct tests that assess thinking ability. The problem is that most teachers lack either the skill or time to construct proper tests. Although important and probably the most common measurement technique used by teachers, testing should be thought of as only one of several techniques that you can implement for obtaining information about student progress. We will deal with test construction in greater detail in Chapter 10.

APPLY AND REFLECT 9.5

Teachers should use multiple sources when evaluating student performance. Why is this necessary? Isn't one test enough to judge student performance? Why or why not?

Objective Observation

Observation can be an effective evaluative technique. But, as noted earlier, observation often lacks reliability and validity. For example, you may view students you like differently from those you dislike, let the time of day affect your observation, or allow your perceptions to change with time. Lack of objective observation can be overcome to some extent through the use of rating scales, checklists, and other written guides that help objectify observations.

A **rating scale** is nothing more than a specific set of characteristics or qualities that are arranged in order of quality. Indications are made along the scale in such a way that a judgment can be made about the degree to which the attribute being assessed is present. For example, a scale for assessing student involvement in a group project might have five steps, with the lowest category labeled "uninvolved" and the highest labeled "involved." It might look like this:

$$\underset{\text{Uninvolved}}{0} \quad 1 \quad 2 \quad 3 \quad 4 \quad \underset{\text{Involved}}{5}$$

The rater would develop the criteria for what to look for in group involvement and would mark students against the criteria. The scale could be modified and additional scales added to construct a more detailed instrument for assessing total group involvement. This instrument might be similar to the one shown in Figure 9.7.

Checklists are similar to rating scales in that both are used for gathering information about physical kinds of student behaviors. However, a **checklist** differs from a rating scale in that it indicates the presence or absence of identified attributes.

A checklist basically is a list of the criteria against which a student's performance or end product is judged. With a checklist, a teacher simply checks off the criteria items that have been met. For example, a checklist for assessing student readiness for a lesson might look like this:

_____ 1. Reading assignment completed.

_____ 2. Completed homework.

_____ 3. Has book, pencil, and paper.

_____ 4. Demonstrates understanding of related vocabulary.

You would simply check those items that had been demonstrated.

Attitudes, feelings, and opinions are often difficult for teachers to evaluate. Indeed, some attitudinal behaviors may not occur on a daily basis. One technique for overcoming this difficulty is to have students complete a questionnaire. **Questionnaires** call on students to examine themselves and react to a series of statements about their attitudes, feelings, and opinions. Because questionnaires require self-reporting of these attributes, it is important that you recognize the potential for persons to choose socially correct responses rather than to indicate true beliefs. Nonetheless, questionnaires, especially those administered anonymously, can provide valuable information. The questionnaire designer decides what information is wanted and then writes statements or questions that will elicit this information. Questionnaires' response styles can vary from simple checklist-type responses to open-ended statements. For example, a checklist-type questionnaire designed to evaluate a science lesson might include statements such as these:

1. The lesson was _____ important.
   _____ interesting.
   _____ boring.
   _____ unimportant.

Figure 9.7
Rating Scale for
Group Involvement

RATING SCALE FOR GROUP INVOLVEMENT

Name _____ Date _____

Directions: Rate the student's involvement on each attribute by placing an X on the appropriate position on the scale.

1. Participation
   ._____._____._____._____._____.
   0   1   2   3   4   5
   Uninvolved   Involved

2. Cooperativeness
   ._____._____._____._____._____.
   0   1   2   3   4   5
   Inadequate   Adequate

3. Productivity
   ._____._____._____._____._____.
   0   1   2   3   4   5
   Inadequate   Adequate

4. Self-Discipline
   ._____._____._____._____._____.
   0   1   2   3   4   5
   Inadequate   Adequate

5. Motivation
   ._____._____._____._____._____.
   0   1   2   3   4   5
   Inadequate   Adequate

2. I find science   _____ fun.
                       _____ exciting.
                       _____ boring.
                       _____ difficult.

The scoring of the checklist type of test is simple. The number of negative statements checked is subtracted from the number of positive statements checked. The result is the positiveness of the attribute being measured.

This concludes the formal discussion of information sources and evaluative instruments. Table 9.4 gives a summary of the information sources and evaluative instruments addressed in this chapter. Review Table 9.4 and complete Review and Reflective Exercise 9.2.

APPLY AND REFLECT 9.6

You should record and organize observational data in a way that ensures accuracy and ready access. How will you do this?

TABLE 9.4   Information Sources and Evaluation Instruments

Concept	Description
Cumulative record	A file that holds information collected on students during the school years
Personal contact	The collection of data through daily interactions and observations of students
Analysis	An examination of students' work
Open-ended themes and diaries	The periodic writing of students on in-school and out-of-school topics
Conferences	A meeting between individuals regarding issues of common concern to both parties
Testing	A task or series of tasks used in obtaining systematic observations
Rating scale	A set of characteristics arranged in order of quality so that performance can be better judged
Checklist	A listing of characteristics used for indicating the presence or absence of identified attributes
Questionnaire	A set of statements to which students react in order to examine their attitudes, feelings, and opinions

REVIEW AND REFLECTIVE EXERCISE 9.2   Describe some ways to obtain evaluative information.

REVIEW

- What kinds of information can be obtained from cumulative records, personal contacts, analysis, themes and diaries, conferences, and testing? Which are valid and reliable?
- Why use rating scales, checklists, and questionnaires?

REFLECTION

- Teachers need evaluative information. In addition to the sources mentioned in this chapter, what other sources of evaluative information would you use in the area you expect to teach? Would rating scales, checklists, and written guides make your evaluative information more accurate?

REFLECTIONS ON TEACHER PRACTICE 9.2   Keeping Up With Students

1. How important is homework in the teaching process? Should you grade all homework?

2. Are the benefits derived from the use of rubrics worth the time and effort it takes to develop them? How else might student learning be assessed and evaluated?

◆ ◆ ◆

Keeping up with all those student papers can be a chore. I find that having a system definitely does help.

Homework Policy: I always make sure that I collect all assignments and let students know that "everything counts." I do want them to take their assignments seriously, so I review all assignments after I collect them, and then assign a letter grade of E, S, or N. If they really appear to get the idea, let's say on a

math sheet, they receive an E. If they appear to be doing reasonably well with the assignment, I assign an S. If they miss the point altogether, I assign an N. Most of my students strive for an E. I let them know that homework is part of their grade. Each week, I assign a grade of 1 to 5 for homework completion. If they miss one assignment in the week, they get a 4. If they miss two, they get a 3, and so on. At the end of the marking period, I use homework completion as a means of deciding whether or not a borderline student can be raised up to the higher grade, or should be dropped down a grade. Quality of homework also enters into the picture when it comes to grading. Shoddy work receives a shoddy grade.

Student Writing: This is the most challenging and time consuming thing to keep up with. You need to obtain or create a rubric for your students' writing exercises. Creating a rubric takes time, but once you have it, you can use it from year to year, and it provides a quick and objective means of grading writing. I created a rubric for each type of writing piece the kids do. I have rubrics for persuasive, expressive, descriptive, narrative, and informative writing. Books like those published by "Teacher's Mailbox" have writing ideas and rubrics to go along with them. These published rubrics can help. I tend to use my own, so that I am meeting state standards. Our students are graded on voice, conventions, organization, and content, so I take these into consideration when I am creating rubrics for my students. In one writing piece, I may not look for *everything*. I may tell the students that they will be graded on organization in a particular writing piece. In another, I may be grading for voice. Toward the end of the school year, I will grade on everything—all domains, and expect them to have the work as "picture perfect" as they can possibly make it.

Tests: I use the tests that come with the text series as often as possible to save myself time, but I do have some of my own quizzes made up. Of course, you probably realize that multiple-choice tests take a great deal less time to grade than essay. But I do believe that students should write in all areas, so I typically assign at least two to three essays with each test I give.

—*CAROLYN, elementary school teacher*

SOURCE: Reprinted with permission from ProTeacher, a professional community for elementary school teachers (http://www.proteacher.net).

ON YOUR OWN 9.3 Reflections on Teacher Practice

Read and reflect on the viewpoints expressed in Keeping Up With Students. Log on to the Web-based student study site at http://www.sagepub.com/eis2study and react to the related activities.

SUMMARY

The Evaluation Process

- Evaluating student learning is a complex endeavor that requires the same careful planning necessary for teaching content. Evaluation helps you become a better planner and to better understand students, their abilities, interests, attitudes, and needs in order to better teach and motivate them.

Evaluation Types

- The three types of evaluation are pretest, formative, and posttest (summative). Pretest evaluation is carried out prior to instruction for placement purposes. Formative evaluation is used during instruction to promote learning. Posttest evaluation follows instruction and is used to judge the end product of learning.

Systems of Evaluation

- Evaluation can be competitive, noncompetitive, or performance based. Competitive evaluation requires that students compete with each other, whereas noncompetitive evaluation requires that students show improvement in their level of achievement. Performance assessment requires that students demonstrate the behavior that the assessor wants to measure.

Measurement Accuracy

- Reliability, validity, and usability are three important qualities of every measurement device.

Information Sources

- Evaluation requires information. This information can be obtained from cumulative records, personal contacts, analysis, opened-ended themes and diaries, conferences, and testing.

DISCUSSION QUESTIONS AND ACTIVITIES

1. **Test-bank critique.** Examine and critique the test materials included in a published program of study for the subject area and grade level you would like to teach. What changes would you make before using the materials?

2. **Evaluation purposes.** List five purposes of evaluation. Why should there be a match between the method of evaluation and the purpose of evaluation?

3. **Conferences.** Plan a general conference with a parent for the first time. Discuss what topics might be important to include in a conference.

4. **Evaluating students.** List all the evaluation practices you think are beneficial to students and their learning. Now list all the practices you think are harmful to students and learning. Reflect on the two lists you have generated.

5. **Testing criticism.** Since paper-and-pencil tests are often criticized as measuring only low-level learning, do you believe that eventually they will no longer be used?

TECHNOLOGY AND EDUCATION

Digital portfolio assessment is a growing form of alternative assessment. Use search tools such as Google or Yahoo to locate examples of digital portfolios. Include such words as *electronic portfolios, digital portfolios,* or *eportfolios* in your search. Develop an overall flexible plan for student digital portfolios at the grade level you expect to teach. What purpose will the portfolio serve? What criteria will be applied for reflection and evaluation?

DECONSTRUCTING THE STANDARDS

Chapter 9 content addresses topics related to INTASC Standards 8 and 9.

 ♦ INTASC Standard 8 states: *Assessment of Student Learning:* The teacher understands and uses formal and informal assessment strategies to evaluate and ensure the continuous intellectual, social, and physical development of the learner.
 ♦ INTASC Standard 9 states: *Professional Commitment and Responsibility:* The teacher is a reflective practitioner who continually evaluates the effects of his or her choices and actions on others (students, parents, and other professionals in the learning community) and who actively seeks out opportunities to grow professionally.

For each of these two standards, write your response to the following:

- Which part(s) of each standard does this chapter address?
- How does this chapter address this standard?
- How will the concepts in this chapter help you apply this standard as a teacher?

PRAXIS CONNECTION

Log on to the Web-based student study site at http://www.sagepub.com/eis2study. Access the Praxis II: Principles of Learning and Teaching assessments and/or state-related exams and complete the Chapter 9 test preparation exercises.

PORTFOLIO CONNECTION

Log on to the Web-based student study site at http://www.sagepub.com/eis2study. Access the Portfolio Connection. Complete the Chapter 9 portfolio link to INTASC activities.

CONNECTION WITH THE FIELD

1. **Teacher interview**. Interview an elementary and secondary teacher.
   a. How important do they feel assessment is for promoting learning?
   b. How often do they test?
   c. How do they prepare students for testing (such as the day before)?
   d. Do they go over tests with students after they give them?

2. **Evaluation systems.** Study the evaluation system of a teacher in the subject area and grade level you would like to teach. Determine the extent to which the teacher uses norm-referenced and criterion-referenced evaluation.

3. **Observation.** Develop a simple observation instrument to keep track of the questions answered by students in a classroom. Use the instrument in an actual classroom. Did your observational instrument make it easier to keep track of the questioning and answering sequence? How would you modify the original instrument?

4. **Rating scales.** Develop a rating scale for assessing a common classroom behavior problem. Use the scale in an actual classroom. How helpful was your rating scale?

CHAPTER 10

Constructing and Grading Tests

Experience is the name everyone gives to their mistakes.

—OSCAR WILDE

OVERVIEW

Most teachers test to some degree. These tests can be commercially produced or teacher made. Therefore, teachers must be aware of how standardized tests are produced, as well as how to write test items and design tests.

The final step in the evaluation process is the interpretation of collected information in determining whether outcomes are met and/or in assigning grades. To do so, teachers must be able to arrange information in an objective and impersonal way.

This chapter was designed to help prospective teachers better understand testing, to improve test construction skills, and to better understand grading and the assignment, recording, and reporting of grades. To these ends, the focus will be on test types, test item construction, and students' grades.

OBJECTIVES

After completing your study of Chapter 10, you should be able to do the following:

- Given the purpose of the test, correctly determine an appropriate test for that purpose.
- Compare and contrast standardized tests and teacher-made tests.
- Compare and contrast the different types of teacher-made test items and the advantages and disadvantages associated with each.
- Construct the different types of items that can be included in teacher-made tests.
- List the purposes for assigning grades.
- Assign letter grades for participating students and provide a valid rationale for this assignment.
- Describe the procedure for teacher recordkeeping and the reporting of student progress.

Most schools put their primary emphasis on learning in the cognitive domain. Although there are a number of ways to measure knowledge in the cognitive domain, the most common is through the use of tests. These tests can be published by commercial testing bureaus, or they can be designed and constructed by individual teachers. Keep in mind, however, that teachers do not need to test, and lack of testing is frequent in early childhood classes, in the arts, in special education, in vocational classes, and in many nontraditional classes.

Tests are designed and administered for various purposes. Some are given for diagnostic (pretest) purposes, whereas others are given for determining grades. As such, tests are sometimes given before instruction; others, after instruction. Indeed, at times, a single test may be given before instruction for diagnosis (pretest) and again after instruction for determining student progress (posttest). Tests are also designed and administered for measuring student achievement. The measured achievement can be used in comparing students' scores with one another (norm-referenced tests) or in comparing students' scores with predetermined criteria (criterion-referenced tests).

As a teacher, you will be responsible for selecting the tests for your classroom. This will not always be easy.

Types of Tests

The compilation of evaluative information requires the use of a data-recording instrument. Of course, the most popular instrument in schools today is the test. Consequently, in this section, we will discuss the general characteristics of two commonly used testing devices: standardized tests and teacher-made tests. Detailed guidelines for constructing these tests are beyond the scope of this book. For more information on test construction, you should consult a basic textbook that details the construction, validation, and administration of tests.

Standardized Tests

Ebel and Frisbie (1991) define a **standardized test** as one that has been constructed by experts with explicit instructions for administration, standard scoring procedures, and tables of norms for interpretation. Standardized tests measure individual performance on a group-administered and group-normed test. Standardization means that the examinees attempt the same questions under the same conditions with the same directions, the time limit for taking the test is the same for everyone, and the results are scored with the same detailed procedure.

The preparation, editing, and analysis of standardized tests are undertaken by experts in the field covered. First, these experts write a battery of content questions related to the subject field that should be answerable by the average, well-informed student at the targeted grade level. These questions are then tried out on a representative sample of students in the subject area at the specified grade level from all kinds of schools in all parts of the country. Based on the results obtained from the representative sample, the test is revised, and a final version of the exam is written. The exam is then administered to a sample of students that is larger and more carefully selected to represent the target subject area and grade level. This latter sample of students forms the norming group against which all subsequent student scores will be compared. The final step in the development of the standardized test is the production of a test manual that provides clear directions for administration and scoring of the test, as well as certain information related to the test characteristics and interpretation of scores.

REFLECTIONS ON TEACHER PRACTICE 10.1 | Preparing for Standards Assessment

1. How is high-stakes testing beneficial to students, families, and society? Do you support high-stakes testing? Why or why not?

2. How concerned should you be regarding students' reading ability and reading comprehension skills?

◆ ◆ ◆

We've just completed standards assessment testing for the state. The experience led me to reflect upon my own teaching practice and to wonder about education in lower socioeconomic areas.

No Child Left Behind (NCLB) says that for our school (which is classified as a "failure" at the moment) to be taken off the failure list, we must raise our test scores at least 6 percentage points every year in order to make the 100-percent pass rate at the end of the time period allowed. We are to do this with no additional help from the government and very little from the district. I, personally, have not been given any additional curriculum (e.g., texts, readings, etc.) or administrative tools (e.g., increased copy machine access to run off the items needed) to ensure my classroom success. At least 40 percent of my students read below grade level but do not have a reading class scheduled in their roster (there are not enough reading specialists in my building to accommodate the need).

How can the students be better prepared for taking a standardized test in general? As an eighth grade teacher, I am not sure how much damage I can undo before they leave me and go to the high school, where the performance bar is raised even higher. I want to raise the bar myself, but I am afraid that it is all for naught. I feel caught in a vicious cycle that I am worried will never end.

The students I teach have poor writing, reading comprehension, and math skills. Why is that? I have seen them struggle through exercises that my 12-year-old (a sixth grader) can handle with ease. It has to boil down to what these students have NOT been getting in their past academic lives. It is obvious to me that they have not been getting a "proper" education. I use the term loosely, as it can mean different things depending on where you are coming from. For example, proper reading skills for my eighth graders would not always include being on grade level. For you and the students you teach, that might be different. Proper reading skills for me would include being able to comprehend what you have just read and apply it to a real-life situation. Remember, I teach 13- and 14-year-olds. I would have thought their prior knowledge base would be wider and deeper than it is. I feel as though I have to reteach ideas that they should already know. Let me give you an example of what I am up against.

We are learning about the frontier West, the pioneers, and the westward expansion of the United States during the years 1840 to 1880. In the first lesson, I wanted to "revisit" (note my word of choice) what the country looked like during this time period and how the geography of the United States played a significant role in being able to settle the West. Our task was to label mountains, plains, rivers, and deserts using our textbook and a student atlas. Well, I could not go further because most of my students did not know what a "plain" was, let alone how it might have been an obstacle in travel plans. And some wanted to know if a desert was the same thing as what you eat at the end of your meal (I kid you not). So instead of moving forward, I had to step back (several steps actually) and teach a lesson on United States geography, which, by the way, is in our sixth grade district curriculum. After they learned terms and applied them to a map of the United States, their assessment was to answer the following question: If you were a pioneer traveling on foot or leading a wagon, what kind of obstacle would a mountain present to you? Then substitute the words plain, river, and desert in the place of mountain and answer the question again. We even had difficulty with this. First, I had to define "obstacle" before we could go further. Most still could not answer the question until I set a scene for them.

I painted a picture. "Okay, you are a person who wants to get to the West before the next winter. You come across a river. How are you going to get across it and not lose your supplies like flour and sugar? You know if they get wet they are ruined and you will likely starve." Or "You are driving a wagon pulled by slow oxen. You have come to the start of a steep climb up a mountain. You are in tall grass and the weather is still warm, but when you look straight up at the mountain, all you see is snow. How are you going to get your wagon up and over before the winter comes? What might you experience on the trail that is going to stop you from getting over the top?" This type of banter is ongoing and seems endless to me. Until we've exhausted every angle of every task, the students seem hard-pressed to begin. To me, this comes back to a basic lack of reading and comprehension skills—which bears on their ability to pass the standardized achievement tests.

(Continued)

(Continued)

What can I do in social studies class to help prepare my students for these kinds of tests? First, I have decided that I need to "mock up" a variety of short reading assignments, create multiple-choice questions to test for understanding and then develop an open-ended question that can help determine if the student has internalized the content. These supplemental reading tasks will then "mirror" the kinds of questions students will encounter on the standardized tests.

This is a daunting task. The textbook is a basic form of reading, not a great deal of depth, but a good survey of content. I have not found any books that I could just purchase and include in my curriculum. There are many reading books that will assist in raising student test scores, but after an exhaustive search I have not found even one book that concentrates on social studies readings.

Second, I will need to beef up my reading comprehension strategies and incorporate them more often into my lessons. I have used them sporadically this year, but I really need to focus more on reading in the content area instead of learning the content—a subtle, but very important difference.

I feel as though my main task as a social studies teacher—whether or not I like it—is to help students figure out what to do with the words they see before them that don't make any sense. I didn't go to graduate school to become a reading specialist. But if I don't develop into one (self-taught, because there's no support for my professional development in this area, either), my students are not going to be able to break the cycle of failure. Once again, I need to rethink and remold my teacher-self into something other than what I thought I should be.

I can see why some teachers find a niche and stay put for years and years. Trying to be an effective teacher is exhausting!

—*CAROLYN, eighth-grade social studies teacher*

SOURCE: www.middleweb.com. Reprinted with permission.

ON YOUR OWN 10.1   Reflections on Teacher Practice

Read and reflect on the viewpoints expressed in Preparing for Standards Assessment. Log on to the Web-based student study site at http://www.sagepub.com/eis2study and react to the related activities.

Standardized tests are particularly useful in comparing the performance of one individual with another, of an individual against a group, or of one group with another group. Such comparisons are possible because of the availability of the norming-group data and the uniformity of the procedures for administration and scoring the test. Thus, you could compare a single school with others schools in a district, compare districts, compare states, or compare students in one state with all students in the nation. For example, suppose a student scored 80% on a physics test. For most purposes, this is sufficient information for evaluation purposes, but at times you might want to know how a physics score of 80% compares to the physics scores of other students in the district, state, or nation.

Standardized tests come in the form of test batteries and single-subject tests. Some standardized tests are used in assessing personality, but the most commonly used standardized test measures knowledge in specific areas, such as English, social studies, psychology, or chemistry. These tests are usually referred to as *achievement tests* because they measure how much a student has learned in a particular subject area. Other standardized tests that are commonly used are those that measure students' aptitudes, or abilities, for performing certain activities. These tests are designed to measure an individual's potential in a given field—such as journalism, mathematics, law, drafting, teaching, or auto mechanics—and are given a variety of labels, including general ability test, intelligence tests, or scholastic aptitude tests.

Standardized test results generally include a percentile norm, an age norm, and a grade-level norm, or a combination of these norms. Teachers are often called upon to interpret these norms for parents. Therefore, you need a basic understanding of their meaning. At the most basic level, a percentile rank (see Chapter 9) of 85 indicates that 85% of the norm group performed more poorly and 15% performed better than the individual in question. An age rank of 15.6 means that, regardless of chronological age, the student got the same number of right answers as did the average 15½-year-old in the norm group: The number to the left of the decimal point represents years, and the number to the right of the decimal point represents months. Grade-level norms are the most widely reported and the least useful of the measures. Grade-level norms are reported as grade-equivalent scores, with the tenths place representing the months in a 10-month school year. The only real value of grade-equivalent scores is to determine if the test was too easy or too difficult for students scoring at a particular level.

Sax (1980) and Ebel and Frisbie (1991) report that standardized achievement tests are most properly used to make decisions about

1. Determining placement in differentiated instructional tracks

2. Individualizing instruction for remediation or acceleration

3. Diagnosing areas of strength and weakness

4. Gauging the effectiveness of an instructional program or group of programs

5. Evaluating the extent of student progress

6. Determining teaching emphasis and effectiveness

Although these reasons present a strong case for the use of standardized tests in educational decision making, it is important to recognize that a too narrow or too broad interpretation of results can lead to oversimplifying a complex situation. For example, one English class performs more poorly on grammar than another. Can you assume that the teacher is doing a poor job of teaching grammar concepts? Probably not, and certainly not without more information about the composition of the two classes. The poor performance could be explained by a large number of mainstreamed special-needs students in the first class or by the fact that all school assemblies and announcements occur during second period, reducing instructional time during that period.

Standardized tests and teacher-made tests are given for different reasons. Standardized tests generally cover a much broader range of a content area than would a teacher-made test, which is designed to measure achievement in a particular unit of work. Thus, achievement tests in the classroom should supplement teacher-made evaluation. The use of standardized tests will continue to play an important role for educational decision making and for public reporting on the state of school learning, but standardized tests are only one method for evaluating learning. The tests can give valuable information on how well your students are doing overall in comparison with other student groups.

Certain limitations are also associated with the use of standardized tests. For example, their validity is often questionable in situations in which they do not measure what was taught; that is, they may not be consistent with the goals and objectives established by the teacher. Moreover, standardized tests are likely to have some social and cultural bias, which means that the test may discriminate against certain social and cultural groups that lack prerequisite language, background experience, or testing experiences.

APPLY AND REFLECT 10.1

Standardized tests are widely used in our schools. Do you think the results should be used to make major educational decisions? Why or why not?

ON YOUR OWN 10.2   **View From the Classroom**

Log on to the Web-based student study site at http://www.sagepub.com/eis2study. Review the Chapter 10 teacher surveys and react to the related activities.

Teacher-Made Tests

For material related to this concept, go to Clip 10.1 on the Student Resource CD bound into the back of your textbook.

Teacher-made tests are the most common of all school evaluative instruments. There are three basic reasons for the popularity of teacher-made tests. First, they can be constructed so they are consistent with classroom goals and objectives. Second, teacher-made tests present the same questions to all students under nearly identical conditions. This means that the test results provide the means and basis for making comparative judgments among students. Third, teacher-made tests generate a product that can be evaluated and easily stored for later use. This means that tests and results can be readily accessible for review by students and parents when explaining how grades were determined. In addition, teacher-made tests are much less expensive to construct and administer.

Although teacher-made tests have their advantages, the bulk of these tests have unknown or low reliability, and most teachers lack the skill for designing valid tests or writing appropriate test items. Teacher-made tests remain, however, an important part of the instructional process. Consequently, you should further develop and refine your skill in test construction.

Teachers have three basic alternatives in constructing tests: They can construct an objective test, an essay test, or a combination. Objective tests comprise alternative-choice, multiple-choice, matching, and completion items, whereas essay tests include supply items. These supply items can be written either as brief- or extended-essay questions; that is, the students must supply short or elaborate responses. Brief-essay items ask students to write a sentence or short paragraph, solve a problem, or give a proof, whereas extended-essay items require that students write at length. The item type or types used in the construction of a particular test depends on your objectives and the nature of the behaviors being measured.

Standardized tests provide valuable information for making curriculum decisions.

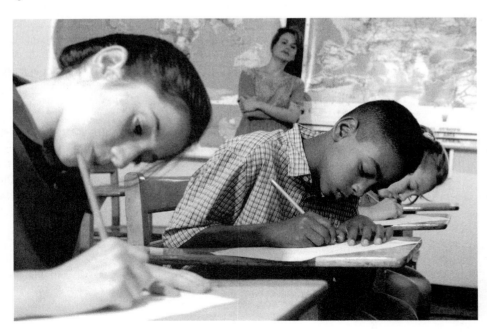

Test items should be written at the taxonomical level of your objectives. Contrary to common belief, this can be accomplished with almost any type of test item—objective or essay. Although it is more difficult to write objective items at the higher levels, it is also difficult to write high-level essay items.

Instructional objectives usually suggest the best type of test item. For example, an objective that involves solving physics problems would probably be best evaluated through the use of brief-essay items, whereas knowledge of the definitions of terms would probably be best evaluated through the use of multiple-choice items. In general, however, when objectives lend themselves to more than one type of test item, most teachers prefer objective items over essay types because of their scoring ease and reliability.

Classroom tests generally should not contain more than two types of test items. Students may have trouble when they must shift to different types of responses. Therefore, if your objectives can be evaluated by one or two test types, then limit your test to these types.

The purpose of testing is to check student mastery of the stated objectives. Therefore, one overall principle applies to the writing of all test items: Every item should separate the students who have mastered the objectives from those who have not. Students who cannot respond should not be able to guess or bluff their way to success on a test. Moreover, "test wiseness" (the ability to answer questions through the use of clues from the question) should be guarded against when constructing a test. Let us now briefly consider the various types of test items commonly used by teachers.

Alternate-Choice Items

The simplest form of objective test item is the alternate-choice type. The true/false format is the most common form of alternate-choice item. Variations on the basic true/false item include yes/no, right/wrong, and agree/disagree items.

Alternate-choice items tend to be popular because they appear to be easy to write. These items, generally, are simple declarative sentences. Unfortunately, writing good alternate-choice items requires skill, if you are to avoid triviality and discourage guessing. Writing good true/false items is difficult because there are few assertions that are unambiguously true or false. Therefore, because of

"I studied for this test, and the ploy paid off."

SOURCE: Created by Martha Campbell.

this particular sensitivity to ambiguity, it is especially crucial that your alternate-choice items be stated as clearly as possible. For instance, consider the following:

Poor: The value of pi is 3.14. T or F

This question is ambiguous; 3.14 is not the exact value of pi, but it is a commonly used value. To be totally clear, the item could be rewritten as follows:

Better: The value of pi rounded to the nearest one hundredth is 3.14. T or F

This question is better because it allows for the small difference between what is commonly used as the value of pi and the "exact" value. Following are some further suggestions for improving the writing of alternate-choice items:

1. Avoid using negative statements and double negatives. Such statements can be confusing and may cause knowledgeable students to get them wrong.

2. Make sure an item is not dependent on insignificant facts. Make sure that your items ask something important and worth remembering. For example, a statement should not be false because an individual's seldom-used first name is asked. Do not use trick items that appear to be true but are false because of an inconspicuous word or phrase.

3. Don't make your false items longer than your true items (or vice versa). If you find it necessary to write a few lengthy true items, make sure that you supply approximately the same number of lengthy false items.

4. Watch for item response patterns. Generally, the proportion of true and false items in a test should not be too different. Similarly, guard against correct/incorrect response patterns—such as T T T F F F or T F T F T F—that could help students achieve a misleading number of correct answers.

5. Be clear and concise. Use simple grammar in item construction. Avoid dependent clauses and compound sentences.

6. Limit each statement to only one central idea. Don't mix true and false ideas in a single statement.

7. Be especially sensitive to the use of certain key words that can divulge the correct response. Words such as *always, never, all,* and *none* indicate sweeping generalizations, which are associated with false items, whereas words like *sometimes, often, probably, usually,* and *generally* are associated with true items.

8. Avoid exact quote statements from the textbook or workbook. Quotations can have different meaning when they are taken out of context or may make students think that you prefer rote learning.

Alternate-choice items permit teachers to take a broad sampling of behaviors in a limited amount of time. Moreover, the scoring of alternate-choice items tends to be quick and simple. But it is often difficult to write good items. Also, some kinds of learning cannot be evaluated easily through alternate-choice items. For example, problem-solving situations often are difficult to evaluate using alternate-choice techniques. Finally, students have a 50% chance of guessing the correct answer, thus giving the items poor reliability and validity.

Multiple-Choice Items

Multiple-choice items are popular and used widely because they have some benefits over other methods. However, they also have limitations. Multiple-choice items can be used successfully in measuring achievement of almost any objective of interest to the teacher. Moreover, like alternative-choice questions, a multiple-choice test enables a teacher to ask many questions and, thus, cover many objectives on the same test. It can be used for measuring almost any type of cognitive behavior, from factual knowledge to the analysis of complex data. Undoubtedly, the multiple-choice format is the most versatile of all objective item formats. Moreover, it has the added advantage of being easy to score.

The basic form of the multiple-choice item is a *stem* or *lead,* which sets up the problem or asks a question to be completed with one of a number of alternative answers or responses (usually three to five). One of the responses is the correct answer; the other alternatives are called *distractors* or *foils* and should be plausible but incorrect. Writing good multiple-choice items is not as easy as many beginning teachers believe. It often takes a substantial amount of patience and creative ability to write good distractors. Unless you know your course content well, the number of items that can be constructed is limited.

Multiple-choice items should be constructed so they are straightforward, clear, and concise. Consider the following example:

Poor: Who was president during the Civil War?
- A. Jefferson Davis
- B. Abraham Lincoln
- C. Ulysses S. Grant
- D. George Washington

The correct response depends on whether you are asking for the president of the United States or of the Confederacy. In other words, there are two possible correct responses to the question. The question, however, could be reworded as follows:

Better: Who was president of the United States during the Civil War?
- A. Jefferson Davis
- B. Abraham Lincoln
- C. Ulysses S. Grant
- D. George Washington

A summary of the guidelines that can be followed to write better multiple-choice items follows:

1. The central issue or problem should be stated clearly in the stem. It should be stated in the form of an incomplete statement or question, and there should be no ambiguity in terminology.

2. Avoid writing a stem at the end of one page and the alternatives on the next page, or placing choices in a linear sequence.

3. Avoid providing grammatical or contextual clues to the correct answer. For example, the use of *an* before the choices suggests that the answer begins with a vowel. Instead, use the form *a(n),* which means "either *a* or *an.*"

4. Use language that even the most unskilled readers will understand. Keep the reading requirement in a question to a minimum. Write concise stems and precise choices.

5. Avoid absolute terms (such as *always, never,* and *none*) in the stem and alternatives. Test-wise individuals are usually sensitive to these terms.

6. Alternatives should be grammatically correct. The use of *is* or *are,* for example, can often help students guess the correct response. All alternatives should fit the stem to avoid giving clues to items that are incorrect.

7. Avoid the use of negatives (such as *not, except,* and *least*) and double negatives in the stem and alternatives. If negatives are used in the stem, put them as near the end of the stem as possible.

8. Avoid giving structural clues. For example, try not to use one letter for the correct response more often than others or create a pattern of correct responses.

9. Use "all of the above" and "none of the above" with care. "All of the above" is usually a poorer response than "none of the above" because all alternatives must be correct answers. It is often difficult to write four or five correct responses to a stem.

10. Avoid pulling statements directly from the textbook. Test students for understanding, not memorization.

11. Alternatives should be plausible to less knowledgeable students. Write distractors that include common errors, errors that are likely, and erroneous commonsense solutions.

Once you have written a pool of multiple-choice items for a unit of instruction, you generally will find it easy to modify the items based on feedback data. Moreover, multiple-choice items are relatively insensitive to guessing; however, they are more sensitive to guessing than are supply items.

Matching

Matching questions are designed to measure students' ability to recall a fairly large amount of factual information. Students are presented two lists of items (phrases, concepts, dates, principles, or names) and asked to select an item from one list that most closely relates to an item from the second list. Essentially, a matching item is an efficient arrangement of a series of multiple-choice items with all stems (sometimes called *premises*) having the same set of possible alternative responses. Thus, matching items can be used anywhere multiple-choice items can be used. They are best suited for measurement of verbal, associative knowledge.

Matching items are relatively easy to construct, especially if they are intended for measuring lower level learning. Conversely, the chief disadvantage is that they are not effective for evaluating higher level thinking.

Writing good matching questions is often difficult. Another problem associated with matching items is the tendency for one part of the item to give away the answer to another part. Consider, for example, the following:

Poor:

1. Alex Haley	A. *Wheels*
2. James A. Michener	B. *The Exorcist*
3. William Golding	C. *Lord of the Flies*
4. William Peter Blatty	D. *Cujo*
5. Arthur Hailey	E. *Centennial*
6. Stephen King	F. *Roots*

There are exactly six premises and six responses. If each statement is to be used only once, the students need only answer five of the premises correctly to correctly identify the sixth response for the last premise. It is better to allow each response to be used more than once or, even better, to add extra responses—for example,

Better:

1. Alex Haley	A. *The Exorcist*
2. James A. Michener	B. *Wheels*

3. William Golding   C. *The Grapes of Wrath*

4. William Peter Blatty   D. *Lord of the Flies*

5. Arthur Hailey   E. *Cujo*

6. Stephen King   F. *Centennial*

                           G. *Roots*

                           H. *1984*

Many multiple-choice questions can be easily converted to matching items. In fact, you should think of matching items as a set of multiple-choice items with the same set of alternatives. Each response is then appropriate for each premise. Also, the following guidelines will aid in the construction of better matching items:

1. Indicate clearly and concisely the basis for matching the premises with the responses.

2. Design the entire matching item so it is contained on one page. That is, don't put the premises on one page and the responses on the back or on the next page.

3. Keep the number of items to be matched short. Limit the number of items to 10 or so. The more premises, the more difficult it is to avoid giving inadvertent clues.

4. Put premises and responses in logical order. That is, be sure that premises and responses are easy for students to find.

5. Be sure items include statements, words, or phrases that have a high degree of homogeneity. Both the premises and the responses should fall in the same general topic or category.

6. Make the length of statements consistent. In fact, longer statements and phrases should be listed in the left column and shorter ones in the right column.

7. If names are to be matched, use complete names. Using only last names sometimes causes confusion.

Completion

Completion items require that students write responses in their own handwriting. They generally ask students to supply a recalled word or phrase. A completion test item usually contains a blank, which the student must fill in correctly with one word or a short phrase.

Completion items are not easy to write. Skill is needed to write such items so that there is only one correct response. Some teachers eliminate this problem by providing students with a selection of answers, some correct and some incorrect, from which students select a response.

Completion items are most useful for the testing of specific facts. They are less powerful than essay items, however, in terms of the kinds of thinking they can evaluate.

Placement of the blank is of prime importance in writing completion items. Consider the following glaring error:

Poor:

_____, _____, and _____ are three large cities in _____.

In general, it is best to use only one blank in a completion item, and it should be placed near the end of the statement. Thus, the example would be better rewritten as follows:

Better:

Dallas, Houston, and Austin are three large cities in the state of _____.

A summary of guidelines associated with writing better completion items follows:

1. Give clear instructions. Indicate how detailed answers should be, whether synonyms will be correct, and whether spelling will be a factor in grading.

2. Be definite enough in the incomplete statement so that only one correct answer is possible.

3. Do not adapt direct statements from the textbook with a word or two missing. Such usage encourages students to memorize the text.

4. Make sure all blanks are of equal length and correspond to the lengths of the desired responses. That is, all blanks for all items should be of equal length and long enough to accommodate the longest response. Young students write big. So, allow sufficient space for your young students to write their answers.

5. Write items that can be completed by a single word or brief phrase.

Some subjects lend themselves better than others to testing through completion items. For example, subjects that focus on the recall of specific unambiguous facts or that require students to perform certain calculations to fill in the blank in the statement are more suited for evaluation through the use of completion items.

Essay

Essay items give students the opportunity to formulate answers to questions in their own words. Essay questions are said to measure what students know because they permit students to select from their own storehouse of knowledge in answering a question. In effect, essay questions can successfully determine students' ability to analyze, synthesize, evaluate, and solve problems. Some specialists advocate using words such as *why, how,* and *what consequences* in essay questions because, they claim, such terms call for a command of essential knowledge of concepts to integrate the subject into an appropriate response. Other test specialists urge teachers to use words such as *discuss, explain,* and *examine* because they prompt responses that provide a glimpse of how students think. Still other specialists advocate more precision and structure through the use of words such as *identify, compare,* and *contrast.*

Essay test items come in two basic forms: brief and extended. The brief-essay item generally requires a short answer or the solution of a problem, whereas the extended-essay item calls for several paragraphs of writing. Because of time constraints, extended essays are seldom used in the classroom. In fact, most teacher-made tests are a combination of objective items and brief-essay items.

Essay items continue to be misused by teachers. Teachers often take less time in writing essay items than objective items. In fact, essay questions appear to be so easy to write that teachers often prepare them too hastily. Consider the following example:

Poor: Discuss Shakespeare's work.

This question is unclear. You should tell students what to discuss, and tell them in descriptive terms. "Describe the use of metaphor in Shakespeare's works" or "Analyze the political ramifications of Shakespeare's works" are more specific statements. Notice that the following phrasing makes the requested task much clearer.

Better: Analyze the use of humor in Shakespeare's *Twelfth Night.*

You should give careful consideration to the construction of essay questions so that students will know what is required of them. The following guidelines should be of further assistance in writing better essay questions:

1. Make directions clear and explicit. If spelling and grammar are to be considered in grading, tell the students. Also, if organization, creativity, and content are to be considered in grading, share this information.

2. Allow ample time for students to answer the questions. If more than one essay question is to be answered during a period, suggest a time allotment for each question.

3. Students should be given a choice of questions. Such choice avoids penalizing students who may know the subject as a whole but have limited knowledge in the particular area of a single question.

4. The worth of each question should be determined as a test is being written. Convey this information in the test instructions, and grade accordingly.

5. Explain your scoring technique to students before you give the test. It should be clear to them what you will be looking for when you grade the test.

A common problem associated with essay tests is content coverage. Because of the time students need to respond to essays, fewer topics can be covered. Realistically, only a few essay items can be included on an exam.

Essay items are difficult to score. There is often no single right answer to a question. Because of this tendency, essay items generally tend to be less reliable and less valid than other types of test items. With care, however, biases associated with essay grading can be controlled to some extent. Several guidelines follow:

1. Write a sample answer to each essay question ahead of time and assign points to various components of your answer.

2. Skim through all responses to a question before beginning the grading of the question. Establish a model answer for each question, and grade each question for all students before proceeding to the next question.

3. Grade essays blindly. Have students write their names on the back of the exam so it can be graded without knowledge of the identity of the respondent.

4. Establish a reasonable page limit and time limit for each essay item. This will indicate the level of detail desired and help students finish the entire test.

5. If time permits, read student responses several times. This will reduce the chances of making serious errors in judgment.

Despite grading drawbacks, unrestricted essay items are usually required to evaluate higher order knowledge and thinking. Therefore, they should be used, but used with care.

APPLY AND REFLECT 10.2	Teacher-made tests can be objective or essay. Which would work best at the grade level you expect to teach? Why?

Authentic Assessment

Authentic assessment is any type of assessment that requires students to demonstrate skills and competencies that realistically represent real-world problems and situations. Students are required to integrate knowledge and to complete tasks that have real-life applications. Authentic assessments can include exhibitions, oral presentations, and other projects. Students might be asked to evaluate case

"It's not easy getting all your homework done between dinner time and prime time."

SOURCE: Created by Martha Campbell.

For material related to this concept, go to Clip 10.2 on the Student Resource CD bound into the back of your textbook.

studies, write definitions and defend them orally, perform role-plays, or have oral readings recorded on tape. They might collect writing folders that include drafts and revisions showing changes in spelling and mechanics, revision strategies, and their history as a writer.

Perhaps the most widely used authentic assessment technique is the portfolio. Portfolios are a collection of learner work over time (see Chapter 9). They may include research papers, book reports, journals, logs, photographs, drawings, video- and audiotapes, abstracts of readings, group projects, software, slides, and test results; in fact, some of the assessments listed earlier could have a place in a portfolio. Portfolios should represent a documented history of learning and an organized demonstration of accomplishment. They can serve as a catalyst for reflection on one's growth as a learner.

Some guidelines for the development of good authentic assessment are the following:

1. Design meaningful and worthy programs or tasks that match the content and outcomes of instruction.

2. Make sure tasks have real-life applicability.

3. Put emphasis on product and process, conveying that both development and achievement matter.

4. Provide opportunities for learner self-evaluation.

5. Develop scoring procedures and their application. Develop rubrics to help establish consistency and fairness.

APPLY AND REFLECT 10.3

Authentic assessment represents an option to objective and essay testing. What problems do you associate with this form of assessment?

Teachers must assess, and this assessment should serve several purposes. Complete Expansion Activity 10.1: Classroom Assessment to further explore the validity of assessment.

EXPANSION ACTIVITY 10.1   Classroom Assessment

Think about the following statement and decide whether you agree or disagree with it.

A teacher should never use a single measure to assess learning.

Why do you agree or disagree with the statement?

Which type of assessment to use is an issue often faced by teachers. As a rule, there are no absolute guidelines relative to the superiority of one type of assessment over another in every situation. In general, the best procedure is to use the best assessment device that will measure the type of objectives the teacher has for a particular lesson or unit and the type of knowledge expected of students. However, in general, lower levels of knowledge (factual and comprehensive) are best measured through objective test items (alternate choice, multiple choice, etc.), whereas essay items do a better job of assessing higher order knowledge (evaluation, synthesis, analysis, etc.). Procedural knowledge (knowing how to do something) is best assessed through performance measures. Moreover, norm-referenced tests may work best when measuring general ability in such areas as algebra, English, general science, or American history, whereas criterion-referenced tests may work best when measuring mastery of basic skills, determining if students have prerequisites to start a new unit, assessing affective and psychomotor objectives, and grouping students for instruction.

This section has focused on several types of test items. Keep in mind, however, that the different kinds of items can be written to sample almost any behavior. Even so, there are certain advantages and disadvantages associated with the various types of teacher-made test items. Table 10.1 illustrates these advantages and disadvantages. To further your test development skills, complete Expansion Activity 10.2: Test Analysis.

Quizzes

Classroom quizzes can be used for evaluating student progress. In fact, quizzes are an excellent way to check homework and find out whether concepts from the preceding lesson were understood.

Teacher quizzes differ from regular teacher-made tests in that they usually consist of three to five questions and are limited to the material taught in the immediate or preceding lesson. They are easy to develop, administer, and grade; thus, they provide prompt evaluative information to both students and teacher.

Quizzes encourage students to keep up with their homework, and they show students their strengths and weaknesses in learning. In addition, quizzes help teachers improve instruction by providing feedback related to their effectiveness. Problems identified through quizzes serve as early warning signals of teaching or learning problems. Early identification allows the teacher to focus on problems before they worsen.

ON YOUR OWN 10.3   Public View of Education

Log on to the Web-based student study site at http://www.sagepub.com/eis2study. Review the public surveys relative to Chapter 10 and react to the related activities.

TABLE 10.1	Advantages and Disadvantages Associated With the Different Types of Test Items	
Type	**Advantages**	**Disadvantages**
Alternate Choice	Large sampling of content Easy to score	Guessing Writing clear items difficult Tends to test memorization
Multiple Choice	Large sampling of content Scoring simple and fast Measures wide range of cognitive levels Reduces guessing	Question construction time-consuming Often used to test trivial content
Matching	Large sampling of content Can test associations Easy to construct and score	Tests for recognition Guessing
Completion	Large sampling of content Easy to construct Limited guessing	Tests for memorization Writing good items difficult Difficult to score
Essay	Measures higher cognitive levels Less time needed to construct	Difficult to score Questions sometimes ambiguous

EXPANSION ACTIVITY 10.2   Test Analysis

Companies that publish textbooks commonly include tests for each chapter in the book. These tests usually include multiple choice, true and false, matching, and other types of questions. Using these tests can save time, but are they appropriate for all classrooms? Select a chapter or unit test furnished by a textbook company for a textbook that you might use in an area you expect to teach. Analyze the test relative to the following questions.

1. Do the test items emphasize the same things emphasized in the chapter or unit objectives?

2. Has an important area of content or any objective been overlooked or underemphasized?

3. Does the test cover all levels of instructional objectives included in the lesson?

4. Does the language of the items correspond to the language and reading level of the intended students?

5. Do questions require students to perform the behaviors they are to be taught?

6. Does the number of items for each objective provide a sufficient sample of pupil performance?

7. Is there a reasonable balance between what the items measure and the amount of time that will be required for students to develop a response?

8. What is your overall evaluation of the test?

Although not technically a teacher-made test item type, quizzes represent an important source of evaluative information to teachers. Moreover, quizzes can often be used to motivate students.

Valid tests are not always easy to construct. It takes time and knowledge of evaluation.

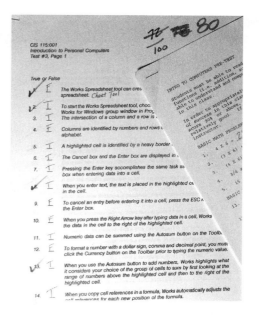

Published Test Banks

Many textbooks and programs of study include publisher-produced test banks. These test banks vary in quality. Some test banks are provided in the form of masters for copying and typically include chapter and unit tests. Many of these tests are geared to factual information and, consequently, ease of grading. If you have planned a set of instructional objectives independent of those suggested in the textbook, it is likely that the published test will fall short of serving your needs.

A more promising development is the advent of test bank databases. Schools that purchase this service for teachers are provided with a phone number that allows teachers to order customized tests from the test bank. Use of this tool certainly requires advance planning. Complete Web Link 10.1: Computer Use in Assessment to identify other resources that will help you in your assessment efforts.

WEB LINK 10.1   *Computer Use in Assessment*

Do an Internet search relative to the use of computers in classroom assessment. What are some appropriate computer uses at the grade level you expect to teach? Share your findings with your class.

A summary of the testing concepts covered to this point is given in Table 10.2. Study Table 10.2 and complete Review and Reflective Exercise 10.1 to check your understanding of the concepts presented in this chapter.

The gathering of data is not the end of the evaluative process. You then must interpret these data and assign grades. The importance of grades cannot be overemphasized because of their influence on students' lives. For example, grades are often used for college entrance, courses of study, and job recommendations.

Table 10.2	Evaluative Instruments
Type	**Description**
Standardized test	A commercially developed test that samples behavior under uniform procedures
Teacher-made test	An evaluative instrument developed and scored by a teacher for classroom assessment
Alternate-choice item	A statement to which respondents react either positively or negatively
Multiple-choice item	A test question with a stem that poses a problem or asks a question to be answered by one of several alternative responses
Matching item	An arranged series of premises, each of which is matched with a specific item from a second list of responses
Completing item	A statement with a missing word or phrase, which must be supplied by the respondent
Brief-essay item	A question to which respondents formulate a short-answer response in their own words or solve a problem
Extended-essay item	A question to which respondents formulate responses of several paragraphs in their own words

REVIEW AND REFLECTIVE EXERCISE 10.1   Describe the different types of tests.

REVIEW

- What is a standardized test? How is it developed?
- Why do most classroom teachers use teacher-made tests?
- Name and describe the kinds of teacher-made tests.
- What is a student work sample?

REFLECTION

- What would be the best type of test to use in the area you expect to teach? Why?
- How can student work samples add validity to the evaluation process?

Grading Systems

Assigning grades is a responsibility most teachers dislike and feel uncomfortable doing. There is no way to assign grades that is fair to all students. Most school districts assign grades of A, B, C, D, and F. Regardless of the system used, however, assigning grades to students' work is inherently subjective.

You will be required to make judgments when grades are assigned. How many tests should be given? How many As, Cs, and Fs should be given? Will grading be absolute or on a curve? Will students be allowed to retake exams? Can students use extra-credit assignments to modify grades and to what extent?

Homework is a special consideration. Should it be counted in the grading system? Who should grade homework—students or teachers? The grading of homework by students provides immediate feedback and allows the teacher to decide what materials need to be retaught. On the other hand, when the teacher grades the homework, workloads are increased and feedback to students is delayed. Moreover, there is some question as to whether homework should be counted in the grading system. Some say no. Indeed, it is generally not a good idea for a teacher to assign a grade to work that has been graded by students; instead, only the fact that the work was completed should be recorded.

A distinction must be made between the grades you give to students on tests, quizzes, and classroom activities and the grades you issue for grade cards. As a teacher, you must grade students' examination and quizzes. Basically, these grades can be assigned in one of two ways: an absolute grading system or a relative grading system.

Absolute Grading Standards

Grades may be given relative to performance against an established set of grading criteria. An illustration of an **absolute grading standard** is shown in Table 10.3. In this system, grades are assigned based on the number of items answered correctly. This system, in theory, makes it possible for all students to make high grades. In fact, each student is potentially capable of achieving any grade; that is, no one needs to fail, and all students can make good grades if they put forth the effort. Grading is simple: A student either does get an established percentage of the responses correct or does not. Student scores depend on the difficulty of the test.

There are major limitations associated with an absolute grading standard: (a) The establishment of a standard for each grade is often difficult; (b) the standard established for each grade may vary from time to time, according to the content being taught and with respect to curriculum changes; (c) teaching effectiveness may vary; and (d) the level of examination difficulty may vary. Despite these limitations, however, most teachers use the absolute standard of grading. The major advantage of such a system is that it puts the control of test scores in the hands of students.

Relative Grading Standards

Teachers frequently use a **relative grading standard,** in which they assess student performance with respect to the performance of other students. Accordingly, they often use a curve when assigning grades. In this type of system, students are compared with each other. Of course, the best-known curve is the normal curve (see Chapter 9). When this curve is used, you would expect to give 3.5% As, 23.8% Bs, 45% Cs, 23.8% Ds, and 3.5% Fs. The normal curve, however, is applicable only when the group is large and diversified. Moreover, when the normal curve is used, some students must get As, some students must fail, and most of the students must be given Cs.

TABLE 10.3	Examples of Absolute Standards of Grading		
Percentage Grade	Correct		Percentage Correct
A	90 to 100		85 to 100
B	80 to 89		75 to 84
C	70 to 79	OR	65 to 74
D	60 to 69		55 to 64
F	Less than 60		Less than 55

Because of its lack of flexibility, few teachers use the normal curve. Instead, they implement a relative grading system based on a simple ranking system. In a ranking system, the teacher establishes a fixed percentage for each assigned grade. For example, you might set up the following curve:

A = Top 10%

B = Next 20%

C = Next 40%

D = Next 20%

F = Next 10%

Another common method of grading with curves is the inspection method. When using this method, a frequency distribution of raw scores is set up on a vertical or horizontal line, as shown in Figure 10.1. Grades are then assigned according to natural breaks in the distribution. It is possible that this type of system will not yield A or F grades. For example, if the lowest grade in Figure 10.1 had been 14, few teachers would assign an F grade for this work. As you see, the inspection method yields different grades for different individuals. There is no correct or incorrect division. Figure 10.2 shows three possible inspection grading patterns for grade distribution.

The relative grading standard has a major limitation in that it does not take into account differences in overall ability of students. Thus, some students will always receive As, and some always get Fs.

Assuming one of the previously mentioned methods is used in arriving at grades, the next task you will face as a teacher is to assign 9-week, or term, grades. As you might imagine, this can represent a real challenge.

Assigning Final Grades

Final term grades are generally determined by combining all the results of students' work for a grading period. There are three major ways of accomplishing this end: a point assignment system, a weighted assignment system, and a percentage assignment system.

Point Grading System

A **point grading system** is fairly simple and easy to use. The importance of each assignment, quiz, or test is reflected in the points allocated. For example, you may decide that assignments will be worth 10 points, quizzes 25 points, and tests 100 points. At the end of the grading period, the points are added up, and grades are assigned according to the established grade range. This system is illustrated in Figure 10.3.

Figure 10.1
The Inspection
Method

Figure 10.2
Examples of Inspection Grade Distributions

Distribution 1			Distribution 2			Distribution 3		
100			100			100		A
95			95			95		
94	(1)	A	94	(1)	A	94	(1)	B
91	(1)		91	(1)		91	(1)	
90	(1)		90	(1)		90	(1)	
85		B	85			85		
81	(2)		81	(2)	B	81	(2)	
75			75			75		
74	(4)	C	74	(4)		74	(4)	C
70	(3)		70	(3)		70	(4)	
65			65		C	65		
64	(2)	D	64	(2)		64	(2)	
60	(1)		60	(1)		60	(1)	
55			55			55		
50			50			50		
45			45		D	45		D
44	(1)	F	44	(1)		44	(1)	
43			43			43		
42			42		F	42		F

Figure 10.3
Example of a Point Grading System

Student Work	Points
Assignments	250 (25 × 10 pts.)
Quizzes	150 (6 × 25 pts.)
Tests	300 (3 × 100 pts.)

Total points possible = 700

Grade Range

A 650 to 700

B 600 to 649

C 550 to 599

D 500 to 549

F 499 or less

Weighted Grading System

A **weighted grading system** is more complex than the point grading system. Every assignment is given a letter grade, and all grades are then weighted to arrive at a final grade. An example of this system is illustrated in Figure 10.4.

The determination of a final grade can be made simpler and more objective by changing grades to numerical values: A = 4; B = 3; C = 2; D = 1; F = 0. Once numerical values are assigned, an average

Figure 10.4
Example of a Weighted
Grading System

Student Work	Weight
Homework assignments	25%
Quizzes (6)	25%
Tests (3)	50%
Total	**100%**

score is calculated for homework, quizzes, and tests. For example, you would calculate a homework average for seven homework assignments with the grades of A, B, B, C, C, D, and A by carrying out the following computation:

$$(4 + 3 + 3 + 2 + 2 + 1 + 4)/7 = 19/7 = 2.71.$$

A quiz average for four quizzes graded B, B, C, and D would be computed as follows:

$$(3 + 3 + 2 + 1)/4 = 9/4 = 2.25.$$

Calculation of a test average for three tests with grades of C, C, and D would result in the following computation:

$$(2 + 2 + 1)/3 = 5/3 = 1.67.$$

Applying the weights outlined in Figure 10.4, you would calculate a final grade as follows:

Homework: $2.71 \times 25\% = 2.71 \times .25 = .68$

Quizzes: $2.25 \times 25\% = 2.25 \times .25 = .56$

Tests: $1.67 \times 50\% = 1.67 \times .50 = .84$

Total numerical grade $= 2.08$

Thus, the final grade for the student would be 2.08 or a C. Of course, if other student exercises—such as class projects, term papers, and group projects—were included in a grading period, they would also be part of the grading system and be accounted for in the weights.

Percentage Grading System

The **percentage grading system** is probably the simplest of all grading systems and the most widely used. The system typically relies on the calculation of the percentage correct of the responses attempted. For example, a student who gets 20 of 25 correct on a homework assignment has a score of 80 written in the grade book, 6 of 8 correct on a quiz has a 75 recorded in the grade book, and 40 of 60 correct on an examination has a 67 written in the grade book. You typically calculate an average of these and other term scores in arriving at a final score on which to base the term grade. The problem with this system is that all student exercises carry the same weight, even though the types of exercises are markedly different—homework, quiz, and examination.

Even with the noted flaw, teachers tend to use the percentage system extensively for two reasons. First, it is simple to use and understand. Second, parents and students prefer the system because of its simplicity and their ability to understand it. Before I finish this chapter on test construction and grading with a discussion of contracting for grades, complete Expansion Activity 10.3: Grading, which will help you develop your philosophy on grading.

EXPANSION ACTIVITY 10.3   Grading

Construct a sound approach to grading. What criteria did you establish for making the approach sound? Share it with your class.

APPLY AND REFLECT 10.4	Because teacher-made tests are seldom designed to give a normal distribution, it usually is unwise to give grades based on the normal curve. Do you agree with this statement? What is your rationale for your decision?

Contracting for Grades

Most schools give teachers considerable freedom in establishing grading standards. Some teachers have used this flexibility in implementing a contract approach to grading. With a contract, the teacher promises to award a specific grade for specified performance. Students know exactly what they must do to receive a certain grade; depending on the amount of work they wish to do, they receive a particular grade. For example, a simple contract follows:

To receive a grade of D, you must satisfactorily complete activities 1 through 6, satisfactorily complete half of the homework, and pass the posttest.

To receive a grade of C, you must complete activities 1 through 6, satisfactorily complete 60% of the homework, do one of the optional activities satisfactorily, and receive at least a C on the posttest.

Assigning grades is not an easy task.

To receive a grade of B, you must complete activities 1 through 6, satisfactorily complete 80% of the homework, do two of the optional activities very well, and receive at least a B on the posttest.

To receive a grade of A, you must complete activities 1 through 6, satisfactorily complete 90% of the homework, do four of the optional activities excellently, complete at least one of the major project activities satisfactorily, and receive at least a B+ on the posttest.

Even though this contract outlines the requirements for a D, it is unlikely that students will want to contract for the low grade. It sets the baseline, however, for the activities required for a higher grade.

When you establish a contract system, you must develop sets of objectives that correspond to specific letter grades. You then decide the activities and assignments that will be required at each level. These objectives, corresponding letter grades, and requirements are shared with students in writing, so students can study them and make decisions on a contract grade.

Some teachers like to write a more detailed contract, which is signed by both student and teacher. A detailed sample contract is illustrated in Chapter 12, Figure 12.2.

REFLECTIONS ON TEACHER PRACTICE 10.2   Giving Marks

1. What do grades really mean to students? How can you better use grades?

2. What forms of grading are better than commonly used letter grades?

◆ ◆ ◆

Grades can be good motivators. I taught grades nine to twelve at a vocational secondary school. As a special education teacher with a specialist in behaviour, I was assigned to help students who got kicked out of their regular classes and were timetabled to work with me to help rescue their credits. I found that I had the best results when I would get students to contract for a mark that they wanted. I had students sign a very formal looking contract printed on special paper with all the expectations outlined in detail. For an A, I will complete . . . , For a B, I will complete . . . etc. I found students responded very well— remember all things are relative—they didn't tell me to "kiss" off when I introduced the contract. I told them they didn't need to worry about getting anything more than a D, (this took them by surprise) although their final mark could be an A, B, C or D. They couldn't contract for less than a D. Failure was not an option. I know we're supposed to aim high, but high for these kids was a pass.

I had it set up so that for a D, the student would have to meet the minimum expectations for that course. The expectations

rose as did the mark. Not surprisingly, most students would contract for the minimum D. But as they became more successful, they would ask to renegotiate the contract for a higher final mark. My department head at that time told me to create assignments that were totally different from those in the regular classroom. He said it was important that the assignments be different so that the students wouldn't be reminded of their failure in the regular classroom. I remember one assignment that I created for a student that had him plan a trip to Florida over March break with his friends. He had to determine the cost of the trip and show the route they would take. It was a good basic math exercise because he had to determine the cost of going from Oakville, Ontario to Fort Lauderdale. He had to determine the cost of getting there by car or plane, the cost of his over night stays, the cost of his food, entertainment etc. He also had to find out the average temperature and rain fall at his destination and plan an appropriate wardrobe to take along. I can still see him sitting at a table with his tough macho exterior colouring a map and highlighting his route while telling me he and his friends would sleep in the car or on the beach so they could save money for lots of beer and still stay within his budget.

Working with those students was a real eye opener. Remember that was early in my career. Now after all these years and after teaching young offenders in open and closed custody

facilities, my eyes are wide open. Nothing, absolutely nothing surprises or shocks me anymore.

—At-risk teacher, secondary

SOURCE: http://www.teachersatrisk.com/category/evaluation. Reprinted with permission.

Recordkeeping

Recordkeeping is often a burden for teachers and is time-consuming. It also requires a great deal of accuracy. Fortunately, the recordkeeping burden can be reduced by computer technology. For example, electronic grade books can keep track of students' assessment data and other classroom information. Most electronic grade books available today can store many types of student information, including test scores, homework grades, project grades, semester averages, teacher judgments, and attendance. Some programs can also handle missing assignments, automatically e-mail parents, and function to keep records of students and parent information such as mailing addresses, phone numbers, locker numbers, book numbers, and other details. Many programs allow each component of the assessment system to be weighted, and the program will then compute the students' 6- or 9-week grades and semester grades based on the formula you create. Some school districts give parents and/or students the opportunity to connect with the school computer, enter a personal identification number and a password, and access the student's grades and teacher assignments and comments.

School attendance is one of the most important school records and must be accurate. Class roll must be taken daily or every period of the day, and all absences and cases of tardiness recorded. These records are used for various purposes, including computing average daily attendance for state funding. Attendance is also sometimes used in court cases to verify a student's presence in school. Complete Web Link 10.2: Electronic Grade Books, which will give you the opportunity to compare a few available electronic grade books.

WEB LINK 10.2 Electronic Grade Books

Sample electronic grade books can be found at http://www.techlearning.com/story/showArticle .php?articleID=15202081 and http://www.electronic-school.com/2001/03/0301poweruser.html. Compare the different grade books and identify the one that you would like to use. Discuss your selection rationale with classmates.

Reporting Student Progress

Most school districts issue report cards four or six times per year, that is, every 6 or 9 weeks. Report card grades are most often derived from some combination of the following:

- Scores on tests
- Scores on homework
- Scores on papers and projects
- Scores on seatwork
- Class participation (academic behavior, classroom involvement, and so on)
- Classroom behavior and attitude

The form of grade cards and the judgment on report cards varies from one school district to another and, in many cases, from one grade level to another. Some report cards convey letter grades (typically A, B, C, D, and F, sometimes also allowing pluses or minuses). Some report cards convey numeral scores (such as 91 in English, 85 in math, and so on). Other report cards have a pass/fail category in one or more subjects. Yet other report cards have checklists indicating skills or outcomes the student has attained. Some report cards have categories for affective characteristics, such as effort, cooperation, attitude, and other appropriate and inappropriate behaviors. Many also have space for a teacher's written comments. Checklists of skills and outcomes are mainly used in lower elementary school grades. In the higher elementary school grade levels and secondary schools, letter grades are mainly used.

Some school districts provide parents with a weekly, biweekly, monthly, or midterm report of the student's progress. These written reports can include the students' performance on tests and quizzes, homework, projects, oral reports, and so on. They can also include information about the students' motivation, behavior, and cooperation, as well as suggestions for how parents can help students. Complete Web Link 10.3: Report Cards, which will give you the opportunity to review various grade cards.

WEB LINK 10.3   Grade Cards

Sample report cards can be found at

http://intranet.cps.k12.il.us/Standards/Student_Report_Cards/2002_Report_Card_Sample.pdf,

http://www.rediker.com/Reports/Samples/ReportCards/RC-graphics-12.html,

http://www.aaps.k12.mi.us/aaps.forparents/k–5_sample_report_cards,

http://www.rediker.com/Reports/Samples/Reportcards/RC-Tri-Valley.html, and

http://www.pacificasd.org/curriculum/reportCard.htm. Review the various report card options. Would you be comfortable using these forms? Share your thoughts with your classmates.

This section has described grading systems and the assigning of grades. But, as noted earlier, grading is a very subjective undertaking. It should be carried out with care and planning. Review Table 10.4 and complete Review and Reflective Exercise 10.2.

APPLY AND REFLECT 10.5	You should make grading procedures explicit. They should be written down and communicated clearly to students early in the year. What procedure and system do you feel best fits the grade level you expect to teach?

TABLE 10.4   Assigning Grades

System	Description
Absolute grading standard	Performance compared with established set of criteria
Relative grading standard	Students' performance compared with that of classmates, including grading on the curve
Point grading system	Student work is allocated points, and grades are assigned according to established grade range
Weighted grading system	Assignments are given a letter grade, and all grades are weighted to determine final grade
Percentage grading system	Percentage correct is recorded for each assignment, and an average is calculated to determine final grade
Grade contract	Written agreement between student and teacher as to what students will do to earn a specific grade

REVIEW AND REFLECTIVE EXERCISE 10.2 Outline techniques for assigning grades.

REVIEW

- What is the purpose of assigning grades?
- Describe the two basic grading systems.
- How are grades usually recorded and reported?

REFLECTION

- Reflect on how the teachers you had over the years assigned grades. Were the systems fair? How would you have changed them?
- How do you plan to assign grades in the area you expect to teach?
- Do you feel comfortable assigning grades?
- How do you plan to record grades?

SUMMARY

Testing and grading represent two important, but unpopular, challenges for teachers.

Types of Tests

- Teachers generally use either standardized tests or teacher-made tests in the classroom. Standardized tests are tests prepared and published by assessment specialists, whereas teacher-made tests are developed by teachers to address specific classroom situations. Standardized tests are used for providing some indication of how individual students and classrooms compare with local, regional, or national averages. Teacher-made tests are used for gathering information and making judgments regarding the achievement of students.

- Widely used teacher-made test formats include alternative-choice tests, multiple-choice tests, matching tests, completion tests, essay (brief and extended) tests, and combinations of these.

Grading Systems

- The absolute grading system and relative grading system are the two principal grading systems commonly used in schools. An absolute standard compares student performance against an established set of criteria, whereas the relative standard compares students with one another.

- Three systems are available to teachers for assigning grades: the point system, the weighted system, and the percentage system.

- Teacher contracts can be used effectively in the grading process. With contract grading, the teacher outlines exactly what students must do to earn specific grades.

- Recordkeeping can be a burden; however, the recordkeeping burden can be reduced through the use of computer technology.

- The form of grade cards and the judgment on report cards varies from one school district to another and often from one grade level to another.

DISCUSSION QUESTIONS AND ACTIVITIES

1. **Standardized tests.** Describe three important characteristics of commonly used standardized tests. Briefly describe at least three standardized tests for a subject area.

2. **Test items.** Make up several examples of alternate-choice, multiple-choice, matching, completion, and essay test items. Ask your class to critique them. Discuss which types of items were most difficult to construct and the least difficult to construct.

3. **Grading systems**. Compare the major advantages and disadvantages associated with absolute and relative grading standards. Do you prefer one system over the other? Defend your choice.

4. **Grading objectivity.** Can a teacher be objective in assigning grades? Explain.

5. **Grading procedures.** Outline a grading procedure you expect to follow and use as a teacher.

TECHNOLOGY AND EDUCATION

Most teachers in today's schools use a wide array of technology and related software programs designed to help record student performance and grades, help generate and score tests, and assist with authentic and performance assessment. Use one or more of the available search engines and conduct a search for software programs relative to the following teacher tools.

1. Electronic Grade Books
2. Test Generators
3. Rubric Generators

Review and analyze the available teacher tools located. Select two or three that you think are best and write a short description of each. Share your descriptions with your instructor and classmates.

DECONSTRUCTING THE STANDARDS

Chapter 10 content addresses topics related to INTASC Standards 8 and 9.

♦ INTASC Standard 8 states: *Assessment of Student Learning:* The teacher understands and uses formal and informal assessment strategies to evaluate and ensure the continuous intellectual, social, and physical development of the learner.
♦ INTASC Standard 9 states: *Professional Commitment and Responsibility:* The teacher is a reflective practitioner who continually evaluates the effects of his or her choices and actions on others (students, parents, and other professionals in the learning community) and who actively seeks out opportunities to grow professionally.

For each of these two standards, write your response to the following:

- Which part(s) of each standard does this chapter address?
- How does this chapter address this standard?
- How will the concepts in this chapter help you apply this standard as a teacher?

PRAXIS CONNECTION

Log on to the Web-based student study site at http://www.sagepub.com/eis2study. Access the Praxis II: Principles of Learning and Teaching assessments and/or state-related exams and complete the Chapter 10 test preparation exercises.

PORTFOLIO CONNECTION

Log on to the Web-based student study site at http://www.sagepub.com/eis2study. Access the Portfolio Connection. Complete the Chapter 10 portfolio link to INTASC activities.

1. **Teacher interviews.** Interview several classroom teachers about their tests and homework. How do the teachers deal with the following issues?
   a. Test construction
   b. Test and homework scoring and grade assignment
   c. Test and homework makeup for absences
   d. Homework for extra credit
   e. Late or missing homework
   f. Recording grades
   g. Reporting student progress

2. **Test construction.** Examine a standardized test and then visit with several classroom teachers relative to their tests. Compare the tests in terms of construction, clarity, and readability. Are there major weaknesses in either test?

LEADING THE DYNAMIC CLASSROOM

O nce lessons have been planned, they must be implemented. Even the best-laid plans, however, can fail in the classroom. A successful teacher is one who can ably communicate, motivate, diagnose, and manage a classroom. Therefore teachers must be aware of the influences that the communication process, motivation, and management skills have on the success of a lesson. Part V focuses on these implementation issues.

Without communication and motivation, there would be no teaching or learning. Chapter 11 deals with the important process of communication. Various verbal and nonverbal techniques are addressed, as well as the often overlooked skill of listening.

Chapter 12 focuses on motivation. Learning will take place only when there is a desire to know, to understand, to learn. Thus, teachers must develop students' desire for learning. They must motivate!

Skillful classroom management is indispensable to a career in the classroom. The establishment of an environment conducive to learning will not be an easy task. If you are to do well, you must have a repertoire of management techniques from which to choose. Chapter 13 outlines several approaches to classroom management. In addition, Chapter 13 looks at leadership and the classroom atmosphere and their effect on behavior.

CHAPTER 11

Communicating With Students and Parents

I have often regretted my speech, never my silence.

—Xenocrates

OVERVIEW

Communication is essential in helping students learn. As a teacher, you must be sensitive to cultivating excellent communication skills and to monitoring the effectiveness of your interactions with students and parents.

Unfortunately, teachers often do most of the talking in classrooms, and students do most of the listening. Perhaps because of this, teachers tend to not really listen to what students are saying or not saying.

Experienced teachers know the importance of open communication and positive dialogue with parents. They make it a point to open channels of communication with parents at the beginning of the school year.

This chapter is about communication. As such, it will address both the sending and receiving of information and messages.

OBJECTIVES

After completing your study of Chapter 11, you should be able to do the following:

- Explain the importance of the communication process.
- Differentiate among the verbal, vocal, and metaverbal components of a message.
- Identify variables associated with the verbal and vocal components of a message.
- Explain the role nonverbal communication plays in the classroom and provide examples of various nonverbal behaviors commonly used in the classroom.
- Identify and explain the four spatial distances.
- Explain how color communicates.
- Explain the importance of listening and define the different types of listening.
- Identify and describe variables that interfere with listening.
- Explain the importance of feedback in the communication process.

Of all the knowledge and skills you possess as a teacher, those concerning communication will be among the most significant and the most useful. Through communication, you interact with students and parents, you teach, and students learn. Without communication, teaching could not occur and a school would not function.

As a practical skill, communication consists of the ability to speak, write, and read. Of equal importance in the communication process, however, is the ability to listen. Most teacher preparatory programs place a great deal of emphasis on the ability to read and write, with little attention put on speaking and almost no attention being given to nonverbal communication and listening. The most persuasive teachers do not rely exclusively on reading and writing; they talk, they observe, and they listen. Thus, the skills I will examine here are verbal and nonverbal communication, as well as the art of listening, which serves an important function in the classroom.

REFLECTIONS ON TEACHER PRACTICE 11.1　Working With Parents

1. What benefit would be gained from extending the school year and student time in school?

2. How are parents unrealistic about the function of schools and what schools can accomplish?

◆　◆　◆

As an educator, I am familiar with the old "boredom" tale from parents. I listen politely without comment. Then I ask them nicely what I can do to make my class more interesting for their child. Usually, they don't have an answer. The real problem is that in this age of instant results, many parents today expect their child's entire education to occur within the 6-hour school day. And they expect it to be individually tailored to their child. Whereas teachers should consider individual needs, it is unrealistic to individualize instruction for all students. I think many parents and educators have lost sight of the original intent of public education in the United States. Public education was set up to provide students with a foundation of skills and opportunities for education. It was assumed that truly interested students would continue learning at home. Now, with most parents working to make ends meet, I believe they have an absolute right to expect more from their child's school. But because most kids are only in school for about 1,200 hours per year, it is unrealistic to expect schools to work miracles. So much has changed in society, but our country's educational system has not yet caught up.

Perhaps we need to restructure our country's educational system to better address the needs of today's parents, who, just trying to survive, are often spread too thin to educate their children at home. If individualized instruction is what we need to have, then perhaps all students should be designated for "special education," with smaller classes of students working toward individual goals. After all, every student has his or her own special needs. As our system works now, only certain "identified" students are having their "special" needs met. Is that really fair?

Perhaps students should be in school for more hours. I feel like I have so much to "cover" for standardized tests that my students don't get the opportunity to practice newly learned skills as much as research says they need to. Of course, changes in our educational system will not happen until teachers are seen (and ultimately paid) as the highly specialized professionals that we are.

—*MARY, elementary school teacher*

SOURCE: Reprinted with permission from ProTeacher, a professional community for elementary school teachers (http://www.proteacher.net).

ON YOUR OWN 11.1　Reflections on Teacher Practice

Read and reflect on the viewpoints expressed in Working With Parents. Log on to the Web-based student study site at http://www.sagepub.com/eis2study and react to the related activities.

For material related to this concept, go to Clip 11.1 on the Student Resource CD bound into the back of your textbook.

Classroom Communication

Communication is the act, by one or more persons, of sending and receiving messages that are distorted by noise, have some effect, and provide some opportunity for feedback. Messages may be sent and received in many forms: verbal, vocal, physical, or situational. Thus, you must be skilled at sending messages through any one or combinations of these modes. But of equal importance is your ability to decode messages (feedback) transmitted by students. This ability is directly related to your listening skill. Before I address listening, let's look at verbal and nonverbal communication.

Cell phones in the classroom can be a problem. Many schools do not allow cell phones in school.

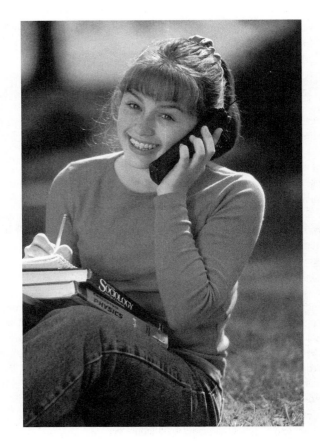

Verbal Communication

Teachers communicate information to students by talking, that is, through **verbal communication.** Learning, however, does not take place only through teacher talk and words. Nonverbal variables sometimes determine whether something is learned.

Goodall (1983, pp. 14–15) breaks spoken messages into three components: verbal, vocal, and metaverbal. The **verbal component** refers to the actual words spoken and their meanings; the **vocal component** includes such variables as voice firmness, modulation, tone, tempo, pitch, and loudness; and the **metaverbal component** refers to what may be implied, or intended, by the spoken words.

The Verbal Component

Words can be interpreted in many ways, and these interpretations can be the basis for misunderstandings. Indeed, the message communicated in any interaction depends on both the words and the meanings attached to the words spoken. These meanings are learned as a result of experiences and, thus, are arbitrary. For example, a class discussion of terms such as *ghost, fear, feminism, religion,* or *democracy* will have varying outcomes, depending on students' experiences. Despite the formal dictionary definitions of such terms, you must make sure that your verbal instructions are related as much as possible to the learners' experiences. This determination calls for your assessment of what students bring to the learning situation—for example, intelligence, learning history, and learning ability. This information may show that the verbal aspects of your messages are outside the experience base of your students. (A word of caution: Don't let your assessment of students influence your expectations of their ability. Students tend to behave in a way congruent with how they are viewed.)

Another problem associated with the use of words is their misuse, which may stem from a lack of knowledge of their meanings. Indeed, it is often possible to talk endlessly about a subject and sound quite knowledgeable when, in fact, you haven't the slightest idea of the word meanings. These bluffing behaviors with words should be avoided in the classroom. Students will usually see through the lack of knowledge, and you will lose their respect.

Hurt, Scott, and McCroskey (1978, p. 76) suggest several other variables that may have some effect on whether a message is received and decoded accurately:

1. *Organization.* Good or well-organized verbal information tends to be learned more thoroughly, as does the information presented first or last in a lesson.

2. *Message sidedness.* Two-sided messages that present opposing views tend to be learned best.

3. *Language intensity.* Verbal information that deviates from a neutral position appears to be learned best.

4. *Concreteness and ambiguity.* The more concrete a message, the better. You must take care, however, that your message isn't made so concrete that the basic concept is lost.

Generally, variables such as those discussed earlier and those suggested by Hurt et al. (1978) tend to increase students' attention, which is your primary aim in the classroom. The increased attention should result in increased learning. Join some classmates to react to Expansion Activity 11.1: Talking to further explore teacher talk in the classroom.

EXPANSION ACTIVITY 11.1   Talking

Talk "with" people, not "to" people.

What does this statement imply? Should you talk "with" or "to" students? Form groups of four or five and react to the statement above. Share your group's reaction with the class.

The Vocal Component

How you say words is extremely important. The voice brings words to life. Changes in tone, voice loudness or strength, rate, inflection, or pitch can change a message emphasis, as well as its very meaning. For example, messages such as "I agree!" or "Yes!" can communicate different meanings, depending on the tone and modulation.

As a teacher, you will interact with groups and will often want to emphasize points with your voice. Therefore, it is essential that you develop and project a strong voice, so that you are heard by all students. This will take practice but is well worth the effort. Often, the practice of talking over a little distance or the practice of inhaling and exhaling air will improve both the strength and projection of your voice.

The rate at which you speak will affect students as well. When you speak rapidly, you might convey the message that the subject isn't really important and should be finished with as soon as possible. In contrast, words spoken at a slower rate can indicate their importance and, therefore, indicate that they should be considered carefully. This fact is important to remember because you might be required to teach subjects that interest you little or to teach in areas in which you lack preparation. With such subjects, you must carefully watch your rate of presentation.

The tone, inflections, and pitch of the voice often affect words. Tone or inflection can communicate word seriousness or validity. For example, the seriousness of such messages as "I mean it!" or "Be quiet!" or even "I am losing my patience!" is affected by your tone and inflection. Moreover, as Hennings (1975) points out, "The high-pitched voice can grate on a decoder's nerves so that the listener turns off to words spoken; the very deep voice can distract from the message" (p. 17). Therefore, you must guard against using an incorrect tone, inflection, or pitch, which might distract from your messages.

Voice volume, rate, tone, inflection, and pitch send emotional information. High levels of loudness, rate, and pitch can communicate excitement or enthusiasm, whereas a slow rate and even pitch can communicate disinterest. Joy, eagerness, anger, wonder, awe, displeasure, determination, and indecisiveness can be communicated through variations in the voice. Skill at using your voice can assist you greatly in keeping students on task and with the general management of the classroom environment. Therefore, practice with your voice; it will continue to serve you in your instruction if you know how to use it effectively.

You must be aware of the effect that a monotone voice can have on students. It can put them to sleep, cause their minds to wander, and, in general, result in a loss of student attention. Diversity in the voice can overcome these negative effects to some extent. Indeed, you can be a more effective teacher and keep students' attention by varying your voice volume, rate, tone, inflection, and pitch.

Classroom communication is a multichannel process. When you communicate with students, all the expressive cues (verbal and nonverbal) converge to communicate one message, positive or negative. Sometimes, however, what is said is not what students are expected to understand.

The Metaverbal Component

When you speak, there is often an implied, or intended, message that cannot be directly attributed to the meaning of the words or the way they are spoken. This is referred to as the metaverbal component of a message. You may, for example, ask a student to drop by after school for a visit about an issue brought up in class, when actually you want to discuss the student's falling grades.

Metaverbal messages are often tricky because you are trying to communicate an implied message. That is, students are being asked to hear beyond the words. Sometimes what you mean to imply when you speak is not how your words and actions are interpreted.

As you teach or listen, all basic components of verbal communication contribute to the messages received by students. Thus, students are hearing what you say at three levels: what is said, how it is said, and why (implied) it is said. Therefore, exercise care in the act of communicating and match your intent with your message.

APPLY AND REFLECT 11.1	More communication is not always best; some things are best left unsaid. What is implied in this statement? Discuss your interpretation with that of your classmates.

Technology can have an impact on a teacher's ability to communicate. Complete Expansion Activity 11.2: Communicating With Technology, which will let you explore this issue.

Nonverbal Communication

Communication can be nonlinguistic. That is, you can send messages without using words. This form of communication is referred to as **nonverbal communication.** Because some researchers in the area of communication claim that more than 80% of our communication is nonverbal in nature, it is important that teachers be proficient with its use (P. W. Miller, 1986; Sathre, Olson, & Whitney, 1977).

You constantly send messages through the way you dress; your posture; the way you look, move, work your voice, and use space; and the way you use words. These nonverbal messages can reinforce, modify, or even contradict your verbal messages, as, for example, when you say with a sigh of relief, "I wish you could stay longer." In fact, the nonverbal part of communication often is more important than the verbal part, in that it expresses real feelings. Sometimes nonverbal information plays a role in determining what our reaction will be in certain situations or in deciding what our future behavior will be. For example, when a friend says, "I'd like to get together again soon," that person may state it in such a way that you suspect otherwise. Thus, actions often do speak much louder than words.

For material related to this concept, go to Clip 11.2 on the Student Resource CD bound into the back of your textbook.

Teacher gestures and movement can improve the communication of classroom concepts.

Sometimes nonverbal communication is designed very carefully for evoking a particular response, whereas at other times it occurs naturally or accidentally. In either case, it can influence perceptions, attitudes, and feelings. These nonverbal cues are often not taken at face value; rather, inferences are made from them in determining what to believe. Thus, teachers and students often unwittingly reveal attitudes and feelings toward each other and toward school in general through nonverbal cues. In other words, you must be alert to your nonverbal expressions and the effects they can have on students. An awareness of nonverbal communications and their consequences is a step toward controlling them. I will now look at some elements of nonverbal communications.

EXPANSION ACTIVITY 11.2   Communicating With Technology

Technology is having a tremendous impact on education and our schools. How can e-mail and technology be used to improve communication within a school? With parents? With students?

"First, you have to get their attention."

Facial Language

The face and eyes are probably the most conspicuous parts of our body, and, as such, we communicate a great deal of information through our facial expressions. In fact, according to P. W. Miller (1986), the face is second only to words in communicating our feelings. Miller further suggests that these facial expressions can be readily visible or fleeting, involuntary or voluntary. Whatever the type, facial expressions can reinforce, modify, and contradict what is said verbally.

Facial expressions that are readily visible are usually intentional. They send a message (e.g., a smile of pleasure) or are used to mask true feelings (e.g., a stern look of displeasure to cover pleasure). These expressions are formed by the movement of facial muscles around the forehead, mouth, eyebrows, chin, cheeks, or nose. Wrinkling the forehead, for example, communicates deep thought, lifting the eyebrows reveals wonder or surprise, a sneer shows anger or displeasure, and a jutting chin demonstrates firmness. Conversely, fleeting facial expressions are often unintentional and are usually quickly covered up with other expressions. For example, you may feel sudden disgust, anger, or dislike for someone you meet but do not want to communicate this to the individual. Therefore, you quickly mask your true feelings or emotions with other, intended expressions.

Involuntary facial expressions usually take place under traumatic or delightful circumstances. Such microexpressions can flash across your face in situations where you are fearful, angry, happy, or surprised. In the classroom, these expressions are often fleeting in that you attempt to cover them up with other expressions as soon as possible. Under certain circumstances, however, you may want to retain such expressions to convey a message to students. For example, teachers often use expressions of displeasure or anger for controlling misbehavior in the classroom and expressions of humor for relieving tension or improving student attention.

Teachers commonly use voluntary facial expressions when communicating with students. In fact, effective teachers have perfected their facial expression. They convey a message with a look—for example, a smile of approval or a frown of displeasure (Ostermeier, 1994).

The eyes can send several kinds of messages. As P. W. Miller (1986) notes, your eyes "can be shifty and evasive, conveying hate, fear, and guilt, or they can express confidence, love, and support" (p. 13).

Also, with eye contact, you can open communication, prolong communication, or cut off communication entirely.

As most teachers know, eye contact can be used in controlling interaction in the classroom. When they want a student to speak, they make direct eye contact with that individual. Conversely, when they want to continue talking, they refrain from making direct eye contact with anyone who may want to speak. Moreover, most of us can remember trying to avoid a question we couldn't answer by glancing away from the teacher. At such times, we became very interested in our textbook or our assignment. Thus, teachers sometimes gauge eye contact in determining when students are lying, when students can't answer a question, or when students have failed to complete their homework. Indeed, you probably have heard it said that, when students are lying or when they haven't done as they should, they avoid direct eye contact. This hypothesis, however, generally hasn't been supported by research. In fact, watch your use of such unproven generalizations, for they may influence you inappropriately. For example, you may tend to distrust students who do not make direct eye contact when speaking to you. But a shy student who does not like or finds it difficult to make direct eye contact may be completely trustworthy.

Very direct eye contact—a stare—can change student behavior. A stare used with silence can be quite effective in gaining the attention of misbehaving or inattentive students. Indeed, the stare alone can result in appropriate student behavior.

Body Language

Kinesics, or the study of body movements and gestures in communication, represents an important source of information. Indeed, gestures with the head, arms, hands, and other body parts are pervasive as nonverbal communicators. Gestures may provide information, as when you point when giving directions; they may communicate feelings, as when you nod your head in agreement as a student speaks; they may emphasize a point, as when you tap something you have written on the chalkboard; they may call for attention, as when you stomp your foot. Indeed, we often interpret an individual's body movements as an indication of his or her character (as in an authoritative or nonchalant walk). Our physical actions, then, are sending information constantly to those who are observant and attentive.

The overuse of body movement and gestures can be a deterrent to effective communication. When you use too many gestures too often, students find it difficult to discern the peaks and cannot really tell what is important in a message. Also, too many gestures can prompt students to attend to the gestures themselves rather than to the message.

Stance and general posture are another type of kinesics communication. A tense, rigid body tends to communicate the desire for distance and insecurity, whereas a relaxed body denotes strength, openness, and friendliness. The way you stand can also communicate information. A body orientation toward the listener tends to suggest security and comfort in the communication interaction.

The use of touch is a very powerful nonverbal communicator. Touch in communication is influenced by who does the touching. Teachers of young children, for example, often use hugs as reinforcement, whereas touch is often inappropriate for use with middle and secondary school students.

Although it is usually unwise for you to touch a student of the opposite sex, remember that an appropriate pat on the back is a good reinforcer for students (Mehrabian, 1968; Ostermeier, 1994). You should use your best judgment as to whether or when to use touch in communicating with your students.

The way you dress sends a variety of messages. It is often difficult to take a speaker seriously, for example, if he or she is dressed in ill-fitting, wrinkled clothing. Conversely, we tend to pay attention to an attractively dressed speaker. Teachers, then, would be well advised to dress as befitting their roles as classroom leaders.

The Language of Space and Motion

The arrangement of your classroom and your use of the space can shape communication. How you place objects within your classroom, as well as where and how you choose to move within the confines of the space, is significant.

The Environment

The physical makeup of the learning environment can create moods and, in doing so, affect the interaction within the environment. Indeed, the attractiveness of a room appears to influence the happiness and energy of people working in it. Such findings are supported by P. W. Miller (1986) in his summary of research related to student reactions in ugly and beautiful classrooms. He states that "subjects in the ugly room had reactions of monotony, fatigue, headache, irritability, and hostility, while subjects in the beautiful room responded favorably with feelings of comfort, pleasure, importance, and enjoyment for completing the assigned tasks" (p. 23). Thus, Miller's findings suggest that a well-decorated, pleasing classroom is more conducive to open communications and is more effective at keeping students on task.

Colors can affect the behavior of students. For example, it has been shown that blue is more soothing and red more active than other colors (Snider & Osgood, 1969). Perhaps color can be used in influencing actions within the classroom. It may be that a combination of such colors as blue and red will result in more productive communication patterns.

Territoriality

Territoriality is commonly observed in the classroom. Indeed, learning environments are too often arranged into territories, with the teacher's desk forming the teacher's territory and each student's seat or desk forming the individual student's territory. Such arrangements can lead to the understanding that each is to remain in his or her own territory. This, too, often leads to a restricted environment, with little interaction. Also, such restricted environments can convey messages of teachers wanting to keep their distance from students.

Territoriality can also be observed in classrooms or other areas where seats are not assigned. For example, when a student takes the seat normally occupied by another student, the regular occupant often becomes disturbed and resentful. Likewise, in a library, you may mark your territory with a jacket or books when you leave the room.

Teacher Motion

Teacher movement within the classroom can aid or hinder the communication process. Movement toward a student who is speaking can, for example, convey a message of interest, whereas movement away from the student can communicate lack of interest. A teacher's movement, then, can often prolong interaction. Indeed, teacher movement throughout different areas in the classroom often helps keep student attention directed toward the teacher (see Chapter 12 for a more detailed discussion of this topic).

Proxemics

Proxemics is the study of the use and meaning of space. Studies (Hall, 1959; Montagu, 1977) indicate that people engaged in interaction tend to choose a particular separation distance, depending on their feeling toward the other person or persons at the time, the context of the conversation, and their personal goals. For example, conversations between intimate people usually take place within 18 inches (intimate distance). Friends in conversation usually stand 3 to 4½ feet apart (personal distance). Business and social interactions usually take place with a separation of 4 to 7 feet (social distance). For most presentations, a distance of 15 feet or more is most common (public distance).

Even though the generalizations about "appropriate" interaction distances are tentative, you should recognize the value of the use of space in your interactions with students. In general, teachers want to work within the personal and social distance ranges in their interactions with students. Interactions with individual students should take place at a personal distance, whereas whole-class interactions usually occur at the social distance.

The Language of Time

Time and its subtleties can be wisely used for successful communication. How you decide to spend class time conveys important attitudinal information. When you spend little time on a topic, or pass it by completely, you communicate that the topic is unimportant or that you have little interest in it. Such actions can unintentionally translate into similar attitudes by students.

Pauses and silence represent another way that time can be used in communicating. For example, pausing just before or after you make a point signifies that the point is important. In addition, pauses can cue students that an important point is going to be made or that the last point made was important enough for them to reflect on it.

Time can also be used to communicate a variety of emotional responses. Silence, for example, can reflect fear, a determination to be uncooperative, or an attempt at defiance. And, of course, silence is often used for showing lack of interest. In fact, your discussions will often result in silence when your topic lacks interest or when you fail to motivate.

Teachers ask many questions; however, they may find it difficult to allow for sufficient time between the asking of their questions and the reception of a student response. Teachers often expect almost instant responses to their questions, and, when not forthcoming, they tend to answer the questions themselves. These teachers must learn to increase their wait time so they can improve classroom interaction (see Chapter 5 for a detailed discussion of wait time).

Finally, reverence for silence and the sense of time vary with different cultures, subcultures, and regions (Berger, 1991; Gilliland, 1988). The Apache, for example, encourage silence. For some African cultures, time is only approximate. The Midwest has a reputation for punctuality. In New York, people are on the go, and time is money; however, punctuality is perhaps not as revered as in the Midwest. Indeed, lateness can be "fashionable" for social gatherings. On the notoriously laidback West Coast, on the other hand, being late is not a serious problem. Teachers then should take a close look at their students' concept of time before they react to situations that involve time. Perhaps their students are running on different clocks.

The Language of the Voice

As mentioned earlier in this chapter, the vocal cues that accompany our spoken language exert a great deal of influence on a listener's perception. Indeed, vocal intonation can reveal prejudices, emotions, and background information about a speaker; it can communicate excitement, fear, or some other strong emotions. These perceptions are generally based on experiences and stereotypes associated with various vocal qualities, intonations, characteristics, and so on.

The adage is often true: "It's not what you say. It's how you say it." A vibrant "That's an excellent idea!" conveys a different message than does a simple monotone "That's an excellent idea." As noted earlier, when a contradiction occurs between a verbal and vocal message, the vocal message is usually believed.

As a teacher, you must watch your vocal messages. Your vocal intonations sometimes will communicate meanings different from those you intend. Your messages can be modified by varying the loudness or softness, by using high pitch or low pitch, and by varying the tone or the quality of speech. You must be aware of and pay attention to the effect of these voice intonations. That is, you must learn to speak so your verbal and vocal messages are congruent.

This concludes the discussion of verbal and nonverbal communication. Table 11.1 summarizes the material presented in this section. Before moving on to communicating with parents, review the summary and complete Review and Reflective Exercise 11.1.

APPLY AND REFLECT 11.2   Make sure your verbal and nonverbal messages are congruent when you interact with students. What habits do you have that might negatively affect this ability?

TABLE 11.1   Communication Process

Type	Description
Verbal communication	Communication with the spoken word through verbal, vocal, or metaverbal components
Nonverbal communication	Nonlinguistic communication, or the sending of messages without words

REVIEW AND REFLECTIVE EXERCISE 11.1   Identify good approaches to communication.

REVIEW

- What are some barriers to effective communication?
- What are some important aspects of nonverbal communication?

REFLECTION

- What are your own communication strengths and weaknesses? What might you do to improve them? How does your ability to speak affect your view of the world?

Communicating With Parents

Veteran teachers stress the importance of communicating with parents and families, but good communication between you and parents will not just happen. It requires work and special skills such as good listening techniques, tact, kindness, consideration, empathy, enthusiasm, and an understanding of parent-child relationships.

You should not wait for parent-teacher conferences to begin communicating with parents. Effective teachers start communicating with parents at the beginning of the school year. This will be a major investment of time, but one that will pay off in the long run. Send a letter of introduction to parents (see Figure 11.1). It doesn't need to be personal, just an overview of what you think the semester or year will look like, an introduction of yourself, and a general invitation to the parents to be involved in your classroom. Make sure to include how parents can best get in contact with you and encourage them to feel free to do so. If you can find out from the students (this is something you should include on their information sheets) what their parents' last names are, it is nice to use a computer to put "Dear Ms. Alvarez" at the top instead of "Dear Parent or Guardian." It is also a good idea to send these letters through the mail rather than via the black holes of students' backpacks and lockers. Complete Expansion Activity 11.3: Introductory Letter to Parents, which will give you the opportunity to draft an introductory letter to the parents of your future students.

EXPANSION ACTIVITY 11.3   Introductory Letter to Parents

Prepare an introductory letter that you might send to parents at the start of the school year. Share it with your instructor and classmates.

Figure 11.1
Sample Letter to
Parents

Jones Elementary School
2004 Elementary School Road
Wichita, KS

September 5, 2004

John and Mary Miller
5555 Springdale Drive
Wichita, KS

Dear Mr. and Mrs. Miller:

I am Larry's new [fourth grade] teacher. I am excited about this year and look forward to working with you to accomplish your child's academic needs. I will use several methods to give feedback to you and your child about his progress. Please note that I use the following:

1. quarterly grade reports will give your child's progress to date

2. graded homework assignments weekly

3. graded quizzes and tests

4. our [fourth grade] Internet school site

I hope you will ask Larry about his homework and weekly grades. Please have him share his work with you. I do schedule parent conferences as needed. If you wish to schedule an appointment with me, please call 471-1234. I am available before and immediately after school. Those hours are 7:30 a.m. to 8:00 a.m. and 3:00 p.m. to 4:00 p.m.

So you will be able to talk with your child about his work this first 9 weeks, the objectives we will cover include

●

●

●

I look forward to meeting you at the open house on September 11 at 7:00 p.m. My room number is 28 and I am located in the north wing.

I look forward to the opportunity of working with you and your child this year. Together we will make a terrific team.

Sincerely,
Jane Zimmerman
Teacher

For material related to this concept, go to Clip 11.3 on the Student Resource CD bound into the back of your textbook.

Invite parents to your classroom. In most schools, there is an open house near the beginning of each year or semester. Take full advantage of this and share your expectations with them. Invite them at other times, too. Invite them to hear student presentations or performances. Have students organize a night at the end of the year to showcase their work and have a little party for their parents.

Use progress reports to really report student progress to parents. While it is much easier to simply average grades and write "85" on a progress report, parents will appreciate it much more if you add a few sentences at the bottom. These should always include some good things before any bad ones. "Mike has turned in almost every assignment and is making good progress, but he did not do quite enough to prepare for his presentation on Mexico. We will be working on research skills before we begin our next unit."

Language and culture will affect the lens through which parents view school in general, and your class. Therefore, it is essential that you have a good understanding of the language differences and the culture of your students' families. Language, how it is used, and mannerisms will contribute to complexities of the communication process in working with parents. In many instances, language cannot be translated (word for word) because meanings can be different. Cultural values must be taken into account as well as how a culture communicates within its own society. For example, different cultures can have different concepts about time (e.g., punctuality), authority, tone of voice, or competition. Likewise, nonverbal messages expressed through touch or gestures, facial expressions, and personal space can have different meanings in different cultures. For example, Japanese tend to be straight-faced when happy and smile to mask unpleasant feelings such as anger or sadness.

When communicating with parents from other cultures, you must try to be more aware of your own automatic responses so that you can learn to keep them in check. Remember always to give parents the benefit of the doubt and assume that their intentions are not unkind.

Each school district that receives Title I, Part A funds must develop a written parental involvement policy that must include a parental involvement plan. The plan must provide opportunities for participation of parents with limited English proficiency, parents with disabilities, parents of migratory children, economically disadvantaged parents, parents of children with limited literacy, and racial or ethnic minorities. These plans shall put into operation activities and procedures for the involvement of parents in all of its schools. These programs, activities, and procedures will be planned and operated with meaningful consultation with parents, teachers, administrators, and community representatives. The plan must be updated periodically to meet the changing needs of parents and schools, as well as be in a format and language readily understood by parents and school personnel. The plan must

1. hold an annual meeting to inform parents of the school's involvement in Title I, explain Title I requirements, and explain parents' rights to be involved;

2. offer, whenever practicable, a number of meetings;

3. involve parents in an organized, ongoing, and timely way, in the planning, review, and improvement of the parent involvement plan;

4. invite parents to attend informational sessions regarding the curriculum, forms of assessment used in the school, and student proficiency level expectations;

5. give parents opportunities to make suggestions and to participate as appropriate in decisions relating to the education of their children.

As more and more school districts across the United States implement school-based management, teachers communicating with school administrators and community leaders will assume greater importance. Indeed, teachers are now finding themselves with the power to be involved in making decisions about how money should be spent at school sites, what the staff mix should be, and what should be taught in classrooms and how. School-based management decentralized control from the central district office to individual schools as a way to give school constituents—principals, teachers, parents, and community members—more control over what happens in schools.

Dealing With Difficult Parents

Sometime during your teaching career, you will have to deal with difficult parents. Therefore, you should be prepared to do so. You should be aware of your school's and district's policies for dealing with parent conflict. What are the approved steps to take when a resolution cannot be reached? What are the policies related to specific situations? Make sure you follow the district's policies, guidelines, and procedures.

When parents contact you with a concern or problem, respond quickly with a phone call or meeting to resolve the situation. Inaction on your part is frequently perceived as lack of interest or caring about the students' and/or parents' concern or problem. Even the shortest delays often lead to more frustration and anger on the parents' part.

When conferencing with a difficult parent, remain at eye level with them and never sit behind your desk. Move your chair out from behind the desk and place it close to and in front of the parent. This sends a strong assertive message to the parent. It says, "I am comfortable and confident in this situation." It is important to really listen to what parents are saying and to not interrupt them. If they are angry, give them time to vent some of their frustrations. However, always keep in mind that you are not anyone's doormat. You should be an active listener so you fully understand their side of the story. Active listening is often difficult when the parent's side of the story is full of misinformation and possible lies. Never underestimate the power of a stern, disapproving look. It can give parents a loud and clear, "BACK OFF." Often, intimidating or bullying parents are less aggressive if you make eye contact with them throughout the meeting. Selective silence is also one of the most effective ways of dealing with difficult parents. It is easy to use and is a very low threat. You must at all times remain calm and retain your composure. If the parents' side seems to be going on and on with no end in sight after a lengthy discussion, ask them what their bottom line is. Ask, "What do you want to happen because of this conference?"

During any meeting with difficult parents, you must remain professional. There is no need to argue with parents. Parents often have a way of sliding the blame away from their own child toward other students or you. It is important to listen to what parents have to say, but remember to keep the parents' focus on their child. Do not be defensive, act confidently, and look them in their eyes as you speak throughout the conference. Some difficult parents are inclined to twist the truth, or they may have a reputation for being volatile. In these cases, it is beneficial to have a third party join you for the meeting. Doing so could prevent a "he said/she said" conflict from occurring after the meeting. Indeed, some parents are not as boisterous or judgmental with a third party present. If the difficult parent tries to verbally bully you, just say, "I am sorry but I don't allow people to treat me this way. Perhaps we can continue this when you have calmed down." Then slowly and calmly walk away.

ON YOUR OWN 11.2   View From the Classroom

Log on to the Web-based student study site at http://www.sagepub.com/eis2study. Review the Chapter 11 teacher surveys and react to the related activities.

This completes my brief discussion on communicating with parents and dealing with difficult parents. But before moving on to the next section, complete Web Link 11.1: Communicating With Parents. In the next section, I will consider another very important topic related to the communication process: the art of listening.

Components of Listening

Hearing and listening are not the same thing. Hearing is an automatic, physical component of listening. **Hearing** occurs when eardrum vibration caused by sound impulses is transmitted to the brain. **Listening** occurs when the brain assigns meaning to the transmitted impulses. Thus, listening is an active process, an art.

Many times, you hear but do not listen. You hear boring lectures, for example, but seldom listen to them. It is hard work to *really* listen—and it is much harder than talking. Although listening takes effort and discipline, the dividends that result will continue to reward you as a teacher, both inside and outside the classroom.

Virtually everyone listens; however, few do it well. Basic to the improvement of your listening ability is awareness of the need for improving the skill. When you compare all the training you receive in reading, writing, and speaking with that provided in listening, you will find your listening training to be lacking. This is ironic when you realize that 60% of your communication involves listening (DeVito, 1985; Friedman, 1986).

Listening requires that you first learn to cut down on your talking. Although when we were younger, we tended to ramble on and on, oblivious to what others around us were saying, we soon learned from adults that others did not look favorably toward those who talked continuously. But cutting down on our talking is only the beginning to becoming a good listener.

Listening is more than just being silent. Like thinking, listening is an intense, active process. It takes concentration and self-discipline. In fact, Barker (1971, p. 4) describes the listening process as having four components: hearing, attending, understanding, and remembering.

Hearing

As previously mentioned, *hearing* is physiological. It is the nonselective process of sound waves striking the eardrums, with the resultant electrochemical impulses being transmitted to the brain. Therefore, any aural information you wish to process and understand is accompanied by noise. This noise masks the desired message. In fact, hearing can be affected by exposure to continuous loud tones or noise. Loud music and city noises can lead to auditory fatigue, a temporary loss of hearing, and even to a permanent loss of hearing.

Attending

Although listening starts with a physiological process of hearing, it quickly becomes a psychological one as students decide whether to focus on, or *attend* to, what you say. This decision is directly related to their needs, wants, desires, and interests, as well as the relevance of the message, the setting, the intensity of the message, the concreteness of the message, and the duration of the message.

Listening involves focusing on the speaker and the message being transmitted. In some cases, listeners may not like what the speaker is saying, or they may not see the importance of the message, but they will never truly know unless they sit it out and listen. Although you cannot control all the variables that affect listening in your classroom, your awareness of such variables can enable you to take a step toward controlling them. You must teach students to focus their attention, stop talking, stop

Communication comes in many forms and can send a variety of messages to different individuals.

fidgeting, and stop letting their minds wander. You must teach them to "lock in" on what you are saying while blocking out everything around them.

Blocking out external stimuli is not an easy task for you and students and, in fact, is not always desirable behavior for teachers, who must be aware of everything that is happening in the classroom. Indeed, teachers must learn to both be aware of what is going on in the classroom and pay attention to students when the situation calls for it.

The way we view a speaker also affects our willingness to listen. If a speaker is described as being very intelligent or as someone of importance, we tend to listen with greater intensity. This tendency also applies to speakers who are attractive and who hold ideas, attitudes, and values similar to our own. Other factors such as size, dress, and name may also have an effect on our capacity for listening. You must control these affecting variables as much as possible if you are to enhance listening in your classroom.

Listening, like talking, consists of both a verbal and nonverbal component. The words we hear are only one aspect of listening. We also gain information through nonverbal means—that is, through the constant interplay of gestures, feelings, body movements, and so on inherent in human interaction. Thus, teachers sometimes believe they are sending one message (verbal), but their voice, choice of words, and gestures (nonverbal) send a completely different message.

Sokolove, Sadker, and Sadker (1986, p. 232) identify four nonverbal cues that will affect communication in your classroom. These writers suggest that attentiveness can be improved by giving special attention to the following:

1. *Eye contact.* Focus your eyes directly on students when they speak, while taking care that the direct contact does not make them uncomfortable.

2. *Facial expressions.* Let your facial expressions show that you are really listening. These expressions should give feedback (positive and negative) to students as to whether the message is being received as intended.

3. *Body posture.* Relax as a listener. This will relax your students and stimulate them to say more. In fact, the teacher who is relaxed and leans toward students when they are speaking communicates interest and involvement.

4. *Physical space.* Locate yourself so that you and student speakers have comfortable separation.

Although much of the nonverbal information you receive will be on a conscious level, you will also glean information from students at the subconscious level—for example, when you know they aren't really interested in what you are saying. This subconscious information will play an important part in shaping your impressions and helps in developing a response to the messages being sent, even though students may not be aware of them. Indeed, inferences—sometimes inaccurate—regarding students are often formed based on the subconscious information you receive.

Understanding

Understanding involves the mental processing of received information. During this phase, students must actively judge the worthiness of the message and the relevance of the information, as well as select and organize the information received (Friedman, 1986). They must consider the information and decide "Am I really interested?" This judgment is based on several elements. First, it involves recognition of the rules of grammar that were used to create the message. Second, judgment is often based on their knowledge about the source of the information—whether the source is reliable, the teacher, a professional, and so on. Third, understanding can hinge on the social context. For example, the same message delivered in the classroom and on the playground would most likely elicit different judgments. Finally, students often judge the merit of a message by their ability to organize it into a recognizable form.

Remembering

Remembering is the fourth component of the listening process. The recall of information is directly related to how the information is evaluated. In other words, before students send the information to long-term memory, they must decide that it is worthy of remembering. In this evaluation process, they are "weighing the message against personal beliefs, questioning the speaker's motives, challenging the ideas presented, suspecting the validity of the message, holding the speaker's ideas up to standards of excellence, wondering what has been omitted, thinking how the message could have been improved, and in other ways evaluating what is being said" (Friedman, 1986, p. 7). This evaluation generally takes place with respect to the internal beliefs and values they hold. They must learn, however, to evaluate information on its own merit. This ability is difficult, and it takes self-discipline, but it will be well worth the effort.

Experiences and internal feelings often have an effect on student evaluation. They all have emotional filters, which affect how they evaluate what they hear. These filters may block words or phrases or, conversely, allow certain words or phrases to rush in and overly impress them. They may at times even change what they hear, as with such words as *homework, test,* or *play.* Like observing, listening can be selective to some degree.

Nichols and Stevens (1957) offer three guidelines for helping students reduce the effects of filters on evaluation. They should do the following:

1. Be self-disciplined. Withhold evaluation until they receive the total message.

2. Hunt for negative evidence related to the received message. Don't take what they hear at face value.

3. Make a realistic self-analysis of the information they hear. Test the information against their biases, values, and feelings.

| APPLY AND REFLECT 11.3 | Be careful not to filter out difficult or undesirable messages. Do you have a tendency to do so? If so, how can you overcome this tendency? |

The ability to recall information is also related to how often students hear the information and whether the information has been rehearsed. Of course, the more times they hear any piece of information, the better they will retain it; similarly, rehearsed information is more often remembered.

Some students are poor listeners because they have developed bad listening habits. These bad habits include the following:

1. *Pseudolistening.* Pseudolistening is an imitation of listening. Good pseudolisteners look you in the eye, nod and smile in agreement, and even answer questions occasionally. In other words, they give the appearance of attentiveness, but, in reality, they are thinking about other things.

2. *Insulated listening.* Some students avoid listening when they do not want to deal with an issue or when it takes mental exertion to understand what is being said. If they have such a habit, you must make special efforts to have them practice listening to difficult-to-understand information.

3. *Selective listening.* Selective listeners attend only to a teacher's remarks that interest them. Such students automatically cease listening when the message is of little interest. They equate "interest" with "value." The fallacy associated with this habit is that the message is often worth listening to. Of course, all students are somewhat selective at times—for instance, when they screen out the class next door and background noise.

4. *Attribute listening.* Attribute listeners are more interested in the delivery and/or the physical appearance of the teacher. These students are often more concerned with criticizing the teacher's style of delivery or physical appearance than with listening to the message. They associate the importance of the message with the way it is delivered or with the appearance of the teacher or speaker. They should remember that the content of most messages is more important than the method of delivery or the appearance of the deliverer.

5. *Stage hogging.* Stage hoggers want to talk. They are interested only in expressing their own ideas. If they allow others to speak, it seems to be only while they catch their breath. Some students and many teachers, for example, want to do all the talking in the classroom. These students and teachers seldom give other students the opportunity to voice their opinions; when they do, they often cut off these student remarks. Teachers must be especially sensitive to the habit of stage hogging. Remember: Stage hogging isn't really conversing; essentially, it's speech making.

6. *Defensive listening.* Defensive listeners take innocent remarks as personal attacks. Teenagers are notorious for being defensive listeners. They often take parental or teacher remarks about their behaviors as being distrustful snooping, and teachers must be aware of this. Similarly, teachers must also realize that many students will be overly sensitive and defensive regarding remarks about their appearance and physical attributes. Children and teenagers can be extremely cruel to each other at times.

In most cases, an awareness of the bad habits associated with the listening process is enough in itself to assist students in overcoming their effects. Still, students should practice working on such bad habits if they are to become better listeners.

Thinking often affects listening. It is a well-established fact that we can process information at a faster pace than it can be delivered to us. Therefore, when students listen, they have time for taking in their environment and for thinking—for meandering off on mental tangents. This extra thinking time would be better used in reflecting on and analyzing what is being said.

Although teachers want students to be better listeners, they often lack the skill. These needed skills might be better understood through an examination of the different styles of listening.

Styles of Listening

We listen for different reasons and with different ends in mind. Indeed, listening does and should vary from situation to situation. Listening to a student recitation, for example, calls for a different style of listening than does helping a student with his or her problems. Here I will address three styles of listening: one-way, two-way, and empathic.

One-Way Listening

One-way listening occurs when you are not actively taking part in the exchange of a message. In a word, it is passive listening. You listen without talking and without giving nonverbal directions to the speaker. One-way listening gives speakers the opportunity to develop their thoughts and ideas without being unduly influenced by the listeners. Common examples of one-way listening are watching television and taking in a lecture.

One-way listening gives a speaker free rein. The listener becomes a sounding board for the speaker's ideas or problems. Students often need such a person, who will just hear them out without giving a reaction. The occasional need for a sounding board explains why some people enjoy talking to inanimate objects or pets.

You are also taking part in one-way listening when you just sit back, relax, and let the auditory input stimulate your senses. Listening to music for the pure enjoyment is an excellent example of this type of listening.

One-way listening has limited value to teachers. Indeed, except for the few cases we have addressed, it isn't very effective for the simple reason that students often misunderstand at least some of a teacher's ideas. For example, messages that are overly vague will often be interpreted incorrectly by students. In other cases, teachers can send incorrect information or a student can simply get the information wrong. Thus, a teacher can say "8 grams" instead of "5," or a student can transform 8 grams into 5. On the whole, although one-way listening has its uses, complete understanding of your message isn't always a sure thing. Fortunately, there are other, better listening styles.

Two-Way Listening

Two-way listening actively involves the listener in the exchange of information. In practice, listeners provide feedback to the speaker by asking for more information or by paraphrasing the speaker's message.

Asking for additional information when a message is unclear is a valuable tool in seeking understanding. Often, you simply ask the student to elaborate on the information presented. For example, you might want a student to provide more details on the method used to solve a math word problem, a student might ask you to repeat your directions for writing a theme, or students might ask you for clarification on how to use a piece of laboratory equipment.

Restating the student's message in your own words is another technique for providing feedback. One example of paraphrasing might be "So you're telling me that you have problems with your parents because they are too restrictive." The thing to remember in restating the student's message is to paraphrase the words, not parrot them.

Although active listening usually involves verbal feedback, the feedback can be nonverbal—for example, a smile or nod of comprehension, or a frown that shows a lack of understanding. If you are observant, active nonverbal listening techniques can be as effective as the more common verbal techniques.

Two-way listening offers some real advantages for teachers. First, it boosts the odds that you will accurately and fully understand what students are telling you. In effect, active listening serves as a double check on the accuracy of your interpretation of student statements. A second advantage of active listening is that it often stimulates students to explore issues in greater depth. Last, your use of listening encourages students to solve their own problems by giving them the opportunity to talk through them.

Empathic Listening

Empathic listening is listening with feeling. It is an earnest attempt to experience what the speaker is experiencing or feeling and to respond to those feelings. Only through such listening can you fully understand another's meaning. Empathic listening calls for careful attention to the speaker's verbal and nonverbal cues. The listener gleans the full meaning of the speaker's message by putting these cues together into a statement that reflects the content as well as the associated feeling.

During the response portion of empathic listening, the listener is attempting to avoid misinterpretation of the speaker or to clarify the message. Sokolove et al. (1986, p. 230) suggest that the teacher's function in empathic listening is like holding up a mirror for the student's words, feelings, and behaviors. Through the process of empathic listening, you try to provide direct feedback regarding the success of student communication. This response can take the form of simple paraphrasing of the student's words or can be an actual interpretation of the student's message as reflected in the verbal and nonverbal behaviors. For example, if a student conveys that he or she dislikes your science class, your reflective response to the content of this message might be, "I believe you are saying that you dislike science because you find the experiments too difficult."

Your response to a student statement can be related to the content component of the message or the affective component of the message. For example, your response to the content of a message might begin with phrases such as "I believe you are saying" or "You appear to think," whereas, with responses that reflect the affective component of a message, you might begin with "I think you are feeling" or "You appear to feel."

There are no quick methods for achieving empathy with your students. But it is important to work toward this end. You must learn to see the student's point of view. For example, if students turn in their work late, you should attempt to put yourself in the students' place in understanding the reasons for the lateness. You will often see behaviors that you will consider foolish and ridiculous. What you need to do, however, is consider such situations from the viewpoint of the students.

In summary, skill in the various types of listening is an essential tool for effective teaching. Indeed, the importance of good listening on the part of teachers has become more acceptable and recognizable today than ever before. Listening skill is now acknowledged as directly related to teacher effectiveness. All teachers must be proficient listeners.

APPLY AND REFLECT 11.4	Listen with an open mind. Withhold judgment until you have all the information. Why is it important that teachers do this? Discuss your reasons with the rest of the class. Do they agree?

Listening Feedback

Classroom communication requires that the specific messages you encode and transmit are received and accurately decoded by students. This is generally continuous and two-way. Students continuously decode the information you send and send you messages in return. These student-feedback messages, in general, are usually nonverbal.

Students are continuously sending nonverbal messages of understanding or uncertainty, agreement or disagreement, liking or distaste, concern or lack of concern, attention or inattention. When you receive this feedback, you should interpret it and incorporate it to modify or clarify your original message; namely, you should respond by reexplaining, offering further examples, or changing your mode of instruction. Identifying and responding to such student feedback is a skill you must master.

The successful use of feedback in the learning environment is an effective way to improve instruction. Many teachers, however, indicate that they rarely, if ever, use feedback as part of their teaching strategy. But feedback is so important to the total learning process that it must not be avoided or ignored.

APPLY AND REFLECT 11.5

Interpretation of feedback isn't always accurate. Check the validity of the feedback you receive. What are some techniques for doing this?

Table 11.2 summarizes the different types of listening. Review the summary and complete Review and Reflective Exercise 11.2.

TABLE 11.2   Listening

Type	Description
One-way	Passive listening with no interaction between speaker and listeners
Two-way	Active listening with exchange between speaker and listeners
Empathic	Listening with an effort to experience the speaker's feelings

REVIEW AND REFLECTIVE EXERCISE 11.2   Identify the components and styles of listening.

REVIEW

- Describe the components and styles of listening.
- Differentiate between one-way and two-way listening.
- What is empathic listening?

REFLECTION

- How difficult do you find it to stop talking and really listen? What does it mean to listen with an open mind? How does your ability to listen affect your view of the world?

REFLECTIONS ON TEACHER PRACTICE 11.2   Teacher Teams

1. Is the establishment of "school building teams" a good idea? If at all, how should they be used?

2. How should "school building teams" be involved in school and/or district policy decisions?

◆ ◆ ◆

One of the most important aspects of "school building teams" is continual communication with the team leaders from the administration of the building. There has to be an open trust and the administration has to be willing to listen to all, while the team leaders have to be willing to provide solutions and suggestions along with their "venting."

Three years ago, we made the conscious decision to look to our team leaders as instructional leaders, and we modeled for them at our team leader meetings open dialogue around instructional issues, not business issues. We then asked them to do this twice a week with their teams. We provided them support by listening, giving them training, and listening some more. We also

shared this expectation with all the team members. It seemed to work, and our school now uses e-mail for MOST of the "business conversations."

The downside of a team is when a group of teachers form a team of friends, but not a team of professionals. Then, they seem to band together around petty issues, instead of the real issues. When we have this happen, we struggle with whether to disband the team or teams that are doing this.

—MICHELLE, middle-level teacher

SOURCE: www.middleweb.com. Reprinted with permission.

SUMMARY

Communication is central to the learning process, for without it, learning could not take place.

The Communication Process

- Classroom exchanges consist of both spoken and nonverbal messages, with the spoken message comprising the verbal, vocal, and metaverbal components. The verbal component of a message is the actual words spoken; the vocal component is the meaning attached to the words, depending on such things as pitch, loudness, tone, and rate; and the metaverbal component is the implied, or intended, message. Students also learn through nonverbal communication; that is, they learn from a teacher's facial language, body language, use of space and motion, use of time, and use of the voice.

Components of Listening

- Teachers and students alike need to develop better listening skills.
- Effective teachers communicate with parents, school administrators, and community leaders.
- Listening is a four-step process: hearing, attending, understanding, and remembering.
- Teachers must overcome bad habits and become proficient at one-way, two-way, and empathic listening.
- Teachers have not learned to use nonverbal communication effectively, and rarely—if at all—have they learned to use feedback and to *really* listen to students.

DISCUSSION QUESTIONS AND ACTIVITIES

1. **The communication process.** Even when effectively carried out, communication can have good or bad results. Recall several incidents in which communication improved a situation and several in which communication made a situation worse.
2. **Listening habits.** Use the bad habits described in this chapter to describe faulty listening behaviors you use daily. In what circumstances are you guilty of these habits? Around whom? In what settings? At what times?

TECHNOLOGY AND EDUCATION

One way that teachers can communicate with students and parents is through the development of Web sites, which can provide a variety of information to students and their parents. Some schools make provisions so that each teacher has a Web page for use for his or her classroom. Teachers may post syllabi, rules and procedures, notices, listing of homework, Web links to useful resources, and much more. In addition, e-mail may be provided. If you had a Web page available for your classroom use at your future school, how might you use it? What information might you post? Would you consider using e-mail?

DECONSTRUCTING THE STANDARDS

Chapter 11 content addresses topics related to INTASC Standards 2 and 6.

- ♦ INTASC Standard 2 states: *Knowledge of Human Development and Learning:* The teacher understands how children learn and develop and can provide learning opportunities that support their intellectual, social, and personal development.

♦ INTASC Standard 6 states: *Communication Skills:* The teacher uses knowledge of effective verbal, nonverbal, and media communication techniques to foster active inquiry, collaboration, and supportive interaction in the classroom.

For each of these two standards, write your response to the following:

- Which part(s) of each standard does this chapter address?
- How does this chapter address this standard?
- How will the concepts in this chapter help you apply this standard as a teacher?

PRAXIS CONNECTION

Log on to the Web-based student study site at http://www.sagepub.com/eis2study. Access the Praxis II: Principles of Learning and Teaching assessments and/or state-related exams and complete the Chapter 11 test preparation exercises.

PORTFOLIO CONNECTION

Log on to the Web-based student study site at http://www.sagepub.com/eis2study. Access the Portfolio Connection. Complete the Chapter 11 portfolio link to INTASC activities.

CONNECTION WITH THE FIELD

1. **Vocal communication.** Listen to the audio portion only of a videotaped instructional episode from a classroom at the level that you expect to teach. List information being exchanged through vocal communication.

2. **Nonverbal communication.** Play the tape in Activity 1 with only video (no audio). List information being exchanged by the teacher or the students through nonverbal communication.

3. **Metaverbal communication.** Play the tape again with audio and video. Did you notice any implied messages? If so, what were they? Give your reasons for making these conclusions.

4. **Classroom observation.** Complete several observations at the grade level you expect to teach. Collect data related to communication acts such as these:
   a. The effective use of verbal communication
   b. The different nonverbal languages used by the teachers
   c. The teachers' listening skills

5. **Parent involvement.** Talk to several teachers about their experiences with parent involvement. Are they successful in getting a great deal of parent involvement? How do these teachers work with parents who resist involvement?

CHAPTER 12

Motivating Students

Whether you think that you can, or that you can't, you are usually right.

—HENRY FORD

OVERVIEW

One of your greatest teaching challenges will be to develop students' desire to learn—that is, to motivate students. The traditional approach to motivation was one of preaching to students about learning and the benefits they would derive as well-informed citizens. Needless to say, this approach was ineffective.

Lack of motivation and problems with classroom management are often cited as the major causes for the apathy. Thus, motivation and classroom management are two keys to effective instruction. Classroom management will be addressed in Chapter 13.

This chapter will focus on the meaning of motivation and will consider three basic orientations: cognitive, stimulation, and reinforcement. Through these three orientations, I will address internal and external factors that affect motivation. Emphasis will be put on techniques that will help keep students interested, involved, and on task.

OBJECTIVES

After completing your study of Chapter 12, you should be able to do the following:

- Describe the concept of motivation from the cognitive, stimulation, and reinforcement points of view, as well as explain the interrelationship among the three viewpoints.
- Identify examples of intrinsic and extrinsic motivation.
- Discuss student attitudes and needs and their motivational effect on learning.
- Explain the possible effects of stimulus variation on learning, as well as techniques for varying the stimuli in the teaching-learning environment.
- Define reinforcement and describe the types of classroom reinforcement.
- Differentiate between the concepts of positive and negative reinforcement.
- Identify and discuss three techniques that can be used in providing feedback to students.
- Describe the characteristics of reward mechanism systems and explain the advantages associated with their use.
- Describe common ways to identify viable reinforcers for use with students.
- Describe contingency contracts and their appropriate classroom use.

Children and adolescents today have been raised with television, high-production movies, and highly stimulating musical productions. Having grown accustomed to such highly stimulating experiences, children often expect such experiences when they enter the classroom. Needless to say, they are too often disappointed and sometimes find the classroom less than exciting. Consequently, there can be limited motivation to learn in many classrooms.

All teachers will undoubtedly agree that motivation is a critical factor in classroom learning. Some students will be naturally enthusiastic about learning, but many need—or expect—their teachers to inspire, challenge, and stimulate them. But what is motivation, and, more important, how do you go about developing students' basic physiological drive to learn? Attempts to explain motivation have led to disagreement because of the complexity of the concept. Let's begin our study of motivation by looking at its source.

Intrinsic Versus Extrinsic Motivation

Motivation can be defined as something that energizes and directs our behaviors. That is, motivated behavior is behavior that is energized, directed, and sustained. In plain language, motivation is what gets you going, keeps you going, and determines where you're trying to go. Motivation can vary in both intensity and direction. Obviously, such influences can come from within (internal) or outside (external) the individual. Internal, or **intrinsic, motivation** is what learners themselves bring into the learning environment—that is, their internal attributes (attitudes, needs, personality factors, and values). I shall refer to the emphasis on these internal factors as a *cognitive* approach to motivation. Essentially, this view is concerned with the unique internal attributes that direct individual behaviors. In contrast, external, or **extrinsic, motivation** originates in the learning environment, where persons are offered the right incentives for doing certain things. This use of rewards represents a *reinforcement* approach to motivation.

Keeping students on task is a challenge in the instructional process.

Figure 12.1
Motivational
Interactions

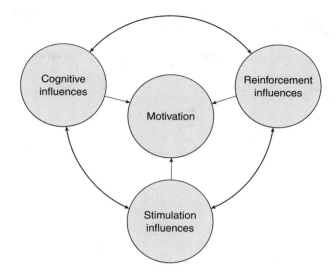

Internal motives often are difficult to change, and, when change does occur, it occurs slowly. Indeed, what with the short time you will have with students, the likelihood of your changing students' internal motivational patterns will be slim at best. Thus, you must learn to stimulate the motivational attributes that already exist.

External motivation makes use of incentives in getting students to modify behaviors. These incentives represent artificially devised techniques for prompting students to work harder. Ideally, incentives should never become the primary reason for doing classroom work; that is, you should use incentives only sparingly and phase them out as soon as possible.

Current evidence strongly favors establishing a classroom climate in which students are intrinsically motivated to learn (Hennessey & Amabile, 1998; Wigfield & Eccles, 2002). Students are more motivated to learn when they are given choices, become absorbed in challenges that match their skills, and receive rewards that have informational value but are not used for control.

Many theorists assume that intrinsic and extrinsic motives are interrelated and will interact. This viewpoint, referred to as the *stimulation* approach to motivation, suggests that external, environmental factors can be used in influencing internal factors. Figure 12.1 shows how the different motivational viewpoints interact to influence student motivation. Let's look at these approaches more closely.

ON YOUR OWN 12.1   Reflections on Teacher Practice

Read and reflect on the viewpoints expressed in Establishing a Token Economy. Log on to the Web-based student study site at http://www.sagepub.com/eis2study and react to the related activities.

The Cognitive Approach to Motivation

Like most people, students have a tendency to react according to their perceptions of events. These perceptions result in differing desires, based on variations in their attitude, need structure, curiosity level, task interest, satisfaction with learning, and sense of well-being. According to the cognitive perspective, students' thoughts guide their motivation. The focus is on such ideas as students' internal motivation

REFLECTIONS ON TEACHER PRACTICE 12.1 — Establishing a Token Economy

1. What are the ethical implications of a token economy system?

2. How well would a token economy system work with elementary school children? Middle school students? High school students?

◆ ◆ ◆

Last year was the first time I used this type of system, and the class loved it! The way I used it required a lot of start-up work, but after that it ran quite smoothly. First of all, I made up a list of classroom jobs, enough for each student to have at least one job. Then the jobs were posted as Mrs. _____'s classified ads. The kids filled out applications that were made to resemble real job applications, with strengths, references, and so on. Then I notified them that they were to come in (usually at lunch or other "free" times) for an interview. They are instructed to dress up a bit, and be polite and businesslike. It's so cute, they get so nervous. Then they are notified about which job they are getting. They are then asked to read and sign a contract, which includes a $10.00 signing bonus.

They are paid every week. Usually each job pays $5.00 or $10.00 per week. I have payroll people (students) who write out the paychecks, with taxes deducted (10 percent to keep it simple). The following day we do our banking. I go to a local bank and get check book covers, and account registers. Each child gets one; they feel so grown up. I copy real bank deposit slips, and the kids fill them out. This takes some time and weekly reinforcement, but once they understand how to do it they are responsible for filling out the deposit slip correctly. If the banker finds an error, the student's bank account is charged a $5.00 fee. I have one or two parents help out on banking day.

We also have a cash system I made up—"Starbucks" in the amounts of $1.00, $5.00, $10.00, and $20.00. The kids can earn money for things such as a good test or quiz score, exceptional behavior, caught being good, asking a really good question, and so on. And they each get $20.00 on their birthday. They can also lose money for things like forgetting homework, needing to go out to their locker, or to their book bag, excessive talking, being out of their seat at inappropriate times, and so on. Throughout the year, the parents are asked to send in anything that they think the kids would like, and we have an auction at the end of each semester (twice a year). Most of the stuff is new, and some is just stuff that their kids don't play with or use anymore. These things don't have to be expensive, just things that kids would like. Some of my most popular and highest auction items came from the dollar store. Grab bags with pop, candy, and chip-type things are really popular, too.

I think our token economy system is a wonderfully worthwhile endeavor; the kids love it and are learning some real-life skills in the process.

—*LIBBY, fifth-grade teacher*

SOURCE: Reprinted with permission from ProTeacher, a professional community for elementary school teachers (http://www.proteacher.net).

to achieve, their attributions (perceptions about the causes of success or failure, especially the perception that effort is an important factor in achievement), and their beliefs that they can effectively control their environment. The cognitive perspective also stresses the importance of goal setting, planning, and monitoring progress toward a goal (Schunk & Ertmer, 2000; Zimmerman & Schunk, 2001).

APPLY AND REFLECT 12.1

You should urge your students to think about and select realistic long-term goals. What kinds of goals do you hope to instill in your students? Why is it a good idea or not a good idea to involve parents in setting student goals?

Students' Attitude

Some students will love school and your subject at the outset, whereas others will hate it all. These predetermined attitudes—or mind-sets toward certain persons, places, and things—are the results of prior experiences with school and similar subjects: Some will love school and your subject because they find it interesting or easy, whereas others will hate school and your subject because they find it boring or difficult. Your job is to deal with negative attitudes and to bring about change. Because you cannot force students to like school or your subject, this task will not be an easy one. Indeed, you cannot compel students to change their attitudes against their will. Your best strategy is to entice change through the use of innovative motivational techniques.

First, it is important that negative mind-sets regarding school and learning be reversed. Thus, you must show students that school is worthwhile. In other words, you must show students that the learning acquired in school is important to the development of life skills and of the skills necessary for accomplishing career goals. One way of accomplishing this task is by inviting respected community leaders and businesspeople into the school for discussion about the importance of school and learning.

Second, students often are concerned with subject relevance. Therefore, you should be prepared to respond to those age-old questions: "Why do we have to learn this stuff?" or "What good is this stuff going to be for me?" If you cannot answer such questions convincingly, perhaps you should reevaluate your course content. You, of all people, should know why your subject is worthwhile.

Finally, if you are going to develop positive attitudes toward school and learning, you must involve students in their own learning and stimulate their interest. We will consider involvement and interest techniques in the next section, when we discuss stimulation motivation.

Student Needs

A *need* can be defined as "any type of deficiency in the human organism or the absence of anything the person requires, or thinks he requires, for his overall wellbeing" (Kolesnik, 1978, p. 149). Obviously, students will enter your class with a wide variety of needs. Indeed, Maslow (1970) has suggested that human needs function on seven hierarchical levels. The first four lower level needs, labeled **deficiency needs,** are the need for survival, safety, belonging, and self-esteem, whereas the three higher level **being needs** are the need for intellectual achievement, aesthetic appreciation, and self-actualization. The being needs, unlike the deficiency needs, are never truly satisfied; that is, the quest for their fulfillment only motivates individuals to seek further fulfillment.

Maslow's needs hierarchy can provide valuable insight into the reasons for some students' behaviors. In a word, students' desire to fulfill lower level needs may interfere with your desire that they achieve higher level goals. A student's longing, for example, to belong to the peer group and maintain self-esteem within the group may interfere with achievement. Indeed, students sometimes break rules, or even openly defy a teacher, simply for peer recognition. Furthermore, the intensity of various needs varies from individual to individual and even changes with time and circumstances.

The need for safety has important ramifications for teachers. Essentially, because it is usually more difficult to learn when there is a feeling of insecurity, you should avoid using fear and excessive anxiety as a motivating device. That is, avoid shaming students when they make mistakes or judgment errors, and avoid overemphasizing tests and grades. Indeed, students are often motivated when they feel secure enough to share their ideals and opinions. An atmosphere tempered with a little anxiety can motivate students, but exercise care when you use fear and anxiety with your students.

For material related to this concept, go to Clip 12.1 on the Student Resource CD bound into the back of your textbook.

Schools now recognize that if students' basic needs are not met, learning will suffer. They have responded by providing free breakfast and lunch programs. The most important deficiency needs, however, are those for love and self-esteem. Students who do not feel that they are loved and that they are capable are unlikely to have a strong motivation to achieve the higher level growth objectives.

All students have the need to achieve and the need to avoid failure. Consequently, the overall tendency (resultant motivation) of students will be to take risks to achieve or to avoid threatening situations that might lead to failure. Therefore, when you plan, consider which students have high achievement needs, low achievement needs, and fear of failure. You may want to provide challenging optional assignments for high achievers and provide encouragement and reinforcement for students with an acute fear of failure.

Natural Motives

By nature, people are curious, are stimulated by suspense, and have a natural desire for action, adventure, and interesting experiences. Therefore, you should harness these **natural motives** in planning your learning activities. For example, educational games, puzzles, computers, and simulations represent viable strategies for capturing the natural motives of most students. Finally, as much as is feasible, select activities that will give students the opportunity to pursue individual interests and desires.

Other incentives include giving students recognition—for example, by displaying their work, giving them a certificate of achievement, placing them on the honor roll, or verbally mentioning their accomplishments. Another type of incentive focuses on allowing students to do something special, such as a desirable activity, as a reward for good work. This might include extra time at recess, playing computer games, a field trip, or even a party.

APPLY AND REFLECT 12.2	Make sure your students have sufficient opportunities for fulfilling their need for affiliation and belonging. What kinds of activities and interactions would you use to help you accomplish this task?

To this point, I have focused on the internal motives of students. Table 12.1 offers a review of the major concepts.

TABLE 12.1 Cognitive Approach to Motivation

Factor	Description
Attitude	Mind-set toward person, place, or thing
Need	Deficiency, real or imaginary, that a person requires for well-being
Natural motives	Internal desires of individual; many are believed to be innate

ON YOUR OWN 12.2 View From the Classroom

Log on to the Web-based student study site at http://www.sagepub.com/eis2study. Review the Chapter 12 teacher surveys and react to the related activities.

What can you do to influence students' perceptions of events? How can you stimulate the internal motives of your students? To answer these questions, we must turn to the stimulation approach to motivation. Before you continue, however, complete Review and Reflective Exercise 12.1, which will check your understanding of the concepts presented to this point.

REVIEW AND REFLECTIVE EXERCISE 12.1   Discuss the key factors in the cognitive view of motivation.

REVIEW

- What is motivated behavior?
- What is the difference between intrinsic and extrinsic motivation? How can extrinsic motivation be used to support achievement?
- Define motivation from the cognitive perspective and describe its key components.
- How would you summarize the cognitive perspective to motivation?

REFLECTION

- Recall a school situation in which you were highly motivated to accomplish something. How would you describe your motivation in terms of the cognitive view of motivation?

- How do motives tend to change as children progress from elementary through high school? Why is intrinsic motivation considered to be more desirable or powerful than extrinsic motivation?

The Stimulation Approach to Motivation

It is rather easy to teach when students are internally motivated to learn. This, however, is usually not the case; most students are not overly excited about learning.

Thus, you must learn to stimulate the desire to learn. Let's look at some techniques that can be used in accomplishing this end.

Classroom Atmosphere

The school and classroom atmosphere often set the tone for learning. Such factors as the physical environment and classroom communication can often make the difference between a motivated learner and a bored, reluctant learner (see Chapter 11).

Will your classroom be attractive and colorful with open communication, or will it be bleak and drab with limited communication? Many classrooms tend to be on the bleak side with little or no communication. An attractive room, however, is more conducive to learning. Compelling bulletin boards and displays can add much to the atmosphere of your classroom. Indeed, they can be designed to be both informative and colorful, and when students are allowed to design and construct them, classroom bulletin boards and displays can be quite motivating.

For material related to this concept, go to Clip 12.2 on the Student Resource CD bound into the back of your textbook.

The arrangement of the classroom, coupled with the seating of students, can also be an effective motivating device. That is, your room arrangement can foster group cohesiveness, which can lead to a high level of group belongingness. Because a sense of belonging is a basic need, it has a positive influence on motivation. Even better, give students an occasional opportunity to rearrange their own seating. When arranging your classroom, however, remember that distractions and disruptions can often occur in high-traffic areas. These include group work areas, students' desks, the teacher's desk, the pencil sharpener, bookshelves, computer stations, and storage location. Separate these areas from each other as much as possible and make sure they are easily accessible.

APPLY AND REFLECT 12.3

Make your classroom physically and psychologically safe. How would you accomplish this task?

Modeling

Modeling is a motivational technique in which people whom students admire demonstrate, through their actions, the values and behaviors you want students to acquire. These actions usually take the form of subtle suggestions that are communicated through noted nonverbal body language. For example, students who role-play or observe others role-play political leaders, musicians, poets, and scientists sometimes develop related interests. Furthermore, students at times serve as role models for each other. That is, when students see certain desirable behaviors in respected or admired peers, they may learn these behaviors themselves. Consequently, group work sometimes results in the transfer of desirable behaviors.

Teacher enthusiasm is a compelling source of motivation.

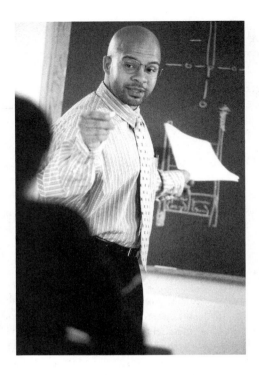

The most notable model in most classrooms will be you, the teacher. Indeed, the enthusiasm and sense of wonder you show for your subject will often be passed on to students. Consequently, if you appear interested and excited about a lesson, students often become transfixed, eager to find out what is so interesting. Indeed, research suggests that enthusiastic teachers produce higher academic achievement by students (Silvernail, 1979, pp. 27–28). Thus, teacher enthusiasm appears to be directly related to students' need for achievement.

Be enthusiastic about your subject. A teacher's enthusiasm is a crucial factor in student motivation. If you become bored or apathetic, students will too. Typically, a teacher's enthusiasm comes from confidence, excitement about the content, and genuine pleasure in teaching. If you find yourself uninterested in the material, think back to what attracted you to the field and bring those aspects of the subject matter to life for your students. Or challenge yourself to devise the most exciting way to present the material, however dull the material itself may seem to you.

APPLY AND REFLECT 12.4

Are you enthusiastic? How would you demonstrate this enthusiasm to your students?

Stimulating Interest

Students naturally seek stimulation as they constantly search for interesting things to do, for variety, for challenge. Thus, students prefer environments rich in stimuli to those that are monotonous and dull; doing *something*—no matter how trivial—generally is more interesting than doing nothing.

The human need for stimulation has important motivational implications. The learning environment typically is under continuous bombardment from such external stimuli as street traffic, hall traffic, and schoolyard conversation. All these stimuli take students' attention and interest away from the classroom to some degree. Therefore, you must compete continuously with irrelevant external stimuli for students' attention. If the students view the irrelevant external stimuli as more interesting or novel than the learning activity, more than likely they will direct their attention and interest toward the external stimuli.

Students are notorious for their inattentiveness and short attention spans. If periodic changes in stimuli do not occur in the learning environment, students lose interest. In other words, unless students are extremely engaged in the class proceedings, their attention soon turns to external stimuli or to their own thoughts. Thus, you must learn to vary your behaviors or your learning activities, so students receive new stimuli that will keep their attention directed toward the lesson. In effect, you must consciously incorporate *stimulus variation* into your lessons for the purpose of gaining, maintaining, and increasing student attention and interest. Allen, Ryan, Bush, and Cooper (1969) suggest several behaviors or behavior patterns that can accomplish this end: gestures, focusing techniques, varied interaction styles, shifts in sensory channels, and movement.

"Of course I believe that a teacher should offer a positive role model; however . . ."

SOURCE: Created by Ford Button.

Gestures can capture and focus our attention. A tap on the desk, a hand movement, or a shift of body position, for instance, is often all that is needed to refocus attention back on a lesson. Such gestural movements represent a change in stimuli to the students, which usually prompts them to direct their attention back to the lesson. Indeed, an added emphasis can be communicated through various general movements of the body, head, and hands. A snap of the fingers or a nod of the head can focus student attention on you as you teach.

Focusing is the technique of directing students' attention to what you have said or will say through verbal statement or gestures. Verbal focusing can be used effectively in directing students to pay closer attention to specifics in a lesson presentation, or it can be used when you notice that student attention is beginning to wander. Examples of verbal statements that are commonly used in focusing

APPLY AND REFLECT 12.5   Make learning fun, and try to have a happy classroom: Use humor once in a while, and try an occasional surprise in your lessons. How would you design a happy classroom, and what occasional surprises would be appropriate for the grade level you plan to teach?

students' attention are "This point is well worth remembering!" and "These are today's major issues!" or even "Make sure you include this point in your notes." Even greater impact can be obtained when a verbal focusing statement is used in conjunction with a gesture—for example, a tap on the chalkboard in conjunction with a verbal statement such as "Remember these definitions!"

You can use any one of four basic interaction styles with your students: teacher-group, teacher-student, student-student, and student-group. The *teacher-group interaction* style should be used when you want to address the class as a whole—for example, when you are giving a lecture or when giving a demonstration. If, on the other hand, you want to address or question a specific student, the *teacher-student interaction* style is appropriate. When used wisely, this style enhances student interest in a lesson through involvement.

Sometimes you may want to redirect a student comment or question to another student for a response or for clarification. Such *student-student interaction* can be used when it is desirable to acknowledge a student's knowledge in the area being discussed or when it is desirable to direct an inattentive student's attention back to the lesson. At other times, you may want to withdraw from a discussion and direct a question or a request for clarification to a student, which would require that the student address the entire group. This *student-group interaction* should be used only with students who can assume a central role in a group discussion; avoid putting your students in uncomfortable situations.

Although most classroom communication is oral, you have four other communication channels: seeing, touching, tasting, and smelling. You can stimulate interest by shifting between these sensory channels. When you make such shifts, you prompt students to make a shift in reception modes, which in turn causes them to refocus their attention. The use of an overhead projector or PowerPoint, for instance, is a typical example of the effective use of refocusing, with students being required to shift their "primary" reception between aural and visual modes.

In most cases, you will be the most significant person in the classroom environment. Thus, any action on your part will draw students' attention. Consequently, you can refocus student attention during your lessons by incorporating simple movement in your teaching actions—for example,

1. Move to the left or to the right within the classroom.

2. Move to the back or to the front within the classroom.

3. Move among the students.

In general, you should avoid remaining stationary (or hiding) behind a podium or desk when you teach. You have probably been exposed to teachers who stood rigidly behind a podium and spoke in a low monotone voice; you probably had trouble maintaining attention and interest. Clearly, such experiences reveal the importance of developing skills in focusing student attention and interest on a lesson.

Finally, teacher enthusiasm should not be overlooked as a focusing technique. When you are enthusiastic, you keep students' attention as a result of your energy and excitement. Although focusing techniques are used for drawing students' attention and interest toward your lessons, they can refocus attention and interest *away* from the lesson if they are overused. That is, if you implement refocusing techniques too often, students may become more interested in the novelty of your presentation rather than in the lesson content. The continual use of "uh" or "okay," pacing, or the tapping of your foot, for example, can detract from your lesson. Indeed, even overly enthusiastic teachers can detract from their lessons when they exhibit excessive emotional behaviors.

Set Induction

Typically, you must get students' attention and interest at the outset of your lessons (see Chapter 4). That is, you must get the undivided attention of every student in your class and prepare them to listen (establish a cognitive set).

Many factors influence student attention and interest at the onset of a lesson—the weather, holidays, school sports, and so on. Therefore, you must develop a repertoire of techniques that will gain student attention and interest. For example, as pointed out in Chapter 4, the act of facing the class in silence is often all that is needed for gaining the attention and interest of your class. This technique is especially effective when you have a small group within the class that is inattentive. Silence and an intense stare in the group's direction will soon get their undivided attention. Silence and pauses are effective tools for gaining student attention.

Another often used method that can foster student attention and interest is to begin your class with a topic that is of vital interest to the class. Indeed, the topic itself need not even be closely related to the lesson of the day. For example, interest in cars can lead into a study of motion or friction. A discussion of the beach can lead into a discussion of the solar system. This technique needs to be developed; it is an art.

Such techniques as the use of gestures, teacher movement, suspense, models, and pictures can be quite effective attention getters. An interesting demonstration, a discrepant event, or a picture will usually attract students' attention. Even better, let your students conduct the introductory demonstration, lead in the discrepant event, or show the pictures. You should experiment with various attention-getting techniques when determining which ones will be the most effective with your students. Classes differ, based on such factors as course content, socioeconomic level, background, motivation, grade level, and class size.

Motivational Methods

Many of the teaching strategies described in Chapters 6 and 7 heighten student motivation through the direct involvement of students in their own learning. In addition, many of the strategies are motivational in that they can influence students' cognitive needs. The need for belonging, for example, can be met through cooperative learning—that is, through a classroom structure in which groups of students work together toward a common goal, with individual group members contributing for the benefit of the individual and the group. The interaction and sharing of responsibility in cooperative learning represents a form of social motivation in that they greatly enhance the sense of belonging. This sense of belonging can be accomplished through many of the instructional strategies that involve experiences that satisfy the need for affiliation and acceptance from others.

Vary your teaching methods. Variety reawakens students' involvement in the subject and their motivation. Break the routine by incorporating a variety of teaching activities and methods in your subject: role-playing, brainstorming, discussions, demonstrations, case studies, audiovisual presentations, guest speakers, or small-group work.

For material related to this concept, go to Clip 12.3 on the Student Resource CD bound into the back of your textbook.

For some students, awards will serve as motivators and will encourage learning and achievement. However, be careful about giving awards or prizes as incentives for top achievers. High-achieving students are usually internally motivated, and poor achievers become frustrated when they must compete against them. One way to overcome this problem is by having students (high and low achievers) compete against their own records instead of against each other. For instance, students can keep charts of their daily or weekly grades and try to show improvement. Another way to avoid the problem is to have groups compete against each other. Students work together as a unit to win rewards with all members winning. Recognition is also an excellent motivator for students at all levels.

When students use their own initiative in exploring concepts and meet with success, a sense of competence (an intrinsic need to cope with the environment) often results and the level of aspiration often rises. Therefore, the use of strategies that maximize student involvement in learning may well stimulate a sense of competence along with a sense of accomplishment. Moreover, if students can help select and plan their own activities, they will find them even more interesting. Consequently, some forms of self-directed learning represent effective motivational strategies.

Make students active participants in the learning process. Students learn by doing, making, writing, designing, creating, and solving. Passivity dampens students' motivation and curiosity. Pose questions. Don't tell students something when you can ask them. Encourage students to suggest approaches to a problem or to guess the results of an experiment. Use small-group work.

Students desire variety, action, excitement, and novelty. Indeed, they would much rather read a story with many subplots or a lot of action than read a slow-moving, single-plot story. Furthermore, they prefer stimuli that are new or represent new experiences to stimuli that are routine or familiar. In other words, you should try to add life to your lessons by keeping your lessons lively; by introducing interesting, stimulating materials and teaching techniques; and by using approaches ranging from pauses to humor. Humor, for example, will give your students a change of pace. The pauses will give students time to think, ponder, and reflect. Complete Expansion Activity 12.1: Motivators to explore motivational strategies at various grade levels.

EXPANSION ACTIVITY 12.1   Motivators

Read the following list of motivational strategies. Which would be effective at the elementary level, secondary level, or at all levels? Discuss your selections with your classmates.

1. Use variety and occasional surprises in your lesson.
2. Challenge motivated students and guarantee success for slow learners.
3. Write messages on the papers you return to students.
4. Teach with popular songs.
5. Let students conduct lessons.
6. Ask students to present daily newscasts.
7. Be enthusiastic.
8. Keep progress records.
9. Videotape special events.
10. Teach with newspapers.
11. Make materials vivid and novel.
12. Allow for learner choice and control.
13. Relate lessons to students' lives.
14. Give class a pizza party if all tests scores are above 80%.

Teacher Expectations

Hold high, but realistic, expectations for your students. Research has shown that a teacher's expectations have a powerful effect on students' performance. If you act as though you expect your students to be motivated, hardworking, and interested in your class, they are more likely to be so. Researchers have found that students who feel they have supportive, caring teachers are more strongly motivated to engage in academic work than students with unsupportive, uncaring teachers (McCombs, 2001; Newman, 2002).

Set realistic expectations for students when you make assignments, give presentations, conduct discussions, and grade examinations. "Realistic" in this context means that your standards are high enough to motivate students to do their best work but not so high that students will inevitably be frustrated in trying to meet those expectations. To develop the drive to achieve, students need to believe that achievement is possible—which means that you need to provide early opportunities for success.

Students tend to perform better and feel more personally adequate when you set high expectations and hold them to these expectations (Good & Brophy, 1987). This **self-fulfilling prophecy** holds important ramifications for teachers; namely, students behave and achieve in accordance with your expectations.

Help your students set achievable goals for themselves. Failure to attain unrealistic goals can disappoint and frustrate students. Encourage students to focus on their continued improvement, not just on their grade on any one test or assignment. Help students evaluate their progress by encouraging them to critique their own work, analyze their strengths, and work on their weaknesses. For example, consider asking students to submit self-evaluation forms with one or two assignments.

Classroom interaction studies suggest that teachers tend to favor students they perceive as high achievers. Indeed, high achievers often receive more time to answer questions and more positive feedback, and they have more and higher quality interaction with their teachers. In fact, Cooper and Good (1983, p. 10) offer several common ways that teachers respond differently to high-achieving students ("highs") than to low-achieving students ("lows").

1. Seating lows far from the teacher

2. Paying less attention to lows in academic situations (using less eye contact, nods, winks, and smiles)

3. Calling on lows less often to answer classroom questions

4. Waiting less time for lows to answer questions

5. Criticizing lows more frequently than highs for incorrect classroom responses

6. Praising lows less frequently than highs after successful classroom responses

7. Praising lows more frequently than highs for marginal or inadequate classroom responses

8. Providing lows with less accurate and less detailed feedback than highs

9. Demanding less work and effort from lows than from highs

10. Interrupting performance of lows more frequently than highs

These findings suggest that teachers tend to give more support to the students they view as more capable. As a result, the interactions between the more capable students and their teachers tend to be more positive.

Students' motivation, aspiration, and self-concept can be affected to a considerable extent by your viewpoints and actions. When you expect students to do poorly, you may unconsciously give them less encouragement, less time to answer questions, and less attention. As this pattern continues over the year, students move closer and closer to your expectations. Be aware, then, that students are using your actions as a mirror of themselves, so challenge your students and communicate a belief in their abilities—and mean it. Complete Expansion Activity 12.2: Classroom Design, which will let you design your own motivationally rich classroom.

This concludes the discussion of the stimulation approach to motivation. Table 12.2 reviews the major concepts covered. Review the table and complete Review and Reflective Exercise 12.2, which will check your understanding of the concepts presented in this section.

TABLE 12.2 Stimulation Approach to Motivation

Factor	Description
Classroom atmosphere	The climate of the classroom, which generally is related to leadership style, environmental arrangement, and communication
Stimulation	Engaging and interesting factors that attract and involve students
Modeling	The demonstration of desired values and behaviors by a person admired by students
Set induction	Gaining students' attention and interest at the outset of a lesson
Teacher expectation	Perception of how well students will do, which often becomes a self-fulfilling prophecy

The Reinforcement Approach to Motivation

Reinforcement, or the rewarding of desired actions, is a long-recognized motivational technique. This technique is based on the principle that actions that induce pleasure tend to be repeated. Essentially, we tend to behave in ways that result in a valued payoff, or reward. Thus, if a student will work at obtaining something, the something (event, object, action, etc.) acts as a reinforcer for that student and will be a motivator. A reinforcer, however, may serve as a motivator for one student, but not for another. In other words, the reinforcement is proven to be a motivator only if the desired behaviors are increased or enhanced. Grades, for example, are not motivators to all students. Any repeated student actions, appropriate or inappropriate, are being reinforced in some way with a payoff; that is, the student is being motivated by a reward to behave as he or she does. Reinforcement, then, can be an effective motivator when used appropriately. Let's now take a close look at teacher reinforcement and its function as a motivator.

Positive Versus Negative Reinforcement

Reinforcement can be positive or negative. **Positive reinforcement** occurs when something valued by the student is presented as a result of some student action. Possible positive reinforcers are grades, praise, and stickers.

Negative reinforcement, on the other hand, involves the removal of an aversive stimulus, such as a test or the threat of detention. In effect, students are placed in an undesirable situation from which they are motivated to escape by means of appropriate actions. Note that the student is in control with negative reinforcement; that is, the negative situation can be escaped with appropriate actions.

REVIEW AND REFLECTIVE EXERCISE 12.2 Discuss the key factors in the stimulation view of motivation.

REVIEW

- Define motivation from the stimulation perspective and describe its key components.
- How would you summarize the stimulation view of motivation?

REFLECTION

- Recall a school situation in which you were highly motivated to accomplish something. How would you describe your motivation in terms of the stimulation view of motivation?
- Think about several of your own past schoolmates who showed low motivation in school. Why do you think they behaved the way they did? What teaching strategies might have helped them?

APPLY AND REFLECT 12.6

You should use a mix of reinforcers, tangible rewards, social rewards, feedback, and teacher actions in your classroom. Make a list of appropriate reinforcers for the grade level you expect to teach.

Reinforcement Techniques

What types of reinforcement typically are best for motivating students? Unfortunately, this is not an easy question to answer. The most effective technique in any given situation depends on such variables as the grade level, the student, the learning activity, and you as the teacher. Four reinforcement sources, however, have proven to be effective at motivating students: teacher approval, observation of other students, knowledge of results, and reward mechanisms.

Teacher approval can take one of two forms: verbal or nonverbal. **Verbal reinforcement** occurs when you follow a student action or response with a positive comment. Typical examples often include one-word "Good!" or brief-phrase comments such as "That's right!" and "Great idea!" You should take care not to overuse such brief-phrase reinforcers, for they can lose their effectiveness if you use a single one exclusively. Therefore, be a wise verbal reinforcer: Choose a variety of comments, and make sure you use them only for appropriate actions or responses.

Two basic questions relative to student motivation are "Where does it come from—within or outside, and how do you get it?" The answers are quite complicated and there are no rigid answers. Most often, reinforcers that are used in schools to motivate students are things given to students. The use of good grades, praise, privileges, games, puzzles, and even candy are commonly used as positive reinforcers, while negative reinforcers commonly include bad grades, punishments, and loss of privileges.

Reward your students' successes. Both positive and negative comments influence motivation, but research consistently indicates that students are more affected by positive feedback and success. Praise builds students' self-confidence, competence, and self-esteem. Recognize sincere efforts even if the product is less than stellar. If a student's performance is weak, let the student know that you believe he or she can improve and succeed over time. Also, don't overlook how student ideas may be used as reinforcers: You should apply, compare, and build on contributions made by students. Consequently, when you show that what students say is important, they are motivated to participate even more.

APPLY AND REFLECT 12.7 Having students keep charts of their daily and weekly grades and encouraging them to show improvement is a good reinforcer. How effective do you think this reinforcer would be at the grade level you expect to teach? Why?

Not all reinforcers have the same effect on every child. You should find out what reinforcers work best with which children—that is, individualize the use of particular reinforcers. For one student it might be praise, for another it might be getting to spend more time participating in a favorite activity, for another it might involve being a hall monitor for a week, and for yet another it could be getting to surf the Internet. Natural reinforcers like praise and privileges are generally recommended over material rewards like candy, stars, and money.

Give students feedback as quickly as possible. Return tests and papers promptly, and reward success publicly and immediately. Give students some indication of how well they have done and how to improve. Rewards can be as simple as saying a student's response was good, with an indication of why it was good, or mentioning the names of contributors: "Robert's point about pollution really synthesized the ideas we had been discussing."

When a physical action is used for sending a message of approval for a student action or response, it is referred to as **nonverbal reinforcement.** A nod of approval, a smile, eye contact, movement toward a student, or any other positive gesture, for example, shows students they are correct or on the right track. Nonverbal reinforcement is a powerful motivator—perhaps even more powerful than verbal reinforcement.

When student actions are only partially acceptable, you want to motivate the student so that he or she will continue to attempt the desired action. For example, you might want to reinforce an attempt at solving a geometry proof or the fact that the procedure used in investigating a problem was correct. In effect, you want to differentially reinforce the acceptable parts of a student action or the attempt itself. In such situations, you are using the technique of **qualified reinforcement.** Qualified reinforcement can be an effective technique for getting your shy and less able students more involved in class activities.

Vicarious Motivation

Seeing other students being reinforced for their actions can motivate students. That is, if a student sees another student reinforced for certain behaviors, he or she tends to act in the same way if the reinforcement is desirable. For example, if a student is given exemption from the unit test for doing well on the chapter tests, that reinforcement may motivate other students to do well on chapter tests. The term applied to this type of motivation is **vicarious motivation.** In effect, the first student serves as a model for the desired behaviors.

Vicarious motivation usually is quite efficient in that desired actions are learned immediately; no teaching is required. Therefore, with properly chosen reinforcers and appropriate application, vicarious motivation can initiate desired new actions and behaviors.

One important principle of behavior is that we can promote less-desired (low-strength) activities by linking them to more-desired activities. In other words, access to something desirable is made contingent on doing something less desirable. For example, a teacher might say, "As soon as you finish your work, you may go outside" or "Clean up your art project, and then I will read you a story." These are examples of the Premack Principle (Premack, 1965). Teachers can use the Premack Principle by alternating more enjoyable activities with less enjoyable ones and making participation in the enjoyable activities depend on successful completion of the less enjoyable ones. For example, in elementary school, it may be a good idea to schedule computer time, which most students consider an enjoyable activity, after completion of a difficult subject.

Consequences that weaken behavior are called punishers. Punishment can take two primary forms: presentation punishment and removal punishment. Presentation punishment is the use of unpleasant consequences, or aversive stimuli, as when a student is scolded. Removal punishment is the withdrawal of a pleasant consequence. Examples include loss of a privilege, having to stay in during recess, or having to stay after school. One frequently used form of removal punishment in classrooms is time-out, in which students who misbehave are required to sit in the corner or in the hall for several minutes.

Feedback as Motivator

Three techniques can be used to provide feedback to students: praise, disclosure of results, and grades. If they are to be effective, these feedback techniques must be carefully and systematically applied. Simply "handing out" positive feedback will, in time, destroy any technique's effectiveness as a motivator. Appropriately used feedback, therefore, is contingent on the desired action, specifies clearly the action being reinforced, and is believable (O'Leary & O'Leary, 1977). In other words, positive feedback should be a sincere recognition of student work that has been well done.

Teachers have long acknowledged and recognized the power of praise as a compelling motivator. Brophy (1981), in a comprehensive analysis of praise, attests to the importance of teacher praise as a reinforcement technique. Indeed, Brophy suggests that praise is more powerful than general reinforcement because it generally calls for teacher attention and energy beyond the use of the standard one-word or short phrase response ("Good," "Fine answer," or "Okay"). To be effective, praise should be specific, attend to students' accomplishments, help students appreciate their accomplishments, and focus attention on task-relevant behavior. Praise that is global and general or that rewards mere participation, compares students with others, or focuses attention on external authority is generally ineffective. Praise can lay the foundation for lasting internal change because it works to improve students' self-esteem. Finally, don't forget to "catch them being good" and praise them.

Providing students with the results of assigned tasks motivates some students because it communicates the correctness of responses. Results that indicate success lead to renewed vigor, whereas

Providing feedback on how well a student did on assigned work is often an effective motivator.

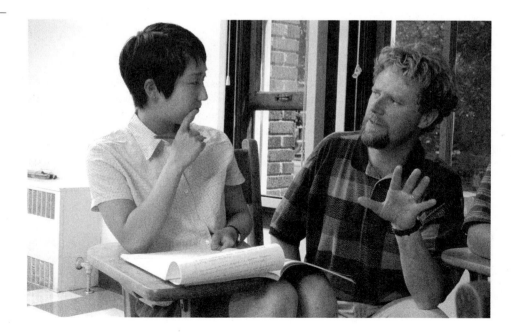

indications of needed corrective measures communicate what actions or efforts are needed for improving performance. If you are to ensure that students benefit from the motivational effects of work results, you must return papers and tests to students immediately—with more than a simple grade marked on them. Indeed, it is suggested that teachers can achieve maximum incentive from marking papers if each returned paper is personalized with comments about strengths and weaknesses. Simple comments written in the margins should be sufficient for offering students needed guidance.

Teachers have always considered tests and grades as highly motivational in nature. Unfortunately, the research does not support the conjecture that tests and grades motivate students to learn but, rather, that tests typically motivate students to cram—that is, learn for the test. Actually, tests and good grades seem to be motivational only to top students, while offering only limited incentive to low-ability students. Therefore, you would be wise not to make grades your primary source of motivation. Instead, you should appeal to students' intrinsic motives and rely more on cooperative and self-directed strategies. Such structures are more likely to be motivational for students.

Reward Mechanisms

As used here, a **reward mechanism** is a more formal system of reinforcement. It is an agreement whereby students earn specified rewards for displaying certain types of behaviors. In one such successful system, students earn tokens, points, stars, or checks—or anything else that seems appropriate—for performing desired academic and classroom behaviors. These tokens are then periodically exchanged for a desirable reward, such as free time, no homework, tangible objects, educational games, or anything desired by the students that is deemed appropriate.

You can also offer a menu of rewards in a reward mechanism system. Students then purchase the rewards for different numbers of tokens—for instance, few tokens yield less desirable rewards, and many tokens yield more desirable rewards. For example, students might be excused from a homework assignment for a few tokens and be allowed to listen to music in class for several tokens.

APPLY AND REFLECT 12.8	Educational games are good reinforcers. What are some games that would be appropriate at the grade level you expect to teach?

An advantage to using the more formal reward mechanism is that students are not inadvertently overlooked from receiving reinforcement. It is, however, sometimes difficult to find adequate reinforcers for students. Two common ways of identifying such reinforcers are simply asking students directly or having them fill out a questionnaire about desired reinforcers. Moreover, simply observing students during their free time or after they finish their work can give you valuable clues as to what can be used for reinforcement. The best reinforcers frequently depend on the students, the subject, and the situation. Complete Expansion Activity 12.3: Motivators to identify classroom motivators and strategies for their use.

EXPANSION ACTIVITY 12.3   Motivators

Make a list of motivators as well as specific strategies that teachers can use to enhance individual and group motivation in their classrooms. Share your list and strategies with your classmates.

1. What evidence suggests that many adolescents are self-centered?

2. If adolescents are self-centered, how would you use this characteristic to make your teaching more effective?

◆ ◆ ◆

Always keep one fact in mind when working with adolescents: developmentally, adolescents ARE self-centered. This is the time they are trying to figure out who they are and how they fit in the world around them. They want to be unique, but they want to fit in. Rather than trying to work against that developmental characteristic, we'd do better to use it to our advantage.

Relevance is a huge issue regardless of what subject or grade level we teach. Most of us have at some point in our lives asked, "Why do I have to learn this?" (I cried it almost daily while taking Geometry in high school; I didn't see relevance until I took Trigonometry.)

I think the key is to NOT water down the curriculum, but, rather, look for ways to bring the curriculum into our kids' real lives. It is a task that really forces us to think outside the box and to get to know our kids and their interests well. For example,

when teaching point of view—specifically the concept of, "How would the story change if this other character told the story?"—I have to start with something they already know, usually what they call "He say—she say" stories. Every time I have skipped that step, they continue to change all the events of the story instead of merely telling it as that other person has interpreted it. Point of view now gets a nod because it makes sense in their own lives.

I think the real key with adolescents is to start with them and move the concept outward. It's not always easy, but my kids are always more successful when I figure out a way to do this.

—*ELLEN, middle-level teacher*

SOURCE: www.middleweb.com. Reprinted with permission.

Contingency Contracts

Contingency contracts are formal, written agreements between a teacher and student that describe exactly what the student must do to earn a desired privilege or reward. These contracts can be written by the teacher and presented to the student for agreement, or the student can work out the contract and present it to the teacher. Contracts are usually best, however, when they are written by the teacher and student together in a negotiating process. Regardless of the contract development process followed, the contract should specify exactly what the student will do to earn the privilege or reward. A sample contingency contract is shown in Figure 12.2.

Contracts should encourage students to make realistic expectations of their abilities. Accordingly, you can stipulate that the contract can be changed, but there should be a built-in penalty for any alterations.

Let us now apply the motivation concepts from this chapter. Complete Web Link 12.1: Motivation, which will let you develop some motivation ideas of your own.

No matter what your specific explanations for the sources of motivation, you should be aware that no one is completely unmotivated. Even doing nothing takes motivation. Table 12.3 gives a review of the major concepts in this section. Review the table and complete Review and Reflective Exercise 12.3, which will check your understanding of this section.

Figure 12.2
A Sample Contract

Read through the listed items and check those you would like to do. Then decide for what grade you would like to contract. Grades will be given as follows:

D—The starred items plus one more from each group

C—The starred items plus two more from each group

B—The starred items plus three more from each group

A—The starred items plus four more from each group

Discuss your choice with your teacher, and sign your name in the proper place.

I, _____ , agree to complete the following work on the unit at a level of _____ or better.
(Grade)

 * Read assigned text chapters

 * Complete in-class and out-of-class assignments

 * Complete unit test at or above contracted grade level

Group I

 * Do one library assignment

 1. Prepare an outline of unit content

 2. Write a one-page paper on a unit topic

 3. Complete an optional writing assignment

 4. Develop an annotated bibliography related to the unit

 5. Review a textbook that addresses the unit topic and write a short report on its contents

Group II

 * Give one class demonstration

 1. Conduct a short project related to the unit content

 2. Lead a class discussion of a topic related to this unit

 3. Locate and present to class unit-related newspaper articles

 4. Draw some conclusions relative to the importance of the unit topic to your everyday life

_____

Date

_____

Student's Signature

_____

Teacher's Signature

TABLE 12.3   Reinforcement Approach to Motivation

Factor	Description
Positive reinforcement	Presentation of a desired stimulus to strengthen the likelihood of a behavior or an event
Negative reinforcement	Removal of an unpleasant stimulus to strengthen the likelihood of a behavior or an event
Verbal reinforcement	Presentation of positive comments as a consequence to strengthen student behavior or an event
Nonverbal reinforcement	Use of a physical action as a positive consequence to strengthen behavior or an event
Vicarious motivation	Strengthening of behavior because of a desire to receive consequences received by others who exhibit that behavior
Feedback	Disclosure of correctness of response
Reward mechanism	Formal system of reinforcement
Contingency contract	Formal, written agreement between student and teacher as to what students will do for receiving a reward

REVIEW AND REFLECTIVE EXERCISE 12.3   Discuss the key factors in the reinforcement view of motivation.

REVIEW

- Describe the different reinforcement types.
- Define motivation from the reinforcement perspective and describe its key components.
- How would you summarize the reinforcement perspective to motivation?
- What is a contingency contract?

REFLECTION

- Explain how motivation has intensity and direction. How would you use rewards, praise, and grades as incentives to enhance individual and group motivation to learn at the grade level you expect to teach? Would you use contingency contract at this grade level?
- Recall a school situation in which you were highly motivated to accomplish something. How would you describe your motivation in terms of the reinforcement view of motivation?

SUMMARY

Motivation is largely influenced by internal factors, the teacher's action, and the physical environment. There is no surefire method of motivating students. Motivation techniques that work in one situation may be totally ineffective in another.

Intrinsic Versus Extrinsic Motivation

- Motivation can come from within (intrinsic motivation) or outside (extrinsic motivation) an individual. Intrinsic motivation is related to an individual's attitudes, needs, personality factors, and values. Extrinsic motivation comes from stimulation within the environment and from the application of desired incentives.

The Cognitive Approach to Motivation

- We are motivated by our perception of events. Our perceptions are related to such internal attributes as attitudes, needs, curiosity, interests, and sense of well-being.
- Central to the desire to attend to the learning process is classroom atmosphere. Teachers should establish a democratic classroom that is attractive and characterized by open communication.

The Stimulation Approach to Motivation

- Teachers must use various stimulus variation techniques for gaining and maintaining student attention. Commonly used techniques for providing the needed changes in stimuli include using gestures, refocusing student attention, varying classroom interaction styles, shifting students' sensory channels, and using teacher movement. Teacher enthusiasm can also be an effective motivator. When you show excitement and interest in your lesson, that excitement is often communicated to students.
- A strong beginning for your lesson is crucial for motivating students' desire to learn. Begin each lesson with an attention-getting device that will stimulate interest in the coming lesson. The beginning of a lesson should be followed up with other stimulating devices that will keep students interested.

The Reinforcement Approach to Motivation

- Reinforcement is a long-recognized technique for motivating students. Teachers should select their reinforcers based on their knowledge of the students and subject.
- Don't rely on grades exclusively for providing feedback; offering praise and disclosing the results of assigned work can also motivate students. Reward mechanism and contingency contracts offer more formal motivational systems.

DISCUSSION QUESTIONS AND ACTIVITIES

1. **Reinforcement menus.** Develop a list of incentives that could be used in the subject and at the grade level you expect to teach. Arrange them in ascending order of value.
2. **Contingency contracts.** Set up a sample contingency contract for a unit in a subject at the grade level you expect to teach.

TECHNOLOGY AND EDUCATION

There are many resources and ideas available to provide guidance for motivating and reinforcing students. Conduct Web searches using available search engines relative to classroom motivation and reinforcement. Identify ideas and techniques you feel would be successful for you in the subject and at the grade level you expect to teach. Share your findings with classmates. Do they agree?

DECONSTRUCTING THE STANDARDS

Chapter 12 content addresses topics related to INTASC Standard 5.

♦ INTASC Standard 5 states: *Classroom Motivation and Management:* The teacher uses an understanding of individual and group motivation and behavior to create a learning environment that encourages positive social interaction, active engagement in learning, and self-motivation.

For Standard 5, write your response to the following:

- Which part(s) of the standard does this chapter address?
- How does this chapter address this standard?
- How will the concepts in this chapter help you apply this standard as a teacher?

PRAXIS CONNECTION

Log on to the Web-based student study site at http://www.sagepub.com/eis2study. Access the Praxis II: Principles of Learning and Teaching assessments and/or state-related exams and complete the Chapter 12 test preparation exercises.

PORTFOLIO CONNECTION

Log on to the Web-based student study site at http://www.sagepub.com/eis2study. Access the Portfolio Connection. Complete the Chapter 12 portfolio link to INTASC activities.

CONNECTION WITH THE FIELD

1. **Interview.** Interview an elementary and a secondary teacher. Ask them to share the strategies they use to motivate their students. How do they compare?
2. **Classroom observation.** Complete several school observations. Plan your visits to collect viable observational data related to motivation:
   a. The use of stimulus variation
   b. The different types of stimulus variation used by the teachers
   c. Examples of teacher enthusiasm displayed
   d. The use of positive and negative reinforcement
   e. The different types of reinforcement used by the teachers
   f. The use of praise and encouragement

3. **Teaching.** Teach a 20-minute minilesson to a group of students or to peers. Try to use as much stimulus variation and as many reinforcement techniques as possible in your lesson. If possible, videotape the lesson.

4. **Teaching analysis.** Study the videotape you made in Activity 3. Record your uses of stimulus variation and reinforcement. Draw some conclusions regarding your proficiency in the use of stimulus variation and reinforcement.

CHAPTER 13

Managing the Classroom Environment

Leadership means not having to be completely in harmony with everyone else.

—WINSTON CHURCHILL

OVERVIEW

Conducting the business of the classroom for the achievement of learning intent is the function of a teacher, and one that requires skill at effective leadership and management. Management is often difficult in the classroom, which is a dynamic system of hundreds of interactions that must be monitored. In other words, classroom management is not an easy task. It takes planning.

All teachers have management problems. Therefore, you must deal effectively with misbehavior if you are to accomplish your instructional goals. How you deal with misbehavior depends on your management philosophy and the approach you tend to endorse. As such, this chapter will examine the principles of three current approaches to classroom management and some illustrative models.

Also, if classroom managers are to function effectively, they require an understanding of misbehavior. Therefore, I will address how to deal with misbehavior. I will examine such issues as ways to start the year off right, the establishment of rules, the effective monitoring of a classroom, and the appropriate use of punishment. Finally, teacher-tested ideas for conducting the business of the classroom will be presented.

OBJECTIVES

After completing your study of Chapter 13, you should be able to do the following:

- Define *classroom management* and identify its various aspects.
- Identify similarities and differences in classroom management at the elementary, middle, and secondary levels.
- Identify and describe the self-discipline, instructional, and desist approaches to classroom management, as well as characteristics of the different illustrative models of discipline associated with each approach.

- Identify and discuss causes of classroom misbehavior.
- Discuss organizational techniques that lead to effective classroom management.
- Identify and discuss teacher-tested techniques for effectively preventing classroom management problems.
- Identify and discuss punishment and its appropriate use in the classroom.

Effective teaching requires effective classroom leadership and management. Indeed, teachers, administrators, parents, and students report that misbehavior interferes a great deal with the ability of a teacher to teach and with the ability of students to learn (Charles, 2002; Evertson, Emmer, & Worsham, 2003; Gallup & Elam, 1988). Although such reports suggest that there are serious management and discipline problems in the public schools, it would be a mistake to assume that schools are out of control.

What is the role of classroom leadership and management? Before we can develop techniques for its improvement, we must know what their functions should be.

The Role of Classroom Leadership

What type of leader do you want to be? Do you want to be stimulating, warm, caring, fair, funny, and interesting? Or would you prefer to be commanding, dominating, sharp, critical, and harsh? Perhaps you choose to be lackadaisical and completely permissive? These characteristics determine your leadership style: authoritarian, democratic, or laissez-faire. The type of leader you become also depends on the policies of the school, your students, and your personality. Some teachers feel students lack the maturity and ability to be involved in decision making; therefore, they rely heavily on the authoritarian style of leadership.

The *authoritarian* style of leadership is characterized by power, domination, pressure, and criticism. The authoritarian teacher assumes the sole responsibility for making all decisions for the class and uses pressure, a sharp voice, and fear in forcing compliance. Accordingly, the authoritarian teacher uses criticism and "putdowns" for motivating students, which often results in an atmosphere of hostility and, for students, feelings of powerlessness, competitiveness, high dependency, and alienation from the subject matter (Schmuck & Schmuck, 1988). Students in this type of atmosphere often develop a fear of failure, low self-esteem, and a defeatist attitude. Consequently, students tend to give up when they encounter a new or difficult task.

The *democratic* teacher is kind, caring, and warm, but also firm. The democratic leader tries to provide stimulation from within through a sharing of responsibility and encouragement, rather than demands. Self-esteem is developed by a sharing of responsibility, and students are encouraged when they make mistakes. The democratic classroom atmosphere is one of openness, friendly communication, and independence, with a resultant high level of productivity and performance.

The *laissez-faire* leader is completely permissive. Anything goes, which generally leads to chaos. The classroom is often disorganized, which causes student frustration, a high level of stress, and a feeling of being totally overwhelmed and lost.

A change from the obsolete authoritarian approach of demanding submission to a more democratic approach based on freedom, choice, and responsibility would do much for helping students develop a positive feeling toward school and your subject. Students might learn to be truly responsible individuals.

Teaching and classroom leadership can be stressful. Indeed, teaching has been rated one of the five most stressful occupations. Teachers report experiencing high stress related to lack of resources and support, high-stakes testing, accountability requirements, hostile parents, inadequate discipline

Making instruction relevant and interesting keeps students on task and curbs potential undesirable behaviors.

policies, noisy students, the attitude and actions of fellow teachers, lack of professional autonomy, moderate pay, and lack of recognition. As in other countries, teacher burnout is a serious problem in the United States. Signs of teacher stress and burnout may include being tired, frustrated, overwhelmed and irritable, and bringing problems home. Teacher stress and burnout doesn't just happen once in a career. So, it is vital to learn how to cope with problems appropriately. Ideas to reduce stress and burnout include the following:

- *Learn to laugh.* Learn to put things in perspective.

- *Prioritize responsibilities.* What are the most important things to get done?

- *Do relaxing exercises.* Walk, concentrate on a hobby, and turn off the news. At school, when you have a few minutes, walk around the classroom, buy a pedometer, and wear it to increase awareness of how much or little you move each day (two to three miles should be a goal).

- *Watch your diet.* Caffeine, sugar, and unbalanced meals create stress on your body and a dependency that, if left unfilled, results in mental stress.

- *Meditation.* Turn off the lights and visualize your plans for the weekend or a vacation. Take deep breaths and relax.

School administrations frequently cause stress when they do not support teachers. Districts need to listen to teachers, make them part of the decision-making teams, and even provide coping strategies.

ON YOUR OWN 13.1   View From the Classroom

Log on to the Web-based student study site at http://www.sagepub.com/eis2study. Review the Chapter 13 teacher surveys and react to the related activities.

For material related to this concept, go to Clip 13.1 on the Student Resource CD bound into the back of your textbook.

The Role of Classroom Management

Classroom management is the process of organizing and conducting the business of the classroom relatively free of behavior problems. Classroom management is often perceived as related to the preservation of order and the maintenance of control. But this view is too simplistic; classroom management means much more. Indeed, it involves the establishment and maintenance of the classroom environment so that educational goals can be accomplished.

REFLECTIONS ON TEACHER PRACTICE 13.1 | Managing the Classroom

1. Why is classroom management a major problem for many teachers?

2. Can teachers really treat all students equally?

◆ ◆ ◆

I believe the selection of a classroom management strategy has to be based on the teacher's personality and the characteristics of the class being managed. To use a system that doesn't fit you will create unnecessary stress and you won't use it well. If it doesn't suit the students, it will not work either. So, I suggest that you study as many strategies as you can and evaluate them in terms of your personality.

My biggest suggestion is, whatever strategy you choose, do not attempt to teach until it is working. If you begin the year insisting on proper discipline and behavior, it will become a habit that will continue through the rest of the year. If you let things slide at the beginning, the students will expect it to last till the end. This doesn't mean that you have to be an ogre until Thanksgiving. It does mean

that you must find a way to create the atmosphere you want before you do any serious amount of teaching.

As for respect, the students will respect you when you are consistent. Students, as a group, don't like surprises. There can be few, if any, exceptions to rules and procedures. If any exceptions should become necessary, you should explain to the students why an exception has been made. The other side of respect is to respect students in return. Whatever forms of respect you demand from your students you should extend to them as well.

—*JOHN VOSE, elementary school teacher*

SOURCE: Reprinted with permission from ProTeacher, a professional community for elementary school teachers (http://www.proteacher.net).

ON YOUR OWN 13.2   Reflections on Teacher Practice

Read and reflect on the viewpoints expressed in Managing the Classroom. Log on to the Web-based student study site at http://www.sagepub.com/eis2study and react to the related activities.

Central to effective management is the ability to provide a positive social and physical environment conducive to the learning process. The way desks, tables, and other classroom materials are arranged has an influence on order in the classroom. There are several aspects of the physical space that must be addressed. First, you need to arrange the floor space for placement of student desks, the teacher's desk, computers, bookcases, filing cabinets, tables, and activity centers. Second, you need to decide how to store classroom materials, including textbooks, resource books, instructional materials, frequently used materials, and equipment. Finally, you must decide how to use wall space and bulletin boards. In thinking about how to organize the classroom physical space, you need to decide what type of instructional activities students will mainly be engaged in (small group, whole class, centers, individual assignments, etc.). Arrange your classroom environment to support that type of activity (Crane, 2001). You should create an environment where students feel valued and comfortable, thus setting the stage for teaching and learning. Keep in mind, however, that your classroom should be enticing, with a cheerful appearance, but not cluttered.

Although not its sole component, another highly important aspect of classroom management is **discipline,** which, as noted earlier, perennially appears as the major concern of teachers, administrators, parents, and students. Discipline should not be viewed as being primarily concerned with punishment. **Punishment** involves the consequences of misbehavior, whereas discipline deals with the prevention of classroom misbehavior as well as the consequences of disruptive actions. This chapter will focus on discipline rather than punishment because your success as a classroom teacher will depend on your adequacy in making sound decisions in both of these areas.

Classroom management experts report changes in thinking about the best way to manage classrooms. The emphasis has been on creating and applying rules to control students' behavior. The newer focus, however, is more on students' needs for nurturing relationships and opportunities for self-regulation (Kennedy et al., 2001). The newer trend places more emphasis on guiding students to become more proficient at self-discipline and less dependent on external control. We will look at some of these models in the next section.

Elementary, middle, and secondary school classrooms involve many similar management issues. At all levels, good classroom managers design the classroom environment for optimal learning, establish and maintain rules, get students to cooperate, effectively deal with problems, and use good communication strategies. Middle and secondary students' problems, however, can be more longstanding and more deeply ingrained and, as such, more difficult to modify than those of younger children. Also, in secondary school, students sometimes are resistant to authority, and discipline problems are frequently more severe and students potentially more unruly and even dangerous. At the same time, some adolescents resist authority and place greater importance on peer norms. Because most middle and secondary students have more advanced reasoning skills than younger students, they generally demand more elaborate and logical explanation of rules and discipline. Keep these differences between elementary, middle, and secondary schools in mind as we explore effective classroom management. Complete Web Link 13.1: Organizing a Classroom, which will give you some tips on organizing your classroom for better on-task behaviors.

WEB LINK 13.1   Organizing a Classroom

Access Web sites: http://www.theteachersguide.com/ClassManagement.htm and http://www.pacificnet.net/~mandel/ClassroomManagement.html. Analyze the ideas presented on organizing a classroom. Discuss the ideas that you think will be useful for you at the grade level you expect to teach with classmates.

As a teacher, you will be expected to provide for all students assigned to you. When special-needs students are assigned to be integrated into your classroom, you must ensure that there is successful integration. This may call for some major modifications or only minor modifications in your classroom management plan. However, only a few accommodations need to be made in your management plan for most special-needs students. Remember that most special-needs students want to be treated like everyone else.

As a teacher, you must be aware of the principles and consequences of any classroom management decisions and strategies you may wish to implement. For an overview of the various strategies, let's take a look at three such management approaches: the self-discipline approach, the instructional approach, and the desist approach.

Approaches to Classroom Management

The three approaches to classroom management form a continuum, from the self-discipline approach at one extreme, to the instructional approach, to the desist approach at the opposite extreme. The representative models to be discussed are depicted in Figure 13.1.

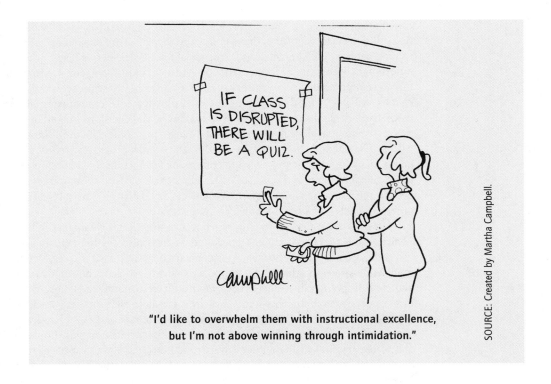

SOURCE: Created by Martha Campbell.

"I'd like to overwhelm them with instructional excellence,
but I'm not above winning through intimidation."

The Self-Discipline Approach

The **self-discipline approach** is built on the premise that students can be trusted to evaluate and change their actions, so their behaviors are beneficial and appropriate to self and to the class as a whole. The approach views classroom management as a function of the teacher's ability to build and establish working teacher-student relationships. In a word, advocates argue that teachers need to recognize the dignity of students and that they must exhibit the attitudinal qualities of realness, trust, acceptance, and empathy. This approach represents the most democratic view of classroom management. With these attitudinal qualities in mind, let's look at four of the more democratic classroom management models.

Reality Therapy

Developed by William Glasser (1965, 1977, 1986), **reality therapy** is a strategy that helps students take the responsibility for examining and solving their own problems. Glasser believes that students are rational beings and can control their behavior if they wish. For example, witness the usual good student behaviors found on the first day of school.

Furthermore, Glasser suggests that students often must be assisted in making good choices rather than bad choices. Indeed, he feels that students must be guided so that they become responsible individuals able to satisfy their needs in the real world. That is to say, they must be guided toward reality. It is the teacher's job to provide the needed guidance so that students make good choices. The teacher must help students examine their behaviors in light of their benefit to self and to the class. If a behavior is found inappropriate, the individual student must be assisted in devising a realistic, written plan for changing the inappropriate behavior. No excuses are acceptable for not carrying out the devised plan. The student has made a commitment and is held to it. If the original plan proves inadequate, it is essential that both the teacher and student be willing to reexamine the plan and to renew or change the commitment. If the student is unwilling to make the commitment, he or she should not be allowed to remain in the classroom.

**Figure 13.1
The Continuum
of Classroom
Management Model**

Note that reality therapy places the responsibility on the student, not the teacher. The teacher does not punish. In fact, Glasser does not believe in punishment. He feels punishment hinders personal development and is ineffective. If a student disrupts the class, he or she simply is removed until a commitment for change has been worked out. Thus, the teacher's function is to assist students in becoming responsible, productive members of the classroom.

Rules that are enforced are essential according to Glasser. Indeed, background and poor upbringing do not make poor behavior acceptable. Student responsibility must be stressed continually. Students are forced to acknowledge their behavior, and they should make value judgments regarding that behavior. For example, when a disruption occurs, the teacher should never ask why a student is doing what he or she is doing; rather, the teacher should ask, "What are you doing?" The emphasis should be put on the *you* so that there is no misinterpretation as to who is responsible. This question should be followed up with queries such as "Is this behavior against the rules?" or "Is this behavior helping you or this class?" If the misbehavior persists, a (private) conference is needed for working out a commitment for change. If the disruptions continue or the commitment is not followed, the consequences should become progressively more severe: principal conference, followed by parent conference, followed by in-school suspension, followed by out-of-school suspension, and finally with permanent exclusion from school.

Classroom meetings are an essential element in addressing problems in the Glasser model. Students sit in a close circle and discuss classroom situations and problems. The teacher's role is to provide background information as needed by the group and to give opinions sparingly. Classroom rules, consequences, and procedures are developed at such meetings, and all students are expected to participate in their formation. All students are expected to observe the agreed-upon rules and consequences. The rules are flexible, however, and could be changed with another meeting as the situation changes.

APPLY AND REFLECT 13.1	You should always stress student responsibility. Emphasize that good behaviors result from good choices. How easy would this be at the grade level you expect to teach?

Teacher Effectiveness Training (TET)

Teacher effectiveness training (TET), conceived by Dr. Thomas Gordon (1974), stresses the establishment of positive working relationships between teachers and students. Gordon believes that teachers can reduce disruptive student behaviors by using clearer, less provocative communication.

Furthermore, he recommends that nonverbal language and listening should be stressed as the teacher interacts with students in an atmosphere of openness and trust.

According to Gordon, the key to teacher effectiveness training is to identify who owns the problem when one develops in the learning environment: teacher or student. If the teacher is blocked from reaching the instructional goals by the student's actions, then the teacher owns the problem. For example, if students continuously talk as the teacher tries to teach, the teacher owns the problem because he or she is kept from reaching the goal of teaching. On the other hand, if the teacher feels annoyed by a student's behavior or if the teacher wishes a student would change his or her behavior, the problem likely belongs to the student. The student who says he or she hates the teacher or hates the subject has a problem.

When the teacher owns the problem, an I-message should be sent. An **I-message** tells the student how you feel about a problem situation and invites the student to change, to correct that situation—for example, "I am angry with this continuous talking in class," "I am disappointed in your behavior at the assembly," or "I can't hear myself think with the noise in this classroom." If the process works, the student (or class) should see the harm being done and change his or her (or their) behavior. If an I-message does not correct the problem, however, the teacher and student (class) are in a conflict situation, which calls for finding a solution through problem solving. When this happens, Gordon recommends that a "no-lose" problem resolution tactic be employed. The no-lose strategy is a six-step form of negotiation in which teacher and student (class) contribute relatively equally. First, the problem or conflict is clearly determined. Second, possible solutions are generated, with the teacher and student (class) presenting an equal number of ideas. These ideas are evaluated in the third step, and those unacceptable are rejected. During the fourth step, the remaining ideas are ranked and the best solution is selected. This is followed by the fifth step, a determination of how to implement the selected solution so that all parties are satisfied. The sixth and final step entails an assessment of how well the solution works. In general, punishment is not recognized as a viable option in the no-lose tactic because the student (class) would be placed in a losing situation.

A student-owned problem calls for active listening (or empathic listening) on the part of the teacher. That is, the teacher should listen carefully and become a counselor and supporter for the student, who should be encouraged to express his or her views. As such, the teacher should reflect back only the student's point of view and help the student find his or her own problem solution. The teacher's function is not to give or impose solutions to students' problems.

Inner Discipline

Inner discipline, developed by Barbara Coloroso (2002), a former nun and now a teacher and author, rejects "quick-fix" solutions to discipline problems. Instead, she suggests you focus on helping children develop their own self-discipline by owning up to their mistakes, thinking through solutions, and correcting their misdeeds while leaving their dignity intact.

Coloroso suggests that teachers treat kids with respect and help them develop inner discipline that will enable them to handle their own problems and to interact successfully with others. She believes that children can develop the ability to handle their own problems and can learn from their successes and mistakes. Coloroso suggests the teacher's role is to help students develop this ability by allowing them to make their own decisions and to grow from the results of those decisions, whatever they may be. It means giving students a sense of power in their own lives and offering them opportunities to make decisions, take responsibility for their actions, and learn from their successes and mistakes. Coloroso contends that students are worth all the effort teachers can expend on them and that school should be neither adult dominated nor student controlled. It should be a place where joint efforts are made to learn, relate, grow, and create community.

Teachers must, however, make sure that student decisions don't lead to situations that are life threatening, morally threatening, or unhealthy. This ability should be developed apart from typical systems of reward and punishment and will then serve individuals for the rest of their lives.

Consequences, natural and reasonable, should be associated with rules and should be allowed or invoked consistently when rules are violated. Students will then develop the inner discipline and self-confidence that will help them grow into responsible, resourceful, and resilient adults.

Coloroso suggests that teachers fall into three categories. "Brickwall teachers" are rigid, use power and coercion to control others, and teach what instead of how to think. They demand that students follow the rules without question. "Jellyfish teachers" provide little structure, consistency, or guidance and rely on putdowns, threats, and bribery to control students. Punishment and rewards are often arbitrary and inconsistent. These teachers are lax in discipline, set few limits, and more or less let students do what they want. "Backbone teachers" provide the support and structure necessary for students to behave creatively, cooperatively, and responsibly, which leads to inner discipline. They use rules that are clear and simple, with consequences that are reasonable, simple, valuable, and purposeful. Students have freedom to pursue opportunities and solve problems within established limits.

Beyond Discipline

In his book, *Beyond Discipline: From Compliance to Community,* Alfie Kohn (1996) questions the assumption that classroom problems are always the fault of students who don't do as they are told. Most teachers work to control children's behavior either by punishment or reward, which is often ineffective. Instead of acknowledging the possible problems of a dull curriculum or poor teaching, teachers place complete blame on students for their negative behavior.

Kohn suggests that our present approaches that are based on reward and punishment are only short-term solutions to classroom problems. He contends that punishment only teaches students that they will suffer dire consequences when they are caught misbehaving, and rewards teach them how to respond positively only in order to win a prize or praise. Therefore, both punishments and rewards do not cultivate long-lasting moral values in students.

Kohn would have teachers do away with classroom discipline and in its place have teachers work to develop a sense of democratic classroom community that recognizes the needs and interests of both teachers and students. A classroom community is a place where students are cared about and care about others, are valued and respected, and think in terms of *we* instead of *I.* Students are involved in the decision-making process and are continually brought into making judgments, expressing their opinions, and working cooperatively toward solutions that benefit the class, which will have a positive impact on students and eliminate behavioral problems. Kohn believes rules are of no practical value in the classroom; rules blind teachers to what students can achieve. When problems arise, the teacher should ask the student, "What do you think we can do to solve this problem?" Class meetings should be used as the forum for addressing questions that affect the class, including problems of behavior.

APPLY AND REFLECT 13.2	Should you ask your students to make value judgments about their personal behavior? Why is it or isn't it a good idea to have students make value judgments about each other's behavior?

The Instructional Approach

The premise that forms the basis for the **instructional approach** to classroom management is that well-planned and well-implemented instruction will prevent most classroom problems. Basically, the assumption is that students will not engage in disruptive behavior when lessons are geared to meet their interests, needs, and abilities. In other words, the instructional approach is predicated on the assumption that well-planned and well-implemented lessons that engage students in their own learning and afford them the opportunity to be successful learners will prevent and solve most management problems. Let's now look at two models of classroom management that focus on the principles of the instructional approach.

The Kounin Model

In a comprehensive comparison of effective and ineffective classroom managers, Jacob Kounin (1970) found that the teachers differed very little in the way they handled classroom problems once they arose. The primary difference was in the things the successful managers did that tended to prevent classroom problems. First, these teachers were environmentally aware. In other words, they knew everything that went on in their classrooms at all times. Second, the effective managers were skilled as group leaders and at keeping activities moving. That is, these teachers had students involved and doing something productive at all times. No one ever just sat and waited for work or watched others. The teachers had lessons that were well planned and conducted at a smooth, even, appropriate pace. Kounin concluded that some teachers are better classroom managers because of skill in four areas: "withitness," overlapping activities, group focusing, and movement management (Charles, 2002).

Withitness is the skill to know what is going on in all parts of the classroom at all times; nothing is missed. "Withit" teachers note and act quickly and accurately in curbing class disturbances. They respond immediately to student misbehavior and know who started what. A major component of withitness is scanning the class frequently and establishing eye contact with individual students. "Withit" teachers communicate to students that they are aware of everything that is happening in the classroom, that they don't miss a thing. "Withit" teachers don't make *timing* errors (waiting too long before intervening) or *target errors* (blaming the wrong person and letting the real perpetrators escape responsibility for misbehavior). "Withit" teachers prevent minor disruptions from becoming major and know who the instigator is in a problem situation. "Withit" teachers appear to have eyes in the back of their head.

Effective classroom managers are also skilled at overlapping. **Overlapping** means handling two or more activities or groups at the same time. Essentially, it is the ability to monitor the whole class at all times. It involves keeping a small group on task, for example, while also helping other students with their seatwork.

Finally, Kounin notes that successful classroom management also depends on movement management and group focus—that is, the ability to make smooth lesson transitions, keep an appropriate pace, and involve all students in a lesson. Moreover, effective managers do not leave a lesson hanging while tending to something else or change back and forth from one subject or activity to another. They keep students alert by holding their attention, by holding them accountable, and by involving all students in the lesson.

The Jones Model

Frederick Jones (1979), in his more than 10 years of researching the problems teachers encounter in the classroom, found that most management problems result from massive time wasting by students. In other words, most classroom problems are a result of students being off task. In fact, Jones estimated that teachers lose 50% or more of their instructional time through students' time wasting (e.g., talking and walking around the room). Jones contends that this wasted instructional time can be reclaimed when teachers correctly implement four strategies: limit setting, good body language, incentive systems, and giving help efficiently.

Limit setting is the establishment of classroom boundaries for appropriate behavior. According to Jones, these **limits** should include the formation of rules of behavior, as well as descriptions of appropriate work behavior, procedures for getting supplies and materials, instruction on what to do when stuck on seatwork, and what to do when finished with assigned seatwork.

Ninety percent of discipline and keeping students on task, Jones contends, involved the skillful use of body language. **Body language** is a set of physical mannerisms that tend to get students back to work, the most effective of which are physical proximity to students, direct eye contact, body position (body orientation toward student), facial expressions, and tone of voice.

Jones contends that **incentive systems** also can be used effectively to keep students on task and to get them to complete their work. Indeed, he suggests that preferred activities, such as time on the computer, free time, use of educational games, and free reading, can serve as motivational rewards for desired behaviors. Furthermore, Jones adds, the use of peer pressure represents a quite effective motivator. For example, time can be deducted from the class-preferred activity time when an individual student misbehaves. The deduction of time can be recorded, as Jones suggests, with a large stopwatch placed at the front of the room, so the whole class can see. If a large stopwatch is not available, a standard amount of time (e.g., one minute) can be deducted for each instance of misbehavior.

Finally, Jones found that *giving help efficiently* is related to time on task. His research revealed that teachers on the average spend 4 minutes helping individual students who are having difficulty with seatwork. Jones recommends that this time be cut to no more than 20 seconds per student. Doing so allows more students to be helped and reduces the tendency for students to work only when the teacher is standing over them.

Setting limits, using body language, implementing an incentive system, and giving help efficiently will not eliminate all behavior problems. When such problems do develop, Jones suggests, a back-up system, such as in-class isolation or removal from the room, is needed.

APPLY AND REFLECT 13.3	It is suggested that you use body language instead of words to show you mean business. How would you do this?

The Desist Approach

The **desist approach** to classroom management gives the teacher full responsibility for regulating the classroom. The teacher enforces a set of specific rules to control student behavior in the classroom. Because the desist approach models of classroom management give teachers power to deal forcefully and quickly with misbehavior, they can be viewed as power systems. The desist approach probably is the most widely used strategy in today's schools. Two common desist models of classroom management are *assertive discipline* and *behavior modification*.

Assertive Discipline

Lee and Marlene Canter (1976) contend that teachers have a basic right to require decent behavior in the classroom. To this end, the Canters advocate **assertive discipline,** which calls for assertive teachers. Assertive teachers clearly and firmly communicate needs and requirements to students, follow up their words with appropriate actions, and respond to students in ways that maximize compliance but in no way violate the best interest of the students (Canter & Canter, 1976, p. 9). Assertive teachers take charge in the classroom in a calm yet forceful way.

Assertive teachers do not tolerate improper behavior that interrupts learning. Commonly used excuses—peer pressure, home environment, and heredity, for example—are not accepted for misbehavior. The assertive teacher establishes rules and limits for behavior, along with consequences for proper behavior and improper behavior. Students who follow the established rules receive positive consequences, such as a material reward, free time, or special privileges, whereas students who break the rules receive negative consequences, such as detention, giving up part of their lunch period, staying after school, or going to the principal's office. The rules, limits, and consequences are communicated to students and parents in clear terms at the beginning of the year.

Assertive teachers insist on decent, responsible behavior from their students. After establishing expectations early in the year, assertive teachers consistently reinforce the established procedures and guidelines. In other words, the teachers make promises, not threats. They do not *threaten* to enforce the rules and guidelines and apply the consequences to misbehavior; they *promise* to do so. It is assumed that all students, if they want, are capable of behaving; it is a matter of choice.

APPLY AND REFLECT 13.4	Make promises, not threats. What does this mean to you?

Behavior Modification

Behavior modification, based on the ideas and work of B. F. Skinner (1968, 1971), is an approach that evolves from the assumptions that students will change their behavior to receive definite rewards.

The basic premise of behavior modification is that student behavior can be changed by altering the consequences that follow their actions and behaviors. Technically, reinforcement principles are used systematically for changing some aspect of educational practice or student behavior. Students who follow established procedures, who follow the rules, or who perform well on required work are given reinforcers, or rewards. The reinforcers may be teacher praise, good grades, or even such tangible items as stickers or appropriate free movies. Students who do not follow the procedures, who misbehave, or who perform poorly are denied desired rewards or are punished in some way.

Basically, there are four general categories of consequences that can follow students' actions: positive reinforcement, negative reinforcement, Punishment I, and Punishment II. As noted in Chapter 12, positive and negative reinforcement are used for maintaining or increasing the occurrence of a desired student behavior. In the case of positive reinforcement, a reward (e.g., praise, grades, or free time) is presented for desired behavior, whereas negative reinforcement involves the removal of an undesired stimulus (e.g., weekend homework, no visiting, or a change in the seating arrangement).

Inappropriate student actions can be discouraged through the use of punishment. Like reinforcement, punishment comes in two categories, simply labeled I and II. Punishment I, the most commonly used form, involves the application of some undesirable stimulus. For example, undesirable student action can be followed by a private reprimand, isolation, or a trip to the principal's office. In contrast, Punishment II involves the removal of a desired stimulus or the withholding of an anticipated positive stimulus. For example, inappropriate student behavior could be followed by a loss of free time, exclusion from a school film, or loss of computer time for a week. If used appropriately, both Punishments I and II should result in the elimination of, or at least a decrease in, undesired student behaviors.

Reinforcement can also be a complex system. For example, one such program is the token reinforcement system, in which students earn tokens for both positive classroom behaviors and academic work. The tokens earned are then periodically exchanged for some desired activity or reward (see Chapter 12).

Management approaches can be studied and analyzed. But you must decide on your own modus operandi with regard to managerial style. These management approaches are summarized in Table 13.1. How you respond to management problems will depend on which approach or approaches along the continuum of management strategies best fits your educational philosophy. Moreover, how you

APPLY AND REFLECT 13.5	Accept no excuses for improper behavior. This is often not an easy task. How would you do so?

respond to student misbehavior should also be related to the cause of the misbehavior. Complete Expansion Activity 13.1: Management Approaches to further address the different approaches to classroom management.

EXPANSION ACTIVITY 13.1   Management Approaches

Form groups of four or five. Discuss the virtues of the self-discipline, instructional, and desist approaches to classroom management. Which approach is most applicable to the elementary classroom? Middle school classroom? Secondary school classroom? Give a rationale for your conclusions.

Let's now look at some of the reasons students misbehave. But, first, review the approach summary and complete Review and Reflective Exercise 13.1.

TABLE 13.1 Management Approaches	
Approach	**Description**
Self-discipline approach	View that students can evaluate and change to appropriate behavior
Instructional approach	View that well-planned and well-implemented instruction will prevent classroom problems
Desist approach	View that the teacher should have full regulatory power in the classroom

---

REVIEW AND REFLECTIVE EXERCISE 13.1   Describe the broad approaches to classroom management.

REVIEW

- Describe the goals and challenges of good classroom management.
- Is good classroom management related to school level (elementary, middle, high school)?
- Outline the major elements of the three broad approaches to classroom management.

REFLECTION

- What elements of the three broad approaches to classroom management would be effective at the grade level you expect to teach? What approaches have your past teachers used? Were they successful? If not, how would you change them?

Causes of Misbehavior

Classroom misbehavior can often be attributed to conditions that are not readily obvious. Therefore, if you are to deal successfully with misbehavior, you must try to identify the deeper problems that are causing the actions. That is, you must get to the root of the problems that are causing students to misbehave. A careful examination of students' classroom behaviors, desirable as well as undesirable, can reveal that they are influenced by forces and pressures inside and outside the classroom.

Home Environment

Relationships with parents and siblings often affect classroom behavior. Parents usually serve as models and communicate important attitudinal ideals and feelings to their children. If these parental influences are negative toward school or learning, a student might develop these same negative ideals and feelings.

Through daily interactions, parents establish the general acceptable conduct of behavior of their children and, therefore, directly influence students' classroom behavior. Consequently, when parents are extremely tolerant and do not teach respect for others, when they allow their children to talk back, or when swearing and fighting are tolerated in the home, these behaviors often carry over into the classroom. Conversely, students who come from homes with overly strict parents may be inclined to be followers who do not question authority, or they may resent anyone in authority—including the teacher. Therefore, you must try to determine the rules of conduct established in the home before you can deal effectively with misbehavior in the classroom.

Students from homes where there is constant family friction and a related lack of parental support sometimes develop discipline problems. Constant involvement in the home's emotional turmoil and a too often associated feeling of rejection can also lead to problems in the classroom. You should be sensitive to abrupt behavioral changes that might be a result of a student's problems at home.

Lack of supervision in the home is a common problem in our society. Many students come from single-parent homes or from homes where both parents are too busy with their own lives to be concerned with the children. Therefore, you may have students who work, who stay out late at night, or who watch television late into the night. These students often fall asleep in class or are inattentive. Other students may live on junk food or come to school without breakfast. These students sometimes lack the energy to carry out assignments or even to pay attention. You need to counsel these students, and perhaps the parents, on the importance of rest and proper diet.

Parental attitudes toward schooling influence students' behavior in the classroom. Parents who put little value on education, for example, often instill these attitudes in their children. Furthermore, parents who communicate negative feelings toward educators (classroom teachers as well as administrators) often pass on such feelings to their children, who, in turn, will have little respect for educators.

Conversely, some parents value education so highly that they establish unreasonable expectations for their children—for example, parents who accept nothing but straight-A work. Similarly, problems may develop when parents have unrealistic goals for their children—for instance, parents who want their sons or daughters to be physicians and so insist that they enroll in advanced science courses. Problems often develop because of lack of interest or lack of academic ability. Both high expectations and unrealistic goals can result in poor motivation, low self-esteem, and behavior problems. Complete Expansion Activity 13.2: Home-Based Reinforcement to brainstorm some more practical ways to involve parents in classroom management.

EXPANSION ACTIVITY 13.2 Home-Based Reinforcement

Home-based reinforcement programs are some of the most practical and effective classroom management methods. Teachers give students a daily or weekly report card to take home, and parents are instructed to provide special privileges or rewards to students on the basis of these reports. Form groups of four and five to explore this concept. Do you think this strategy would be effective at all grade levels? Why or why not? What kinds of privileges and rewards could be used effectively at the grade level you expect to teach?

The Teacher

Teachers who do not plan have trouble with class control. Teachers who do not start class when the bell rings, who are sidetracked from their lessons into unrelated talk, or who are not sure where they are going next in their lessons communicate disorder to their students. Too often, such a message of disorder leads to disrespect toward the teacher and a dislike of the subject.

Student busing often impacts what teachers can do in the classroom.

Teachers must teach at the level of their students' ability. Lessons aimed too low bore and irritate bright students, whereas lessons geared too high frustrate low-ability students. But the teacher who focuses on the average students, as many teachers do, are still not challenging the bright students and are not giving low-ability students a reasonable opportunity to be successful. As a result, both groups can become mischievous, inattentive, and interruptive in class. In short, you must design lessons that offer challenge to your bright students but, at the same time, give low-ability students reasonable opportunities for success.

Teachers must show respect for students as individuals with rights, values, and feelings. They must exercise control and refrain from ridiculing them, both in front of their peers and in private. Ridicule and sarcasm back students into a defensive position to save face with peers, which can cause problems. Also, teachers should refrain from demanding an unreasonable degree of inactivity from students. Some talking, scuffling of feet, and paper shuffling is unavoidable. Remember that students need some outlets for their energy. In fact, students often find it difficult to be perfectly quiet, inactive, and attentive in the classroom for extended periods of time, as some teachers insist. In short, don't be oversensitive to noise in the classroom, but let common sense be your guide. Establish your limits, however, and don't tolerate all the desires of students in your classroom.

Personality and Health Problems

Some student classroom problems can be attributed to immaturity and/or problems related to health. Immaturity is especially a problem with elementary school students.

Older students often feel insecure about their appearance, lack of peer recognition, and lack of parental respect. Such feelings may stem from a lack of self-respect and self-control, which results in

APPLY AND REFLECT 13.6

You should establish procedures for starting and ending (dismissing) your classes. What will yours be?

constant talking, no consideration for others, immature actions, and a lack of responsibility. These behaviors, although usually viewed as minor, when exhibited daily should be addressed at once so that their escalation into more serious problems can be averted.

More serious problems, such as cheating on tests and talking back to teachers, often can be traced back to the home environment or even to some deep, underlying causes, which may require expert assistance. Keep in mind, however, that some students go to such extreme measures to obtain attention from their parents, teachers, or classmates.

Some students present problems to the teacher because of health problems. Allergies, poor eyesight, respiratory ailments, and poor hearing can affect classroom behavior. It is difficult to concentrate when you have trouble breathing, or seeing, or hearing. Indeed, an illness may be so severe that students are not able to exert the energy needed for classroom activities or homework exercises. It is important that you be sensitive to the health problems of students and refer those with such problems to the school nurse, principal, and/or parents so they become aware of the problem.

Once a philosophy of classroom management has been formulated and the cause of misbehavior understood, your managerial style must be implemented in such a way that it prevents problems from developing and deals with the misbehavior that does take place. This requires that you organize for the prevention of problems, as well as deal with the ongoing management of the class.

Organizing for Effective Management

For material related to this concept, go to Clip 13.2 on the Student Resource CD bound into the back of your textbook.

Effective classroom management takes organization. Walter Doyle (1986) describes six characteristics that reflect the complexity and potential for classroom problems:

• *Classrooms are multidimensional.* Classrooms are the setting for many activities that must be managed and supervised. Teachers must also keep records and keep students on task and on a schedule. Students have individual needs that the teacher must take into account.

• *Activities occur simultaneously.* Many classroom activities occur at the same time and must be monitored.

• *Things happen quickly.* Events often occur rapidly in classrooms and frequently require an immediate teacher response.

• *Events are often unpredictable.* Even though you plan carefully and are well organized, events will occur that you never expected. These unexpected events must be addressed.

• *There is little privacy.* Classrooms are public places where students observe how the teacher handles unexpected events and discipline problems.

• *Classrooms have histories.* Students have memories of what happened earlier in their classrooms. They remember how you handled discipline problems earlier in the year, how you treated other students, which students get privileges, and whether you keep promises.

As you can see, the often crowded, complex nature of most classrooms calls for effective organizational skills.

Much of what we have covered in this chapter should prove useful in organizing your classroom for effective management. The three approaches to classroom management have their advantages and limitations. However, teachers do not have to select one approach over another. In fact, research has shown that effective classroom managers are able to blend together the best parts of different approaches. Basically, effective managers must be able to build trusting relations with students, prevent misbehavior, redirect minor misbehavior, stop major disruptive behavior, and teach self-control. Such techniques as motivation and variety in instructional planning represent major factors in the prevention of management problems. Let's look, however, at some other key classroom problem prevention areas.

Planning

Obviously, classroom order takes planning. Plans must be devised such that classroom problems are minimized and learning time is maximized. In other words, if you are to be effective, you should be well prepared: You should know exactly what and how you will teach and have all required materials ready for students. In fact, you should overestimate what can be accomplished in the allowed time. It can be extremely frustrating and embarrassing to find yourself with 15 to 20 minutes of class time and nothing to do. Needless to say, problems often develop. Therefore, overplan—with activities that are interesting, stimulating, and relevant—and keep your lessons moving at a brisk but appropriate pace. Finally, it is good practice to have alternative activities planned and available in case they are needed.

The school calendar should be consulted when planning, because certain days or weeks require special steps to avoid potential behavior problems. For instance, the day before a major holiday, the day of an afternoon assembly or pep rally, the day of a big football or basketball game, and the week before Christmas or spring break are apt to require special attention and preparation. At such times, it is essential that students be involved in highly motivating and interesting activities that will compete successfully with other, external events.

Effective planning is often the key to a smooth-running classroom.

The Establishment of Routines

Many school and classroom activities are basically routine—for example, the taking and reporting of attendance, the issuing of passes for students to leave the room or building, and the distribution and collection of papers. Some of these routines are established by the school for all teachers, whereas others are established by individual teachers. Teachers often spend too much time on simple classroom routines. For example, some elementary teachers spend much time getting students ready for lunch, recess, and dismissal because they call students by name, one at a time. This time wasting is unnecessary. Many teachers establish routines early in the year that require an entire row or table to be quiet and ready to go before students are called to line up. Lining up then takes seconds, not minutes. Other such procedures should also become routine for students.

What are the standard school operating procedures and routines? To find out, you should consult the school handbook and talk with your department head, other teachers, and the principal. In most schools, routines and procedures are established for (a) taking and keeping of attendance, (b) dealing with tardy students, (c) issuing passes to leave the classroom or building, (d) having students in after school, (e) recording and reporting grades, (f) using the school library, (g) dealing with ill students, (h) issuing failing notices, and (i) conducting parental conferences. Such school routines and procedures must be adhered to by all teachers, because if each teacher were to establish individual school routines and procedures, the results would more than likely be student uncertainty and discipline problems. Therefore, you should find out the established school routines and procedures *prior* to the reporting of students to class.

Routines and procedures must also be established for the classroom. Routines and procedures should be established for activities such as entering the classroom and starting class, checking attendance, passing out materials, and collecting and checking homework. You should, for instance, have a short activity ready when students enter the classroom (e.g., a problem or question on the overhead or a few pages to read) that they will complete as you take care of routine activities.

Attendance represents a problem area for many teachers in that they will spend as much as 10 minutes calling roll. Students usually use this wasted time at the beginning of the period for talking and other mischievous activities. Instead of calling roll, you should prepare a seating chart for each class (see Figure 13.2). A pocket-type seating chart works best, because you or your students will request some changes in seating during the year. During the first class meeting, students should be given the opportunity to select a seat. Once the selection has been made, have students write their names—or you write their names—on slips, which are placed in the appropriate slots. You may have to change some seat assignments later, but in the beginning give them their choice.

The collection and distribution of papers should be streamlined as much as possible. Unnecessary amounts of time spent on such tasks often lead to student misbehavior. Collecting and passing out materials can be accomplished by passing to, or from, the front of the class seating rows. In other seating arrangements, a similar technique—for instance, assigning one student per group to collect or pass out materials—can be used.

Taking care of excused absences is another time-consuming administrative chore. In handling these, you must, of course, sign the admission slip, but you must also bring the student up-to-date as to missed classroom activities and assignments. When several students have been absent on a given day, the handling of missed work can often delay the start of class considerably. This delay usually will result in talking and general student misbehavior. A monthly calendar, such as that shown in Figure 13.3, can be helpful in dealing with absences. Students know what classroom activities were completed on a given day; they know what assignment was given. The calendar also gives your better students the opportunity to work ahead so they can work on other individual projects. Indeed, announcements, messages of recognition, and motivational messages (e.g., awards, birthdays, and accomplishments) can be shared with the class through the class calendar. Computer programs are available to make the construction of class calendars a relatively easy task.

Figure 13.2
Seating Chart

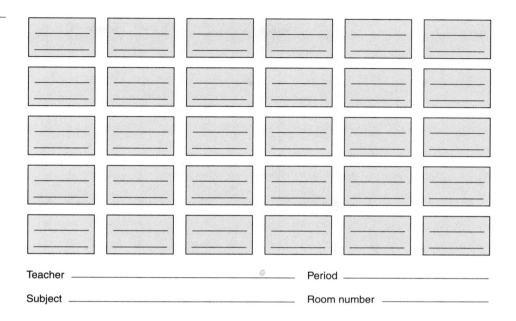

Teacher _____   Period _____

Subject _____   Room number _____

Oftentimes, teachers find it necessary to use specialized techniques to monitor and modify the classroom environment for special-needs students. For example, special-needs students may have difficulty working in groups or working on new tasks or making transitions from one activity to another. Therefore, teachers must provide the structure and support special-needs students require to be successful in the regular classroom. Special-needs students respond most favorably to an environment that is structured, predictable, and orderly.

You should never become a slave to routine; however, when routines will be of assistance in carrying out classroom business efficiently, they should be used. You should determine and use the routines and procedures that are appropriate for your particular classroom.

APPLY AND REFLECT 13.7	Set up a class routine or activity for the first 4 or 5 minutes of class. Share it.

Managing Space

Your classroom should be arranged to be an environment in which it is easy for you and students to work and so that it does not encourage misbehavior. The pencil sharpener, for example, should not be positioned in a place where students must pass close to other students when going to use it. Students often can't leave each other alone as they pass nearby. In addition, it is usually unwise to place the wastebasket at the front of the room; it is an inviting target for basketball practice.

Most classrooms today have moveable chairs. Therefore, don't get in the habit of seating students only in straight rows. You should try different seating arrangements (e.g., circles, semicircles, U-shapes, and squares). In fact, arrange your seating according to the activity to be completed by students. Experiment with various arrangements and see what works best with your students.

Figure 13.3
Monthly Calendar

S	M	T	W	T	F	S
1 Welcome back to class, Jesse.	**2** Text pages 450–451. Do practice 1–10. Do pages 452–453: Apply section.	**3** Text pages 454–455. Do practice work 1–10. Persevere, you can do it!	**4** Text 456–457. Do all practice work.	**5** Text pages 458–459. Do all practice work. This one is a "piece of cake."	**6** Spelling test. All assignments must be in baskets today!	**7** Birthdays this month are: Kevin, Kendra, Thomas, Alison, Jennifer, and Hope!
8 Failing notices go out Friday. Don't be caught off balance. Turn in all work NOW.	**9** Spelling. Text pages 462–463. Do all practice work.	**10** Text pages 464–465. Do all practice work. Stretch your neck out and try Part C.**	**11** Text pages 468–469. Do A&B.	**12** Text pages 470–471. Do all practice work.	**13** NO SCHOOL TODAY!	**14** ALCOHOL IS A DRUG.
15 Welcome back to class, Carlos.	**16** Tune into Spelling! 50 words this week for the spelling spin-off on Friday.	**17** Text pages 472–475. Do all practice work. Challenge** Try the Apply*	**18** Film today on preparing speeches!	**19** TIME FOR TALK. DISCUSS TOPIC FOR SPEECHES TODAY.	**20** SPELLING SPIN-OFF** Today!	**21** Character Comes from the Heart! Students Persevere** **************
22 "Write On" with Learning. Essay winners this month are Jay and Natalie****	**23** Library to begin research.	**24** Library work. Bibliography due end of class today. See page 339.	**25** Library work. Topic outlines due today!! See page 340 for help.	**26** Library work. Rough drafts due today. See page 343 for help.	**27** Library work. Final drafts due today. See pages 347–349 for help.	**28** Remember to say "NO" to drugs.
29 Don't forget to vote this month for the most improved student in your class.	**30** Text Pages 502–504. Do all practice work.					

Constructive use of wall space makes a classroom more conducive to learning and evokes a more positive climate. For example, walls can display motivational statements, materials to spark interest in a topic, or classroom procedures. Moreover, before school begins, put up a bulletin board and be prepared to change it periodically. Make your bulletin boards attractive, interesting, and colorful so they help promote a positive attitude toward your room and subject. You might also want to devote one bulletin board to announcements, such as the bell schedule, the weekly lunch menu, news items of interest to the class, and classroom rules and consequences.

Establishing Usable Limits

Limits specify the expected and forbidden actions in the classroom. Students need and want limits (rules); that is, they want to know what is expected of them and why. Teachers who try to avoid setting limits and imposing necessary structure will often find that chaos results. But don't establish rules for the sake of having rules. Indeed, you should take care not to have too many rules, unenforceable rules, and unnecessary rules; only essential rules and limits should be set.

Clarity and consistency are vital in the establishment of rules. Your rules should always reinforce the basic idea that students are in school to study and learn. When no longer needed, a rule should be discarded or changed. But, as long as they are retained, rules must be enforced. You should always explain and discuss with students why certain rules are necessary. You may even want to spend time negotiating the establishment of certain rules with students at the beginning of the year.

It is often better to have five or six general rules that cover many specifics, rather than to list all the specifics. But if specific actions represent a problem area (e.g., chewing gum or using reference books), then a rule should cover the specific problem. Examples of appropriate general rules that might be established and discussed are these:

1. *Be prepared with books, paper, pencil, and so on when you come to class.* You should discuss exactly what is to be brought to class.

2. *Be in your seat and ready to work when the bell rings.* You may want students to begin working on a warm-up activity that is written on the overhead, you may require that they have homework ready to be checked, or you may ask that they have notebooks open and ready to take notes when the bell rings.

3. *Take care of your classroom and respect other people's property.* This means school, teacher, and fellow student property is to be left alone.

4. *Be polite and respectful.* This conduct covers verbal abuse, fighting, talking back, and general conduct.

5. *Obtain permission before speaking or leaving your seat.* Address exceptions to this rule—such as when to sharpen pencils, throw trash away, and go to the teacher's desk for assistance.

Again, your rules should always be discussed with and taught to students. In fact, some teachers require that students pass a test about classroom regulations at the beginning of the year. Specific behaviors that are included and excluded in each general rule should be explained and discussed at the beginning of the year. Indeed, you might be wise to have students record the rules for future reference. You should also consider sending parents a copy of your classroom rules.

APPLY AND REFLECT 13.8	Will you have rules in your class? If yes, why do you think you will need them? If not, why not?

As soon as you have established your rules, you must decide on the consequences for breaking a rule. It is often rather difficult to make this decision at the time the rule is broken. The appropriate response is often to have the student "do it right." For example, messes can be cleaned up, incomplete papers can be finished or redone, and broken property can be replaced.

When you have established the rules for your classroom and the consequences for breaking the rules, you have taken the first step in making students aware of what will and will not be tolerated in the classroom. You must now think about managing the classroom on a daily basis. Complete Expansion Activity 13.3: Misbehaving Students to explore some common classroom problems.

Managing the Class

Effective classroom management is a daily and essential challenge to teachers. Managing a class basically involves getting off to a good start, then keeping the class moving smoothly toward established goals.

Sharing Control

Controlling the students is one of the biggest concerns of most teachers. They fear classroom chaos. They fear open defiance. Moreover, new teachers tend to be worried about basic classroom survival.

Some experts believe that the best way to avoid many of the classroom fears and concerns is through shared control. That is, the teacher should give students a voice in decision making. Students can be given the opportunity to provide input in establishing classroom rules and in curriculum decisions. This shared decision making gives students a stake in the educational process and a sense of ownership. You do not rely on "blind obedience" but, instead, "negotiate the learning space together."

Shared control does not mean students do whatever they want. Limits are established, but students participate in the setting of these limits. In so doing, they discuss appropriate and inappropriate classroom behaviors and ways to address classroom problems. The process gives students some ownership of the classroom environment. It places more of the burden on students for controlling their own behaviors, but the teacher still sets and guards the boundaries beyond which students may not transgress.

APPLY AND REFLECT 13.9	It is often suggested that you involve students as much as possible in the establishment of classroom rules and consequences. Do you think this is feasible in most classrooms? Why or why not?

Getting Started

Wong and Wong (1998) contend that the first days of school can make or break a teacher. They suggest that the first few days—or even the first few minutes—of school or a class will determine your success or failure for the rest of the school year. During these initial days, it is essential that you establish your credibility as a manager. In fact, student respect for you as a teacher will often be established during the first few days.

What do effective classroom managers do during those first critical days? Experienced teachers begin the first day of school or a class with an activity. Inexperienced teachers often want to begin that first day or class with a fun activity. This is not recommended. Effective managers begin with classroom management procedures. School should be viewed as a serious place to learn, not a place to go to have fun. You can make learning fun at times, but you can't make learning fun all the time.

EXPANSION ACTIVITY 13.3   Misbehaving Students

Some students will misbehave or show off in class in an attempt to gain peer recognition and approval. Others will misbehave just for the sake of misbehaving. Some will deliberately not follow classroom procedures or break classroom rules in an attempt to challenge your authority or to find out how far they can push you. How would you go about getting the classroom cooperation of students without constant nagging and reminders? What about students who fail to get assignments turned in or turn in assignments late or poorly done? How would you address these problems?

Experienced teachers suggest the secret to successful management is organization. The focus during the first few days of school should be on the making and teaching of rules, the organizational system, classroom procedures, and expectations. Feedback on appropriateness of actions is essential in these early stages. In other words, you should create a positive classroom environment and establish rules and consequences. Planning is the key to management: Make sure your content is interesting and meaningful to students. Moreover, it is important that you clearly communicate standards for academic work and establish an atmosphere of free exchange. Indeed, involve students as much as possible in the learning process. Finally, monitor student behavior closely, and deal with misbehavior quickly and firmly.

Making full and meaningful use of time on the first day is especially critical. Therefore, it might be helpful to plan, using the following:

1. *Seating slips.* Pass out seating slips and have students sign them. Collect them in order, separating each row with a paper clip. It is often wise to count and inspect the slips as they are collected. If you don't, you may find slips signed by "Snow White" or not signed at all.

2. *Books.* Assign books to students, keeping an accurate record of assigned book numbers. Books sometimes get lost or stolen. Remember, you or the student will replace any unreturned book. Have a short activity for students to do as you distribute books.

3. *Assignment sheet.* Distribute an assignment sheet with at least one week's work on it. Explain it to students. Make your first assignment short, interesting, involving, and not dependent on the textbook.

4. *Class discussion.* Discuss unique contributions of your subject that make it important and relevant to them.

5. *Homework.* Discuss assigned homework topic. Pose some provocative questions.

6. *Marking system.* Give a brief explanation of your grading system, of when you collect homework, of when tests are administered, and so on.

Completing all of these tasks will be difficult on the first day, but accomplishing a great deal the first day may serve you well. Students will be impressed with your organization and businesslike manner, and first impressions are important.

EXPANSION ACTIVITY 13.4   Getting Started

The first few weeks of schools are critical to a smooth-running classroom. What would you do to start the year to accomplish this task? How would you communicate your expectations to students? How would you make sure they understood your expectations? Share your thoughts with classmates.

Finally, leave 2 or 3 minutes at the end of the period for closure. That is, save some time at the end of the period for needed cleanup and for giving assignments. When—and only when—you are ready, you should dismiss the class. Don't let the bell dismiss (or start) the class. This should be understood from the first day. Complete Expansion Activity 13.4: Getting Started to generate ideas for starting the school year at the grade level you expect to teach.

Getting to Know the Students

Your relationship with students is of primary importance in classroom management. Students can usually tell if you truly care about them and want to help. Remember that students are unique in terms of personality, experience, language facility, academic potential, attitude, and home environment.

Therefore, try to learn something about their home environment, their special needs and problems, and what interests them. They will also appreciate your recognition of their successes and achievements.

It is good practice to know as much as possible about your students. Of course, middle school and secondary teachers may have 25 to 30 students per class and up to 150 students total in all classes. Just learning names can be a chore. Learning names as soon as possible, however, shows definite interest. A seating chart is helpful in remembering names.

It is advisable to know more about students than just their names. An information card (Figure 13.4), completed during the first class period, can provide some of this information. If more information is needed, student files are usually available to teachers. Information on students often proves helpful in understanding why students act the way they do.

Bored students often cause problems for teachers.

Enforcement of Rules

Lax enforcement of established rules makes them worthless. In fact, students like to know where they stand and will periodically test your enforcement of the rules.

When this happens, quick and firm application of the consequences should follow. If a student tries you—and one always will—you cannot ignore the breaking of the rules because the behavior will ripple to other students, and they will also want to test you. Conversely, if you are firm when a student tests you, this action, too, will ripple out to other students, and they will be less likely to test you in the future.

The use of the **ripple effect** is especially effective with high-status students. Consequently, you should be firm with these students, and other students will give you fewer problems.

Be consistent and fair in your enforcement of the rules. Treat all students the same, but be humane. Sometimes you must consider the reasons for misbehavior and make exceptions with regard to punishment. But make sure the class as a whole understands the reason for an exception.

APPLY AND REFLECT 13.10   Effective managers use the "ripple effect" to their advantage. How would you do so?

Figure 13.4
Information Card

Family Name: _____ First Name: _____

Address: _____ Telephone: _____

Homeroom Teacher: _____

Father's First Name: _____

Occupation: _____

Mother's First Name: _____

Occupation: _____

Number of Siblings: _____

Interests (hobbies, clubs, sports, other activities): _____

_____

_____

_____

Monitoring the Classroom

You should be aware of what is going on in the classroom at all times. Therefore, room arrangement is an important part of your ability to monitor the classroom: You must be able to monitor all areas of the classroom from your desk and from any other classroom area. When a potential problem is spotted, a simple pause in conjunction with eye contact (a stare) usually curbs the inappropriate activity.

Two aspects of room arrangement are critical to effective monitoring: your ability to see students at all times and the traffic patterns within the room. Your capacity for seeing students and moving quickly to be in proximity of a potential problem will often control the misbehavior. Therefore, apply careful thought to your room arrangement. Eliminate barriers that may keep you from seeing certain areas of the room.

Monitoring the classroom as you teach is not an easy task. You must be well prepared, know your content thoroughly, and maintain contact with all areas of the classroom at all times. If you are uncertain about what you are to teach or if there are dead spots in your lesson, students may recognize the insecurity and become inattentive.

Resolving Conflict

Modern society glamorizes violence. It portrays heroes as people who win through violence. In doing so, it teaches children to be violent. They are learning to inflict pain, to destroy, to kill one another with no apparent remorse. No school appears to be immune to the violence problem.

Violence, however, is preventable. Young people must realize that they have many choices for dealing with conflict other than passivity and aggression. They need to learn conflict resolution skills. Conflict resolution encourages young people to openly discuss their conflicts. Young people must also learn the skills needed to make choices in light of their understanding and appreciation of their own and other cultures. A supportive atmosphere must be established to support these conflict resolution skills.

For material related to this concept, go to Clip 13.3 on the Student Resource CD bound into the back of your textbook.

Teachers, too, must learn and apply a new set of skills for heading off and resolving conflict. Teachers must learn to share their power with students, so that they can help deal with their own disputes. To this end, training in a peer mediation system can be indispensable (Johnson, Johnson, Stevahn, & Hodne, 1997). Peer mediation teaches young people how to engage in problem-solving negotiations and how to mediate schoolmates' conflicts.

Using Punishment

Sooner or later, no matter how well you plan to prevent problems, student misbehavior is going to demand that you administer punishment. Some student behavior will be so severe that some kind of adverse stimulus must be employed to decrease the occurrence of the behavior. You must be aware, however, that what is considered punishment by one individual might not be considered punishment by another—in fact, it may even be considered rewarding. Also, when applying adverse consequences for misbehavior, be sure that you communicate to students that they have chosen the consequence. They should understand that by choosing to misbehave, they have also chosen the consequences.

The most common consequence used for curbing disruptive behavior is probably the verbal reprimand. But, all too often, these reprimands become mere nagging. As a rule, older students are at an age when they react negatively to being treated other than as adults. Efforts to apply adverse stimulus such as criticism may provoke hostility. Indeed, the student may blow up and say something unintentional. Thus, criticizing, ridiculing, or embarrassing a student can result in a power struggle between the student and teacher, which does little for resolving the long-term behavior problem.

One way of avoiding a confrontation with offending students is to administer the reprimand privately rather than publicly. In this way, the student "saves face," and there is no need to engage in a power struggle. Moreover, a private talk gives you the opportunity to develop a closer personal relationship with the misbehaving student. If the private talk fails to solve the problem, more severe consequences must be administered. Other consequences often applied when severe misbehavior occurs are, in order of severity, loss of privileges, detention, in-school suspension, and out-of-school suspension.

Loss of privileges is a common and effective form of punishment. Examples are the loss of free time, the loss of time on the computer, the loss of a weekend free of homework, or the loss of any other preferred activities. Other options include requiring students to stay in the classroom when others attend an assembly or pep rally. Unfortunately, the problem with this form of punishment is the lack of privileges commonly available for use in most classrooms and, consequently, the shortage of privilege to be denied.

Detention is one of the most frequently used means of punishment, which generally comes in two forms. One type requires that all students serving detention report to a detention hall at a specified time (e.g., Monday after school or Saturday morning). The other kind requires that the students report back to the teacher's classroom after or before school. But because many students ride buses or work, many teachers have students return to the classroom during a break during the day (e.g., part of their lunch break). When using detention as a punishment option, the student should be required to complete a serious academic task. Moreover, you should avoid engaging in conversation with students serving detention. Conversation with the teacher may be perceived as enjoyable, and, hence, the misbehavior might be repeated for more of the "enjoyable" detention.

On occasion, misbehavior becomes so serious or persistent that you must solicit outside assistance. As a general rule, assistance comes from two sources: the school administration (e.g., the vice principal or principal) and parents. When a student is sent to the principal's office, you should phone or send a message to the office, reporting that a student is being sent and why. A call to parents about a behavior problem usually has positive results. Most parents are concerned about the behavior and progress of their children and are willing to work cooperatively in correcting any misbehavior. There are exceptions; some parents feel that taking care of school misbehavior is your job.

WEB LINK 13.2   Classroom Discipline Techniques

Access the following two Internet URL sites: www.teachnet.com/how-to/manage and www.theteacher scorner.net/resources/websites.htm. Review and analyze the techniques for better classroom discipline. Write a short paper on techniques that will and will not work with the age group of students you expect to teach. Share your findings with your class.

In-school suspension is becoming very common. This technique involves removing misbehaving students from a class and placing them in a special area, where they do their schoolwork. They generally are placed in a bare room, furnished with only a table and chair. They report to this room at the beginning of the school day and remain until the end of the day. Meals are sent in, and teachers send in the class work for the day. If the in-school suspension does not correct the misbehavior, out-of-school suspension usually follows. But, out-of-school suspension should be used with extreme cases and as a last resort.

Assigning extra work or deducting from academic grades for misbehavior should be avoided. Associating grades and subject work with punishment only creates a dislike for the subject. It is often good policy, however, to request that students redo sloppy or incorrect work. Indeed, accepting sloppy work or incorrect work only encourages more of the same.

Punishment of the whole class for the misbehavior of one or two students sometimes creates negative effects. Indeed, such an approach may curb the inappropriate behavior, but other students often feel the teacher is unfair and, as a result, will develop a negative attitude toward that teacher. On the other hand, if the teacher is well respected and viewed as fair, the use of peer pressure can be an effective approach to discipline.

To this point, I have not mentioned the use of corporal punishment as an option. First of all, it is illegal in most states for teachers to administer corporal punishment. Second, some students are too old for corporal punishment. Moreover, corporal punishment often fails to address the long-term problem. In short, corporal punishment has proven to be ineffective. Also, other techniques can be more effective with older students. And corporal punishment can lay you open to accusations of brutality and legal difficulties.

APPLY AND REFLECT 13.11   The use of corporal punishment is not advised. Do you agree? Why?

When used, punishment should be administered immediately after the misbehavior, and it should be fair—that is, the punishment should fit the crime. Certainly, the same punishment should not be administered for constant talking as for constant harm to other students. Of course, all misbehavior must be dealt with. Therefore, keep your emotions under control and deal with problems consistently, fairly, and professionally. In other words, when you do use punishment, make it swift, sure, and impressive.

When administered appropriately, punishment can be an effective deterrent to misbehavior. Punishment should only be used, however, when no other alternatives are available. If the misbehavior is not severe, a warning should first be issued. If a warning does not work, you should consider punishment.

This completes our study of classroom management. Complete Web Link 13.2: Classroom Discipline Techniques and Web Link 13.3: Discipline Problems, which will let you explore some of the problems you may encounter as a teacher.

REFLECTIONS ON TEACHER PRACTICE 13.2 | Classroom Management

1. Is prevention or the cure most important in classroom management? Why?

2. What procedures will you establish in your classroom to prevent management problems?

◆　◆　◆

Prevention is sooo much better than a cure! There are so many things that can be prevented if you start with the end in mind. Let me give you an example:

The room I teach in has a front door and a back door. During class change, the doorway was always jammed with kids going out and kids coming in. Chaos resulted (you know the kind . . . pushing, shoving, louder voices, someone falls on the floor etc) and by the time my in-coming Grade 6/7 classes got in, everyone was hyper, unfocused maybe even wounded! Part way through the year (I'm a slow learner!) it occurred to me that maybe if the kids always went out the back door and came in the front, the traffic jam problem would disappear. I was right, except I discovered another "truth"—it's hard to establish new procedures part way through the year!

I finally gave up trying to change them that year, however the next fall, right off the bat I established the "In the front, out the back" procedure. It was no big deal to implement . . . but I held rigidly to it for two weeks. After that, it was a non-issue and I can't tell you what a difference it made. The beginnings and ends of my classes flowed without a hitch. No one questioned the procedure at all!

The next thing I noticed, though, was the amount of wasted time that occurred at the beginning of each class. It was sort of "dead" time (I'm taking attendance, answering a question, grabbing a coffee, looking for my materials . . . you know how it is!) that had the potential to set the attitude for the rest of the class. It was during this "dead" 5 minutes that kids started goofing off and by the time I was ready to start, no one had their binders/books open . . . and what class were they in anyway?

Once again, last fall I started a new procedure (although my new kids didn't know it was new). At the beginning of each class they came to expect a short "something" on the board or overhead projector to do "as soon" as they stepped in the room. Sometimes I'd have the lights low and the overhead projector flashing the "Do Now" (an idea I read on a Listserv) on the wall. The kids had an actual "Do Now" scribbler that had to be dated, completed in the time allotted, marked and corrected . . . each report card I gathered them in advantage of the learning/review that accompanied it.

Although these two procedures may not seem like discipline approaches, they actually are because they prevent many issues from even starting. There are enough unexpected "issues" requiring some discipline procedures so if we can anticipate problems, put procedures in place that support correct behavior we'll actually set the students up for success!

Both these ideas may seem obvious to many of you, but I humbly admit that I never used them (or even thought about them) until the last three years (and I've taught since 1975!).

Hope these thoughts turn the lights on for someone else too!

—BRENDA, middle-level teacher

SOURCE: www.middleweb.com. Reprinted with permission.

WEB LINK 13.3 | Discipline Problems

Access Internet URL site www.disciplinehelp.com. The site gives a list of 117 problem behaviors and suggestions for handling the problems. Select five of the problems that you think will cause you concern at the grade level you expect to teach. Analyze the Web site's advice for the five problems and write a summary of your conclusions. Present your five problems and analysis to the class.

Table 13.2 summarizes the control aspect of classroom management. Review the summary and complete Review and Reflective Exercise 13.2.

TABLE 13.2 Control Techniques

Element	Description
Routines	Classroom activities that are repetitive and follow a common procedure
Limits	The accepted and nonaccepted actions in the classroom
Monitoring	Being aware of what is taking place in the classroom
Punishment	The application of a negative stimulus or removal of a positive stimulus for inappropriate behavior

REVIEW AND REFLECTIVE EXERCISE 13.2 Formulate techniques for effective classroom management.

REVIEW
- Describe classroom characteristics that represent potential for classroom problems.
- What elements contribute to an effective learning environment?
- What strategies are most likely to get the school year off to the right start for a teacher?
- Describe how you would prevent serious discipline problems.

REFLECTION
- How worried are you about problem behaviors among the students you plan to teach? In view of your own current skills, how prepared are you for dealing with these problem behaviors?
- Based on your personal experiences and classroom observations, which would probably be easier for you to manage—an elementary school classroom, a middle school classroom, or a high school classroom? Why? What standards of "good" behavior would be nonnegotiable? Would you be flexible about some things? Explain.

SUMMARY

A classroom must be organized and orderly, and it must run smoothly for learning to take place. Positive management strategies are essential to effective teaching and learning.

The Role of Classroom Leadership

- The three styles of classroom leadership are authoritarian, democratic, and laissez-faire.
- Teaching and classroom leadership is stressful.

The Role of Classroom Management

- Three common schools of thought on classroom management are the self-discipline approach, the instructional approach, and the desist approach.

Approaches to Classroom Management

- Principles of the self-discipline approach to classroom management are supported by the Glasser reality therapy model, Gordon teacher effectiveness training (TET) model, Coloroso inner discipline model, and Kohn beyond discipline model.
- Principles of the instructional approach to classroom management are emphasized by the Kounin model and the Jones model.
- Principles of the desist approach to classroom management are integral components of assertive discipline and behavioral modification.

Causes of Misbehavior

- Misbehavior sometimes can be attributed to influences outside the classroom, such as the home environment or the community, and by attributes associated with the teacher or with students themselves.

Organizing for Effective Management

- Characteristics that represent potential for classroom problems include classrooms are multidimensional, activities occur simultaneously, things happen quickly, events are often unpredictable, there is little privacy, and classrooms have histories.
- Effective management calls for planning well, establishing routines, arranging your room to avoid problems, and formulating limits.

Managing a Class

- Teachers must establish credibility at the beginning of the year—and then keep it. They must be fair, firm, and consistent with students. They must monitor their classrooms and apply the consequences to misbehavior.
- Teachers should use punishment only as a last resort. They should establish a positive classroom atmosphere, where students have an opportunity to develop a sense of self-discipline.

DISCUSSION QUESTIONS AND ACTIVITIES

1. **Discipline approaches.** Analyze the three approaches to classroom management. Which approach, if any, do you prefer? Can you put together parts of the different approaches and

come up with an eclectic approach that you think would work for you? Can you identify some basic concepts that appear to be true of all three approaches?

2. **Causes of misbehavior.** Think back over the classes you have attended in which there have been disciplinary incidents. List the possible causes for any such misbehavior. How might knowledge of the causes of these incidents influence a teacher's actions? Some behavior problems are teacher created and some are student centered. Can you think of examples?

3. **Planning.** Plan a first day for a class you may teach. What activities would you try on the first day? What rules and consequences would you plan to implement and discuss?

4. **Rules and consequences.** Prepare a list of rules for a classroom at the grade level you expect to teach. After you have established a set of rules, prepare a list of consequences for breaking the rules.

5. **Maintaining control.** What types of procedures would you use to maintain control throughout the year? What measures would you take for severe misbehavior problems?

TECHNOLOGY AND EDUCATION

Many computer programs exist to help teachers manage their classroom. Typical tools include standard forms, student home-based reinforcement programs, student reports, letters to parents, locating information, e-mail, scheduling, classroom arrangement, and complete management systems. Conduct Web searches using one of the available search engines for these and other classroom management tools that would be useful at the grade level you expect to teach. Share your finding with classmates.

DECONSTRUCTING THE STANDARDS

Chapter 13 content addresses topics related to INTASC Standard 5.

♦ INTASC Standard 5 states: *Classroom Motivation and Management:* The teacher uses an understanding of individual and group motivation and behavior to create a learning environment that encourages positive social interaction, active engagement in learning, and self-motivation.

For Standard 5, write your response to the following:

- Which part(s) of the standard does this chapter address?
- How does this chapter address this standard?
- How will the concepts in this chapter help you apply this standard as a teacher?

PRAXIS CONNECTION

Log on to the Web-based student study site at http://www.sagepub.com/eis2study. Access the Praxis II: Principles of Learning and Teaching assessments and/or state-related exams and complete the Chapter 13 test preparation exercises.

PORTFOLIO CONNECTION

Log on to the Web-based student study site at http://www.sagepub.com/eis2study. Access the Portfolio Connection. Complete the Chapter 13 portfolio link to INTASC activities.

CONNECTION WITH THE FIELD

1. **Behavior observation.** Complete several observations in various classrooms at different grade levels. How do the observed teachers control behavior? Observe the students as well, as you consider these questions:
   a. Do students seat themselves when the bell rings? Is there a warm-up activity?
   b. Do the students raise their hands before speaking?
   c. Do the students refrain from speaking during class?
   d. Do the students hand in papers in an orderly manner?

2. **Teacher interviews.** Interview several teachers at different grade levels. Do they have management problems? If so, how do they handle these problems? Do they support the self-discipline, instructional, or desist approach to classroom management? Make a list of ideas you can use when you become a teacher.

3. **Interview counselors.** Interview school counselors at elementary, middle, and high schools. Ask them to describe the discipline policies at their schools and how well they work. Could you support any or all of the policies?

4. **Student handbooks.** Examine and compare several student handbooks from different school districts. Discuss similarities and differences with your classmates.

Appendix A

Laboratory Experiences

Microteaching and Reflective Teaching

The primary purpose of teacher education is to prepare novice teachers for the classroom. Because teaching is such a highly complex series of acts, however, becoming a skillful teacher takes practice. Furthermore, teacher preparation cannot be accomplished through the application of a formula or recipe. In short, teacher effectiveness is best developed through application-type experiences. In general, there are two ways such practice can be provided: laboratory and field-based experiences.

Laboratory experiences usually take place on campuses, whereas field-based experiences generally take place in public or private school classrooms. Of course, field-based experiences would provide the most realistic experiences and thus would be more desirable. But because public or private school classrooms are not readily available to most methods classes for practice purposes, application-type experiences are most commonly achieved through laboratory practice. Laboratory experiences come in two forms: microteaching and reflective teaching.

Essentially, microteaching and reflective teaching differ only in the complexity of the experience. Whereas *microteaching* is concerned with the practice of a limited number of skills or behaviors, *reflective* teaching deals with the total teaching act.

Microteaching

Microteaching is a scaled-down sample of teaching in which a small group of four to six students are taught a 5- to 10-minute minilesson demonstrating one or more specific skills. In effect, microteaching provides a close simulation of public or private classroom teaching for the purpose of practicing designated skills and behaviors.

Microteaching is often an integral component of methods classes in teacher preparatory programs, whereby the various skills and behaviors addressed are practiced and demonstrated. Microteaching is a technique through which preservice teachers can home in on a particular aspect of teaching by placing it "under a microscope" for close examination. Each session focuses on a specific skill or behavior until a satisfactory level of mastery is demonstrated. Demonstration lessons usually are videotaped and critiqued by the teacher trainee and the instructor.

Microteaching simplifies the task of teaching by subdividing multifaceted teaching acts into simpler, less complex components. Because the teacher trainee is teaching a shorter, less complex lesson, he or she can better manage the lesson and focus it on a few major skills in the planning process. In addition, microteaching provides an opportunity for self-analysis and allows for constructive feedback from both the students being taught and an instructor. Videotaping the microteaching lesson offers a further advantage because the tape can be replayed as many times as necessary, and the viewer can focus on different aspects of a lesson with each viewing.

Microteaching does not just involve getting up in front of a small group and teaching. The experience must be carefully planned. First, the skills or behaviors that will and can be practiced in the short time span must be selected with care. For example, the teacher trainee may want to work on effective questioning techniques, the appropriate application of reinforcement, the effective use of stimulus variation, the implementation of a specific teaching method (discussion, lecture, inquiry, discovery, exposition with interaction, etc.), or some combination of these skills or behaviors.

Second, a topic must be selected that will be appropriate for demonstrating the selected skills or behaviors. Not every topic is automatically appropriate for being taught by any method. For example, time constraints dictate that the topic be somewhat narrow—a single concept or subconcept that can be taught in a 5- to 10-minute time span. Therefore, the topic concept must be analyzed carefully in relation to the proposed method and procedure to be used, as well as with regard to the allotted time.

Third, the teacher trainee should narrow the topic to a single concept or subconcept. Once the concept or subconcept has been determined, a limited number of objectives (perhaps only one) must be specified.

The Microteaching Preparation Form in this appendix can be used by the teacher trainee in developing a microteaching lesson. Remember to limit your teaching time to no more than 10 minutes.

Finally, a form must be developed that contains an appropriate set of criteria against which mastery of the desired skill(s) or behavior(s) will be judged. The Microteaching Evaluation Form and Microteaching Self-Analysis Form are examples of such evaluation forms and may be of some assistance in the design of similar evaluative instruments. The Microteaching Evaluation Form can be completed by the students taught and the instructor. The feedback obtained from the completed forms should be analyzed by the teacher trainee and the instructor with respect to mastery of stated skill(s) or behavior(s). The Microteaching Self-Analysis Form should be completed by the teacher trainee, and perhaps the instructor, as a videotape of the microteaching session is replayed for analysis. Such an analysis will help in identifying specific teaching skills that need improvement.

Reflective Teaching

Reflective teaching was developed by Cruickshank (1987) as a result of a desire to provide on-campus laboratory and clinical teaching practice. Essentially, reflective teaching is a modified form of microteaching in that prospective teachers engage in the whole act of teaching; that is, they plan, teach, execute, and evaluate. Special emphasis is placed on a knowledge of whether the learners (peers) actually learned and how satisfied they were with the instruction. In effect, the potential teacher is called on to analyze and reflect on the teaching act itself.

Specifically, as conceived by Cruickshank, reflective teaching has the following components and characteristics:

1. The total class is divided into groups of four to six students.

2. One student from each group is selected (designated) to teach the group.

3. Designated teachers teach toward *identical* instructional objectives, using their own choice of teaching methods.

4. Designated teachers teach at the same time, either in nearby classrooms or in different parts of the same classroom, and are required to finish within the same period of time (usually 15 to 20 minutes).

5. Designated teachers focus on two things: learner achievement and learner satisfaction.

6. Learners (peers) are asked to be themselves and not to play the role of school-age students.

7. There must be a measurable product (evaluation) resulting from the teaching experience, so that teaching and learning can be determined.

8. A learner satisfaction form is completed by the learners following the administration of the evaluation.

9. A large-group discussion follows the reflective teaching experience. That is, the total class reflects on and discusses the different teaching acts that took place.

10. The next teacher is selected (designated), and the cycle repeats.

The goal of reflective teaching is to teach and improve teaching skills through reflection on what was taught and how well it was taught. Each learner's achievement evaluation and lesson satisfaction are analyzed to elicit information relative to the effectiveness of the designated teacher. Reflection on this information is very instructive to the total class because the students can compare the different methodological approaches and become aware that the effectiveness of the approach depends on the objective(s) and the teacher.

Because practice of the total teaching act is the ultimate goal of reflective teaching, students should be responsible for the development and presentation of a complete lesson. Thus, when planning for a reflective teaching session, the instructor should provide the instructional objective and, in most cases, a common evaluative instrument. The designated teachers, however, should plan a total lesson using a form similar to the Lesson Plan Format in this appendix.

Feedback to the designated teachers is a major component in reflective teaching. It should be given as soon as possible after the teaching session, and it must be objective. If it is to be objective, the evaluation instrument used should be based on identified effective teaching skills. An example of such an instrument is shown in the Teaching Evaluation Form. Feedback can be provided by having the instructor and learners complete and share the evaluative information with the designated teachers. Moreover, if the lesson can be videotaped, the designated teachers can complete an evaluation of their own teaching. Learners also should be asked to complete a Learner Satisfaction Form like the one in this appendix. Feedback on lesson satisfaction can be used in addressing the areas that the learners found inappropriate in a lesson presentation.

Finally, grades are an important ingredient in any teacher preparatory program. Thus, the Teaching Evaluation Form should be based on the program criteria for effective teaching. As such, the instructor's, learner's, and designated teacher's self-evaluation of a teaching session can provide input for grades.

MICROTEACHING PREPARATION FORM

Microteacher:_____ Date: _____

Course Title: _____

Use this form for preparation of your lesson. Prepare a copy for your instructor.

1. Concept to teach: _____

_____

2. Skill(s) or behavior(s) to demonstrate: _____

_____

3. Specific instructional objective(s): _____

_____

_____

4. Focusing activity: _____

_____

_____

5. Instructional procedure: _____

_____

_____

6. Closure: _____

_____

_____

7. Audiovisual materials and equipment needed:_____

_____

_____

8. Notes and comments: _____

_____

_____

MICROTEACHING EVALUATION FORM

Microteacher: _____ Date: _____

Subject: _____ Tape No.: _____

Rate the teacher trainee on each skill area. Code: 5 or 4, mastery of skill demonstrated; 3 or 2, some skill refinement needed; or 1 or 0, much skill refinement needed.

Organization of Lesson

5 4 3 2 1 0   Lesson preparation

5 4 3 2 1 0   Focusing activity

5 4 3 2 1 0   First skill/Behavior _____

5 4 3 2 1 0   Second skill/Behavior _____

5 4 3 2 1 0   Closure

5 4 3 2 1 0   Subject-matter knowledge

Comments: _____

_____

_____

_____

_____

_____

_____

MICROTEACHING SELF-ANALYSIS FORM

Microteacher: _____ Date: _____

Concept taught: _____ Tape No.: _____

Replay the tape of your microteaching session as needed to collect data for the following items. Analyze the collected data and draw conclusions with respect to the behavior addressed in each item.

1. Teacher talk versus student talk. Set up a small chart as follows:

   Teacher talk: _____

   Student talk: _____

   Silence or confusion: _____

As you view your microteaching tape, place a tally on the chart to represent who was talking approximately every 3 seconds. If no one was talking or if many people were talking simultaneously, then place a tally in the silence or confusion category. When you have finished, count the number of tallies in each category as well as the total number of tallies in the categories teacher talk and student talk combined. Use the following formulas to determine the percentage of teacher talk and student talk:

$$\text{Percentage of teacher talk} = \frac{\text{Tallies in teacher talk category}}{\text{Total tallies in teacher talk} + \text{student talk categories}} \times 100$$

$$\text{Percentage of student talk} = \frac{\text{Tallies in student talk category}}{\text{Total tallies in teacher talk} + \text{student talk categories}} \times 100$$

2. Filler words. Record the filler words or sounds ("okay," "you know," or "uh") and the number of times each was used:

   _____

   _____

   _____

   _____

   _____

3. Questions. Record the number of questions asked:

   Convergent: _____

   Divergent: _____

4. Student names. Record the number of times students are addressed by name:

   _____

   _____

   _____

   _____

   _____

5. Pauses. Record the number of times pauses are used to give students time to think:

   _____

   _____

   _____

   _____

   _____

6. Reinforcement. Record the number of times reinforcement is used:

   Verbal Reinforcement: _____

   Nonverbal Reinforcement: _____

7. Sensory channels. Record the number of times students are required to change sensory channels:

   _____

   _____

   _____

   _____

   _____

LESSON PLAN FORMAT

Teacher: _____ Date: _____

Course Title: _____

Topic: _____

Instructional objective(s): _____

_____

_____

Focusing activity: _____

_____

_____

Content	Instructional Procedures
	a.
	b.
	c.
	d.
	e.
	f.

Closure: _____

_____

_____

Evaluation procedure: _____

_____

_____

Instructional materials: _____

_____

_____

Notes and comments: _____

_____

_____

TEACHING EVALUATION FORM

Teacher:_____   Date: _____

Subject: _____   Tape No.: _____

Rate the teacher trainee on each skill area. Code: 5 or 4, mastery of skill demonstrated; 3 or 2, some skill refinement needed; or 1 or 0, much skill refinement needed.

Organization of Lesson

5 4 3 2 1 0   Lesson preparation

5 4 3 2 1 0   Focusing activity

5 4 3 2 1 0   Closure

5 4 3 2 1 0   Subject-matter knowledge

Comments: _____

_____

_____

_____

_____

Lesson Presentation

5 4 3 2 1 0   Audience contact

5 4 3 2 1 0   Enthusiasm

5 4 3 2 1 0   Speech quality and delivery

5 4 3 2 1 0   Audience involvement

5 4 3 2 1 0   Verbal behaviors

5 4 3 2 1 0   Nonverbal behaviors

5 4 3 2 1 0   Use of questions and questioning techniques

5 4 3 2 1 0   Directions and pacing

5 4 3 2 1 0   Use of reinforcement

5 4 3 2 1 0   Use of aids and materials

Comments: _____

_____

_____

_____

_____

LEARNER SATISFACTION FORM

Teacher:_____   Date: _____

Subject: _____   Tape No.: _____

1. During the lesson, how satisfied were you as a learner (Rate your satisfaction by placing an X on the following scale)?

   Very satisfied   Satisfied   Very unsatisfied

   <----------------------.----------------------.----------------------.----------------------.----------------------.---------------------->

2. What would have increased your satisfaction? _____

   _____

   _____

   _____

   _____

   _____

   _____

   _____

   _____

   _____

APPENDIX B

State Licensure/Certification and Reciprocity

Students and teachers often need information related to licensure/certification as they prepare for a teaching career or as they relocate after obtaining certification in a state. Licensure/certification regulations vary a great deal among states. Some states offer relatively few licenses; others offer many. Most states require applicants to pass examinations such as the Praxis II or a state-developed exam before applicants can be granted a regular license. Although some states will grant a temporary license to an applicant licensed in another state, the applicant often has to fulfill additional requirements, such as a specific test or additional courses, to obtain a regular license.

Many changes can be anticipated in the licensing of teachers in the next few years. Indeed, most states are experimenting with and implementing alternative means of authorizing people to teach. Many mid-career professionals are showing interest in pursuing second careers in education. These older applicants have a college education and life experiences that make them attractive as teachers. Requirements for alternative routes to teacher licensure vary greatly with some preparing excellent teachers, whereas others are preparing teachers who leave the profession after a short stay. Below are resources to help you find state teacher certification addresses, telephone numbers, and Web sites, as well as general information on state reciprocity.

State Teacher Certification Addresses

Many states continually revise and pass new legislation relative to the licensure/certification of teachers. State departments also continuously update and revise their Web sites. Therefore, instead of providing often outdated state department information in this appendix, I am providing Web sites with the latest addresses, telephone numbers, state teacher certification requirements, and links to state departments of education. This information is provided at the following sites.

http://www.education-world.com/jobs/state_certification.shtml

http://www.uky.edu/Education/TEP/usacert.html

These sites should provide the information students and teachers need as they consider relocating or as they move from state to state and seek licensure/certification information.

Reciprocity

Due to the growing teacher shortage, some state policy makers are mandating that their state accept out-of-state licenses without additional subsequent requirements. These reciprocity agreements between states, whereby one state recognizes the validity of another state's teacher certification program and grants equivalent certification to teachers who have moved from a cooperating state, are not practiced in the same way. Nor do all states have reciprocity. Other states have mandated that their state accept certificates issued by the National Board for Professional Teaching Standards (NBPTS).

Many states have signed reciprocity agreements, which allow individuals certified in one state to be certified in others. However, certain requirements such as state or national examinations or state history are not waived. Candidates are usually given provisional certification, which is good for 1 year, and applicants must meet all state requirements during the provisional year before a standard certificate is issued. Reciprocity does not always guarantee that a license will transfer directly from state to state but generally guarantees individuals will be awarded the closest comparable areas.

APPENDIX C

Praxis II Case Histories Format

Based on knowledge and skills that states commonly require of beginning teachers, the Praxis Series was developed by the Educational Testing Service (ETS). The ETS Praxis Series assesses individual development at the entering education level (Praxis I), subject matter knowledge level (Praxis II), and classroom performance level (Praxis III). Many states have implemented one or more of these assessment levels. Test questions cover the breadth of materials new teachers need to know and assess knowledge of both principles and processes of teaching. The exams consist of two formats, multiple choice and case history. The case history format poses particular problems that teachers routinely face in the classroom, and more important, many are based on authentic real-world example of students working in the context of the subject matter.

ETS has developed four Tests at a Glance sites to give teacher education candidates practice with the Praxis II: Principles of Learning and Teaching (PLT) Assessments. These sites have been designed for early childhood (test 0521), Grades K–6 (test 0522), Grades 5–9 (test 0523), and Grades 7–12 (test 0524) candidates. The four Web site addresses are given below. Review of the site at the grade levels you expect to teach and completion of the site sample exercises will give you the opportunity to become familiar with the PLT format.

PLT: Early Childhood: ftp://ftp.ets.org/pub/tandl/0521.pdf

PLT: Grades K–6: ftp://ftp.ets.org/pub/tandl/0522.pdf

PLT: Grades 5–9: ftp://ftp.ets.org/pub/tandl/0523.pdf

PLT: Grades 7–12: ftp://ftp.ets.org/pub/tandl/0524.pdf

Review and completion of the above applicable Test at a Glance will help prepare you for the case history component of the Praxis II: Principles of Learning and Teaching Assessments. The Praxis II Connection for each text chapter on the Web-based student study site (www.sagepub.com/eis2study) will further assist you in preparing for the Praxis II and/or state exam.

GLOSSARY

A

Absolute grading standard: Student grades given relative to performance against an established criterion—for example, 90% to 100%, A; 80% to 89%, B; 70% to 79%, C; and 60% to 69%, D.

Academic learning time: The time in class during which students are actively engaged in academic tasks that result in performance being at the 80% level or better.

Accountability: Holding schools and teachers responsible for what is taught and what students learn.

Accreditation: Procedure for verifying school programs and course quality and uniformity.

Active learning: Learning by doing with students engaged in reading, writing, discussing, and problem solving.

Advance organizer: An introductory statement, before instruction begins, that provides a structure for new information that is to be presented.

Affective domain: Learning domain in Benjamin Bloom's Taxonomy concerned with values, attitudes, feelings, and emotions.

Allocated time: Time appropriated for students to engage in school activities such as classes, lunch, announcements, and so on.

Assertive discipline: A classroom management approach developed by Lee and Marlene Canter that stresses the need for and rights of teachers to communicate classroom needs and requirements in clear, firm, nonhostile terms and that stresses the rights of students to learn.

Assessment: Process of collecting a full range of information about students and classrooms for the purpose of making educational decisions.

Attention-deficit/hyperactivity disorder (ADHD): A learning disability characterized by difficulty in remaining still so that one can concentrate on learning.

Attitudes: Mind-sets toward a person, place, or thing.

B

Behavior modification: Shaping behavior by altering the consequences, outcomes, or rewards that follow the behavior.

Being needs: The three higher levels of Abraham Maslow's need hierarchy: intellectual achievement, aesthetic appreciation, and self-actualization.

Block scheduling: An instructional delivery pattern that divides school time into instructional blocks ranging from 20 to 110 minutes.

Body language: Physical mannerisms that communicate and can be used to prompt students to stay attentive and on task—such as physical proximity, eye contact, body position, facial expressions, and tone of voice.

Brainstorming: Instructional technique in which small groups of students generate ideas, solutions, or comments relative to an assigned topic. All answers, no matter how wrong they may seem to the teacher or other students, are accepted as possibilities related to the assigned task.

Buzz group: Instructional technique in which a small work group is formed for a short duration to share opinions, viewpoints, or reactions.

C

Checklist: List of criteria or characteristics against which a performance or an end product is to be judged.

Classroom management: Process of organizing and conducting the business of the classroom to keep it relatively free of behavior problems.

Closure: Activity used for pulling a lesson together so concepts make sense and bringing it to a logical conclusion.

Cognitive domain: Learning domain in Benjamin Bloom's Taxonomy that focuses on information, thinking, and reasoning ability.

Cognitive set: Predisposition to act or behave in a certain way.

Cognitive style: The means by which individuals process and think about what they learn.

Communication: The process by which information and feelings are shared by people through an exchange of verbal and nonverbal messages.

Competitive evaluation: Evaluation that forces students to compete with each other.

Computer-based instruction (CBI): Use of computers for presenting instructional information, asking questions, and interacting with students. Individualized instruction administered by a computer.

Computers: Electronic devices that can store and manipulate information, as well as interact with users; commonplace in many classrooms and in everyday life.

Concept attainment: Strategy designed to teach concepts through the presentation of examples and nonexamples.

Constructivist approach: Approach to learning that emphasizes that individuals actively construct knowledge and understanding.

Contingency contract: Grading system in which a formal, written agreement between students and a teacher is drawn up as to what students will do to receive a specified reward.

Convergent questions: Questions that allow for only a few right responses.

Cooperative learning: Instructional technique in which students of mixed abilities work together as a team on an assigned task. Interdependence and support for all members of the group is stressed.

Course planning: Broadest and most general type of instruction planning, usually divided into a sequence of units of study.

Creative thinking: Process of assembling information to develop a whole new understanding of a concept or idea. Four stages generally associated with creative thought are preparation, incubation, illumination, and verification.

Creativity: Capacity for producing imaginative, original products, or ways of solving problems.

Criterion-referenced test: Testing in which interpretations are made by comparing a student's score against a predetermined standard.

Critical thinking: Analyzing complex situations critically, using standards of objectivity and consistency, and arriving at tentative conclusions.

Cumulative record: File that holds information collected on students over a period of school years.

Curriculum: Systematic plan of instruction for a school system. The learning, intended and unintended, that takes place under the sponsorship of the school.

Curriculum integration: Form of teaching and learning that draws upon the knowledge and skills of a variety of discipline areas as they become necessary in problem solving.

D

Daily lesson plan: A detailed outline used to structure instructional activities for a single day and to help with the flow of the instruction.

Decision making: Thinking that asks students to choose the best response from several options.

Deductive thinking: Thinking that asks students to consider given generalizations and provide supporting data.

Deficiency needs: The four lowest levels of Abraham Maslow's need hierarchy: survival, safety, belonging, and self-esteem.

Demonstration: Instructional method in which the teacher or some other designated individual stands before a class, shows something, and tells what is happening or what has happened or asks students to discuss what has happened.

Desist approach: Method of classroom management that gives the teacher full responsibility for regulating the classroom.

Diagnostic evaluation: Evaluation administered prior to instruction to assess students' knowledge and abilities so that appropriate instruction can be provided.

Diagnostic pretest evaluation: See *Diagnostic evaluation.*

Differentiated instruction: A teaching theory based on the premise that instructional approaches should vary and be adapted in relation to individual and diverse students in the classroom.

Direct teaching: A structured, teacher-centered approach that is characterized by teacher direction and control, higher teacher expectations for students' progress, maximizing time students spend on academic tasks, and efforts by the teacher to keep negative affect to a minimum.

Disabled: Having an inability to do something.

Discipline: Dealing with the prevention of classroom misbehavior, as well as reacting to consequences of disruptive actions.

Discovery learning: Instructional method that focuses on intentional learning through supervised problem solving according to the scientific method. Students are encouraged to learn concepts and principles through their own exploration.

Discussion: Instructional method in which students exchange and share ideas relative to an assigned topic. Can take the form of either a small-group or whole-group activity.

Divergent questions: Questions that allow for many right responses.

Drill: Fixation of specific associations for automatic recall.

E

Educational games: See *Simulation.*

Empathic listening: Listening with feeling. An attempt to experience what a speaker is experiencing or feeling and responding to those feelings.

Empirical questions: Questions that require students to integrate or analyze remembered or given information and supply a single, correct predictable answer.

Engaged time: Actual time individual students are engaged in purposeful classroom learning.

English as a second language (ESL): English language training for students whose first language is not English. Training is designed to help participants learn English reading, writing, listening, and speaking skills.

English language learners (ELL): Learners who are beginning to learn English as a new language or have already gained some proficiency in English.

Evaluation: Process of obtaining available information about students and using it to ascertain the degree of change in students' performance.

Evaluative questions: Questions that require that a judgment be made or a value be put on something.

Exposition teaching: Teaching method in which some authority—teacher, textbook, film, or micro-computer—presents information without overt interaction taking place between the authority and the students.

Exposition with interaction teaching: Authority-presented instruction followed by questioning that ascertains whether information has been comprehended.

Extrinsic motivation: Motivation created by events or rewards outside the individual.

F

Factual questions: Questions that require the recall of information through the mental processes of recognition and rote memory.

Focusing questions: Questions used to direct students' attention to a lesson or to the content of a lesson.

Formal curriculum: School learning experiences that are intentional.

Formative evaluation: Use of evaluation information for supplying feedback to students before or during the learning process and for promoting learning.

G

Gifted and talented (G/T) students: Learners with exceptional general intellect, specific academic ability, creative productive thinking, leadership ability, or visual and performing arts talents.

Goals: Broad statements of instructional intent that describe the general purpose of instruction.

Graphic organizers: Pictorial or graphical ways to organize written or oral information.

H

Halting time: Teacher's pause in talking, used for giving students time to think about presented materials and directions.

Handicapped: Possessing an impairment that limits one's activities.

Hearing: Transmission of eardrum vibration caused by sound impulses to the brain.

Heuristic approach: Active, reflective teaching methods that involve students in problem solving and comprise modes of discovery, inquiry (including Richard Suchman inquiry), and simulations and games.

I

I-messages: Teacher messages that tell students how the teacher feels about problem situations and implicitly ask for corrected behavior.

Incentive systems: Systems that offer preferred activities or items for motivational purposes or for keeping students on task.

Independent study: Instructional method in which students are involved in activities carried out with little or no guidance.

Individualized instruction: Instructional method in which instruction is tailored to interests, needs, and abilities of individual students.

Inductive thinking: Thinking that asks students to make generalizations based on knowledge of specific examples and details.

Informational objectives: Statements of instructional intent that are an abbreviation of instructional objectives with only the performance and product specified.

Infusion approach: Method of teaching thinking skills in which desired skill is used in conjunction with and incorporated into regular curriculum.

Inner discipline: Ability to control one's own behavior and make responsible decisions.

Inquiry: Instructional method that focuses on the flexible yet systematic process of problem solving.

Inquiry demonstration: Instructional method in which students are asked only to observe in silence.

Instructional approach: Method of classroom management based on the premise that well-planned and well-implemented instruction will prevent most classroom problems.

Instructional objective: Narrow four-component statement of learning intent. The components are the performance, a product, the conditions, and the criterion.

Instructional strategy: The global plan for teaching a particular lesson consisting of the methodology to be used and the sequence of steps to be followed for implementing the lesson activities.

Instructional time: Amount of allocated time available for learning.

Internet: System established to let computers communicate with each other.

Intrinsic motivation: Stimulation of student learning that comes from activities that are rewarding in themselves.

L

Learning: Relatively permanent change in an individual's capacity for performance as a result of experience or practice.

Learning style: The set of cognitive, affective, and physiological behaviors through which an individual learns most effectively; determined by a combination of hereditary and environmental influences.

Lecture: Teacher presents information with no overt interaction with students.

Lecture recitation: Instructional technique in which the teacher makes a clear presentation, followed by student responses centered on the ideas that were presented by the teacher.

Lesson procedure: Sequence of steps designed to lead students to the acquisition of the desired learning.

Limited English proficient (LEP): A designation for students with limited ability to understand, read, speak, or write English whose first or primary language isn't English.

Limits: Accepted and nonaccepted actions in the classroom.

Listening: Active process of assigning meaning to what is heard, or the brain giving meaning to impulses transmitted from the eardrum to the brain. Larry L. Barker defines four components of listening as hearing, attending, understanding, and remembering. Listening styles can be one-way, two-way, or empathic.

M

Mandated time: Total time available for all activities carried out in school.

Mastery curriculum: Learning considered essential for all students to know.

Mastery learning: Diagnostic-corrective-enrichment instructional model in which students work on objectives until mastery is achieved. It is based on the assumption that every student is capable of achieving most of the course objectives if given the time and appropriate experiences.

Measurement: Assignment of numerical values to objects, events, performances, or products to indicate the degree to which they possess the characteristics being measured.

Mental Operation system: Four-category question model composed of factual, empirical, productive, and evaluative questions.

Metacognition: Cognition about cognition, or "knowing about knowing."

Metaverbal component: Underlying, or hidden, message that cannot be directly attributed to the meaning of the words or how they are spoken.

Methodology: Planned patterned behaviors that are definite steps through which the teacher influences learning.

Microteaching: Technique of practicing teaching skills and processes in scaled-down and simulated situations.

Middle schools: Schools designed to meet unique needs of preadolescents, usually for Grades 5 or 6 through 7 or 8.

Minimum competency tests: Exit tests designed to ascertain whether students have achieved basic levels of performance in basic skill areas—such as reading, writing, and computation—before they can graduate or continue to the next level.

Modeling: Person demonstrating or acting as one wants others to act and communicating examples of the values, ideas, and behaviors to be acquired by students.

Motivation: Influences of needs, desires, and drives on the intensity and direction of behaviors.

Multiple intelligences: A proposition by Howard Gardner asserting that traditional measures of intelligence are limited and that individuals possess different types of intelligences. These intelligences include spatial, bodily-kinesthetic, musical, linguistic, logical-mathematical, interpersonal, intrapersonal, and naturalistic intelligences.

N

Natural motives: Individuals' internal desires. Many natural motives are believed to be innate.

Needs: Deficiencies or requirements in the individual or the absence of anything the person requires, or thinks he or she requires, for overall well-being.

Negative reinforcement: Strengthening the likelihood of a behavior or event by the removal of an unpleasant stimulus.

Noncompetitive evaluation: Evaluation that does not force students to compete with each other.

Nonverbal communication: Nonlingustic communication or the sending of messages without the use of words. Comprises facial language, body language (kinesics), use of the voice, and use of space, motion, and time.

Nonverbal reinforcement: Use of physical action as a positive consequence to strengthen behavior or event.

Normal curve: Bell-shaped distribution. Mathematical construct divided into equal segments that reflect the natural distribution of all sorts of things in nature.

Norm-referenced test: Test interpretation made by comparing a student's score with that of a norm group (a large representative sample) to obtain meaning.

O

Objective: Anticipated result or product of instruction. Unambiguous statement of instructional intent.

Overlapping: Engaging in or supervising several activities simultaneously.

P

Panels: Instructional technique in which five to eight students prepare and discuss a topic in front of a class. Also known as a *roundtable*.

Percentage grading system: Percentage correct is recorded for each assignment, and an average is calculated to determine a final grade.

Percentile score: Derived score on a distribution of scores below which a given percentage of raw scores fall.

Performance assessment: Assessment in which students demonstrate the behaviors to be measured.

PL 94–142: Federal law requiring provision of special education services to eligible students.

Point grading system: Student work is allocated points and grades are assigned according to an established grade range.

Portfolio: Systematic, organized collection of evidence (e.g., projects, written work, and video demonstrations of skills) that documents growth and development and that represents progress made toward reaching specified goals and objectives.

Positive reinforcement: Strengthening the likelihood of occurrence of a behavior or an event by presenting a desired stimulus.

Posttest evaluation: Evaluation completed after instruction to determine the extent of student learning.

Practice: Repeating of specified tasks or skills for the purpose of improvement.

Probing questions: Questions that follow a student response and require the student to think and respond more thoroughly than in the initial response.

Problem solving: Instructional technique that focuses on the intentional elimination of uncertainty or doubt through direct experiences and under supervision.

Procedure: Sequence of steps designed to lead students to the acquisition of the desired learning.

Productive questions: Broad, open-ended questions with many correct responses that require students to use their imagination, think creatively, and produce something unique.

Prompting questions: Questions that include the use of hints to aid students in answering or in correcting an initial response.

Psychomotor domain: Learning domain concerned with muscular abilities and skills on a continuum ranging from the simple to the complex.

Punishment: Application of a negative stimulus or removal of a positive stimulus as a result of inappropriate behavior.

Q

Qualified reinforcement: Differential reinforcement of acceptable parts of student actions or attempts.

Questionnaire: Lists of written statements regarding attitudes, feelings, and opinions to which the reader must respond.

R

Rating scale: Scale of values, arranged in order of quality, describing someone or something being evaluated.

Reality therapy: William Glasser's personality theory of therapy in which individuals are helped to become responsible and able to satisfy their needs in the real world.

Redirecting: Asking different individuals to respond to a question in light of, or to add new insight to, the previous responses.

Reflective teaching: Teacher as an informed and thoughtful decision maker, who analyzes past experiences in planning and teaching and in promoting thinking about the nature of teaching and learning.

Reinforcement: Theory that says the consequences of an action strengthen or weaken the likelihood of the behavior or event. Rewarding of desired actions.

Reinforcer: Anything found pleasurable by individuals.

Relative grading standard: Student's grades given relative to performance of other students. Grading on the curve.

Reliability: Extent to which individual responses are measured consistently. The coefficient of stability of scores.

Responsibility: State of being accountable or answerable for one's actions. Ability to meet obligations or to act without direct guidance.

Reward mechanism: A formal system of reinforcement.

Ripple effect: Spread of behaviors from one individual to others through imitation.

Role-playing: Instructional technique designed to let students assume the role(s) of individuals in a re-creation of an event or situation.

Roundtable: See *Panels.*

Rubric: A scoring guide that helps establish uniformity in an evaluation of a student.

S

Self-discipline approach: Method of classroom management built on the premise that students can be trusted to evaluate and change their actions so their behaviors are beneficial and appropriate to the self and to the class as a whole.

Self-fulfilling prophecy: Phenomenon in which believing that something will happen causes it to occur.

Separate approach: View suggested by Reuven Feuerstein that students need special, focused instruction on thinking skills.

Set induction: Something a teacher does at the outset of a lesson to get students' undivided attention, arouse their interest, and establish a conceptual framework.

Simulation: Instructional technique in which students are involved in models of artificial situations and/or events designed to provide no-risk experiences for students. Also referred to as *educational games.*

Socratic method: Instructional method in which a questioning-and-interaction sequence is used to draw information out of students.

Standard deviation: Extent to which scores are spread out around the mean.

Standardized test: Commercially developed test that samples behavior under uniform procedures.

Standard scores: Scores based on individuals' variance from the mean expressed in standard deviations.

Stimulus variation: Actions, behaviors, or behavior patterns designed to gain and maintain student attention during a lesson.

Strategy: Methodology and procedure of a lesson.

Student-centered curriculum: Activity curriculum that focuses on student needs and interests.

Student work sample: Collection of students' work over period of time that offers credible evidence of student learning and teacher effectiveness.

Subject-centered curriculum: School curriculum patterns wherein subjects are separated into distinct courses of study.

Suchman inquiry: Inquiry approach developed by Richard Suchman whereby students are presented and asked to explain discrepant events.

T

Task group: Instructional technique in which a group of four to eight students is formed to solve a problem or complete a project.

Teacher effectiveness training (TET): Self-discipline approach to classroom management conceived by Thomas Gordon that stresses establishment of positive working relationships between teachers and students. Key is based on who owns the problem when one develops—teacher or student.

Teacher-made tests: Evaluative instruments developed and scored by a teacher for classroom assessment.

Teacher-student planning: Participatory process that directly involves students in instructional planning.

Teacher testing: Requirement, usually legislatively mandated, that teachers pass a test prior to certification.

Teaching: Actions of someone who is trying to assist others to reach their fullest potential in all aspects of development.

Team planning: Coordination of teachers' instructional approaches among disciplines.

Technology literacy: Basic understanding of the general principles of technology and the application of technology.

Telelecture: Lecture transmitted from a central studio classroom to distant classrooms.

Test: Task or series of tasks used to obtain systematic observations regarding ability, skill, knowledge, or performance.

Textbook recitation: Instructional method in which students are assigned content to read and study in a textbook and are then questioned on what has been read and studied.

Thematic unit: Unit of instruction planned by a team of teachers that is organized for interdisciplinary/cross-curricular teaching over a block of time.

Thinking: Withholding judgment to use past knowledge and experience in finding new information, concepts, or conclusions.

Time on task: See *Engaged time.*

Transfer: Ability to use classroom-acquired information outside the classroom or in different subjects.

U

Unit plan: Plan that links goals and objectives, content, activities, resources and materials, and evaluation for a particular unit of study for a course.

Usability: Suitability of a measurement device to collect desired data.

V

Validity: Ability of a test to measure what it purports to measure.

Verbal communication: Communication through use of spoken words.

Verbal component: Actual words and meaning of a spoken message.

Verbal reinforcement: Presentation of positive comments to strengthen student behavior or event.

Vicarious motivation: Strengthening of behavior because of desire to receive consequences received by others who exhibit that behavior.

Vocal component: Meaning attached to a spoken message, resulting from such variables as voice firmness, modulation, tone, tempo, pitch, and loudness.

W

Wait time: Time needed for students to consider their responses to questions. *Wait time 1* is the initial time a teacher waits following a question before calling for the response. *Wait time 2* is the total time a teacher waits for all students to respond to the same question or for students to respond to each other's responses to a question.

Weekly plan: Condensed version of a week's daily lesson plans, written on a short form provided by the school.

Weighted grading system: Assignments are given a letter grade, and all grades are weighted in determining the final grade.

Withitness: Ability of a teacher to be aware of what is going on in all parts of the classroom and the ability to communicate this awareness.

REFERENCES

A

Airasian, P. W. (2001). *Classroom assessment: Concepts and applications* (4th ed.). New York: McGraw-Hill.

Alexander, G. A., Graham, S., & Harris, K. R. (1998). A perspective on strategy research: Progress and prospects. *Educational Psychology Review, 10*(2), 129–154.

Allen, D. W., Ryan, K. A., Bush, R. N., & Cooper, J. M. (1969). *Questioning skills.* Stanford, CA: General Learning Corporation.

Alvermann, D. E., Moore, D. E., & Conley, M. W. (Eds.). (1987). *Research within reach, secondary school reading: A research guided response to concerns of reading educators.* Newark, DE: International Reading Association.

Anderson, J. R., Greeno, J. G., Reder, L. M., & Simon, H. A. (2000). Perspectives on learning, thinking, and activity. *Educational Researcher, 29*(4), 11–13.

Anderson, L. W., & Krathwohl, D. R. (Eds.). (2001). *A taxonomy for learning, teaching, and assessing: A revision of Bloom's Taxonomy of educational objectives.* New York: Longman.

Armstrong, D. G. (2002). *Curriculum today.* Englewood Cliffs, NJ: Prentice Hall.

Armstrong, T. (1994). *Multiple intelligences in the classroom.* Alexandria, VA: Association for Supervision and Curriculum Development.

Arons, A. B. (1988, April 9). *What current research in teaching and learning says to the practicing teacher.* Robert Karplus Lecture presented at the National Convention of the National Science Teacher Association, St. Louis, MO.

Ashton, P. (1988). *Teaching higher-order thinking and content: An essential ingredient in teacher preparation.* Gainesville: University of Florida Press.

Association for Supervision and Curriculum Development (ASCO). (1990). *Teaching thinking skills* [Video]. Alexandria, VA: Author.

Ausubel, D. P. (1963). *The psychology of meaningful verbal learning: An introduction to school learning.* New York: Grune and Stratton.

Aviram, A. (2000). From "computers in the classroom" to mindful radical adaptation by education systems to the emerging cyber culture. *Journal of Educational Change, 1*(4), 331–352.

B

Banks, J. A. (2002). *An introduction to multicultural education* (3rd ed.). Boston: Allyn & Bacon.

Barker, L. L. (1971). *Listening behavior.* Englewood Cliffs, NJ: Prentice Hall.

Batsche, G., Elliott, J., Graden, J. L., Grimes, J., Kovaleski, J. F., Prasse, D., et al. (2005). *Response to intervention: Policy considerations and implementation.* Alexandria, VA: National Association of State Directors of Special Education, Inc.

Beane, J. A. (1995). Curriculum integration and the disciplines of knowledge. *Phi Delta Kappan, 76*(8), 616–622.

Becher, H. J., & Ravitz, J. L. (April, 2001). *Computer use by teachers: Are Cuban's predictions correct?* Paper presented at the annual meeting of the American Educational Research Association, Seattle, WA.

Beisser, S. R. (1998, March). Parent to parent: ABC's of parenting your gifted child. *Parenting for High Potential,* p. 25.

Berger, E. H. (1991). *Parents as partners in education* (3rd ed.). New York: Merrill.

Berliner, D. (1987). Simple views of effective teaching and simple theory of classroom instruction. In D. Berliner & B. Rosenshire (Eds.), *Talks to teachers* (pp. 93–110). New York: Random House.

Beyer, B. K. (1984). Improving thinking skills: Practical approaches. *Phi Delta Kappan, 65,* 556–560.

Beyer, B. K. (1988). *Developing a thinking skills program.* Boston: Allyn & Bacon.

Block, J. H., Efthim, H. E., & Burns, R. B. (1989). *Building effective mastery learning schools.* New York: Longman.

Bloom, B. S., Engelhart, M. D., Furst, E. J., Hill, W. H., & Krathwohl, D. R. (Eds.). (1956). *Taxonomy of educational objectives: Handbook I. Cognitive domain.* New York: David McKay.

Boyer, E. L. (1983). *High school.* New York: Harper & Row.

Brookfield, S. D. (1987). *Developing critical thinkers.* San Francisco: Jossey-Bass.

Brooks, J. G., & Brooks, M. G. (1999). *In search of understanding: The case for constructivist classrooms* (2nd ed.). Alexandria, VA: Association for Supervision and Curriculum Development.

Brophy, J. (1981). Teacher praise: A functional analysis. *Review of Educational Research, 51,* 5–32.

Brown, F. (2004). The road to Brown, its leaders, and the future. *Education & Urban Society, 36*(3), 255–266.

Bruner, J. (2004). *Toward a theory of instruction.* Cambridge, MA: Belknap.

Bruner, J. S. (1977). *The process of education.* Cambridge, MA: Harvard University Press.

Butler, D. L., & Winne, P. H. (1995). Feedback and self-regulated learning: A theoretical synthesis. *Review of Educational Research, 65,* 245–282.

C

Campbell, D. (2000). *Choosing democracy* (2nd ed.). Upper Saddle River, NJ: Merrill/Prentice Hall.

Canter, L., & Canter, M. (1976). *Assertive discipline: A take-charge approach for today's educator.* Los Angeles: Canter and Associates.

Charles, C. M. (2002). *Building classroom discipline* (6th ed.). New York: Longman.

Checkley, K. (1997). The first seven . . . and the eighth: A conversation with Howard Gardner. *Educational Leadership, 55*(1), 8–13.

Coloroso, B. (2002). *Kids are worth it! Giving your child the gift of inner discipline.* New York: HarperCollins.

Cooper, H., & Good, T. L. (1983). *Pygmalion grows up.* New York: Longman.

Countryman, L. L., & Schroeder, M. (1996). When students lead parent-teacher conferences. *Education Leadership, 53*(7), 64–68.

Crane, C. (2001). General classroom space. *School Planning and Management, 40,* 54–55.

Cruickshank, D. R. (1987). *Reflection teaching.* Reston, VA: Association of Teacher Educators.

Cuban, L. (2001). *Oversold and underused: Reforming schools through technology, 1980–2000.* Cambridge, MA: Harvard University Press.

D

Danielson, C. (1996). *Enhancing professional practice: A framework for teaching.* Alexandria, VA: Association for Supervision and Curriculum Development.

Davidson, N., & O'Leary, P. W. (1990, February). How cooperative learning can enhance mastery teaching. *Educational Leadership, 47*(5), 30–33.

DeVito, J. A. (1985). *Communication.* New York: Harper & Row.

Dillion, J. (1987). *Classroom questions and discussions.* Norwood, NJ: Ablex.

Doyle, W. (1986). Classroom organization and management. In M. C. Wittrock (Ed.), *Handbook of research on teaching* (4th ed., pp. 392–431). New York: Macmillan.

Drafke, M. (1993). *Graphic organizers.* Retrieved from http://www.cod.edu/people/faculty/drafke/graphic%20organizers.htm

Dunn, R., & Dunn, K. (1993). *Teaching secondary students through their individual learning styles: Practical approach for Grades 7–12.* Boston: Allyn & Bacon.

E

Ebel, R. L., & Frisbie, D. A. (1991). *Essentials of educational measurement* (5th ed.). Englewood Cliffs, NJ: Prentice Hall.

Ellis, A. K. (2001). Cooperative learning. In A. K. Ellis (Ed.), *Research on educational innovations* (pp. 216–229). Larchmont, NY: Eye on Education.

Evertson, C. M., Emmer, E. T., Clements, B. S., Sanford, J. P., & Worsham, M. E. (1994). *Classroom management for elementary teachers* (3rd ed.). Boston: Allyn & Bacon.

Evertson, C. M., Emmer, E. T., & Worsham, M. E. (2003). *Classroom management for elementary teachers* (6th ed.). Boston: Allyn & Bacon.

F

Fantini, M. D. (1986). *Regaining excellence in education.* Columbus, OH: Merrill.

Friedman, P. G. (1986). *Listening processes: Attention, understanding, evaluation.* Washington, DC: National Education Association.

G

Gagne, N. L. (1985). *Hard gains in the soft sciences: The case of pedagogy.* Bloomington, IN: Center on Evaluation, Development, and Research.

Gallup, A. M., & Elam, S. M. (1988). The annual Gallup Poll of the public attitude toward the public schools. *Phi Delta Kappan, 70*(1), 33–46.

Gardner, H. (2003, April). *Multiple intelligences after twenty years.* Paper presented at the annual conference of the American Educational Research Association, Chicago.

Gibran, K. (1989). *The prophet.* New York: Knopf. (Original work published 1923)

Gilliland, H. (Ed.). (1988). *Teaching the Native American.* Dubuque, IA: Kendall/Hunt.

Gilstrap, R. L., & Martin, W. R. (1975). *Current strategies for teachers: A resource for personalizing education.* Pacific Palisades, CA: Goodyear.

Glasser, W. (1965). *Reality therapy: A new approach to psychiatry.* New York: Harper & Row.

Glasser, W. (1977). 10 steps to good discipline. *Today's Education, 66,* 61–63.

Glasser, W. (1986). *Control therapy in the classroom.* New York: Harper & Row.

Glatthorn, A. (1987). Cooperative professional development: Peer-centered options for teacher growth. *Educational Leadership, 44,* 31–35.

Good, T. L., & Brophy, J. E. (1987). *Looking in classrooms* (4th ed.). New York: Harper & Row.

Goodall, H. L., Jr. (1983). *Human communication.* Dubuque, IA: William C. Brown.

Goodlad, J. I. (1984). *A place called school: Prospects for the future.* New York: McGraw-Hill.

Gordon, T. (1974). *Teacher effectiveness training.* New York: David McKay.

Green, F. R. (1999). Brain and learning research: Implications for meeting the needs of diverse learners. *Education, 119*(4), 682.

Gronlund, N. E. (1999). *How to write and use instructional objectives* (6th ed.). Englewood Cliffs, NJ: Prentice Hall.

H

Hall, E. T. (1959). *The silent language.* Greenwich, CT: Fawcett.

Haller, E. P., Child, D. A., & Walberg, H. J. (1988). Can comprehension be taught? A quantitative synthesis of "metacognitve" studies. *Educational Researcher, 17*(9), 5–8.

Hannaford, C. (1995). *Smart moves.* Arlington, VA: Great Ocean.

Harrow, A. J. (1972). *Taxonomy of the psychomotor domain: A guide for developing behavior objectives.* New York: David McKay.

Healy, J. (1998). *Failure to connect.* New York: Simon & Schuster.

Hennessey, B. A., & Amabile, T. M. (1998). Reward, intrinsic motivation, and creativity. *American Psychologist, 53,* 674–675.

Hennings, D. G. (1975). *Mastering classroom communications: What interaction analysis tells the teacher.* Pacific Palisades, CA: Goodyear.

Hollingsworth, H. (2005, January 8). School funding popular problem. *Times Record* (Fort Smith, AR), p. 5A.

Hunter, M. (1980). *Teach more—faster.* El Segundo, CA: TIP Publications.

Hunter, M. (1995). Mastery teaching. In J. H. Block, S. T. Everson, & T. R. Guskey (Eds.), *School improvement programs* (pp. 181–204). New York: Scholastic.

Hurt, H. T., Scott, M. D., & McCroskey, J. C. (1978). *Communications in the classroom.* Menlo Park, CA: Addison-Wesley.

I

Idol, L. (1997). Key questions related to building collaborative and inclusive schools. *Journal of Learning Disabilities, 30,* 384–394.

J

Jacobs, H. H. (1997). *Mapping the big picture: Integrating curriculum & assessment K–12.* Alexandria, VA: Association for Supervision and Curriculum Development.

Jacobson, D., Eggen, P., & Kauchak, D. (1989). *Methods for teaching: A skills approach* (3rd ed.). Columbus, OH: Merrill.

Jensen, E. (2005). *Teaching with the brain in mind* (2nd ed.). Alexandria, VA: Association for Supervision and Curriculum Development.

Jewett, A. E., & Mullan, M. R. (1977). Movement process categories in physical education in teaching-learning. In *Curriculum design: Purposes and processes in physical education teaching-learning.* Washington, DC: American Alliance for Health, Physical Education and Recreation.

Johnson, D. W., & Johnson, R. T. (1985). The internal dynamics of cooperative learning groups. In R. Slavin, S. Sharan, S. Kagan, C. Webb, & R. Schmuck (Eds.), *Learning to cooperate, cooperating to learn* (pp. 103–124). New York: Plenum.

Johnson, D. W., & Johnson, R. T. (1999). *Learning together and along: Cooperation, competition, and individualization* (5th ed.). Boston: Allyn & Bacon.

Johnson, D. W., & Johnson, R. T. (2002). *Meaningful assessment: A meaningful and cooperative process.* Boston: Allyn & Bacon.

Johnson, D. W., Johnson, R. T., Stevahn, L., & Hodne, P. (1997). The three Cs of safe schools. *Educational Leadership, 55*(2), 8–13.

Jones, F. (1979, June). The gentle art of classroom discipline. *National Elementary Principal, 58,* 26–32.

Joyce, B., & Weil, M. (1996). *Models of teaching* (5th ed.). New York: McGraw-Hill.

Joyce, B., Weil, M., & Calhoun, E. (2003). *Models of teaching* (7th ed.). Boston: Allyn & Bacon.

K

Kagan, S. (1990). The structural approach to cooperative learning. *Educational Leadership, 47*(4), 12–15.

Karnes, F. A., & Bean, S. M. (Eds.). (2000). *Methods & materials for teaching the gifted.* Waco, TX: Prufrock.

Kaufman, R., Westland, C., & Engvall, R. (1997). The dichotomy between the concept of professionalism and the reality of sexism in teaching. *Journal of Teacher Education, 48*(2), 118–128.

Kavale, K. A., Holdnack, J. A., & Mostert, M. P. (2005). Responsiveness to intervention and the identification of specific learning disability: A critique and alternative proposal. *Learning Disability Quarterly, 28,* 2.

Kennedy, C. H., Long, T., Kristine, J., Cox, M. J., Tang, J., & Thompson, T. (2001). Facilitating general education participation for students with behavior problems by linking positive behavior supports and person-centered planning. *Journal of Emotional and Behavioral Disorders, 9,* 146–160.

Kirkpatrick, H., & Cuban, L. (1998). Computers make kids smarter—right? *TECHNOS Quarterly, 7*(2), 26–31.

Kohn, A. (1996). *Beyond discipline: From compliance to community.* Alexandria, VA: Association for Supervision and Curriculum Development.

Kolesnik, W. B. (1978). *Motivation: Understanding and influencing human behavior.* Boston: Allyn & Bacon.

Kounin, J. S. (1970). *Discipline and group management in classrooms.* New York: Holt, Rinehart & Winston.

Krathwohl, D. R., Bloom, B. S., & Masia, B. B. (1964). *Taxonomy of educational objectives: Handbook II. Affective domain.* New York: David McKay.

Kulik, J. A., & Kulik, C. C. (1992). Meta-analytic findings on grouping programs. *Gifted Child Quarterly, 36*(2), 73–77.

L

Lewin, L. (2001). *Using the Internet to strengthen curriculum.* Alexandria, VA: Association of Supervision and Curriculum Development.

Linn, M. C., & Slotta, J. D. (2000). WISE science. *Educational Leadership, 58*(2), 29–32.

Lipman, M. (1988a, September). Critical thinking—What can it be? *Educational Leadership,* 38–43.

Lipman, M. (1988b). *Philosophy goes to school.* Philadelphia: Temple University Press.

Looney, S. D. (2004). *Education and the legal system.* Upper Saddle River, NJ: Pearson Education, Inc.

Lyman, H. B. (1991). *Test scores & what they mean* (5th ed.). Englewood Cliffs, NJ: Prentice Hall.

M

Mager, R. F. (1997). *Preparing instructional objectives: A critical tool in the development of effective instruction.* Atlanta, GA: Center for Effective Performance.

Martinez, M. E. (1998). What is problem solving? *Phi Delta Kappan, 70*(8), 605–609.

Maslow, A. H. (1970). *Motivation and personality* (2nd ed.). New York: Harper & Row.

Mayer, R. E., & Wittrock, M. C. (1996). Problem-solving transfer. In D. C. Berliner & R. C. Calfee (Eds.), *Handbook of educational psychology* (pp. 47–62). New York: Macmillan.

McCall, A. L. (1995). Constructing conceptions of multicultural teaching: Preservice teachers' life experiences and teacher education. *Journal of Teacher Education, 46*(5), 340–350.

McCombs, B. L. (2001, April). *What do we know about learners and learning? The learner-centered framework.* Paper presented at the meeting of the American Educational Research Association, Seattle, WA.

Mehrabian, A. (1968). Communication without words. *Psychology Today, 2,* 53–55.

Meyer, C. A. (1992). What's the difference between authentic and performance assessment? *Educational Leadership, 49*(8), 39–40.

Miller, A. D., Barbetta, P. M., & Heron, T. E. (1994). START tutoring: Designing, training, implementing, adapting, and evaluating tutoring program for school and home settings. In R. Gardner, D. M. Sainatok, J. O. Cooper, T. E. Heron, W. L. Heward, J. Eshleman, & T. A. Grossi (Eds.), *Behavior analysis in education: Focus on measurably superior instruction* (pp. 265–282). Monterey, CA: Brooks/Cole.

Miller, P. W. (1986). *Nonverbal communications.* Washington, DC: National Educational Association.

Montagu, A. (1977). The skin, touch, and human development. *Somatics, 3,* 3–8.

Moore, K. D. (2001). *Classroom teaching skills* (5th ed.). New York: McGraw-Hill.

Murphy, K. R., & Davidshofer, C. O. (1991). *Psychological testing* (2nd ed.). Englewood Cliffs, NJ: Prentice Hall.

N

National Commission on Teaching & America's Future. (1996, September). *What matters most: Teaching for America's future.* New York: Author.

Newman, R. S. (2002). What do I need to succeed? . . . When I don't understand what I'm doing!?: Developmental influences on students' adaptive help seeking. In A. Wigfield & J. S. Eccles (Eds.), *Development of achievement motivation* (pp. 33–53). San Diego: Academic Press.

Nichols, R. G., & Stevens, L. A. (1957). *Are you listening?* New York: McGraw-Hill.

Nickerson, R. (1985). Understanding understanding. *American Journal of Education, 93,* 201–239.

O

O'Donnell, A. M. (1996). Effects of explicit incentives on scripted and unscripted cooperation. *Journal of Educational Psychology, 88*(1), 74–86.

O'Leary, K. D., & O'Leary, S. (Eds.). (1977). *Classroom management: The successful use of behavior modification* (2nd ed.). Elmsford, NY: Pergamon.

Oliva, P. F. (2000). *Developing the curriculum* (5th ed.). Boston: Allyn & Bacon.

Orlich, D. C., Harder, R. J., Callahan, R. C., Kauchak, D. P., Pendergrass, R. A., Keough, A. J., et al. (1990). *Teaching strategies* (3rd ed.). Lexington, MA: D. C. Heath.

Ostermeier, T. H. (1994, March). *Differences in meanings for nonverbal cues and ease/difficulty in intercultural listening.* Paper presented at the annual meeting of the International Listening Association Convention, Boston. (ERIC Document Reproduction Service No. ED 371 404)

Overturf, B. J. (1997). Reading portfolios reveal new dimensions of students. *Middle School Journal, 28*(3), 45–50.

P

Padron, Y. N. (1994). Teaching and learning risks associated with limited cognitive mastery in science and mathematics for limited English proficient students. In *Proceedings of the Third National Research Symposium on Limited English Proficient Student Issues: Focus on Middle and High Schools: Vol. 2.* Washington, DC: U.S. Department of Education.

Paul, R. (1993). *Critical thinking: How to prepare students for a rapidly changing world.* Santa Rosa, CA: Foundation for Critical Thinking.

Posner, G. J., & Rudnitsky, A. N. (2000) *Course design.* New York: Addison-Wesley.

Prawat, R. S. (1991). The value of ideas: The immersion approach to the development of thinking. *Educational Researcher, 20*(2), 3–10, 30.

Premack, D. (1965). Reinforcement theory. In D. Levine (Ed.), *Nebraska Symposium on Motivation* (Vol. 13, pp. 123–180). Lincoln: University of Nebraska Press.

R

Raths, L. E., Wassermann, S., Jonas, A., & Rothstein, A. M. (1986). *Teaching for thinking: Theory, strategies, and activities for the classroom.* New York: Teachers College Press.

Rea, P. J., McLaughlin, V. L., & Walther-Thomas, C. (2002). Outcomes of students with learning disabilities in inclusive and pullout programs. *Exceptional Children, 68,* 203–222.

Reese, P. (2005, February 11). Corporal punishment in state schools declines. *Arkansas Democrat Gazette* (Little Rock, AR), p. 16A.

Renzulli, J. S., Gentry, M., & Reis, S. M. (2003). *Enrichment clusters: A practical plan for real-world, student-driven learning.* Mansfield Center, CT: Creative Learning Press.

Renzulli, J. S., & Reis, S. M. (1997). *The schoolwide enrichment model: A how-to guide for educational excellence.* Mansfield Center, CT: Creative Learning Press.

Riding, R. J., & Rayner, S. G. (1998). *Cognitive styles and learning strategies: Understanding style differences in learning behaviour.* London: David Fulton Publishers.

Roberts, P., & Kellough, D. (2003). *A guide for developing interdisciplinary thematic units* (3rd ed.). Englewood Cliffs, NJ: Prentice Hall.

Rosenshine, B., & Stevens, R. (1986). Teaching functions. In M. Wittrock (Ed.), *Handbook of research on teaching* (3rd ed., pp. 376–391). New York: Macmillan.

Ross, A., & Olsen, K. (1993). *The way we were . . . the way we can be: A vision for the middle school through integrated thematic instruction* (2nd ed.). Kent, WA: Books for Educators. (ERIC Document Reproduction Service No. ED371906)

Rowe, M. B. (1974a). Relation of wait time and rewards to the development of language, logic, and fate control: Part two. Rewards. *Journal of Research in Science Teaching, 11*(4), 291–308.

Rowe, M. B. (1974b). Wait time and rewards as instructional variables, their influence on language, logic, and fate control: Part one. Wait time. *Journal of Research in Science Teaching, 11*(2), 81–94.

Rowe, M. B. (1978). Wait, wait, wait. *School Science and Mathematics, 78,* 207–216.

S

Sadker, M., & Sadker, D. (1994). *Failing at fairness: How America's schools cheat girls.* New York: Scribner's.

Sadler, W. A., & Whimbey, A. (1985). A holistic approach to improving thinking skills. *Phi Delta Kappan, 67*(3), 199–203.

Salpeter, J. (2000, June). What does research say about technology's impact on education: Interview with Larry Cuban. *Technology and Learning.* Retrieved from http://techlearning.com/db_area/archives/TL/062000/archives/cuban/php

Sathre, F. S., Olson, R. W., & Whitney, C. I. (1977). *Let's talk.* Glenview, IL: Scott, Foresman.

Sax, G. (1980). *Principles of educational and psychological measurement and evaluation* (2nd ed.). Belmont, CA: Wadsworth.

Schmuck, R. A., & Schmuck, P. A. (1988). *Group processes in the classroom* (5th ed.). Dubuque, IA: William C. Brown.

Schunk, D. H. (2000). *Learning theories: An educational perspective* (3rd ed.). Columbus, OH: Merrill/Prentice Hall.

Schunk, D. H., & Ertmer, P. A. (2000). Self-regulation and academic learning: Self-efficacy enhancing intervention. In M. Boekarts, P. Pintrich, & M. Zeidner (Eds.), *Handbook of self-regulation* (pp. 631–649). San Diego: Academic Press.

Schunk, D. H., & Zimmerman, B. J. (1997). Social origins of self-regulatory competence. *Educational Psychologist, 32*(4), 195–208.

Shaughnessy, M. F. (1998). An interview with Rita Dunn about learning styles. *The Clearing House, 71*(3), 141–146.

Shulman, L. (1987). Knowledge and teaching: Foundations of the new reform. *Harvard Educational Review, 57,* 1–22.

Silverman, L. K. (1986). Parenting young gifted children. *Journal of Children in Contemporary Society, 18,* 73–87.

Silvernail, D. L. (1979). *Teaching styles as related to student achievement.* Washington, DC: National Education Association.

Skinner, B. F. (1968). *The technology of teaching.* New York: Appleton-Century-Crofts.

Skinner, B. F. (1971). *Beyond freedom and dignity.* New York: Knopf.

Slavin, R. E. (1995). *Cooperative learning* (2nd ed.). Boston: Allyn & Bacon.

Snider, J., & Osgood, C. E. (Eds.). (1969). *Semantic differential technique: A sourcebook.* Chicago: Aldine.

Sokolove, S., Sadker, D., & Sadker, M. (1986). Interpersonal communication skills. In J. M. Cooper (Ed.), *Classroom teaching skills* (3rd ed., pp. 233–278). Lexington, MA: D. C. Heath.

Stein, J. (Editor in Chief). (1984). *The Random House college dictionary.* New York: Random House.

Sternberg, R. (1998). Principles of teaching for successful intelligence. *Educational Psychologist, 33*(1), 65–72.

Stone, R. (2002). *Best practices for high school classrooms: What award-winning secondary teachers do.* Thousand Oaks, CA: Corwin Press.

Suchman, J. R. (1961). Inquiry training: Building skills for autonomous discovery. *Merrill-Palmer Quarterly of Behavior and Development, 7,* 147–169.

Suchman, J. R. (1966). *Inquiry development program in physical science.* Chicago: Science Research Associates.

T

TenBrink, T. D. (2003). Assessment. In J. M. Cooper (Ed.), *Classroom teaching skills* (7th ed., pp. 311–353). Lexington, MA: D. C. Heath.

Tishman, S., Perkins, D. N., & Jay, E. (1995). *The thinking classroom.* Boston: Allyn & Bacon.

Tomlinson, C. A. (1995). *How to differentiate instruction in mixed-ability classrooms.* Alexandria, VA: Association for Supervision and Curriculum Development.

Tomlinson, C. A. (1999). *The differentiated classroom: Responding to the needs of all learners.* Alexandria, VA: Association for Supervision and Curriculum Development.

Torrance, E. P. (1983). *Creativity in the classroom.* Washington, DC: Library of Congress.

U

U.S. Department of Education (2004). Retrieved from http://www.ed.gov/teachers/nclbguide/nclb_teachers-toolkit.pdfx

V

Vaughn, S., & Fuchs, L. S. (2003). Redefining learning disabilities as inadequate response to instruction: The promise and potential problems. *Learning Disabilities: Research & Practice, 18,* 137–146.

W

Walsh, D., & Paul, R. (1988). *The goal of critical thinking: From educational ideal to educational reality.* Washington, DC: American Federation of Teachers.

Waxman, H., Padron, Y., & Arnold, K. (2001). Effective instructional practices for students placed at risk of academic failure. In G. Borman, S. Stringfield, & R. Slavin (Eds.), *Title I: Compensatory education at the crossroads* (pp. 137–170). Mahwah, NJ: Lawrence Erlbaum.

Wigfield, A., & Eccles, J. S. (2002). Students' motivation during the middle school years. In J. Aronson (Ed.), *Improving academic development: Impact of psychological factors in education* (pp. 201–223). New York: Academic Press.

Wiggins, G., & McTighe, J. (2005). *Understanding by design* (2nd ed.). Alexandria, VA: Association for Supervision and Curriculum Development.

Winebrenner, S. (2002). *Teaching gifted kids in the regular classroom: Strategies and techniques every teacher can use to meet the academic needs of the gifted and talented.* Minneapolis, MN: Free Spirit.

Wittrock, M. (Ed.). (1986). *Handbook of research on teaching* (3rd ed.). New York: Macmillan.

Wong, H. K., & Wong, R. T. (1998). *The first days of school.* Mountain View, CA: Harry K. Wong.

Wulf, K. M., & Schane, B. (1984). *Curriculum design.* Glenview, IL: Scott, Foresman.

Z

Zimmerman, B. J. (1998, April). *Achieving academic excellence: The role of perceived efficacy and self-regulatory skill.* Paper presented at the annual meeting of the American Educational Research Association, San Diego.

Zimmerman, B. J., & Schunk, D. H. (Eds.). (2001). *Self-regulated learning and academic achievement: Theoretical perspectives* (2nd ed.). Mahwah, NJ: Lawrence Erlbaum.

Zuckerbrod, N. (2007, January 14). Education law under review. *Times Record* (Fort Smith, AR), p. 10A.

Index

Brief-essay item, 290, 296 (table)
Brookfield, S. D., 232, 233
Brophy, J., 349
Brown v. Board of Education of Topeka, 20
Bruner, J. S., 202
Buckley Amendment, 21
Burnout, 359
Bush, R. N., 341
Buzz group, 172, 175

Calhoun, E., 7
Callahan, R. C., 83, 105, 127, 129
Campbell, D., 45
Canter, L., 367
Canter, M., 367
Certification requirements, 16, 22–23, 399
    alternative certification, 16, 23
    assessment of teaching standards and, 17–18
    provisional certification, 400
    reciprocity arrangements, 400
    state certification addresses, 399–400
    teacher portfolios and, 259
    teacher testing requirement and, 16–17
Characterization by value/value complex objectives, 85 (table), 86
Checkley, K., 50
Checklists, 272
Child, D. A., 83
Child abuse/neglect law, 20–21
Child Abuse Prevention and Treatment Act (CAPTA) of 1996, 20
Child Protective Service (CPS) agency, 20
Civil Rights Act of 1964, 20
Classroom context:
    communication process and, 312–320, 320 (table)
    engaged time, 31, 31 (figure)
    indirect teaching methods and, 170, 173, 191–192
    motivated learning and, 339
    organizational effectiveness and, 8
    positive classroom environment, 9–10, 11
    research-based teaching and, xvi, 10
    teacher withitness and, 366
    See also Assessment; Classroom management; Curriculum design; Instructional practice; Teaching
Classroom management, 357, 358, 360, 384
    administrative chores and, 374–375, 375–376 (figures)
    approaches to, 361–369, 363 (figure), 369 (table)
    assertive discipline and, 367–368
    back-up systems and, 367
    behavior modification and, 368
    beyond discipline approach and, 365
    body language and, 366
    conflict resolution and, 381–382
    corporal punishment and, 21–22
    dehydration and, 35
    desist approach to, 363 (figure), 367–369, 369 (table)
    discipline, definition of, 361
    effective management principles and, 360–361, 372–384, 385 (table)
    enforcement of rules, 380

    inner discipline approach and, 364–365
    instructional approach to, 363 (figure), 365–367, 369 (table)
    Jones Model of, 366–367
    Kounin Model of, 366
    leadership, role of, 358–359
    limits on behavior/rules and, 366, 371, 376–377, 380
    misbehavior, causes of, 369–372, 378
    monitoring classroom activities and, 381
    overlapping activities and, 366
    peer mediation system and, 382
    planning for, 373
    punishment and, 361, 368, 382–383
    reality therapy approach and, 362–363
    ripple effect and, 380
    routines, maintenance of, 374–375, 375–376 (figures)
    self-discipline approach to, 362–365, 363 (figure), 369 (table)
    sharing control and, 378
    space management and, 375–376
    start-of-school activities, 378–379
    stress management strategies and, 359
    student information and, 379–380, 381 (figure)
    teacher effectiveness training and, 363–364
    time wasting actions and, 31–32, 366, 374
    transition management and, 366
    withitness and, 366
    See also Incentive systems; Punishment
Classroom modification plans, 62, 65 (figure)
Closure activities, 132
    cueing, 133
    demonstration/application of knowledge, 132, 133
    lectures and, 149
    new/prior knowledge, connection of, 133
    planning for, 133
    summary questions and, 133
    See also Lesson plans
Cognitive domain objectives, 80–83, 82 (table), 83–84 (figures), 85 (table), 90 (table), 280
Cognitive set, 125
Cognitive style, 47–48
Coloroso, B., 364, 365
Communication, 310, 311
    classroom communication, 312–320, 320 (table)
    computer-based communication, 53
    decoding messages, 312, 313, 329
    definition of, 312
    difficult parents and, 323
    limited English proficient students and, 64
    listening, components of, 324–327
    listening, styles of, 328–329
    multicultural competency and, 321
    nonverbal communication, 315–317, 325–326
    parent-school communication, 320–324, 322 (figure)
    physical learning environment and, 318
    proxemics and, 318
    school-based management and, 321, 323
    silence and, 319, 323
    space/motion, language of, 317–318

About the Author

Kenneth D. Moore (Henderson State University—retired) grew up in Wichita, Kansas, where he attended Wichita North High School and later taught in the Texas public schools. He received his EdD degree in Curriculum and Instruction from the University of Houston. Dr. Moore has been involved in teacher education for more than 35 years at both the public school and higher education levels. During his tenure in higher education, he served as dean of teacher education for 12 years and worked closely with school administrators, classroom teachers, student teachers, and teacher education candidates. He has traveled extensively, serving as accreditation consultant and conducting workshops. Dr. Moore has authored three books, numerous journal publications, and an ERIC monograph, and he has presented many papers at regional and national conventions. He has also served as director of the Southwest Regional Association of Teachers of Science, President of the Oklahoma Association of Teacher Educators, President of the Oklahoma Association of Colleges for Teacher Education, and President of the Arkansas Association of Colleges for Teacher Education. He is past member of the National Council for Accreditation of Teacher Education (NCATE) Board of Examiners (BOE). The texts he has authored include *Classroom Teaching Skills 6/e, Clinical Supervision: A Practical Guide to Student Teacher Supervision* (coauthored), and *Middle and Secondary Instructional Methods*. Currently, Dr. Moore is semiretired and lives with his wife Susan in Van Buren, Arkansas, where he pursues his favorite projects, serves as an educational consultant, and continues to write.